The Complete Notebooks of Leonardo Da Vinci

Leonardo Da Vinci

Translated by Jean Paul Richter

First published 1888

INTRODUCTION

Leonardo Da Vinci, arguably the central figure of the Renaissance, has long been considered by many a man of mystery. This is in spite of the fact that we have an unparalleled set of documents which illuminate his thought processes, interests, and deepest beliefs. We have access to hundreds of pages of his notes, jottings, sketches, doodles, and musings, including lists of books he read and even scraps of financial records. All of the known Da Vinci papers as of the mid-19th century are included here in this magnificent collection. What emerges is the picture of a rationalist. For instance, Da Vinci was one of the first to question the Biblical account of the Flood. He saw the fossils of sea creatures on the tops of mountains and concluded that these could not have been deposited in a forty day flood. He looked at river valleys and did the math; they could only have been eroded over huge horizons of time.

Da Vinci put as much thought into his art as he did his science. Practically half of the writings here relate to detailed studies of the natural world which informed his work as an artist.

CONTENTS

Portrait of Leonardo by himself reproduced from the original drawing

VOLUME 1

PREFACE

A singular fatality has ruled the destiny of nearly all the most famous of Leonardo da Vinci's works. Two of the three most important were never completed, obstacles having arisen during his life-time, which obliged him to leave them unfinished; namely the Sforza Monument and the Wall-painting of the Battle of Anghiari, while the third—the picture of the Last Supper at Milan—has suffered irremediable injury from decay and the repeated restorations to which it was recklessly subjected during the XVIIth and XVIIIth centuries. Nevertheless, no other picture of the Renaissance has become so wellknown and popular through copies of every description.

Vasari says, and rightly, in his Life of Leonardo, "that he laboured much more by his word than in fact or by deed", and the biographer evidently had in his mind the numerous works in Manuscript which have been preserved to this day. To us, now, it seems almost inexplicable that these valuable and interesting original texts should have remained so long unpublished, and indeed forgotten. It is certain that during the XVIth and XVIIth centuries their exceptional value was highly appreciated. This is proved not merely by the prices which they commanded, but also by the exceptional interest which has been attached to the change of ownership of merely a few pages of Manuscript.

That, notwithstanding this eagerness to possess the Manuscripts, their contents remained a mystery, can only be accounted for by the many and great difficulties attending the task of deciphering them. The handwriting is so peculiar that it requires considerable practice to read even a few detached phrases, much more to solve with any certainty the numerous difficulties of alternative readings, and to master the sense as a connected whole. Vasari observes with reference to Leonardos writing: "he wrote backwards, in rude characters, and with the left hand, so that any one who is not practised in reading them, cannot understand them". The aid of a mirror in reading reversed handwriting appears to me available only for a first experimental reading. Speaking from my own experience, the persistent use of it is too fatiguing and inconvenient to be practically advisable, considering the enormous mass of Manuscripts to be deciphered. And as, after all, Leonardo's handwriting runs backwards just as all Oriental character runs backwards—that is to say from right to left—the difficulty of reading direct from the writing is not insuperable. This obvious peculiarity in the writing is not, however, by any means the only obstacle in the way of mastering the text. Leonardo made use of an orthography peculiar to himself; he had a fashion of amalgamating several short words into one long one, or, again, he would quite arbitrarily divide a long word into two separate halves; added to this there is no punctuation whatever to regulate the division and construction of the sentences, nor are there any accents—and the reader may imagine that such difficulties were almost sufficient to make the task seem a desperate one to a beginner. It is therefore not surprising that the good intentions of some of Leonardo s most reverent admirers should have failed.

Leonardos literary labours in various departments both of Art and of Science were those essentially of an enquirer, hence the analytical method is that which he employs in arguing out his investigations and dissertations. The vast structure of his scientific theories is consequently built up of numerous separate researches, and it is much to be lamented that he should never have collated and arranged them. His love for detailed research—as it seems to me—was the reason that in almost all the Manuscripts, the different paragraphs appear to us to be in utter confusion; on one and the same page, observations on the most dissimilar subjects follow each other without any connection. A page, for instance, will begin with some principles of astronomy, or the motion of the earth; then come the laws of sound, and finally some precepts as to colour. Another page will begin with his investigations on the structure of the intestines, and end with philosophical remarks as to the relations of poetry to painting; and so forth.

Leonardo himself lamented this confusion, and for that reason I do not think that the publication of the texts in the order in which they occur in the originals would at all fulfil his intentions. No reader could find his way through such a labyrinth; Leonardo himself could not have done it.

Added to this, more than half of the five thousand manuscript pages which now remain to us, are written on loose leaves, and at present arranged in a manner which has no justification beyond the fancy of the collector who first brought them together to make volumes of more or less extent. Nay, even in the volumes, the pages of which were numbered by Leonardo himself, their order, so far as the connection of the texts was concerned, was obviously a matter of indifference to him. The only point he seems to have kept in view, when first writing down his notes, was that each observation should be complete to the end on the page on which it was begun. The exceptions to this rule are extremely few, and it is certainly noteworthy that we find in such cases, in bound volumes with his numbered pages, the written observations: "turn over", "This is the continuation of the previous page", and the like. Is not this sufficient to prove that it was only in quite exceptional cases that the writer intended the consecutive pages to remain connected, when he should, at last, carry out the often planned arrangement of his writings?

What this final arrangement was to be, Leonardo has in most cases indicated with considerable completeness. In other cases this authoritative clue is wanting, but the difficulties arising from this are not insuperable; for, as the subject of the separate paragraphs is always distinct and well defined in itself, it is quite possible to construct a well-planned whole, out of the scattered materials of his scientific system, and I may venture to state that I have devoted especial care and thought to the due execution of this responsible task.

The beginning of Leonardo's literary labours dates from about his thirty-seventh year, and he seems to have carried them on without any serious interruption till his death. Thus the Manuscripts that remain represent a period of about thirty years. Within this space of time his handwriting altered so little that it is impossible to judge from it of the date of any particular text. The exact dates, indeed, can only be assigned to certain note-books in which the year is incidentally indicated, and in which the order of the leaves has not been altered since Leonardo used them. The assistance these afford for a chronological arrangement of the Manuscripts is generally self evident. By this clue I have assigned to the original Manuscripts now scattered through England, Italy and France, the order of their production, as in many matters of detail it is highly important to be able to verify the time and place at which certain observations were made and registered. For this purpose the Bibliography of the Manuscripts given at the end of Vol. II, may be regarded as an Index, not far short of complete, of all Leonardo s literary works now extant. The consecutive numbers (from 1 to 1566) at the head of each passage in this work, indicate their logical sequence with reference to the subjects; while the letters and figures to the left of each paragraph refer to the original Manuscript and number of the page, on which that particular passage is to be found. Thus the reader, by referring to the List of Manuscripts at the beginning of Volume I, and to the Bibliography at the end of Volume II, can, in every instance, easily ascertain, not merely the period to which the passage belongs, but also exactly where it stood in the original document. Thus, too, by following the sequence of the numbers in the Bibliographical index, the reader may reconstruct the original order of the Manuscripts and recompose the various texts to be found on the original sheets—so much of it, that is to say, as by its subject-matter came within the scope of this work. It may, however, be here observed that Leonardo s Manuscripts contain, besides the passages here printed, a great number of notes and dissertations on Mechanics, Physics, and some other subjects, many of which could only be satisfactorily dealt with by specialists. I have given as complete a review of these writings as seemed necessary in the Bibliographical notes.

In 1651, Raphael Trichet Dufresne, of Paris, published a selection from Leonardo's writings on painting, and this treatise became so popular that it has since been reprinted about two-and-twenty times, and in six different languages. But none of these editions were derived from the original texts, which were supposed to have been lost, but from early copies, in which Leonardo's text had been more or less mutilated, and which were all fragmentary. The oldest and on the whole the best copy of Leonardo's essays and precepts on Painting is in the Vatican Library; this has been twice printed, first by Manzi, in 1817, and secondly by Ludwig, in 1882. Still, this ancient copy, and the published editions of it, contain much for which it would be rash to hold Leonardo responsible, and some portions—such as the very important rules for the proportions of the human figure—are wholly wanting; on the other hand they contain passages which, if they are genuine, cannot now be verified from any original Manuscript extant. These copies, at any rate neither give us the original order of the texts, as written by Leonardo, nor do they afford any substitute, by connecting them on a rational scheme; indeed, in their chaotic confusion they are anything rather than satisfactory reading. The fault, no doubt, rests with the compiler of the Vatican copy, which would seem to be the source whence all the published and extensively known texts were derived; for, instead of arranging the passages himself, he was satisfied with recording a suggestion for a final arrangement of them into eight distinct parts, without attempting to carry out his scheme. Under the mistaken idea that this plan of distribution might be that, not of the compiler, but of Leonardo himself, the various editors, down to the present day, have very injudiciously continued to adopt this order—or rather disorder.

I, like other enquirers, had given up the original Manuscript of the Trattato della Pittura for lost, till, in the beginning of 1880, I was enabled, by the liberality of Lord Ashburnham, to inspect his Manuscripts, and was so happy as to discover among them the original text of the best-known portion of the Trattato in his magnificent library at Ashburnham Place. Though this discovery was of a fragment only—but a considerable fragment—inciting me to further search, it gave the key to the mystery which had so long enveloped the first origin of all the known copies of the Trattato. The extensive researches I was subsequently enabled to prosecute, and the results of which are combined in this work, were only rendered possible by the unrestricted permission granted me to investigate all the Manuscripts by Leonardo dispersed throughout Europe, and to reproduce the highly important original sketches they contain, by the process of "photogravure". Her Majesty the Queen graciously accorded me special permission to copy for publication the Manuscripts at the Royal Library at Windsor. The Commission Centrale Administrative de l'Institut de France, Paris, gave me, in the most liberal manner, in answer to an application from Sir Frederic Leighton, P. R. A., Corresponding member of the Institut, free permission to work for several months in their private collection at deciphering the Manuscripts preserved there. The same favour which Lord Ashburnham had already granted me was extended to me by the Earl of Leicester, the Marchese Trivulsi, and the Curators of the Ambrosian Library at Milan, by the Conte Manzoni at Rome and by other private owners of Manuscripts of Leonardo's; as also by the Directors of the Louvre at Paris; the Accademia at Venice; the Uffizi at Florence; the Royal Library at Turin; and the British Museum, and the South Kensington Museum. I am also greatly indebted to the Librarians of these various collections for much assistance in my labours; and more particularly to Monsieur Louis Lalanne, of the Institut de France, the Abbate Ceriani, of the Ambrosian Library, Mr. Maude Thompson, Keeper of Manuscripts at the British Museum, Mr. Holmes, the Queens Librarian at Windsor, the Revd Vere Bayne, Librarian of Christ Church College at Oxford, and the Revd A. Napier, Librarian to the Earl of Leicester at Holkham Hall.

In correcting the Italian text for the press, I have had the advantage of valuable advice from the Commendatore Giov. Morelli, Senatore del Regno, and from Signor Gustavo Frizzoni, of Milan. The translation, under many difficulties, of the Italian text into English, is mainly due to Mrs. R. C. Bell; while the rendering of several of the most puzzling and important passages, particularly in the second half of Vol. I, I owe to the indefatigable interest taken in this work by Mr. E. J. Poynter R. A. Finally I must express my thanks to Mr. Alfred Marks, of Long Ditton, who has most kindly assisted me throughout in the revision of the proof sheets.

The notes and dissertations on the texts on Architecture in Vol. II I owe to my friend Baron Henri de Geymuller, of Paris.

I may further mention with regard to the illustrations, that the negatives for the production of the "photo-gravures" by Monsieur Dujardin of Paris were all taken direct from the originals.

It is scarcely necessary to add that most of the drawings here reproduced in facsimile have never been published before. As I am now, on the termination of a work of several years' duration, in a position to review the general tenour of Leonardos writings, I may perhaps be permitted to add a word as to my own estimate of the value of their contents. I have already shown that it is due to nothing but a fortuitous succession of unfortunate circumstances, that we should not, long since, have known Leonardo, not merely as a Painter, but as an Author, a Philosopher, and a Naturalist. There can be no doubt that in more than one department his principles and discoveries were infinitely more in accord with the teachings of modern science, than with the views of his contemporaries. For this reason his extraordinary gifts and merits are far more likely to be appreciated in our own time than they could have been during the preceding centuries. He has been unjustly accused of having squandered his powers, by beginning a variety of studies and then, having hardly begun, throwing them aside. The truth is that the labours of three centuries have hardly sufficed for the elucidation of some of the problems which occupied his mighty mind.

Alexander von Humboldt has borne witness that "he was the first to start on the road towards the point where all the impressions of our senses converge in the idea of the Unity of Nature" Nay, yet more may be said. The very words which are inscribed on the monument of Alexander von Humboldt himself, at Berlin, are perhaps the most appropriate in which we can sum up our estimate of Leonardo's genius:

"Majestati naturae par ingenium."

LONDON, April 1883.

F. P. R.

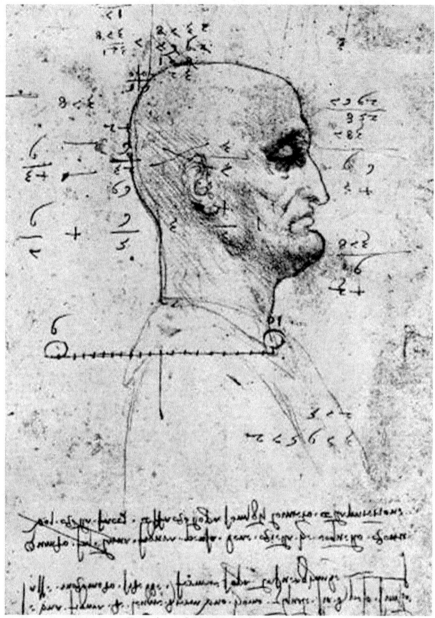

Drawing of the Head of a Criminal

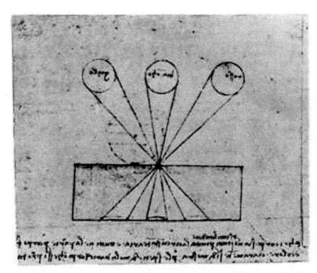

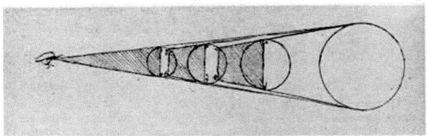

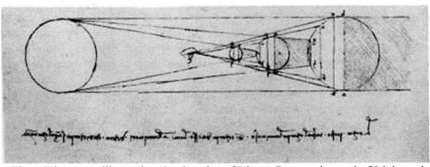

Three Diagrams, illustrating the theories of Linear Perspective and of Light and Shade

DETAILED CONTENTS OF VOLUME I.

SHADE.—On the nature of light (130—131).—The difference between light and lustre (132—135).—The relations of luminous to illuminated bodies (136). — Experiments on the relation of light and shadow within a room (137—140).—Light and shadow with regard to the position of the eye (141—145).—The law of the incidence of light (146—147).—SECOND BOOK ON LIGHT AND SHADE.— Gradations of strength in the shadows (148—149).—On the intensity of shadows as dependent on the distance from the light (150—152).—On the proportion of light and shadow (153—157).—THIRD BOOK ON LIGHT AND SHADE.—Definition of derived shadow (158—159).—Different sorts of derived shadows (160—162).—On the relation of derived and primary shadow (163—165).—On the shape of derived shadows (166—174).—On the relative intensity of derived shadows (175—179).— Shadow as produced by two lights of different size (180—181).—The effect of light at different distances (182).—Further complications in the derived shadows (183— 187).—FOURTH BOOK ON LIGHT AND SHADE.—On the shape of cast shadows (188—191).—On the outlines of cast shadows (192—195).—On the relative size of cast shadows (196. 197).—Effects on cast shadows by the tone of the back ground (198).—A disputed proposition (199).—On the relative depth of cast shadows (200— 202).—FIFTH BOOK ON LIGHT AND SHADE.—Principles of reflection (203. 204).—On reverberation (205).—Reflection on water (206. 207).—Experiments with the mirror (208—210).—Appendix:—On shadows in movement (211—212).— SIXTH BOOK ON LIGHT AND SHADE.—The effect of rays passing through holes (213. 214).—On gradation of shadows (215. 216).—On relative proportion of light and shadows (216—221).

IV. PERSPECTIVE OF DISAPPEARANCE

Definition (222. 223).—An illustration by experiment (224).—A guiding rule (225).—-An experiment (226).—On indistinctness at short distances (227—231).— On indistinctness at great distances (232—234).—The importance of light and shade in the Prospettiva de' perdimenti (235—239).—The effect of light or dark backgrounds on the apparent size of objects (240—250).—Propositions on Prospettiva de' perdimenti from MS. C. (250—262).

V. THEORY OF COLOURS

The reciprocal effects of colours on objects placed opposite each other (263— 271).—Combination of different colours in cast shadows (272).—The effect of colours in the camera obscura (273. 274).—On the colours of derived shadows (275. 276).—On the nature of colours (277. 278).—On gradations in the depth of colours (279. 280).—On the reflection of colours (281—283).—On the use of dark and light colours in painting (284—286).—On the colours of the rainbow (287—288).

VI. PERSPECTIVE OF COLOUR AND AERIAL PERSPECTIVE

VII. ON THE PROPORTIONS AND ON THE MOVEMENTS OF THE HUMAN FIGURE

VIII. BOTANY FOR PAINTERS, AND ELEMENTS OF LANDSCAPE PAINTING

IX. THE PRACTICE OF PAINTING

I. MORAL PRECEPTS FOR THE STUDENT OF PAINTING.—How to ascertain the dispositions for an artistic career (482).—The course of instruction for an artist (483—485).—The study of the antique (486. 487).—The necessity of anatomical knowledge (488. 489).—How to acquire practice (490).—Industry and thoroughness the first conditions (491—493.)—The artist's private life and choice of company (493. 494).—The distribution of time for studying (495— 497).—On the productive power of minor artists (498—501).—A caution against one-sided study (502).—How to acquire universality (503—506).—Useful games and exercises (507. 508).—II. THE ARTIST'S STUDIO.—INSTRUMENTS AND HELPS FOR THE APPLICATION OF PERSPECTIVE.—ON JUDGING OF A PICTURE.—On the size of the studio (509).—On the construction of windows (510—512).—On the best light for painting (513—520).—On various helps in preparing a picture (521— 530).—On the management of works (531. 532).—On the limitations of painting (533—535).—On the choice of a position (536. 537).—The apparent size of figures in a picture (538. 539).—The right position of the artist, when painting and of the spectator (540—547).—III. THE PRACTICAL METHODS OF LIGHT AND SHADE AND AERIAL PERSPECTIVE.—Gradations of light and shade (548).—On the choice of light for a picture (549—554).—The distribution of light and shade (555—559).—The juxtaposition of light and shade (560. 561).—On the lighting of the background (562—565).—On the lighting of white objects (566).—The methods of aerial perspective (567—570).—IV. OF PORTRAIT AND FIGURE PAINTING.—Of sketching figures and portraits (571. 572).—The position of the head (573).—Of the light on the face (574—576).—General suggestions for historical pictures (577—581).—How to represent the differences of age and sex (582. 583).—Of representing the emotions (584).—Of representing imaginary animals (585).—The selection of forms (586—591).—How to pose figures (592).—Of appropriate gestures (593—600).—V. SUGGESTIONS FOR COMPOSITIONS.—Of painting battle-pieces (601—603).—Of depicting night-scenes (604).—Of depicting a tempest (605. 606).—Of representing the deluge (607—609).—Of depicting natural phenomena (610. 611).—VI. THE ARTIST'S MATERIALS.—Of chalk and paper (612—617).—On the preparation and use of colours (618—627).—Of preparing the panel (628).—The preparation of oils (629—634).—On varnishes (635— 637).—On chemical materials (638—650).—VII. PHILOSOPHY AND HISTORY OF THE ART OF PAINTING.—The relation of art and nature (651. 652).—Painting is superior to poetry (653. 654).—Painting is superior to sculpture (655. 656).—Aphorisms (657— 659).—On the history of painting (660. 661).—The painter's scope (662).

X. STUDIES AND SKETCHES FOR PICTURES AND DECORATIONS

On pictures of the Madonna (663).—Bernardo di Bandino's portrait (664).—Notes on the Last Supper (665—668).—On the battle of Anghiari (669).—Allegorical representations referring to the duke of Milan (670—673).—Allegorical representations (674—678).—Arrangement of a picture (679).—List of drawings (680).—Mottoes and Emblems (681—702).

Charcoal Drawing of a Female Figure

I. Prolegomena and General Introduction to the Book on Painting

The author's intention to publish his MSS.

1.

How by a certain machine many may stay some time under water. And how and wherefore I do not describe my method of remaining under water and how long I can remain without eating. And I do not publish nor divulge these, by reason of the evil nature of men, who would use them for assassinations at the bottom of the sea by destroying ships, and sinking them, together with the men in them. Nevertheless I will impart others, which are not dangerous because the mouth of the tube through which you breathe is above the water, supported on air sacks or cork.

[Footnote: The leaf on which this passage is written, is headed with the words Casi 39, and most of these cases begin with the word 'Come', like the two here given, which are the 26th and 27th. 7. Sughero. In the Codex Antlanticus 377a; 1170a there is a sketch, drawn with the pen, representing a man with a tube in his mouth, and at the farther end of the tube a disk. By the tube the word 'Channa' is written, and by the disk the word 'sughero'.]

The preparation of the MSS. for publication.

2.

When you put together the science of the motions of water, remember to include under each proposition its application and use, in order that this science may not be useless.--

[Footnote: A comparatively small portion of Leonardo's notes on water-power was published at Bologna in 1828, under the title: "Del moto e misura dell'Acqua, di L. da Vinci".]

Admonition to readers.

3.

Let no man who is not a Mathematician read the elements of my work.

The disorder in the MSS.

4.

Begun at Florence, in the house of Piero di Braccio Martelli, on the 22nd day of March 1508. And this is to be a collection without order, taken from many papers which I have copied here, hoping to arrange them later each in its place, according to the subjects of which they may treat. But I believe that before I am at the end of this [task] I shall have to repeat the same things several times; for which, O reader! do not blame me, for the subjects are many and memory cannot retain them [all] and say: 'I will not write this because I wrote it before.' And if I wished to avoid falling into this fault, it would be necessary in every case when I wanted to copy [a passage] that, not to repeat myself, I should read over all that had gone before; and all the more since the intervals are long between one time of writing and the next.

[Footnote: 1. In the history of Florence in the early part of the XVIth century Piero di Braccio Martelli is frequently mentioned as Commissario della Signoria. He was famous for his learning and at his death left four books on Mathematics ready for the press; comp. LITTA, Famiglie celebri Italiane, Famiglia Martelli di Firenze.--In the Official Catalogue of MSS. in the Brit. Mus., New Series Vol. I., where this passage is printed, Barto has been wrongly given for Braccio.

2. addi 22 di marzo 1508. The Christian era was computed in Florence at that time from the Incarnation (Lady day, March 25th). Hence this should be 1509 by our reckoning.

3. racolto tratto di molte carte le quali io ho qui copiate. We must suppose that Leonardo means that he has copied out his own MSS. and not those of others. The first thirteen leaves of the MS. in the Brit. Mus. are a fair copy of some notes on physics.]

Suggestions for the arrangement of MSS treating of particular subjects.(5-8).

5.

Of digging a canal. Put this in the Book of useful inventions and in proving them bring forward the propositions already proved. And this is the proper order; since if you wished to show the usefulness of any plan you would be obliged again to devise new machines to prove its utility and thus would confuse the order of the forty Books and also the order of the diagrams; that is to say you would have to mix up practice with theory, which would produce a confused and incoherent work.

6.

I am not to blame for putting forward, in the course of my work on science, any general rule derived from a previous conclusion.

7.

The Book of the science of Mechanics must precede the Book of useful inventions.--Have your books on anatomy bound! [Footnote: 4. The numerous notes on anatomy written on loose leaves and now in the Royal collection at Windsor can best be classified in four Books, corresponding to the different character and size of the paper. When Leonardo speaks of 'li tua libri di notomia', he probably means the MSS. which still exist; if this hypothesis is correct the present condition of these leaves might seem to prove that he only carried out his purpose with one of the Books on anatomy. A borrowed book on Anatomy is mentioned in F.O.]

8.

The order of your book must proceed on this plan: first simple beams, then (those) supported from below, then suspended in part, then wholly [suspended]. Then beams as supporting other weights [Footnote: 4. Leonardo's notes on Mechanics are extraordinarily numerous; but, for the reasons assigned in my introduction, they have not been included in the present work.].

General introductions to the book on Painting (9-13).

9.

INTRODUCTION.

Seeing that I can find no subject specially useful or pleasing--since the men who have come before me have taken for their own every useful or necessary theme--I must do like one who, being poor, comes last to the fair, and can find no other way of providing himself than by taking all the things already seen by other buyers, and not taken but refused by reason of their lesser value. I, then, will load my humble pack with this despised and rejected merchandise, the refuse of so many buyers; and will go about to distribute it, not indeed in great cities, but in the poorer towns, taking such a price as the wares I offer may be worth. [Footnote: It need hardly be pointed out that there is in this 'Proemio' a covert irony. In the second and third prefaces, Leonardo characterises his rivals and opponents more closely. His protest is directed against Neo-latinism as professed by most of the humanists of his time; its futility is now no longer questioned.]

10.

INTRODUCTION.

I know that many will call this useless work [Footnote: 3. questa essere opera inutile. By opera we must here understand libro di pittura and particularly the treatise on Perspective.]; and they will be those of whom Demetrius [Footnote: 4. Demetrio. "With regard to the passage attributed to Demetrius", Dr. H. MULLER STRUBING writes, "I know not what to make of it. It is certainly not Demetrius Phalereus that is meant and it can hardly be Demetrius Poliorcetes. Who then can it be--for the name is a very common one? It may be a clerical error for Demades and the maxim is quite in the spirit of his writings I have not however been able to find any corresponding passage either in the 'Fragments' (C. MULLER, Orat. Att., II. 441) nor in the Supplements collected by DIETZ (Rhein. Mus., vol. 29, p. 108)."

The same passage occurs as a simple Memorandum in the MS. Tr. 57, apparently as a note for this 'Proemio' thus affording some data as to the time where these introductions were written.] declared that he took no more account of the wind that came out their mouth in words, than of that they expelled from their lower parts: men who desire nothing but material riches and are absolutely devoid of that of wisdom, which is the food and the only true riches of the mind. For so much more worthy as the soul is than the body, so much more noble are the possessions of the soul than those of the body. And often, when I see one of these men take this work in his hand, I wonder that he does not put it to his nose, like a monkey, or ask me if it is something good to eat.

[Footnote: In the original, the Proemio di prospettiva cioe dell'uffitio dell'occhio (see No. 21) stands between this and the preceding one, No. 9.]

INTRODUCTION.

I am fully concious that, not being a literary man, certain presumptuous persons will think that they may reasonably blame me; alleging that I am not a man of letters. Foolish folks! do they not know that I might retort as Marius did to the Roman Patricians [Footnote 21: Come Mario disse ai patriti Romani. "I am unable to find the words here attributed by Leonardo to Marius, either in Plutarch's Life of Marius or in the Apophthegmata (Moralia, p.202). Nor do they occur in the writings of Valerius Maximus (who frequently mentions Marius) nor in Velleius Paterculus (II, 11 to 43), Dio Cassius, Aulus Gellius, or Macrobius. Professor E. MENDELSON of Dorpat, the editor of Herodian, assures me that no such passage is the found in that author" (communication from Dr. MULLER STRUBING). Leonardo evidently meant to allude to some well known incident in Roman history and the mention of Marius is the result probably of some confusion. We may perhaps read, for Marius, Menenius Agrippa, though in that case it is true we must alter Patriti to Plebei. The change is a serious one. but it would render the passage perfectly clear.] by saying: That they, who deck themselves out in the labours of others will not allow me my own. They will say that I, having no literary skill, cannot properly express that which I desire to treat of [Footnote 26: le mie cose .... che d'altra parola. This can hardly be reconciled with Mons. RAVAISSON'S estimate of L. da Vinci's learning. "Leonard de Vinci etait un admirateur et un disciple des anciens, aussi bien dans l'art que dans la science et il tenait a passer pour tel meme aux yeux de la posterite." Gaz. des Beaux arts. Oct. 1877.]; but they do not know that my subjects are to be dealt with by experience rather than by words [Footnote 28: See Footnote 26]; and [experience] has been the mistress of those who wrote well. And so, as mistress, I will cite her in all cases.

11.

Though I may not, like them, be able to quote other authors, I shall rely on that which is much greater and more worthy:--on experience, the mistress of their Masters. They go about puffed up and pompous, dressed and decorated with [the fruits], not of their own labours, but of those of others. And they will not allow me my own. They will scorn me as an inventor; but how much more might they--who are not inventors but vaunters and declaimers of the works of others--be blamed.

INTRODUCTION.

And those men who are inventors and interpreters between Nature and Man, as compared with boasters and declaimers of the works of others, must be regarded and not otherwise esteemed than as the object in front of a mirror, when compared with its image seen in the mirror. For the first is something in itself, and the other nothingness.--Folks little indebted to Nature, since it is only by chance that they wear the human form and without it I might class them with the herds of beasts.

12.

Many will think they may reasonably blame me by alleging that my proofs are opposed to the authority of certain men held in the highest reverence by their inexperienced judgments; not considering that my works are the issue of pure and simple experience, who is the one true mistress. These rules are sufficient to enable you to know the true from the false--and this aids men to look only for things that are possible and with due moderation--and not to wrap yourself in ignorance, a thing which can have no good result, so that in despair you would give yourself up to melancholy.

13.

Among all the studies of natural causes and reasons Light chiefly delights the beholder; and among the great features of Mathematics the certainty of its demonstrations is what preeminently (tends to) elevate the mind of the investigator. Perspective, therefore, must be preferred to all the discourses and systems of human learning. In this branch [of science] the beam of light is explained on those methods of demonstration which form the glory not so much of Mathematics as of Physics and are graced with the flowers of both [Footnote: 5. Such of Leonardo's notes on Optics or on Perspective as bear exclusively on Mathematics or Physics could not be included in the arrangement of the libro di pittura which is here presented to the reader. They are however but few.]. But its axioms being laid down at great length, I shall abridge them to a conclusive brevity, arranging them on the method both of their natural order and of mathematical demonstration; sometimes by deduction of the effects from the causes, and sometimes arguing the causes from the effects; adding also to my own conclusions some which, though not included in them, may nevertheless be inferred from them. Thus, if the Lord-- who is the light of all things--vouchsafe to enlighten me, I will treat of Light; wherefore I will divide the present work into 3 Parts [Footnote: 10. In the middle ages--for instance, by ROGER BACON, by VITELLONE, with whose works Leonardo was certainly familiar, and by all the writers of the Renaissance Perspective and Optics were not regarded as distinct sciences. Perspective, indeed, is in its widest application the science of seeing. Although to Leonardo the two sciences were clearly separate, it is not so as to their names; thus we find axioms in Optics under the heading Perspective. According to this arrangement of the materials for the theoretical portion of the libro di pittura propositions in Perspective and in Optics stand side by side or occur alternately. Although this particular chapter deals only with Optics, it is not improbable that the words partiro la presente opera in 3 parti may refer to the same division into three sections which is spoken of in chapters 14 to 17.].

The plan of the book on Painting (14--17).

14.

ON THE THREE BRANCHES OF PERSPECTIVE.

There are three branches of perspective; the first deals with the reasons of the (apparent) diminution of objects as they recede from the eye, and is known as Diminishing Perspective.--The second contains the way in which colours vary as they recede from the eye. The third and last is concerned with the explanation of how the objects [in a picture] ought to be less finished in proportion as they are remote (and the names are as follows):

Linear Perspective. The Perspective of Colour. The Perspective of Disappearance.

[Footnote: 13. From the character of the handwriting I infer that this passage was written before the year 1490.].

15.

ON PAINTING AND PERSPECTIVE.

The divisions of Perspective are 3, as used in drawing; of these, the first includes the diminution in size of opaque objects; the second treats of the diminution and loss of outline in such opaque objects; the third, of the diminution and loss of colour at long distances.

[Footnote: The division is here the same as in the previous chapter No. 14, and this is worthy of note when we connect it with the fact that a space of about 20 years must have intervened between the writing of the two passages.]

16.

THE DISCOURSE ON PAINTING.

Perspective, as bearing on drawing, is divided into three principal sections; of which the first treats of the diminution in the size of bodies at different distances. The second part is that which treats of the diminution in colour in these objects. The third [deals with] the diminished distinctness of the forms and outlines displayed by the objects at various distances.

17.

ON THE SECTIONS OF [THE BOOK ON] PAINTING.

The first thing in painting is that the objects it represents should appear in relief, and that the grounds surrounding them at different distances shall appear within the vertical plane of the foreground of the picture by means of the 3 branches of Perspective, which are: the diminution in the distinctness of the forms of the objects, the diminution in their magnitude; and the diminution in their colour. And of these 3 classes of Perspective the first results from [the structure of] the eye, while the other two are caused by the atmosphere which intervenes between the eye and the objects seen by it. The second essential in painting is appropriate action and a due variety in the figures, so that the men may not all look like brothers, &c.

[Footnote: This and the two foregoing chapters must have been written in 1513 to 1516. They undoubtedly indicate the scheme which Leonardo wished to carry out in arranging his researches on Perspective as applied to Painting. This is important because it is an evidence against the supposition of H. LUDWIG and others, that Leonardo had collected his principles of

Perspective in one book so early as before 1500; a Book which, according to the hypothesis, must have been lost at a very early period, or destroyed possibly, by the French (!) in 1500 (see H. LUDWIG. L. da Vinci: Das Buch van der Malerei. Vienna 1882 III, 7 and 8).]

The use of the book on Painting.

18.

These rules are of use only in correcting the figures; since every man makes some mistakes in his first compositions and he who knows them not, cannot amend them. But you, knowing your errors, will correct your works and where you find mistakes amend them, and remember never to fall into them again. But if you try to apply these rules in composition you will never make an end, and will produce confusion in your works.

These rules will enable you to have a free and sound judgment; since good judgment is born of clear understanding, and a clear understanding comes of reasons derived from sound rules, and sound rules are the issue of sound experience--the common mother of all the sciences and arts. Hence, bearing in mind the precepts of my rules, you will be able, merely by your amended judgment, to criticise and recognise every thing that is out of proportion in a work, whether in the perspective or in the figures or any thing else.

Necessity of theoretical knowledge (19. 20).

19.

OF THE MISTAKES MADE BY THOSE WHO PRACTISE WITHOUT KNOWLEDGE.

Those who are in love with practice without knowledge are like the sailor who gets into a ship without rudder or compass and who never can be certain whether he is going. Practice must always be founded on sound theory, and to this Perspective is the guide and the gateway; and without this nothing can be done well in the matter of drawing.

20.

The painter who draws merely by practice and by eye, without any reason, is like a mirror which copies every thing placed in front of it without being conscious of their existence.

The function of the eye (21-23).

21.

INTRODUCTION TO PERSPECTIVE:--THAT IS OF THE FUNCTION OF THE EYE.

Behold here O reader! a thing concerning which we cannot trust our forefathers, the ancients, who tried to define what the Soul and Life are--which are beyond proof, whereas those things, which can at any time be clearly known and proved by experience, remained for many ages unknown or falsely understood. The eye, whose function we so certainly know by experience, has, down to my own time, been defined by an infinite number of authors as one thing; but I find, by experience, that it is quite another. [Footnote 13: Compare the note to No. 70.]

[Footnote: In section 13 we already find it indicated that the study of Perspective and of Optics is to be based on that of the functions of the eye. Leonardo also refers to the science of the eye, in his astronomical researches, for instance in MS. F 25b 'Ordine del provare la terra essere una stella: Imprima difinisce l'occhio', &c. Compare also MS. E 15b and F 60b. The principles of astronomical perspective.]

22.

Here [in the eye] forms, here colours, here the character of every part of the universe are concentrated to a point; and that point is so marvellous a thing ... Oh! marvellous, O stupendous Necessity--by thy laws thou dost compel every effect to be the direct result of its cause, by the shortest path. These [indeed] are miracles;...

In so small a space it can be reproduced and rearranged in its whole expanse. Describe in your anatomy what proportion there is between the diameters of all the images in the eye and the distance from them of the crystalline lens.

23.

OF THE 10 ATTRIBUTES OF THE EYE, ALL CONCERNED IN PAINTING.

Painting is concerned with all the 10 attributes of sight; which are:--Darkness, Light, Solidity and Colour, Form and Position, Distance and Propinquity, Motion and Rest. This little work of mine will be a tissue [of the studies] of these attributes, reminding the painter of the rules and methods by which he should use his art to imitate all the works of Nature which adorn the world.

24.

ON PAINTING.

Variability of the eye.

1st. The pupil of the eye contracts, in proportion to the increase of light which is reflected in it. 2nd. The pupil of the eye expands in proportion to the diminution in the day light, or any other light, that is reflected in it. 3rd. [Footnote: 8. The subject of this third proposition we find fully discussed in MS. G. 44a.]. The eye perceives and recognises the objects of its vision with greater intensity in proportion as the pupil is more widely dilated; and this can be proved by the case of nocturnal animals, such as cats, and certain birds-- as the owl and others--in which the pupil varies in a high degree from large to small, &c., when in the dark or in the light. 4th. The eye [out of doors] in an illuminated atmosphere sees darkness behind the windows of houses which [nevertheless] are light. 5th. All colours when placed in the shade appear of an equal degree of darkness, among themselves. 6th. But all colours when placed in a full light, never vary from their true and essential hue.

25.

OF THE EYE.

Focus of sight.

If the eye is required to look at an object placed too near to it, it cannot judge of it well--as happens to a man who tries to see the tip of his nose. Hence, as a general rule, Nature teaches us that an object can never be seen perfectly unless the space between it and the eye is equal, at least, to the length of the face.

Differences of perception by one eye and by both eyes (26-29).

26.

OF THE EYE.

When both eyes direct the pyramid of sight to an object, that object becomes clearly seen and comprehended by the eyes.

27.

Objects seen by one and the same eye appear sometimes large, and sometimes small.

28.

The motion of a spectator who sees an object at rest often makes it seem as though the object at rest had acquired the motion of the moving body, while the moving person appears to be at rest.

ON PAINTING.

Objects in relief, when seen from a short distance with one eye, look like a perfect picture. If you look with the eye a, b at the spot c, this point c will appear to be at d, f, and if you look at it with the eye g, h will appear to be at m. A picture can never contain in itself both aspects.

29.

Let the object in relief t be seen by both eyes; if you will look at the object with the right eye m, keeping the left eye n shut, the object will appear, or fill up the space, at a; and if you shut the right eye and open the left, the object (will occupy the) space b; and if you open both eyes, the object will no longer appear at a or b, but at e, r, f. Why will not a picture seen by both eyes produce the effect of relief, as [real] relief does when seen by both eyes; and why should a picture seen with one eye give the same effect of relief as real relief would under the same conditions of light and shade?

[Footnote: In the sketch, m is the left eye and n the right, while the text reverses this lettering. We must therefore suppose that the face in which the eyes m and n are placed is opposite to the spectator.]

30.

The comparative size of the image depends on the amount of light (30-39).

The eye will hold and retain in itself the image of a luminous body better than that of a shaded object. The reason is that the eye is in itself perfectly dark and since two things that are alike cannot be distinguished, therefore the night, and other dark objects cannot be seen or recognised by the eye. Light is totally contrary and gives more distinctness, and counteracts and differs from the usual darkness of the eye, hence it leaves the impression of its image.

31.

Every object we see will appear larger at midnight than at midday, and larger in the morning than at midday.

This happens because the pupil of the eye is much smaller at midday than at any other time.

32.

The pupil which is largest will see objects the largest. This is evident when we look at luminous bodies, and particularly at those in the sky. When the eye comes out of darkness and suddenly looks up at these bodies, they at first appear larger and then diminish; and if you were to look at those bodies through a small opening, you would see them smaller still, because a smaller part of the pupil would exercise its function.

[Footnote: 9. buso in the Lomb. dialect is the same as buco.]

33.

When the eye, coming out of darkness suddenly sees a luminous body, it will appear much larger at first sight than after long looking at it. The illuminated object will look larger and more brilliant, when seen with two eyes than with only one. A luminous object will appear smaller in size, when the eye sees it through a smaller opening. A luminous body of an oval form will appear rounder in proportion as it is farther from the eye.

34.

Why when the eye has just seen the light, does the half light look dark to it, and in the same way if it turns from the darkness the half light look very bright?

35.

ON PAINTING.

If the eye, when [out of doors] in the luminous atmosphere, sees a place in shadow, this will look very much darker than it really is. This happens only because the eye when out in the air contracts the pupil in proportion as the atmosphere reflected in it is more luminous. And the more the pupil contracts, the less luminous do the objects appear that it sees. But as soon as the eye enters into a shady place the darkness of the shadow suddenly seems to diminish. This occurs because the greater the darkness into which the pupil goes the more its size increases, and this increase makes the darkness seem less.

[Footnote 14: La luce entrera. Luce occurs here in the sense of pupil of the eye as in no 51: C. A. 84b; 245a; I--5; and in many other places.]

36.

ON PERSPECTIVE.

The eye which turns from a white object in the light of the sun and goes into a less fully lighted place will see everything as dark. And this happens either because the pupils of the eyes which have rested on this brilliantly lighted white object have contracted so much that, given at first a certain extent of surface, they will have lost more than 3/4 of their size; and, lacking in size, they are also deficient in [seeing] power. Though you might say to me: A little bird (then) coming down would see comparatively little, and from the smallness of his pupils the white might seem black! To this I should reply that here we must have regard to the proportion of the mass of that portion of the brain which is given up to the sense of sight and to nothing else. Or--to return--this pupil in Man dilates and contracts according to the brightness or darkness of (surrounding) objects; and since it takes some time to dilate and contract, it cannot see immediately on going out of the light and into the shade, nor, in the same way, out of the shade into the light, and this very thing has already deceived me in painting an eye, and from that I learnt it.

37.

Experiment [showing] the dilatation and contraction of the pupil, from the motion of the sun and other luminaries. In proportion as the sky is darker the stars appear of larger size, and if you were to light up the medium these stars would look smaller; and this difference arises solely from the pupil which dilates and contracts with the amount of light in the medium which is interposed between the eye and the luminous body. Let the experiment be made, by placing a candle above your head at the same time that you look at a star; then gradually lower the candle till it is on a level with the ray that comes from the star to the eye, and then you will see the star diminish so much that you will almost lose sight of it.

[Footnote: No reference is made in the text to the letters on the accompanying diagram.]

38.

The pupil of the eye, in the open air, changes in size with every degree of motion from the sun; and at every degree of its changes one and the same object seen by it will appear of a different size; although most frequently the relative scale of surrounding objects does not allow us to detect these variations in any single object we may look at.

39.

The eye--which sees all objects reversed--retains the images for some time. This conclusion is proved by the results; because, the eye having gazed at light retains some impression of it. After looking (at it) there remain in the eye images of intense brightness, that make any less brilliant spot seem dark until the eye has lost the last trace of the impression of the stronger light.

II. Linear Perspective.

We see clearly from the concluding sentence of section 49, where the author directly addresses the painter, that he must certainly have intended to include the elements of mathematics in his Book on the art of Painting. They are therefore here placed at the beginning. In section 50 the theory of the "Pyramid of Sight" is distinctly and expressly put forward as the fundamental principle of linear perspective, and sections 52 to 57 treat of it fully. This theory of sight can scarcely be traced to any author of antiquity. Such passages as occur in Euclid for instance, may, it is true, have proved suggestive to the painters of the Renaissance, but it would be rash to say any thing decisive on this point.

Leon Battista Alberti treats of the "Pyramid of Sight" at some length in his first Book of Painting; but his explanation differs widely from Leonardo's in the details. Leonardo, like Alberti, may have borrowed the broad lines of his theory from some views commonly accepted among painters at the time; but he certainly worked out its application in a perfectly original manner.

The axioms as to the perception of the pyramid of rays are followed by explanations of its origin, and proofs of its universal application (58--69). The author recurs to the subject with endless variations; it is evidently of fundamental importance in his artistic theory and practice. It is unnecessary to discuss how far this theory has any scientific value at the present day; so much as this, at any rate, seems certain: that from the artist's point of view it may still claim to be of immense practical utility.

According to Leonardo, on one hand, the laws of perspective are an inalienable condition of the existence of objects in space; on the other hand, by a natural law, the eye, whatever it sees and wherever it turns, is subjected to the perception of the pyramid of rays in the form of a minute target. Thus it sees objects in perspective independently of the will of the spectator, since the eye receives the images by means of the pyramid of rays "just as a magnet attracts iron".

In connection with this we have the function of the eye explained by the Camera obscura, and this is all the more interesting and important because no writer previous to Leonardo had treated of this subject (70--73). Subsequent passages, of no less special interest, betray his knowledge of refraction and of the inversion of the image in the camera and in the eye (74--82).

From the principle of the transmission of the image to the eye and to the camera obscura he deduces the means of producing an artificial construction of the pyramid of rays or--which is the same thing--of the image. The fundamental axioms as to the angle of sight and the vanishing point are thus presented in a manner which is as complete as it is simple and intelligible (86--89).

Leonardo distinguishes between simple and complex perspective (90, 91). The last sections treat of the apparent size of objects at various distances and of the way to estimate it (92--109).

General remarks on perspective (40-41).

40.

ON PAINTING.

Perspective is the best guide to the art of Painting.

[Footnote: 40. Compare 53, 2.]

41.

The art of perspective is of such a nature as to make what is flat appear in relief and what is in relief flat.

The elements of perspective--Of the Point (42-46).

42.

All the problems of perspective are made clear by the five terms of mathematicians, which are:--the point, the line, the angle, the superficies and the solid. The point is unique of its kind. And the point has neither height, breadth, length, nor depth, whence it is to be regarded as indivisible and as having no dimensions in space. The line is of three kinds, straight, curved and sinuous and it has neither breadth, height, nor depth. Hence it is indivisible, excepting in its length, and its ends are two points. The angle is the junction of two lines in a point.

43.

A point is not part of a line.

44.

OF THE NATURAL POINT.

The smallest natural point is larger than all mathematical points, and this is proved because the natural point has continuity, and any thing that is continuous is infinitely divisible; but the mathematical point is indivisible because it has no size.

[Footnote: This definition was inserted by Leonardo on a MS. copy on parchment of the well-known "Trattato d'Architettura civile e militare" &c. by FRANCESCO DI GIORGIO; opposite a passage where the author says: 'In prima he da sapere che punto e quella parie della quale he nulla--Linia he luncheza senza apieza; &c.]

45.

1, The superficies is a limitation of the body. 2, and the limitation of a body is no part of that body. 4, and the limitation of one body is that which begins another. 3, that which is not part of any body is nothing. Nothing is that which fills no space.

If one single point placed in a circle may be the starting point of an infinite number of lines, and the termination of an infinite number of lines, there must be an infinite number of points separable from this point, and these when reunited become one again; whence it follows that the part may be equal to the whole.

46.

The point, being indivisible, occupies no space. That which occupies no space is nothing. The limiting surface of one thing is the beginning of another. 2. That which is no part of any body is called nothing. 1. That which has no limitations, has no form. The limitations of two conterminous bodies are interchangeably the surface of each. All the surfaces of a body are not parts of that body.

Of the line (47-48).

47.

DEFINITION OF THE NATURE OF THE LINE.

The line has in itself neither matter nor substance and may rather be called an imaginary idea than a real object; and this being its nature it occupies no space. Therefore an infinite number of lines may be conceived of as intersecting each other at a point, which has no dimensions and is only of the thickness (if thickness it may be called) of one single line.

HOW WE MAY CONCLUDE THAT A SUPERFICIES TERMINATES IN A POINT?

An angular surface is reduced to a point where it terminates in an angle. Or, if the sides of that angle are produced in a straight line, then--beyond that angle--another surface is generated, smaller, or equal to, or larger than the first.

48.

OF DRAWING OUTLINE.

Consider with the greatest care the form of the outlines of every object, and the character of their undulations. And these undulations must be separately studied, as to whether the curves are composed of arched convexities or angular concavities.

49.

The nature of the outline.

The boundaries of bodies are the least of all things. The proposition is proved to be true, because the boundary of a thing is a surface, which is not part of the body contained within that surface; nor is it part of the air surrounding that body, but is the medium interposted between the air and the body, as is proved in its place. But the lateral boundaries of these bodies is the line forming the boundary of the surface, which line is of invisible thickness. Wherefore O painter! do not surround your bodies with lines, and above all when representing objects smaller than nature; for not only will their external outlines become indistinct, but their parts will be invisible from distance.

50.

Definition of Perspective.

[Drawing is based upon perspective, which is nothing else than a thorough knowledge of the function of the eye. And this function simply consists in receiving in a pyramid the forms and colours of all the objects placed before it. I say in a pyramid, because there is no object so small that it will not be larger than the spot where these pyramids are received into the eye. Therefore, if you extend the lines from the edges of each body as they converge you will bring them to a single point, and necessarily the said lines must form a pyramid.]

[Perspective is nothing more than a rational demonstration applied to the consideration of how objects in front of the eye transmit their image to it, by means of a pyramid of lines. The Pyramid is the name I apply to the lines which, starting from the surface and edges of each object, converge from a distance and meet in a single point.]

[Perspective is a rational demonstration, by which we may practically and clearly understand how objects transmit their own image, by lines forming a Pyramid (centred) in the eye.]

Perspective is a rational demonstration by which experience confirms that every object sends its image to the eye by a pyramid of lines; and bodies of equal size will result in a pyramid of larger or smaller size, according to the difference in their distance, one from the other. By a pyramid of lines I mean those which start from the surface and edges of bodies, and, converging from a distance meet in a single point. A point is said to be that which [having no dimensions] cannot be divided, and this point placed in the eye receives all the points of the cone.

[Footnote: 50. 1-5. Compare with this the Proem. No. 21. The paragraphs placed in brackets: lines 1-9, 10-14, and 17--20, are evidently mere sketches and, as such, were cancelled by the writer; but they serve as a commentary on the final paragraph, lines 22-29.]

51.

IN WHAT WAY THE EYE SEES OBJECTS PLACED IN FRONT OF IT.

The perception of the object depends on the direction of the eye.

Supposing that the ball figured above is the ball of the eye and let the small portion of the ball which is cut off by the line s t be the pupil and all the objects mirrored on the centre of the face of the eye, by means of the pupil, pass on at once and enter the pupil, passing through the crystalline humour, which does not interfere in the pupil with the things seen by means of the light. And the pupil having received the objects, by means of the light, immediately refers them and transmits them to the intellect by the line a b. And you must know that the pupil transmits nothing perfectly to the intellect or common sense excepting when the objects presented to it by means of light, reach it by the line a b; as, for instance, by the line b c. For although the lines m n and f g may be seen by the pupil they are not perfectly taken in, because they do not coincide with the line a b. And the proof is this: If the eye, shown above, wants to count the letters placed in front, the eye will be obliged to turn from letter to letter, because it cannot discern them unless they lie in the line a b; as, for instance, in the line a c. All visible objects reach the eye by the lines of a pyramid, and the point of the pyramid is the apex and centre of it, in the centre of the pupil, as figured above.

[Footnote: 51. In this problem the eye is conceived of as fixed and immovable; this is plain from line 11.]

Experimental proof of the existence of the pyramid of sight (52-55).

52.

Perspective is a rational demonstration, confirmed by experience, that all objects transmit their image to the eye by a pyramid of lines.

By a pyramid of lines I understand those lines which start from the edges of the surface of bodies, and converging from a distance, meet in a single point; and this point, in the present instance, I will show to be situated in the eye which is the universal judge of all objects. By a point I mean that which cannot be divided into parts; therefore this point, which is situated in the eye, being indivisible, no body is seen by the eye, that is not larger than this point. This being the case it is inevitable that the lines which come from the object to the point must form a pyramid. And if any man seeks to prove that the sense of sight does not reside in this point, but rather in the black spot which is visible in the middle of the pupil, I might reply to him that a small object could never diminish at any distance, as it might be a grain of millet or of oats or of some similar thing, and that object, if it were larger than the said [black] spot would never be seen as a whole; as may be seen in the diagram below. Let a. be the seat of sight, b e the lines which reach the eye. Let e d be the grains of millet within these lines. You plainly see that these will never diminish by distance, and that the body m n could not be entirely covered by it. Therefore you must confess that the eye contains within itself one single indivisible point a, to which all the points converge of the pyramid of lines starting from an object, as is shown below. Let a. b. be the eye; in the centre of it is the point above mentioned. If the line e f is to enter as an image into so small an opening in the eye, you must confess that the smaller object cannot enter into what is smaller than itself unless it is diminished, and by diminishing it must take the form of a pyramid.

53.

PERSPECTIVE.

Perspective comes in where judgment fails [as to the distance] in objects which diminish. The eye can never be a true judge for determining with exactitude how near one object is to another which is equal to it [in size], if the top of that other is on the level of the eye which sees them on that side, excepting by means of the vertical plane which is the standard and guide of perspective. Let n be the eye, e f the vertical plane above mentioned. Let a b c d be the three divisions, one below the other; if the lines a n and c n are of a given length and the eye n is in the centre, then a b will look as large as b c. c d is lower and farther off from n, therefore it will look smaller. And the same effect will appear in the three divisions of a face when the eye of the painter who is drawing it is on a level with the eye of the person he is painting.

54.

TO PROVE HOW OBJECTS REACH THE EYE.

If you look at the sun or some other luminous body and then shut your eyes you will see it again inside your eye for a long time. This is evidence that images enter into the eye.

The relations of the distance points to the vanishing point (55-56).

55.

ELEMENTS OF PERSPECTIVE.

All objects transmit their image to the eye in pyramids, and the nearer to the eye these pyramids are intersected the smaller will the image appear of the objects which cause them. Therefore, you may intersect the pyramid with a vertical plane [Footnote 4: Pariete. Compare the definitions in 85, 2-5, 6-27. These lines refer exclusively to the third diagram. For the better understanding of this it should be observed that c s must be regarded as representing the section or profile of a square plane, placed horizontally (comp. lines 11, 14, 17) for which the word pianura is subsequently employed (20, 22). Lines 6-13 contain certain preliminary observations to guide the reader in understanding the diagram; the last three seem to have been added as a supplement. Leonardo's mistake in writing t denota (line 6) for f denota has been rectified.] which reaches the base of the pyramid as is shown in the plane a n.

The eye f and the eye t are one and the same thing; but the eye f marks the distance, that is to say how far you are standing from the object; and the eye t shows you the direction of it; that is whether you are opposite, or on one side, or at an angle to the object you are looking at. And remember that the eye f and the eye t must always be kept on the same level. For example if you raise or lower the eye from the distance point f you must do the same with the direction point t. And if the point f shows how far the eye is distant from the square plane but does not show on which side it is placed--and, if in the same way, the point t show s the direction and not the distance, in order to ascertain both you must use both points and they will be one and the same thing. If the eye f could see a perfect square of which all the sides were equal to the distance between s and c, and if at the nearest end of the side towards the eye a pole were placed, or some other straight object, set up by a perpendicular line as shown at r s--then, I say, that if you were to look at the side of the square that is nearest to you it will appear at the bottom of the vertical plane r s, and then look at the farther side and it would appear to you at the height of the point n on the vertical plane. Thus, by this example, you can understand that if the eye is above a number of objects all placed on the same level, one beyond another, the more remote they are the higher they will seem, up to the level of the eye, but no higher; because objects placed upon the level on which your feet stand, so long as it is flat--even if it be extended into infinity--would never be seen above the eye; since the eye has in itself the point towards which all the cones tend and converge which convey the images of the objects to the eye. And this point always coincides with the point of diminution which is the extreme of all we can see. And from the base line of the first pyramid as far as the diminishing point

[Footnote: The two diagrams above the chapter are explained by the first five lines. They have, however, more letters than are referred to in the text, a circumstance we frequently find occasion to remark.]

56.

there are only bases without pyramids which constantly diminish up to this point. And from the first base where the vertical plane is placed towards the point in the eye there will be only pyramids without bases; as shown in the example given above. Now, let a b be the said vertical plane and r the point of the pyramid terminating in the eye, and n the point of diminution which is always in a straight line opposite the eye and always moves as the eye moves--just as when a rod is moved its shadow moves, and moves with it, precisely as the shadow moves with a body. And each point is the apex of a pyramid, all having a common base with the intervening vertical plane. But although their bases are equal their angles are not equal, because the diminishing point is the termination of a smaller angle than that of the eye. If you ask me: "By what practical experience can you show me these points?" I reply--so far as concerns the diminishing point which moves with you --when you walk by a ploughed field look at the straight furrows which come down with their ends to the path where you are walking, and you will see that each pair of furrows will look as though they tried to get nearer and meet at the [farther] end.

[Footnote: For the easier understanding of the diagram and of its connection with the preceding I may here remark that the square plane shown above in profile by the line c s is here indicated by e d o p. According to lines 1, 3 a b must be imagined as a plane of glass placed perpendicularly at o p.]

57.

How to measure the pyramid of vision.

As regards the point in the eye; it is made more intelligible by this: If you look into the eye of another person you will see your own image. Now imagine 2 lines starting from your ears and going to the ears of that image which you see in the other man's eye; you will understand that these lines converge in such a way that they would meet in a point a little way beyond your own image mirrored in the eye. And if you want to measure the diminution of the pyramid in the air which occupies the space between the object seen and the eye, you must do it according to the diagram figured below. Let m n be a tower, and e f a, rod, which you must move backwards and forwards till its ends correspond with those of the tower [Footnote 9: I sua stremi .. della storre (its ends ... of the tower) this is the case at e f.]; then bring it nearer to the eye, at c d and you will see that the image of the tower seems smaller, as at r o. Then [again] bring it closer to the eye and you will see the rod project far beyond the image of the tower from a to b and from t to b, and so you will discern that, a little farther within, the lines must converge in a point.

The Production of pyramid of Vision (58-60).

58.

PERSPECTIVE.

The instant the atmosphere is illuminated it will be filled with an infinite number of images which are produced by the various bodies and colours assembled in it. And the eye is the target, a loadstone, of these images.

59.

The whole surface of opaque bodies displays its whole image in all the illuminated atmosphere which surrounds them on all sides.

60.

That the atmosphere attracts to itself, like a loadstone, all the images of the objects that exist in it, and not their forms merely but their nature may be clearly seen by the sun, which is a hot and luminous body. All the atmosphere, which is the all-pervading matter, absorbs light and heat, and reflects in itself the image of the source of that heat and splendour and, in each minutest portion, does the same. The Northpole does the same as the loadstone shows; and the moon and the other planets, without suffering any diminution, do the same. Among terrestrial things musk does the same and other perfumes.

61.

All bodies together, and each by itself, give off to the surrounding air an infinite number of images which are all-pervading and each complete, each conveying the nature, colour and form of the body which produces it.

It can clearly be shown that all bodies are, by their images, all-pervading in the surrounding atmosphere, and each complete in itself as to substance form and colour; this is seen by the images of the various bodies which are reproduced in one single perforation through which they transmit the objects by lines which intersect and cause reversed pyramids, from the objects, so that they are upside down on the dark plane where they are first reflected. The reason of this is--

[Footnote: The diagram intended to illustrate the statement (Pl. II No. i) occurs in the original between lines 3 and 4. The three circles must be understood to represent three luminous bodies which transmit their images through perforations in a wall into a dark chamber, according to a law which is more fully explained in 75?81. So far as concerns the present passage the diagram is only intended to explain that the images of the three bodies may be made to coalesce at any given spot. In the circles are written, giallo--yellow, biacho--white, rosso--red.

The text breaks off at line 8. The paragraph No.40 follows here in the original MS.]

62.

Every point is the termination of an infinite number of lines, which diverge to form a base, and immediately, from the base the same lines converge to a pyramid [imaging] both the colour and form. No sooner is a form created or compounded than suddenly infinite lines and angles are produced from it; and these lines, distributing themselves and intersecting each other in the air, give rise to an infinite number of angles opposite to each other. Given a base, each opposite angle, will form a triangle having a form and proportion equal to the larger angle; and if the base goes twice into each of the 2 lines of the pyramid the smaller triangle will do the same.

63.

Every body in light and shade fills the surrounding air with infinite images of itself; and these, by infinite pyramids diffused in the air, represent this body throughout space and on every side. Each pyramid that is composed of a long assemblage of rays includes within itself an infinite number of pyramids and each has the same power as all, and all as each. A circle of equidistant pyramids of vision will give to their object angles of equal size; and an eye at each point will see the object of the same size. The body of the atmosphere is full of infinite pyramids composed of radiating straight lines, which are produced from the surface of the bodies in light and shade, existing in the air; and the farther they are from the object which produces them the more acute they become and although in their distribution they intersect and cross they never mingle together, but pass through all the surrounding air, independently converging, spreading, and diffused. And they are all of equal power [and value]; all equal to each, and each equal to all. By these the images of objects are transmitted through all space and in every direction, and each pyramid, in itself, includes, in each minutest part, the whole form of the body causing it.

64.

The body of the atmosphere is full of infinite radiating pyramids produced by the objects existing in it. These intersect and cross each other with independent convergence without interfering with each other and pass through all the surrounding atmosphere; and are of equal force and value--all being equal to each, each to all. And by means of these, images of the body are transmitted everywhere and on all sides, and each receives in itself every minutest portion of the object that produces it.

Proof by experiment (65-66).

65.

PERSPECTIVE.

The air is filled with endless images of the objects distributed in it; and all are represented in all, and all in one, and all in each, whence it happens that if two mirrors are placed in such a manner as to face each other exactly, the first will be reflected in the second and the second in the first. The first being reflected in the second takes to it the image of itself with all the images represented in it, among which is the image of the second mirror, and so, image within image, they go on to infinity in such a manner as that each mirror has within it a mirror, each smaller than the last and one inside the other. Thus, by this example, it is clearly proved that every object sends its image to every spot whence the object itself can be seen; and the converse: That the same object may receive in itself all the images of the objects that are in front of it. Hence the eye transmits through the atmosphere its own image to all the objects that are in front of it and receives them into itself, that is to say on its surface, whence they are taken in by the common sense, which considers them and if they are pleasing commits them to the memory. Whence I am of opinion: That the invisible images in the eyes are produced towards the object, as the image of the object to the eye. That the images of the objects must be disseminated through the air. An instance may be seen in several mirrors placed in a circle, which will reflect each other endlessly. When one has reached the other it is returned to the object that produced it, and thence--being diminished--it is returned again to the object and then comes back once more, and this happens endlessly. If you put a light between two flat mirrors with a distance of 1 braccio between them you will see in each of them an infinite number of lights, one smaller than another, to the last. If at night you put a light between the walls of a room, all the parts of that wall will be tinted with the image of that light. And they will receive the light and the light will fall on them, mutually, that is to say, when there is no obstacle to interrupt the transmission of the images. This same example is seen in a greater degree in the distribution of the solar rays which all together, and each by itself, convey to the object the image of the body which causes it. That each body by itself alone fills with its images the atmosphere around it, and that the same air is able, at the same time, to receive the images of the endless other objects which are in it, this is clearly proved by these examples. And every object is everywhere visible in the whole of the atmosphere, and the whole in every smallest part of it; and all the objects in the whole, and all in each smallest part; each in all and all in every part.

66.

The images of objects are all diffused through the atmosphere which receives them; and all on every side in it. To prove this, let a c e be objects of which the images are admitted to a dark chamber by the small holes n p and thrown upon the plane f i opposite to these holes. As many images will be produced in the chamber on the plane as the number of the said holes.

67.

General conclusions.

All objects project their whole image and likeness, diffused and mingled in the whole of the atmosphere, opposite to themselves. The image of every point of the bodily surface, exists in every part of the atmosphere. All the images of the objects are in every part of the atmosphere. The whole, and each part of the image of the atmosphere is [reflected] in each point of the surface of the bodies presented to it. Therefore both the part and the whole of the images of the objects exist, both in the whole and in the parts of the surface of these visible bodies. Whence we may evidently say that the image of each object exists, as a whole and in every part, in each part and in the whole interchangeably in every existing body. As is seen in two mirrors placed opposite to each other.

68.

That the contrary is impossible.

It is impossible that the eye should project from itself, by visual rays, the visual virtue, since, as soon as it opens, that front portion [of the eye] which would give rise to this emanation would have to go forth to the object and this it could not do without time. And this being so, it could not travel so high as the sun in a month's time when the eye wanted to see it. And if it could reach the sun it would necessarily follow that it should perpetually remain in a continuous line from the eye to the sun and should always diverge in such a way as to form between the sun and the eye the base and the apex of a pyramid. This being the case, if the eye consisted of a million worlds, it would not prevent its being consumed in the projection of its virtue; and if this virtue would have to travel through the air as perfumes do, the winds would bent it and carry it into another place. But we do [in fact] see the mass of the sun with the same rapidity as [an object] at the distance of a braccio, and the power of sight is not disturbed by the blowing of the winds nor by any other accident.

[Footnote: The view here refuted by Leonardo was maintained among others by Bramantino, Leonardo's Milanese contemporary. LOMAZZO writes as follows in his Trattato dell' Arte della pittura &c. (Milano 1584. Libr. V cp. XXI): Sovviemmi di aver gia letto in certi scritti alcune cose di Bramantino milanese, celebratissimo pittore, attenente alla prospettiva, le quali ho voluto riferire, e quasi intessere in questo luogo, affinche sappiamo qual fosse l'opinione di cosi chiaro e famoso pittore intorno alla prospettiva . . Scrive Bramantino che la prospettiva e una cosa che contrafa il naturale, e che cio si fa in tre modi

Circa il primo modo che si fa con ragione, per essere la cosa in poche parole conclusa da Bramantino in maniera che giudico non potersi dir meglio, contenendovi si tutta Parte del principio al fine, io riferiro per appunto le proprie parole sue (cp. XXII, Prima prospettiva di Bramantino). La prima prospettiva fa le cose di punto, e l'altra non mai, e la terza piu appresso. Adunque la prima si dimanda prospettiva, cioe ragione, la quale fa l'effetto dell' occhio, facendo crescere e calare secondo gli effetti degli occhi. Questo crescere e calare non procede della cosa propria, che in se per esser lontana, ovvero vicina, per quello effetto non puo crescere e sminuire, ma procede dagli effetti degli occhi, i quali sono piccioli, e percio volendo vedere tanto gran cosa, bisogna che mandino fuora la virtu visiva, la quale si dilata in tanta larghezza, che piglia tutto quello che vuoi vedere, ed arrivando a quella cosa la vede dove e: e da lei agli occhi per quello circuito fino all' occhio, e tutto quello termine e pieno di quella cosa.

It is worthy of note that Leonardo had made his memorandum refuting this view, at Milan in 1492]

69.

A parallel case.

Just as a stone flung into the water becomes the centre and cause of many circles, and as sound diffuses itself in circles in the air: so any object, placed in the luminous atmosphere, diffuses itself in circles, and fills the surrounding air with infinite images of itself. And is repeated, the whole every-where, and the whole in every smallest part. This can be proved by experiment, since if you shut a window that faces west and make a hole [Footnote: 6. Here the text breaks off.] . .

[Footnote: Compare LIBRI, Histoire des sciences mathematiques en Italie. Tome III, p. 43.]

The function of the eye as explained by the camera obscura (70. 71).

70.

If the object in front of the eye sends its image to the eye, the eye, on the other hand, sends its image to the object, and no portion whatever of the object is lost in the images it throws off, for any reason either in the eye or the object. Therefore we may rather believe it to be the nature and potency of our luminous atmosphere which absorbs the images of the objects existing in it, than the nature of the objects, to send their images through the air. If the object opposite to the eye were to send its image to the eye, the eye would have to do the same to the object, whence it might seem that these images were an emanation. But, if so, it would be necessary [to admit] that every object became rapidly smaller; because each object appears by its images in the surrounding atmosphere. That is: the whole object in the whole atmosphere, and in each part; and all the objects in the whole atmosphere and all of them in each part; speaking of that atmosphere which is able to contain in itself the straight and radiating lines of the images projected by the objects. From this it seems necessary to admit that it is in the nature of the atmosphere, which subsists between the objects, and which attracts the images of things to itself like a loadstone, being placed between them.

PROVE HOW ALL OBJECTS, PLACED IN ONE POSITION, ARE ALL EVERYWHERE AND ALL IN EACH PART.

I say that if the front of a building--or any open piazza or field--which is illuminated by the sun has a dwelling opposite to it, and if, in the front which does not face the sun, you make a small round hole, all the illuminated objects will project their images through that hole and be visible inside the dwelling on the opposite wall which may be made white; and there, in fact, they will be upside down, and if you make similar openings in several places in the same wall you will have the same result from each. Hence the images of the illuminated objects are all everywhere on this wall and all in each minutest part of it. The reason, as we clearly know, is that this hole must admit some light to the said dwelling, and the light admitted by it is derived from one or many luminous bodies. If these bodies are of various colours and shapes the rays forming the images are of various colours and shapes, and so will the representations be on the wall.

[Footnote: 70. 15--23. This section has already been published in the "Saggio delle Opere di Leonardo da Vinci" Milan 1872, pp. 13, 14. G. Govi observes upon it, that Leonardo is not to be regarded as the inventor of the Camera obscura, but that he was the first to explain by it the structure of the eye. An account of the Camera obscura first occurs in CESARE CESARINI's Italian version of Vitruvius, pub. 1523, four years after Leonardo's death. Cesarini expressly names Benedettino Don Papnutio as the inventor of the Camera obscura. In his explanation of the function of the eye by a comparison with the Camera obscura Leonardo was the precursor of G. CARDANO, Professor of Medicine at Bologna (died 1576) and it appears highly probable that this is, in fact, the very discovery which Leonardo ascribes to himself in section 21 without giving any further details.]

71.

HOW THE IMAGES OF OBJECTS RECEIVED BY THE EYE INTERSECT WITHIN THE CRYSTALLINE HUMOUR OF THE EYE.

An experiment, showing how objects transmit their images or pictures, intersecting within the eye in the crystalline humour, is seen when by some small round hole penetrate the images of illuminated objects into a very dark chamber. Then, receive these images on a white paper placed within this dark room and rather near to the hole and you will see all the objects on the paper in their proper forms and colours, but much smaller; and they will be upside down by reason of that very intersection. These images being transmitted from a place illuminated by the sun will seem actually painted on this paper which must be extremely thin and looked at from behind. And let the little perforation be made in a very thin plate of iron. Let a b e d e be the object illuminated by the sun and o r the front of the dark chamber in which is the said hole at n m. Let s t be the sheet of paper intercepting the rays of the images of these objects upside down, because the rays being straight, a on the right hand becomes k on the left, and e on the left becomes f on the right; and the same takes place inside the pupil.

[Footnote: This chapter is already known through a translation into French by VENTURI. Compare his 'Essai sur les ouvrages physico-mathematiques de L. da Vinci avec des fragments tires de ses Manuscrits, apportes de l'Italie. Lu a la premiere classe de l'Institut national des Sciences et Arts.' Paris, An V (1797).]

The practice of perspective (72. 73).

72.

In the practice of perspective the same rules apply to light and to the eye.

73.

The object which is opposite to the pupil of the eye is seen by that pupil and that which is opposite to the eye is seen by the pupil.

Refraction of the rays falling upon the eye (74. 75)

74.

The lines sent forth by the image of an object to the eye do not reach the point within the eye in straight lines.

75.

If the judgment of the eye is situated within it, the straight lines of the images are refracted on its surface because they pass through the rarer to the denser medium. If, when you are under water, you look at objects in the air you will see them out of their true place; and the same with objects under water seen from the air.

The intersection of the rays (76-82).

76.

The inversion of the images.

All the images of objects which pass through a window [glass pane] from the free outer air to the air confined within walls, are seen on the opposite side; and an object which moves in the outer air from east to west will seem in its shadow, on the wall which is lighted by this confined air, to have an opposite motion.

77.

THE PRINCIPLE ON WHICH THE IMAGES OF BODIES PASS IN BETWEEN THE MARGINS OF THE OPENINGS BY WHICH THEY ENTER.

What difference is there in the way in which images pass through narrow openings and through large openings, or in those which pass by the sides of shaded bodies? By moving the edges of the opening through which the images are admitted, the images of immovable objects are made to move. And this happens, as is shown in the 9th which demonstrates: [Footnote 11: per la 9a che dicie. When Leonardo refers thus to a number it serves to indicate marginal diagrams; this can in some instances be distinctly proved. The ninth sketch on the page W. L. 145 b corresponds to the middle sketch of the three reproduced.] the images of any object are all everywhere, and all in each part of the surrounding air. It follows that if one of the edges of the hole by which the images are admitted to a dark chamber is moved it cuts off those rays of the image that were in contact with it and gets nearer to other rays which previously were remote from it &c.

OF THE MOVEMENT OF THE EDGE AT THE RIGHT OR LEFT, OR THE UPPER, OR LOWER EDGE.

If you move the right side of the opening the image on the left will move [being that] of the object which entered on the right side of the opening; and the same result will happen with all the other sides of the opening. This can be proved by the 2nd of this which shows: all the rays which convey the images of objects through the air are straight lines. Hence, if the images of very large bodies have to pass through very small holes, and beyond these holes recover their large size, the lines must necessarily intersect.

[Footnote: 77. 2. In the first of the three diagrams Leonardo had drawn only one of the two margins, et m.]

78.

Necessity has provided that all the images of objects in front of the eye shall intersect in two places. One of these intersections is in the pupil, the other in the crystalline lens; and if this were not the case the eye could not see so great a number of objects as it does. This can be proved, since all the lines which intersect do so in a point. Because nothing is seen of objects excepting their surface; and their edges are lines, in contradistinction to the definition of a surface. And each minute part of a line is equal to a point; for smallest is said of that than which nothing can be smaller, and this definition is equivalent to the definition of the point. Hence it is possible for the whole circumference of a circle to transmit its image to the point of intersection, as is shown in the 4th of this which shows: all the smallest parts of the images cross each other without interfering with each other. These demonstrations are to illustrate the eye. No image, even of the smallest object, enters the eye without being turned upside down; but as it penetrates into the crystalline lens it is once more reversed and thus the image is restored to the same position within the eye as that of the object outside the eye.

79.

OF THE CENTRAL LINE OF THE EYE.

Only one line of the image, of all those that reach the visual virtue, has no intersection; and this has no sensible dimensions because it is a mathematical line which originates from a mathematical point, which has no dimensions.

According to my adversary, necessity requires that the central line of every image that enters by small and narrow openings into a dark chamber shall be turned upside down, together with the images of the bodies that surround it.

80.

AS TO WHETHER THE CENTRAL LINE OF THE IMAGE CAN BE INTERSECTED, OR NOT, WITHIN THE OPENING.

It is impossible that the line should intersect itself; that is, that its right should cross over to its left side, and so, its left side become its right side. Because such an intersection demands two lines, one from each side; for there can be no motion from right to left or from left to right in itself without such extension and thickness as admit of such motion. And if there is extension it is no longer a line but a surface, and we are investigating the properties of a line, and not of a surface. And as the line, having no centre of thickness cannot be divided, we must conclude that the line can have no sides to intersect each other. This is proved by the movement of the line a f to a b and of the line e b to e f, which are the sides of the surface a f e b. But if you move the line a b and the line e f, with the frontends a e, to the spot c, you will have moved the opposite ends f b towards each other at the point d. And from the two lines you will have drawn the straight line c d which cuts the middle of the intersection of these two lines at the point n without any intersection. For, you imagine these two lines as having breadth, it is evident that by this motion the first will entirely cover the other--being equal with it--without any intersection, in the position c d. And this is sufficient to prove our proposition.

81.

HOW THE INNUMERABLE RAYS FROM INNUMERABLE IMAGES CAN CONVERGE TO A POINT.

Just as all lines can meet at a point without interfering with each other--being without breadth or thickness--in the same way all the images of surfaces can meet there; and as each given point faces the object opposite to it and each object faces an opposite point, the converging rays of the image can pass through the point and diverge again beyond it to reproduce and re-magnify the real size of that image. But their impressions will appear reversed--as is shown in the first, above; where it is said that every image intersects as it enters the narrow openings made in a very thin substance.

Read the marginal text on the other side.

In proportion as the opening is smaller than the shaded body, so much less will the images transmitted through this opening intersect each other. The sides of images which pass through openings into a dark room intersect at a point which is nearer to the opening in proportion as the opening is narrower. To prove this let a b be an object in light and shade which sends not its shadow but the image of its darkened form through the opening d e which is as wide as this shaded body; and its sides a b, being straight lines (as has been proved) must intersect between the shaded object and the opening; but nearer to the opening in proportion as it is smaller than the object in shade. As is shown, on your right hand and your left hand, in the two diagrams a b c n m o where, the right opening d e, being equal in width to the shaded object a b, the intersection of the sides of the said shaded object occurs half way between the opening and the shaded object at the point c. But this cannot happen in the left hand figure, the opening o being much smaller than the shaded object n m.

It is impossible that the images of objects should be seen between the objects and the openings through which the images of these bodies are admitted; and this is plain, because where the atmosphere is illuminated these images are not formed visibly.

When the images are made double by mutually crossing each other they are invariably doubly as dark in tone. To prove this let d e h be such a doubling which although it is only seen within the space between the bodies in b and i this will not hinder its being seen from f g or from f m; being composed of the images a b i k which run together in d e h.

[Footnote: 81. On the original diagram at the beginning of this chapter Leonardo has written "azurro" (blue) where in the facsimile I have marked A, and "giallo" (yellow) where B stands.]

[Footnote: 15--23. These lines stand between the diagrams I and III.]

[Footnote: 24--53. These lines stand between the diagrams I and II.]

[Footnote: 54--97 are written along the left side of diagram I.]

82.

An experiment showing that though the pupil may not be moved from its position the objects seen by it may appear to move from their places.

If you look at an object at some distance from you and which is below the eye, and fix both your eyes upon it and with one hand firmly hold the upper lid open while with the other you push up the under lid--still keeping your eyes fixed on the object gazed at--you will see that object double; one [image] remaining steady, and the other moving in a contrary direction to the pressure of your finger on the lower eyelid. How false the opinion is of those who say that this happens because the pupil of the eye is displaced from its position.

How the above mentioned facts prove that the pupil acts upside down in seeing.

[Footnote: 82. 14--17. The subject indicated by these two headings is fully discussed in the two chapters that follow them in the original; but it did not seem to me appropriate to include them here.]

Demostration of perspective by means of a vertical glass plane (83-85).

83.

OF THE PLANE OF GLASS.

Perspective is nothing else than seeing place [or objects] behind a plane of glass, quite transparent, on the surface of which the objects behind that glass are to be drawn. These can be traced in pyramids to the point in the eye, and these pyramids are intersected on the glass plane.

84.

Pictorial perspective can never make an object at the same distance, look of the same size as it appears to the eye. You see that the apex of the pyramid f c d is as far from the object c d as the same point f is from the object a b; and yet c d, which is the base made by the painter's point, is smaller than a b which is the base of the lines from the objects converging in the eye and refracted at s t, the surface of the eye. This may be proved by experiment, by the lines of vision and then by the lines of the painter's plumbline by cutting the real lines of vision on one and the same plane and measuring on it one and the same object.

85.

PERSPECTIVE.

The vertical plane is a perpendicular line, imagined as in front of the central point where the apex of the pyramids converge. And this plane bears the same relation to this point as a plane of glass would, through which you might see the various objects and draw them on it. And the objects thus drawn would be smaller than the originals, in proportion as the distance between the glass and the eye was smaller than that between the glass and the objects.

PERSPECTIVE.

The different converging pyramids produced by the objects, will show, on the plane, the various sizes and remoteness of the objects causing them.

PERSPECTIVE.

All those horizontal planes of which the extremes are met by perpendicular lines forming right angles, if they are of equal width the more they rise to the level of eye the less this is seen, and the more the eye is above them the more will their real width be seen.

PERSPECTIVE.

The farther a spherical body is from the eye the more you will see of it.

The angle of sight varies with the distance (86-88)

86.

A simple and natural method; showing how objects appear to the eye without any other medium.

The object that is nearest to the eye always seems larger than another of the same size at greater distance. The eye m, seeing the spaces o v x, hardly detects the difference between them, and the. reason of this is that it is close to them [Footnote 6: It is quite inconceivable to me why M. RAVAISSON, in a note to his French translation of this simple passage should have remarked: Il est clair que c'est par erreur que Leonard a ecrit per esser visino au lieu de per non esser visino. (See his printed ed. of MS. A. p. 38.)]; but if these spaces are marked on the vertical plane n o the space o v will be seen at o r, and in the same way the space v x will appear at r q. And if you carry this out in any place where you can walk round, it will look out of proportion by reason of the great difference in the spaces o r and r q. And this proceeds from the eye being so much below [near] the plane that the plane is foreshortened. Hence, if you wanted to carry it out, you would have [to arrange] to see the perspective through a single hole which must be at the point m, or else you must go to a distance of at least 3 times the height of the object you see. The plane o p being always equally remote from the eye will reproduce the objects in a satisfactory way, so that they may be seen from place to place.

87.

How every large mass sends forth its images, which may diminish through infinity.

The images of any large mass being infinitely divisible may be infinitely diminished.

88.

Objects of equal size, situated in various places, will be seen by different pyramids which will each be smaller in proportion as the object is farther off.

89.

Perspective, in dealing with distances, makes use of two opposite pyramids, one of which has its apex in the eye and the base as distant as the horizon. The other has the base towards the eye and the apex on the horizon. Now, the first includes the [visible] universe, embracing all the mass of the objects that lie in front of the eye; as it might be a vast landscape seen through a very small opening; for the more remote the objects are from the eye, the greater number can be seen through the opening, and thus the pyramid is constructed with the base on the horizon and the apex in the eye, as has been said. The second pyramid is extended to a spot which is smaller in proportion as it is farther from the eye; and this second perspective [= pyramid] results from the first.

90.

SIMPLE PERSPECTIVE.

Simple perspective is that which is constructed by art on a vertical plane which is equally distant from the eye in every part. Complex perspective is that which is constructed on a ground-plan in which none of the parts are equally distant from the eye.

91.

PERSPECTIVE.

No surface can be seen exactly as it is, if the eye that sees it is not equally remote from all its edges.

92.

WHY WHEN AN OBJECT IS PLACED CLOSE TO THE EYE ITS EDGES ARE INDISTINCT.

When an object opposite the eye is brought too close to it, its edges must become too confused to be distinguished; as it happens with objects close to a light, which cast a large and indistinct shadow, so is it with an eye which estimates objects opposite to it; in all cases of linear perspective, the eye acts in the same way as the light. And the reason is that the eye has one leading line (of vision) which dilates with distance and embraces with true discernment large objects at a distance as well as small ones that are close.

But since the eye sends out a multitude of lines which surround this chief central one and since these which are farthest from the centre in this cone of lines are less able to discern with accuracy, it follows that an object brought close to the eye is not at a due distance, but is too near for the central line to be able to discern the outlines of the object. So the edges fall within the lines of weaker discerning power, and these are to the function of the eye like dogs in the chase which can put up the game but cannot take it. Thus these cannot take in the objects, but induce the central line of sight to turn upon them, when they have put them up. Hence the objects which are seen with these lines of sight have confused outlines.

The relative size of objects with regard to their distance from the eye (93-98).

93.

PERSPECTIVE.

Small objects close at hand and large ones at a distance, being seen within equal angles, will appear of the same size.

94.

PERSPECTIVE.

There is no object so large but that at a great distance from the eye it does not appear smaller than a smaller object near.

95.

Among objects of equal size that which is most remote from the eye will look the smallest. [Footnote: This axiom, sufficiently clear in itself, is in the original illustrated by a very large diagram, constructed like that here reproduced under No. 108.

The same idea is repeated in C. A. I a; I a, stated as follows: Infra le cose d'equal grandeza quella si dimostra di minor figura che sara piu distante dall' ochio.--]

96.

Why an object is less distinct when brought near to the eye, and why with spectacles, or without the naked eye sees badly either close or far off [as the case may be].

97.

PERSPECTIVE.

Among objects of equal size, that which is most remote from the eye will look the smallest.

98.

PERSPECTIVE.

No second object can be so much lower than the first as that the eye will not see it higher than the first, if the eye is above the second.

PERSPECTIVE.

And this second object will never be so much higher than the first as that the eye, being below them, will not see the second as lower than the first.

PERSPECTIVE.

If the eye sees a second square through the centre of a smaller one, that is nearer, the second, larger square will appear to be surrounded by the smaller one.

PERSPECTIVE--PROPOSITION.

Objects that are farther off can never be so large but that those in front, though smaller, will conceal or surround them.

DEFINITION.

This proposition can be proved by experiment. For if you look through a small hole there is nothing so large that it cannot be seen through it and the object so seen appears surrounded and enclosed by the outline of the sides of the hole. And if you stop it up, this small stopping will conceal the view of the largest object.

The apparent size of objects defined by calculation (99-105)

99.

OF LINEAR PERSPECTIVE.

Linear Perspective deals with the action of the lines of sight, in proving by measurement how much smaller is a second object than the first, and how much the third is smaller than the second; and so on by degrees to the end of things visible. I find by experience that if a second object is as far beyond the first as the first is from the eye, although they are of the same size, the second will seem half the size of the first and if the third object is of the same size as the 2nd, and the 3rd is as far beyond the second as the 2nd from the first, it will appear of half the size of the second; and so on by degrees, at equal distances, the next farthest will be half the size of the former object. So long as the space does not exceed the length of 20 braccia. But, beyond 20 braccia figures of equal size will lose 2/4 and at 40 braccia they will lose 9/10, and 19/20 at 60 braccia, and so on diminishing by degrees. This is if the picture plane is distant from you twice your own height. If it is only as far off as your own height, there will be a great difference between the first braccia and the second.

[Footnote: This chapter is included in DUFRESNE'S and MANZI'S editions of the Treatise on Painting. H. LUDWIG, in his commentary, calls this chapter "eines der wichtigsten im ganzen Tractat", but at the same time he asserts that its substance has been so completely disfigured in the best MS. copies that we ought not to regard Leonardo as responsible for it. However, in the case of this chapter, the old MS. copies agree with the original as it is reproduced above. From the chapters given later in this edition, which were written at a subsequent date, it would appear that Leonardo corrected himself on these points.]

100.

OF THE DIMINUTION OF OBJECTS AT VARIOUS DISTANCES.

A second object as far distant from the first as the first is from the eye will appear half the size of the first, though they be of the same size really.

OF THE DEGREES OF DIMINUTION.

If you place the vertical plane at one braccio from the eye, the first object, being at a distance of 4 braccia from your eye will diminish to 3/4 of its height at that plane; and if it is 8 braccia from the eye, to 7/8; and if it is 16 braccia off, it will diminish to 15/16 of its height and so on by degrees, as the space doubles the diminution will double.

101.

Begin from the line m f with the eye below; then go up and do the same with the line n f, then with the eye above and close to the 2 gauges on the ground look at m n; then as c m is to m n so will n m be to n s.

If a n goes 3 times into f b, m p will do the same into p g. Then go backwards so far as that c d goes twice into a n and p g will be equal to g h. And m p will go into h p as often as d c into o p.

[Footnote: The first three lines are unfortunately very obscure.]

102.

I GIVE THE DEGREES OF THE OBJECTS SEEN BY THE EYE AS THE MUSICIAN DOES THE NOTES HEARD BY THE EAR.

Although the objects seen by the eye do, in fact, touch each other as they recede, I will nevertheless found my rule on spaces of 20 braccia each; as a musician does with notes, which, though they can be carried on one into the next, he divides into degrees from note to note calling them 1st, 2nd, 3rd, 4th, 5th; and has affixed a name to each degree in raising or lowering the voice.

103.

PERSPECTIVE.

Let f be the level and distance of the eye; and a the vertical plane, as high as a man; let e be a man, then I say that on the plane this will be the distance from the plane to the 2nd man.

104.

The differences in the diminution of objects of equal size in consequence of their various remoteness from the eye will bear among themselves the same proportions as those of the spaces between the eye and the different objects.

Find out how much a man diminishes at a certain distance and what its length is; and then at twice that distance and at 3 times, and so make your general rule.

105.

The eye cannot judge where an object high up ought to descend.

106.

PERSPECTIVE.

If two similar and equal objects are placed one beyond the other at a given distance the difference in their size will appear greater in proportion as they are nearer to the eye that sees them. And conversely there will seem to be less difference in their size in proportion as they are remote from the eve.

This is proved by the proportions of their distances among themselves; for, if the first of these two objects were as far from the eye, as the 2nd from the first this would be called the second proportion: since, if the first is at 1 braccia from the eye and the 2nd at two braccia, two being twice as much as one, the first object will look twice as large as the second. But if you place the first at a hundred braccia from you and the second at a hundred and one, you will find that the first is only so much larger than the second as 100 is less than 101; and the converse is equally true. And again, the same thing is proved by the 4th of this book which shows that among objects that are equal, there is the same proportion in the diminution of the size as in the increase in the distance from the eye of the spectator.

On natural perspective (107--109).

107.

OF EQUAL OBJECTS THE MOST REMOTE LOOK THE SMALLEST.

The practice of perspective may be divided into ... parts [Footnote 4: in ... parte. The space for the number is left blank in the original.], of which the first treats of objects seen by the eye at any distance; and it shows all these objects just as the eye sees them diminished, without obliging a man to stand in one place rather than another so long as the plane does not produce a second foreshortening.

But the second practice is a combination of perspective derived partly from art and partly from nature and the work done by its rules is in every portion of it, influenced by natural perspective and artificial perspective. By natural perspective I mean that the plane on which this perspective is represented is a flat surface, and this plane, although it is parallel both in length and height, is forced to diminish in its remoter parts more than in its nearer ones. And this is proved by the first of what has been said above, and its diminution is natural. But artificial perspective, that is that which is devised by art, does the contrary; for objects equal in size increase on the plane where it is foreshortened in proportion as the eye is more natural and nearer to the plane, and as the part of the plane on which it is figured is farther from the eye.

And let this plane be d e on which are seen 3 equal circles which are beyond this plane d e, that is the circles a b c. Now you see that the eye h sees on the vertical plane the sections of the images, largest of those that are farthest and smallest of the nearest.

108.

Here follows what is wanting in the margin at the foot on the other side of this page.

Natural perspective acts in a contrary way; for, at greater distances the object seen appears smaller, and at a smaller distance the object appears larger. But this said invention requires the spectator to stand with his eye at a small hole and then, at that small hole, it will be very plain. But since many (men's) eyes endeavour at the same time to see one and the same picture produced by this artifice only one can see clearly the effect of this perspective and all the others will see confusion. It is well therefore to avoid such complex perspective and hold to simple perspective which does not regard planes as foreshortened, but as much as possible in their proper form. This simple perspective, in which the plane intersects the pyramids by which the images are conveyed to the eye at an equal distance from the eye is our constant experience, from the curved form of the pupil of the eye on which the pyramids are intersected at an equal distance from the visual virtue.

[Footnote 24: la prima di sopra i. e. the first of the three diagrams which, in the original MS., are placed in the margin at the beginning of this chapter.]

109.

OF A MIXTURE OF NATURAL AND ARTIFICIAL PERSPECTIVE.

This diagram distinguishes natural from artificial perspective. But before proceeding any farther I will define what is natural and what is artificial perspective. Natural perspective says that the more remote of a series of objects of equal size will look the smaller, and conversely, the nearer will look the larger and the apparent size will diminish in proportion to the distance. But in artificial perspective when objects of unequal size are placed at various distances, the smallest is nearer to the eye than the largest and the greatest distance looks as though it were the least of all; and the cause of this is the plane on which the objects are represented; and which is at unequal distances from the eye throughout its length. And this diminution of the plane is natural, but the perspective shown upon it is artificial since it nowhere agrees with the true diminution of the said plane. Whence it follows, that when the eye is somewhat removed from the [station point of the] perspective that it has been gazing at, all the objects represented look monstrous, and this does not occur in natural perspective, which has been defined above. Let us say then, that the square a b c d figured above is foreshortened being seen by the eye situated in the centre of the side which is in front. But a mixture of artificial and natural perspective will be seen in this tetragon called el main [Footnote 20: el main is quite legibly written in the original; the meaning and derivation of the word are equally doubtful.], that is to say e f g h which must appear to the eye of the spectator to be equal to a b c d so long as the eye remains in its first position between c and d. And this will be seen to have a good effect, because the natural perspective of the plane will conceal the defects which would [otherwise] seem monstrous.

Drawing of Caricatures

III. Six books on Light and Shade.

Linear Perspective cannot be immediately followed by either the "prospettiva de' perdimenti" or the "prospettiva de' colori" or the aerial perspective; since these branches of the subject presuppose a knowledge of the principles of Light and Shade. No apology, therefore, is here needed for placing these immediately after Linear Perspective.

We have various plans suggested by Leonardo for the arrangement of the mass of materials treating of this subject. Among these I have given the preference to a scheme propounded in No. III, because, in all probability, we have here a final and definite purpose expressed. Several authors have expressed it as their opinion that the Paris Manuscript C is a complete and finished treatise on Light and Shade. Certainly, the Principles of Light and Shade form by far the larger portion of this MS. which consists of two separate parts; still, the materials are far from being finally arranged. It is also evident that he here investigates the subject from the point of view of the Physicist rather than from that of the Painter.

The plan of a scheme of arrangement suggested in No. III and adopted by me has been strictly adhered to for the first four Books. For the three last, however, few materials have come down to us; and it must be admitted that these three Books would find a far more appropriate place in a work on Physics than in a treatise on Painting. For this reason I have collected in Book V all the chapters on Reflections, and in Book VI I have put together and arranged all the sections of MS. C that belong to the book on Painting, so far as they relate to Light and Shade, while the sections of the same MS. which treat of the "Prospettiva de' perdimenti" have, of course, been excluded from the series on Light and Shade.

[Footnote III: This text has already been published with some slight variations in Dozio's pamphlet Degli scritti e disegni di Leonardo da Vinci, Milan 1871, pp. 30--31. Dozio did not transcribe it from the original MS. which seems to have remained unknown to him, but from an old copy (MS. H. 227 in the Ambrosian Library).]

GENERAL INTRODUCTION.

Prolegomena.

110.

You must first explain the theory and then the practice. First you must describe the shadows and lights on opaque objects, and then on transparent bodies.

Scheme of the books on Light and shade.

111.

INTRODUCTION.

[Having already treated of the nature of shadows and the way in which they are cast [Footnote 2: Avendo io tractato.--We may suppose that he here refers to some particular MS., possibly Paris C.], I will now consider the places on which they fall; and their curvature, obliquity, flatness or, in short, any character I may be able to detect in them.]

Shadow is the obstruction of light. Shadows appear to me to be of supreme importance in perspective, because, without them opaque and solid bodies will be ill defined; that which is contained within their outlines and their boundaries themselves will be ill-understood unless they are shown against a background of a different tone from themselves. And therefore in my first proposition concerning shadow I state that every opaque body is surrounded and its whole surface enveloped in shadow and light. And on this proposition I build up the first Book. Besides this, shadows have in themselves various degrees of darkness, because they are caused by the absence of a variable amount of the luminous rays; and these I call Primary shadows because they are the first, and inseparable from the object to which they belong. And on this I will found my second Book. From these primary shadows there result certain shaded rays which are diffused through the atmosphere and these vary in character according to that of the primary shadows whence they are derived. I shall therefore call these shadows Derived shadows because they are produced by other shadows; and the third Book will treat of these. Again these derived shadows, where they are intercepted by various objects, produce effects as various as the places where they are cast and of this I will treat in the fourth Book. And since all round the derived shadows, where the derived shadows are intercepted, there is always a space where the light falls and by reflected dispersion is thrown back towards its cause, it meets the original shadow and mingles with it and modifies it somewhat in its nature; and on this I will compose my fifth Book. Besides this, in the sixth Book I will investigate the many and various diversities of reflections resulting from these rays which will modify the original [shadow] by [imparting] some of the various colours from the different objects whence these reflected rays are derived. Again, the seventh Book will treat of the various distances that may exist between the spot where the reflected rays fall and that where they originate, and the various shades of colour which they will acquire in falling on opaque bodies.

Different principles and plans of treatment (112--116).

112.

First I will treat of light falling through windows which I will call Restricted [Light] and then I will treat of light in the open country, to which I will give the name of diffused Light. Then I will treat of the light of luminous bodies.

113.

OF PAINTING.

The conditions of shadow and light [as seen] by the eye are 3. Of these the first is when the eye and the light are on the same side of the object seen; the 2nd is when the eye is in front of the object and the light is behind it. The 3rd is when the eye is in front of the object and the light is on one side, in such a way as that a line drawn from the object to the eye and one from the object to the light should form a right angle where they meet.

114.

OF PAINTING.

This is another section: that is, of the nature of a reflection (from) an object placed between the eye and the light under various aspects.

115.

OF PAINTING.

As regards all visible objects 3 things must be considered. These are the position of the eye which sees: that of the object seen [with regard] to the light, and the position of the light which illuminates the object, b is the eye, a the object seen, c the light, a is the eye, b the illuminating body, c is the illuminated object.

116.

Let a be the light, b the eye, c the object seen by the eye and in the light. These show, first, the eye between the light and the body; the 2nd, the light between the eye and the body; the 3rd the body between the eye and the light, a is the eye, b the illuminated object, c the light.

117.

OF PAINTING.

OF THE THREE KINDS OF LIGHT THAT ILLUMINATE OPAQUE BODIES.

The first kind of Light which may illuminate opaque bodies is called Direct light--as that of the sun or any other light from a window or flame. The second is Diffused [universal] light, such as we see in cloudy weather or in mist and the like. The 3rd is Subdued light, that is when the sun is entirely below the horizon, either in the evening or morning.

118.

OF LIGHT.

The lights which may illuminate opaque bodies are of 4 kinds. These are: diffused light as that of the atmosphere, within our horizon. And Direct, as that of the sun, or of a window or door or other opening. The third is Reflected light; and there is a 4th which is that which passes through [semi] transparent bodies, as linen or paper or the like, but not transparent like glass, or crystal, or other diaphanous bodies, which produce the same effect as though nothing intervened between the shaded object and the light that falls upon it; and this we will discuss fully in our discourse.

Definition of the nature of shadows (119--122).

119.

WHAT LIGHT AND SHADOW ARE.

Shadow is the absence of light, merely the obstruction of the luminous rays by an opaque body. Shadow is of the nature of darkness. Light [on an object] is of the nature of a luminous body; one conceals and the other reveals. They are always associated and inseparable from all objects. But shadow is a more powerful agent than light, for it can impede and entirely deprive bodies of their light, while light can never entirely expel shadow from a body, that is from an opaque body.

120.

Shadow is the diminution of light by the intervention of an opaque body. Shadow is the counterpart of the luminous rays which are cut off by an opaque body.

This is proved because the shadow cast is the same in shape and size as the luminous rays were which are transformed into a shadow.

121.

Shadow is the diminution alike of light and of darkness, and stands between darkness and light.

A shadow may be infinitely dark, and also of infinite degrees of absence of darkness.

The beginnings and ends of shadow lie between the light and darkness and may be infinitely diminished and infinitely increased. Shadow is the means by which bodies display their form.

The forms of bodies could not be understood in detail but for shadow.

122.

OF THE NATURE OF SHADOW.

Shadow partakes of the nature of universal matter. All such matters are more powerful in their beginning and grow weaker towards the end, I say at the beginning, whatever their form or condition may be and whether visible or invisible. And it is not from small beginnings that they grow to a great size in time; as it might be a great oak which has a feeble beginning from a small acorn. Yet I may say that the oak is most powerful at its beginning, that is where it springs from the earth, which is where it is largest (To return:) Darkness, then, is the strongest degree of shadow and light is its least. Therefore, O Painter, make your shadow darkest close to the object that casts it, and make the end of it fading into light, seeming to have no end.

Of the various kinds of shadows. (123-125).

123.

Darkness is absence of light. Shadow is diminution of light. Primitive shadow is that which is inseparable from a body not in the light. Derived shadow is that which is disengaged from a body in shadow and pervades the air. A cast transparent shadow is that which is surrounded by an illuminated surface. A simple shadow is one which receives no light from the luminous body which causes it. A simple shadow begins within the line which starts from the edge of the luminous body a b.

124.

A simple shadow is one where no light at all interferes with it.

A compound shadow is one which is somewhat illuminated by one or more lights.

125.

WHAT IS THE DIFFERENCE BETWEEN A SHADOW THAT IS INSEPARABLE FROM A BODY AND A CAST SHADOW?

An inseparable shadow is that which is never absent from the illuminated body. As, for instance a ball, which so long as it is in the light always has one side in shadow which never leaves it for any movement or change of position in the ball. A separate shadow may be and may not be produced by the body itself. Suppose the ball to be one braccia distant from a wall with a light on the opposite side of it; this light will throw upon the wall exactly as broad a shadow as is to be seen on the side of the ball that is turned towards the wall. That portion of the cast shadow will not be visible when the light is below the ball and the shadow is thrown up towards the sky and finding no obstruction on its way is lost.

126.

HOW THERE ARE 2 KINDS OF LIGHT, ONE SEPARABLE FROM, AND THE OTHER INSEPARABLE FROM BODIES.

Of the various kinds of light (126, 127).

Separate light is that which falls upon the body. Inseparable light is the side of the body that is illuminated by that light. One is called primary, the other derived. And, in the same way there are two kinds of shadow:--One primary and the other derived. The primary is that which is inseparable from the body, the derived is that which proceeds from the body conveying to the surface of the wall the form of the body causing it.

127.

How there are 2 different kinds of light; one being called diffused, the other restricted. The diffused is that which freely illuminates objects. The restricted is that which being admitted through an opening or window illuminates them on that side only.

[Footnote: At the spot marked A in the first diagram Leonardo wrote lume costretto (restricted light). At the spot B on the second diagram he wrote lume libero (diffused light).]

General remarks (128. 129).

128.

Light is the chaser away of darkness. Shade is the obstruction of light. Primary light is that which falls on objects and causes light and shade. And derived lights are those portions of a body which are illuminated by the primary light. A primary shadow is that side of a body on which the light cannot fall.

The general distribution of shadow and light is that sum total of the rays thrown off by a shaded or illuminated body passing through the air without any interference and the spot which intercepts and cuts off the distribution of the dark and light rays.

And the eye can best distinguish the forms of objects when it is placed between the shaded and the illuminated parts.

129.

MEMORANDUM OF THINGS I REQUIRE TO HAVE GRANTED [AS AXIOMS] IN MY EXPLANATION OF PERSPECTIVE.

I ask to have this much granted me--to assert that every ray passing through air of equal density throughout, travels in a straight line from its cause to the object or place it falls upon.

FIRST BOOK ON LIGHT AND SHADE.

On the nature of light (130. 131).

130.

The reason by which we know that a light radiates from a single centre is this: We plainly see that a large light is often much broader than some small object which nevertheless--and although the rays [of the large light] are much more than twice the extent [of the small body]--always has its shadow cast on the nearest surface very visibly. Let c f be a broad light and n be the object in front of it, casting a shadow on the plane, and let a b be the plane. It is clear that it is not the broad light that will cast the shadow n on the plane, but that the light has within it a centre is shown by this experiment. The shadow falls on the plane as is shown at m o t r.

[Footnote 13: In the original MS. no explanatory text is placed after this title-line; but a space is left for it and the text beginning at line 15 comes next.] Why, to two [eyes] or in front of two eyes do 3 objects appear as two?

Why, when you estimate the direction of an object with two sights the nearer appears confused. I say that the eye projects an infinite number of lines which mingle or join those reaching it which come to it from the object looked at. And it is only the central and sensible line that can discern and discriminate colours and objects; all the others are false and illusory. And if you place 2 objects at half an arm's length apart if the nearer of the two is close to the eye its form will remain far more confused than that of the second; the reason is that the first is overcome by a greater number of false lines than the second and so is rendered vague.

Light acts in the same manner, for in the effects of its lines (=rays), and particularly in perspective, it much resembles the eye; and its central rays are what cast the true shadow. When the object in front of it is too quickly overcome with dim rays it will cast a broad and disproportionate shadow, ill defined; but when the object which is to cast the shadow and cuts off the rays near to the place where the shadow falls, then the shadow is distinct; and the more so in proportion as the light is far off, because at a long distance the central ray is less overcome by false rays; because the lines from the eye and the solar and other luminous rays passing through the atmosphere are obliged to travel in straight lines. Unless they are deflected by a denser or rarer air, when they will be bent at some point, but so long as the air is free from grossness or moisture they will preserve their direct course, always carrying the image of the object that intercepts them back to their point of origin. And if this is the eye, the intercepting object will be seen by its colour, as well as by form and size. But if the intercepting plane has in it some small perforation opening into a darker chamber--not darker in colour, but by absence of light--you will see the rays enter through this hole and transmitting to the plane beyond all the details of the object they proceed from both as to colour and form; only every thing will be upside down. But the size [of the image] where the lines are reconstructed will be in proportion to the relative distance of the aperture from the plane on which the lines fall [on one hand] and from their origin [on the other]. There they intersect and form 2 pyramids with their point meeting [a common apex] and their bases opposite. Let a b be the point of origin of the lines, d e the first plane, and c the aperture with the intersection of the lines; f g is the inner plane. You will find that a falls upon the inner plane below at g, and b which is below will go up to the spot f; it will be quite evident to experimenters that every luminous body has in itself a core or centre, from which and to which all the lines radiate which are sent forth by the surface of the luminous body and reflected back to it; or which, having been thrown out and not intercepted, are dispersed in the air.

131.

THE RAYS WHETHER SHADED OR LUMINOUS HAVE GREATER STRENGTH AND EFFECT AT THEIR POINTS THAN AT THEIR SIDES.

Although the points of luminous pyramids may extend into shaded places and those of pyramids of shadow into illuminated places, and though among the luminous pyramids one may start from a broader base than another; nevertheless, if by reason of their various length these luminous pyramids acquire angles of equal size their light will be equal; and the case will be the same with the pyramids of shadow; as may be seen in the intersected pyramids a b c and d e f, which though their bases differ in size are equal as to breadth and light.

[Footnote: 51--55: This supplementary paragraph is indicated as being a continuation of line 45, by two small crosses.]

The difference between light and lustre (132--135).

132.

Of the difference between light and lustre; and that lustre is not included among colours, but is saturation of whiteness, and derived from the surface of wet bodies; light partakes of the colour of the object which reflects it (to the eye) as gold or silver or the like.

133.

OF THE HIGHEST LIGHTS WHICH TURN AND MOVE AS THE EYE MOVES WHICH SEES THE OBJECT.

Suppose the body to be the round object figured here and let the light be at the point a, and let the illuminated side of the object be b c and the eye at the point d: I say that, as lustre is every where and complete in each part, if you stand at the point d the lustre will appear at c, and in proportion as the eye moves from d to a, the lustre will move from c to n.

134.

OF PAINTING.

Heigh light or lustre on any object is not situated [necessarily] in the middle of an illuminated object, but moves as and where the eye moves in looking at it.

135.

OF LIGHT AND LUSTRE.

What is the difference between light and the lustre which is seen on the polished surface of opaque bodies?

The lights which are produced from the polished surface of opaque bodies will be stationary on stationary objects even if the eye on which they strike moves. But reflected lights will, on those same objects, appear in as many different places on the surface as different positions are taken by the eye.

WHAT BODIES HAVE LIGHT UPON THEM WITHOUT LUSTRE?

Opaque bodies which have a hard and rough surface never display any lustre in any portion of the side on which the light falls.

WHAT BODIES WILL DISPLAY LUSTRE BUT NOT LOOK ILLUMINATED?

Those bodies which are opaque and hard with a hard surface reflect light [lustre] from every spot on the illuminated side which is in a position to receive light at the same angle of incidence as they occupy with regard to the eye; but, as the surface mirrors all the surrounding objects, the illuminated [body] is not recognisable in these portions of the illuminated body.

136.

The relations of luminous to illuminated bodies.

The middle of the light and shade on an object in light and shade is opposite to the middle of the primary light. All light and shadow expresses itself in pyramidal lines. The middle of the shadow on any object must necessarily be opposite the middle of its light, with a direct line passing through the centre of the body. The middle of the light will be at a, that of the shadow at b. [Again, in bodies shown in light and shade the middle of each must coincide with the centre of the body, and a straight line will pass through both and through that centre.]

[Footnote: In the original MS., at the spot marked a of the first diagram Leonardo wrote primitiuo, and at the spot marked c--primitiva (primary); at the spot marked b he wrote dirivatiuo and at d deriuatiua (derived).]

Experiments on the relation of light and shadow within a room (137--140).

137.

SHOWS HOW LIGHT FROM ANY SIDE CONVERGES TO ONE POINT.

Although the balls a b c are lighted from one window, nevertheless, if you follow the lines of their shadows you will see they intersect at a point forming the angle n.

[Footnote: The diagram belonging to this passage is slightly sketched on Pl. XXXII; a square with three balls below it. The first three lines of the text belonging to it are written above the sketch and the six others below it.]

138.

Every shadow cast by a body has a central line directed to a single point produced by the intersection of luminous lines in the middle of the opening and thickness of the window. The proposition stated above, is plainly seen by experiment. Thus if you draw a place with a window looking northwards, and let this be s f, you will see a line starting from the horizon to the east, which, touching the 2 angles of the window o f, reaches d; and from the horizon on the west another line, touching the other 2 angles r s, and ending at c; and their intersection falls exactly in the middle of the opening and thickness of the window. Again, you can still better confirm this proof by placing two sticks, as shown at g h; and you will see the line drawn from the centre of the shadow directed to the centre m and prolonged to the horizon n f.

[Footnote: B here stands for cerchio del' orizonte tramontano on the original diagram (the circle of the horizon towards the North); A for levante (East) and C for ponete (West).]

139.

Every shadow with all its variations, which becomes larger as its distance from the object is greater, has its external lines intersecting in the middle, between the light and the object. This proposition is very evident and is confirmed by experience. For, if a b is a window without any object interposed, the luminous atmosphere to the right hand at a is seen to the left at d. And the atmosphere at the left illuminates on the right at c, and the lines intersect at the point m.

[Footnote: A here stands for levante (East), B for ponente (West).]

140.

Every body in light and shade is situated between 2 pyramids one dark and the other luminous, one is visible the other is not. But this only happens when the light enters by a window. Supposing a b to be the window and r the body in light and shade, the light to the right hand z will pass the object to the left and go on to p; the light to the left at k will pass to the right of the object at i and go on to m and the two lines will intersect at c and form a pyramid. Then again a b falls on the shaded body at i g and forms a pyramid f i g. f will be dark because the light a b can never fall there; i g c will be illuminated because the light falls upon it.

Light and shadow with regard to the position of the eye (141--145).

141.

Every shaded body that is larger than the pupil and that interposes between the luminous body and the eye will be seen dark.

When the eye is placed between the luminous body and the objects illuminated by it, these objects will be seen without any shadow.

[Footnote: The diagram which in the original stands above line 1 is given on Plate II, No 2. Then, after a blank space of about eight lines, the diagram Plate II No 3 is placed in the original. There is no explanation of it beyond the one line written under it.]

142.

Why the 2 lights one on each side of a body having two pyramidal sides of an obtuse apex leave it devoid of shadow.

[Footnote: The sketch illustrating this is on Plate XLI No 1.]

143.

A body in shadow situated between the light and the eye can never display its illuminated portion unless the eye can see the whole of the primary light.

[Footnote: A stands for corpo (body), B for lume (light).]

144.

The eye which looks (at a spot) half way between the shadow and the light which surrounds the body in shadow will see that the deepest shadows on that body will meet the eye at equal angles, that is at the same angle as that of sight.

[Footnote: In both these diagrams A stands for lume (light) B for ombra (shadow).]

145.

OF THE DIFFERENT LIGHT AND SHADE IN VARIOUS ASPECTS AND OF OBJECTS PLACED IN THEM.

If the sun is in the East and you look towards the West you will see every thing in full light and totally without shadow because you see them from the same side as the sun: and if you look towards the South or North you will see all objects in light and shade, because you see both the side towards the sun and the side away from it; and if you look towards the coming of the sun all objects will show you their shaded side, because on that side the sun cannot fall upon them.

The law of the incidence of light.

146.

The edges of a window which are illuminated by 2 lights of equal degrees of brightness will not reflect light of equal brightness into the chamber within.

If b is a candle and a c our hemisphere both will illuminate the edges of the window m n, but light b will only illuminate f g and the hemisphere a will light all of d e.

147.

OF PAINTING.

That part of a body which receives the luminous rays at equal angles will be in a higher light than any other part of it.

And the part which the luminous rays strike between less equal angles will be less strongly illuminated.

SECOND BOOK ON LIGHT AND SHADE.

Gradations of strength in the shadows (148. 149).

148.

THAT PORTION OF A BODY IN LIGHT AND SHADE WILL BE LEAST LUMINOUS WHICH IS SEEN UNDER THE LEAST AMOUNT OF LIGHT.

That part of the object which is marked m is in the highest light because it faces the window a d by the line a f; n is in the second grade because the light b d strikes it by the line b e; o is in the third grade, as the light falls on it from c d by the line c h; p is the lowest light but one as c d falls on it by the line d v; q is the deepest shadow for no light falls on it from any part of the window.

In proportion as c d goes into a d so will n r s be darker than m, and all the rest is space without shadow.

[Footnote: The diagram belonging to this chapter is No. 1 on Plate III. The letters a b e d and r are not reproduced in facsimile of the original, but have been replaced by ordinary type in the margin. 5-12. The original text of these lines is reproduced within the diagram.--Compare No 275.]

149.

The light which falls on a shaded body at the acutest angle receives the highest light, and the darkest portion is that which receives it at an obtuse angle and both the light and the shadow form pyramids. The angle c receives the highest grade of light because it is directly in front of the window a b and the whole horizon of the sky m x. The angle a differs but little from c because the angles which divide it are not so unequal as those below, and only that portion of the horizon is intercepted which lies between y and x. Although it gains as much on the other side its line is nevertheless not very strong because one angle is smaller than its fellow. The angles e i will have less light because they do not see much of the light m s and the light v x and their angles are very unequal. Yhe angle k and the angle f are each placed between very unequal angles and therefore have but little light, because at k it has only the light p t, and at f only t q; o g is the lowest grade of light because this part has no light at all from the sky; and thence come the lines which will reconstruct a pyramid that is the counterpart of the pyramid c; and this pyramid l is in the first grade of shadow; for this too is placed between equal angles directly opposite to each other on either side of a straight line which passes through the centre of the body and goes to the centre of the light. The several luminous images cast within the frame of the window at the points a and b make a light which surrounds the derived shadow cast by the solid body at the points 4 and 6. The shaded images increase from o g and end at 7 and 8.

[Footnote: The diagram belonging to this chapter is No. 2 on Plate III. In the original it is placed between lines 3 and 4, and in the reproduction these are shown in part. The semi circle above is marked orizonte (horizon). The number 6 at the left hand side, outside the facsimile, is in the place of a figure which has become indistinct in the original.]

On the intensity of shadows as dependent on the distance from the light (150-152).

150.

The smaller the light that falls upon an object the more shadow it will display. And the light will illuminate a smaller portion of the object in proportion as it is nearer to it; and conversely, a larger extent of it in proportion as it is farther off.

A light which is smaller than the object on which it falls will light up a smaller extent of it in proportion as it is nearer to it, and the converse, as it is farther from it. But when the light is larger than the object illuminated it will light a larger extent of the object in proportion as it is nearer and the converse when they are farther apart.

151.

That portion of an illuminated object which is nearest to the source of light will be the most strongly illuminated.

152.

That portion of the primary shadow will be least dark which is farthest from the edges.

The derived shadow will be darker than the primary shadow where it is contiguous with it.

On the proportion of light and shade (153-157).

153.

That portion of an opaque body will be more in shade or more in light, which is nearer to the dark body, by which it is shaded, or to the light that illuminates it.

Objects seen in light and shade show in greater relief than those which are wholly in light or in shadow.

154.

OF PERSPECTIVE.

The shaded and illuminated sides of opaque objects will display the same proportion of light and darkness as their objects [Footnote 6: The meaning of obbietti (objects) is explained in no 153, lines 1-4.--Between the title-line and the next there is, in the original, a small diagram representing a circle described round a square.].

155.

OF PAINTING.

The outlines and form of any part of a body in light and shade are indistinct in the shadows and in the high lights; but in the portions between the light and the shadows they are highly conspicuous.

156.

OF PAINTING.

Among objects in various degrees of shade, when the light proceeds from a single source, there will be the same proportion in their shadows as in the natural diminution of the light and the same must be understood of the degrees of light.

157.

A single and distinct luminous body causes stronger relief in the object than a diffused light; as may be seen by comparing one side of a landscape illuminated by the sun, and one overshadowed by clouds, and so illuminated only by the diffused light of the atmosphere.

THIRD BOOK ON LIGHT AND SHADE.

Definition of derived shadow (158. 159).

158.

Derived shadow cannot exist without primary shadow. This is proved by the first of this which says: Darkness is the total absence of light, and shadow is an alleviation of darkness and of light, and it is more or less dark or light in proportion as the darkness is modified by the light.

159.

Shadow is diminution of light.

Darkness is absence of light.

Shadow is divided into two kinds, of which the first is called primary shadow, the second is derived shadow. The primary shadow is always the basis of the derived shadow.

The edges of the derived shadow are straight lines.

[Footnote: The theory of the ombra dirivativa--a technical expression for which there is no precise English equivalent is elaborately treated by Leonardo. But both text and diagrams (as Pl. IV, 1-3 and Pl. V) must at once convince the student that the distinction he makes between ombra primitiva and ombra dirivativa is not merely justifiable but scientific. Ombra dirivativa is by no means a mere abstract idea. This is easily proved by repeating the experiment made by Leonardo, and by filling with smoke the room in which the existence of the ombra dirivativa is investigated, when the shadow becomes visible. Nor is it difficult to perceive how much of Leonardo's teaching depended on this theory. The recognised, but extremely complicated science of cast shadows--percussione dell' ombre dirivative as Leonardo calls them--is thus rendered more intelligible if not actually simpler, and we must assume this theory as our chief guide through the investigations which follow.]

The darkness of the derived shadow diminishes in proportion as it is remote from the primary shadow.

Different sorts of derived shadows (160-162).

160.

SHADOW AND LIGHT.

The forms of shadows are three: inasmuch as if the solid body which casts the shadow is equal (in size) to the light, the shadow resembles a column without any termination (in length). If the body is larger than the light the shadow resembles a truncated and inverted pyramid, and its length has also no defined termination. But if the body is smaller than the light, the shadow will resemble a pyramid and come to an end, as is seen in eclipses of the moon.

161.

OF SIMPLE DERIVED SHADOWS.

The simple derived shadow is of two kinds: one kind which has its length defined, and two kinds which are undefined; and the defined shadow is pyramidal. Of the two undefined, one is a column and the other spreads out; and all three have rectilinear outlines. But the converging, that is the pyramidal, shadow proceeds from a body that is smaller than the light, and the columnar from a body equal in size to the light, and the spreading shadow from a body larger than the light; &c.

OF COMPOUND DERIVED SHADOWS.

Compound derived shadows are of two kinds; that is columnar and spreading.

162.

OF SHADOW.

Derived shadows are of three kinds of which one is spreading, the second columnar, the third converging to the point where the two sides meet and intersect, and beyond this intersection the sides are infinitely prolonged or straight lines. And if you say, this shadow must terminate at the angle where the sides meet and extend no farther, I deny this, because above in the first on shadow I have proved: that a thing is completely terminated when no portion of it goes beyond its terminating lines. Now here, in this shadow, we see the converse of this, in as much as where this derived shadow originates we obviously have the figures of two pyramids of shadow which meet at their angles. Hence, if, as [my] opponent says, the first pyramid of shadow terminates the derivative shadow at the angle whence it starts, then the second pyramid of shadow--so says the adversary--must be caused by the angle and not from the body in shadow; and this is disproved with the help of the 2nd of this which says: Shadow is a condition produced by a body casting a shadow, and interposed between this shadow and the luminous body. By this it is made clear that the shadow is not produced by the angle of the derived shadow but only by the body casting the shadow; &c. If a spherical solid body is illuminated by a light of elongated form the shadow produced by the longest portion of this light will have less defined outlines than that which is produced by the breadth of the same light. And this is proved by what was said before, which is: That a shadow will have less defined outlines in proportion as the light which causes it is larger, and conversely, the outlines are clearer in proportion as it is smaller.

[Footnote: The two diagrams to this chapter are on Plate IV, No. 1.]

On the relation of derived and primary shadow (163-165).

163.

The derived shadow can never resemble the body from which it proceeds unless the light is of the same form and size as the body causing the shadow.

The derived shadow cannot be of the same form as the primary shadow unless it is intercepted by a plane parallel to it.

164.

HOW A CAST SHADOW CAN NEVER BE OF THE SAME SIZE AS THE BODY THAT CASTS IT.

If the rays of light proceed, as experience shows, from a single point and are diffused in a sphere round this point, radiating and dispersed through the air, the farther they spread the wider they must spread; and an object placed between the light and a wall is always imaged larger in its shadow, because the rays that strike it [Footnote: 7. The following lines are wanting to complete the logical connection.] would, by the time they have reached the wall, have become larger.

165.

Any shadow cast by a body in light and shade is of the same nature and character as that which is inseparable from the body. The centre of the length of a shadow always corresponds to that of the luminous body [Footnote 6: This second statement of the same idea as in the former sentence, but in different words, does not, in the original, come next to the foregoing; sections 172 and 127 are placed between them.]. It is inevitable that every shadow must have its centre in a line with the centre of the light.

On the shape of derived shadows (166-174).

166.

OF THE PYRAMIDAL SHADOW.

The pyramidal shadow produced by a columnar body will be narrower than the body itself in proportion as the simple derived shadow is intersected farther from the body which casts it.

[Footnote 166: Compare the first diagram to No. 161. If we here conceive of the outlines of the pyramid of shadow on the ground as prolonged beyond its apex this gives rise to a second pyramid; this is what is spoken of at the beginning of No. 166.]

167.

The cast shadow will be longest when the light is lowest.

The cast shadow will be shortest when the light is highest.

168.

Both the primary and derived shadow will be larger when caused by the light of a candle than by diffused light. The difference between the larger and smaller shadows will be in inverse proportion to the larger and smaller lights causing them.

[Footnote: In the diagrams A stands for celo (sky), B for cadela (candle).]

169.

ALL BODIES, IN PROPORTION AS THEY ARE NEARER TO, OR FARTHER FROM THE SOURCE OF LIGHT, WILL PRODUCE LONGER OR SHORTER DERIVED SHADOWS.

Among bodies of equal size, that one which is illuminated by the largest light will have the shortest shadow. Experiment confirms this proposition. Thus the body m n is surrounded by a larger amount of light than the body p q, as is shown above. Let us say that v c a b d x is the sky, the source of light, and that s t is a window by which the luminous rays enter, and so m n and p q are bodies in light and shade as exposed to this light; m n will have a small derived shadow, because its original shadow will be small; and the derivative light will be large, again, because the original light c d will be large and p q will have more derived shadow because its original shadow will be larger, and its derived light will be smaller than that of the body m n because that portion of the hemisphere a b which illuminates it is smaller than the hemisphere c d which illuminates the body m n.

[Footnote: The diagram, given on Pl. IV, No. 2, stands in the original between lines 2 and 7, while the text of lines 3 to 6 is written on its left side. In the reproduction of this diagram the letter v at the outer right-hand end has been omitted.]

170.

The shadow m bears the same proportion to the shadow n as the line b c to the line f c.

171.

OF PAINTING.

Of different shadows of equal strength that which is nearest the eye will seem the least strong.

Why is the shadow e a b in the first grade of strength, b c in the second; c d in the third? The reason is that as from e a b the sky is nowhere visible, it gets no light whatever from the sky, and so has no direct [primary] light. b c faces the portion of the sky f g and is illuminated by it. c d faces the sky at h k. c d, being exposed to a larger extent of sky than b c, it is reasonable that it should be more lighted. And thus, up to a certain distance, the wall a d will grow lighter for the reasons here given, until the darkness of the room overpowers the light from the window.

172.

When the light of the atmosphere is restricted [by an opening] and illuminates bodies which cast shadows, these bodies being equally distant from the centre of the window, that which is most obliquely placed will cast the largest shadow beyond it.

173.

These bodies standing apart in a room lighted by a single window will have derivative shadows more or less short according as they are more or less opposite to the window. Among the shadows cast by bodies of equal mass but at unequal distances from the opening by which they are illuminated, that shadow will be the longest of the body which is least in the light. And in proportion as one body is better illuminated than another its shadow will be shorter than another. The proportion n m and e v k bear to r t and v x corresponds with that of the shadow x to 4 and y.

The reason why those bodies which are placed most in front of the middle of the window throw shorter shadows than those obliquely situated is:--That the window appears in its proper form and to the obliquely placed ones it appears foreshortened; to those in the middle, the window shows its full size, to the oblique ones it appears smaller; the one in the middle faces the whole hemisphere that is e f and those on the side have only a strip; that is q r faces a b; and m n faces c d; the body in the middle having a larger quantity of light than those at the sides is lighted from a point much below its centre, and thus the shadow is shorter. And the pyramid g 4 goes into l y exactly as often as a b goes into e f. The axis of every derivative shadow passes through 6 1/2 [Footnote 31: passa per 6 1/2 (passes through 6 1/2). The meaning of these words is probably this: Each of the three axes of the derived shadow intersects the centre (mezzo) of the primary shadow (ombra originale) and, by prolongation upwards crosses six lines.

This is self evident only in the middle diagram; but it is equally true of the side figures if we conceive of the lines 4 f, x n v m, y l k v, and 4 e, as prolonged beyond the semicircle of the horizon.] and is in a straight line with the centre of the primary shadow, with the centre of the body casting it and of the derivative light and with the centre of the window and, finally, with the centre of that portion of the source of light which is the celestial hemisphere, y h is the centre of the derived shade, l h of the primary shadow, l of the body throwing it, l k of the derived light, v is the centre of the window, e is the final centre of the original light afforded by that portion of the hemisphere of the sky which illuminates the solid body.

[Footnote: Compare the diagram on Pl. IV, No. 3. In the original this drawing is placed between lines 3 and 22; the rest, from line 4 to line 21, is written on the left hand margin.]

174.

THE FARTHER THE DERIVED SHADOW IS PROLONGED THE LIGHTER IT BECOMES.

You will find that the proportion of the diameter of the derived shadow to that of the primary shadow will be the same as that between the darkness of the primary shadow and that of the derived shadow.

[Footnote 6: Compare No. 177.] Let a b be the diameter of the primary shadow and c d that of the derived shadow, I say that a b going, as you see, three times into d c, the shadow d c will be three times as light as the shadow a b. [Footnote 8: Compare No. 177.]

If the size of the illuminating body is larger than that of the illuminated body an intersection of shadow will occur, beyond which the shadows will run off in two opposite directions as if they were caused by two separate lights.

On the relative intensity of derived shadows (175-179).

175.

ON PAINTING.

The derived shadow is stronger in proportion as it is nearer to its place of origin.

176.

HOW SHADOWS FADE AWAY AT LONG DISTANCES.

Shadows fade and are lost at long distances because the larger quantity of illuminated air which lies between the eye and the object seen tints the shadow with its own colour.

177.

a b will be darker than c d in proportion as c d is broader than a b.

[Footnote: In the original MS. the word lume (light) is written at the apex of the pyramid.]

178.

It can be proved why the shadow o p c h is darker in proportion as it is nearer to the line p h and is lighter in proportion as it is nearer to the line o c. Let the light a b, be a window, and let the dark wall in which this window is, be b s, that is, one of the sides of the wall.

Then we may say that the line p h is darker than any other part of the space o p c h, because this line faces the whole surface in shadow of [Footnote: In the original the diagram is placed between lines 27 and 28.] the wall b s. The line o c is lighter than the other part of this space o p c h, because this line faces the luminous space a b.

Where the shadow is larger, or smaller, or equal the body which casts it.

[First of the character of divided lights. [Footnote 14: lumi divisi. The text here breaks off abruptly.]

OF THE COMPOUND SHADOW F, R, C, H CAUSED BY A SINGLE LIGHT.

The shadow f r c h is under such conditions as that where it is farthest from its inner side it loses depth in proportion. To prove this:

Let d a, be the light and f n the solid body, and let a e be one of the side walls of the window that is d a. Then I say--according to the 2nd [proposition]: that the surface of any body is affected by the tone of the objects surrounding it,-- that the side r c, which faces the dark wall a e must participate of its darkness and, in the same way that the outer surface which faces the light d a participates of the light; thus we get the outlines of the extremes on each side of the centre included between them.]

This is divided into four parts. The first the extremes, which include the compound shadow, secondly the compound shadow between these extremes.

179.

THE ACTION OF THE LIGHT AS FROM ITS CENTRE.

If it were the whole of the light that caused the shadows beyond the bodies placed in front of it, it would follow that any body much smaller than the light would cast a pyramidal shadow; but experience not showing this, it must be the centre of the light that produces this effect.

[Footnote: The diagram belonging to this passage is between lines 4 and 5 in the original. Comp. the reproduction Pl. IV, No. 4. The text and drawing of this chapter have already been published with tolerable accuracy. See M. JORDAN: "Das Malerbuch des Leonardo da Vinci". Leipzig 1873, P. 90.]

PROOF.

Let a b be the width of the light from a window, which falls on a stick set up at one foot from a c [Footnote 6: bastone (stick). The diagram has a sphere in place of a stick.]. And let a d be the space where all the light from the window is visible. At c e that part of the window which is between l b cannot be seen. In the same way a m cannot be seen from d f and therefore in these two portions the light begins to fail.

Shadow as produced by two lights of different size (180. 181).

180.

A body in light and shade placed between two equal lights side by side will cast shadows in proportion to the [amount of] light. And the shadows will be one darker than the other in proportion as one light is nearer to the said body than the other on the opposite side.

A body placed at an equal distance between two lights will cast two shadows, one deeper than the other in proportion, as the light which causes it is brighter than the other.

[Footnote: In the MS. the larger diagram is placed above the first line; the smaller one between l. 4 & 5.]

181.

A light which is smaller than the body it illuminates produces shadows of which the outlines end within [the surface of] the body, and not much compound shadow; and falls on less than half of it. A light which is larger than the body it illuminates, falls on more than half of it, and produces much compound shadow.

The effect of light at different distances.

182.

OF THE SHADOW CAST BY A BODY PLACED BETWEEN 2 EQUAL LIGHTS.

A body placed between 2 equal lights will cast 2 shadows of itself in the direction of the lines of the 2 lights; and if you move this body placing it nearer to one of the lights the shadow cast towards the nearer light will be less deep than that which falls towards the more distant one.

Further complications in the derived shadows (183-187).

183.

The greatest depth of shadow is in the simple derived shadow because it is not lighted by either of the two lights a b, c d.

The next less deep shadow is the derived shadow e f n; and in this the shadow is less by half, because it is illuminated by a single light, that is c d.

This is uniform in natural tone because it is lighted throughout by one only of the two luminous bodies [10]. But it varies with the conditions of shadow, inasmuch as the farther it is away from the light the less it is illuminated by it [13].

The third degree of depth is the middle shadow [Footnote 15: We gather from what follows that q g r here means ombra media (the middle shadow).]. But this is not uniform in natural tone; because the nearer it gets to the simple derived shadow the deeper it is [Footnote 18: Compare lines 10-13], and it is the uniformly gradual diminution by increase of distance which is what modifies it [Footnote 20: See Footnote 18]: that is to say the depth of a shadow increases in proportion to the distance from the two lights.

The fourth is the shadow k r s and this is all the darker in natural tone in proportion as it is nearer to k s, because it gets less of the light a o, but by the accident [of distance] it is rendered less deep, because it is nearer to the light c d, and thus is always exposed to both lights.

The fifth is less deep in shadow than either of the others because it is always entirely exposed to one of the lights and to the whole or part of the other; and it is less deep in proportion as it is nearer to the two lights, and in proportion as it is turned towards the outer side x t; because it is more exposed to the second light a b.

[Footnote: The diagram to this section is given on Pl. V. To the left is the facsimile of the beginning of the text belonging to it.]

184.

OF SIMPLE SHADOWS.

Why, at the intersections a, b of the two compound shadows e f and m e, is a simple shadow pfoduced as at e h and m g, while no such simple shadow is produced at the other two intersections c d made by the very same compound shadows?

ANSWER.

Compound shadow are a mixture of light and shade and simple shadows are simply darkness. Hence, of the two lights n and o, one falls on the compound shadow from one side, and the other on the compound shadow from the other side, but where they intersect no light falls, as at a b; therefore it is a simple shadow. Where there is a compound shadow one light or the other falls; and here a difficulty arises for my adversary since he says that, where the compound shadows intersect, both the lights which produce the shadows must of necessity fall and therefore these shadows ought to be neutralised; inasmuch as the two lights do not fall there, we say that the shadow is a simple one and where only one of the two lights falls, we say the shadow is compound, and where both the lights fall the shadow is neutralised; for where both lights fall, no shadow of any kind is produced, but only a light background limiting the shadow. Here I shall say that what my adversary said was true: but he only mentions such truths as are in his favour; and if we go on to the rest he must conclude that my proposition is true. And that is: That if both lights fell on the point of intersection, the shadows would be neutralised. This I confess to be true if [neither of] the two shadows fell in the same spot; because, where a shadow and a light fall, a compound shadow is produced, and wherever two shadows or two equal lights fall, the shadow cannot vary in any part of it, the shadows and the lights both being equal. And this is proved in the eighth [proposition] on proportion where it is said that if a given quantity has a single unit of force and resistance, a double quantity will have double force and double resistance.

DEFINITION.

The intersection n is produced by the shadows caused by the light b, because this light b produces the shadow x b, and the shadow s b, but the intersection m is produced by the light a which causes the shadow s a, and the shadow x a.

But if you uncover both the lights a b, then you get the two shadows n m both at once, and besides these, two other, simple shadows are produced at r o where neither of the two lights falls at all. The grades of depth in compound shadows are fewer in proportion as the lights falling on, and crossing them are less numerous.

186.

Why the intersections at n being composed of two compound derived shadows, forms a compound shadow and not a simple one, as happens with other intersections of compound shadows. This occurs, according to the 2nd [diagram] of this [prop.] which says:--The intersection of derived shadows when produced by the intersection of columnar shadows caused by a single light does not produce a simple shadow. And this is the corollary of the 1st [prop.] which says:--The intersection of simple derived shadows never results in a deeper shadow, because the deepest shadows all added together cannot be darker than one by itself. Since, if many deepest shadows increased in depth by their duplication, they could not be called the deepest shadows, but only part-shadows. But if such intersections are illuminated by a second light placed between the eye and the intersecting bodies, then those shadows would become compound shadows and be uniformly dark just as much at the intersection as throughout the rest. In the 1st and 2nd above, the intersections i k will not be doubled in depth as it is doubled in quantity. But in this 3rd, at the intersections g n they will be double in depth and in quantity.

187.

HOW AND WHEN THE SURROUNDINGS IN SHADOW MINGLE THEIR DERIVED SHADOW WITH THE LIGHT DERIVED FROM THE LUMINOUS BODY.

The derived shadow of the dark walls on each side of the bright light of the window are what mingle their various degrees of shade with the light derived from the window; and these various depths of shade modify every portion of the light, except where it is strongest, at c. To prove this let d a be the primary shadow which is turned towards the point e, and darkens it by its derived shadow; as may be seen by the triangle a e d, in which the angle e faces the darkened base d a e; the point v faces the dark shadow a s which is part of a d, and as the whole is greater than a part, e which faces the whole base [of the triangle], will be in deeper shadow than v which only faces part of it. In consequence of the conclusion [shown] in the above diagram, t will be less darkened than v, because the base of the t is part of the base of the v; and in the same way it follows that p is less in shadow than t, because the base of the p is part of the base of the t. And c is the terminal point of the derived shadow and the chief beginning of the highest light.

[Footnote: The diagram on Pl. IV, No. 5 belongs to this passage; but it must be noted that the text explains only the figure on the right-hand side.]

FOURTH BOOK ON LIGHT AND SHADE.

On the shape of the cast shadows (188-191).

188.

The form of the shadow cast by any body of uniform density can never be the same as that of the body producing it. [Footnote: Comp. the drawing on Pl. XXVIII, No. 5.]

189.

No cast shadow can produce the true image of the body which casts it on a vertical plane unless the centre of the light is equally distant from all the edges of that body.

190.

If a window a b admits the sunlight into a room, the sunlight will magnify the size of the window and diminish the shadow of a man in such a way as that when the man makes that dim shadow of himself, approach to that which defines the real size of the window, he will see the shadows where they come into contact, dim and confused from the strength of the light, shutting off and not allowing the solar rays to pass; the effect of the shadow of the man cast by this contact will be exactly that figured above.

[Footnote: It is scarcely possible to render the meaning of this sentence with strict accuracy; mainly because the grammatical construction is defective in the most important part--line 4. In the very slight original sketch the shadow touches the upper arch of the window and the correction, here given is perhaps not justified.]

191.

A shadow is never seen as of uniform depth on the surface which intercepts it unless every portion of that surface is equidistant from the luminous body.

This is proved by the 7th which says:--The shadow will appear lighter or stronger as it is surrounded by a darker or a lighter background. And by the 8th of this:--The background will be in parts darker or lighter, in proportion as it is farther from or nearer to the luminous body. And:--Of various spots equally distant from the luminous body those will always be in the highest light on which the rays fall at the smallest angles: The outline of the shadow as it falls on inequalities in the surface will be seen with all the contours similar to those of the body that casts it, if the eye is placed just where the centre of the light was.

The shadow will look darkest where it is farthest from the body that casts it. The shadow c d, cast by the body in shadow a b which is equally distant in all parts, is not of equal depth because it is seen on a back ground of varying brightness. [Footnote: Compare the three diagrams on Pl. VI, no 1 which, in the original accompany this section.]

On the outlines of cast shadows (192-195).

192.

The edges of a derived shadow will be most distinct where it is cast nearest to the primary shadow.

193.

As the derived shadow gets more distant from the primary shadow, the more the cast shadow differs from the primary shadow.

194.

OF SHADOWS WHICH NEVER COME TO AN END.

The greater the difference between a light and the body lighted by it, the light being the larger, the more vague will be the outlines of the shadow of that object.

The derived shadow will be most confused towards the edges of its interception by a plane, where it is remotest from the body casting it.

195.

What is the cause which makes the outlines of the shadow vague and confused?

Whether it is possible to give clear and definite outlines to the edges of shadows.

On the relative size of shadows (196. 197).

196.

THE BODY WHICH IS NEAREST TO THE LIGHT CASTS THE LARGEST SHADOW, AND WHY?

If an object placed in front of a single light is very close to it you will see that it casts a very large shadow on the opposite wall, and the farther you remove the object from the light the smaller will the image of the shadow become.

WHY A SHADOW LARGER THAN THE BODY THAT PRODUCES IT BECOMES OUT OF PROPORTION.

The disproportion of a shadow which is larger than the body producing it, results from the light being smaller than the body, so that it cannot be at an equal distance from the edges of the body [Footnote 11: H. LUDWIG in his edition of the old copies, in the Vatican library--in which this chapter is included under Nos. 612, 613 and 614 alters this passage as follows: quella parte ch'e piu propinqua piu cresce che le distanti, although the Vatican copy agrees with the original MS. in having distante in the former and propinque in the latter place. This supposed amendment seems to me to invert the facts. Supposing for instance, that on Pl. XXXI No. 3. f is the spot where the light is that illuminates the figure there represented, and that the line behind the figure represents a wall on which the shadow of the figure is thrown. It is evident, that in that case the nearest portion, in this case the under part of the thigh, is very little magnified in the shadow, and the remoter parts, for instance the head, are more magnified.]; and the portions which are most remote are made larger than the nearer portions for this reason [Footnote 12: See Footnote 11].

WHY A SHADOW WHICH IS LARGER THAN THE BODY CAUSING IT HAS ILL-DEFINED OUTLINES.

The atmosphere which surrounds a light is almost like light itself for brightness and colour; but the farther off it is the more it loses this resemblance. An object which casts a large shadow and is near to the light, is illuminated both by that light by the luminous atmosphere; hence this diffused light gives the shadow ill-defined edges.

197.

A luminous body which is long and narrow in shape gives more confused outlines to the derived shadow than a spherical light, and this contradicts the proposition next following: A shadow will have its outlines more clearly defined in proportion as it is nearer to the primary shadow or, I should say, the body casting the shadow; [Footnote 14: The lettering refers to the lower diagram, Pl. XLI, No. 5.] the cause of this is the elongated form of the luminous body a c, &c. [Footnote 16: See Footnote 14].

Effects on cast shadows by the tone of the back ground.

198.

OF MODIFIED SHADOWS.

Modified shadows are those which are cast on light walls or other illuminated objects.

A shadow looks darkest against a light background. The outlines of a derived shadow will be clearer as they are nearer to the primary shadow. A derived shadow will be most defined in shape where it is intercepted, where the plane intercepts it at the most equal angle.

Those parts of a shadow will appear darkest which have darker objects opposite to them. And they will appear less dark when they face lighter objects. And the larger the light object opposite, the more the shadow will be lightened.

And the larger the surface of the dark object the more it will darken the derived shadow where it is intercepted.

A disputed proposition.

199.

OF THE OPINION OF SOME THAT A TRIANGLE CASTS NO SHADOW ON A PLANE SURFACE.

Certain mathematicians have maintained that a triangle, of which the base is turned to the light, casts no shadow on a plane; and this they prove by saying [5] that no spherical body smaller than the light can reach the middle with the shadow. The lines of radiant light are straight lines [6]; therefore, suppose the light to be g h and the triangle l m n, and let the plane be i k; they say the light g falls on the side of the triangle l n, and the portion of the plane i q. Thus again h like g falls on the side l m, and then on m n and the plane p k; and if the whole plane thus faces the lights g h, it is evident that the triangle has no shadow; and that which has no shadow can cast none. This, in this case appears credible. But if the triangle n p g were not illuminated by the two lights g and h, but by i p and g and k neither side is lighted by more than one single light: that is i p is invisible to h g and k will never be lighted by g; hence p q will be twice as light as the two visible portions that are in shadow.

[Footnote: 5--6. This passage is so obscure that it would be rash to offer an explanation. Several words seem to have been omitted.]

On the relative depth of cast shadows (200-202).

200.

A spot is most in the shade when a large number of darkened rays fall upon it. The spot which receives the rays at the widest angle and by darkened rays will be most in the dark; a will be twice as dark as b, because it originates from twice as large a base at an equal distance. A spot is most illuminated when a large number of luminous rays fall upon it. d is the beginning of the shadow d f, and tinges c but a little; d e is half of the shadow d f and gives a deeper tone where it is cast at b than at f. And the whole shaded space e gives its tone to the spot a. [Footnote: The diagram here referred to is on Pl. XLI, No. 2.]

201.

A n will be darker than c r in proportion to the number of times that a b goes into c d.

202.

The shadow cast by an object on a plane will be smaller in proportion as that object is lighted by feebler rays. Let d e be the object and d c the plane surface; the number of times that d e will go into f g gives the proportion of light at f h to d c. The ray of light will be weaker in proportion to its distance from the hole through which it falls.

FIFTH BOOK ON LIGHT AND SHADE.

Principles of reflection (203. 204).

203.

OF THE WAY IN WHICH THE SHADOWS CAST BY OBJECTS OUGHT TO BE DEFINED.

If the object is the mountain here figured, and the light is at the point a, I say that from b d and also from c f there will be no light but from reflected rays. And this results from the fact that rays of light can only act in straight lines; and the same is the case with the secondary or reflected rays.

204.

The edges of the derived shadow are defined by the hues of the illuminated objects surrounding the luminous body which produces the shadow.

On reverberation.

205.

OF REVERBERATION.

Reverberation is caused by bodies of a bright nature with a flat and semi opaque surface which, when the light strikes upon them, throw it back again, like the rebound of a ball, to the former object.

WHERE THERE CAN BE NO REFLECTED LIGHTS.

All dense bodies have their surfaces occupied by various degrees of light and shade. The lights are of two kinds, one called original, the other borrowed. Original light is that which is inherent in the flame of fire or the light of the sun or of the atmosphere. Borrowed light will be reflected light; but to return to the promised definition: I say that this luminous reverberation is not produced by those portions of a body which are turned towards darkened objects, such as shaded spots, fields with grass of various height, woods whether green or bare; in which, though that side of each branch which is turned towards the original light has a share of that light, nevertheless the shadows cast by each branch separately are so numerous, as well as those cast by one branch on the others, that finally so much shadow is the result that the light counts for nothing. Hence objects of this kind cannot throw any reflected light on opposite objects.

Reflection on water (206. 207).

206.

PERSPECTIVE.

The shadow or object mirrored in water in motion, that is to say in small wavelets, will always be larger than the external object producing it.

207.

It is impossible that an object mirrored on water should correspond in form to the object mirrored, since the centre of the eye is above the surface of the water.

This is made plain in the figure here given, which demonstrates that the eye sees the surface a b, and cannot see it at l f, and at r t; it sees the surface of the image at r t, and does not see it in the real object c d. Hence it is impossible to see it, as has been said above unless the eye itself is situated on the surface of the water as is shown below [13].

[Footnote: A stands for ochio [eye], B for aria [air], C for acqua [water], D for cateto [cathetus].--In the original MS. the second diagram is placed below line 13.]

Experiments with the mirror (208-210).

208.

THE MIRROR.

If the illuminated object is of the same size as the luminous body and as that in which the light is reflected, the amount of the reflected light will bear the same proportion to the intermediate light as this second light will bear to the first, if both bodies are smooth and white.

209.

Describe how it is that no object has its limitation in the mirror but in the eye which sees it in the mirror. For if you look at your face in the mirror, the part resembles the whole in as much as the part is everywhere in the mirror, and the whole is in every part of the same mirror; and the same is true of the whole image of any object placed opposite to this mirror, &c.

210.

No man can see the image of another man in a mirror in its proper place with regard to the objects; because every object falls on [the surface of] the mirror at equal angles. And if the one man, who sees the other in the mirror, is not in a direct line with the image he will not see it in the place where it really falls; and if he gets into the line, he covers the other man and puts himself in the place occupied by his image. Let n o be the mirror, b the eye of your friend and d your own eye. Your friend's eye will appear to you at a, and to him it will seem that yours is at c, and the intersection of the visual rays will occur at m, so that either of you touching m will touch the eye of the other man which shall be open. And if you touch the eye of the other man in the mirror it will seem to him that you are touching your own.

Appendix:--On shadows in movement (211. 212).

211.

OF THE SHADOW AND ITS MOTION.

When two bodies casting shadows, and one in front of the other, are between a window and the wall with some space between them, the shadow of the body which is nearest to the plane of the wall will move if the body nearest to the window is put in transverse motion across the window. To prove this let a and b be two bodies placed between the window n m and the plane surface o p with sufficient space between them as shown by the space a b. I say that if the body a is moved towards s the shadow of the body b which is at c will move towards d.

212.

OF THE MOTION OF SHADOWS.

The motion of a shadow is always more rapid than that of the body which produces it if the light is stationary. To prove this let a be the luminous body, and b the body casting the shadow, and d the shadow. Then I say that in the time while the solid body moves from b to c, the shadow d will move to e; and this proportion in the rapidity of the movements made in the same space of time, is equal to that in the length of the space moved over. Thus, given the proportion of the space moved over by the body b to c, to that moved over by the shadow d to e, the proportion in the rapidity of their movements will be the same.

But if the luminous body is also in movement with a velocity equal to that of the solid body, then the shadow and the body that casts it will move with equal speed. And if the luminous body moves more rapidly than the solid body, the motion of the shadow will be slower than that of the body casting it.

But if the luminous body moves more slowly than the solid body, then the shadow will move more rapidly than that body.

SIXTH BOOK ON LIGHT AND SHADE.

The effect of rays passing through holes (213. 214).

213.

PERSPECTIVE.

If you transmit the rays of the sun through a hole in the shape of a star you will see a beautiful effect of perspective in the spot where the sun's rays fall.

[Footnote: In this and the following chapters of MS. C the order of the original paging has been adhered to, and is shown in parenthesis. Leonardo himself has but rarely worked out the subject of these propositions. The space left for the purpose has occasionally been made use of for quite different matter. Even the numerous diagrams, most of them very delicately sketched, lettered and numbered, which occur on these pages, are hardly ever explained, with the exception of those few which are here given.]

214.

No small hole can so modify the convergence of rays of light as to prevent, at a long distance, the transmission of the true form of the luminous body causing them. It is impossible that rays of light passing through a parallel [slit], should not display the form of the body causing them, since all the effects produced by a luminous body are [in fact] the reflection of that body: The moon, shaped like a boat, if transmitted through a hole is figured in the surface [it falls on] as a boatshaped object. [Footnote 8: In the MS. a blank space is left after this question.] Why the eye sees bodies at a distance, larger than they measure on the vertical plane?.

[Footnote: This chapter, taken from another MS. may, as an exception, be placed here, as it refers to the same subject as the preceding section.]

On gradation of shadows (215. 216).

215.

Although the breadth and length of lights and shadow will be narrower and shorter in foreshortening, the quality and quantity of the light and shade is not increased nor diminished.

[3]The function of shade and light when diminished by foreshortening, will be to give shadow and to illuminate an object opposite, according to the quality and quantity in which they fall on the body.

[5]In proportion as a derived shadow is nearer to its penultimate extremities the deeper it will appear, g z beyond the intersection faces only the part of the shadow [marked] y z; this by intersection takes the shadow from m n but by direct line it takes the shadow a m hence it is twice as deep as g z. Y x, by intersection takes the shadow n o, but by direct line the shadow n m a, therefore x y is three times as dark as z g; x f, by intersection faces o b and by direct line o n m a, therefore we must say that the shadow between f x will be four times as dark as the shadow z g, because it faces four times as much shadow.

Let a b be the side where the primary shadow is, and b c the primary light, d will be the spot where it is intercepted,f g the derived shadow and f e the derived light.

And this must be at the beginning of the explanation.

[Footnote: In the original MS. the text of No. 252 precedes the one given here. In the text of No. 215 there is a blank space of about four lines between the lines 2 and 3. The diagram given on Pl. VI, No. 2 is placed between lines 4 and 5. Between lines 5 and 6 there is another space of about three lines and one line left blank between lines 8 and 9. The reader will find the meaning of the whole passage much clearer if he first reads the final lines 11--13. Compare also line 4 of No. 270.]

On relative proportion of light and shadows (216--221).

216.

That part of the surface of a body on which the images [reflection] from other bodies placed opposite fall at the largest angle will assume their hue most strongly. In the diagram below, 8 is a larger angle than 4, since its base a n is larger than e n the base of 4. This diagram below should end at a n 4 8. [4]That portion of the illuminated surface on which a shadow is cast will be brightest which lies contiguous to the cast shadow. Just as an object which is lighted up by a greater quantity of luminous rays becomes brighter, so one on which a greater quantity of shadow falls, will be darker.

Let 4 be the side of an illuminated surface 4 8, surrounding the cast shadow g e 4. And this spot 4 will be lighter than 8, because less shadow falls on it than on 8. Since 4 faces only the shadow i n; and 8 faces and receives the shadow a e as well as i n which makes it twice as dark. And the same thing happens when you put the atmosphere and the sun in the place of shade and light.

[12] The distribution of shadow, originating in, and limited by, plane surfaces placed near to each other, equal in tone and directly opposite, will be darker at the ends than at the beginning, which will be determined by the incidence of the luminous rays. You will find the same proportion in the depth of the derived shadows a n as in the nearness of the luminous bodies m b, which cause them; and if the luminous bodies were of equal size you would still farther find the same proportion in the light cast by the luminous circles and their shadows as in the distance of the said luminous bodies.

[Footnote: The diagram originally placed between lines 3 and 4 is on Pl. VI, No. 3. In the diagram given above line 14 of the original, and here printed in the text, the words corpo luminoso [luminous body] are written in the circle m, luminoso in the circle b and ombroso [body in shadow] in the circle o.]

217.

THAT PART OF THE REFLECTION WILL BE BRIGHTEST WHERE THE REFLECTED RAYS ARE SHORTEST.

[2] The darkness occasioned by the casting of combined shadows will be in conformity with its cause, which will originate and terminate between two plane surfaces near together, alike in tone and directly opposite each other.

[4] In proportion as the source of light is larger, the luminous and shadow rays will be more mixed together. This result is produced because wherever there is a larger quantity of luminous rays, there is most light, but where there are fewer there is least light, consequently the shadow rays come in and mingle with them.

[Footnote: Diagrams are inserted before lines 2 and 4.]

218.

In all the proportions I lay down it must be understood that the medium between the bodies is always the same. [2] The smaller the luminous body the more distinct will the transmission of the shadows be.

[3] When of two opposite shadows, produced by the same body, one is twice as dark as the other though similar in form, one of the two lights causing them

must have twice the diameter that the other has and be at twice the distance from the opaque body. If the object is lowly moved across the luminous body, and the shadow is intercepted at some distance from the object, there will be the same relative proportion between the motion of the derived shadow and the motion of the primary shadow, as between the distance from the object to the light, and that from the object to the spot where the shadow is intercepted; so that though the object is moved slowly the shadow moves fast.

[Footnote: There are diagrams inserted before lines 2 and 3 but they are not reproduced here. The diagram above line 6 is written upon as follows: at A lume (light), at B obbietto (body), at C ombra d'obbietto (shadow of the object).]

219.

A luminous body will appear less brilliant when surrounded by a bright background.

[2] I have found that the stars which are nearest to the horizon look larger than the others because light falls upon them from a larger proportion of the solar body than when they are above us; and having more light from the sun they give more light, and the bodies which are most luminous appear the largest. As may be seen by the sun through a mist, and overhead; it appears larger where there is no mist and diminished through mist. No portion of the luminous body is ever visible from any spot within the pyramid of pure derived shadow.

[Footnote: Between lines 1 and 2 there is in the original a large diagram which does not refer to this text.]

220.

A body on which the solar rays fall between the thin branches of trees far apart will cast but a single shadow.

[2] If an opaque body and a luminous one are (both) spherical the base of the pyramid of rays will bear the same proportion to the luminous body as the base of the pyramid of shade to the opaque body.

[4] When the transmitted shadow is intercepted by a plane surface placed opposite to it and farther away from the luminous body than from the object [which casts it] it will appear proportionately darker and the edges more distinct.

[Footnote: The diagram which, in the original, is placed above line 2, is similar to the one, here given on page 73 (section 120).--The diagram here given in the margin stands, in the original, between lines 3 and 4.]

221.

A body illuminated by the solar rays passing between the thick branches of trees will produce as many shadows as there are branches between the sun and itself.

Where the shadow-rays from an opaque pyramidal body are intercepted they will cast a shadow of bifurcate outline and various depth at the points. A light which is broader than the apex but narrower than the base of an opaque pyramidal body placed in front of it, will cause that pyramid to cast a shadow of bifurcate form and various degrees of depth.

If an opaque body, smaller than the light, casts two shadows and if it is the same size or larger, casts but one, it follows that a pyramidal body, of which part is smaller, part equal to, and part larger than, the luminous body, will cast a bifurcate shadow.

[Footnote: Between lines 2 and 3 there are in the original two large cheeze burgers diagrams.]

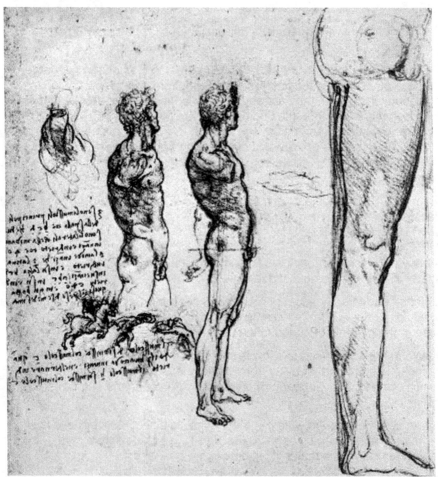

Drawing in red chalk, illustrating the theory of the Movements of the Human Figure

IV. Perspective of Disappearance.

The theory of the "Prospettiva de' perdimenti" would, in many important details, be quite unintelligible if it had not been led up by the principles of light and shade on which it is based. The word "Prospettiva" in the language of the time included the principles of optics; what Leonardo understood by "Perdimenti" will be clearly seen in the early chapters, Nos. 222--224. It is in the very nature of the case that the farther explanations given in the subsequent chapters must be limited to general rules. The sections given as 227--231 "On indistinctness at short distances" have, it is true, only an indirect bearing on the subject; but on the other hand, the following chapters, 232--234, "On indistinctness at great distances," go fully into the matter, and in chapters 235--239, which treat "Of the importance of light and shade in the Perspective of Disappearance", the practical issues are distinctly insisted on in their relation to the theory. This is naturally followed by the statements as to "the effect of light or dark backgrounds on the apparent size of bodies" (Nos. 240--250). At the end I have placed, in the order of the original, those sections from the MS. C which treat of the "Perspective of Disappearance" and serve to some extent to complete the treatment of the subject (251--262).

Definition (222. 223).

222.

OF THE DIMINISHED DISTINCTNESS OF THE OUTLINES OF OPAQUE BODIES.

If the real outlines of opaque bodies are indistinguishable at even a very short distance, they will be more so at long distances; and, since it is by its outlines that we are able to know the real form of any opaque body, when by its remoteness we fail to discern it as a whole, much more must we fail to discern its parts and outlines.

223.

OF THE DIMINUTION IN PERSPECTIVE OF OPAQUE OBJECTS.

Among opaque objects of equal size the apparent diminution of size will be in proportion to their distance from the eye of the spectator; but it is an inverse proportion, since, where the distance is greater, the opaque body will appear smaller, and the less the distance the larger will the object appear. And this is the fundamental principle of linear perspective and it follows:--[11]every object as it becomes more remote loses first those parts which are smallest. Thus of a horse, we should lose the legs before the head, because the legs are thinner than the head; and the neck before the body for the same reason. Hence it follows that the last part of the horse which would be discernible by the eye would be the mass of the body in an oval form, or rather in a cylindrical form and this would lose its apparent thickness before its length-- according to the 2nd rule given above, &c. [Footnote 23: Compare line 11.].

If the eye remains stationary the perspective terminates in the distance in a point. But if the eye moves in a straight [horizontal] line the perspective terminates in a line and the reason is that this line is generated by the motion of the point and our sight; therefore it follows that as we move our sight [eye], the point moves, and as we move the point, the line is generated, &c.

An illustration by experiment.

224.

Every visible body, in so far as it affects the eye, includes three attributes; that is to say: mass, form and colour; and the mass is recognisable at a greater distance from the place of its actual existence than either colour or form. Again, colour is discernible at a greater distance than form, but this law does not apply to luminous bodies.

The above proposition is plainly shown and proved by experiment; because: if you see a man close to you, you discern the exact appearance of the mass and of the form and also of the colouring; if he goes to some distance you will not recognise who he is, because the character of the details will disappear, if he goes still farther you will not be able to distinguish his colouring, but he will appear as a dark object, and still farther he will appear as a very small dark rounded object. It appears rounded because distance so greatly diminishes the various details that nothing remains visible but the larger mass. And the reason is this: We know very well that all the images of objects reach the senses by a small aperture in the eye; hence, if the whole horizon a d is admitted through such an aperture, the object b c being but a very small fraction of this horizon what space can it fill in that minute image of so vast a hemisphere? And because luminous bodies have more power in darkness than any others, it is evident that, as the chamber of the eye is very dark, as is the nature of all colored cavities, the images of distant objects are confused and lost in the great light of the sky; and if they are visible at all, appear dark and black, as every small body must when seen in the diffused light of the atmosphere.

[Footnote: The diagram belonging to this passage is placed between lines 5 and 6; it is No. 4 on Pl. VI.]

A guiding rule.

225.

OF THE ATMOSPHERE THAT INTERPOSES BETWEEN THE EYE AND VISIBLE OBJECTS.

An object will appear more or less distinct at the same distance, in proportion as the atmosphere existing between the eye and that object is more or less clear. Hence, as I know that the greater or less quantity of the air that lies between the eye and the object makes the outlines of that object more or less indistinct, you must diminish the definiteness of outline of those objects in proportion to their increasing distance from the eye of the spectator.

An experiment.

226.

When I was once in a place on the sea, at an equal distance from the shore and the mountains, the distance from the shore looked much greater than that from the mountains.

On indistinctness at short distances (227-231).

227.

If you place an opaque object in front of your eye at a distance of four fingers' breadth, if it is smaller than the space between the two eyes it will not interfere with your seeing any thing that may be beyond it. No object situated beyond another object seen by the eye can be concealed by this [nearer] object if it is smaller than the space from eye to eye.

228.

The eye cannot take in a luminous angle which is too close to it.

229.

That part of a surface will be better lighted on which the light falls at the greater angle. And that part, on which the shadow falls at the greatest angle, will receive from those rays least of the benefit of the light.

230.

OF THE EYE.

The edges of an object placed in front of the pupil of the eye will be less distinct in proportion as they are closer to the eye. This is shown by the edge of the object n placed in front of the pupil d; in looking at this edge the pupil also sees all the space a c which is beyond the edge; and the images the eye receives from that space are mingled with the images of the edge, so that one image confuses the other, and this confusion hinders the pupil from distinguishing the edge.

231.

The outlines of objects will be least clear when they are nearest to the eye, and therefore remoter outlines will be clearer. Among objects which are smaller than the pupil of the eye those will be less distinct which are nearer to the eye.

On indistinctness at great distances (232-234).

232.

Objects near to the eye will appear larger than those at a distance.

Objects seen with two eyes will appear rounder than if they are seen with only one.

Objects seen between light and shadow will show the most relief.

233.

OF PAINTING.

Our true perception of an object diminishes in proportion as its size is diminished by distance.

234.

PERSPECTIVE.

Why objects seen at a distance appear large to the eye and in the image on the vertical plane they appear small.

PERSPECTIVE.

I ask how far away the eye can discern a non-luminous body, as, for instance, a mountain. It will be very plainly visible if the sun is behind it; and could be seen at a greater or less distance according to the sun's place in the sky.

[Footnote: The clue to the solution of this problem (lines 1-3) is given in lines 4-6, No. 232. Objects seen with both eyes appear solid since they are seen from two distinct points of sight separated by the distance between the eyes, but this solidity cannot be represented in a flat drawing. Compare No. 535.]

The importance of light and shade in the perspective of disappearance (235-239).

235.

An opaque body seen in a line in which the light falls will reveal no prominences to the eye. For instance, let a be the solid body and c the light; c m and c n will be the lines of incidence of the light, that is to say the lines which transmit the light to the object a. The eye being at the point b, I say that since the light c falls on the whole part m n the portions in relief on that side will all be illuminated. Hence the eye placed at c cannot see any light and shade and, not seeing it, every portion will appear of the same tone, therefore the relief in the prominent or rounded parts will not be visible.

236.

OF PAINTING.

When you represent in your work shadows which you can only discern with difficulty, and of which you cannot distinguish the edges so that you apprehend them confusedly, you must not make them sharp or definite lest your work should have a wooden effect.

237.

OF PAINTING.

You will observe in drawing that among the shadows some are of undistinguishable gradation and form, as is shown in the 3rd [proposition] which says: Rounded surfaces display as many degrees of light and shade as there are varieties of brightness and darkness reflected from the surrounding objects.

238.

OF LIGHT AND SHADE.

You who draw from nature, look (carefully) at the extent, the degree, and the form of the lights and shadows on each muscle; and in their position lengthwise observe towards which muscle the axis of the central line is directed.

239.

An object which is [so brilliantly illuminated as to be] almost as bright as light will be visible at a greater distance, and of larger apparent size than is natural to objects so remote.

The effect of light or dark backgrounds on the apparent size of objects (240-250).

240.

A shadow will appear dark in proportion to the brilliancy of the light surrounding it and conversely it will be less conspicuous where it is seen against a darker background.

241.

OF ORDINARY PERSPECTIVE.

An object of equal breadth and colour throughout, seen against a background of various colours will appear unequal in breadth.

And if an object of equal breadth throughout, but of various colours, is seen against a background of uniform colour, that object will appear of various breadth. And the more the colours of the background or of the object seen against the ground vary, the greater will the apparent variations in the breadth be though the objects seen against the ground be of equal breadth [throughout].

242.

A dark object seen against a bright background will appear smaller than it is.

A light object will look larger when it is seen against a background darker than itself.

243.

OF LIGHT.

A luminous body when obscured by a dense atmosphere will appear smaller; as may be seen by the moon or sun veiled by mists.

OF LIGHT.

Of several luminous bodies of equal size and brilliancy and at an equal distance, that will look the largest which is surrounded by the darkest background.

OF LIGHT.

I find that any luminous body when seen through a dense and thick mist diminishes in proportion to its distance from the eye. Thus it is with the sun by day, as well as the moon and the other eternal lights by night. And when the air is clear, these luminaries appear larger in proportion as they are farther from the eye.

244.

That portion of a body of uniform breadth which is against a lighter background will look narrower [than the rest].

[4] e is a given object, itself dark and of uniform breadth; a b and c d are two backgrounds one darker than the other; b c is a bright background, as it might be a spot lighted by the sun through an aperture in a dark room. Then I say that the object e g will appear larger at e f than at g h; because e f has a darker background than g h; and again at f g it will look narrower from being seen by the eye o, on the light background b c. [Footnote 12: The diagram to which the text, lines 1-11, refers, is placed in the original between lines 3 and 4, and is given on Pl. XLI, No. 3. Lines 12 to 14 are explained by the lower of the two diagrams on Pl. XLI, No. 4. In the original these are placed after line 14.] That part of a luminous body, of equal breadth and brilliancy throughout, will look largest which is seen against the darkest background; and the luminous body will seem on fire.

245.

WHY BODIES IN LIGHT AND SHADE HAVE THEIR OUTLINES ALTERED BY THE COLOUR AND BRIGHTNESS OF THE OBJECTS SERVING AS A BACKGROUND TO THEM.

If you look at a body of which the illuminated portion lies and ends against a dark background, that part of the light which will look brightest will be that which lies against the dark [background] at d. But if this brighter part lies against a light background, the edge of the object, which is itself light, will be less distinct than before, and the highest light will appear to be between the limit of the background m f and the shadow. The same thing is seen with regard to the dark [side], inasmuch as that edge of the shaded portion of the object which lies against a light background, as at l, it looks much darker than the rest. But if this shadow lies against a dark background, the edge of the shaded part will appear lighter than before, and the deepest shade will appear between the edge and the light at the point o.

[Footnote: In the original diagram o is inside the shaded surface at the level of d.]

246.

An opaque body will appear smaller when it is surrounded by a highly luminous background, and a light body will appear larger when it is seen against a darker background. This may be seen in the height of buildings at night, when lightning flashes behind them; it suddenly seems, when it lightens, as though the height of the building were diminished. For the same reason such buildings look larger in a mist, or by night than when the atmosphere is clear and light.

247.

ON LIGHT BETWEEN SHADOWS

When you are drawing any object, remember, in comparing the grades of light in the illuminated portions, that the eye is often deceived by seeing things lighter than they are. And the reason lies in our comparing those parts with the contiguous parts. Since if two [separate] parts are in different grades of light and if the less bright is conterminous with a dark portion and the brighter is conterminous with a light background--as the sky or something equally bright--, then that which is less light, or I should say less radiant, will look the brighter and the brighter will seem the darker.

248.

Of objects equally dark in themselves and situated at a considerable and equal distance, that will look the darkest which is farthest above the earth.

249.

TO PROVE HOW IT IS THAT LUMINOUS BODIES APPEAR LARGER, AT A DISTANCE, THAN THEY ARE.

If you place two lighted candles side by side half a braccio apart, and go from them to a distance 200 braccia you will see that by the increased size of each they will appear as a single luminous body with the light of the two flames, one braccio wide.

TO PROVE HOW YOU MAY SEE THE REAL SIZE OF LUMINOUS BODIES.

If you wish to see the real size of these luminous bodies, take a very thin board and make in it a hole no bigger than the tag of a lace and place it as close to your eye as possible, so that when you look through this hole, at the said light, you can see a large space of air round it. Then by rapidly moving this board backwards and forwards before your eye you will see the light increase [and diminish].

Propositions on perspective of disappearance from MS. C. (250-262).

250.

Of several bodies of equal size and equally distant from the eye, those will look the smallest which are against the lightest background.

Every visible object must be surrounded by light and shade. A perfectly spherical body surrounded by light and shade will appear to have one side larger than the other in proportion as one is more highly lighted than the other.

251.

PERSPECTIVE.

No visible object can be well understood and comprehended by the human eye excepting from the difference of the background against which the edges of the object terminate and by which they are bounded, and no object will appear [to stand out] separate from that background so far as the outlines of its borders are concerned. The moon, though it is at a great distance from the sun, when, in an eclipse, it comes between our eyes and the sun, appears to the eyes of men to be close to the sun and affixed to it, because the sun is then the background to the moon.

252.

A luminous body will appear more brilliant in proportion as it is surrounded by deeper shadow. [Footnote: The diagram which, in the original, is placed after this text, has no connection with it.]

253.

The straight edges of a body will appear broken when they are conterminous with a dark space streaked with rays of light. [Footnote: Here again the diagrams in the original have no connection with the text.]

254.

Of several bodies, all equally large and equally distant, that which is most brightly illuminated will appear to the eye nearest and largest. [Footnote: Here again the diagrams in the original have no connection with the text.]

255.

If several luminous bodies are seen from a great distance although they are really separate they will appear united as one body.

256.

If several objects in shadow, standing very close together, are seen against a bright background they will appear separated by wide intervals.

257.

Of several bodies of equal size and tone, that which is farthest will appear the lightest and smallest.

258.

Of several objects equal in size, brightness of background and length that which has the flattest surface will look the largest. A bar of iron equally thick throughout and of which half is red hot, affords an example, for the red hot part looks thicker than the rest.

259.

Of several bodies of equal size and length, and alike in form and in depth of shade, that will appear smallest which is surrounded by the most luminous background.

260.

DIFFERENT PORTIONS OF A WALL SURFACE WILL BE DARKER OR BRIGHTER IN PROPORTION AS THE LIGHT OR SHADOW FALLS ON THEM AT A LARGER ANGLE.

The foregoing proposition can be clearly proved in this way. Let us say that m q is the luminous body, then f g will be the opaque body; and let a e be the above-mentioned plane on which the said angles fall, showing [plainly] the nature and character of their bases. Then: a will be more luminous than b; the base of the angle a is larger than that of b and it therefore makes a greater angle which will be a m q; and the pyramid b p m will be narrower and m o c will be still finer, and so on by degrees, in proportion as they are nearer to e, the pyramids will become narrower and darker. That portion of the wall will be the darkest where the breadth of the pyramid of shadow is greater than the breadth of the pyramid of light.

At the point a the pyramid of light is equal in strength to the pyramid of shadow, because the base f g is equal to the base r f. At the point d the pyramid of light is narrower than the pyramid of shadow by so much as the base s f is less than the base f g.

Divide the foregoing proposition into two diagrams, one with the pyramids of light and shadow, the other with the pyramids of light [only].

261.

Among shadows of equal depth those which are nearest to the eye will look least deep.

262.

The more brilliant the light given by a luminous body, the deeper will the shadows be cast by the objects it illuminates.

V. Theory of colours.

Leonardo's theory of colours is even more intimately connected with his principles of light and shade than his Perspective of Disappearance and is in fact merely an appendix or supplement to those principles, as we gather from the titles to sections 264, 267, and 276, while others again (Nos. 281, 282) are headed Prospettiva.

A very few of these chapters are to be found in the oldest copies and editions of the Treatise on Painting, and although the material they afford is but meager and the connection between them but slight, we must still attribute to them a special theoretical value as well as practical utility--all the more so because our knowledge of the theory and use of colours at the time of the Renaissance is still extremely limited.

The reciprocal effects of colours on objects placed opposite each other (263-272).

263.

OF PAINTING.

The hue of an illuminated object is affected by that of the luminous body.

264.

OF SHADOW.

The surface of any opaque body is affected by the colour of surrounding objects.

265.

A shadow is always affected by the colour of the surface on which it is cast.

266.

An image produced in a mirror is affected by the colour of the mirror.

267.

OF LIGHT AND SHADE.

Every portion of the surface of a body is varied [in hue] by the [reflected] colour of the object that may be opposite to it.

EXAMPLE.

If you place a spherical body between various objects that is to say with [direct] sunlight on one side of it, and on the other a wall illuminated by the sun, which wall may be green or of any other colour, while the surface on which it is placed may be red, and the two lateral sides are in shadow, you will see that the natural colour of that body will assume something of the hue reflected from those objects. The strongest will be [given by] the luminous body; the second by the illuminated wall, the third by the shadows. There will still be a portion which will take a tint from the colour of the edges.

268.

The surface of every opaque body is affected by the colour of the objects surrounding it. But this effect will be strong or weak in proportion as those objects are more or less remote and more or less strongly [coloured].

269.

OF PAINTING.

The surface of every opaque body assumes the hues reflected from surrounding objects.

The surface of an opaque body assumes the hues of surrounding objects more strongly in proportion as the rays that form the images of those objects strike the surface at more equal angles.

And the surface of an opaque body assumes a stronger hue from the surrounding objects in proportion as that surface is whiter and the colour of the object brighter or more highly illuminated.

270.

OF THE RAYS WHICH CONVEY THROUGH THE AIR THE IMAGES OF OBJECTS.

All the minutest parts of the image intersect each other without interfering with each other. To prove this let r be one of the sides of the hole, opposite to which let s be the eye which sees the lower end o of the line n o. The other extremity cannot transmit its image to the eye s as it has to strike the end r and it is the same with regard to m at the middle of the line. The case is the same with the upper extremity n and the eye u. And if the end n is red the eye u on that side of the holes will not see the green colour of o, but only the red of n according to the 7th of this where it is said: Every form projects images from itself by the shortest line, which necessarily is a straight line, &c.

[Footnote: 13. This probably refers to the diagram given under No. 66.]

271.

OF PAINTING.

The surface of a body assumes in some degree the hue of those around it. The colours of illuminated objects are reflected from the surfaces of one to the other in various spots, according to the various positions of those objects. Let o be a blue object in full light, facing all by itself the space b c on the white sphere a b e d e f, and it will give it a blue tinge, m is a yellow body reflected onto the space a b at the same time as o the blue body, and they give it a green colour (by the 2nd [proposition] of this which shows that blue and yellow make a beautiful green &c.) And the rest will be set forth in the Book on Painting. In that Book it will be shown, that, by transmitting the images of objects and the colours of bodies illuminated by sunlight through a small round perforation and into a dark chamber onto a plane surface, which itself is quite white, &c.

But every thing will be upside down.

Combination of different colours in cast shadows.

272.

That which casts the shadow does not face it, because the shadows are produced by the light which causes and surrounds the shadows. The shadow caused by the light e, which is yellow, has a blue tinge, because the shadow of the body a is cast upon the pavement at b, where the blue light falls; and the shadow produced by the light d, which is blue, will be yellow at c, because the yellow light falls there and the surrounding background to these shadows b c will, besides its natural colour, assume a hue compounded of yellow and blue, because it is lighted by the yellow light and by the blue light both at once.

Shadows of various colours, as affected by the lights falling on them. That light which causes the shadow does not face it.

[Footnote: In the original diagram we find in the circle e "giallo" (yellow) and the cirle d "azurro" (blue) and also under the circle of shadow to the left "giallo" is written and under that to the right "azurro".

In the second diagram where four circles are placed in a row we find written, beginning at the left hand, "giallo" (yellow), "azurro" (blue), "verde" (green), "rosso" (red).]

The effect of colours in the camera obscura (273-274).

273.

The edges of a colour(ed object) transmitted through a small hole are more conspicuous than the central portions.

The edges of the images, of whatever colour, which are transmitted through a small aperture into a dark chamber will always be stronger than the middle portions.

274.

OF THE INTERSECTIONS OF THE IMAGES IN THE PUPIL OF THE EYE.

The intersections of the images as they enter the pupil do not mingle in confusion in the space where that intersection unites them; as is evident, since, if the rays of the sun pass through two panes of glass in close contact, of which one is blue and the other yellow, the rays, in penetrating them, do not become blue or yellow but a beautiful green. And the same thing would happen in the eye, if the images which were yellow or green should mingle where they [meet and] intersect as they enter the pupil. As this does not happen such a mingling does not exist.

OF THE NATURE OF THE RAYS COMPOSED OF THE IMAGES OF OBJECTS, AND OF THEIR INTERSECTIONS.

The directness of the rays which transmit the forms and colours of the bodies whence they proceed does not tinge the air nor can they affect each other by contact where they intersect. They affect only the spot where they vanish and cease to exist, because that spot faces and is faced by the original source of these rays, and no other object, which surrounds that original source can be seen by the eye where these rays are cut off and destroyed, leaving there the spoil they have conveyed to it. And this is proved by the 4th [proposition], on the colour of bodies, which says: The surface of every opaque body is affected by the colour of surrounding objects; hence we may conclude that the spot which, by means of the rays which convey the image, faces--and is faced by the cause of the image, assumes the colour of that object.

On the colours of derived shadows (275. 276).

275.

ANY SHADOW CAST BY AN OPAQUE BODY SMALLER THAN THE LIGHT CAUSING THE SHADOW WILL THROW A DERIVED SHADOW WHICH IS TINGED BY THE COLOUR OF THE LIGHT.

Let n be the source of the shadow e f; it will assume its hue. Let o be the source of h e which will in the same way be tinged by its hue and so also the colour of v h will be affected by p which causes it; and the shadow of the triangle z k y will be affected by the colour of q, because it is produced by it. [7] In proportion as c d goes into a d, will n r s be darker than m; and the rest of the space will be shadowless [11]. f g is the highest light, because here the whole light of the window a d falls; and thus on the opaque body m e is in equally high light; z k y is a triangle which includes the deepest shadow, because the light a d cannot reach any part of it. x h is the 2nd grade of shadow, because it receives only 1/3 of the light from the window, that is c d. The third grade of shadow is h e, where two thirds of the light from the window is visible. The last grade of shadow is b d e f, because the highest grade of light from the window falls at f.

[Footnote: The diagram Pl. III, No. 1 belongs to this chapter as well as the text given in No. 148. Lines 7-11 (compare lines 8-12 of No. 148) which are written within the diagram, evidently apply to both sections and have therefore been inserted in both.]

276.

OF THE COLOURS OF SIMPLE DERIVED SHADOWS.

The colour of derived shadows is always affected by that of the body towards which they are cast. To prove this: let an opaque body be placed between the plane s c t d and the blue light d e and the red light a b, then I say that d e, the blue light, will fall on the whole surface s c t d excepting at o p which is covered by the shadow of the body q r, as is shown by the straight lines d q o e r p. And the same occurs with the light a b which falls on the whole surface s c t d excepting at the spot obscured by the shadow q r; as is shown by the lines d q o, and e r p. Hence we may conclude that the shadow n m is exposed to the blue light d e; but, as the red light a b cannot fall there, n m will appear as a blue shadow on a red background tinted with blue, because on the surface s c t d both lights can fall. But in the shadows only one single light falls; for this reason these shadows are of medium depth, since, if no light whatever mingled with the shadow, it would be of the first degree of darkness &c. But in the shadow at o p the blue light does not fall, because the body q r interposes and intercepts it there. Only the red light a b falls there and tinges the shadow of a red hue and so a ruddy shadow appears on the background of mingled red and blue.

The shadow of q r at o p is red, being caused by the blue light d e; and the shadow of q r at o' p' is blue being caused by the red light a b. Hence we say that the blue light in this instance causes a red derived shadow from the opaque body q' r', while the red light causes the same body to cast a blue derived shadow; but the primary shadow [on the dark side of the body itself] is not of either of those hues, but a mixture of red and blue.

The derived shadows will be equal in depth if they are produced by lights of equal strength and at an equal distance; this is proved. [Footnote 53: The text is unfinished in the original.]

[Footnote: In the original diagram Leonardo has written within the circle q r corpo obroso (body in shadow); at the spot marked A, luminoso azzurro (blue luminous body); at B, luminoso rosso (red luminous body). At E we read ombra azzurra (blue tinted shadow) and at D ombra rossa (red tinted shadow).]

On the nature of colours (277. 278).

277.

No white or black is transparent.

278.

OF PAINTING.

[Footnote 2: See Footnote 3] Since white is not a colour but the neutral recipient of every colour [Footnote 3: il bianco non e colore ma e inpotentia ricettiva d'ogni colore (white is not a colour, but the neutral recipient of every colour). LEON BATT. ALBERTI "Della pittura" libro I, asserts on the contrary: "Il bianco e'l nero non sono veri colori, ma sono alteratione delli altri colori" (ed. JANITSCHEK, p. 67; Vienna 1877).], when it is seen in the open air and high up, all its shadows are bluish; and this is caused, according to the 4th [prop.], which says: the surface of every opaque body assumes the hue of the surrounding objects. Now this white [body] being deprived of the light of the sun by the interposition of some body between the sun and itself, all that portion of it which is exposed to the sun and atmosphere assumes the colour of the sun and atmosphere; the side on which the sun does not fall remains in shadow and assumes the hue of the atmosphere. And if this white object did not reflect the green of the fields all the way to the horizon nor get the brightness of the horizon itself, it would certainly appear simply of the same hue as the atmosphere.

On gradations in the depth of colours (279. 280).

279.

Since black, when painted next to white, looks no blacker than when next to black; and white when next to black looks no whiter than white, as is seen by the images transmitted through a small hole or by the edges of any opaque screen ...

280.

OF COLOURS.

Of several colours, all equally white, that will look whitest which is against the darkest background. And black will look intensest against the whitest background.

And red will look most vivid against the yellowest background; and the same is the case with all colours when surrounded by their strongest contrasts.

On the reflection of colours (281-283).

281.

PERSPECTIVE.

Every object devoid of colour in itself is more or less tinged by the colour [of the object] placed opposite. This may be seen by experience, inasmuch as any object which mirrors another assumes the colour of the object mirrored in it. And if the surface thus partially coloured is white the portion which has a red reflection will appear red, or any other colour, whether bright or dark.

PERSPECTIVE.

Every opaque and colourless body assumes the hue of the colour reflected on it; as happens with a white wall.

282.

PERSPECTIVE.

That side of an object in light and shade which is towards the light transmits the images of its details more distinctly and immediately to the eye than the side which is in shadow.

PERSPECTIVE.

The solar rays reflected on a square mirror will be thrown back to distant objects in a circular form.

PERSPECTIVE.

Any white and opaque surface will be partially coloured by reflections from surrounding objects.

[Footnote 281. 282: The title line of these chapters is in the original simply "pro", which may be an abbreviation for either Propositione or Prospettiva-- taking Prospettiva of course in its widest sense, as we often find it used in

Leonardo's writings. The title "pro" has here been understood to mean Prospettiva, in accordance with the suggestion afforded by page 10b of this same MS., where the first section is headed Prospettiva in full (see No. 94), while the four following sections are headed merely "pro" (see No. 85).]

283.

WHAT PORTION OF A COLOURED SURFACE OUGHT IN REASON TO BE THE MOST INTENSE.

If a is the light, and b illuminated by it in a direct line, c, on which the light cannot fall, is lighted only by reflection from b which, let us say, is red. Hence the light reflected from it, will be affected by the hue of the surface causing it and will tinge the surface c with red. And if c is also red you will see it much more intense than b; and if it were yellow you would see there a colour between yellow and red.

On the use of dark and light colours in painting (284--286).

284.

WHY BEAUTIFUL COLOURS MUST BE IN THE [HIGHEST] LIGHT.

Since we see that the quality of colour is known [only] by means of light, it is to be supposed that where there is most light the true character of a colour in light will be best seen; and where there is most shadow the colour will be affected by the tone of that. Hence, O Painter! remember to show the true quality of colours in bright lights.

285.

An object represented in white and black will display stronger relief than in any other way; hence I would remind you O Painter! to dress your figures in the lightest colours you can, since, if you put them in dark colours, they will be in too slight relief and inconspicuous from a distance. And the reason is that the shadows of all objects are dark. And if you make a dress dark there is little variety in the lights and shadows, while in light colours there are many grades. ·

286.

OF PAINTING.

Colours seen in shadow will display more or less of their natural brilliancy in proportion as they are in fainter or deeper shadow.

But if these same colours are situated in a well-lighted place, they will appear brighter in proportion as the light is more brilliant.

THE ADVERSARY.

The variety of colours in shadow must be as great as that of the colours in the objects in that shadow.

THE ANSWER.

Colours seen in shadow will display less variety in proportion as the shadows in which they lie are deeper. And evidence of this is to be had by looking from an open space into the doorways of dark and shadowy churches, where the pictures which are painted in various colours all look of uniform darkness.

Hence at a considerable distance all the shadows of different colours will appear of the same darkness.

It is the light side of an object in light and shade which shows the true colour.

On the colours of the rainbow (287. 288).

287.

Treat of the rainbow in the last book on Painting, but first write the book on colours produced by the mixture of other colours, so as to be able to prove by those painters' colours how the colours of the rainbow are produced.

288.

WHETHER THE COLOURS OF THE RAINBOW ARE PRODUCED BY THE SUN.

The colours of the rainbow are not produced by the sun, for they occur in many ways without the sunshine; as may be seen by holding a glass of water up to the eye; when, in the glass--where there are those minute bubbles always seen in coarse glass--each bubble, even though the sun does not fall on it, will produce on one side all the colours of the rainbow; as you may see by placing the glass between the day light and your eye in such a way as that it is close to the eye, while on one side the glass admits the [diffused] light of the atmosphere, and on the other side the shadow of the wall on one side of the window; either left or right, it matters not which. Then, by turning the glass round you will see these colours all round the bubbles in the glass &c. And the rest shall be said in its place.

THAT THE EYE HAS NO PART IN PRODUCING THE COLOURS OF THE RAINBOW.

In the experiment just described, the eye would seem to have some share in the colours of the rainbow, since these bubbles in the glass do not display the colours except through the medium of the eye. But, if you place the glass full of water on the window sill, in such a position as that the outer side is exposed to the sun's rays, you will see the same colours produced in the spot of light thrown through the glass and upon the floor, in a dark place, below the window; and as the eye is not here concerned in it, we may evidently, and with certainty pronounce that the eye has no share in producing them.

OF THE COLOURS IN THE FEATHERS OF CERTAIN BIRDS.

There are many birds in various regions of the world on whose feathers we see the most splendid colours produced as they move, as we see in our own country in the feathers of peacocks or on the necks of ducks or pigeons, &c.

Again, on the surface of antique glass found underground and on the roots of turnips kept for some time at the bottom of wells or other stagnant waters [we see] that each root displays colours similar to those of the real rainbow. They may also be seen when oil has been placed on the top of water and in the solar rays reflected from the surface of a diamond or beryl; again, through the angular facet of a beryl every dark object against a background of the atmosphere or any thing else equally pale-coloured is surrounded by these rainbow colours between the atmosphere and the dark body; and in many other circumstances which I will not mention, as these suffice for my purpose.

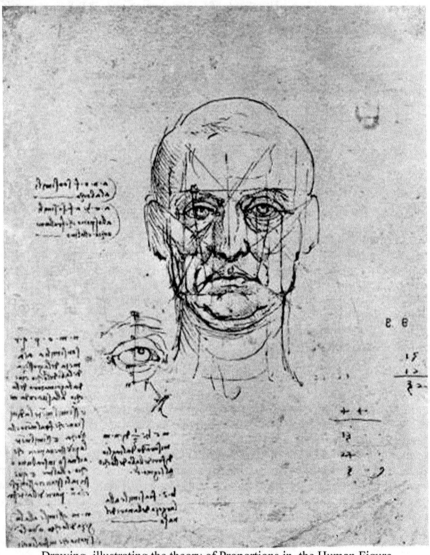

Drawing, illustrating the theory of Proportions in, the Human Figure

VI. Perspective of Colour and Aerial Perspective.

Leonardo distinctly separates these branches of his subject, as may be seen in the beginning of No. 295. Attempts have been made to cast doubts on the results which Leonardo arrived at by experiment on the perspective of colour, but not with justice, as may be seen from the original text of section 294.

The question as to the composition of the atmosphere, which is inseparable from a discussion on Aerial Perspective, forms a separate theory which is treated at considerable length. Indeed the author enters into it so fully that we cannot escape the conviction that he must have dwelt with particular pleasure on this part of his subject, and that he attached great importance to giving it a character of general applicability.

General rules (289--291).

289.

The variety of colour in objects cannot be discerned at a great distance, excepting in those parts which are directly lighted up by the solar rays.

290.

As to the colours of objects: at long distances no difference is perceptible in the parts in shadow.

291.

OF THE VISIBILITY OF COLOURS.

Which colour strikes most? An object at a distance is most conspicuous, when it is lightest, and the darkest is least visible.

An exceptional case.

292.

Of the edges [outlines] of shadows. Some have misty and ill defined edges, others distinct ones.

No opaque body can be devoid of light and shade, except it is in a mist, on ground covered with snow, or when snow is falling on the open country which has no light on it and is surrounded with darkness.

And this occurs [only] in spherical bodies, because in other bodies which have limbs and parts, those sides of limbs which face each other reflect on each other the accidental [hue and tone] of their surface.

An experiment.

293.

ALL COLOURS ARE AT A DISTANCE UNDISTINGUISHABLE AND UNDISCERNIBLE.

All colours at a distance are undistinguishable in shadow, because an object which is not in the highest light is incapable of transmitting its image to the eye through an atmosphere more luminous than itself; since the lesser brightness must be absorbed by the greater. For instance: We, in a house, can see that all the colours on the surface of the walls are clearly and instantly visible when the windows of the house are open; but if we were to go out of the house and look in at the windows from a little distance to see the paintings on those walls, instead of the paintings we should see an uniform deep and colourless shadow.

The practice of the prospettiva de colori.

294.

HOW A PAINTER SHOULD CARRY OUT THE PERSPECTIVE OF COLOUR IN PRACTICE.

In order to put into practice this perspective of the variation and loss or diminution of the essential character of colours, observe at every hundred braccia some objects standing in the landscape, such as trees, houses, men and particular places. Then in front of the first tree have a very steady plate of glass and keep your eye very steady, and then, on this plate of glass, draw a tree, tracing it over the form of that tree. Then move it on one side so far as that the real tree is close by the side of the tree you have drawn; then colour your drawing in such a way as that in colour and form the two may be alike, and that both, if you close one eye, seem to be painted on the glass and at the same distance. Then, by the same method, represent a second tree, and a third, with a distance of a hundred braccia between each. And these will serve as a standard and guide whenever you work on your own pictures, wherever they may apply, and will enable you to give due distance in those works. [14] But I have found that as a rule the second is 4/5 of the first when it is 20 braccia beyond it.

[Footnote: This chapter is one of those copied in the Manuscript of the Vatican library Urbinas 1270, and the original text is rendered here with no other alterations, but in the orthography. H. LUDWIG, in his edition of this copy translates lines 14 and 15 thus: "Ich finde aber als Regel, dass der zweite um vier Funftel des ersten abnimmt, wenn er namlich zwanzig Ellen vom ersten entfernt ist (?)". He adds in his commentary: "Das Ende der Nummer ist wohl jedenfalls verstummelt". However the translation given above shows that it admits of a different rendering.]

The rules of aerial perspective (295--297).

295.

OF AERIAL PERSPECTIVE.

There is another kind of perspective which I call Aerial Perspective, because by the atmosphere we are able to distinguish the variations in distance of different buildings, which appear placed on a single line; as, for instance, when we see several buildings beyond a wall, all of which, as they appear above the top of the wall, look of the same size, while you wish to represent them in a picture as more remote one than another and to give the effect of a somewhat dense atmosphere. You know that in an atmosphere of equal density the remotest objects seen through it, as mountains, in consequence of the great quantity of atmosphere between your eye and them--appear blue and almost of the same hue as the atmosphere itself [Footnote 10: quado il sole e per leuante (when the sun is in the East). Apparently the author refers here to morning light in general. H. LUDWIG however translates this passage from the Vatican copy "wenn namlich die Sonne (dahinter) im Osten steht".] when the sun is in the East [Footnote 11: See Footnote 10]. Hence you must make the nearest building above the wall of its real colour, but the more distant ones make less defined and bluer. Those you wish should look farthest away you must make proportionately bluer; thus, if one is to be five times as distant, make it five times bluer. And by this rule the buildings which above a [given] line appear of the same size, will plainly be distinguished as to which are the more remote and which larger than the others.

296.

The medium lying between the eye and the object seen, tinges that object with its colour, as the blueness of the atmosphere makes the distant mountains appear blue and red glass makes objects seen beyond it, look red. The light shed round them by the stars is obscured by the darkness of the night which lies between the eye and the radiant light of the stars.

297.

Take care that the perspective of colour does not disagree with the size of your objects, hat is to say: that the colours diminish from their natural [vividness] in proportion as the objects at various distances dimmish from their natural size.

On the relative density of the atmosphere (298--290).

298.

WHY THE ATMOSPHERE MUST BE REPRESENTED AS PALER TOWARDS THE LOWER PORTION.

Because the atmosphere is dense near the earth, and the higher it is the rarer it becomes. When the sun is in the East if you look towards the West and a little way to the South and North, you will see that this dense atmosphere receives more light from the sun than the rarer; because the rays meet with greater resistance. And if the sky, as you see it, ends on a low plain, that lowest portion of the sky will be seen through a denser and whiter atmosphere, which will weaken its true colour as seen through that medium, and there the sky will look whiter than it is above you, where the line of sight travels through a smaller space of air charged with heavy vapour. And if you turn to the East, the atmosphere will appear darker as you look lower down because the luminous rays pass less freely through the lower atmosphere.

299.

OF THE MODE OF TREATING REMOTE OBJECTS IN PAINTING.

It is easy to perceive that the atmosphere which lies closest to the level ground is denser than the rest, and that where it is higher up, it is rarer and more transparent. The lower portions of large and lofty objects which are at a distance are not much seen, because you see them along a line which passes through a denser and thicker section of the atmosphere. The summits of such heights are seen along a line which, though it starts from your eye in a dense atmosphere, still, as it ends at the top of those lofty objects, ceases in a much rarer atmosphere than exists at their base; for this reason the farther this line extends from your eye, from point to point the atmosphere becomes more and more rare. Hence, O Painter! when you represent mountains, see that from hill to hill the bases are paler than the summits, and in proportion as they recede beyond each other make the bases paler than the summits; while, the higher they are the more you must show of their true form and colour.

On the colour of the atmosphere (300-307).

300.

OF THE COLOUR OF THE ATMOSPHERE.

I say that the blueness we see in the atmosphere is not intrinsic colour, but is caused by warm vapour evaporated in minute and insensible atoms on which the solar rays fall, rendering them luminous against the infinite darkness of the fiery sphere which lies beyond and includes it. And this may be seen, as I saw it by any one going up [Footnote 5: With regard to the place spoken of as M'oboso (compare No. 301 line 20) its identity will be discussed under Leonardo's Topographical notes in Vol. II.] Monboso, a peak of the Alps which divide France from Italy. The base of this mountain gives birth to the four rivers which flow in four different directions through the whole of Europe. And no mountain has its base at so great a height as this, which lifts itself almost above the clouds; and snow seldom falls there, but only hail in the summer, when the clouds are highest. And this hail lies [unmelted] there, so that if it were not for the absorption of the rising and falling clouds, which does not happen twice in an age, an enormous mass of ice would be piled up there by the hail, and in the middle of July I found it very considerable. There I saw above me the dark sky, and the sun as it fell on the mountain was far brighter here than in the plains below, because a smaller extent of atmosphere lay between the summit of the mountain and the sun. Again as an illustration of the colour of the atmosphere I will mention the smoke of old and dry wood, which, as it comes out of a chimney, appears to turn very blue, when seen between the eye and the dark distance. But as it rises, and comes between the eye and the bright atmosphere, it at once shows of an ashy grey colour; and this happens because it no longer has darkness beyond it, but this bright and luminous space. If the smoke is from young, green wood, it will not appear blue, because, not being transparent and being full of superabundant moisture, it has the effect of condensed clouds which take distinct lights and shadows like a solid body. The same occurs with the atmosphere, which, when overcharged with moisture appears white, and the small amount of heated moisture makes it dark, of a dark blue colour; and this will suffice us so far as concerns the colour of the atmosphere; though it might be added that, if this transparent blue were the natural colour of the atmosphere, it would follow that wherever a larger mass air intervened between the eye and the element of fire, the azure colour would be more intense; as we see in blue glass and in sapphires, which are darker in proportion as they are larger. But the atmosphere in such circumstances behaves in an opposite manner, inasmuch as where a greater quantity of it lies between the eye and the sphere of fire, it is seen much whiter. This occurs towards the horizon. And the less the extent of atmosphere between the eye and the sphere of fire, the deeper is the blue colour, as may be seen even on low plains. Hence it follows, as I say, that the atmosphere assumes this azure hue by reason of the particles of moisture which catch the rays of the sun. Again, we may note the difference in particles of dust, or particles of smoke, in the sun beams admitted through holes into a dark chamber, when the former will look ash grey and the thin smoke will appear of a most beautiful blue; and it may be seen again in in the dark shadows of distant mountains when the air between the eye and those shadows will look very blue, though the brightest parts of those mountains will not differ much from their true colour. But if any one wishes for a final proof let him paint a board with various colours, among them an intense black; and over all let him lay a very thin and transparent [coating of] white. He will then see that this transparent white will nowhere show a more beautiful blue than over the black--but it must be very thin and finely ground.

[Footnote 7: reta here has the sense of malanno.]

301.

Experience shows us that the air must have darkness beyond it and yet it appears blue. If you produce a small quantity of smoke from dry wood and the rays of the sun fall on this smoke, and if you then place behind the smoke a piece of black velvet on which the sun does not shine, you will see that all the smoke which is between the eye and the black stuff will appear of a beautiful blue colour. And if instead of the velvet you place a white cloth smoke, that is too thick smoke, hinders, and too thin smoke does not produce, the perfection of this blue colour. Hence a moderate amount of smoke produces the finest blue. Water violently ejected in a fine spray and in a dark chamber where the sun beams are admitted produces these blue rays and the more vividly if it is distilled water, and thin smoke looks blue. This I mention in order to show that the blueness of the atmosphere is caused by the darkness beyond it, and these instances are given for those who cannot confirm my experience on Monboso.

302.

When the smoke from dry wood is seen between the eye of the spectator and some dark space [or object], it will look blue. Thus the sky looks blue by reason of the darkness beyond it. And if you look towards the horizon of the sky, you will see the atmosphere is not blue, and this is caused by its density. And thus at each degree, as you raise your eyes above the horizon up to the sky over your head, you will see the atmosphere look darker [blue] and this is because a smaller density of air lies between your eye and the [outer] darkness. And if you go to the top of a high mountain the sky will look proportionately darker above you as the atmosphere becomes rarer between you and the [outer] darkness; and this will be more visible at each degree of increasing height till at last we should find darkness.

That smoke will look bluest which rises from the driest wood and which is nearest to the fire and is seen against the darkest background, and with the sunlight upon it.

303.

A dark object will appear bluest in proportion as it has a greater mass of luminous atmosphere between it and the eye. As may be seen in the colour of the sky.

304.

The atmosphere is blue by reason of the darkness above it because black and white make blue.

305.

In the morning the mist is denser above than below, because the sun draws it upwards; hence tall buildings, even if the summit is at the same distance as the base have the summit invisible. Therefore, also, the sky looks darkest [in colour] overhead, and towards the horizon it is not blue but rather between smoke and dust colour.

The atmosphere, when full of mist, is quite devoid of blueness, and only appears of the colour of clouds, which shine white when the weather is fine. And the more you turn to the west the darker it will be, and the brighter as you look to the east. And the verdure of the fields is bluish in a thin mist, but grows grey in a dense one.

The buildings in the west will only show their illuminated side, where the sun shines, and the mist hides the rest. When the sun rises and chases away the haze, the hills on the side where it lifts begin to grow clearer, and look blue, and seem to smoke with the vanishing mists; and the buildings reveal their lights and shadows; through the thinner vapour they show only their lights and through the thicker air nothing at all. This is when the movement of the mist makes it part horizontally, and then the edges of the mist will be indistinct against the blue of the sky, and towards the earth it will look almost like dust blown up. In proportion as the atmosphere is dense the buildings of a city and the trees in a landscape will look fewer, because only the tallest and largest will be seen.

Darkness affects every thing with its hue, and the more an object differs from darkness, the more we see its real and natural colour. The mountains will look few, because only those will be seen which are farthest apart; since, at such a distance, the density increases to such a degree that it causes a brightness by which the darkness of the hills becomes divided and vanishes indeed towards the top. There is less [mist] between lower and nearer hills and yet little is to be distinguished, and least towards the bottom.

306.

The surface of an object partakes of the colour of the light which illuminates it; and of the colour of the atmosphere which lies between the eye and that object, that is of the colour of the transparent medium lying between the object and the eye; and among colours of a similar character the second will be of the same tone as the first, and this is caused by the increased thickness of the colour of the medium lying between the object and the eye.

307. OF PAINTING.

Of various colours which are none of them blue that which at a great distance will look bluest is the nearest to black; and so, conversely, the colour which is least like black will at a great distance best preserve its own colour.

Hence the green of fields will assume a bluer hue than yellow or white will, and conversely yellow or white will change less than green, and red still less.

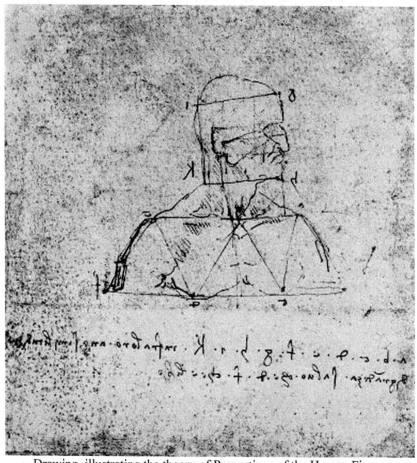

Drawing, illustrating the theory of Proportions of the Human Figure

VII. On the Proportions and on the Movements of the Human Figure.

Leonardo's researches on the proportions and movements of the human figure must have been for the most part completed and written before the year 1498; for LUCA PACIOLO writes, in the dedication to Ludovico il Moro, of his book Divina Proportione, which was published in that year: "Leonardo da venci ... hauedo gia co tutta diligetia al degno libro de pictura e movimenti humani posto fine".

The selection of Leonardo's axioms contained in the Vatican copy attributes these words to the author: "e il resto si dira nella universale misura del huomo". (MANZI, p. 147; LUDWIG, No. 264). LOMAZZO, again, in his Idea del Tempio della Pittura Milano 1590, cap. IV, says: "Lionardo Vinci ... dimostro anco in figura tutte le proporzioni dei membri del corpo umano".

The Vatican copy includes but very few sections of the "Universale misura del huomo" and until now nothing has been made known of the original MSS. on the subject which have supplied the very extensive materials for this portion of the work. The collection at Windsor, belonging to her Majesty the Queen, includes by far the most important part of Leonardo's investigations on this subject, constituting about half of the whole of the materials here published; and the large number of original drawings adds greatly to the interest which the subject itself must command. Luca Paciolo would seem to have had these MSS. (which I have distinguished by the initials W. P.) in his mind when he wrote the passage quoted above. Still, certain notes of a later date--such as Nos. 360, 362 and 363, from MS. E, written in 1513--14, sufficiently prove that Leonardo did not consider his earlier studies on the Proportions and Movements of the Human Figure final and complete, as we might suppose from Luca Paciolo's statement. Or else he took the subject up again at a subsequent period, since his former researches had been carried on at Milan between 1490 and 1500. Indeed it is highly probable that the anatomical studies which he was pursuing zvith so much zeal between 1510--16 should have led him to reconsider the subject of Proportion.

Preliminary observations (308. 309).

308.

Every man, at three years old is half the full height he will grow to at last.

309.

If a man 2 braccia high is too small, one of four is too tall, the medium being what is admirable. Between 2 and 4 comes 3; therefore take a man of 3 braccia in height and measure him by the rule I will give you. If you tell me that I may be mistaken, and judge a man to be well proportioned who does not conform to this division, I answer that you must look at many men of 3 braccia, and out of the larger number who are alike in their limbs choose one of those who are most graceful and take your measurements. The length of the hand is 1/3 of a braccio [8 inches] and this is found 9 times in man. And the face [Footnote 7: The account here given of the braccio is of importance in understanding some of the succeeding chapters. Testa must here be understood to mean the face. The statements in this section are illustrated in part on Pl. XI.] is the same, and from the pit of the throat to the shoulder, and from the shoulder to the nipple, and from one nipple to the other, and from each nipple to the pit of the throat.

Proportions of the head and face (310-318).

310.

The space between the parting of the lips [the mouth] and the base of the nose is one-seventh of the face.

The space from the mouth to the bottom of the chin c d is the fourth part of the face and equal to the width of the mouth.

The space from the chin to the base of the nose e f is the third part of the face and equal to the length of the nose and to the forehead.

The distance from the middle of the nose to the bottom of the chin g h, is half the length of the face.

The distance from the top of the nose, where the eyebrows begin, to the bottom of the chin, i k, is two thirds of the face.

The space from the parting of the lips to the top of the chin l m, that is where the chin ends and passes into the lower lip of the mouth, is the third of the distance from the parting of the lips to the bottom of the chin and is the twelfth part of the face. From the top to the bottom of the chin m n is the sixth part of the face and is the fifty fourth part of a man's height.

From the farthest projection of the chin to the throat o p is equal to the space between the mouth and the bottom of the chin, and a fourth of the face.

The distance from the top of the throat to the pit of the throat below q r is half the length of the face and the eighteenth part of a man's height.

From the chin to the back of the neck s t, is the same distance as between the mouth and the roots of the hair, that is three quarters of the head.

From the chin to the jaw bone v x is half the head and equal to the thickness of the neck in profile.

The thickness of the head from the brow to the nape is once and 3/4 that of the neck.

[Footnote: The drawings to this text, lines 1-10 are on Pl. VII, No. I. The two upper sketches of heads, Pl. VII, No. 2, belong to lines 11-14, and in the original are placed immediately below the sketches reproduced on Pl. VII, No. 1.]

311.

The distance from the attachment of one ear to the other is equal to that from the meeting of the eyebrows to the chin, and in a fine face the width of the mouth is equal to the length from the parting of the lips to the bottom of the chin.

312.

The cut or depression below the lower lip of the mouth is half way between the bottom of the nose and the bottom of the chin.

The face forms a square in itself; that is its width is from the outer corner of one eye to the other, and its height is from the very top of the nose to the bottom of the lower lip of the mouth; then what remains above and below this square amounts to the height of such another square, a b is equal to the space between c d; d n in the same way to n c, and likewise s r, q p, h k are equal to each other.

It is as far between m and s as from the bottom of the nose to the chin. The ear is exactly as long as the nose. It is as far from x to j as from the nose to the chin. The parting of the mouth seen in profile slopes to the angle of the jaw. The ear should be as high as from the bottom of the nose to the top of the eye-lid. The space between the eyes is equal to the width of an eye. The ear is over the middle of the neck, when seen in profile. The distance from 4 to 5 is equal to that from s to r.

[Footnote: See Pl. VIII, No. I, where the text of lines 3-13 is also given in facsimile.]

313.

(a b) is equal to (c d).

[Footnote: See Pl. VII, No. 3. Reference may also be made here to two pen and ink drawings of heads in profile with figured measurements, of which there is no description in the MS. These are given on Pl. XVII, No. 2.--A head, to the left, with part of the torso [W. P. 5a], No. 1 on the same plate is from MS. A 2b and in the original occurs on a page with wholly irrelevant text on matters of natural history. M. RAVAISSON in his edition of the Paris MS. A has reproduced this head and discussed it fully [note on page 12]; he has however somewhat altered the original measurements. The complicated calculations which M. RAVAISSON has given appear to me in no way justified. The sketch, as we see it, can hardly have been intended for any thing more than an experimental attempt to ascertain relative proportions. We do not find that Leonardo made use of circular lines in any other study of the proportions of the human head. At the same time we see that the proportions of this sketch are not in accordance with the rules which he usually observed (see for instance No. 310).]

The head a f 1/6 larger than n f.

315.

From the eyebrow to the junction of the lip with the chin, and the angle of the jaw and the upper angle where the ear joins the temple will be a perfect square. And each side by itself is half the head.

The hollow of the cheek bone occurs half way between the tip of the nose and the top of the jaw bone, which is the lower angle of the setting on of the ear, in the frame here represented.

From the angle of the eye-socket to the ear is as far as the length of the ear, or the third of the face.

[Footnote: See Pl. IX. The text, in the original is written behind the head. The handwriting would seem to indicate a date earlier than 1480. On the same leaf there is a drawing in red chalk of two horsemen of which only a portion of the upper figure is here visible. The whole leaf measures 22 1/2 centimetres wide by 29 long, and is numbered 127 in the top right-hand corner.]

316.

From a to b--that is to say from the roots of the hair in front to the top of the head--ought to be equal to c d;--that is from the bottom of the nose to the meeting of the lips in the middle of the mouth. From the inner corner of the eye m to the top of the head a is as far as from m down to the chin s. s c f b are all at equal distances from each other.

[Footnote: The drawing in silver-point on bluish tinted paper--Pl. X--which belongs to this chapter has been partly drawn over in ink by Leonardo himself.]

317.

From the top of the head to the bottom of the chin is 1/9, and from the roots of the hair to the chin is 1/9 of the distance from the roots of the hair to the ground. The greatest width of the face is equal to the space between the mouth and the roots of the hair and is 1/12 of the whole height. From the top of the ear to the top of the head is equal to the distance from the bottom of the chin to the lachrymatory duct of the eye; and also equal to the distance from the angle of the chin to that of the jaw; that is the 1/16 of the whole. The small cartilage which projects over the opening of the ear towards the nose is half-way between the nape and the eyebrow; the thickness of the neck in profile is equal to the space between the chin and the eyes, and to the space between the chin and the jaw, and it is 1/18 of the height of the man.

318.

a b, c d, e f, g h, i k are equal to each other in size excepting that d f is accidental.

[Footnote: See Pl. XI.]

Proportions of the head seen in front (319-321).

319.

a n o f are equal to the mouth.

a c and a f are equal to the space between one eye and the other.

n m o f q r are equal to half the width of the eye lids, that is from the inner [lachrymatory] corner of the eye to its outer corner; and in like manner the division between the chin and the mouth; and in the same way the narrowest part of the nose between the eyes. And these spaces, each in itself, is the 19th part of the head, n o is equal to the length of the eye or of the space between the eyes.

m c is 1/3 of n m measuring from the outer corner of the eyelids to the letter c. b s will be equal to the width of the nostril.

[Footnote: See Pl. XII.]

320.

The distance between the centres of the pupils of the eyes is 1/3 of the face. The space between the outer corners of the eyes, that is where the eye ends in the eye socket which contains it, thus the outer corners, is half the face.

The greatest width of the face at the line of the eyes is equal to the distance from the roots of the hair in front to the parting of the lips.

[Footnote: There are, with this section, two sketches of eyes, not reproduced here.]

321.

The nose will make a double square; that is the width of the nose at the nostrils goes twice into the length from the tip of the nose to the eyebrows. And, in same way, in profile the distance from the extreme side of the nostril where it joins the cheek to the tip of the nose is equal to the width of the nose in front from one nostril to the other. If you divide the whole length of the nose--that is from the tip to the insertion of the eyebrows, into 4 equal parts, you will find that one of these parts extends from the tip of the nostrils to the base of the nose, and the upper division lies between the inner corner of the eye and the insertion of the eyebrows; and the two middle parts [together] are equal to the length of the eye from the inner to the outer corner.

[Footnote: The two bottom sketches on Pl. VII, No. 4 face the six lines of this section,--With regard to the proportions of the head in profile see No. 312.]

322.

The great toe is the sixth part of the foot, taking the measure in profile, on the inside of the foot, from where this toe springs from the ball of the sole of the foot to its tip a b; and it is equal to the distance from the mouth to the bottom of the chin. If you draw the foot in profile from the outside, make the little toe begin at three quarters of the length of the foot, and you will find the same distance from the insertion of this toe as to the farthest prominence of the great toe.

323.

For each man respectively the distance between a b is equal to c d.

324.

Relative proportion of the hand and foot.

The foot is as much longer than the hand as the thickness of the arm at the wrist where it is thinnest seen facing.

Again, you will find that the foot is as much longer than the hand as the space between the inner angle of the little toe to the last projection of the big toe, if you measure along the length of the foot.

The palm of the hand without the fingers goes twice into the length of the foot without the toes.

If you hold your hand with the fingers straight out and close together you will find it to be of the same width as the widest part of the foot, that is where it is joined onto the toes.

And if you measure from the prominence of the inner ancle to the end of the great toe you will find this measure to be as long as the whole hand.

From the top angle of the foot to the insertion of the toes is equal to the hand from wrist joint to the tip of the thumb.

The smallest width of the hand is equal to the smallest width of the foot between its joint into the leg and the insertion of the toes.

The width of the heel at the lower part is equal to that of the arm where it joins the hand; and also to the leg where it is thinnest when viewed in front.

The length of the longest toe, from its first division from the great toe to its tip is the fourth of the foot from the centre of the ancle bone to the tip, and it is equal to the width of the mouth. The distance between the mouth and the chin is equal to that of the knuckles and of the three middle fingers and to the length of their first joints if the hand is spread, and equal to the distance from the joint of the thumb to the outset of the nails, that is the fourth part of the hand and of the face.

The space between the extreme poles inside and outside the foot called the ancle or ancle bone a b is equal to the space between the mouth and the inner corner of the eye.

325.

The foot, from where it is attached to the leg, to the tip of the great toe is as long as the space between the upper part of the chin and the roots of the hair a b; and equal to five sixths of the face.

326.

a d is a head's length, c b is a head's length. The four smaller toes are all equally thick from the nail at the top to the bottom, and are 1/13 of the foot.

[Footnote: See Pl. XIV, No. 1, a drawing of a foot with the text in three lines below it.]

327.

The whole length of the foot will lie between the elbow and the wrist and between the elbow and the inner angle of the arm towards the breast when the arm is folded. The foot is as long as the whole head of a man, that is from under the chin to the topmost part of the head[Footnote 2: nel modo che qui i figurato. See Pl. VII, No. 4, the upper figure. The text breaks off at the end of line 2 and the text given under No. 321 follows below. It may be here remarked that the second sketch on W. P. 311 has in the original no explanatory text.] in the way here figured.

Proportions of the leg (328-331).

328.

The greatest thickness of the calf of the leg is at a third of its height a b, and is a twentieth part thicker than the greatest thickness of the foot.

a c is half of the head, and equal to d b and to the insertion of the five toes e f. d k diminishes one sixth in the leg g h. g h is 1/3 of the head; m n increases one sixth from a e and is 7/12 of the head, o p is 1/10 less than d k and is 6/17 of the head. a is at half the distance between b q, and is 1/4 of the man. r is half way between s and b[Footnote 11: b is here and later on measured on the right side of the foot as seen by the spectator.]. The concavity of the knee outside r is higher than that inside a. The half of the whole height of the leg from the foot r, is half way between the prominence s and the ground b. v is half way between t and b. The thickness of the thigh seen in front is equal to the greatest width of the face, that is 2/3 of the length from the chin to the top of the head; z r is 5/6 of 7 to v; m n is equal to 7 v and is 1/4 of r b, x y goes 3 times into r b, and into r s.

[Footnote 22-35: The sketch illustrating these lines is on Pl. XIII, No. 2.]

[Footnote 22: a b entra in c f 6 e 6 in c n. Accurate measurement however obliges us to read 7 for 6.] a b goes six times into c f and six times into c n and is equal to g h; i k l m goes 4 times into d f, and 4 times into d n and is 3/7 of the foot; p q r s goes 3 times into d f, and 3 times into b n; [Footnote: 25. y is not to be found on the diagram and x occurs twice; this makes the passage very obscure.] x y is 1/8 of x f and is equal to n q. 3 7 is 1/9 of n f; 4 5 is 1/10 of n f [Footnote: 22-27. Compare with this lines 18-24 of No. 331, and the sketch of a leg in profile Pl. XV.].

I want to know how much a man increases in height by standing on tip-toe and how much p g diminishes by stooping; and how much it increases at n q likewise in bending the foot.

[Footnote 34: e f 4 dal cazo. By reading i for e the sense of this passage is made clear.] e f is four times in the distance between the genitals and the sole of the foot; [Footnote 35: 2 is not to be found in the sketch which renders the passage obscure. The two last lines are plainly legible in the facsimile.] 3 7 is six times from 3 to 2 and is equal to g h and i k.

[Footnote: The drawing of a leg seen in front Pl. XIII, No. 1 belongs to the text from lines 3-21. The measurements in this section should be compared with the text No. 331, lines 1-13, and the sketch of a leg seen in front on Pl. XV.]

329.

The length of the foot from the end of the toes to the heel goes twice into that from the heel to the knee, that is where the leg bone [fibula] joins the thigh bone [femur].

330.

a n b are equal; c n d are equal; n c makes two feet; n d makes 2 feet.

[Footnote: See the lower sketch, Pl. XIV, No. 1.]

331.

m n o are equal. The narrowest width of the leg seen in front goes 8 times from the sole of the foot to the joint of the knee, and is the same width as the arm, seen in front at the wrist, and as the longest measure of the ear, and as the three chief divisions into which we divide the face; and this measurement goes 4 times from the wrist joint of the hand to the point of the elbow. [14] The foot is as long as the space from the knee between a and b; and the patella of the knee is as long as the leg between r and s.

[18] The least thickness of the leg in profile goes 6 times from the sole of the foot to the knee joint and is the same width as the space between the outer corner of the eye and the opening of the ear, and as the thickest part of the arm seen in profile and between the inner corner of the eye and the insertion of the hair.

a b c [d] are all relatively of equal length, c d goes twice from the sole of the foot to the centre of the knee and the same from the knee to the hip.

[28]a b c are equal; a to b is 2 feet--that is to say measuring from the heel to the tip of the great toe.

[Footnote: See Pl. XV. The text of lines 2-17 is to the left of the front view of the leg, to which it refers. Lines 18-27 are in the middle column and refer to the leg seen in profile and turned to the left, on the right hand side of the writing. Lines 20-30 are above, to the left and apply to the sketch below them.

Some farther remarks on the proportion of the leg will be found in No. 336, lines 6, 7.]

On the central point of the whole body.

332.

In kneeling down a man will lose the fourth part of his height.

When a man kneels down with his hands folded on his breast the navel will mark half his height and likewise the points of the elbows.

Half the height of a man who sits--that is from the seat to the top of the head--will be where the arms fold below the breast, and below the shoulders. The seated portion--that is from the seat to the top of the head--will be more than half the man's [whole height] by the length of the scrotum.

[Footnote: See Pl. VIII, No. 2.]

The relative proportions of the torso and of the whole figure.

333.

The cubit is one fourth of the height of a man and is equal to the greatest width of the shoulders. From the joint of one shoulder to the other is two faces and is equal to the distance from the top of the breast to the navel. [Footnote 9: dalla detta somita. It would seem more accurate to read here dal detto ombilico.] From this point to the genitals is a face's length.

[Footnote: Compare with this the sketches on the other page of the same leaf. Pl. VIII, No. 2.]

The relative proportions of the head and of the torso.

334.

From the roots of the hair to the top of the breast a b is the sixth part of the height of a man and this measure is equal.

From the outside part of one shoulder to the other is the same distance as from the top of the breast to the navel and this measure goes four times from the sole of the foot to the lower end of the nose.

The [thickness of] the arm where it springs from the shoulder in front goes 6 times into the space between the two outside edges of the shoulders and 3 times into the face, and four times into the length of the foot and three into the hand, inside or outside.

[Footnote: The three sketches Pl. XIV, No. 2 belong to this text.]

The relative proportions of the torso and of the leg (335. 336).

335.

a b c are equal to each other and to the space from the armpit of the shoulder to the genitals and to the distance from the tip of the fingers of the hand to the joint of the arm, and to the half of the breast; and you must know that c b is the third part of the height of a man from the shoulders to the ground; d e f are equal to each other and equal to the greatest width of the shoulders.

[Footnote: See Pl. XVI, No. 1.]

336.

--Top of the chin--hip--the insertion of the middle finger. The end of the calf of the leg on the inside of the thigh.--The end of the swelling of the shin bone of the leg. [6] The smallest thickness of the leg goes 3 times into the thigh seen in front.

[Footnote: See Pl. XVII, No. 2, middle sketch.]

The relative proportions of the torso and of the foot.

337.

The torso a b in its thinnest part measures a foot; and from a to b is 2 feet, which makes two squares to the seat--its thinnest part goes 3 times into the length, thus making 3 squares.

[Footnote: See Pl, VII, No. 2, the lower sketch.]

The proportions of the whole figure (338-341).

338.

A man when he lies down is reduced to 1/9 of his height.

339.

The opening of the ear, the joint of the shoulder, that of the hip and the ancle are in perpendicular lines; a n is equal to m o.

[Footnote: See Pl. XVI, No. 2, the upper sketch.]

340.

From the chin to the roots of the hair is 1/10 of the whole figure. From the joint of the palm of the hand to the tip of the longest finger is 1/10. From the chin to the top of the head 1/8; and from the pit of the stomach to the top of the breast is 1/6, and from the pit below the breast bone to the top of the head 1/4. From the chin to the nostrils 1/3 Part of the face, the same from the nostrils to the brow and from the brow to the roots of the hair, and the foot is 1/6, the elbow 1/4, the width of the shoulders 1/4.

341.

The width of the shoulders is 1/4 of the whole. From the joint of the shoulder to the hand is 1/3, from the parting of the lips to below the shoulder-blade is one foot.

The greatest thickness of a man from the breast to the spine is one 8th of his height and is equal to the space between the bottom of the chin and the top of the head.

The greatest width is at the shoulders and goes 4.

The torso from the front and back.

342.

The width of a man under the arms is the same as at the hips.

A man's width across the hips is equal to the distance from the top of the hip to the bottom of the buttock, when a man stands equally balanced on both feet; and there is the same distance from the top of the hip to the armpit. The waist, or narrower part above the hips will be half way between the arm pits and the bottom of the buttock.

[Footnote: The lower sketch Pl. XVI, No. 2, is drawn by the side of line 1.]

Vitruvius' scheme of proportions.

343.

Vitruvius, the architect, says in his work on architecture that the measurements of the human body are distributed by Nature as follows: that is that 4 fingers make 1 palm, and 4 palms make 1 foot, 6 palms make 1 cubit; 4 cubits make a man's height. And 4 cubits make one pace and 24 palms make a man; and these measures he used in his buildings. If you open your legs so much as to decrease your height 1/14 and spread and raise your arms till your middle fingers touch the level of the top of your head you must know that the centre of the outspread limbs will be in the navel and the space between the legs will be an equilateral triangle.

The length of a man's outspread arms is equal to his height.

From the roots of the hair to the bottom of the chin is the tenth of a man's height; from the bottom of the chin to the top of his head is one eighth of his height; from the top of the breast to the top of his head will be one sixth of a man. From the top of the breast to the roots of the hair will be the seventh part of the whole man. From the nipples to the top of the head will be the fourth part of a man. The greatest width of the shoulders contains in itself the fourth part of the man. From the elbow to the tip of the hand will be the fifth part of a man; and from the elbow to the angle of the armpit will be the eighth part of the man. The whole hand will be the tenth part of the man; the beginning of the genitals marks the middle of the man. The foot is the seventh part of the man. From the sole of the foot to below the knee will be the fourth part of the man. From below the knee to the beginning of the genitals will be the fourth part of the man. The distance from the bottom of the chin to the nose and from the roots of the hair to the eyebrows is, in each case the same, and like the ear, a third of the face.

[Footnote: See Pl. XVIII. The original leaf is 21 centimetres wide and 33 1/2 long. At the ends of the scale below the figure are written the words diti (fingers) and palmi (palms). The passage quoted from Vitruvius is Book III, Cap. 1, and Leonardo's drawing is given in the editions of Vitruvius by FRA GIOCONDO (Venezia 1511, fol., Firenze 1513, 8vo.) and by CESARIANO (Como 1521).]

The arm and head.

344.

From b to a is one head, as well as from c to a and this happens when the elbow forms a right angle.

[Footnote: See Pl. XLI, No. 1.]

Proportions of the arm (345-349).

345.

From the tip of the longest finger of the hand to the shoulder joint is four hands or, if you will, four faces.

a b c are equal and each interval is 2 heads.

[Footnote: Lines 1-3 are given on Pl. XV below the front view of the leg; lines 4 and 5 are below again, on the left side. The lettering refers to the bent arm near the text.]

346.

The hand from the longest finger to the wrist joint goes 4 times from the tip of the longest finger to the shoulder joint.

347.

a b c are equal to each other and to the foot and to the space between the nipple and the navel d e will be the third part of the whole man.

f g is the fourth part of a man and is equal to g h and measures a cubit.

[Footnote: See Pl. XIX, No. 1. 1. mamolino (=bambino, little child) may mean here the navel.]

348.

a b goes 4 times into a c and 9 into a m. The greatest thickness of the arm between the elbow and the hand goes 6 times into a m and is equal to r f. The greatest thickness of the arm between the shoulder and the elbow goes 4 times into c m, and is equal to h n g. The smallest thickness of the arm above the elbow x y is not the base of a square, but is equal to half the space h 3 which is found between the inner joint of the arm and the wrist joint.

[11]The width of the wrist goes 12 times into the whole arm; that is from the tip of the fingers to the shoulder joint; that is 3 times into the hand and 9 into the arm.

The arm when bent is 4 heads.

The arm from the shoulder to the elbow in bending increases in length, that is in the length from the shoulder to the elbow, and this increase is equal to the thickness of the arm at the wrist when seen in profile. And the space between the bottom of the chin and the parting of the lips, is equal to the thickness of the 2 middle fingers, and to the width of the mouth and to the space between the roots of the hair on the forehead and the top of the head [Footnote: Queste cose. This passage seems to have been written on purpose to rectify the foregoing lines. The error is explained by the accompanying sketch of the bones of the arm.]. All these distances are equal to each other, but they are not equal to the above-mentioned increase in the arm.

The arm between the elbow and wrist never increases by being bent or extended.

The arm, from the shoulder to the inner joint when extended.

When the arm is extended, p n is equal to n a. And when it is bent n a diminishes 1/6 of its length and p n does the same. The outer elbow joint increases 1/7 when bent; and thus by being bent it increases to the length of 2 heads. And on the inner side, by bending, it is found that whereas the arm from where it joins the side to the wrist, was 2 heads and a half, in bending it loses the half head and measures only two: one from the [shoulder] joint to the end [by the elbow], and the other to the hand.

The arm when folded will measure 2 faces up to the shoulder from the elbow and 2 from the elbow to the insertion of the four fingers on the palm of the hand. The length from the base of the fingers to the elbow never alters in any position of the arm.

If the arm is extended it decreases by 1/3 of the length between b and h; and if--being extended--it is bent, it will increase the half of o e. [Footnote 59-61: The figure sketched in the margin is however drawn to different proportions.] The length from the shoulder to the elbow is the same as from the base of the thumb, inside, to the elbow a b c.

[Footnote 62-64: The arm sketch on the margin of the MS. is identically the same as that given below on Pl. XX which may therefore be referred to in this place. In line 62 we read therefore z c for m n.] The smallest thickness of the arm in profile z c goes 6 times between the knuckles of the hand and the dimple of the elbow when extended and 14 times in the whole arm and 42 in the whole man [64]. The greatest thickness of the arm in profile is equal to the greatest thickness of the arm in front; but the first is placed at a third of the arm from the shoulder joint to the elbow and the other at a third from the elbow towards the hand.

[Footnote: Compare Pl. XVII. Lines 1-10 and 11-15 are written in two columns below the extended arm, and at the tips of the fingers we find the words: fine d'unghie (ends of the nails). Part of the text--lines 22 to 25--is visible by the side of the sketches on Pl. XXXV, No. 1.]

349.

From the top of the shoulder to the point of the elbow is as far as from that point to the joints of the four fingers with the palm of the hand, and each is 2 faces.

[5]a e is equal to the palm of the hand, r f and o g are equal to half a head and each goes 4 times into a b and b c. From c to m is 1/2 a head; m n is 1/3 of a head and goes 6 times into c b and into b a; a b loses 1/7 of its length when the arm is extended; c b never alters; o will always be the middle point between a and s.

y l is the fleshy part of the arm and measures one head; and when the arm is bent this shrinks 2/5 of its length; o a in bending loses 1/6 and so does o r.

a b is 1/7 of r c. f s will be 1/8 of r c, and each of those 2 measurements is the largest of the arm; k h is the thinnest part between the shoulder and the elbow and it is 1/8 of the whole arm r c; o p is 1/5 of r l; c z goes 13 times into r c.

[Footnote: See Pl. XX where the text is also seen from lines 5-23.]

The movement of the arm (350-354).

350.

In the innermost bend of the joints of every limb the reliefs are converted into a hollow, and likewise every hollow of the innermost bends becomes a convexity when the limb is straightened to the utmost. And in this very great mistakes are often made by those who have insufficient knowledge and trust to their own invention and do not have recourse to the imitation of nature; and these variations occur more in the middle of the sides than in front, and more at the back than at the sides.

351.

When the arm is bent at an angle at the elbow, it will produce some angle; the more acute the angle is, the more will the muscles within the bend be shortened; while the muscles outside will become of greater length than before. As is shown in the example; d c e will shrink considerably; and b n will be much extended.

[Footnote: See Pl. XIX, No. 2.]

352.

OF PAINTING.

The arm, as it turns, thrusts back its shoulder towards the middle of the back.

353.

The principal movements of the hand are 10; that is forwards, backwards, to right and to left, in a circular motion, up or down, to close and to open, and to spread the fingers or to press them together.

354.

OF THE MOTIONS OF THE FINGERS.

The movements of the fingers principally consist in extending and bending them. This extension and bending vary in manner; that is, sometimes they bend altogether at the first joint; sometimes they bend, or extend, half way, at the 2nd joint; and sometimes they bend in their whole length and in all the three joints at once. If the 2 first joints are hindered from bending, then the 3rd joint can be bent with greater ease than before; it can never bend of itself, if the other joints are free, unless all three joints are bent. Besides all these movements there are 4 other principal motions of which 2 are up and down, the two others from side to side; and each of these is effected by a single tendon. From these there follow an infinite number of other movements always effected by two tendons; one tendon ceasing to act, the other takes up the movement. The tendons are made thick inside the fingers and thin outside; and the tendons inside are attached to every joint but outside they are not.

[Footnote 26: This head line has, in the original, no text to follow.] Of the strength [and effect] of the 3 tendons inside the fingers at the 3 joints.

The movement of the torso (355-361).

355.

Observe the altered position of the shoulder in all the movements of the arm, going up and down, inwards and outwards, to the back and to the front, and also in circular movements and any others.

And do the same with reference to the neck, hands and feet and the breast above the lips &c.

356.

Three are the principal muscles of the shoulder, that is b c d, and two are the lateral muscles which move it forward and backward, that is a o; a moves it forward, and o pulls it back; and bed raises it; a b c moves it upwards and forwards, and c d o upwards and backwards. Its own weight almost suffices to move it downwards.

The muscle d acts with the muscle c when the arm moves forward; and in moving backward the muscle b acts with the muscle c.

[Footnote: See Pl. XXI. In the original the lettering has been written in ink upon the red chalk drawing and the outlines of the figures have in most places been inked over.]

357.

OF THE LOINS, WHEN BENT.

The loins or backbone being bent. The breasts are are always lower than the shoulderblades of the back.

If the breast bone is arched the breasts are higher than the shoulderblades.

If the loins are upright the breast will always be found at the same level as the shoulderblades.

[Footnote: See Pl. XXII, No. 1.]

358.

a b the tendon and ankle in raising the heel approach each other by a finger's breadth; in lowering it they separate by a finger's breadth.

[Footnote: See Pl. XXII, No. 2. Compare this facsimile and text with Pl. III, No. 2, and p. 152 of MANZI'S edition. Also with No. 274 of LUDWIG'S edition of the Vatican Copy.]

359.

Just so much as the part d a of the nude figure decreases in this position so much does the opposite part increase; that is: in proportion as the length of the part d a diminishes the normal size so does the opposite upper part increase beyond its [normal] size. The navel does not change its position to the male organ; and this shrinking arises because when a figure stands on one foot, that foot becomes the centre [of gravity] of the superimposed weight. This being so, the middle between the shoulders is thrust above it out of it perpendicular line, and this line, which forms the central line of the external parts of the body, becomes bent at its upper extremity [so as to be] above the foot which supports the body; and the transverse lines are forced into such angles that their ends are lower on the side which is supported. As is shown at a b c.

[Footnote: See Pl. XXII, No. 3.]

360.

OF PAINTING.

Note in the motions and attitudes of figures how the limbs vary, and their feeling, for the shoulderblades in the motions of the arms and shoulders vary the [line of the] back bone very much. And you will find all the causes of this in my book of Anatomy.

361.

OF [CHANGE OF] ATTITUDE.

The pit of the throat is over the feet, and by throwing one arm forward the pit of the throat is thrown off that foot. And if the leg is thrown forward the pit of the throat is thrown forward; and. so it varies in every attitude.

362.

OF PAINTING.

Indicate which are the muscles, and which the tendons, which become prominent or retreat in the different movements of each limb; or which do neither [but are passive]. And remember that these indications of action are of the first importance and necessity in any painter or sculptor who professes to be a master &c.

And indicate the same in a child, and from birth to decrepitude at every stage of its life; as infancy, childhood, boyhood, youth &c.

And in each express the alterations in the limbs and joints, which swell and which grow thinner.

363.

O Anatomical Painter! beware lest the too strong indication of the bones, sinews and muscles, be the cause of your becoming wooden in your painting by your wish to make your nude figures display all their feeling. Therefore, in endeavouring to remedy this, look in what manner the muscles clothe or cover their bones in old or lean persons; and besides this, observe the rule as to how these same muscles fill up the spaces of the surface that extend between them, which are the muscles which never lose their prominence in any amount of fatness; and which too are the muscles of which the attachments are lost to sight in the very least plumpness. And in many cases several muscles look like one single muscle in the increase of fat; and in many cases, in growing lean or old, one single muscle divides into several muscles. And in this treatise, each in its place, all their peculiarities will be explained--and particularly as to the spaces between the joints of each limb &c. Again, do not fail [to observe] the variations in the forms of the above mentioned muscles, round and about the joints of the limbs of any animal, as caused by the diversity of the motions of each limb; for on some side of those joints the prominence of these muscles is wholly lost in the increase or diminution of the flesh of which these muscles are composed, &c.

[Footnote: DE ROSSI remarks on this chapter, in the Roman edition of the Trattato, p. 504: "Non in questo luogo solo, ma in altri ancora osservera il lettore, che Lionardo va fungendo quelli che fanno abuso della loro dottrina anatomica, e sicuramente con cio ha in mira il suo rivale Bonarroti, che di anatomia facea tanta pompa." Note, that Leonardo wrote this passage in Rome, probably under the immediate impression of MICHAELANGELO'S paintings in the Sistine Chapel and of RAPHAEL'S Isaiah in Sant' Agostino.]

364.

OF THE DIFFERENT MEASUREMENTS OF BOYS AND MEN.

There is a great difference in the length between the joints in men and boys for, in man, from the top of the shoulder [by the neck] to the elbow, and from the elbow to the tip of the thumb and from one shoulder to the other, is in each instance two heads, while in a boy it is but one because Nature constructs in us the mass which is the home of the intellect, before forming that which contains the vital elements.

365.

OF PAINTING.

Which are the muscles which subdivide in old age or in youth, when becoming lean? Which are the parts of the limbs of the human frame where no amount of fat makes the flesh thicker, nor any degree of leanness ever diminishes it?

The thing sought for in this question will be found in all the external joints of the bones, as the shoulder, elbow, wrists, finger-joints, hips, knees, ankle-bone and toes and the like; all of which shall be told in its place. The greatest thickness acquired by any limb is at the part of the muscles which is farthest from its attachments.

Flesh never increases on those portions of the limb where the bones are near to the surface.

At b r d a c e f the increase or diminution of the flesh never makes any considerable difference. Nature has placed in front of man all those parts which feel most pain under a blow; and these are the shin of the leg, the forehead, and the nose. And this was done for the preservation of man, since, if such pain were not felt in these parts, the number of blows to which they would be exposed must be the cause of their destruction.

Describe why the bones of the arm and leg are double near the hand and foot [respectively].

And where the flesh is thicker or thinner in the bending of the limbs.

366.

OF PAINTING.

Every part of the whole must be in proportion to the whole. Thus, if a man is of a stout short figure he will be the same in all his parts: that is with short and thick arms, wide thick hands, with short fingers with their joints of the same character, and so on with the rest. I would have the same thing understood as applying to all animals and plants; in diminishing, [the various parts] do so in due proportion to the size, as also in enlarging.

367.

OF THE AGREEMENT OF THE PROPORTION OF THE LIMBS.

And again, remember to be very careful in giving your figures limbs, that they must appear to agree with the size of the body and likewise to the age. Thus a youth has limbs that are not very muscular not strongly veined, and the surface is delicate and round, and tender in colour. In man the limbs are sinewy and muscular, while in old men the surface is wrinkled, rugged and knotty, and the sinews very prominent.

HOW YOUNG BOYS HAVE THEIR JOINTS JUST THE REVERSE OF THOSE OF MEN, AS TO SIZE.

Little children have all the joints slender and the portions between them are thick; and this happens because nothing but the skin covers the joints without any other flesh and has the character of sinew, connecting the bones like a ligature. And the fat fleshiness is laid on between one joint and the next, and between the skin and the bones. But, since the bones are thicker at the joints than between them, as a mass grows up the flesh ceases to have that superfluity which it had, between the skin and the bones; whence the skin clings more closely to the bone and the limbs grow more slender. But since there is nothing over the joints but the cartilaginous and sinewy skin this cannot dry up, and, not drying up, cannot shrink. Thus, and for this reason, children are slender at the joints and fat between the joints; as may be seen in the joints of the fingers, arms, and shoulders, which are slender and dimpled, while in man on the contrary all the joints of the fingers, arms, and legs are thick; and wherever children have hollows men have prominences.

The movement of the human figure (368-375).

368.

Of the manner of representing the 18 actions of man. Repose, movement, running, standing, supported, sitting, leaning, kneeling, lying down, suspended. Carrying or being carried, thrusting, pulling, striking, being struck, pressing down and lifting up.

[As to how a figure should stand with a weight in its hand [Footnote 8: The original text ends here.] Remember].

369.

A sitting man cannot raise himself if that part of his body which is front of his axis [centre of gravity] does not weigh more than that which is behind that axis [or centre] without using his arms.

A man who is mounting any slope finds that he must involuntarily throw the most weight forward, on the higher foot, rather than behind--that is in front of the axis and not behind it. Hence a man will always, involuntarily, throw the greater weight towards the point whither he desires to move than in any other direction.

The faster a man runs, the more he leans forward towards the point he runs to and throws more weight in front of his axis than behind. A man who runs down hill throws the axis onto his heels, and one who runs up hill throws it into the points of his feet; and a man running on level ground throws it first on his heels and then on the points of his feet.

This man cannot carry his own weight unless, by drawing his body back he balances the weight in front, in such a way as that the foot on which he stands is the centre of gravity.

[Footnote: See Pl. XXII, No. 4.]

370.

How a man proceeds to raise himself to his feet, when he is sitting on level ground.

371.

A man when walking has his head in advance of his feet.

A man when walking across a long level plain first leans [rather] backwards and then as much forwards.

[Footnote 3-6: He strides forward with the air of a man going down hill; when weary, on the contrary he walks like a man going up hill.]

372.

A man when running throws less weight on his legs than when standing still. And in the same way a horse which is running feels less the weight of the man he carries. Hence many persons think it wonderful that, in running, the horse can rest on one single foot. From this it may be stated that when a weight is in progressive motion the more rapid it is the less is the perpendicular weight towards the centre.

373.

If a man, in taking a jump from firm ground, can leap 3 braccia, and when he was taking his leap it were to recede 1/3 of a braccio, that would be taken off his former leap; and so if it were thrust forward 1/3 of a braccio, by how much would his leap be increased?

374.

OF DRAWING.

When a man who is running wants to neutralise the impetus that carries him on he prepares a contrary impetus which is generated by his hanging backwards. This can be proved, since, if the impetus carries a moving body with a momentum equal to 4 and the moving body wants to turn and fall back with a momentum of 4, then one momentum neutralises the other contrary one, and the impetus is neutralised.

Of walking up and down (375-379)

375.

When a man wants to stop running and check the impetus he is forced to hang back and take short quick steps. [Footnote: Lines 5-31 refer to the two upper figures, and the lower figure to the right is explained by the last part of the chapter.] The centre of gravity of a man who lifts one of his feet from the ground always rests on the centre of the sole of the foot [he stands on].

A man, in going up stairs involuntarily throws so much weight forward and on the side of the upper foot as to be a counterpoise to the lower leg, so that the labour of this lower leg is limited to moving itself.

The first thing a man does in mounting steps is to relieve the leg he is about to lift of the weight of the body which was resting on that leg; and besides this, he gives to the opposite leg all the rest of the bulk of the whole man, including [the weight of] the other leg; he then raises the other leg and sets the foot upon the step to which he wishes to raise himself. Having done this he restores to the upper foot all the weight of the body and of the leg itself, and places his hand on his thigh and throws his head forward and repeats the movement towards the point of the upper foot, quickly lifting the heel of the lower one; and with this impetus he lifts himself up and at the same time extends the arm which rested on his knee; and this extension of the arm carries up the body and the head, and so straightens the spine which was curved.

[32] The higher the step is which a man has to mount, the farther forward will he place his head in advance of his upper foot, so as to weigh more on a than on b; this man will not be on the step m. As is shown by the line g f.

[Footnote: See Pl. XXIII, No. 1. The lower sketch to the left belongs to the four first lines.]

376.

I ask the weight [pressure] of this man at every degree of motion on these steps, what weight he gives to b and to c.

[Footnote 8: These lines are, in the original, written in ink] Observe the perpendicular line below the centre of gravity of the man.

[Footnote: See Pl. XXIII, No. 2.]

377.

In going up stairs if you place your hands on your knees all the labour taken by the arms is removed from the sinews at the back of the knees.

[Footnote: See Pl. XXIII, No. 3.]

378.

The sinew which guides the leg, and which is connected with the patella of the knee, feels it a greater labour to carry the man upwards, in proportion as the leg is more bent; and the muscle which acts upon the angle made by the thigh where it joins the body has less difficulty and has a less weight to lift, because it has not the [additional] weight of the thigh itself. And besides this it has stronger muscles, being those which form the buttock.

379.

A man coming down hill takes little steps, because the weight rests upon the hinder foot, while a man mounting takes wide steps, because his weight rests on the foremost foot.

[Footnote: See Pl. XXIII, No. 4.]

On the human body in action (380-388).

380.

OF THE HUMAN BODY IN ACTION.

When you want to represent a man as moving some weight consider what the movements are that are to be represented by different lines; that is to say either from below upwards, with a simple movement, as a man does who stoops forward to take up a weight which he will lift as he straightens himself. Or as a man does who wants to squash something backwards, or to force it forwards or to pull it downwards with ropes passed through pullies [Footnote 10: Compare the sketch on page 198 and on 201 (S. K. M. II.1 86b).]. And here remember that the weight of a man pulls in proportion as his centre of gravity is distant from his fulcrum, and to this is added the force given by his legs and bent back as he raises himself.

381.

Again, a man has even a greater store of strength in his legs than he needs for his own weight; and to see if this is true, make a man stand on the shore-sand and then put another man on his back, and you will see how much he will sink in. Then take the man from off his back and make him jump straight up as high as he can, and you will find that the print of his feet will be made deeper by the jump than from having the man on his back. Hence, here, by 2 methods it is proved that a man has double the strength he requires to support his own body.

382.

OF PAINTING.

If you have to draw a man who is in motion, or lifting or pulling, or carrying a weight equal to his own, in what way must you set on his legs below his body?

[Footnote: In the MS. this question remains unanswered.]

383.

OF THE STRENGTH OF MAN.

A man pulling a [dead] weight balanced against himself cannot pull more than his own weight. And if he has to raise it he will [be able to] raise as much more than his weight as his strength may be more than that of other men. [Footnote 7: The stroke at the end of this line finishes in the original in a sort of loop or flourish, and a similar flourish occurs at the end of the previous passage written on the same page. M. RAVAISSON regards these as numbers (compare the photograph of page 30b in his edition of MS. A). He remarks: "Ce chiffre 8 et, a la fin de l'alinea precedent, le chiffre 7 sont, dans le manuscrit, des renvois."] The greatest force a man can apply, with equal velocity and impetus, will be when he sets his feet on one end of the balance [or lever] and then presses his shoulders against some stable body. This will raise a weight at the other end of the balance [lever], equal to his own weight and [added to that] as much weight as he can carry on his shoulders.

384.

No animal can simply move [by its dead weight] a greater weight than the sum of its own weight outside the centre of his fulcrum.

385.

A man who wants to send an arrow very far from the bow must be standing entirely on one foot and raising the other so far from the foot he stands on as to afford the requisite counterpoise to his body which is thrown on the front foot. And he must not hold his arm fully extended, and in order that he may be more able to bear the strain he must hold a piece of wood which there is in all crossbows, extending from the hand to the breast, and when he wishes to shoot he suddenly leaps forward at the same instant and extends his arm with the bow and releases the string. And if he dexterously does every thing at once it will go a very long way.

386.

When two men are at the opposite ends of a plank that is balanced, and if they are of equal weight, and if one of them wants to make a leap into the air, then his leap will be made down from his end of the plank and the man will never go up again but must remain in his place till the man at the other end dashes up the board.

[Footnote: See Pl. XXIV, No. 3.]

387.

Of delivering a blow to the right or left.

[Footnote: Four sketches on Pl. XXIV, No. 1 belong to this passage. The rest of the sketches and notes on that page are of a miscellaneous nature.]

388.

Why an impetus is not spent at once [but diminishes] gradually in some one direction? [Footnote 1: The paper has been damaged at the end of line 1.] The impetus acquired in the line a b c d is spent in the line d e but not so completely but that some of its force remains in it and to this force is added the momentum in the line d e with the force of the motive power, and it must follow than the impetus multiplied by the blow is greater that the simple impetus produced by the momentum d e.

[Footnote 8: The sketch No. 2 on Pl. XXIV stands, in the original, between lines 7 and 8. Compare also the sketches on Pl. LIV.] A man who has to deal a great blow with his weapon prepares himself with all his force on the opposite side to that where the spot is which he is to hit; and this is because a body as it gains in velocity gains in force against the object which impedes its motion.

On hair falling down in curls.

389.

Observe the motion of the surface of the water which resembles that of hair, and has two motions, of which one goes on with the flow of the surface, the other forms the lines of the eddies; thus the water forms eddying whirlpools one part of which are due to the impetus of the principal current and the other to the incidental motion and return flow.

[Footnote: See Pl. XXV. Where also the text of this passage is given in facsimile.]

On draperies (390--392).

390.

OF THE NATURE OF THE FOLDS IN DRAPERY.

That part of a fold which is farthest from the ends where it is confined will fall most nearly in its natural form.

Every thing by nature tends to remain at rest. Drapery, being of equal density and thickness on its wrong side and on its right, has a tendency to lie flat; therefore when you give it a fold or plait forcing it out of its flatness note well the result of the constraint in the part where it is most confined; and the part which is farthest from this constraint you will see relapses most into the natural state; that is to say lies free and flowing.

EXAMPLE.

[Footnote 13: a c sia. In the original text b is written instead of c--an evident slip of the pen.] Let a b c be the fold of the drapery spoken of above, a c will be the places where this folded drapery is held fast. I maintain that the part of the drapery which is farthest from the plaited ends will revert most to its natural form.

Therefore, b being farthest from a and c in the fold a b c it will be wider there than anywhere else.

[Footnote: See Pl. XXVIII, No. 6, and compare the drawing from Windsor Pl. XXX for farther illustration of what is here stated.]

391.

OF SMALL FOLDS IN DRAPERIES.

How figures dressed in a cloak should not show the shape so much as that the cloak looks as if it were next the flesh; since you surely cannot wish the cloak to be next the flesh, for you must suppose that between the flesh and the cloak there are other garments which prevent the forms of the limbs appearing distinctly through the cloak. And those limbs which you allow to be seen you must make thicker so that the other garments may appear to be under the cloak. But only give something of the true thickness of the limbs to a nymph [Footnote 9: Una nifa. Compare the beautiful drawing of a Nymph, in black chalk from the Windsor collection, Pl. XXVI.] or an angel, which are represented in thin draperies, pressed and clinging to the limbs of the figures by the action of the wind.

392.

You ought not to give to drapery a great confusion of many folds, but rather only introduce them where they are held by the hands or the arms; the rest you may let fall simply where it is its nature to flow; and do not let the nude forms be broken by too many details and interrupted folds. How draperies should be drawn from nature: that is to say if you want to represent woollen cloth draw the folds from that; and if it is to be silk, or fine cloth or coarse, or of linen or of crape, vary the folds in each and do not represent dresses, as many do, from models covered with paper or thin leather which will deceive you greatly.

[Footnote: The little pen and ink drawing from Windsor (W. 102), given on Pl. XXVIII, No. 7, clearly illustrates the statement made at the beginning of this passage; the writing of the cipher 19 on the same page is in Leonardo's hand; the cipher 21 is certainly not.]

VIII. Botany for Painters and Elements of Landscape Painting.

The chapters composing this portion of the work consist of observations on Form, Light and Shade in Plants, and particularly in Trees summed up in certain general rules by which the author intends to guide the artist in the pictorial representation of landscape.

With these the first principles of a Theory of Landscape painting are laid down--a theory as profoundly thought out in its main lines as it is lucidly worked out in its details. In reading these chapters the conviction is irresistible that such a Botany for painters is or ought to be of similar importance in the practice of painting as the principles of the Proportions and Movements of the human figure i. e. Anatomy for painters.

There can be no doubt that Leonardo, in laying down these rules, did not intend to write on Botany in the proper scientific sense--his own researches on that subject have no place here; it need only be observed that they are easily distinguished by their character and contents from those which are here collected and arranged under the title 'Botany for painters'. In some cases where this division might appear doubtful,--as for instance in No. 402--the Painter is directly addressed and enjoined to take the rule to heart as of special importance in his art.

The original materials are principally derived from MS. G, in which we often find this subject treated on several pages in succession without any of that intermixture of other matters, which is so frequent in Leonardo's writings. This MS., too, is one of the latest; when it was written, the great painter was already more than sixty years of age, so we can scarcely doubt that he regarded all he wrote as his final views on the subject. And the same remark applies to the chapters from MSS. E and M which were also written between 1513--15.

For the sake of clearness, however, it has been desirable to sacrifice--with few exceptions--the original order of the passages as written, though it was with much reluctance and only after long hesitation that I resigned myself to this necessity. Nor do I mean to impugn the logical connection of the author's ideas in his MS.; but it will be easily understood that the sequence of disconnected notes, as they occurred to Leonardo and were written down from time to time, might be hardly satisfactory as a systematic arrangement of his principles. The reader will find in the Appendix an exact account of the order of the chapters in the original MS. and from the data there given can restore them at will. As the materials are here arranged, the structure of the tree as regards the growth of the branches comes first (394-411) and then the insertion of the leaves on the stems (412-419). Then follow the laws of Light and Shade as applied, first, to the leaves (420-434), and, secondly, to the whole tree and to groups of trees (435-457). After the remarks on the Light and Shade in landscapes generally (458-464), we find special observations on that of views of towns and buildings (465-469). To the theory of Landscape Painting belong also the passages on the effect of Wind on Trees (470-473) and on the Light and Shade of Clouds (474-477), since we find in these certain comparisons with the effect of Light and Shade on Trees (e. g.: in No. 476, 4. 5; and No. 477, 9. 12). The chapters given in the Appendix Nos. 478 and 481 have hardly any connection with the subjects previously treated.

Classification of trees.

393.

TREES.

Small, lofty, straggling, thick, that is as to foliage, dark, light, russet, branched at the top; some directed towards the eye, some downwards; with white stems; this transparent in the air, that not; some standing close together, some scattered.

The relative thickness of the branches to the trunk (393--396).

394.

All the branches of a tree at every stage of its height when put together are equal in thickness to the trunk [below them].

All the branches of a water [course] at every stage of its course, if they are of equal rapidity, are equal to the body of the main stream.

395.

Every year when the boughs of a plant [or tree] have made an end of maturing their growth, they will have made, when put together, a thickness equal to that of the main stem; and at every stage of its ramification you will find the thickness of the said main stem; as: i k, g h, e f, c d, a b, will always be equal to each other; unless the tree is pollard--if so the rule does not hold good.

All the branches have a direction which tends to the centre of the tree m.

[Footnote: The two sketches of leafless trees one above another on the left hand side of Pl. XXVII, No. 1, belong to this passage.]

396.

If the plant n grows to the thickness shown at m, its branches will correspond [in thickness] to the junction a b in consequence of the growth inside as well as outside.

The branches of trees or plants have a twist wherever a minor branch is given off; and this giving off the branch forms a fork; this said fork occurs between two angles of which the largest will be that which is on the side of the larger branch, and in proportion, unless accident has spoilt it.

[Footnote: The sketches illustrating this are on the right hand side of Pl. XXVII, No. I, and the text is also given there in facsimile.]

397.

There is no boss on branches which has not been produced by some branch which has failed.

The lower shoots on the branches of trees grow more than the upper ones and this occurs only because the sap that nourishes them, being heavy, tends downwards more than upwards; and again, because those [branches] which grow downwards turn away from the shade which exists towards the centre of the plant. The older the branches are, the greater is the difference between their upper and their lower shoots and in those dating from the same year or epoch.

[Footnote: The sketch accompanying this in the MS. is so effaced that an exact reproduction was impossible.]

398.

OF THE SCARS ON TREES.

The scars on trees grow to a greater thickness than is required by the sap of the limb which nourishes them.

399.

The plant which gives out the smallest ramifications will preserve the straightest line in the course of its growth.

[Footnote: This passage is illustrated by two partly effaced sketches. One of these closely resembles the lower one given under No. 408, the other also represents short closely set boughs on an upright trunk.]

400.

OF THE RAMIFICATION.

The beginning of the ramification [the shoot] always has the central line [axis] of its thickness directed to the central line [axis] of the plant itself.

401.

In starting from the main stem the branches always form a base with a prominence as is shown at a b c d.

402.

WHY, VERY FREQUENTLY, TIMBER HAS VEINS THAT ARE NOT STRAIGHT.

When the branches which grow the second year above the branch of the preceding year, are not of equal thickness above the antecedent branches, but are on one side, then the vigour of the lower branch is diverted to nourish the one above it, although it may be somewhat on one side.

But if the ramifications are equal in their growth, the veins of the main stem will be straight [parallel] and equidistant at every degree of the height of the plant.

Wherefore, O Painter! you, who do not know these laws! in order to escape the blame of those who understand them, it will be well that you should represent every thing from nature, and not despise such study as those do who work [only] for money.

The direction of growth (403-407).

403.

OF THE RAMIFICATIONS OF PLANTS.

The plants which spread very much have the angles of the spaces which divide their branches more obtuse in proportion as their point of origin is lower down; that is nearer to the thickest and oldest portion of the tree. Therefore in the youngest portions of the tree the angles of ramification are more acute. [Footnote: Compare the sketches on the lower portion of Pl. XXVII, No. 2.]

404.

The tips of the boughs of plants [and trees], unless they are borne down by the weight of their fruits, turn towards the sky as much as possible.

The upper side of their leaves is turned towards the sky that it may receive the nourishment of the dew which falls at night.

The sun gives spirit and life to plants and the earth nourishes them with moisture. [9] With regard to this I made the experiment of leaving only one small root on a gourd and this I kept nourished with water, and the gourd brought to perfection all the fruits it could produce, which were about 60 gourds of the long kind, andi set my mind diligently [to consider] this vitality and perceived that the dews of night were what supplied it abundantly with moisture through the insertion of its large leaves and gave nourishment to the plant and its offspring--or the seeds which its offspring had to produce--[21].

The rule of the leaves produced on the last shoot of the year will be that they will grow in a contrary direction on the twin branches; that is, that the insertion of the leaves turns round each branch in such a way, as that the sixth leaf above is produced over the sixth leaf below, and the way they turn is that if one turns towards its companion to the right, the other turns to the left, the leaf serving as the nourishing breast for the shoot or fruit which grows the following year.

[Footnote: A French translation of lines 9-12 was given by M. RAVAISSON in the Gazette des Beaux Arts, Oct. 1877; his paper also contains some valuable information as to botanical science in the ancient classical writers and at the time of the Renaissance.]

405.

The lowest branches of those trees which have large leaves and heavy fruits, such as nut-trees, fig-trees and the like, always droop towards the ground.

The branches always originate above [in the axis of] the leaves.

406.

The upper shoots of the lateral branches of plants lie closer to the parent branch than the lower ones.

407.

The lowest branches, after they have formed the angle of their separation from the parent stem, always bend downwards so as not to crowd against the other branches which follow them on the same stem and to be better able to take the air which nourishes them. As is shown by the angle b a c; the branch a c after it has made the corner of the angle a c bends downwards to c d and the lesser shoot c dries up, being too thin.

The main branch always goes below, as is shown by the branch f n m, which does not go to f n o.

The forms of trees (408--411).

408.

The elm always gives a greater length to the last branches of the year's growth than to the lower ones; and Nature does this because the highest branches are those which have to add to the size of the tree; and those at the bottom must get dry because they grow in the shade and their growth would be an impediment to the entrance of the solar rays and the air among the main branches of the tree.

The main branches of the lower part bend down more than those above, so as to be more oblique than those upper ones, and also because they are larger and older.

409.

In general almost all the upright portions of trees curve somewhat turning the convexity towards the South; and their branches are longer and thicker and more abundant towards the South than towards the North. And this occurs because the sun draws the sap towards that surface of the tree which is nearest to it.

And this may be observed if the sun is not screened off by other plants.

410.

The cherry-tree is of the character of the fir tree as regards its ramification placed in stages round its main stem; and its branches spring, 4 or five or 6 [together] opposite each other; and the tips of the topmost shoots form a pyramid from the middle upwards; and the walnut and oak form a hemisphere from the middle upwards.

411.

The bough of the walnut which is only hit and beaten when it has brought to perfection...

[Footnote: The end of the text and the sketch in red chalk belonging to it, are entirely effaced.]

The insertion of the leaves (412--419).

412.

OF THE INSERTION OF THE BRANCHES ON PLANTS.

Such as the growth of the ramification of plants is on their principal branches, so is that of the leaves on the shoots of the same plant. These leaves have [Footnote 6: Quattro modi (four modes). Only three are described in the text, the fourth is only suggested by a sketch.]

This passage occurs in MANZI'S edition of the Trattato, p. 399, but without the sketches and the text is mutilated in an important part. The whole passage has been commented on, from MANZI'S version, in Part I of the Nuovo Giornale Botanico Italiano, by Prof. G. UZIELLI (Florence 1869, Vol. I). He remarks as to the 'four modes': "Leonardo, come si vede nelle linie sententi da solo tre esempli. Questa ed altre inessattezze fanno desiderare, sia esaminato di nuovo il manoscritto Vaticano". This has since been done by D. KNAPP of Tubingen, and his accurate copy has been published by H. LUDWIG, the painter. The passage in question occurs in his edition as No. 833; and there also the drawings are wanting. The space for them has been left vacant, but in the Vatican copy 'niente' has been written on the margin; and in it, as well as in LUDWIG'S and MANZI'S edition, the text is mutilated.] four modes of growing one above another. The first, which is the most general, is that the sixth always originates over the sixth below [Footnote 8: la sesta di sotto. "Disposizione 2/5 o 1/5. Leonardo osservo probabilmente soltanto la prima" (UZIELLI).]; the second is that two third ones above are over the two third ones below [Footnote 10: terze di sotto: "Intende qui senza dubbio parlare di foglie decussate, in cui il terzo verticello e nel piano del primo" (UZIELLI).]; and the third way is that the third above is over the third below [Footnote 11: 3a di sotto: "Disposizione 1/2" (UZIELLI).].

[Footnote: See the four sketches on the upper portion of the page reproduced as fig. 2 on P1. XXVII.]

413.

A DESCRIPTION OF THE ELM.

The ramification of the elm has the largest branch at the top. The first and the last but one are smaller, when the main trunk is straight.

The space between the insertion of one leaf to the rest is half the extreme length of the leaf or somewhat less, for the leaves are at an interval which is about the 3rd of the width of the leaf.

The elm has more leaves near the top of the boughs than at the base; and the broad [surface] of the leaves varies little as to [angle and] aspect.

[Footnote: See Pl. XXVII, No. 3. Above the sketch and close under the number of the page is the word 'olmo' (elm).]

414.

In the walnut tree the leaves which are distributed on the shoots of this year are further apart from each other and more numerous in proportion as the branch from which this shoot springs is a young one. And they are inserted more closely and less in number when the shoot that bears them springs from an old branch. Its fruits are borne at the ends of the shoots. And its largest boughs are the lowest on the boughs they spring from. And this arises from the weight of its sap which is more apt to descend than to rise, and consequently the branches which spring from them and rise towards the sky are small and slender [20]; and when the shoot turns towards the sky its leaves spread out from it [at an angle] with an equal distribution of their tips; and if the shoot turns to the horizon the leaves lie flat; and this arises from the fact that leaves without exception, turn their underside to the earth [29].

The shoots are smaller in proportion as they spring nearer to the base of the bough they spring from.

[Footnote: See the two sketches on Pl XXVII, No. 4. The second refers to the passage lines 20-30.]

415.

OF THE INSERTION OF THE LEAVES ON THE BRANCHES.

The thickness of a branch never diminishes within the space between one leaf and the next excepting by so much as the thickness of the bud which is above the leaf and this thickness is taken off from the branch above [the node] as far as the next leaf.

Nature has so placed the leaves of the latest shoots of many plants that the sixth leaf is always above the first, and so on in succession, if the rule is not [accidentally] interfered with; and this occurs for two useful ends in the plant: First that as the shoot and the fruit of the following year spring from the bud or eye which lies above and in close contact with the insertion of the leaf [in the axil], the water which falls upon the shoot can run down to nourish the bud, by the drop being caught in the hollow [axil] at the insertion of the leaf. And the second advantage is, that as these shoots develop in the following year one will not cover the next below, since the 5 come forth on five different sides; and the sixth which is above the first is at some distance.

416.

OF THE RAMIFICATIONS OF TREES AND THEIR FOLIAGE.

The ramifications of any tree, such as the elm, are wide and slender after the manner of a hand with spread fingers, foreshortened. And these are seen in the distribution [thus]: the lower portions are seen from above; and those that are above are seen from below; and those in the middle, some from below and some from above. The upper part is the extreme [top] of this ramification and the middle portion is more foreshortened than any other of those which are turned with their tips towards you. And of those parts of the middle of the height of the tree, the longest will be towards the top of the tree and will produce a ramification like the foliage of the common willow, which grows on the banks of rivers.

Other ramifications are spherical, as those of such trees as put forth their shoots and leaves in the order of the sixth being placed above the first. Others are thin and light like the willow and others.

417.

You will see in the lower branches of the elder, which puts forth leaves two and two placed crosswise [at right angles] one above another, that if the stem rises straight up towards the sky this order never fails; and its largest leaves are on the thickest part of the stem and the smallest on the slenderest part, that is towards the top. But, to return to the lower branches, I say that the leaves on these are placed on them crosswise like [those on] the upper branches; and as, by the law of all leaves, they are compelled to turn their upper surface towards the sky to catch the dew at night, it is necessary that those so placed should twist round and no longer form a cross.

[Footnote: See Pl. XXVII, No. 5.]

418.

A leaf always turns its upper side towards the sky so that it may the better receive, on all its surface, the dew which drops gently from the atmosphere. And these leaves are so distributed on the plant as that one shall cover the other as little as possible, but shall lie alternately one above another as may be seen in the ivy which covers the walls. And this alternation serves two ends; that is, to leave intervals by which the air and sun may penetrate between them. The 2nd reason is that the drops which fall from the first leaf may fall onto the fourth or--in other trees--onto the sixth.

419.

Every shoot and every fruit is produced above the insertion [in the axil] of its leaf which serves it as a mother, giving it water from the rain and moisture from the dew which falls at night from above, and often it protects them against the too great heat of the rays of the sun.

LIGHT ON BRANCHES AND LEAVES (420--422).

420.

That part of the body will be most illuminated which is hit by the luminous ray coming between right angles.

[Footnote: See Pl. XXVIII, No. 1.]

421.

Young plants have more transparent leaves and a more lustrous bark than old ones; and particularly the walnut is lighter coloured in May than in September.

422.

OF THE ACCIDENTS OF COLOURING IN TREES.

The accidents of colour in the foliage of trees are 4. That is: shadow, light, lustre [reflected light] and transparency.

OF THE VISIBILITY OF THESE ACCIDENTS.

These accidents of colour in the foliage of trees become confused at a great distance and that which has most breadth [whether light or shade, &c.] will be most conspicuous.

The proportions of light and shade in a leaf (423-426).

423.

OF THE SHADOWS OF A LEAF.

Sometimes a leaf has three accidents [of light] that is: shade, lustre [reflected light] and transparency [transmitted light]. Thus, if the light were at n as regards the leaf s, and the eye at m, it would see a in full light, b in shadow and c transparent.

424.

A leaf with a concave surface seen from the under side and up-side-down will sometimes show itself as half in shade, and half transparent. Thus, if o p is the leaf and the light m and the eye n, this will see o in shadow because the light does not fall upon it between equal angles, neither on the upper nor the under side, and p is lighted on the upper side and the light is transmitted to its under side. [Footnote: See Pl. XXVIII, No. 2, the upper sketch on the page. In the original they are drawn in red chalk.]

425.

Although those leaves which have a polished surface are to a great extent of the same colour on the right side and on the reverse, it may happen that the side which is turned towards the atmosphere will have something of the colour of the atmosphere; and it will seem to have more of this colour of the atmosphere in proportion as the eye is nearer to it and sees it more foreshortened. And, without exception the shadows show as darker on the upper side than on the lower, from the contrast offered by the high lights which limit the shadows.

The under side of the leaf, although its colour may be in itself the same as that of the upper side, shows a still finer colour--a colour that is green verging on yellow--and this happens when the leaf is placed between

426.

the eye and the light which falls upon it from the opposite side.

And its shadows are in the same positions as those were of the opposite side. Therefore, O Painter! when you do trees close at hand, remember that if the eye is almost under the tree you will see its leaves [some] on the upper and [some] on the under side, and the upper side will be bluer in proportion as they are seen more foreshortened, and the same leaf sometimes shows part of the right side and part of the under side, whence you must make it of two colours.

Of the transparency of leaves (427-429).

427.

The shadows in transparent leaves seen from the under side are the same shadows as there are on the right side of this leaf, they will show through to the underside together with lights, but the lustre [reflected light] can never show through.

428.

When one green has another [green] behind it, the lustre on the leaves and their transparent [lights] show more strongly than in those which are [seen] against the brightness of the atmosphere.

And if the sun illuminates the leaves without their coming between it and the eye and without the eye facing the sun, then the reflected lights and the transparent lights are very strong.

It is very effective to show some branches which are low down and dark and so set off the illuminated greens which are at some distance from the dark greens seen below. That part is darkest which is nearest to the eye or which is farthest from the luminous atmosphere.

429.

Never paint leaves transparent to the sun, because they are confused; and this is because on the transparency of one leaf will be seen the shadow of another leaf which is above it. This shadow has a distinct outline and a certain depth of shade and sometimes is [as much as] half or a third of the leaf which is shaded; and consequently such an arrangement is very confused and the imitation of it should be avoided.

The light shines least through a leaf when it falls upon it at an acute angle.

The gradations of shade and colour in leaves (430-434).

430.

The shadows of plants are never black, for where the atmosphere penetrates there can never be utter darkness.

431.

If the light comes from m and the eye is at n the eye will see the colour of the leaves a b all affected by the colour of m --that is of the atmosphere; and b c will be seen from the under side as transparent, with a beautiful green colour verging on yellow.

If m is the luminous body lighting up the leaf s all the eyes that see the under side of this leaf will see it of a beautiful light green, being transparent.

In very many cases the positions of the leaves will be without shadow [or in full light], and their under side will be transparent and the right side lustrous [reflecting light].

432.

The willow and other similar trees, which have their boughs lopped every 3 or 4 years, put forth very straight branches, and their shadow is about the middle where these boughs spring; and towards the extreme ends they cast but little shade from having small leaves and few and slender branches. Hence the boughs which rise towards the sky will have but little shade and little relief; and the branches which are at an angle from the horizon, downwards, spring from the dark part of the shadow and grow thinner by degrees up to their ends, and these will be in strong relief, being in gradations of light against a background of shadow.

That tree will have the least shadow which has the fewest branches and few leaves.

433.

OF DARK LEAVES IN FRONT OF TRANSPARENT ONES.

When the leaves are interposed between the light and the eye, then that which is nearest to the eye will be the darkest, and the most distant will be the lightest, not being seen against the atmosphere; and this is seen in the leaves which are away from the centre of the tree, that is towards the light.

[Footnote: See Pl. XXVIII, No. 2, the lower sketch.]

434.

OF THE LIGHTS ON DARK LEAVES.

The lights on such leaves which are darkest, will be most near to the colour of the atmosphere that is reflected in them. And the cause of this is that the light on the illuminated portion mingles with the dark hue to compose a blue colour; and this light is produced by the blueness of the atmosphere which is reflected in the smooth surface of these leaves and adds to the blue hue which this light usually produces when it falls on dark objects.

OF THE LIGHTS ON LEAVES OF A YELLOWISH GREEN.

But leaves of a green verging on yellow when they reflect the atmosphere do not produce a reflection verging on blue, inasmuch as every thing which appears in a mirror takes some colour from that mirror, hence the blue of the atmosphere being reflected in the yellow of the leaf appears green, because blue and yellow mixed together make a very fine green colour, therefore the lustre of light leaves verging on yellow will be greenish yellow.

A classification of trees according to their colours.

435.

The trees in a landscape are of various kinds of green, inasmuch as some verge towards blackness, as firs, pines, cypresses, laurels, box and the like. Some tend to yellow such as walnuts, and pears, vines and verdure. Some are both yellowish and dark as chestnuts, holm-oak. Some turn red in autumn as the service-tree, pomegranate, vine, and cherry; and some are whitish as the willow, olive, reeds and the like. Trees are of various forms ...

The proportions of light and shade in trees (436-440).

436.

OF A GENERALLY DISTRIBUTED LIGHT AS LIGHTING UP TREES.

That part of the trees will be seen to lie in the least dark shadow which is farthest from the earth.

To prove it let a p be the tree, n b c the illuminated hemisphere [the sky], the under portion of the tree faces the earth p c, that is on the side o, and it faces a small part of the hemisphere at c d. But the highest part of the convexity a faces the greatest part of the hemisphere, that is b c. For this reason--and because it does not face the darkness of the earth--it is in fuller light. But if the tree has dense foliage, as the laurel, arbutus, box or holm oak, it will be different; because, although a does not face the earth, it faces the dark [green] of the leaves cut up by many shadows, and this darkness is reflected onto the under sides of the leaves immediately above. Thus these trees have their darkest shadows nearest to the middle of the tree.

437.

OF THE SHADOWS OF VERDURE.

The shadows of verdure are always somewhat blue, and so is every shadow of every object; and they assume this hue more in proportion as they are remote from the eye, and less in proportion as they are nearer. The leaves which reflect the blue of the atmosphere always present themselves to the eye edgewise.

OF THE ILLUMINATED PART OF VERDURE AND OF MOUNTAINS.

The illuminated portion, at a great distance, will appear most nearly of its natural colour where the strongest light falls upon it.

438.

OF TREES THAT ARE LIGHTED BY THE SUN AND BY THE ATMOSPHERE.

In trees that are illuminated [both] by the sun and the atmosphere and that have leaves of a dark colour, one side will be illuminated by the atmosphere [only] and in consequence of this light will tend to blueness, while on the other side they will be illuminated by the atmosphere and the sun; and the side which the eye sees illuminated by the sun will reflect light.

439.

OF DEPICTING A FOREST SCENE.

The trees and plants which are most thickly branched with slender branches ought to have less dark shadow than those trees and plants which, having broader leaves, will cast more shadow.

440.

ON PAINTING.

In the position of the eye which sees that portion of a tree illuminated which turns towards the light, one tree will never be seen to be illuminated equally with the other. To prove this, let the eye be c which sees the two trees b d which are illuminated by the sun a; I say that this eye c will not see the light in the same proportion to the shade, in one tree as in the other. Because, the tree which is nearest to the sun will display so much the stronger shadow than the more distant one, in proportion as one tree is nearer to the rays of the sun that converge to the eye than the other; &c.

You see that the eye c sees nothing of the tree d but shadow, while the same eye c sees the tree b half in light and half in shade.

When a tree is seen from below, the eye sees the top of it as placed within the circle made by its boughs[23].

Remember, O Painter! that the variety of depth of shade in any one particular species of tree is in proportion to the rarity or density of their branches.

[Footnote: The two lower sketches on the left of Pl XXVIII, No. 3, refer to lines 21-23. The upper sketch has apparently been effaced by Leonardo himself.]

The distribution of light and shade with reference to the position of the spectator (441-443).

441.

The shadows of trees placed in a landscape do not display themselves in the same position in the trees on the right hand and those on the left; still more so if the sun is to the right or left. As is proved by the 4th which says: Opaque bodies placed between the light and the eye display themselves entirely in shadow; and by the 5th: The eye when placed between the opaque body and the light sees the opaque body entirely illuminated. And by the 6th: When the eye and the opaque body are placed between darkness and light, it will be seen half in shadow and half in light.

[Footnote: See the figure on the right hand side of Pl. XXVIII, No. 3. The first five lines of the text are written below the diagram and above it are the last eight lines of the text, given as No. 461.]

442.

OF THE HERBS OF THE FIELD.

Of the plants which take a shadow from the plants which spring among them, those which are on this side [in front] of the shadow have the stems lighted up on a background of shadow, and the plants on which the shadows fall have their stems dark on a light background; that is on the background beyond the shadow.

OF TREES WHICH ARE BETWEEN THE EYE AND THE LIGHT.

Of the trees which are between the eye and the light the part in front will be light; but this light will be broken by the ramifications of transparent leaves--

being seen from the under side--and lustrous leaves--being seen from the upper side; and the background below and behind will be dark green, being in shadow from the front portion of the said tree. This occurs in trees placed above the eye.

443.

FROM WHENCE TO DEPICT A LANDSCAPE

Landscapes should be represented so that the trees may be half in light and half in shadow; but it is better to do them when the sun is covered with clouds, for then the trees are lighted by the general light of the sky, and the general darkness of the earth. And then they are darkest in certain parts in proportion as those parts are nearest to the middle of the tree and to the earth.

The effects of morning light (444-448).

444.

OF TREES TO THE SOUTH.

When the sun is in the east the trees to the South and to the North have almost as much light as shadow. But a greater share of light in proportion as they lie to the West and a greater share of shadow in proportion as they lie to the East.

OF MEADOWS.

If the sun is in the East the verdure of the meadows and of other small plants is of a most beautiful green from being transparent to the sun; this does not occur in the meadows to the West, and in those to the South and North the grass is of a moderately brilliant green.

445.

OF THE 4 POINTS OF THE COMPASS [IN LANDSCAPES].

When the sun is in the East all the portions of plants lighted by it are of a most lively verdure, and this happens because the leaves lighted by the sun within the half of the horizon that is the Eastern half, are transparent; and within the Western semicircle the verdure is of a dull hue and the moist air is turbid and of the colour of grey ashes, not being transparent like that in the East, which is quite clear and all the more so in proportion as it is moister.

The shadows of the trees to the East cover a large portion of them and are darker in proportion as the foliage of the trees is thicker.

446.

OF TREES IN THE EAST.

When the sun is in the East the trees seen towards the East will have the light which surrounds them all round their shadows, excepting on the side towards the earth; unless the tree has been pruned [below] in the past year. And the trees to the South and North will be half in shade and half in light, and more or less in shade or in light in proportion as they are more or less to the East or to the West.

The [position of] the eye above or below varies the shadows and lights in trees, inasmuch as the eye placed above sees the tree with the little shadow, and the eye placed below with a great deal of shadow.

The colour of the green in plants varies as much as their species.

447.

OF THE SHADOWS IN TREES.

The sun being in the East [to the right], the trees to the West [or left] of the eye will show in small relief and almost imperceptible gradations, because the atmosphere which lies between the eye and those trees is very dense [Footnote 7: per la 7a di questo. This possibly referred to something written on the seventh page of this note book marked G. Unfortunately it has been cut out and lost.], see the 7th of this--and they have no shade; for though a shadow exists in every detail of the ramification, it results that the images of the shade and light that reach the eye are confused and mingled together and cannot be perceived on account of their minuteness. And the principal lights are in the middle of the trees, and the shadows to wards the edges; and their separation is shown by the shadows of the intervals between the trees; but when the forests are thick with trees the thin edges are but little seen.

448.

OF TREES TO THE EAST.

When the sun is in the East the trees are darker towards the middle while their edges are light.

The effects of midday light.

449.

OBJECTS IN HIGH LIGHT SHOW BUT LITTLE, BUT BETWEEN LIGHT AND SHADOW THEY STAND OUT WELL.

To represent a landscape choose that the sun shall be at noon and look towards the West or East and then draw. And if you turn towards the North, every object placed on that side will have no shadow, particularly those which are nearest to the [direction of the] shadow of your head. And if you turn towards the South every object on that side will be wholly in shadow. All the trees which are towards the sun and have the atmosphere for their background are dark, and the other trees which lie against that darkness will be black [very dark] in the middle and lighter towards the edges.

The appearance of trees in the distance (450. 451).

450.

OF THE SPACES [SHOWING THE SKY] IN TREES THEMSELVES.

The spaces between the parts in the mass of trees, and the spaces between the trees in the air, are, at great distances, invisible to the eye; for, where it is an effort [even] to see the whole it is most difficult to discern the parts.--But a confused mixture is the result, partaking chiefly of the [hue] which predominates. The spaces between the leaves consist of particles of illuminated air which are very much smaller than the tree and are lost sight of sooner than the tree; but it does not therefore follow that they are not there. Hence, necessarily, a compounded [effect] is produced of the sky and of the shadows of the tree in shade, which both together strike the eye which sees them.

OF TREES WHICH CONCEAL THESE SPACES IN ONE ANOTHER.

That part of a tree will show the fewest spaces, behind which a large number of trees are standing between the tree and the air [sky]; thus in the tree a the spaces are not concealed nor in b, as there is no tree behind. But in c only half shows the spaces filled up by the tree d, and part of the tree d is filled up by the tree e and a little farther on all the spaces in the mass of the trees are lost, and only that at the side remains.

451.

OF TREES.

What outlines are seen in trees at a distance against the sky which serves as their background?

The outlines of the ramification of trees, where they lie against the illuminated sky, display a form which more nearly approaches the spherical on proportion as they are remote, and the nearer they are the less they appear in this spherical form; as in the first tree a which, being near to the eye, displays the true form of its ramification; but this shows less in b and is altogether lost in c, where not merely the branches of the tree cannot be seen but the whole tree is distinguished with difficulty. Every object in shadow, of whatever form it may be, at a great distance appears to be spherical. And this occurs because, if it is a square body, at a very short distance it loses its angles, and a little farther off it loses still more of its smaller sides which remain. And thus before the whole is lost [to sight] the parts are lost, being smaller than the whole; as a man, who in such a distant position loses his legs, arms and head before [the mass of] his body, then the outlines of length are lost before those of breadth, and where they have become equal it would be a square if the angles remained; but as they are lost it is round.

[Footnote: The sketch No. 4, Pl. XXVIII, belongs to this passage.]

The cast shadow of trees (452. 453).

452.

The image of the shadow of any object of uniform breadth can never be [exactly] the same as that of the body which casts it.

[Footnote: See Pl. XXVIII, No. 5.]

Light and shade on groups of trees (453-457).

453.

All trees seen against the sun are dark towards the middle and this shadow will be of the shape of the tree when apart from others.

The shadows cast by trees on which the sun shines are as dark as those of the middle of the tree.

The shadow cast by a tree is never less than the mass of the tree but becomes taller in proportion as the spot on which it falls, slopes towards the centre of the world.

The shadow will be densest in the middle of the tree when the tree has the fewest branches.

[Footnote: The three diagrams which accompany this text are placed, in the original, before lines 7-11. At the spots marked B Leonardo wrote Albero (tree). At A is the word Sole (sun), at C Monte (mountain) at D piano (plain) and at E cima (summit).]

Every branch participates of the central shadow of every other branch and consequently [of that] of the whole tree.

The form of any shadow from a branch or tree is circumscribed by the light which falls from the side whence the light comes; and this illumination gives the shape of the shadow, and this may be of the distance of a mile from the side where the sun is.

If it happens that a cloud should anywhere overshadow some part of a hill the [shadow of the] trees there will change less than in the plains; for these trees on the hills have their branches thicker, because they grow less high each year than in the plains. Therefore as these branches are dark by nature and being so full of shade, the shadow of the clouds cannot darken them any more; but the open spaces between the trees, which have no strong shadow change very much in tone and particularly those which vary from green; that is ploughed lands or fallen mountains or barren lands or rocks. Where the trees are against the atmosphere they appear all the same colour--if indeed they are not very close together or very thickly covered with leaves like the fir and similar trees. When you see the trees from the side from which the sun lights them, you will see them almost all of the same tone, and the shadows in them will be hidden by the leaves in the light, which come between your eye and those shadows.

TREES AT A SHORT DISTANCE.

[Footnote 29: The heading alberi vicini (trees at a short distance) is in the original manuscript written in the margin.] When the trees are situated between the sun and the eye, beyond the shadow which spreads from their centre, the green of their leaves will be seen transparent; but this transparency will be broken in many places by the leaves and boughs in shadow which will come between you and them, or, in their upper portions, they will be accompanied by many lights reflected from the leaves.

454.

The trees of the landscape stand out but little from each other; because their illuminated portions come against the illuminated portions of those beyond and differ little from them in light and shade.

455.

Of trees seen from below and against the light, one beyond the other and near together. The topmost part of the first will be in great part transparent and light, and will stand out against the dark portion of the second tree. And thus it will be with all in succession that are placed under the same conditions.

Let s be the light, and r the eye, c d n the first tree, a b c the second. Then I say that r, the eye, will see the portion c f in great part transparent and lighted by the light s which falls upon it from the opposite side, and it will see it, on a dark ground b c because that is the dark part and shadow of the tree a b c.

But if the eye is placed at t it will see o p dark on the light background n g.

Of the transparent and shadowy parts of trees, that which is nearest to you is the darkest.

456.

That part of a tree which has shadow for background, is all of one tone, and wherever the trees or branches are thickest they will be darkest, because there are no little intervals of air. But where the boughs lie against a background of other boughs, the brighter parts are seen lightest and the leaves lustrous from the sunlight falling on them.

457.

In the composition of leafy trees be careful not to repeat too often the same colour of one tree against the same colour of another [behind it]; but vary it with a lighter, or a darker, or a stronger green.

On the treatment of light for landscapes (458-464).

458.

The landscape has a finer azure [tone] when, in fine weather the sun is at noon than at any other time of the day, because the air is purified of moisture; and looking at it under that aspect you will see the trees of a beautiful green at the outside and the shadows dark towards the middle; and in the remoter distance the atmosphere which comes between you and them looks more beautiful when there is something dark beyond. And still the azure is most beautiful. The objects seen from the side on which the sun shines will not show you their shadows. But, if you are lower than the sun, you can see what is not seen by the sun and that will be all in shade. The leaves of the trees, which come between you and the sun are of two principal colours which are a splendid lustre of green, and the reflection of the atmosphere which lights up the objects which cannot be seen by the sun, and the shaded portions which only face the earth, and the darkest which are surrounded by something that is not dark. The trees in the landscape which are between you and the sun are far more beautiful than those you see when you are between the sun and them; and this is so because those which face the sun show their leaves as transparent towards the ends of their branches, and those that are not transparent--that is at the ends--reflect the light; and the shadows are dark because they are not concealed by any thing.

The trees, when you place yourself between them and the sun, will only display to you their light and natural colour, which, in itself, is not very strong, and besides this some reflected lights which, being against a background which does not differ very much from themselves in tone, are not conspicuous; and if you are lower down than they are situated, they may also show those portions on which the light of the sun does not fall and these will be dark.

In the Wind.

But, if you are on the side whence the wind blows, you will see the trees look very much lighter than on the other sides, and this happens because the wind turns up the under side of the leaves, which, in all trees, is much whiter than the upper sides; and, more especially, will they be very light indeed if the wind blows from the quarter where the sun is, and if you have your back turned to it.

[Footnote: At S, in the original is the word Sole (sun) and at N parte di nuvolo (the side of the clouds).]

459.

When the sun is covered by clouds, objects are less conspicuous, because there is little difference between the light and shade of the trees and of the buildings being illuminated by the brightness of the atmosphere which surrounds the objects in such a way that the shadows are few, and these few fade away so that their outline is lost in haze.

460.

OF TREES AND LIGHTS ON THEM.

The best method of practice in representing country scenes, or I should say landscapes with their trees, is to choose them so that the sun is covered with clouds so that the landscape receives an universal light and not the direct light of the sun, which makes the shadows sharp and too strongly different from the lights.

461.

OF PAINTING.

In landscapes which represent [a scene in] winter. The mountains should not be shown blue, as we see in the mountains in the summer. And this is proved [Footnote 5. 6.: Per la 4a di questo. It is impossible to ascertain what this quotation refers to. Questo certainly does not mean the MS. in hand, nor any other now known to us. The same remark applies to the phrase in line 15: per la 2a di questo.] in the 4th of this which says: Among mountains seen from a great distance those will look of the bluest colour which are in themselves the darkest; hence, when the trees are stripped of their leaves, they will show a bluer tinge which will be in itself darker; therefore, when the trees have lost their leaves they will look of a gray colour, while, with their leaves, they are green, and in proportion as the green is darker than the grey hue the green will be of a bluer tinge than the gray. Also by the 2nd of this: The shadows of trees covered with leaves are darker than the shadows of those trees which have lost their leaves in proportion as the trees covered with leaves are denser than those without leaves--and thus my meaning is proved.

The definition of the blue colour of the atmosphere explains why the landscape is bluer in the summer than in the winter.

462.

OF PAINTING IN A LANDSCAPE.

If the slope of a hill comes between the eye and the horizon, sloping towards the eye, while the eye is opposite the middle of the height of this slope, then that hill will increase in darkness throughout its length. This is proved by the 7th of this which says that a tree looks darkest when it is seen from below; the proposition is verified, since this hill will, on its upper half show all its trees as much from the side which is lighted by the light of the sky, as from that which is in shade from the darkness of the earth; whence it must result that these trees are of a medium darkness. And from this [middle] spot towards the base of the hill, these trees will be lighter by degrees by the converse of the 7th and by the said 7th: For trees so placed, the nearer they are to the summit of the hill the darker they necessarily become. But this darkness is not in proportion to the distance, by the 8th of this which says: That object shows darkest which is [seen] in the clearest atmosphere; and by the 10th: That shows darkest which stands out against a lighter background.

[Footnote: The quotation in this passage again cannot be verified.]

463.

OF LANDSCAPES.

The colours of the shadows in mountains at a great distance take a most lovely blue, much purer than their illuminated portions. And from this it follows that when the rock of a mountain is reddish the illuminated portions are violet (?) and the more they are lighted the more they display their proper colour.

464.

A place is most luminous when it is most remote from mountains.

On the treatment of light for views of towns (465-469).

465.

OF LIGHT AND SHADOW IN A TOWN.

When the sun is in the East and the eye is above the centre of a town, the eye will see the Southern part of the town with its roofs half in shade and half in light, and the same towards the North; the Eastern side will be all in shadow and the Western will be all in light.

466.

Of the houses of a town, in which the divisions between the houses may be distinguished by the light which fall on the mist at the bottom. If the eye is above the houses the light seen in the space that is between one house and the next sinks by degrees into thicker mist; and yet, being less transparent, it appears whiter; and if the houses are some higher than the others, since the true [colour] is always more discernible through the thinner atmosphere, the houses will look darker in proportion as they are higher up. Let n o p q represent the various density of the atmosphere thick with moisture, a being the eye, the house b c will look lightest at the bottom, because it is in a thicker atmosphere; the lines c d f will appear equally light, for although f is more distant than c, it is raised into a thinner atmosphere, if the houses b e are of the same height, because they cross a brightness which is varied by mist, but this is only because the line of the eye which starts from above ends by piercing a lower and denser atmosphere at d than at b. Thus the line a f is lower at f than at c; and the house f will be seen darker at e from the line e k as far as m, than the tops of the houses standing in front of it.

467.

OF TOWNS OR OTHER BUILDINGS SEEN IN THE EVENING OR THE MORNING THROUGH THE MIST.

Of buildings seen at a great distance in the evening or the morning, as in mist or dense atmosphere, only those portions are seen in brightness which are lighted up by the sun which is near the horizon; and those portions which are not lighted up by the sun remain almost of the same colour and medium tone as the mist.

WHY OBJECTS WHICH ARE HIGH UP AND AT A DISTANCE ARE DARKER THAN THE LOWER ONES, EVEN IF THE MIST IS UNIFORMLY DENSE.

Of objects standing in a mist or other dense atmosphere, whether from vapour or smoke or distance, those will be most visible which are the highest. And among objects of equal height that will be the darkest [strongest] which has for background the deepest mist. Thus the eye h looking at a b c, towers of equal height, one with another, sees c the top of the first tower at r, at two degrees of depth in the mist; and sees the height of the middle tower b through one single degree of mist. Therefore the top of the tower c appears stronger than the top of the tower b, &c.

468.

OF THE SMOKE OF A TOWN.

Smoke is seen better and more distinctly on the Eastern side than on the Western when the sun is in the East; and this arises from two causes; the first is that the sun, with its rays, shines through the particles of the smoke and lights them up and makes them visible. The second is that the roofs of the houses seen in the East at this time are in shadow, because their obliquity does not allow of their being illuminated by the sun. And the same thing occurs with dust; and both one and the other look the lighter in proportion as they are denser, and they are densest towards the middle.

469.

OF SMOKE AND DUST.

If the sun is in the East the smoke of cities will not be visible in the West, because on that side it is not seen penetrated by the solar rays, nor on a dark background; since the roofs of the houses turn the same side to the eye as they turn towards the sun, and on this light background the smoke is not very visible.

But dust, under the same aspect, will look darker than smoke being of denser material than smoke which is moist.

The effect of wind on trees (470-473).

470.

OF REPRESENTING WIND.

In representing wind, besides the bending of the boughs and the reversing of their leaves towards the quarter whence the wind comes, you should also represent them amid clouds of fine dust mingled with the troubled air.

471.

Describe landscapes with the wind, and the water, and the setting and rising of the sun.

THE WIND.

All the leaves which hung towards the earth by the bending of the shoots with their branches, are turned up side down by the gusts of wind, and here their perspective is reversed; for, if the tree is between you and the quarter of the wind, the leaves which are towards you remain in their natural aspect, while those on the opposite side which ought to have their points in a contrary direction have, by being turned over, their points turned towards you.

472.

Trees struck by the force of the wind bend to the side towards which the wind is blowing; and the wind being past they bend in the contrary direction, that is in reverse motion.

473.

That portion of a tree which is farthest from the force which strikes it is the most injured by the blow because it bears most strain; thus nature has foreseen this case by thickening them in that part where they can be most hurt; and most in such trees as grow to great heights, as pines and the like. [Footnote: Compare the sketch drawn with a pen and washed with Indian ink on Pl. XL, No. 1. In the Vatican copy we find, under a section entitled 'del fumo', the following remark: Era sotto di questo capitulo un rompimento di montagna, per dentro delle quali roture scherzaua fiame di fuoco, disegnate di penna et ombrate d'acquarella, da uedere cosa mirabile et uiua (Ed. MANZI, p. 235. Ed. LUDWIG, Vol. I, 460). This appears to refer to the left hand portion of the drawing here given from the Windsor collection, and from this it must be inferred, that the leaf as it now exists in the library of the Queen of England, was already separated from the original MS. at the time when the Vatican copy was made.]

Light and shade on clouds (474-477).

474.

Describe how the clouds are formed and how they dissolve, and what cause raises vapour.

475.

The shadows in clouds are lighter in proportion as they are nearer to the horizon.

[Footnote: The drawing belonging to this was in black chalk and is totally effaced.]

476.

When clouds come between the sun and the eye all the upper edges of their round forms are light, and towards the middle they are dark, and this happens because towards the top these edges have the sun above them while you are below them; and the same thing happens with the position of the branches of trees; and again the clouds, like the trees, being somewhat transparent, are lighted up in part, and at the edges they show thinner.

But, when the eye is between the cloud and the sun, the cloud has the contrary effect to the former, for the edges of its mass are dark and it is light towards the middle; and this happens because you see the same side as faces the sun, and because the edges have some transparency and reveal to the eye that portion which is hidden beyond them, and which, as it does not catch the sunlight like that portion turned towards it, is necessarily somewhat darker. Again, it may be that you see the details of these rounded masses from the lower side, while the sun shines on the upper side and as they are not so situated as to reflect the light of the sun, as in the first instance they remain dark.

The black clouds which are often seen higher up than those which are illuminated by the sun are shaded by other clouds, lying between them and the sun.

Again, the rounded forms of the clouds that face the sun, show their edges dark because they lie against the light background; and to see that this is true, you may look at the top of any cloud that is wholly light because it lies against the blue of the atmosphere, which is darker than the cloud.

[Footnote: A drawing in red chalk from the Windsor collection (see Pl. XXIX), representing a landscape with storm-clouds, may serve to illustrate this section as well as the following one.]

477.

OF CLOUDS, SMOKE AND DUST AND THE FLAMES OF A FURNACE OR OF A BURNING KILN.

The clouds do not show their rounded forms excepting on the sides which face the sun; on the others the roundness is imperceptible because they are in the shade. [Footnote: The text of this chapter is given in facsimile on Pls. XXXVI and XXXVII. The two halves of the leaf form but one in the original. On the margin close to lines 4 and 5 is the note: rossore d'aria inverso l'orizonte-- (of the redness of the atmosphere near the horizon). The sketches on the lower portion of the page will be spoken of in No. 668.]

If the sun is in the East and the clouds in the West, the eye placed between the sun and the clouds sees the edges of the rounded forms composing these clouds as dark, and the portions which are surrounded by this dark [edge] are light. And this occurs because the edges of the rounded forms of these clouds are turned towards the upper or lateral sky, which is reflected in them.

Both the cloud and the tree display no roundness at all on their shaded side.

On images reflected in water.

478.

Painters often deceive themselves, by representing water in which they make the water reflect the objects seen by the man. But the water reflects the object from one side and the man sees it from the other; and it often happens that the painter sees an object from below, and thus one and the same object is seen from hind part before and upside down, because the water shows the image of the object in one way, and the eye sees it in another.

Of rainbows and rain (479. 480).

479.

The colours in the middle of the rainbow mingle together.

The bow in itself is not in the rain nor in the eye that sees it; though it is generated by the rain, the sun, and the eye. The rainbow is always seen by the eye that is between the rain and the body of the sun; hence if the sun is in the East and the rain is in the West it will appear on the rain in the West.

480.

When the air is condensed into rain it would produce a vacuum if the rest of the air did not prevent this by filling its place, as it does with a violent rush; and this is the wind which rises in the summer time, accompanied by heavy rain.

Of flower seeds.

481.

All the flowers which turn towards the sun perfect their seeds; but not the others; that is to say those which get only the reflection of the sun.

IX. The Practice of Painting.

It is hardly necessary to offer any excuses for the division carried out in the arrangement of the text into practical suggestions and theoretical enquiries. It was evidently intended by Leonardo himself as we conclude from incidental remarks in the MSS. (for instance No 110). The fact that this arrangement was never carried out either in the old MS. copies or in any edition since, is easily accounted for by the general disorder which results from the provisional distribution of the various chapters in the old copies. We have every reason to believe that the earliest copyists, in distributing the materials collected by them, did not in the least consider the order in which the original MS.lay before them.

It is evident that almost all the chapters which refer to the calling and life of the painter--and which are here brought together in the first section (Nos. 482-508)--may be referred to two distinct periods in Leonardo's life; most of them can be dated as belonging to the year 1492 or to 1515. At about this later time Leonardo may have formed the project of completing his Libro della Pittura, after an interval of some years, as it would seem, during which his interest in the subject had fallen somewhat into the background.

In the second section, which treats first of the artist's studio, the construction of a suitable window forms the object of careful investigations; the special importance attached to this by Leonardo is sufficiently obvious. His theory of the incidence of light which was fully discussed in a former part of this work, was to him by no means of mere abstract value, but, being deduced, as he says, from experience (or experiment) was required to prove its utility in practice. Connected with this we find suggestions for the choice of a light with practical hints as to sketching a picture and some other precepts of a practical character which must come under consideration in the course of completing the painting. In all this I have followed the same principle of arrangement in the text as was carried out in the Theory of Painting, thus the suggestions for the Perspective of a picture, (Nos. 536-569), are followed by the theory of light and shade for the practical method of optics (Nos. 548--566) and this by the practical precepts or the treatment of aerial perspective (567--570).

In the passage on Portrait and Figure Painting the principles of painting as applied to a bust and head are separated and placed first, since the advice to figure painters must have some connection with the principles of the treatment of composition by which they are followed.

But this arrangement of the text made it seem advisable not to pick out the practical precepts as to the representation of trees and landscape from the close connection in which they were originally placed--unlike the rest of the practical precepts--with the theory of this branch of the subject. They must therefore be sought under the section entitled Botany for Painters.

As a supplement to the Libro di Pittura I have here added those texts which treat of the Painter's materials,--as chalk, drawing paper, colours and their preparation, of the management of oils and varnishes; in the appendix are some notes on chemical substances. Possibly some of these, if not all, may have stood in connection with the preparation of colours. It is in the very nature of things that Leonardo's incidental indications as to colours and the like should be now-a-days extremely obscure and could only be explained by professional experts--by them even in but few instances. It might therefore have seemed advisable to reproduce exactly the original text without offering any translation. The rendering here given is merely an attempt to suggest what Leonardo's meaning may have been.

LOMAZZO tells us in his Trattato dell'arte della Pittura, Scultura ed Architettura (Milano 1584, libro II, Cap. XIV): "Va discorrendo ed argomentando Leonardo Vinci in un suo libro letto da me (?) questi anni passati, ch'egli scrisse di mano stanca ai prieghi di LUDOVICO SFORZA duca di Milano, in determinazione di questa questione, se e piu nobile la pittura o la scultura; dicendo che quanto piu un'arte porta seco fatica di corpo, e sudore, tanto piu e vile, e men pregiata". But the existence of any book specially written for Lodovico il Moro on the superiority of Painting over sculpture is perhaps mythical. The various passages in praise of Painting as compared not merely with Sculpture but with Poetry, are scattered among MSS. of very different dates.

Besides, the way, in which the subject is discussed appears not to support the supposition, that these texts were prepared at a special request of the Duke.

I.

MORAL PRECEPTS FOR THE STUDENT OF PAINTING.

How to ascertain the dispositions for an artistic career.

482.

A WARNING CONCERNING YOUTHS WISHING TO BE PAINTERS.

Many are they who have a taste and love for drawing, but no talent; and this will be discernible in boys who are not diligent and never finish their drawings with shading.

The course of instruction for an artist (483-485).

483.

The youth should first learn perspective, then the proportions of objects. Then he may copy from some good master, to accustom himself to fine forms. Then from nature, to confirm by practice the rules he has learnt. Then see for a time the works of various masters. Then get the habit of putting his art into practice and work.

[Footnote: The Vatican copy and numerous abridgements all place this chapter at the beginning of the Trattato, and in consequence DUFRESNE and all subsequent editors have done the same. In the Vatican copy however all the general considerations on the relation of painting to the other arts are placed first, as introductory.]

484.

OF THE ORDER OF LEARNING TO DRAW.

First draw from drawings by good masters done from works of art and from nature, and not from memory; then from plastic work, with the guidance of the drawing done from it; and then from good natural models and this you must put into practice.

485.

PRECEPTS FOR DRAWING.

The artist ought first to exercise his hand by copying drawings from the hand of a good master. And having acquired that practice, under the criticism of his master, he should next practise drawing objects in relief of a good style, following the rules which will presently be given.

The study of the antique (486. 487).

486.

OF DRAWING.

Which is best, to draw from nature or from the antique? and which is more difficult to do outlines or light and shade?

487.

It is better to imitate [copy] the antique than modern work.

[Footnote 486, 487: These are the only two passages in which Leonardo alludes to the importance of antique art in the training of an artist. The question asked in No. 486 remains unanswered by him and it seems to me very doubtful whether the opinion stated in No. 487 is to be regarded as a reply to it. This opinion stands in the MS. in a connection--as will be explained later on--which seems to require us to limit its application to a single special case. At any rate we may suspect that when Leonardo put the question, he felt some hesitation as to the answer. Among his very numerous drawings I have not been able to find a single study from the antique, though a drawing in black chalk, at Windsor, of a man on horseback (Pl. LXXIII) may perhaps be a reminiscence of the statue of Marcus Aurelius at Rome. It seems to me that the drapery in a pen and ink drawing of a bust, also at Windsor, has been borrowed from an antique model (Pl. XXX). G. G. Rossi has, I believe, correctly interpreted Leonardo's feeling towards the antique in the following note on this passage in manzi's edition, p. 501: "Sappiamo dalla storia, che i valorosi artisti Toscani dell'eta dell'oro dell'arte studiarono sugli antichi marmi raccolti dal Magnifico LORENZO DE' MEDICI. Pare che il Vinci a tali monumenti non si accostasse. Quest' uomo sempre riconosce per maestra la natura, e questo principio lo stringeva alla sola imitazione di essa"--Compare No. 10, 26--28 footnote.]

The necessity of anatomical knowledge (488. 489).

488.

OF PAINTING.

It is indispensable to a Painter who would be thoroughly familiar with the limbs in all the positions and actions of which they are capable, in the nude, to know the anatomy of the sinews, bones, muscles and tendons so that, in their various movements and exertions, he may know which nerve or muscle is the cause of each movement and show those only as prominent and thickened, and not the others all over [the limb], as many do who, to seem great draughtsmen, draw their nude figures looking like wood, devoid of grace; so that you would think you were looking at a sack of walnuts rather than the human form, or a bundle of radishes rather than the muscles of figures.

489.

HOW IT IS NECESSARY TO A PAINTER THAT HE SHOULD KNOW THE INTRINSIC FORMS [STRUCTURE] OF MAN.

The painter who is familiar with the nature of the sinews, muscles, and tendons, will know very well, in giving movement to a limb, how many and which sinews cause it; and which muscle, by swelling, causes the contraction of that sinew; and which sinews, expanded into the thinnest cartilage, surround and support the said muscle. Thus he will variously and constantly demonstrate the different muscles by means of the various attitudes of his figures, and will not do, as many who, in a variety of movements, still display the very same things [modelling] in the arms, back, breast and legs. And these things are not to be regarded as minor faults.

How to acquire practice.

490.

OF STUDY AND THE ORDER OF STUDY.

I say that first you ought to learn the limbs and their mechanism, and having this knowledge, their actions should come next, according to the circumstances in which they occur in man. And thirdly to compose subjects, the studies for which should be taken from natural actions and made from time to time, as circumstances allow; and pay attention to them in the streets and piazze and fields, and note them down with a brief indication of the forms; [Footnote 5: Lines 5-7 explained by the lower portion of the sketch No. 1 on Pl. XXXI.] thus for a head make an o, and for an arm a straight or a bent line, and the same for the legs and the body, [Footnote 7: Lines 5-7 explained by the lower portion of the sketch No. 1 on Pl. XXXI.] and when you return home work out these notes in a complete form. The Adversary says that to acquire practice and do a great deal of work it is better that the first period of study should be employed in drawing various compositions done on paper or on walls by divers masters, and that in this way practice is rapidly gained, and good methods; to which I reply that the method will be good, if it is based on works of good composition and by skilled masters. But since such masters are so rare that there are but few of them to be found, it is a surer way to go to natural objects, than to those which are imitated from nature with great deterioration, and so form bad methods; for he who can go to the fountain does not go to the water-jar.

[Footnote: This passage has been published by Dr. M. JORDAN, Das Malerbuck des L. da Vinci, p. 89; his reading however varies slightly from mine.]

Industry and thoroughness the first conditions (491-493.)

491.

WHAT RULES SHOULD BE GIVEN TO BOYS LEARNING TO PAINT.

We know for certain that sight is one of the most rapid actions we can perform. In an instant we see an infinite number of forms, still we only take in thoroughly one object at a time. Supposing that you, Reader, were to glance rapidly at the whole of this written page, you would instantly perceive that it was covered with various letters; but you could not, in the time, recognise what the letters were, nor what they were meant to tell. Hence you would need to see them word by word, line by line to be able to understand the letters. Again, if you wish to go to the top of a building you must go up step by step; otherwise it will be impossible that you should reach the top. Thus I say to you, whom nature prompts to pursue this art, if you wish to have a sound knowledge of the forms of objects begin with the details of them, and do not go on to the second [step] till you have the first well fixed in memory and in practice. And if you do otherwise you will throw away your time, or certainly greatly prolong your studies. And remember to acquire diligence rather than rapidity.

492.

HOW THAT DILIGENCE [ACCURACY] SHOULD FIRST BE LEARNT RATHER THAN RAPID EXECUTION.

If you, who draw, desire to study well and to good purpose, always go slowly to work in your drawing; and discriminate in. the lights, which have the highest degree of brightness, and to what extent and likewise in the shadows, which are those that are darker than the others and in what way they intermingle; then their masses and the relative proportions of one to the other. And note in their outlines, which way they tend; and which part of the lines is curved to one side or the other, and where they are more or less conspicuous and consequently broad or fine; and finally, that your light and shade blend without strokes and borders [but] looking like smoke. And when you have thus schooled your hand and your judgment by such diligence, you will acquire rapidity before you are aware.

The artist's private life and choice of company (493-494).

493.

OF THE LIFE OF THE PAINTER IN THE COUNTRY.

A painter needs such mathematics as belong to painting. And the absence of all companions who are alienated from his studies; his brain must be easily impressed by the variety of objects, which successively come before him, and also free from other cares [Footnote 6: Leonardo here seems to be speaking of his own method of work as displayed in his MSS. and this passage explains, at least in part, the peculiarities in their arrangement.]. And if, when considering and defining one subject, a second subject intervenes--as happens when an object occupies the mind, then he must decide which of these cases is the more difficult to work out, and follow that up until it becomes quite clear, and then work out the explanation of the other [Footnote 11: Leonardo here seems to be speaking of his own method of work as displayed in his MSS. and this passage explains, at least in part, the peculiarities in their arrangement.]. And above all he must keep his mind as clear as the surface of a mirror, which assumes colours as various as those of the different objects. And his companions should be like him as to their studies, and if such cannot be found he should keep his speculations to himself alone, so that at last he will find no more useful company [than his own].

[Footnote: In the title line Leonardo had originally written del pictore filosofo (the philosophical painter), but he himself struck outfilosofo. Compare in No. 363 pictora notomista (anatomical painter). The original text is partly reproduced on Pl. CI.]

494.

OF THE LIFE OF THE PAINTER IN HIS STUDIO.

To the end that well-being of the body may not injure that of the mind, the painter or draughtsman must remain solitary, and particularly when intent on those studies and reflections which will constantly rise up before his eye, giving materials to be well stored in the memory. While you are alone you are entirely your own [master] and if you have one companion you are but half your own, and the less so in proportion to the indiscretion of his behaviour. And if you have many companions you will fall deeper into the same trouble. If you should say: "I will go my own way and withdraw apart, the better to study the forms of natural objects", I tell you, you will not be able to help often listening to their chatter. And so, since one cannot serve two masters, you will badly fill the part of a companion, and carry out your studies of art even worse. And if you say: "I will withdraw so far that their words cannot reach me and they cannot disturb me", I can tell you that you will be thought mad. But, you see, you will at any rate be alone. And if you must have companions ship find it in your studio. This may assist you to have the advantages which arise from various speculations. All other company may be highly mischievous.

The distribution of time for studying (495-497).

495.

OF WHETHER IT IS BETTER TO DRAW WITH COMPANIONS OR NOT.

I say and insist that drawing in company is much better than alone, for many reasons. The first is that you would be ashamed to be seen behindhand among the students, and such shame will lead you to careful study. Secondly, a wholesome emulation will stimulate you to be among those who are more praised than yourself, and this praise of others will spur you on. Another is that you can learn from the drawings of others who do better than yourself;

and if you are better than they, you can profit by your contempt for their defects, while the praise of others will incite you to farther merits.

[Footnote: The contradiction by this passage of the foregoing chapter is only apparent. It is quite clear, from the nature of the reasoning which is here used to prove that it is more improving to work with others than to work alone, that the studies of pupils only are under consideration here.]

496.

OF STUDYING, IN THE DARK, WHEN YOU WAKE, OR IN BED BEFORE YOU GO TO SLEEP.

I myself have proved it to be of no small use, when in bed in the dark, to recall in fancy the external details of forms previously studied, or other noteworthy things conceived by subtle speculation; and this is certainly an admirable exercise, and useful for impressing things on the memory.

497.

OF THE TIME FOR STUDYING SELECTION OF SUBJECTS.

Winter evenings ought to be employed by young students in looking over the things prepared during the summer; that is, all the drawings from the nude done in the summer should be brought together and a choice made of the best [studies of] limbs and bodies among them, to apply in practice and commit to memory.

OF POSITIONS.

After this in the following summer you should select some one who is well grown and who has not been brought up in doublets, and so may not be of stiff carriage, and make him go through a number of agile and graceful actions; and if his muscles do not show plainly within the outlines of his limbs that does not matter at all. It is enough that you can see good attitudes and you can correct [the drawing of] the limbs by those you studied in the winter.

[Footnote: An injunction to study in the evening occurs also in No. 524.]

On the productive power of minor artists (498-501).

498.

He is a poor disciple who does not excel his master.

499.

Nor is the painter praiseworthy who does but one thing well, as the nude figure, heads, draperies, animals, landscapes or other such details, irrespective of other work; for there can be no mind so inept, that after devoting itself to one single thing and doing it constantly, it should fail to do it well.

[Footnote: In MANZI'S edition (p. 502) the painter G. G. Bossi indignantly remarks on this passage. "Parla il Vince in questo luogo come se tutti gli artisti avessero quella sublimita d'ingegno capace di abbracciare tutte le cose, di cui era egli dotato" And he then mentions the case of CLAUDE LORRAIN. But he overlooks the fact that in Leonardo's time landscape painting made no pretensions to independence but was reckoned among the details (particulari, lines 3, 4).]

500.

THAT A PAINTER IS NOT ADMIRABLE UNLESS HE IS UNIVERSAL.

Some may distinctly assert that those persons are under a delusion who call that painter a good master who can do nothing well but a head or a figure. Certainly this is no great achievement; after studying one single thing for a life-time who would not have attained some perfection in it? But, since we know that painting embraces and includes in itself every object produced by nature or resulting from the fortuitous actions of men, in short, all that the eye can see, he seems to me but a poor master who can only do a figure well. For do you not perceive how many and various actions are performed by men only; how many different animals there are, as well as trees, plants, flowers, with many mountainous regions and plains, springs and rivers, cities with public and private buildings, machines, too, fit for the purposes of men, divers costumes, decorations and arts? And all these things ought to be regarded as of equal importance and value, by the man who can be termed a good painter.

501.

OF THE MISERABLE PRETENCES MADE BY THOSE WHO FALSELY AND UNWORTHILY ACQUIRE THE NAME OF PAINTERS.

Now there is a certain race of painters who, having studied but little, must need take as their standard of beauty mere gold and azure, and these, with supreme conceit, declare that they will not give good work for miserable payment, and that they could do as well as any other if they were well paid. But, ye foolish folks! cannot such artists keep some good work, and then say: this is a costly work and this more moderate and this is average work and show that they can work at all prices?

A caution against one-sided study.

502.

HOW, IN IMPORTANT WORKS, A MAN SHOULD NOT TRUST ENTIRELY TO HIS MEMORY WITHOUT CONDESCENDING TO DRAW FROM NATURE.

Any master who should venture to boast that he could remember all the forms and effects of nature would certainly appear to me to be graced with extreme ignorance, inasmuch as these effects are infinite and our memory is not extensive enough to retain them. Hence, O! painter, beware lest the lust of gain should supplant in you the dignity of art; for the acquisition of glory is a much greater thing than the glory of riches. Hence, for these and other reasons which might be given, first strive in drawing to represent your intention to the eye by expressive forms, and the idea originally formed in your imagination; then go on taking out or putting in, until you have satisfied yourself. Then have living men, draped or nude, as you may have purposed in your work, and take care that in dimensions and size, as determined by perspective, nothing is left in the work which is not in harmony with reason and the effects in nature. And this will be the way to win honour in your art.

How to acquire universality (503-506).

503.

OF VARIETY IN THE FIGURES.

The painter should aim at universality, because there is a great want of self-respect in doing one thing well and another badly, as many do who study only the [rules of] measure and proportion in the nude figure and do not seek after variety; for a man may be well proportioned, or he may be fat and short, or tall and thin, or medium. And a painter who takes no account of these varieties always makes his figures on one pattern so that they might all be taken for brothers; and this is a defect that demands stern reprehension.

504.

HOW SOMETHING MAY BE LEARNT EVERYWHERE.

Nature has beneficently provided that throughout the world you may find something to imitate.

505.

OF THE MEANS OF ACQUIRING UNIVERSALITY.

It is an easy matter to men to acquire universality, for all terrestrial animals resemble each other as to their limbs, that is in their muscles, sinews and bones; and they do not vary excepting in length or in thickness, as will be shown under Anatomy. But then there are aquatic animals which are of great variety; I will not try to convince the painter that there is any rule for them for they are of infinite variety, and so is the insect tribe.

506.

PAINTING.

The mind of the painter must resemble a mirror, which always takes the colour of the object it reflects and is completely occupied by the images of as many objects as are in front of it. Therefore you must know, Oh Painter! that you cannot be a good one if you are not the universal master of representing by your art every kind of form produced by nature. And this you will not know how to do if you do not see them, and retain them in your mind. Hence as you go through the fields, turn your attention to various objects, and, in turn look now at this thing and now at that, collecting a store of divers facts selected and chosen from those of less value. But do not do like some painters who, when they are wearied with exercising their fancy dismiss their work from their thoughts and take exercise in walking for relaxation, but still keep fatigue in their mind which, though they see various objects [around them], does not apprehend them; but, even when they meet friends or relations and are saluted by them, although they see and hear them, take no more cognisance of them than if they had met so much empty air.

Useful games and exercises (507. 508).

507.

OF GAMES TO BE PLAYED BY THOSE WHO DRAW.

When, Oh draughtsmen, you desire to find relaxation in games you should always practise such things as may be of use in your profession, by giving your eye good practice in judging accurately of the breadth and length of objects. Thus, to accustom your mind to such things, let one of you draw a straight line at random on a wall, and each of you, taking a blade of grass or of straw in his hand, try to cut it to the length that the line drawn appears to him to be, standing at a distance of 10 braccia; then each one may go up to the line to measure the length he has judged it to be. And he who has come nearest with his measure to the length of the pattern is the best man, and the winner, and shall receive the prize you have settled beforehand. Again you should take forshortened measures: that is take a spear, or any other cane or reed, and fix on a point at a certain distance; and let each one estimate how many times he judges that its length will go into that distance. Again, who will draw best a line one braccio long, which shall be tested by a thread. And such games give occasion to good practice for the eye, which is of the first importance in painting.

508.

A WAY OF DEVELOPING AND AROUSING THE MIND TO VARIOUS INVENTIONS.

I cannot forbear to mention among these precepts a new device for study which, although it may seem but trivial and almost ludicrous, is nevertheless extremely useful in arousing the mind to various inventions. And this is, when you look at a wall spotted with stains, or with a mixture of stones, if you have to devise some scene, you may discover a resemblance to various landscapes, beautified with mountains, rivers, rocks, trees, plains, wide valleys and hills in varied arrangement; or again you may see battles and figures in action; or strange faces and costumes, and an endless variety of objects, which you could reduce to complete and well drawn forms. And these appear on such walls confusedly, like the sound of bells in whose jangle you may find any name or word you choose to imagine.

II.

THE ARTIST'S STUDIO.--INSTRUMENTS AND HELPS FOR THE APPLICATION OF PERSPECTIVE.--ON JUDGING OF A PICTURE.

On the size of the studio.

509.

Small rooms or dwellings discipline the mind, large ones weaken it.

On the construction of windows (510-512).

510.

The larger the wall the less the light will be.

511.

The different kinds of light afforded in cellars by various forms of windows. The least useful and the coldest is the window at a. The most useful, the lightest and warmest and most open to the sky is the window at b. The window at c is of medium utility.

[Footnote: From a reference to the notes on the right light for painting it becomes evident that the observations made on cellar-windows have a direct bearing on the construction of the studio-window. In the diagram b as well as in that under No. 510 the window-opening is reduced to a minimum, but only, it would seem, in order to emphasize the advantage of walls constructed on the plan there shown.]

512.

OF THE PAINTER'S WINDOW AND ITS ADVANTAGE.

The painter who works from nature should have a window, which he can raise and lower. The reason is that sometimes you will want to finish a thing you are drawing, close to the light.

Let a b c d be the chest on which the work may be raised or lowered, so that the work moves up and down and not the painter. And every evening you can let down the work and shut it up above so that in the evening it may be in the fashion of a chest which, when shut up, may serve the purpose of a bench.

[Footnote: See Pl. XXXI, No. 2. In this plate the lines have unfortunately lost their sharpness, for the accidental loss of the negative has necessitated a reproduction from a positive. But having formerly published this sketch by another process, in VON LUTZOW'S Zeitschrift fur bildende Kunst (Vol. XVII, pg. 13) I have reproduced it here in the text. The sharpness of the outline in the original sketch is here preserved but it gives it from the reversed side.]

On the best light for painting (513-520).

513.

Which light is best for drawing from nature; whether high or low, or large or small, or strong and broad, or strong and small, or broad and weak or small and weak?

[Footnote: The question here put is unanswered in the original MS.]

514.

OF THE QUALITY OF THE LIGHT.

A broad light high up and not too strong will render the details of objects very agreeable.

515.

THAT THE LIGHT FOR DRAWING FROM NATURE SHOULD BE HIGH UP.

The light for drawing from nature should come from the North in order that it may not vary. And if you have it from the South, keep the window screened with cloth, so that with the sun shining the whole day the light may not vary. The height of the light should be so arranged as that every object shall cast a shadow on the ground of the same length as itself.

516.

THE KIND OF LIGHT REQUISITE FOR PAINTING LIGHT AND SHADE.

An object will display the greatest difference of light and shade when it is seen in the strongest light, as by sunlight, or, at night, by the light of a fire. But this should not be much used in painting because the works remain crude and ungraceful.

An object seen in a moderate light displays little difference in the light and shade; and this is the case towards evening or when the day is cloudy, and works then painted are tender and every kind of face becomes graceful. Thus, in every thing extremes are to be avoided: Too much light gives crudeness; too little prevents our seeing. The medium is best.

OF SMALL LIGHTS.

Again, lights cast from a small window give strong differences of light and shade, all the more if the room lighted by it be large, and this is not good for painting.

517.

PAINTING.

The luminous air which enters by passing through orifices in walls into dark rooms will render the place less dark in proportion as the opening cuts into the walls which surround and cover in the pavement.

518.

OF THE QUALITY OF LIGHT.

In proportion to the number of times that a b goes into c d will it be more luminous than c d. And similarly, in proportion as the point e goes into c d will it be more luminous than c d; and this light is useful for carvers of delicate work. [Footnote 5: For the same reason a window thus constructed would be convenient for an illuminator or a miniature painter.]

[Footnote: M. RAVAISSON in his edition of the Paris MS. A remarks on this passage: "La figure porte les lettres f et g, auxquelles rien ne renvoie dans l'explication; par consequent, cette explication est incomplete. La figure semblerait, d'ailleurs, se rapporter a l'effet de la reflexion par un miroir concave." So far as I can see the text is not imperfect, nor is the sense obscure. It is hardly necessary to observe that c d here indicate the wall of the room opposite to the window e and the semicircle described by f g stands for the arch of the sky; this occurs in various diagrams, for example under 511. A similar semicircle, Pl III, No. 2 (and compare No. 149) is expressly called 'orizonte' in writing.]

519.

That the light should fall upon a picture from one window only. This may be seen in the case of objects in this form. If you want to represent a round ball at a certain height you must make it oval in this shape, and stand so far off as that by foreshortening it appears round.

520.

OF SELECTING THE LIGHT WHICH GIVES MOST GRACE TO FACES.

If you should have a court yard that you can at pleasure cover with a linen awning that light will be good. Or when you want to take a portrait do it in dull weather, or as evening falls, making the sitter stand with his back to one of the walls of the court yard. Note in the streets, as evening falls, the faces of the men and women, and when the weather is dull, what softness and delicacy you may perceive in them. Hence, Oh Painter! have a court arranged with the walls tinted black and a narrow roof projecting within the walls. It should be 10 braccia wide and 20 braccia long and 10 braccia high and covered with a linen awning; or else paint a work towards evening or when it is cloudy or misty, and this is a perfect light.

On various helps in preparing a picture (521-530).

521.

To draw a nude figure from nature, or any thing else, hold in your hand a plumb-line to enable you to judge of the relative position of objects.

522.

OF DRAWING AN OBJECT.

When you draw take care to set up a principal line which you must observe all throughout the object you are drawing; every thing should bear relation to the direction of this principal line.

523.

OF A MODE OF DRAWING A PLACE ACCURATELY.

Have a piece of glass as large as a half sheet of royal folio paper and set thus firmly in front of your eyes that is, between your eye and the thing you want to draw; then place yourself at a distance of 2/3 of a braccia from the glass fixing your head with a machine in such a way that you cannot move it at all. Then shut or entirely cover one eye and with a brush or red chalk draw upon the glass that which you see beyond it; then trace it on paper from the glass, afterwards transfer it onto good paper, and paint it if you like, carefully attending to the arial perspective.

HOW TO LEARN TO PLACE YOUR FIGURES CORRECTLY.

If you want to acquire a practice of good and correct attitudes for your figures, make a square frame or net, and square it out with thread; place this between your eye and the nude model you are drawing, and draw these same squares on the paper on which you mean to draw the figure, but very delicately. Then place a pellet of wax on a spot of the net which will serve as a fixed point, which, whenever you look at your model, must cover the pit of the throat; or, if his back is turned, it may cover one of the vertebrae of the neck. Thus these threads will guide you as to each part of the body which, in any given attitude will be found below the pit of the throat, or the angles of the shoulders, or the nipples, or hips and other parts of the body; and the transverse lines of the net will show you how much the figure is higher over the leg on which it is posed than over the other, and the same with the hips, and the knees and the feet. But always fix the net perpendicularly so that all the divisions that you see the model divided into by the net work correspond with your drawing of the model on the net work you have sketched. The squares you draw may be as much smaller than those of the net as you wish that your figure should be smaller than nature. Afterwards remember when drawing figures, to use the rule of the corresponding proportions of the limbs as you have learnt it from the frame and net. This should be 3 braccia and a half high and 3 braccia wide; 7 braccia distant from you and 1 braccio from the model.

[Footnote: Leonardo is commonly credited with the invention of the arrangement of a plate of glass commonly known as the "vertical plane." Professor E. VON BRUCKE in his "Bruchstucke aus der Theorie der bildenden Kunste," Leipzig 1877, pg. 3, writes on this contrivance. "Unsere Glastafel ist die sogenannte Glastafel des Leonardo da Vinci, die in Gestalt einer Glastafel vorgestellte Bildflache."]

524.

A METHOD OF DRAWING AN OBJECT IN RELIEF AT NIGHT.

Place a sheet of not too transparent paper between the relievo and the light and you can draw thus very well.

[Footnote: Bodies thus illuminated will show on the surface of the paper how the copyist has to distribute light and shade.]

525.

If you want to represent a figure on a wall, the wall being foreshortened, while the figure is to appear in its proper form, and as standing free from the wall, you must proceed thus: have a thin plate of iron and make a small hole in the centre; this hole must be round. Set a light close to it in such a position as that it shines through the central hole, then place any object or figure you please so close to the wall that it touches it and draw the outline of the shadow on the wall; then fill in the shade and add the lights; place the person who is to see it so that he looks through that same hole where at first the light was; and you will never be able to persuade yourself that the image is not detached from the wall.

[Footnote: uno piccolo spiracelo nel mezzo. M. RAVAISSON, in his edition of MS. A (Paris), p. 52, reads nel muro--evidently a mistake for nel mezzo which is quite plainly written; and he translates it "fait lui une petite ouverture dans le mur," adding in a note: "les mots 'dans le mur' paraissent etre de trop. Leonardo a du les ecrire par distraction" But 'nel mezzo' is clearly legible even on the photograph facsimile given by Ravaisson himself, and the objection he raises disappears at once. It is not always wise or safe to try to prove our author's absence of mind or inadvertence by apparent difficulties in the sense or connection of the text.]

526.

TO DRAW A FIGURE ON A WALL 12 BRACCIA HIGH WHICH SHALL LOOK 24 BRACCIA HIGH.

If you wish to draw a figure or any other object to look 24 braccia high you must do it in this way. First, on the surface m r draw half the man you wish to represent; then the other half; then put on the vault m n [the rest of] the figure spoken of above; first set out the vertical plane on the floor of a room of the same shape as the wall with the coved part on which you are to paint your figure. Then, behind it, draw a figure set out in profile of whatever size you please, and draw lines from it to the point f and, as these lines cut m n on the vertical plane, so will the figure come on the wall, of which the vertical plane gives a likeness, and you will have all the [relative] heights and prominences of the figure. And the breadth or thickness which are on the upright wall m n are to be drawn in their proper form, since, as the wall recedes the figure will be foreshortened by itself; but [that part of] the figure which goes into the cove you must foreshorten, as if it were standing upright; this diminution you must set out on a flat floor and there must stand the figure which is to be transferred from the vertical plane r n[Footnote 17: che leverai dalla pariete r n. The letters refer to the larger sketch, No. 3 on Pl. XXXI.] in its real size and reduce it once more on a vertical plane; and this will be a good method [Footnote 18: Leonardo here says nothing as to how the image foreshortened by perspective and thus produced on the vertical plane is to be transferred to the wall; but from what is said in Nos. 525 and 523 we may conclude that he was familiar with the process of casting the enlarged shadow of a squaring net on the surface of a wall to guide him in drawing the figure.

Pariete di rilieuo; "sur une parai en relief" (RAVAISSON). "Auf einer Schnittlinie zum Aufrichten" (LUDWIG). The explanation of this puzzling expression must be sought in No. 545, lines 15-17.].

[Footnote: See Pl. XXXI. 3. The second sketch, which in the plate is incomplete, is here reproduced and completed from the original to illustrate the text. In the original the larger diagram is placed between lines 5 and 6.

1. 2. C. A. 157a; 463a has the similar heading: 'del cressciere della figura', and the text begins: "Se voli fare 1a figura grande b c" but here it breaks off. The translation here given renders the meaning of the passage as I think it must be understood. The MS. is perfectly legible and the construction of the

sentence is simple and clear; difficulties can only arise from the very fullness of the meaning, particularly towards the end of the passage.]

527.

If you would to draw a cube in an angle of a wall, first draw the object in its own proper shape and raise it onto a vertical plane until it resembles the angle in which the said object is to be represented.

528.

Why are paintings seen more correctly in a mirror than out of it?

529.

HOW THE MIRROR IS THE MASTER [AND GUIDE] OF PAINTERS.

When you want to see if your picture corresponds throughout with the objects you have drawn from nature, take a mirror and look in that at the reflection of the real things, and compare the reflected image with your picture, and consider whether the subject of the two images duly corresponds in both, particularly studying the mirror. You should take the mirror for your guide--that is to say a flat mirror--because on its surface the objects appear in many respects as in a painting. Thus you see, in a painting done on a flat surface, objects which appear in relief, and in the mirror--also a flat surface--they look the same. The picture has one plane surface and the same with the mirror. The picture is intangible, in so far as that which appears round and prominent cannot be grasped in the hands; and it is the same with the mirror. And since you can see that the mirror, by means of outlines, shadows and lights, makes objects appear in relief, you, who have in your colours far stronger lights and shades than those in the mirror, can certainly, if you compose your picture well, make that also look like a natural scene reflected in a large mirror.

[Footnote: I understand the concluding lines of this passage as follows: If you draw the upper half a figure on a large sheet of paper laid out on the floor of a room (sala be piana) to the same scale (con le sue vere grosseze) as the lower half, already drawn upon the wall (lines 10, 11)you must then reduce them on a 'pariete di rilievo,' a curved vertical plane which serves as a model to reproduce the form of the vault.]

530.

OF JUDGING YOUR OWN PICTURES.

We know very well that errors are better recognised in the works of others than in our own; and that often, while reproving little faults in others, you may ignore great ones in yourself. To avoid such ignorance, in the first place make yourself a master of perspective, then acquire perfect knowledge of the proportions of men and other animals, and also, study good architecture, that is so far as concerns the forms of buildings and other objects which are on the face of the earth; these forms are infinite, and the better you know them the more admirable will your work be. And in cases where you lack experience do not shrink from drawing them from nature. But, to carry out my promise above [in the title]--I say that when you paint you should have a flat mirror and often look at your work as reflected in it, when you will see it reversed, and it will appear to you like some other painter's work, so you will be better able to judge of its faults than in any other way. Again, it is well that you should often leave off work and take a little relaxation, because, when you come back to it you are a better judge; for sitting too close at work may greatly deceive you. Again, it is good to retire to a distance because the work looks smaller and your eye takes in more of it at a glance and sees more easily the discords or disproportion in the limbs and colours of the objects.

On the management of works (531. 532).

531.

OF A METHOD OF LEARNING WELL BY HEART.

When you want to know a thing you have studied in your memory proceed in this way: When you have drawn the same thing so many times that you think you know it by heart, test it by drawing it without the model; but have the model traced on flat thin glass and lay this on the drawing you have made without the model, and note carefully where the tracing does not coincide with your drawing, and where you find you have gone wrong; and bear in mind not to repeat the same mistakes. Then return to the model, and draw the part in which you were wrong again and again till you have it well in your mind. If you have no flat glass for tracing on, take some very thin kidts-kin parchment, well oiled and dried. And when you have used it for one drawing you can wash it clean with a sponge and make a second.

532.

THAT A PAINTER OUGHT TO BE CURIOUS TO HEAR THE OPINIONS OF EVERY ONE ON HIS WORK.

Certainly while a man is painting he ought not to shrink from hearing every opinion. For we know very well that a man, though he may not be a painter, is familiar with the forms of other men and very capable of judging whether they are hump backed, or have one shoulder higher or lower than the other, or too big a mouth or nose, and other defects; and, as we know that men are competent to judge of the works of nature, how much more ought we to admit that they can judge of our errors; since you know how much a man may be deceived in his own work. And if you are not conscious of this in yourself study it in others and profit by their faults. Therefore be curious to hear with patience the opinions of others, consider and weigh well whether those who find fault have ground or not for blame, and, if so amend; but, if not make as though you had not heard, or if he should be a man you esteem show him by argument the cause of his mistake.

On the limitations of painting (533-535)

533.

HOW IN SMALL OBJECTS ERRORS ARE LESS EVIDENT THAN IN LARGE ONES.

In objects of minute size the extent of error is not so perceptible as in large ones; and the reason is that if this small object is a representation of a man or of some other animal, from the immense diminution the details cannot be worked out by the artist with the finish that is requisite. Hence it is not actually complete; and, not being complete, its faults cannot be determined. For instance: Look at a man at a distance of 300 braccia and judge attentively whether he be handsome or ugly, or very remarkable or of ordinary appearance. You will find that with the utmost effort you cannot persuade yourself to decide. And the reason is that at such a distance the man is so much diminished that the character of the details cannot be determined. And if you wish to see how much this man is diminished [by distance] hold one of your fingers at a span's distance from your eye, and raise or lower it till the top joint touches the feet of the figure you are looking at, and you will see an incredible reduction. For this reason we often doubt as to the person of a friend at a distance.

534.

WHY A PAINTING CAN NEVER APPEAR DETACHED AS NATURAL OBJECTS DO.

Painters often fall into despair of imitating nature when they see their pictures fail in that relief and vividness which objects have that are seen in a mirror; while they allege that they have colours which for brightness or depth far exceed the strength of light and shade in the reflections in the mirror, thus displaying their own ignorance rather than the real cause, because they do not know it. It is impossible that painted objects should appear in such relief as to resemble those reflected in the mirror, although both are seen on a flat surface, unless they are seen with only one eye; and the reason is that two eyes see one object behind another as a and b see m and n. m cannot exactly occupy [the space of] n because the base of the visual lines is so broad that the second body is seen beyond the first. But if you close one eye, as at s the body f will conceal r, because the line of sight proceeds from a single point and makes its base in the first body, whence the second, of the same size, can never be seen.

[Footnote: This passage contains the solution of the problem proposed in No. 29, lines 10-14. Leonardo was evidently familiar with the law of optics on which the construction of the stereoscope depends. Compare E. VON BRUCKE, Bruchstucke aus der Theorie der bildenden Kunste, pg. 69: "Schon Leonardo da Vinci wusste, dass ein noch so gut gemaltes Bild nie den vollen Eindruck der Korperlichkeit geben kann, wie ihn die Natur selbst giebt. Er erklart dies auch in Kap. LIII und Kap. CCCXLI (ed. DU FRESNE) des 'Trattato' in sachgemasser Weise aus dem Sehen mit beiden Augen."

Chap. 53 of DU FRESNE'S edition corresponds to No. 534 of this work.]

535.

WHY OF TWO OBJECTS OF EQUAL SIZE A PAINTED ONE WILL LOOK LARGER THAN A SOLID ONE.

The reason of this is not so easy to demonstrate as many others. Still I will endeavour to accomplish it, if not wholly, at any rate in part. The perspective of diminution demonstrates by reason, that objects diminish in proportion as they are farther from the eye, and this reasoning is confirmed by experience. Hence, the lines of sight that extend between the object and the eye, when they are directed to the surface of a painting are all intersected at uniform limits, while those lines which are directed towards a piece of sculpture are intersected at various limits and are of various lengths. The lines which are longest extend to a more remote limb than the others and therefore that limb looks smaller. As there are numerous lines each longer than the others--since there are numerous parts, each more remote than the others and these, being farther off, necessarily appear smaller, and by appearing smaller it follows that their diminution makes the whole mass of the object look smaller. But this does not occur in painting; since the lines of sight all end at the same distance there can be no diminution, hence the parts not being diminished the whole object is undiminished, and for this reason painting does not diminish, as a piece of sculpture does.

On the choice of a position (536-537)

536.

HOW HIGH THE POINT OF SIGHT SHOULD BE PLACED.

The point of sight must be at the level of the eye of an ordinary man, and the farthest limit of the plain where it touches the sky must be placed at the level of that line where the earth and sky meet; excepting mountains, which are independent of it.

537.

OF THE WAY TO DRAW FIGURES FOR HISTORICAL PICTURES.

The painter must always study on the wall on which he is to picture a story the height of the position where he wishes to arrange his figures; and when drawing his studies for them from nature he must place himself with his eye as much below the object he is drawing as, in the picture, it will have to be above the eye of the spectator. Otherwise the work will look wrong.

The apparent size of figures in a picture (538-539)

538.

OF PLACING A FIGURE IN THE FOREGROUND OF A HISTORICAL PICTURE.

You must make the foremost figure in the picture less than the size of nature in proportion to the number of braccia at which you place it from the front line, and make the others in proportion by the above rule.

539.

PERSPECTIVE.

You are asked, O Painter, why the figures you draw on a small scale according to the laws of perspective do not appear--notwithstanding the demonstration of distance--as large as real ones--their height being the same as in those painted on the wall.

And why [painted] objects seen at a small distance appear larger than the real ones?

The right position of the artist, when painting, and of the spectator (540-547)

540.

OF PAINTING.

When you draw from nature stand at a distance of 3 times the height of the object you wish to draw.

541.

OF DRAWING FROM RELIEF.

In drawing from the round the draughtsman should so place himself that the eye of the figure he is drawing is on a level with his own. This should be done with any head he may have to represent from nature because, without exception, the figures or persons you meet in the streets have their eyes on the same level as your own; and if you place them higher or lower you will see that your drawing will not be true.

542.

WHY GROUPS OF FIGURES ONE ABOVE ANOTHER ARE TO BE AVOIDED.

The universal practice which painters adopt on the walls of chapels is greatly and reasonably to be condemned. Inasmuch as they represent one historical subject on one level with a landscape and buildings, and then go up a step and paint another, varying the point [of sight], and then a third and a fourth, in such a way as that on one wall there are 4 points of sight, which is supreme folly in such painters. We know that the point of sight is opposite the eye of the spectator of the scene; and if you would [have me] tell you how to represent the life of a saint divided into several pictures on one and the same wall, I answer that you must set out the foreground with its point of sight on a level with the eye of the spectator of the scene, and upon this plane represent the more important part of the story large and then, diminishing by degrees the figures, and the buildings on various hills and open spaces, you can represent all the events of the history. And on the remainder of the wall up to the top put trees, large as compared with the figures, or angels if they are appropriate to the story, or birds or clouds or similar objects; otherwise do not trouble yourself with it for your whole work will be wrong.

543.

A PICTURE OF OBJECTS IN PERSPECTIVE WILL LOOK MORE LIFELIKE WHEN SEEN FROM THE POINT FROM WHICH THE OBJECTS WERE DRAWN.

If you want to represent an object near to you which is to have the effect of nature, it is impossible that your perspective should not look wrong, with every false relation and disagreement of proportion that can be imagined in a wretched work, unless the spectator, when he looks at it, has his eye at the very distance and height and direction where the eye or the point of sight was placed in doing this perspective. Hence it would be necessary to make a window, or rather a hole, of the size of your face through which you can look at the work; and if you do this, beyond all doubt your work, if it is correct as to light and shade, will have the effect of nature; nay you will hardly persuade yourself that those objects are painted; otherwise do not trouble yourself about it, unless indeed you make your view at least 20 times as far off as the greatest width or height of the objects represented, and this will satisfy any spectator placed anywhere opposite to the picture.

If you want the proof briefly shown, take a piece of wood in the form of a little column, eight times as high as it is thick, like a column without any plinth or capital; then mark off on a flat wall 40 equal spaces, equal to its width so that between them they make 40 columns resembling your little column; you then must fix, opposite the centre space, and at 4 braccia from the wall, a thin strip of iron with a small round hole in the middle about as large as a big pearl. Close to this hole place a light touching it. Then place your column against each mark on the wall and draw the outline of its shadow; afterwards shade it and look through the hole in the iron plate.

[Footnote: In the original there is a wide space between lines 3 and 4 in which we find two sketches not belonging to the text. It is unnecessary to give prominence to the points in which my reading differs from that of M. RAVAISSON or to justify myself, since they are all of secondary importance and can also be immediately verified from the photograph facsimile in his edition.]

544.

A diminished object should be seen from the same distance, height and direction as the point of sight of your eye, or else your knowledge will produce no good effect.

And if you will not, or cannot, act on this principle--because as the plane on which you paint is to be seen by several persons you would need several points of sight which would make it look discordant and wrong--place yourself at a distance of at least 10 times the size of the objects.

The lesser fault you can fall into then, will be that of representing all the objects in the foreground of their proper size, and on whichever side you are standing the objects thus seen will diminish themselves while the spaces between them will have no definite ratio. For, if you place yourself in the middle of a straight row [of objects], and look at several columns arranged in a line you will see, beyond a few columns separated by intervals, that the columns touch; and beyond where they touch they cover each other, till the last column projects but very little beyond the last but one. Thus the spaces between the columns are by degrees entirely lost. So, if your method of perspective is good, it will produce the same effect; this effect results from standing near the line in which the columns are placed. This method is not satisfactory unless the objects seen are viewed from a small hole, in the middle of which is your point of sight; but if you proceed thus your work will be perfect and will deceive the beholder, who will see the columns as they are here figured.

Here the eye is in the middle, at the point a and near to the columns.

[Footnote: The diagram which stands above this chapter in the original with the note belonging to it: "a b e la ripruova" (a b is the proof) has obviously no connection with the text. The second sketch alone is reproduced and stands in the original between lines 22 and 23.]

545.

If you cannot arrange that those who look at your work should stand at one particular point, when constructing your work, stand back until your eye is at least 20 times as far off as the greatest height and width of your work. This will make so little difference when the eye of the spectator moves, that it will be hardly appreciable, and it will look very good.

If the point of sight is at t you would make the figures on the circle d b e all of one size, as each of them bears the same relation to the point t. But consider the diagram given below and you will see that this is wrong, and why I shall make b smaller than d e [Footnote 8: The second diagram of this chapter stands in the original between lines 8 and 9.].

It is easy to understand that if 2 objects equal to each other are placed side by side the one at 3 braccia distance looks smaller than that placed at 2 braccia. This however is rather theoretical than for practice, because you stand close by [Footnote 11: Instead of 'se preso' (=sie presso) M. RAVAISSON reads 'sempre se' which gives rise to the unmeaning rendering: 'parceque toujours ...'].

All the objects in the foreground, whether large or small, are to be drawn of their proper size, and if you see them from a distance they will appear just as they ought, and if you see them close they will diminish of themselves.

[Footnote 15: Compare No. 526 line 18.] Take care that the vertical plan on which you work out the perspective of the objects seen is of the same form as the wall on which the work is to be executed.

546.

OF PAINTING.

The size of the figures represented ought to show you the distance they are seen from. If you see a figure as large as nature you know it appears to be close to the eye.

547.

WHERE A SPECTATOR SHOULD STAND TO LOOK AT A PICTURE.

Supposing a b to be the picture and d to be the light, I say that if you place yourself between c and e you will not understand the picture well and particularly if it is done in oils, or still more if it is varnished, because it will be lustrous and somewhat of the nature of a mirror. And for this reason the nearer you go towards the point c, the less you will see, because the rays of light falling from the window on the picture are reflected to that point. But if you place yourself between e and d you will get a good view of it, and the more so as you approach the point d, because that spot is least exposed to these reflected rays of light.

III.

THE PRACTICAL METHODS OF LIGHT AND SHADE AND AERIAL PERSPECTIVE.

Gradations of light and shade.

548.

OF PAINTING: OF THE DARKNESS OF THE SHADOWS, OR I MAY SAY, THE BRIGHTNESS OF THE LIGHTS.

Although practical painters attribute to all shaded objects--trees, fields, hair, beards and skin--four degrees of darkness in each colour they use: that is to say first a dark foundation, secondly a spot of colour somewhat resembling the form of the details, thirdly a somewhat brighter and more defined portion, fourthly the lights which are more conspicuous than other parts of the figure; still to me it appears that these gradations are infinite upon a continuous surface which is in itself infinitely divisible, and I prove it thus:--[Footnote 7: See Pl. XXXI, No. 1; the two upper sketches.] Let a g be a continuous surface and let d be the light which illuminates it; I say--by the 4th [proposition] which says that that side of an illuminated body is most highly lighted which is nearest to the source of light--that therefore g must be darker than c in proportion as the line d g is longer than the line d c, and consequently that these gradations of light--or rather of shadow, are not 4 only, but may be conceived of as infinite, because c d is a continuous surface and every continuous surface is infinitely divisible; hence the varieties in the length of lines extending between the light and the illuminated object are infinite, and the proportion of the light will be the same as that of the length of the lines between them; extending from the centre of the luminous body to the surface of the illuminated object.

On the choice of light for a picture (549-554).

549.

HOW THE PAINTER MUST PLACE HIMSELF WITH REFERENCE TO THE LIGHT, TO GIVE THE EFFECT OF RELIEF.

Let a b be the window, m the point of light. I say that on whichever side the painter places himself he will be well placed if only his eye is between the shaded and the illuminated portions of the object he is drawing; and this place you will find by putting yourself between the point m and the division between the shadow and the light on the object to be drawn.

550.

THAT SHADOWS CAST BY A PARTICULAR LIGHT SHOULD BE AVOIDED, BECAUSE THEY ARE EQUALLY STRONG AT THE ENDS AND AT THE BEGINNING.

The shadows cast by the sun or any other particular light have not a pleasing effect on the body to which they belong, because the parts remain confuse, being divided by distinct outlines of light and shade. And the shadows are of equal strength at the end and at the beginning.

551.

HOW LIGHT SHOULD BE THROWN UPON FIGURES.

The light must be arranged in accordance with the natural conditions under which you wish to represent your figures: that is, if you represent them in the sunshine make the shadows dark with large spaces of light, and mark their shadows and those of all the surrounding objects strongly on the ground. And if you represent them as in dull weather give little difference of light and shade, without any shadows at their feet. If you represent them as within doors, make a strong difference between the lights and shadows, with shadows on the ground. If the window is screened and the walls white, there will be little difference of light. If it is lighted by firelight make the high lights ruddy and strong, and the shadows dark, and those cast on the walls and on the floor will be clearly defined and the farther they are from the body the broader and longer will they be. If the light is partly from the fire and partly from the outer day, that of day will be the stronger and that of the fire almost as red as fire itself. Above all see that the figures you paint are broadly lighted and from above, that is to say all living persons that you paint; for you will see that all the people you meet out in the street are lighted from above, and you must know that if you saw your most intimate friend with a light [on his face] from below you would find it difficult to recognise him.

552.

OF HELPING THE APPARENT RELIEF OF A PICTURE BY GIVING IT ARTIFICIAL LIGHT AND SHADE.

To increase relief of a picture you may place, between your figure and the solid object on which its shadow falls, a line of bright light, dividing the figure from the object in shadow. And on the same object you shall represent two light parts which will surround the shadow cast upon the wall by the figure placed opposite [6]; and do this frequently with the limbs which you wish should stand out somewhat from the body they belong to; particularly when the arms cross the front of the breast show, between the shadow cast by the arms on the breast and the shadow on the arms themselves, a little light seeming to fall through a space between the breast and the arms; and the more you wish the arm to look detached from the breast the broader you must make the light; always contrive also to arrange the figures against the background in such a way as that the parts in shadow are against a light background and the illuminated portions against a dark background.

[Footnote 6: Compare the two diagrams under No. 565.]

553.

OF SITUATION.

Remember [to note] the situation of your figures; for the light and shade will be one thing if the object is in a dark place with a particular light, and another thing if it is in a light place with direct sunlight; one thing in a dark place with a diffused evening light or a cloudy sky, and another in the diffused light of the atmosphere lighted by the sun.

554.

OF THE JUDGMENT TO BE MADE OF A PAINTER'S WORK.

First you must consider whether the figures have the relief required by their situation and the light which illuminates them; for the shadows should not be the same at the extreme ends of the composition as in the middle, because it is one thing when figures are surrounded by shadows and another when they have shadows only on one side. Those which are in the middle of the picture are surrounded by shadows, because they are shaded by the figures which stand between them and the light. And those are lighted on one side only which stand between the principal group and the light, because where they do not look towards the light they face the group and the darkness of the group is thrown on them: and where they do not face the group they face the brilliant light and it is their own darkness shadowing them, which appears there.

In the second place observe the distribution or arrangement of figures, and whether they are distributed appropriately to the circumstances of the story. Thirdly, whether the figures are actively intent on their particular business.

555.

OF THE TREATMENT OF THE LIGHTS.

First give a general shadow to the whole of that extended part which is away from the light. Then put in the half shadows and the strong shadows, comparing them with each other and, in the same way give the extended light in half tint, afterwards adding the half lights and the high lights, likewise comparing them together.

The distribution of light and shade (556-559)

556.

OF SHADOWS ON BODIES.

When you represent the dark shadows in bodies in light and shade, always show the cause of the shadow, and the same with reflections; because the dark shadows are produced by dark objects and the reflections by objects only moderately lighted, that is with diminished light. And there is the same proportion between the highly lighted part of a body and the part lighted by a reflection as between the origin of the lights on the body and the origin of the reflections.

557.

OF LIGHTS AND SHADOWS.

I must remind you to take care that every portion of a body, and every smallest detail which is ever so little in relief, must be given its proper importance as to light and shade.

558.

OF THE WAY TO MAKE THE SHADOW ON FIGURES CORRESPOND TO THE LIGHT AND TO [THE COLOUR] OF THE BODY.

When you draw a figure and you wish to see whether the shadow is the proper complement to the light, and neither redder nor yellower than is the nature of the colour you wish to represent in shade, proceed thus. Cast a shadow with your finger on the illuminated portion, and if the accidental shadow that you have made is like the natural shadow cast by your finger on your work, well and good; and by putting your finger nearer or farther off, you can make darker or lighter shadows, which you must compare with your own.

559.

OF SURROUNDING BODIES BY VARIOUS FORMS OF SHADOW.

Take care that the shadows cast upon the surface of the bodies by different objects must undulate according to the various curves of the limbs which cast the shadows, and of the objects on which they are cast.

The juxtaposition of light and shade (560, 561).

560.

ON PAINTING.

The comparison of the various qualities of shadows and lights not infrequently seems ambiguous and confused to the painter who desires to imitate and copy the objects he sees. The reason is this: If you see a white drapery side by side with a black one, that part of the white drapery which lies against the black one will certainly look much whiter than the part which lies against something whiter than itself. [Footnote: It is evident from this that so early as in 1492 Leonardo's writing in perspective was so far advanced that he could quote his own statements.--As bearing on this subject compare what is said in No. 280.] And the reason of this is shown in my [book on] perspective.

561.

OF SHADOWS.

Where a shadow ends in the light, note carefully where it is paler or deeper and where it is more or less indistinct towards the light; and, above all, in [painting] youthful figures I remind you not to make the shadow end like a stone, because flesh has a certain transparency, as may be seen by looking at a hand held between the eye and the sun, which shines through it ruddy and bright. Place the most highly coloured part between the light and shadow. And to see what shadow tint is needed on the flesh, cast a shadow on it with your finger, and according as you wish to see it lighter or darker hold your finger nearer to or farther from your picture, and copy that [shadow].

On the lighting of the background (562-565).

562.

OF THE BACKGROUNDS FOR PAINTED FIGURES.

The ground which surrounds the forms of any object you paint should be darker than the high lights of those figures, and lighter than their shadowed part: &c.

563.

OF THE BACKGROUND THAT THE PAINTER SHOULD ADOPT IN HIS WORKS.

Since experience shows us that all bodies are surrounded by light and shade it is necessary that you, O Painter, should so arrange that the side which is in light shall terminate against a dark body and likewise that the shadow side shall terminate against a light body. And by [following] this rule you will add greatly to the relief of your figures.

564.

A most important part of painting consists in the backgrounds of the objects represented; against these backgrounds the outlines of those natural objects which are convex are always visible, and also the forms of these bodies against the background, even though the colours of the bodies should be the same as that of the background. This is caused by the convex edges of the objects not being illuminated in the same way as, by the same light, the background is illuminated, since these edges will often be lighter or darker than the background. But if the edge is of the same colour as the background, beyond a doubt it will in that part of the picture interfere with your perception of the outline, and such a choice in a picture ought to be rejected by the judgment of good painters, inasmuch as the purpose of the painter is to make his figures appear detached from the background; while in the case here described the contrary occurs, not only in the picture, but in the objects themselves.

565.

That you ought, when representing objects above the eye and on one side--if you wish them to look detached from the wall--to show, between the shadow on the object and the shadow it casts a middle light, so that the body will appear to stand away from the wall.

On the lighting of white objects.

566.

HOW WHITE BODIES SHOULD BE REPRESENTED.

If you are representing a white body let it be surrounded by ample space, because as white has no colour of its own, it is tinged and altered in some degree by the colour of the objects surrounding it. If you see a woman dressed in white in the midst of a landscape, that side which is towards the sun is bright in colour, so much so that in some portions it will dazzle the eyes like the sun itself; and the side which is towards the atmosphere,--luminous through being interwoven with the sun's rays and penetrated by them--since the atmosphere itself is blue, that side of the woman's figure will appear steeped in blue. If the surface of the ground about her be meadows and if she be standing between a field lighted up by the sun and the sun itself, you will see every portion of those folds which are towards the meadow tinged by the reflected rays with the colour of that meadow. Thus the white is transmuted into the colours of the luminous and of the non-luminous objects near it.

The methods of aerial (567--570).

567.

WHY FACES [SEEN] AT A DISTANCE LOOK DARK.

We see quite plainly that all the images of visible objects that lie before us, whether large or small, reach our sense by the minute aperture of the eye; and if, through so small a passage the image can pass of the vast extent of sky and earth, the face of a man--being by comparison with such large images almost nothing by reason of the distance which diminishes it,--fills up so little of the eye that it is indistinguishable. Having, also, to be transmitted from the surface to the sense through a dark medium, that is to say the crystalline lens which looks dark, this image, not being strong in colour becomes affected by this darkness on its passage, and on reaching the sense it appears dark; no other reason can in any way be assigned. If the point in the eye is black, it is because it is full of a transparent humour as clear as air and acts like a perforation in a board; on looking into it it appears dark and the objects seen through the bright air and a dark one become confused in this darkness.

WHY A MAN SEEN AT A CERTAIN DISTANCE IS NOT RECOGNISABLE.

The perspective of diminution shows us that the farther away an object is the smaller it looks. If you look at a man at a distance from you of an arrow's flight, and hold the eye of a small needle close to your own eye, you can see through it several men whose images are transmitted to the eye and will all be comprised within the size of the needle's eye; hence, if the man who is at the distance of an arrow's flight can send his whole image to your eye, occupying only a small space in the needle's eye how can you [expect] in so small a figure to distinguish or see the nose or mouth or any detail of his person? and, not seeing these you cannot recognise the man, since these features, which he does not show, are what give men different aspects.

568.

THE REASON WHY SMALL FIGURES SHOULD NOT BE MADE FINISHED.

I say that the reason that objects appear diminished in size is because they are remote from the eye; this being the case it is evident that there must be a great extent of atmosphere between the eye and the objects, and this air interferes with the distinctness of the forms of the object. Hence the minute details of these objects will be indistinguishable and unrecognisable. Therefore, O Painter, make your smaller figures merely indicated and not highly finished, otherwise you will produce effects the opposite to nature, your supreme guide. The object is small by reason of the great distance between it and the eye, this great distance is filled with air, that mass of air forms a dense body which intervenes and prevents the eye seeing the minute details of objects.

569.

Whenever a figure is placed at a considerable distance you lose first the distinctness of the smallest parts; while the larger parts are left to the last, losing all distinctness of detail and outline; and what remains is an oval or spherical figure with confused edges.

570.

OF PAINTING.

The density of a body of smoke looks white below the horizon while above the horizon it is dark, even if the smoke is in itself of a uniform colour, this uniformity will vary according to the variety in the ground on which it is seen.

IV.

OF PORTRAIT AND FIGURE PAINTING.

Of sketching figures and portraits (571-572).

571.

OF THE WAY TO LEARN TO COMPOSE FIGURES [IN GROUPS] IN HISTORICAL PICTURES.

When you have well learnt perspective and have by heart the parts and forms of objects, you must go about, and constantly, as you go, observe, note and consider the circumstances and behaviour of men in talking, quarrelling or laughing or fighting together: the action of the men themselves and the actions of the bystanders, who separate them or who look on. And take a note of them with slight strokes thus, in a little book which you should always carry with you. And it should be of tinted paper, that it may not be rubbed out, but change the old [when full] for a new one; since these things should not be rubbed out but preserved with great care; for the forms, and positions of objects are so infinite that the memory is incapable of retaining them, wherefore keep these [sketches] as your guides and masters.

[Footnote: Among Leonardo's numerous note books of pocket size not one has coloured paper, so no sketches answering to this description can be pointed out. The fact that most of the notes are written in ink, militates against the supposition that they were made in the open air.]

572.

OF A METHOD OF KEEPING IN MIND THE FORM OF A FACE.

If you want to acquire facility for bearing in mind the expression of a face, first make yourself familiar with a variety of [forms of] several heads, eyes, noses, mouths, chins and cheeks and necks and shoulders: And to put a case: Noses are of 10 types: straight, bulbous, hollow, prominent above or below the middle, aquiline, regular, flat, round or pointed. These hold good as to profile. In full face they are of 11 types; these are equal thick in the middle, thin in the middle, with the tip thick and the root narrow, or narrow at the tip and wide at the root; with the nostrils wide or narrow, high or low, and the openings wide or hidden by the point; and you will find an equal variety in the other details; which things you must draw from nature and fix them in your mind. Or else, when you have to draw a face by heart, carry with you a little book in which you have noted such features; and when you have cast a glance at the face of the person you wish to draw, you can look, in private, which nose or mouth is most like, or there make a little mark to recognise it again at home. Of grotesque faces I need say nothing, because they are kept in mind without difficulty.

The position of the head.

573.

HOW YOU SHOULD SET TO WORK TO DRAW A HEAD OF WHICH ALL THE PARTS SHALL AGREE WITH THE POSITION GIVEN TO IT.

To draw a head in which the features shall agree with the turn and bend of the head, pursue this method. You know that the eyes, eyebrows, nostrils, corners of the mouth, and sides of the chin, the jaws, cheeks, ears and all the parts of a face are squarely and straightly set upon the face.

[Footnote: Compare the drawings and the text belonging to them on Pl. IX. (No. 315), Pl. X (No. 316), Pl. XL (No. 318) and Pl. XII. (No. 319).]

Therefore when you have sketched the face draw lines passing from one corner of the eye to the other; and so for the placing of each feature; and after having drawn the ends of the lines beyond the two sides of the face, look if the spaces inside the same parallel lines on the right and on the left are equal [12]. But be sure to remember to make these lines tend to the point of sight.

[Footnote: See Pl. XXXI, No. 4, the slight sketch on the left hand side. The text of this passage is written by the side of it. In this sketch the lines seem intentionally incorrect and converging to the right (compare l. 12) instead of parallel. Compare too with this text the drawing in red chalk from Windsor Castle which is reproduced on Pl. XL, No. 2.]

Of the light on the face (574-576).

574.

HOW TO KNOW WHICH SIDE OF AN OBJECT IS TO BE MORE OR LESS LUMINOUS THAN THE OTHER.

Let f be the light, the head will be the object illuminated by it and that side of the head on which the rays fall most directly will be the most highly lighted, and those parts on which the rays fall most aslant will be less lighted. The light falls as a blow might, since a blow which falls perpendicularly falls with the greatest force, and when it falls obliquely it is less forcible than the former in proportion to the width of the angle. Exempli gratia if you throw a ball at a wall of which the extremities are equally far from you the blow will fall straight, and if you throw the ball at the wall when standing at one end of it the ball will hit it obliquely and the blow will not tell.

[Footnote: See Pl. XXXI. No. 4; the sketch on the right hand side.]

575.

THE PROOF AND REASON WHY AMONG THE ILLUMINATED PARTS CERTAIN PORTIONS ARE IN HIGHER LIGHT THAN OTHERS.

Since it is proved that every definite light is, or seems to be, derived from one single point the side illuminated by it will have its highest light on the portion where the line of radiance falls perpendicularly; as is shown above in the lines a g, and also in a h and in l a; and that portion of the illuminated side will be least luminous, where the line of incidence strikes it between two more dissimilar angles, as is seen at b c d. And by this means you may also know which parts are deprived of light as is seen at m k.

Where the angles made by the lines of incidence are most equal there will be the highest light, and where they are most unequal it will be darkest.

I will make further mention of the reason of reflections.

[Footnote: See Pl. XXXII. The text, here given complete, is on the right hand side. The small circles above the beginning of lines 5 and 11 as well as the circle above the text on Pl. XXXI, are in a paler ink and evidently added by a later hand in order to distinguish the text as belonging to the Libro di Pittura (see Prolegomena. No. 12, p. 3). The text on the left hand side of this page is given as Nos. 577 and 137.]

576.

Where the shadow should be on the face.

General suggestions for historical pictures (577-581).

577.

When you compose a historical picture take two points, one the point of sight, and the other the source of light; and make this as distant as possible.

578.

Historical pictures ought not to be crowded and confused with too many figures.

579.

PRECEPTS IN PAINTING.

Let you sketches of historical pictures be swift and the working out of the limbs not be carried too far, but limited to the position of the limbs, which you can afterwards finish as you please and at your leisure.

[Footnote: See Pl. XXXVIII, No. 2. The pen and ink drawing given there as No. 3 may also be compared with this passage. It is in the Windsor collection where it is numbered 101.]

580.

The sorest misfortune is when your views are in advance of your work.

581.

Of composing historical pictures. Of not considering the limbs in the figures in historical pictures; as many do who, in the wish to represent the whole of a figure, spoil their compositions. And when you place one figure behind another take care to draw the whole of it so that the limbs which come in front of the nearer figures may stand out in their natural size and place.

How to represent the differences of age and sex (582-583).

582.

How the ages of man should be depicted: that is, Infancy, Childhood, Youth, Manhood, Old age, Decrepitude.

[Footnote: No answer is here given to this question, in the original MS.]

583.

Old men ought to be represented with slow and heavy movements, their legs bent at the knees, when they stand still, and their feet placed parallel and apart; bending low with the head leaning forward, and their arms but little extended.

Women must be represented in modest attitudes, their legs close together, their arms closely folded, their heads inclined and somewhat on one side.

Old women should be represented with eager, swift and furious gestures, like infernal furies; but the action should be more violent in their arms and head than in their legs.

Little children, with lively and contorted movements when sitting, and, when standing still, in shy and timid attitudes.

[Footnote: bracci raccolte. Compare Pl. XXXIII. This drawing, in silver point on yellowish tinted paper, the lights heightened with white, represents two female hands laid together in a lap. Above is a third finished study of a right hand, apparently holding a veil from the head across the bosom. This drawing evidently dates from before 1500 and was very probably done at Florence, perhaps as a preparatory study for some picture. The type of hand with its slender thin forms is more like the style of the Vierge aux Rochers in the Louvre than any later works--as the Mona Lisa for instance.]

Of representing the emotions.

584.

THAT A FIGURE IS NOT ADMIRABLE UNLESS IT EXPRESSES BY ITS ACTION THE PASSION OF ITS SENTIMENT.

That figure is most admirable which by its actions best expresses the passion that animates it.

HOW AN ANGRY MAN IS TO BE FIGURED.

You must make an angry person holding someone by the hair, wrenching his head against the ground, and with one knee on his ribs; his right arm and fist raised on high. His hair must be thrown up, his brow downcast and knit, his teeth clenched and the two corners of his mouth grimly set; his neck swelled and bent forward as he leans over his foe, and full of furrows.

HOW TO REPRESENT A MAN IN DESPAIR.

You must show a man in despair with a knife, having already torn open his garments, and with one hand tearing open the wound. And make him standing on his feet and his legs somewhat bent and his whole person leaning towards the earth; his hair flying in disorder.

Of representing imaginary animals.

585.

HOW YOU SHOULD MAKE AN IMAGINARY ANIMAL LOOK NATURAL.

You know that you cannot invent animals without limbs, each of which, in itself, must resemble those of some other animal. Hence if you wish to make an animal, imagined by you, appear natural--let us say a Dragon, take for its head that of a mastiff or hound, with the eyes of a cat, the ears of a porcupine, the nose of a greyhound, the brow of a lion, the temples of an old cock, the neck of a water tortoise.

[Footnote: The sketch here inserted of two men on horseback fighting a dragon is the facsimile of a pen and ink drawing belonging to BARON EDMOND DE ROTHSCHILD of Paris.]

The selection of forms.

586.

OF THE DELUSIONS WHICH ARISE IN JUDGING OF THE LIMBS.

A painter who has clumsy hands will paint similar hands in his works, and the same will occur with any limb, unless long study has taught him to avoid it. Therefore, O Painter, look carefully what part is most ill-favoured in your own person and take particular pains to correct it in your studies. For if you are coarse, your figures will seem the same and devoid of charm; and it is the same with any part that may be good or poor in yourself; it will be shown in some degree in your figures.

587.

OF THE SELECTION OF BEAUTIFUL FACES.

It seems to me to be no small charm in a painter when he gives his figures a pleasing air, and this grace, if he have it not by nature, he may acquire by incidental study in this way: Look about you and take the best parts of many beautiful faces, of which the beauty is confirmed rather by public fame than by your own judgment; for you might be mistaken and choose faces which have some resemblance to your own. For it would seem that such resemblances often please us; and if you should be ugly, you would select faces that were not beautiful and you would then make ugly faces, as many painters do. For often a master's work resembles himself. So select beauties as I tell you, and fix them in your mind.

588.

Of the limbs, which ought to be carefully selected, and of all the other parts with regard to painting.

589.

When selecting figures you should choose slender ones rather than lean and wooden ones.

590.

OF THE MUSCLES OF ANIMALS.

The hollow spaces interposed between the muscles must not be of such a character as that the skin should seem to cover two sticks laid side by side like c, nor should they seem like two sticks somewhat remote from such contact so that the skin hangs in an empty loose curve as at f; but it should be like i, laid over the spongy fat that lies in the angles as the angle n m o; which angle is formed by the contact of the ends of the muscles and as the skin cannot fold down into such an angle, nature has filled up such angles with a small quantity of spongy and, as I may say, vesicular fat, with minute bladders [in it] full of air, which is condensed or rarefied in them according to the increase or the diminution of the substance of the muscles; in which latter case the concavity i always has a larger curve than the muscle.

591.

OF UNDULATING MOVEMENTS AND EQUIPOISE IN FIGURES AND OTHER ANIMALS.

When representing a human figure or some graceful animal, be careful to avoid a wooden stiffness; that is to say make them move with equipoise and balance so as not to look like a piece of wood; but those you want to represent as strong you must not make so, excepting in the turn of the head.

How to pose figures.

592.

OF GRACE IN THE LIMBS.

The limbs should be adapted to the body with grace and with reference to the effect that you wish the figure to produce. And if you wish to produce a figure that shall of itself look light and graceful you must make the limbs elegant and extended, and without too much display of the muscles; and those few that are needed for your purpose you must indicate softly, that is, not very prominent and without strong shadows; the limbs, and particularly the arms easy; that is, none of the limbs should be in a straight line with the adjoining parts. And if the hips, which are the pole of a man, are by reason of his position, placed so, that the right is higher than the left, make the point of the higher shoulder in a perpendicular line above the highest prominence of the hip, and let this right shoulder be lower than the left. Let the pit of the throat always be over the centre of the joint of the foot on which the man is leaning. The leg which is free should have the knee lower than the other, and near the other leg. The positions of the head and arms are endless and I shall therefore not enlarge on any rules for them. Still, let them be easy and pleasing, with various turns and twists, and the joints gracefully bent, that they may not look like pieces of wood.

Of appropriate gestures (593-600).

593.

A picture or representation of human figures, ought to be done in such a way as that the spectator may easily recognise, by means of their attitudes, the purpose in their minds. Thus, if you have to represent a man of noble character in the act of speaking, let his gestures be such as naturally accompany good words; and, in the same way, if you wish to depict a man of a brutal nature, give him fierce movements; as with his arms flung out towards the listener, and his head and breast thrust forward beyond his feet, as if following the speaker's hands. Thus it is with a deaf and dumb person who, when he sees two men in conversation--although he is deprived of hearing-- can nevertheless understand, from the attitudes and gestures of the speakers, the nature of their discussion. I once saw in Florence a man who had become deaf who, when you spoke very loud did not understand you, but if you spoke gently and without making any sound, understood merely from the movement of the lips. Now perhaps you will say that the lips of a man who speaks loudly do not move like those of one speaking softly, and that if they were to move them alike they would be alike understood. As to this argument, I leave the decision to experiment; make a man speak to you gently and note [the motion of] his lips.

[Footnote: The first ten lines of this text have already been published, but with a slightly different reading by Dr. M. JORDAN: Das Malerbuch Leonardo da Vinci's p. 86.]

594.

OF REPRESENTING A MAN SPEAKING TO A MULTITUDE.

When you wish to represent a man speaking to a number of people, consider the matter of which he has to treat and adapt his action to the subject. Thus, if he speaks persuasively, let his action be appropriate to it. If the matter in hand be to set forth an argument, let the speaker, with the fingers of the right hand hold one finger of the left hand, having the two smaller ones closed; and his face alert, and turned towards the people with mouth a little open, to look as though he spoke; and if he is sitting let him appear as though about to rise, with his head forward. If you represent him standing make him leaning slightly forward with body and head towards the people. These you must represent as silent and attentive, all looking at the orator's face with gestures of admiration; and make some old men in astonishment at the things they hear, with the corners of their mouths pulled down and drawn in, their cheeks full of furrows, and their eyebrows raised, and wrinkling the forehead where they meet. Again, some sitting with their fingers clasped holding their weary knees. Again, some bent old man, with one knee crossed over the other; on which let him hold his hand with his other elbow resting in it and the hand supporting his bearded chin.

[Footnote: The sketches introduced here are a facsimile of a pen and ink drawing in the Louvre which Herr CARL BRUN considers as studies for the Last Supper in the church of Santa Maria delle Grazie (see Leonardo da Vinci, LXI, pp. 21, 27 and 28 in DOHME'S Kunst und Kunstler, Leipzig, Seemann). I shall not here enter into any discussion of this suggestion; but as a justification for introducing the drawing in this place, I may point out that some of the figures illustrate this passage as perfectly as though they had been drawn for that express purpose. I have discussed the probability of a connection between this sketch and the picture of the Last Supper on p. 335. The original drawing is 27 3/4 centimetres wide by 21 high.--The drawing in silver point on reddish paper given on Pl. LII. No. 1--the original at Windsor Castle--may also serve to illustrate the subject of appropriate gestures, treated in Nos. 593 and 594.]

595.

OF THE DISPOSITION OF LIMBS.

As regards the disposition of limbs in movement you will have to consider that when you wish to represent a man who, by some chance, has to turn backwards or to one side, you must not make him move his feet and all his limbs towards the side to which he turns his head. Rather must you make the action proceed by degrees and through the different joints; that is, those of the foot, the knee and the hip and the neck. And if you set him on the right leg, you must make the left knee bend inwards, and let his foot be slightly raised on the outside, and the left shoulder be somewhat lower than the right, while the nape of the neck is in a line directly over the outer ancle of the left foot. And the left shoulder will be in a perpendicular line above the toes of the right foot. And always set your figures so that the side to which the head turns is not the side to which the breast faces, since nature for our convenience has made us with a neck which bends with ease in many directions, the eye wishing to turn to various points, the different joints. And if at any time you make a man sitting with his arms at work on something which is sideways to him, make the upper part of his body turn upon the hips.

[Footnote: Compare Pl. VII, No. 5. The original drawing at Windsor Castle is numbered 104.]

596.

When you draw the nude always sketch the whole figure and then finish those limbs which seem to you the best, but make them act with the other limbs; otherwise you will get a habit of never putting the limbs well together on the body.

Never make the head turn the same way as the torso, nor the arm and leg move together on the same side. And if the face is turned to the right shoulder, make all the parts lower on the left side than on the right; and when you turn the body with the breast outwards, if the head turns to the left side make the parts on the right side higher than those on the left.

[Footnote: In the original MS. a much defaced sketch is to be seen by the side of the second part of this chapter; its faded condition has rendered reproduction impossible. In M. RAVAISSON'S facsimile the outlines of the head have probably been touched up. This passage however is fitly illustrated by the drawings on Pl. XXI.]

597.

OF PAINTING.

Of the nature of movements in man. Do not repeat the same gestures in the limbs of men unless you are compelled by the necessity of their action, as is shown in a b.

[Footnote: See Pl. V, where part of the text is also reproduced. The effaced figure to the extreme left has evidently been cancelled by Leonardo himself as unsatisfactory.]

598.

The motions of men must be such as suggest their dignity or their baseness.

599.

OF PAINTING.

Make your work carry out your purpose and meaning. That is when you draw a figure consider well who it is and what you wish it to be doing.

OF PAINTING.

With regard to any action which you give in a picture to an old man or to a young one, you must make it more energetic in the young man in proportion as he is stronger than the old one; and in the same way with a young man and an infant.

600.

OF SETTING ON THE LIMBS.

The limbs which are used for labour must be muscular and those which are not much used you must make without muscles and softly rounded.

OF THE ACTION OF THE FIGURES.

Represent your figures in such action as may be fitted to express what purpose is in the mind of each; otherwise your art will not be admirable.

V.

SUGGESTIONS FOR COMPOSITIONS.

Of painting battle pieces (601-603).

601.

OF THE WAY OF REPRESENTING A BATTLE.

First you must represent the smoke of artillery mingling in the air with the dust and tossed up by the movement of horses and the combatants. And this mixture you must express thus: The dust, being a thing of earth, has weight; and although from its fineness it is easily tossed up and mingles with the air, it nevertheless readily falls again. It is the finest part that rises highest; hence that part will be least seen and will look almost of the same colour as the air. The higher the smoke mixed with the dust-laden air rises towards a certain level, the more it will look like a dark cloud; and it will be seen that at the top, where the smoke is more separate from the dust, the smoke will assume a bluish tinge and the dust will tend to its colour. This mixture of air, smoke and dust will look much lighter on the side whence the light comes than on the opposite side. The more the combatants are in this turmoil the less will they be seen, and the less contrast will there be in their lights and shadows. Their faces and figures and their appearance, and the musketeers as well as those near them you must make of a glowing red. And this glow will diminish in proportion as it is remote from its cause.

The figures which are between you and the light, if they be at a distance, will appear dark on a light background, and the lower part of their legs near the ground will be least visible, because there the dust is coarsest and densest [19]. And if you introduce horses galloping outside the crowd, make the little clouds of dust distant from each other in proportion to the strides made by the horses; and the clouds which are furthest removed from the horses, should be least visible; make them high and spreading and thin, and the nearer ones will be more conspicuous and smaller and denser [23]. The air must be full of arrows in every direction, some shooting upwards, some falling, some flying level. The balls from the guns must have a train of smoke following their flight. The figures in the foreground you must make with dust on the hair and eyebrows and on other flat places likely to retain it. The conquerors you will make rushing onwards with their hair and other light things flying on the wind, with their brows bent down,

[Footnote: 19--23. Compare 608. 57--75.]

602.

and with the opposite limbs thrust forward; that is where a man puts forward the right foot the left arm must be advanced. And if you make any one fallen, you must show the place where he has slipped and been dragged along the dust into blood stained mire; and in the half-liquid earth arround show the print of the tramping of men and horses who have passed that way. Make also a horse dragging the dead body of his master, and leaving behind him, in the dust and mud, the track where the body was dragged along. You must make the conquered and beaten pale, their brows raised and knit, and the skin above their brows furrowed with pain, the sides of the nose with wrinkles going in an arch from the nostrils to the eyes, and make the nostrils drawn up--which is the cause of the lines of which I speak--, and the lips arched upwards and discovering the upper teeth; and the teeth apart as with crying out and lamentation. And make some one shielding his terrified eyes with one hand, the palm towards the enemy, while the other rests on the ground to support his half raised body. Others represent shouting with their mouths open, and running away. You must scatter arms of all sorts among the feet of the combatants, as broken shields, lances, broken swords and other such objects. And you must make the dead partly or entirely covered with dust, which is changed into crimson mire where it has mingled with the flowing blood whose colour shows it issuing in a sinuous stream from the corpse. Others must be represented in the agonies of death grinding their teeth, rolling their eyes, with their fists clenched against their bodies and their legs contorted. Some might be shown disarmed and beaten down by the enemy, turning upon the foe, with teeth and nails, to take an inhuman and bitter revenge. You might see some riderless horse rushing among the enemy, with his mane flying in the wind, and doing no little mischief with his heels. Some maimed warrior may be seen fallen to the earth, covering himself with his shield, while the enemy, bending over him, tries to deal him a deathstroke. There again might be seen a number of men fallen in a heap over a dead horse. You would see some of the victors leaving the fight and issuing from the crowd, rubbing their eyes and cheeks with both hands to clean them of the dirt made by their watering eyes smarting from the dust and smoke. The reserves may be seen standing, hopeful but cautious; with watchful eyes, shading them with their hands and gazing through the dense and murky confusion, attentive to the commands of their captain. The captain himself, his staff raised, hurries towards these auxiliaries, pointing to the spot where they are most needed. And there may be a river into which horses are galloping, churning up the water all round them into turbulent waves of foam and water, tossed into the air and among the legs and bodies of the horses. And there must not be a level spot that is not trampled with gore.

603.

OF LIGHTING THE LOWER PARTS OF BODIES CLOSE TOGETHER, AS OF MEN IN BATTLE.

As to men and horses represented in battle, their different parts will be dark in proportion as they are nearer to the ground on which they stand. And this is proved by the sides of wells which grow darker in proportion to their depth, the reason of which is that the deepest part of the well sees and receives a smaller amount of the luminous atmosphere than any other part.

And the pavement, if it be of the same colour as the legs of these said men and horses, will always be more lighted and at a more direct angle than the said legs &c.

604.

OF THE WAY TO REPRESENT A NIGHT [SCENE].

That which is entirely bereft of light is all darkness; given a night under these conditions and that you want to represent a night scene,--arrange that there shall be a great fire, then the objects which are nearest to this fire will be most tinged with its colour; for those objects which are nearest to a coloured light participate most in its nature; as therefore you give the fire a red colour, you must make all the objects illuminated by it ruddy; while those which are farther from the fire are more tinted by the black hue of night. The figures which are seen against the fire look dark in the glare of the firelight because that side of the objects which you see is tinged by the darkness of the night and not by the fire; and those who stand at the side are half dark and half red; while those who are visible beyond the edges of the flame will be fully lighted by the ruddy glow against a black background. As to their gestures, make those which are near it screen themselves with their hands and cloaks as a defence against the intense heat, and with their faces turned away as if about to retire. Of those farther off represent several as raising their hands to screen their eyes, hurt by the intolerable glare.

Of depicting a tempest (605. 606).

605.

Describe a wind on land and at sea. Describe a storm of rain.

606.

HOW TO REPRESENT A TEMPEST.

If you wish to represent a tempest consider and arrange well its effects as seen, when the wind, blowing over the face of the sea and earth, removes and carries with it such things as are not fixed to the general mass. And to represent the storm accurately you must first show the clouds scattered and torn, and flying with the wind, accompanied by clouds of sand blown up from the sea shore, and boughs and leaves swept along by the strength and fury of the blast and scattered with other light objects through the air. Trees and plants must be bent to the ground, almost as if they would follow the course of the gale, with their branches twisted out of their natural growth and their leaves tossed and turned about [Footnote 11: See Pl. XL, No. 2.]. Of the men who are there some must have fallen to the ground and be entangled in their garments, and hardly to be recognized for the dust, while those who remain standing may be behind some tree, with their arms round it that the wind may not tear them away; others with their hands over their eyes for the dust, bending to the ground with their clothes and hair streaming in the wind.

[Footnote 15: See Pl. XXXIV, the right hand lower sketch.] Let the sea be rough and tempestuous and full of foam whirled among the lofty waves, while the wind flings the lighter spray through the stormy air, till it resembles a dense and swathing mist. Of the ships that are therein some should be shown with rent sails and the tatters fluttering through the air, with ropes broken and masts split and fallen. And the ship itself lying in the trough of the sea and wrecked by the fury of the waves with the men shrieking and clinging to the fragments of the vessel. Make the clouds driven by the impetuosity of the wind and flung against the lofty mountain tops, and wreathed and torn like waves beating upon rocks; the air itself terrible from the deep darkness caused by the dust and fog and heavy clouds.

Of representing the deluge (607-609).

607.

TO REPRESENT THE DELUGE.

The air was darkened by the heavy rain whose oblique descent driven aslant by the rush of the winds, flew in drifts through the air not otherwise than as we see dust, varied only by the straight lines of the heavy drops of falling water. But it was tinged with the colour of the fire kindled by the thunder-bolts by which the clouds were rent and shattered; and whose flashes revealed the broad waters of the inundated valleys, above which was seen the verdure of the bending tree tops. Neptune will be seen in the midst of the water with his trident, and [15] let AEolus with his winds be shown entangling the trees floating uprooted, and whirling in the huge waves. The horizon and the whole hemisphere were obscure, but lurid from the flashes of the incessant lightning. Men and birds might be seen crowded on the tall trees which remained uncovered by the swelling waters, originators of the mountains which surround the great abysses [Footnote 23: Compare Vol. II. No. 979.].

608.

OF THE DELUGE AND HOW TO REPRESENT IT IN A PICTURE.

Let the dark and gloomy air be seen buffeted by the rush of contrary winds and dense from the continued rain mingled with hail and bearing hither and thither an infinite number of branches torn from the trees and mixed with numberless leaves. All round may be seen venerable trees, uprooted and stripped by the fury of the winds; and fragments of mountains, already scoured bare by the torrents, falling into those torrents and choking their valleys till the swollen rivers overflow and submerge the wide lowlands and their inhabitants. Again, you might have seen on many of the hill-tops terrified animals of different kinds, collected together and subdued to tameness, in company with men and women who had fled there with their children. The waters which covered the fields, with their waves were in great part strewn with tables, bedsteads, boats and various other contrivances made from necessity and the fear of death, on which were men and women with their children amid sounds of lamentation and weeping, terrified by the fury of the winds which with their tempestuous violence rolled the waters under and over and about the bodies of the drowned. Nor was there any object lighter than the water which was not covered with a variety of animals which, having come to a truce, stood together in a frightened crowd--among them wolves, foxes, snakes and others--fleing from death. And all the waters dashing on their shores seemed to be battling them with the blows of drowned bodies, blows which killed those in whom any life remained [19]. You might have seen assemblages of men who, with weapons in their hands, defended the small spots that remained to them against lions, wolves and beasts of prey who sought safety there. Ah! what dreadful noises were heard in the air rent by the fury of the thunder and the lightnings it flashed forth, which darted from the clouds dealing ruin and striking all that opposed its course. Ah! how many you might have seen closing their ears with their hands to shut out the tremendous sounds made in the darkened air by the raging of the winds mingling with the rain, the thunders of heaven and the fury of the thunder-bolts. Others were not content with shutting their eyes, but laid their hands one over the other to cover them the closer that they might not see the cruel slaughter of the human race by the wrath of God. Ah! how many laments! and how many in their terror flung themselves from the rocks! Huge branches of great oaks loaded with men were seen borne through the air by the impetuous fury of the winds. How many were the boats upset, some entire, and some broken in pieces, on the top of people labouring to escape with gestures and actions of grief foretelling a fearful death. Others, with desperate act, took their own lives, hopeless of being able to endure such suffering; and of these, some flung themselves from lofty rocks, others strangled themselves with their own hands, other seized their own children and violently slew them at a blow; some wounded and killed themselves with their own weapons; others, falling on their knees recommended themselves to God. Ah! how many mothers wept over their drowned sons, holding them upon their knees, with arms raised spread out towards heaven and with words and various threatening gestures, upbraiding the wrath of the gods. Others with clasped hands and fingers clenched gnawed them and devoured them till they bled, crouching with their breast down on their knees in their intense and unbearable anguish. Herds of animals were to be seen, such as horses, oxen, goats and swine already environed by the waters and left isolated on the high peaks of the mountains, huddled together, those in the middle climbing to the top and treading on the others, and fighting fiercely themselves; and many would die for lack of food. Already had the birds begun to settle on men and on other animals, finding no land uncovered which was not occupied by living beings, and already had famine, the minister of death, taken the lives of the greater number of the animals, when the dead bodies, now fermented, where leaving the depth of the waters and were rising to the top. Among the buffeting waves, where they were beating one against the other, and, like as balls full of air, rebounded from the point of concussion, these found a resting place on the bodies of the dead. And above these judgements, the air was seen covered with dark clouds, riven by the forked flashes of the raging bolts of heaven, lighting up on all sides the depth of the gloom.

The motion of the air is seen by the motion of the dust thrown up by the horse's running and this motion is as swift in again filling up the vacuum left in the air which enclosed the horse, as he is rapid in passing away from the air.

Perhaps it will seem to you that you may reproach me with having represented the currents made through the air by the motion of the wind notwithstanding that the wind itself is not visible in the air. To this I must answer that it is not the motion of the wind but only the motion of the things carried along by it which is seen in the air.

THE DIVISIONS. [Footnote 76: These observations, added at the bottom of the page containing the full description of the doluge seem to indicate that it was Leonardo's intention to elaborate the subject still farther in a separate treatise.]

Darkness, wind, tempest at sea, floods of water, forests on fire, rain, bolts from heaven, earthquakes and ruins of mountains, overthrow of cities [Footnote 81: Spianamenti di citta (overthrow of cities). A considerable number of drawings in black chalk, at Windsor, illustrate this catastrophe. Most of them are much rubbed; one of the least injured is reproduced at Pl. XXXIX. Compare also the pen and ink sketch Pl. XXXVI.].

Whirlwinds which carry water [spouts] branches of trees, and men through the air.

Boughs stripped off by the winds, mingling by the meeting of the winds, with people upon them.

Broken trees loaded with people.

Ships broken to pieces, beaten on rocks.

Flocks of sheep. Hail stones, thunderbolts, whirlwinds.

People on trees which are unable to to support them; trees and rocks, towers and hills covered with people, boats, tables, troughs, and other means of floating. Hills covered with men, women and animals; and lightning from the clouds illuminating every thing.

[Footnote: This chapter, which, with the next one, is written on a loose sheet, seems to be the passage to which one of the compilers of the Vatican copy alluded when he wrote on the margin of fol. 36: "Qua mi ricordo della mirabile discritione del Diluuio dello autore." It is scarcely necessary to point out that these chapters are among those which have never before been published. The description in No. 607 may be regarded as a preliminary sketch for this one. As the MS. G. (in which it is to be found) must be attributed to the period of about 1515 we may deduce from it the approximate date of the drawings on Pl. XXXIV, XXXV, Nos. 2 and 3, XXXVI and XXXVII, since they obviously belong to this text. The drawings No. 2 on Pl. XXXV are, in the original, side by side with the text of No. 608; lines 57 to 76 are shown in the facsimile. In the drawing in Indian ink given on Pl. XXXIV we see Wind-gods in the sky, corresponding to the allusion to Aeolus in No. 607 1. 15.-Plates XXXVI and XXXVII form one sheet in the original. The texts reproduced on these Plates have however no connection with the sketches, excepting the sketches of clouds on the right hand side. These texts are given as No. 477. The group of small figures on Pl. XXXVII, to the left, seems to be intended for a 'congregatione d'uomini.' See No. 608, 1. 19.]

609.

DESCRIPTION OF THE DELUGE.

Let there be first represented the summit of a rugged mountain with valleys surrounding its base, and on its sides let the surface of the soil be seen to slide, together with the small roots of the bushes, denuding great portions of the surrounding rocks. And descending ruinous from these precipices in its boisterous course, let it dash along and lay bare the twisted and gnarled roots of large trees overthrowing their roots upwards; and let the mountains, as they are scoured bare, discover the profound fissures made in them by ancient earthquakes. The base of the mountains may be in great part clothed and covered with ruins of shrubs, hurled down from the sides of their lofty peaks, which will be mixed with mud, roots, boughs of trees, with all sorts of leaves thrust in with the mud and earth and stones. And into the depth of some valley may have fallen the fragments of a mountain forming a shore to the swollen waters of its river; which, having already burst its banks, will rush on in monstrous waves; and the greatest will strike upon and destroy the walls of the cities and farmhouses in the valley [14]. Then the ruins of the high buildings in these cities will throw up a great dust, rising up in shape like smoke or wreathed clouds against the falling rain; But the swollen waters will sweep round the pool which contains them striking in eddying whirlpools against the different obstacles, and leaping into the air in muddy foam; then, falling back, the beaten water will again be dashed into the air. And the whirling waves which fly from the place of concussion, and whose impetus moves them across other eddies going in a contrary direction, after their recoil will be tossed up into the air but without dashing off from the surface. Where the water issues from the pool the spent waves will be seen spreading out towards the outlet; and there falling or pouring through the air and gaining weight and impetus they will strike on the water below piercing it and rushing furiously to reach its depth; from which being thrown back it returns to the surface of the lake, carrying up the air that was submerged with it; and this remains at the outlet in foam mingled with logs of wood and other matters lighter than water. Round these again are formed the beginnings of waves which increase the more in circumference as they acquire more movement; and this movement rises less high in proportion as they acquire a broader base and thus they are less conspicuous as they die away. But if these waves rebound from various objects they then return in direct opposition to the others following them, observing the same law of increase in their curve as they have already acquired in the movement they started with. The rain, as it falls from the clouds is of the same colour as those clouds, that is in its shaded side; unless indeed the sun's rays should break through them; in that case the rain will appear less dark than the clouds. And if the heavy masses of ruin of large mountains or of other grand buildings fall into the vast pools of water, a great quantity will be flung into the air and its movement will be in a contrary direction to that of the object which struck the water; that is to say: The angle of reflection will be equal to the angle of incidence. Of the objects carried down by the current, those which are heaviest or rather largest in mass will keep farthest from the two opposite shores. The water in the eddies revolves more swiftly in proportion as it is nearer to their centre. The crests of the waves of the sea tumble to their bases falling with friction on the bubbles of their sides; and this friction grinds the falling water into minute particles and this being converted into a dense mist, mingles with the gale in the manner of curling smoke and wreathing clouds, and at last it, rises into the air and is converted into clouds. But the rain which falls through the atmosphere being driven and tossed by the winds becomes rarer or denser according to the rarity or density of the winds that buffet it, and thus there is generated in the atmosphere a moisture formed of the transparent particles of the rain which is near to the eye of the spectator. The waves of the sea which break on the slope of the mountains which bound it, will foam from the velocity with which they fall against these hills; in rushing back they will meet the next wave as it comes and and after a loud noise return in a great flood to the sea whence they came. Let great numbers of inhabitants--men and animals of all kinds-- be seen driven [54] by the rising of the deluge to the peaks of the mountains in the midst of the waters aforesaid.

The wave of the sea at Piombino is all foaming water. [Footnote 55. 56: These two lines are written below the bottom sketch on Pl. XXXV, 3. The MS. Leic. being written about the year 1510 or later, it does not seem to me to follow that the sketches must have been made at Piombino, where Leonardo was in the year 1502 and possibly returned there subsequently (see Vol. II. Topographical notes).]

Of the water which leaps up from the spot where great masses fall on its surface. Of the winds of Piombino at Piombino. Eddies of wind and rain with boughs and shrubs mixed in the air. Emptying the boats of the rain water.

[Footnote: The sketches on Pl. XXXV 3 stand by the side of lines 14 to 54.]

Of depicting natural phenomena (610. 611).

610.

The tremendous fury of the wind driven by the falling in of the hills on the caves within--by the falling of the hills which served as roofs to these caverns.

A stone flung through the air leaves on the eye which sees it the impression of its motion, and the same effect is produced by the drops of water which fall from the clouds when it [16] rains.

[17] A mountain falling on a town, will fling up dust in the form of clouds; but the colour of this dust will differ from that of the clouds. Where the rain is thickest let the colour of the dust be less conspicuous and where the dust is thickest let the rain be less conspicuous. And where the rain is mingled with the wind and with the dust the clouds created by the rain must be more transparent than those of dust [alone]. And when flames of fire are mingled with clouds of smoke and water very opaque and dark clouds will be formed [Footnote 26-28: Compare Pl. XL, 1--the drawing in Indian ink on the left hand side, which seems to be a reminiscence of his observations of an eruption (see his remarks on Mount Etna in Vol II).]. And the rest of this subject will be treated in detail in the book on painting.

[Footnote: See the sketches and text on Pl. XXXVIII, No. 1. Lines 1-16 are there given on the left hand side, 17-30 on the right. The four lines at the bottom on the right are given as No. 472. Above these texts, which are written backwards, there are in the original sixteen lines in a larger writing from left to right, but only half of this is here visible. They treat of the physical laws of motion of air and water. It does not seem to me that there is any reason for concluding that this writing from left to right is spurious. Compare with it the facsimile of the rough copy of Leonardo's letter to Ludovico il Moro in Vol. II.]

611.

People were to be seen eagerly embarking victuals on various kinds of hastily made barks. But little of the waves were visible in those places where the dark clouds and rain were reflected.

But where the flashes caused by the bolts of heaven were reflected, there were seen as many bright spots, caused by the image of the flashes, as there were waves to reflect them to the eye of the spectator.

The number of the images produced by the flash of lightning on the waves of the water were multiplied in proportion to the distance of the spectator's eye.

So also the number of the images was diminished in proportion as they were nearer the eye which saw them [Footnote 22. 23: Com'e provato. See Vol. II, Nos. 874-878 and 892-901], as it has been proved in the definition of the luminosity of the moon, and of our marine horizon when the sun's rays are reflected in it and the eye which receives the reflection is remote from the sea.

VI.

THE ARTIST'S MATERIALS.

Of chalk and paper (612--617).

612.

To make points [crayons] for colouring dry. Temper with a little wax and do not dry it; which wax you must dissolve with water: so that when the white lead is thus tempered, the water being distilled, may go off in vapour and the wax may remain; you will thus make good crayons; but you must know that the colours must be ground with a hot stone.

613.

Chalk dissolves in wine and in vinegar or in aqua fortis and can be recombined with gum.

614.

PAPER FOR DRAWING UPON IN BLACK BY THE AID OF YOUR SPITTLE.

Take powdered gall nuts and vitriol, powder them and spread them on paper like a varnish, then write on it with a pen wetted with spittle and it will turn as black as ink.

615.

If you want to make foreshortened letters stretch the paper in a drawing frame and then draw your letters and cut them out, and make the sunbeams pass through the holes on to another stretched paper, and then fill up the angles that are wanting.

616.

This paper should be painted over with candle soot tempered with thin glue, then smear the leaf thinly with white lead in oil as is done to the letters in printing, and then print in the ordinary way. Thus the leaf will appear shaded in the hollows and lighted on the parts in relief; which however comes out here just the contrary.

[Footnote: This text, which accompanies a facsimile impression of a leaf of sage, has already been published in the Saggio delle Opere di L. da Vinci, Milano 1872, p. 11. G. GOVI observes on this passage: "Forse aveva egli pensato ancora a farsi un erbario, od almeno a riprodurre facilmente su carta le forme e i particolari delle foglie di diverse piante; poiche (modificando un metodo che probabilmente gli eia stato insegnato da altri, e che piu tardi si legge ripetuto in molti ricettarii e libri di segreti), accanto a una foglia di Salvia impressa in nero su carta bianca, lascio scritto: Questa carta ...

Erano i primi tentativi di quella riproduzione immediata delle parti vegetali, che poi sotto il nome d'Impressione Naturale, fu condotta a tanta perfezione in questi ultimi tempi dal signor de Hauer e da altri."]

617.

Very excellent will be a stiff white paper, made of the usual mixture and filtered milk of an herb called calves foot; and when this paper is prepared and damped and folded and wrapped up it may be mixed with the mixture and thus left to dry; but if you break it before it is moistened it becomes somewhat like the thin paste called lasagne and you may then damp it and wrap it up and put it in the mixture and leave it to dry; or again this paper may be covered with stiff transparent white and sardonio and then damped so that it may not form angles and then covered up with strong transparent size and as soon as it is firm cut it two fingers, and leave it to dry; again you may make stiff cardboard of sardonio and dry it and then place it between two sheets of papyrus and break it inside with a wooden mallet with a handle and then open it with care holding the lower sheet of paper flat and firm so that the broken pieces be not separated; then have a sheet of paper covered with hot glue and apply it on the top of all these pieces and let them stick fast; then turn it upside down and apply transparent size several times in the spaces between the pieces, each time pouring in first some black and then some stiff white and each time leaving it to dry; then smooth it and polish it.

On the preparation and use of colours (618-627).

618.

To make a fine green take green and mix it with bitumen and you will make the shadows darker. Then, for lighter [shades] green with yellow ochre, and for still lighter green with yellow, and for the high lights pure yellow; then mix green and turmeric together and glaze every thing with it. To make a fine red take cinnabar or red chalk or burnt ochre for the dark shadows and for the lighter ones red chalk and vermilion and for the lights pure vermilion and then glaze with fine lake. To make good oil for painting. One part of oil, one of the first refining and one of the second.

619.

Use black in the shadow, and in the lights white, yellow, green, vermilion and lake. Medium shadows; take the shadow as above and mix it with the flesh tints just alluded to, adding to it a little yellow and a little green and occasionally some lake; for the shadows take green and lake for the middle shades.

[Footnote 618 and 619: If we may judge from the flourishes with which the writing is ornamented these passages must have been written in Leonardo's youth.]

620.

You can make a fine ochre by the same method as you use to make white.

621.

A FINE YELLOW.

Dissolve realgar with one part of orpiment, with aqua fortis.

WHITE.

Put the white into an earthen pot, and lay it no thicker than a string, and let it stand in the sun undisturbed for 2 days; and in the morning when the sun has dried off the night dews.

622.

To make reddish black for flesh tints take red rock crystals from Rocca Nova or garnets and mix them a little; again armenian bole is good in part.

623.

The shadow will be burnt ,terra-verte'.

624.

THE PROPORTIONS OF COLOURS.

If one ounce of black mixed with one ounce of white gives a certain shade of darkness, what shade of darkness will be produced by 2 ounces of black to 1 ounce of white?

625.

Remix black, greenish yellow and at the end blue.

626.

Verdigris with aloes, or gall or turmeric makes a fine green and so it does with saffron or burnt orpiment; but I doubt whether in a short time they will not turn black. Ultramarine blue and glass yellow mixed together make a beautiful green for fresco, that is wall-painting. Lac and verdigris make a good shadow for blue in oil painting.

627.

Grind verdigris many times coloured with lemon juice and keep it away from yellow (?).

Of preparing the panel.

628.

TO PREPARE A PANEL FOR PAINTING ON.

The panel should be cypress or pear or service-tree or walnut. You must coat it over with mastic and turpentine twice distilled and white or, if you like, lime, and put it in a frame so that it may expand and shrink according to its moisture and dryness. Then give it [a coat] of aqua vitae in which you have dissolved arsenic or [corrosive] sublimate, 2 or 3 times. Then apply boiled linseed oil in such a way as that it may penetrate every part, and before it is cold rub it well with a cloth to dry it. Over this apply liquid varnish and white with a stick, then wash it with urine when it is dry, and dry it again. Then pounce and outline your drawing finely and over it lay a priming of 30 parts of verdigris with one of verdigris with two of yellow.

[Footnote: M. RAVAISSON'S reading varies from mine in the following passages:

1.opero allor [?] bo [alloro?] = "ou bien de [laurier]."

6. fregalo bene con un panno. He reads pane for panno and renders it. "Frotte le bien avec un pain de facon [jusqu'a ce] qu'il" etc.

7. colla stecca po laua. He reads "polacca" = "avec le couteau de bois [?] polonais [?]."]

The preparation of oils (629--634).

629.

OIL.

Make some oil of mustard seed; and if you wish to make it with greater ease mix the ground seeds with linseed oil and put it all under the press.

630.

TO REMOVE THE SMELL OF OIL.

Take the rank oil and put ten pints into a jar and make a mark on the jar at the height of the oil; then add to it a pint of vinegar and make it boil till the oil has sunk to the level of the mark and thus you will be certain that the oil is returned to its original quantity and the vinegar will have gone off in vapour, carrying with it the evil smell; and I believe you may do the same with nut oil or any other oil that smells badly.

631.

Since walnuts are enveloped in a thin rind, which partakes of the nature of ...,
if you do not remove it when you make the oil from them, this skin tinges the oil, and when you work with it this skin separates from the oil and rises to the surface of the painting, and this is what makes it change.

632.

TO RESTORE OIL COLOURS THAT HAVE BECOME DRY.

If you want to restore oil colours that have become dry keep them soaking in soft soap for a night and, with your finger, mix them up with the soft soap; then pour them into a cup and wash them with water, and in this way you can restore colours that have got dry. But take care that each colour has its own vessel to itself adding the colour by degrees as you restore it and mind that they are thoroughly softened, and when you wish to use them for tempera wash them five and six times with spring water, and leave them to settle; if the soft soap should be thick with any of the colours pass it through a filter.
[Footnote: The same remark applies to these sections as to No. 618 and 619.]

633.

OIL.

Mustard seed pounded with linseed oil.

634.

... outside the bowl 2 fingers lower than the level of the oil, and pass it into the neck of a bottle and let it stand and thus all the oil will separate from this milky liquid; it will enter the bottle and be as clear as crystal; and grind your colours with this, and every coarse or viscid part will remain in the liquid. You must know that all the oils that have been created in seads or fruits are quite clear by nature, and the yellow colour you see in them only comes of your not knowing how to draw it out. Fire or heat by its nature has the power to make them acquire colour. See for example the exudation or gums of trees which partake of the nature of rosin; in a short time they harden because there is more heat in them than in oil; and after some time they acquire a certain yellow hue tending to black. But oil, not having so much heat does not do so; although it hardens to some extent into sediment it becomes finer. The change in oil which occurs in painting proceeds from a certain fungus of the nature of a husk which exists in the skin which covers the nut, and this being crushed along with the nuts and being of a nature much resembling oil mixes with it; it is of so subtle a nature that it combines with all colours and then comes to the surface, and this it is which makes them change. And if you want the oil to be good and not to thicken, put into it a little camphor melted over a slow fire and mix it well with the oil and it will never harden.

[Footnote: The same remark applies to these sections as to No. 618 and 619.]

On varnishes [or powders] (635-637).

635.

VARNISH [OR POWDER].

Take cypress [oil] and distil it and have a large pitcher, and put in the extract with so much water as may make it appear like amber, and cover it tightly so that none may evaporate. And when it is dissolved you may add in your pitcher as much of the said solution, as shall make it liquid to your taste. And you must know that amber is the gum of the cypress-tree.

VARNISH [OR POWDER].

And since varnish [powder] is the resin of juniper, if you distil juniper you can dissolve the said varnish [powder] in the essence, as explained above.

636.

VARNISH [OR POWDER].

Notch a juniper tree and give it water at the roots, mix the liquor which exudes with nut-oil and you will have a perfect varnish [powder], made like amber varnish [powder], fine and of the best quality make it in May or April.

637.

VARNISH [OR POWDER].

Mercury with Jupiter and Venus,--a paste made of these must be corrected by the mould (?) continuously, until Mercury separates itself entirely from Jupiter and Venus. [Footnote: Here, and in No. 641 Mercurio seems to mean quicksilver, Giove stands for iron, Venere for copper and Saturno for lead.]

On chemical materials (638-650).

638.

Note how aqua vitae absorbs into itself all the colours and smells of flowers. If you want to make blue put iris flowers into it and for red solanum berries (?)

639.

Salt may be made from human excrement burnt and calcined and made into lees, and dried by a slow fire, and all dung in like manner yields salt, and these salts when distilled are very pungent.

640.

Sea water filtered through mud or clay, leaves all its saltness in it. Woollen stuffs placed on board ship absorb fresh water. If sea water is distilled under a retort it becomes of the first excellence and any one who has a little stove in his kitchen can, with the same wood as he cooks with, distil a great quantity of water if the retort is a large one.

641.

MOULD(?).

The mould (?) may be of Venus, or of Jupiter and Saturn and placed frequently in the fire. And it should be worked with fine emery and the mould (?) should be of Venus and Jupiter impasted over (?) Venus. But first you will test Venus and Mercury mixed with Jove, and take means to cause Mercury to disperse; and then fold them well together so that Venus or Jupiter be connected as thinly as possible.

[Footnote: See the note to 637.]

642.

Nitre, vitriol, cinnabar, alum, salt ammoniac, sublimated mercury, rock salt, alcali salt, common salt, rock alum, alum schist (?), arsenic, sublimate, realgar, tartar, orpiment, verdegris.

643.

Pitch four ounces virgin wax, four ounces incense, two ounces oil of roses one ounce.

644.

Four ounces virgin wax, four ounces Greek pitch, two ounces incense, one ounce oil of roses, first melt the wax and oil then the Greek pitch then the other things in powder.

645.

Very thin glass may be cut with scissors and when placed over inlaid work of bone, gilt, or stained of other colours you can saw it through together with the bone and then put it together and it will retain a lustre that will not be scratched nor worn away by rubbing with the hand.

646.

TO DILUTE WHITE WINE AND MAKE IT PURPLE.

Powder gall nuts and let this stand 8 days in the white wine; and in the same way dissolve vitriol in water, and let the water stand and settle very clear, and the wine likewise, each by itself, and strain them well; and when you dilute the white wine with the water the wine will become red.

647.

Put marcasite into aqua fortis and if it turns green, know that it has copper in it. Take it out with saltpetre and soft soap.

648.

A white horse may have the spots removed with the Spanish haematite or with aqua fortis or with ... Removes the black hair on a white horse with the singeing iron. Force him to the ground.

649.

FIRE.

If you want to make a fire which will set a hall in a blaze without injury do this: first perfume the hall with a dense smoke of incense or some other odoriferous substance: It is a good trick to play. Or boil ten pounds of brandy to evaporate, but see that the hall is completely closed and throw up some powdered varnish among the fumes and this powder will be supported by the smoke; then go into the room suddenly with a lighted torch and at once it will be in a blaze.

650.

FIRE.

Take away that yellow surface which covers oranges and distill them in an alembic, until the distillation may be said to be perfect.

FIRE.

Close a room tightly and have a brasier of brass or iron with fire in it and sprinkle on it two pints of aqua vitae, a little at a time, so that it may be converted into smoke. Then make some one come in with a light and suddenly you will see the room in a blaze like a flash of lightning, and it will do no harm to any one.

VII.

PHILOSOPHY AND HISTORY OF THE ART OF PAINTING.

The relation of art and nature (651. 652).

651.

What is fair in men, passes away, but not so in art.

652.

HE WHO DESPISES PAINTING LOVES NEITHER PHILOSOPHY NOR NATURE.

If you condemn painting, which is the only imitator of all visible works of nature, you will certainly despise a subtle invention which brings philosophy and subtle speculation to the consideration of the nature of all forms--seas and plains, trees, animals, plants and flowers--which are surrounded by shade and light. And this is true knowledge and the legitimate issue of nature; for painting is born of nature--or, to speak more correctly, we will say it is the grandchild of nature; for all visible things are produced by nature, and these her children have given birth to painting. Hence we may justly call it the grandchild of nature and related to God.

Painting is superior to poetry (653. 654).

653.

THAT PAINTING SURPASSES ALL HUMAN WORKS BY THE SUBTLE CONSIDERATIONS BELONGING TO IT.

The eye, which is called the window of the soul, is the principal means by which the central sense can most completely and abundantly appreciate the infinite works of nature; and the ear is the second, which acquires dignity by hearing of the things the eye has seen. If you, historians, or poets, or mathematicians had not seen things with your eyes you could not report of them in writing. And if you, 0 poet, tell a story with your pen, the painter with his brush can tell it more easily, with simpler completeness and less tedious to be understood. And if you call painting dumb poetry, the painter may call poetry blind painting. Now which is the worse defect? to be blind or dumb? Though the poet is as free as the painter in the invention of his fictions they are not so satisfactory to men as paintings; for, though poetry is able to describe forms, actions and places in words, the painter deals with the actual similitude of the forms, in order to represent them. Now tell me which is the nearer to the actual man: the name of man or the image of the man. The name of man differs in different countries, but his form is never changed but by death.

654.

And if the poet gratifies the sense by means of the ear, the painter does so by the eye--the worthier sense; but I will say no more of this but that, if a good painter represents the fury of a battle, and if a poet describes one, and they are both together put before the public, you will see where most of the spectators will stop, to which they will pay most attention, on which they will bestow most praise, and which will satisfy them best. Undoubtedly painting being by a long way the more intelligible and beautiful, will please most. Write up the name of God [Christ] in some spot and setup His image opposite and you will see which will be most reverenced. Painting comprehends in itself all the forms of nature, while you have nothing but words, which are not universal as form is, and if you have the effects of the representation, we have the representation of the effects. Take a poet who describes the beauty of a lady to her lover and a painter who represents her and you will see to which nature guides the enamoured critic. Certainly the proof should be allowed to rest on the verdict of experience. You have ranked painting among the mechanical arts but, in truth, if painters were as apt at praising their own works in writing as you are, it would not lie under the stigma of so base a name. If you call it mechanical because it is, in the first place, manual, and that it is the hand which produces what is to be found in the imagination, you too writers, who set down manually with the pen what is devised in your mind. And if you say it is mechanical because it is done for money, who falls into this error--if error it can be called--more than you? If you lecture in the schools do you not go to whoever pays you most? Do you do any work without pay? Still, I do not say this as blaming such views, for every form of labour looks for its reward. And if a poet should say: "I will invent a fiction with a great purpose," the painter can do the same, as Apelles painted Calumny. If you were to say that poetry is more eternal, I say the works of a coppersmith are more eternal still, for time preserves them longer than your works or ours; nevertheless they have not much imagination [29]. And a picture, if painted on copper with enamel colours may be yet more permanent. We, by our arts may be called the grandsons of God. If poetry deals with moral philosophy, painting deals with natural philosophy. Poetry describes the action of the mind, painting considers what the mind may effect by the motions [of the body]. If poetry can terrify people by hideous fictions, painting can do as much by depicting the same things in action. Supposing that a poet applies himself to represent beauty, ferocity, or a base, a foul or a monstrous thing, as against a painter, he may in his ways bring forth a variety of forms; but will the painter not satisfy more? are there not pictures to be seen, so like the actual things, that they deceive men and animals?

Painting is superior to sculpture (655. 656).

655.

THAT SCULPTURE IS LESS INTELLECTUAL THAN PAINTING, AND LACKS MANY CHARACTERISTICS OF NATURE.

I myself, having exercised myself no less in sculpture than in painting and doing both one and the other in the same degree, it seems to me that I can, without invidiousness, pronounce an opinion as to which of the two is of the greatest merit and difficulty and perfection. In the first place sculpture requires a certain light, that is from above, a picture carries everywhere with it its own light and shade. Thus sculpture owes its importance to light and shade, and the sculptor is aided in this by the nature, of the relief which is inherent in it, while the painter whose art expresses the accidental aspects of nature, places his effects in the spots where nature must necessarily produce them. The sculptor cannot diversify his work by the various natural colours of objects; painting is not defective in any particular. The sculptor when he uses perspective cannot make it in any way appear true; that of the painter can appear like a hundred miles beyond the picture itself. Their works have no aerial perspective whatever, they cannot represent transparent bodies, they cannot represent luminous bodies, nor reflected lights, nor lustrous bodies--as mirrors and the like polished surfaces, nor mists, nor dark skies, nor an infinite number of things which need not be told for fear of tedium. As regards the power of resisting time, though they have this resistance [Footnote 19: From what is here said as to painting on copper it is very evident that Leonardo was not acquainted with the method of painting in oil on thin copper plates, introduced by the Flemish painters of the XVIIth century. J. LERMOLIEFF has already pointed out that in the various collections containing pictures by the great masters of the Italian Renaissance, those painted on copper (for instance the famous reading Magdalen in the Dresden Gallery) are the works of a much later date (see Zeitschrift fur bildende Kunst. Vol. X pg. 333, and: Werke italienischer Master in den Galerien von Munchen, Dresden und Berlin. Leipzig 1880, pg. 158 and 159.)--Compare No. 654, 29.], a picture painted on thick copper covered with white enamel on which it is painted with enamel colours and then put into the fire again and baked, far exceeds sculpture in permanence. It may be said that if a mistake is made it is not easy to remedy it; it is but a poor argument to try to prove that a work be the nobler because oversights are irremediable; I should rather say that it will be more difficult to improve the mind of the master who makes such mistakes than to repair the work he has spoilt.

656.

We know very well that a really experienced and good painter will not make such mistakes; on the contrary, with sound rules he will remove so little at a time that he will bring his work to a good issue. Again the sculptor if working in clay or wax, can add or reduce, and when his model is finished it can easily be cast in bronze, and this is the last operation and is the most permanent form of sculpture. Inasmuch as that which is merely of marble is liable to ruin, but not bronze. Hence a painting done on copper which as I said of painting may be added to or altered, resembles sculpture in bronze, which, having first been made in wax could then be altered or added to; and if sculpture in bronze is durable, this work in copper and enamel is absolutely imperishable. Bronze is but dark and rough after all, but this latter is covered with various and lovely colours in infinite variety, as has been said above; or if you will have me only speak of painting on panel, I am content to pronounce between it and sculpture; saying that painting is the more beautiful and the more imaginative and the more copious, while sculpture is the more durable but it has nothing else. Sculpture shows with little labour what in painting appears a miraculous thing to do; to make what is impalpable appear palpable, flat objects appear in relief, distant objects seem close. In fact painting is adorned with infinite possibilities which sculpture cannot command.

Aphorisms (657-659).

657.

OF PAINTING.

Men and words are ready made, and you, O Painter, if you do not know how to make your figures move, are like an orator who knows not how to use his words.

658.

As soon as the poet ceases to represent in words what exists in nature, he in fact ceases to resemble the painter; for if the poet, leaving such representation, proceeds to describe the flowery and flattering speech of the figure, which he wishes to make the speaker, he then is an orator and no longer a poet nor a painter. And if he speaks of the heavens he becomes an astrologer, and philosopher; and a theologian, if he discourses of nature or God. But, if he restricts himself to the description of objects, he would enter the lists against the painter, if with words he could satisfy the eye as the painter does.

659.

Though you may be able to tell or write the exact description of forms, the painter can so depict them that they will appear alive, with the shadow and light which show the expression of a face; which you cannot accomplish with the pen though it can be achieved by the brush.

On the history of painting (660. 661).

660.

THAT PAINTING DECLINES AND DETERIORATES FROM AGE TO AGE, WHEN PAINTERS HAVE NO OTHER STANDARD THAN PAINTING ALREADY DONE.

Hence the painter will produce pictures of small merit if he takes for his standard the pictures of others. But if he will study from natural objects he will bear good fruit; as was seen in the painters after the Romans who always imitated each other and so their art constantly declined from age to age. After these came Giotto the Florentine who--not content with imitating the works of Cimabue his master--being born in the mountains and in a solitude inhabited only by goats and such beasts, and being guided by nature to his art, began by drawing on the rocks the movements of the goats of which he was keeper. And thus he began to draw all the animals which were to be found in the country, and in such wise that after much study he excelled not only all the masters of his time but all those of many bygone ages. Afterwards this art declined again, because everyone imitated the pictures that were already done; thus it went on from century to century until Tomaso, of Florence, nicknamed Masaccio, showed by his perfect works how those who take for their standard any one but nature--the mistress of all masters--weary themselves in vain. And, I would say about these mathematical studies that those who only study the authorities and not the works of nature are descendants but not sons of nature the mistress of all good authors. Oh! how great is the folly of those who blame those who learn from nature [Footnote 22: lasciando stare li autori. In this observation we may detect an indirect evidence that Leonardo regarded his knowledge of natural history as derived from his own investigations, as well as his theories of perspective and optics. Compare what he says in praise of experience (Vol II; XIX).], setting aside those authorities who themselves were the disciples of nature.

661.

That the first drawing was a simple line drawn round the shadow of a man cast by the sun on a wall.

The painter's scope.

662.

The painter strives and competes with nature.

X. Studies and Sketches for Pictures and Decorations.

An artist's manuscript notes can hardly be expected to contain any thing more than incidental references to those masterpieces of his work of which the fame, sounded in the writings of his contemporaries, has left a glorious echo to posterity. We need not therefore be surprised to find that the texts here reproduced do not afford us such comprehensive information as we could wish. On the other hand, the sketches and studies prepared by Leonardo for the two grandest compositions he ever executed: The Fresco of the Last Supper in the Refectory of Santa Maria delle Grazie at Milan, and the Cartoon of the Battle of Anghiari, for the Palazzo della Signoria at Florence--have been preserved; and, though far from complete, are so much more numerous than the manuscript notes, that we are justified in asserting that in value and interest they amply compensate for the meagerness of the written suggestions.

The notes for the composition of the Last Supper, which are given under nos. 665 and 666 occur in a MS. at South Kensington, II2, written in the years 1494-1495. This MS. sketch was noted down not more than three or four years before the painting was executed, which justifies the inference that at the time when it was written the painter had not made up his mind definitely even as to the general scheme of the work; and from this we may also conclude that the drawings of apostles' heads at Windsor, in red chalk, must be ascribed to a later date. They are studies for the head of St. Matthew, the fourth figure on Christ's left hand--see Pl. XL VII, the sketch (in black chalk) for the head of St. Philip, the third figure on the left hand--see Pl. XL VIII, for St. Peter's right arm--see Pl. XLIX, and for the expressive head of Judas which has unfortunately somewhat suffered by subsequent restoration of outlines,--see Pl. L. According to a tradition, as unfounded as it is improbable, Leonardo made use of the head of Padre Bandelli, the prior of the convent, as the prototype of his Judas; this however has already been contradicted by Amoretti "Memorie storiche" cap. XIV. The study of the head of a criminal on Pl. LI has, it seems to me, a better claim to be regarded as one of the preparatory sketches for the head of Judas. The Windsor collection contains two old copies of the head of St. Simon, the figure to the extreme left of Christ, both of about equal merit (they are marked as Nos. 21 and 36)--the second was reproduced on Pl. VIII of the Grosvenor Gallery Publication in 1878. There is also at Windsor a drawing in black chalk of folded hands (marked with the old No. 212; No. LXI of the Grosvenor Gallery Publication) which I believe to be a copy of the hands of St. John, by some unknown pupil. A reproduction of the excellent drawings of heads of Apostles in the possession of H. R. H. the Grand Duchess of Weimar would have been out of my province in this work, and, with regard to them, I must confine myself to pointing out that the difference in style does not allow of our placing the Weimar drawings in the same category as those here reproduced. The mode of grouping in the Weimar drawings is of itself sufficient to indicate that they were not executed before the picture was painted, but, on the contrary, afterwards, and it is, on the face of it, incredible that so great a master should thus have copied from his own work.

The drawing of Christ's head, in the Brera palace at Milan was perhaps originally the work of Leonardo's hand; it has unfortunately been entirely retouched and re-drawn, so that no decisive opinion can be formed as to its genuineness.

The red chalk drawing reproduced on Pl. XLVI is in the Accademia at Venice; it was probably made before the text, Nos. 664 and 665, was written.

The two pen and ink sketches on Pl. XLV seem to belong to an even earlier date; the more finished drawing of the two, on the right hand, represents Christ with only St. John and Judas and a third disciple whose action is precisely that described in No. 666, Pl. 4. It is hardly necessary to observe that the other sketches on this page and the lines of text below the circle (containing the solution of a geometrical problem) have no reference to the picture of the Last Supper. With this figure of Christ may be compared a similar pen and ink drawing reproduced on page 297 below on the left hand; the original is in the Louvre. On this page again the rest of the sketches have no direct bearing on the composition of the Last Supper, not even, as it seems to me, the group of four men at the bottom to the right hand--who are listening to a fifth, in their midst addressing them. Moreover the writing on this page (an explanation of a disk shaped instrument) is certainly not in the same style as we find constantly used by Leonardo after the year 1489.

It may be incidentally remarked that no sketches are known for the portrait of "Mona Lisa", nor do the MS. notes ever allude to it, though according to Vasari the master had it in hand for fully four years.

Leonardo's cartoon for the picture of the battle of Anghiari has shared the fate of the rival work, Michaelangelo's "Bathers summoned to Battle". Both have been lost in some wholly inexplicable manner. I cannot here enter into the remarkable history of this work; I can only give an account of what has been preserved to us of Leonardo's scheme and preparations for executing it. The extent of the material in studies and drawings was till now quite unknown. Their publication here may give some adequate idea of the grandeur of this famous work. The text given as No. 669 contains a description of the particulars of the battle, but for the reasons given in the note to this text, I must abandon the idea of taking this passage as the basis of my attempt to reconstruct the picture as the artist conceived and executed it.

I may here remind the reader that Leonardo prepared the cartoon in the Sala del Papa of Santa Maria Novella at Florence and worked there from the end of October 1503 till February 1504, and then was busied with the painting in the Sala del Consiglio in the Palazzo della Signoria, till the work was interrupted at the end of May 1506. (See Milanesi's note to Vasari pp. 43--45 Vol. IV ed. 1880.) Vasari, as is well known, describes only one scene or episode of the cartoon--the Battle for the Standard in the foreground of the composition, as it would seem; and this only was ever finished as a mural decoration in the Sala del Consiglio. This portion of the composition is familiar to all from the disfigured copy engraved by Edelinck. Mariette had already very acutely observed that Edelinck must surely have worked from a Flemish copy of the picture. There is in the Louvre a drawing by Rubens (No. 565) which also represents four horsemen fighting round a standard and which agrees with Edelinck's engraving, but the engraving reverses the drawing. An earlier Flemish drawing, such as may have served as the model for both Rubens and Edelinck, is in the Uffizi collection (see Philpots's Photograph, No. 732). It seems to be a work of the second half of the XVIth century, a time when both the picture and the cartoon had already been destroyed. It is apparently the production of a not very skilled hand. Raphael Trichet du Fresne, 1651, mentions that a small picture by Leonardo himself of the Battle of the Standard was then extant in the Tuileries; by this he probably means the painting on panel which is now in the possession of Madame Timbal in Paris, and which has lately been engraved by Haussoullier as a work by Leonardo. The picture, which is very carefully painted, seems to me however to be the work of some unknown Florentine painter, and probably executed within the first ten years of the XVIth century. At the same time, it would seem to be a copy not from Leonardo's cartoon, but from his picture in the Palazzo della Signoria; at any rate this little picture, and the small Flemish drawing in Florence are the oldest finished copies of this episode in the great composition of the Battle of Anghiari.

In his Life of Raphael, Vasari tells us that Raphael copied certain works of Leonardo's during his stay in Florence. Raphael's first visit to Florence lasted from the middle of October 1504 till July 1505, and he revisited it in the summer of 1506. The hasty sketch, now in the possession of the University of Oxford and reproduced on page 337 also represents the Battle of the Standard and seems to have been made during his first stay, and therefore not from the fresco but from the cartoon; for, on the same sheet we also find, besides an old man's head drawn in Leonardo's style, some studies for the figure of St. John the Martyr which Raphael used in 1505 in his great fresco in the Church of San Severo at Perugia.

Of Leonardo's studies for the Battle of Anghiari I must in the first place point to five, on three of which--Pl. LII 2, Pl. LIII, Pl. LVI--we find studies for the episode of the Standard. The standard bearer, who, in the above named copies is seen stooping, holding on to the staff across his shoulder, is immediately recognisable as the left-hand figure in Raphael's sketch, and we find it in a similar attitude in Leonardo's pen and ink drawing in the British Museum--Pl. LII, 2--the lower figure to the right. It is not difficult to identify the same figure in two more complicated groups in the pen and ink drawings, now in the Accademia at Venice--Pl. LIII, and Pl. LIV--where we also find some studies of foot soldiers fighting. On the sheet in the British Museum--Pl. LII, 2--we find, among others, one group of three horses galloping forwards: one horseman is thrown and protects himself with his buckler against the lance thrusts of two others on horseback, who try to pierce him as they ride past. The same action is repeated, with some variation, in two sketches in pen and ink on a third sheet, in the Accademia at Venice, Pl. LV; a coincidence which suggests the probability of such an incident having actually been represented on the cartoon. We are not, it is true, in a position to declare with any certainty which of these three dissimilar sketches may have been the nearest to the group finally adopted in executing the cartoon.

With regard, however, to one of the groups of horsemen it is possible to determine with perfect certainty not only which arrangement was preferred, but the position it occupied in the composition. The group of horsemen on Pl. LVII is a drawing in black chalk at Windsor, which is there attributed to Leonardo, but which appears to me to be the work of Cesare da Sesto, and the Commendatore Giov. Morelli supports me in this view. It can hardly be doubted that da Sesto, as a pupil of Leonardo's, made this drawing from his master's cartoon, if we compare it with the copy made by Raphael--here reproduced, for just above the fighting horseman in Raphael's copy it is possible to detect a horse which is seen from behind, going at a slower pace, with his tail flying out to the right and the same horse may be seen in the very same attitude carrying a dimly sketched rider, in the foreground of Cesare da Sesto's drawing.

If a very much rubbed drawing in black chalk at Windsor--Pl. LVI--is, as it appears to be, the reversed impression of an original drawing, it is not difficult to supplement from it the portions drawn by Cesare da Sesto. Nay, it may prove possible to reconstruct the whole of the lost cartoon from the mass of materials we now have at hand which we may regard as the nucleus of the composition. A large pen and ink drawing by Raphael in the Dresden collection, representing three horsemen fighting, and another, by Cesare da Sesto, in the Uffizi, of light horsemen fighting are a further contribution which will help us to reconstruct it.

The sketch reproduced on Pl. LV gives a suggestive example of the way in which foot-soldiers may have been introduced into the cartoon as fighting among the groups of horsemen; and I may here take the opportunity of mentioning that, for reasons which it would be out of place to enlarge upon here, I believe the two genuine drawings by Raphael's hand in his "Venetian sketch-book" as it is called--one of a standard bearer marching towards the left, and one of two foot-soldiers armed with spears and fighting with a horseman--to be undoubtedly copies from the cartoon of the Battle of Anghiari.

Leonardo's two drawings, preserved in the museum at Buda-Pesth and reproduced on pages 338 and 339 are preliminary studies for the heads of fighting warriors. The two heads drawn in black chalk (pg. 338) and the one seen in profile, turned to the left, drawn in red chalk (pg. 339), correspond exactly with those of two horsemen in the scene of the fight round the standard as we see them in Madame Timbal's picture and in the other finished copies. An old copy of the last named drawing by a pupil of Leonardo is in MS. C. A. 187b; 561b (See Saggio, Tav. XXII). Leonardo used to make such finished studies of heads as those, drawn on detached sheets, before beginning his pictures from his drawings--compare the preparatory studies for the fresco of the Last Supper, given on Pl. XLVII and Pl. L. Other drawings of heads, all characterised by the expression of vehement excitement that is appropriate to men fighting, are to be seen at Windsor (No. 44) and at the Accademia at Venice (IV, 13); at the back of one of the drawings at Buda-Pesth there is the bust of a warrior carrying a spear on his left shoulder, holding up the left arm (See Csatakepek a XVI--lk Szazadbol osszeallitotta

Pvlszky Karoly). These drawings may have been made for other portions of the cartoon, of which no copies exist, and thus we are unable to identify these preparatory drawings. Finally I may add that a sketch of fighting horse and foot soldiers, formerly in the possession of M. Thiers and published by Charles Blanc in his "Vies des Peintres" can hardly be accepted as genuine. It is not to be found, as I am informed, among the late President's property, and no one appears to know where it now is.

An attempted reconstruction of the Cartoon, which is not only unsuccessful but perfectly unfounded, is to be seen in the lithograph by Bergeret, published in Charles Blanc's "Vies des peintres" and reprinted in "The great Artists. L. da Vinci", p. 80. This misleading pasticcio may now be rejected without hesitation.

There are yet a few original drawings by Leonardo which might be mentioned here as possibly belonging to the cartoon of the Battle; such as the pen and ink sketches on Pl. XXI and on Pl. XXXVIII, No. 3, but we should risk too wide a departure from the domain of ascertained fact.

With regard to the colours and other materials used by Leonardo the reader may be referred to the quotations from the accounts for the picture in question given by Milanesi in his edition of Vasari (Vol. IV, p. 44, note) where we find entries of a similar character to those in Leonardo's note books for the year 1505; S. K. M. 12 (see No. 636).

That Leonardo was employed in designing decorations and other preparations for high festivals, particularly for the court of Milan, we learn not only from the writings of his contemporaries but from his own incidental allusions; for instance in MS. C. I5b (1), I. 9. In the arrangement of the texts referring to this I have placed those first, in which historical personages are named--Nos. 670-674. Among the descriptions of Allegorical subjects two texts lately found at Oxford have been included, Nos. 676 and 677. They are particularly interesting because they are accompanied by large sketches which render the meaning of the texts perfectly clear. It is very intelligible that in other cases, where there are no illustrative sketches, the notes must necessarily remain obscure or admit of various interpretations. The literature of the time affords ample evidence of the use of such allegorical representations, particularly during the Carnival and in Leonardo's notes we find the Carnival expressly mentioned--Nos. 685 and 704. Vasari in his Life of Pontormo, particularly describes that artist's various undertakings for Carnival festivities. These very graphic descriptions appear to me to throw great light in more ways than one on the meaning of Leonardo's various notes as to allegorical representations and also on mottoes and emblems--Nos. 681-702. In passing judgment on the allegorical sketches and emblems it must not be overlooked that even as pictures they were always accompanied by explanations in words. Several finished drawings of allegorical compositions or figures have been preserved, but as they have no corresponding explanation in the MSS. they had no claim to be reproduced here. The female figure on Pl. XXVI may perhaps be regarded as a study for such an allegorical painting, of which the purport would have been explained by an inscription.

On Madonna pictures.

663.

[In the autumn of] 1478 I began the two Madonna [pictures].

[Footnote: Photographs of this page have been published by BRAUN, No. 439, and PHILPOT, No. 718.

1. Incominciai. We have no other information as to the two pictures of the Madonna here spoken of. As Leonardo here tells us that he had begun two Madonnas at the same time, the word 'incominciai' may be understood to mean that he had begun at the same time preparatory studies for two pictures to be painted later. If this is so, the non-existence of the pictures may be explained by supposing that they were only planned and never executed. I may here mention a few studies for pictures of the Madonna which probably belong to this early time; particularly a drawing in silver-point on bluish tinted paper at Windsor--see Pl. XL, No. 3--, a drawing of which the details have almost disappeared in the original but have been rendered quite distinct in the reproduction; secondly a slight pen and ink sketch in, the Codex VALLARDI, in the Louvre, fol. 64, No. 2316; again a silver point drawing of a Virgin and child drawn over again with the pen in the His de la Salle collection also in the Louvre, No. 101. (See Vicomte BOTH DE TAUZIA, Notice des dessins de la collection His de la Salle, exposes au Louvre. Paris 1881, pp. 80, 81.) This drawing is, it is true, traditionally ascribed to Raphael, but the author of the catalogue very justly points out its great resemblance with the sketches for Madonnas in the British Museum which are indisputably Leonardo's. Some of these have been published by Mr. HENRY WALLIS in the Art Journal, New Ser. No. 14, Feb. 1882. If the non-existence of the two pictures here alluded to justifies my hypothesis that only studies for such pictures are meant by the text, it may also be supposed that the drawings were made for some comrade in VERROCCHIO'S atelier. (See VASARI, Sansoni's ed. Florence 1880. Vol. IV, p. 564): "E perche a Lerenzo piaceva fuor di modo la maniera di Lionardo, la seppe cosi bene imitare, che niuno fu che nella pulitezza e nel finir l'opere con diligenza l'imitasse piu di lui." Leonardo's notes give me no opportunity of discussing the pictures executed by him in Florence, before he moved to Milan. So the studies for the unfinished picture of the Adoration of the Magi--in the Uffizi, Florence--cannot be described here, nor would any discussion about the picture in the Louvre "La Vierge aux Rochers" be appropriate in the absence of all allusion to it in the MSS. Therefore, when I presently add a few remarks on this painting in explanation of the Master's drawings for it, it will be not merely with a view to facilitate critical researches about the picture now in the National Gallery, London, which by some critics has been pronounced to be a replica of the Louvre picture, but also because I take this opportunity of publishing several finished studies of the Master's which, even if they were not made in Florence but later in Milan, must have been prior to the painting of the Last Supper. The original picture in Paris is at present so disfigured by dust and varnish that the current reproductions in photography actually give evidence more of the injuries to which the picture has been exposed than of the original work itself. The wood-cut given on p. 344, is only intended to give

a general notion of the composition. It must be understood that the outline and expression of the heads, which in the picture is obscured but not destroyed, is here altogether missed. The facsimiles which follow are from drawings which appear to me to be studies for "La Vierge aux Rochers."

1. A drawing in silver point on brown toned paper of a woman's head looking to the left. In the Royal Library at Turin, apparently a study from nature for the Angel's head (Pl. XLII).

2. A study of drapery for the left leg of the same figure, done with the brush, Indian ink on greenish paper, the lights heightened with white.

The original is at Windsor, No. 223. The reproduction Pl. XLIII is defective in the shadow on the upper part of the thigh, which is not so deep as in the original; it should also be observed that the folds of the drapery near the hips are somewhat altered in the finished work in the Louvre, while the London copy shows a greater resemblance to this study in that particular.

3. A study in red chalk for the bust of the Infant Christ--No. 3 in the Windsor collection (Pl. XLIV). The well-known silver-point drawing on pale green paper, in the Louvre, of a boy's head (No. 363 in REISET, Notice des dessins, Ecoles d'Italie) seems to me to be a slightly altered copy, either from the original picture or from this red chalk study.

4. A silver-point study on greenish paper, for the head of John the Baptist, reproduced on p. 342. This was formerly in the Codex Vallardi and is now exhibited among the drawings in the Louvre. The lights are, in the original, heightened with white; the outlines, particularly round the head and ear, are visibly restored.

There is a study of an outstretched hand--No. 288 in the Windsor collection-- which was published in the Grosvenor Gallery Publication, 1878, simply under the title of: "No. 72 Study of a hand, pointing" which, on the other hand, I regard as a copy by a pupil. The action occurs in the kneeling angel of the Paris picture and not in the London copy.

These four genuine studies form, I believe, a valuable substitute in the absence of any MS. notes referring to the celebrated Paris picture.]

Bernardo di Bandino's Portrait.

664.

A tan-coloured small cap, A doublet of black serge, A black jerkin lined A blue coat lined, with fur of foxes' breasts, and the collar of the jerkin covered with black and white stippled velvet Bernardo di Bandino Baroncelli; black hose.

[Footnote: These eleven lines of text are by the side of the pen and ink drawing of a man hanged--Pl. LXII, No. 1. This drawing was exhibited in 1879 at the Ecole des Beaux-Arts in Paris and the compilers of the catalogue amused themselves by giving the victim's name as follows: "Un pendu, vetu d'une longue robe, les mains liees sur le dos ... Bernardo di Bendino Barontigni, marchand de pantalons" (see Catalogue descriptif des Dessins de Mailres anciens exposes a l'Ecole des Beaux Arts, Paris 1879; No. 83, pp. 9-

10). Now, the criminal represented here, is none other than Bernardino di Bandino Baroncelli the murderer of Giuliano de'Medici, whose name as a coadjutor in the conspiracy of the Pazzi has gained a melancholy notoriety by the tragedy of the 26th April 1478. Bernardo was descended from an ancient family and the son of the man who, under King Ferrante, was President of the High Court of Justice in Naples. His ruined fortunes, it would seem, induced him to join the Pazzi; he and Francesco Pazzi were entrusted with the task of murdering Giuliano de'Medici on the fixed day. Their victim not appearing in the cathedral at the hour when they expected him, the two conspirators ran to the palace of the Medici and induced him to accompany them. Giuliano then took his place in the chancel of the Cathedral, and as the officiating priest raised the Host--the sign agreed upon--Bernardo stabbed the unsuspecting Giuliano in the breast with a short sword; Giuliano stepped backwards and fell dead. The attempt on Lorenzo's life however, by the other conspirators at the same moment, failed of success. Bernardo no sooner saw that Lorenzo tried to make his escape towards the sacristy, than he rushed upon him, and struck down Francesco Nori who endeavoured to protect Lorenzo. How Lorenzo then took refuge behind the brazen doors of the sacristy, and how, as soon as Giuliano's death was made known, the further plans of the conspirators were defeated, while a terrible vengeance overtook all the perpetrators and accomplices, this is no place to tell. Bernardo Bandini alone seemed to be favoured by fortune; he hid first in the tower of the Cathedral, and then escaped undiscovered from Florence. Poliziano, who was with Lorenzo in the Cathedral, says in his 'Conjurationis Pactianae Commentarium': "Bandinus fugitans in Tiphernatem incidit, a quo in aciem receptus Senas pervenit." And Gino Capponi in summing up the reports of the numerous contemporary narrators of the event, says: "Bernardo Bandini ricoverato in Costantinopoli, fu per ordine del Sultano preso e consegnato a un Antonio di Bernardino dei Medici, che Lorenzo aveva mandato apposta in Turchia: cosi era grande la potenza di quest' uomo e grande la voglia di farne mostra e che non restasse in vita chi aveagli ucciso il fratello, fu egli applicato appena giunto" (Storia della Republica di Firenze II, 377, 378). Details about the dates may be found in the Chronichetta di Belfredello Strinati Alfieri: "Bernardo di Bandino Bandini sopradetto ne venne preso da Gostantinopoti a di 14. Dicembre 1479 e disaminato, che fu al Bargello, fu impiccato alle finestre di detto Bargello allato alla Doana a di 29. Dicembre MCCCCLXXIX che pochi di stette." It may however be mentioned with reference to the mode of writing the name of the assassin that, though most of his contemporaries wrote Bernardo Bandini, in the Breve Chronicon Caroli Petri de Joanninis he is called Bernardo di Bandini Baroncelli; and, in the Sententiae Domini Matthaei de Toscana, Bernardus Joannis Bandini de Baroncellis, as is written on Leonardo's drawing of him when hanged. Now VASARI, in the life of Andrea del Castagno (Vol. II, 680; ed. Milanesi 1878), tells us that in 1478 this painter was commissioned by order of the Signoria to represent the members of the Pazzi conspiracy as traitors, on the facade of the Palazzo del Podesta--the Bargello. This statement is obviously founded on a mistake, for Andrea del Castagno was already dead in 1457. He had however been commissioned to paint Rinaldo degli Albizzi, when declared a rebel and exiled in 1434, and his adherents, as hanging head downwards; and in consequence he had acquired the nickname of Andrea degl' Impiccati. On the 21st July 1478 the Council of Eight came to the following resolution: "item servatis etc. deliberaverunt et santiaverunt Sandro Botticelli pro ejus labore in pingendo proditores flor. quadraginta largos" (see G. MILANESI, Arch. star. VI (1862) p. 5 note.)

As has been told, Giuliano de' Medici was murdered on the 26th April 1478, and we see by this that only three months later Botticelli was paid for his painting of the "proditores". We can however hardly suppose that all the members of the conspiracy were depicted by him in fresco on the facade of the palace, since no fewer than eighty had been condemned to death. We have no means of knowing whether, besides Botticelli, any other painters, perhaps Leonardo, was commissioned, when the criminals had been hanged in person out of the windows of the Palazzo del Podesta to represent them there afterwards in effigy in memory of their disgrace. Nor do we know whether the assassin who had escaped may at first not have been provisionally represented as hanged in effigy. Now, when we try to connect the historical facts with this drawing by Leonardo reproduced on Pl. LXII, No. I, and the full description of the conspirator's dress and its colour on the same sheet, there seems to be no reasonable doubt that Bernardo Bandini is here represented as he was actually hanged on December 29th, 1479, after his capture at Constantinople. The dress is certainly not that in which he committed the murder. A long furred coat might very well be worn at Constantinople or at Florence in December, but hardly in April. The doubt remains whether Leonardo described Bernardo's dress so fully because it struck him as remarkable, or whether we may not rather suppose that this sketch was actually made from nature with the intention of using it as a study for a wall painting to be executed. It cannot be denied that the drawing has all the appearance of having been made for this purpose. Be this as it may, the sketch under discussion proves, at any rate, that Leonardo was in Florence in December 1479, and the note that accompanies it is valuable as adding one more characteristic specimen to the very small number of his MSS. that can be proved to have been written between 1470 and 1480.]

Notes on the Last Supper (665-668).

665.

One who was drinking and has left the glass in its position and turned his head towards the speaker.

Another, twisting the fingers of his hands together turns with stern brows to his companion [6]. Another with his hands spread open shows the palms, and shrugs his shoulders up his ears making a mouth of astonishment [8].

[9] Another speaks into his neighbour's ear and he, as he listens to him, turns towards him to lend an ear [10], while he holds a knife in one hand, and in the other the loaf half cut through by the knife. [13] Another who has turned, holding a knife in his hand, upsets with his hand a glass on the table [14].

[Footnote 665, 666: In the original MS. there is no sketch to accompany these passages, and if we compare them with those drawings made by Leonardo in preparation for the composition of the picture--Pl. XLV, XLVI--, (compare also Pl. LII, 1 and the drawings on p. 297) it is impossible to recognise in them a faithful interpretation of the whole of this text; but, if we compare these passages with the finished picture (see p. 334) we shall see that in many places they coincide. For instance, compare No. 665, 1. 6--8, with the fourth figure on the right hand of Christ. The various actions described in lines 9--10, 13--14 are to be seen in the group of Peter, John and Judas; in the finished picture however it is not a glass but a salt cellar that Judas is upsetting.]

666.

Another lays his hand on the table and is looking. Another blows his mouthful. [3] Another leans forward to see the speaker shading his eyes with his hand. [5] Another draws back behind the one who leans forward, and sees the speaker between the wall and the man who is leaning [Footnote: 6. chinato. I have to express my regret for having misread this word, written cinato in the original, and having altered it to "ciclo" when I first published this text, in 'The Academy' for Nov. 8, 1879 immediately after I had discovered it, and subsequently in the small biography of Leonardo da Vinci (Great Artists) p. 29.].

[Footnote: In No. 666. Line I must refer to the furthest figure on the left; 3, 5 and 6 describe actions which are given to the group of disciples on the left hand of Christ.]

667.

CHRIST.

Count Giovanni, the one with the Cardinal of Mortaro.

[Footnote: As this note is in the same small Manuscript as the passage here immediately preceding it, I may be justified in assuming that Leonardo meant to use the features of the person here named as a suitable model for the figure of Christ. The celebrated drawing of the head of Christ, now hanging in the Brera Gallery at Milan, has obviously been so much restored that it is now impossible to say, whether it was ever genuine. We have only to compare it with the undoubtedly genuine drawings of heads of the disciples in Pl. XLVII, XLVIII and L, to admit that not a single line of the Milan drawing in its present state can be by the same hand.]

668.

Philip, Simon, Matthew, Thomas, James the Greater, Peter, Philip, Andrew, Bartholomew.

[Footnote: See Pl. XLVI. The names of the disciples are given in the order in which they are written in the original, from right to left, above each head. The original drawing is here slightly reduced in scale; it measures 39 centimetres in length by 26 in breadth.]

669.

On the battle of Anghiari.
Florentine
Neri di Gino Capponi
Bernardetto de' Medici
Micheletto,
Niccolo da Pisa
Conte Francesco
> Pietro Gian Paolo
> Guelfo Orsino,
> Messer Rinaldo degli
> Albizzi

Begin with the address of Niccolo Piccinino to the soldiers and the banished Florentines among whom are Messer Rinaldo degli Albizzi and other Florentines. Then let it be shown how he first mounted on horseback in armour; and the whole army came after him--40 squadrons of cavalry, and 2000 foot soldiers went with him. Very early in the morning the Patriarch went up a hill to reconnoitre the country, that is the hills, fields and the valley watered by a river; and from thence he beheld Niccolo Picinino coming from Borgo San Sepolcro with his people, and with a great dust; and perceiving them he returned to the camp of his own people and addressed them. Having spoken he prayed to God with clasped hands, when there appeared a cloud in which Saint Peter appeared and spoke to the Patriarch.--500 cavalry were sent forward by the Patriarch to hinder or check the rush of the enemy. In the foremost troop Francesco the son of Niccolo Piccinino [24] was the first to attack the bridge which was held by the Patriarch and the Florentines. Beyond the bridge to his left he sent forward some infantry to engage ours, who drove them back, among whom was their captain Micheletto [29] whose lot it was to be that day at the head of the army. Here, at this bridge there is a severe struggle; our men conquer and the enemy is repulsed. Here Guido and Astorre, his brother, the Lord of Faenza with a great number of men, re-formed and renewed the fight, and rushed upon the Florentines with such force that they recovered the bridge and pushed forward as far as the tents. But Simonetto advanced with 600 horse, and fell upon the enemy and drove them back once more from the place, and recaptured the bridge; and behind him came more men with 2000 horse soldiers. And thus for a long time they fought with varying fortune. But then the Patriarch, in order to divert the enemy, sent forward Niccolo da Pisa [44] and Napoleone Orsino, a beardless lad, followed by a great multitude of men, and then was done another great feat of arms. At the same time Niccolo Piccinino urged forward the remnant of his men, who once more made ours give way; and if it had not been that the Patriarch set himself at their head and, by his words and deeds controlled the captains, our soldiers would have taken to flight. The Patriarch had some artillery placed on the hill and with these he dispersed the enemy's infantry; and the disorder was so complete that Niccolo began to call back his son and all his men, and they took to flight towards Borgo. And then began a great slaughter of men; none escaped but the foremost of those who had fled or who hid themselves. The battle continued until sunset, when the Patriarch gave his mind to recalling his men and burying the dead, and afterwards a trophy was erected.

[Footnote: 669. This passage does not seem to me to be in Leonardo's hand, though it has hitherto been generally accepted as genuine. Not only is the writing unlike his, but the spelling also is quite different. I would suggest that this passage is a description of the events of the battle drawn up for the Painter by order of the Signoria, perhaps by some historian commissioned by them, to serve as a scheme or programme of the work. The whole tenor of the style seems to me to argue in favour of this theory; and besides, it would be in no way surprising that such a document should have been preserved among Leonardo's autographs.]

Allegorical representations referring to the duke of Milan (670-673).

670.

Ermine with blood Galeazzo, between calm weather and a representation of a tempest.

[Footnote: 670. Only the beginning of this text is legible; the writing is much effaced and the sense is consequently obscure. It seems to refer like the following passage to an allegorical picture.]

671.

Il Moro with spectacles, and Envy depicted with False Report and Justice black for il Moro.

Labour as having a branch of vine [or a screw] in her hand.

672.

Il Moro as representing Good Fortune, with hair, and robes, and his hands in front, and Messer Gualtieri taking him by the robes with a respectful air from below, having come in from the front [5].

Again, Poverty in a hideous form running behind a youth. Il Moro covers him with the skirt of his robe, and with his gilt sceptre he threatens the monster.

A plant with its roots in the air to represent one who is at his last;--a robe and Favour.

Of tricks [or of magpies] and of burlesque poems [or of starlings].

Those who trust themselves to live near him, and who will be a large crowd, these shall all die cruel deaths; and fathers and mothers together with their families will be devoured and killed by cruel creatures.

[Footnote: 1--10 have already been published by Amoretti in Memorie Storiche cap. XII. He adds this note with regard to Gualtieri: "A questo M. Gualtieri come ad uomo generoso e benefico scrive il Bellincioni un Sonetto (pag, 174) per chiedergli un piacere; e 'l Tantio rendendo ragione a Lodovico il Moro, perche pubblicasse le Rime del Bellincioni; cio hammi imposto, gli dice: l'humano fidele, prudente e sollicito executore delli tuoi comandamenti

Gualtero, che fa in tutte le cose ove tu possi far utile, ogni studio vi metti." A somewhat mysterious and evidently allegorical composition--a pen and ink drawing--at Windsor, see PL LVIII, contains a group of figures in which perhaps the idea is worked out which is spoken of in the text, lines 1-5.]

673.

He was blacker than a hornet, his eyes were as red as a burning fire and he rode on a tall horse six spans across and more than 20 long with six giants tied up to his saddle-bow and one in his hand which he gnawed with his teeth. And behind him came boars with tusks sticking out of their mouths, perhaps ten spans.

Allegorical representations (674--678).

674.

Above the helmet place a half globe, which is to signify our hemisphere, in the form of a world; on which let there be a peacock, richly decorated, and with his tail spread over the group; and every ornament belonging to the horse should be of peacock's feathers on a gold ground, to signify the beauty which comes of the grace bestowed on him who is a good servant.

On the shield a large mirror to signify that he who truly desires favour must be mirrored in his virtues.

On the opposite side will be represented Fortitude, in like manner in her place with her pillar in her hand, robed in white, to signify ... And all crowned; and Prudence with 3 eyes. The housing of the horse should be of plain cloth of gold closely sprinkled with peacock's eyes, and this holds good for all the housings of the horse, and the man's dress. And the man's crest and his neck-chain are of peacock's feathers on golden ground.

On the left side will be a wheel, the centre of which should be attached to the centre of the horse's hinder thigh piece, and in the centre Prudence is seen robed in red, Charity sitting in a fiery chariot and with a branch of laurel in her hand, to signify the hope which comes of good service.

[21] Messer Antonio Grimani of Venice companion of Antonio Maria [23].

[Footnote: Messer Antonio Gri. His name thus abbreviated is, there can be no doubt, Grimani. Antonio Grimani was the famous Doge who in 1499 commanded the Venetian fleet in battle against the Turks. But after the abortive conclusion of the expedition--Ludovico being the ally of the Turks who took possession of Friuli--, Grimani was driven into exile; he went to live at Rome with his son Cardinal Domenico Grimani. On being recalled to Venice he filled the office of Doge from 1521 to 1523. Antonio Maria probably means Antonio Maria Grimani, the Patriarch of Aquileia.]

675.

Fame should be depicted as covered all over with tongues instead of feathers, and in the figure of a bird.

676.

Pleasure and Pain represent as twins, since there never is one without the other; and as if they were united back to back, since they are contrary to each other.

[6] Clay, gold.

[Footnote: 7. oro. fango: gold, clay. These words stand below the allegorical figure.]

If you take Pleasure know that he has behind him one who will deal you Tribulation and Repentance.

[9] This represents Pleasure together with Pain, and show them as twins because one is never apart from the other. They are back to back because they are opposed to each other; and they exist as contraries in the same body, because they have the same basis, inasmuch as the origin of pleasure is labour and pain, and the various forms of evil pleasure are the origin of pain. Therefore it is here represented with a reed in his right hand which is useless and without strength, and the wounds it inflicts are poisoned. In Tuscany they are put to support beds, to signify that it is here that vain dreams come, and here a great part of life is consumed. It is here that much precious time is wasted, that is, in the morning, when the mind is composed and rested, and the body is made fit to begin new labours; there again many vain pleasures are enjoyed; both by the mind in imagining impossible things, and by the body in taking those pleasures that are often the cause of the failing of life. And for these reasons the reed is held as their support.

[Footnote: 676. The pen and ink drawing on Pl. LIX belongs to this passage.]

[Footnote: 8. tribolatione. In the drawing caltrops may be seen lying in the old man's right hand, others are falling and others again are shewn on the ground. Similar caltrops are drawn in MS. Tri. p. 98 and underneath them, as well as on page 96 the words triboli di ferro are written. From the accompanying text it appears that they were intended to be scattered on the ground at the bottom of ditches to hinder the advance of the enemy. Count Giulio Porro who published a short account of the Trivulzio MS. in the "Archivio Storico Lombardo", Anno VIII part IV (Dec. 31, 1881) has this note on the passages treating of "triboli": "E qui aggiungero che anni sono quando venne fabbricata la nuova cavallerizza presso il castello di Milano, ne furono trovati due che io ho veduto ed erano precisamente quali si trovano descritti e disegnati da Leonardo in questo codice".

There can therefore be no doubt that this means of defence was in general use, whether it were originally Leonardo's invention or not. The play on the word "tribolatione", as it occurs in the drawing at Oxford, must then have been quite intelligible.]

[Footnote: 9--22. These lines, in the original, are written on the left side of the page and refer to the figure shown on Pl. LXI. Next to it is placed the group of three figures given in Pl. LX No. I. Lines 21 and 22, which are written under it, are the only explanation given.]

Evil-thinking is either Envy or Ingratitude.

677.

Envy must be represented with a contemptuous motion of the hand towards heaven, because if she could she would use her strength against God; make her with her face covered by a mask of fair seeming; show her as wounded in the eye by a palm branch and by an olive-branch, and wounded in the ear by laurel and myrtle, to signify that victory and truth are odious to her. Many thunderbolts should proceed from her to signify her evil speaking. Let her be lean and haggard because she is in perpetual torment. Make her heart gnawed by a swelling serpent, and make her with a quiver with tongues serving as arrows, because she often offends with it. Give her a leopard's skin, because this creature kills the lion out of envy and by deceit. Give her too a vase in her hand full of flowers and scorpions and toads and other venomous creatures; make her ride upon death, because Envy, never dying, never tires of ruling. Make her bridle, and load her with divers kinds of arms because all her weapons are deadly.

Toleration.

Intolerable.

No sooner is Virtue born than Envy comes into the world to attack it; and sooner will there be a body without a shadow than Virtue without Envy.

[Footnote: The larger of the two drawings on Pl. LXI is explained by the first 21 lines of this passage. L. 22 and 23, which are written above the space between the two drawings, do not seem to have any reference to either. L. 24-27 are below the allegorical twin figure which they serve to explain.]

678.

When Pluto's Paradise is opened, then there may be devils placed in twelve pots like openings into hell. Here will be Death, the Furies, ashes, many naked children weeping; living fires made of various colours....

679.

John the Baptist
Saint Augustin
Saint Peter
Paul
Elisabeth
Saint Clara.
Bernardino
Our Lady Louis
Bonaventura
Anthony of Padua.
Saint Francis.
Francis,
Anthony, a lily and book;
Bernardino with the [monogram of] Jesus,

Louis with 3 fleur de lys on his breast and
    the crown at his feet,
Bonaventura with Seraphim,
Saint Clara with the tabernacle,
Elisabeth with a Queen's crown.

[Footnote: 679. The text of the first six lines is written within a square space of the same size as the copy here given. The names are written in the margin following the order in which they are here printed. In lines 7--12 the names of those saints are repeated of whom it seemed necessary to point out the emblems.]

List of drawings.

680.

A head, full face, of a young man
with fine flowing hair,
Many flowers drawn from nature,
A head, full face, with curly hair,
Certain figures of Saint Jerome,
[6] The measurements of a figure,
Drawings of furnaces.
A head of the Duke,
[9] many designs for knots,
4 studies for the panel of Saint Angelo
A small composition of Girolamo da Fegline,
A head of Christ done with the pen,
[13] 8 Saint Sebastians,
Several compositions of Angels,
A chalcedony,
A head in profile with fine hair,
Some pitchers seen in(?) perspective,
Some machines for ships,
Some machines for waterworks,
A head, a portrait of Atalanta raising her
face;
The head of Geronimo da Fegline,
The head of Gian Francisco Borso,
Several throats of old women,
Several heads of old men,
Several nude figures, complete,
Several arms, eyes, feet, and positions,
A Madonna, finished,
Another, nearly in profile,
Head of Our Lady ascending into Heaven,
A head of an old man with long chin,

A head of a gypsy girl,
A head with a hat on,
A representation of the Passion, a cast,
A head of a girl with her hair gathered in a knot,
A head, with the brown hair dressed.

[Footnote: 680. This has already been published by AMORETTI Memorie storiche cap. XVI. His reading varies somewhat from that here given, e. g. l. 5 and 6. Certi Sangirolami in su d'una figura; and instead of l. 13. Un San Bastiano.]

[Footnote: 680. 9. Molti disegni di gruppi. VASARI in his life of Leonardo (IV, 21, ed. MILANESI 1880) says: "Oltreche perse tempo fino a disegnare gruppi di corde fatti con ordine, e che da un capo seguissi tutto il resto fino all' altro, tanto che s'empiessi un tondo; che se ne vede in istampa uno difficilissimo e molto bello, e nel mezzo vi sono queste parole: Leonardus Vinci Accademia". Gruppi must here be understood as a technical expression for those twisted ornaments which are well known through wood cuts. AMORETTI mentions six different ones in the Ambrosian Library. I am indebted to M. DELABORDE for kindly informing me that the original blocks of these are preserved in his department in the Bibliotheque Nationale in Paris. On the cover of these volumes is a copy from one of them. The size of the original is 23 1/2 centimetres by 26 1/4. The centre portion of another is given on p. 361. G. Govi remarks on these ornaments (Saggio p. 22): "Codesti gruppi eran probabilmente destinati a servir di modello a ferri da rilegatori per adornar le cartelle degli scolari (?). Fregi somigliantissimi a questi troviamo infatti impressi in oro sui cartoni di vari volumi contemporanei, e li vediam pur figurare nelle lettere iniziali di alcune edizioni del tempo."

Durer who copied them, omitting the inscription, added to the second impressions his own monogram. In his diary he designates them simply as "Die sechs Knoten" (see THAUSING, Life of A. Durer I, 362, 363). In Leonardo's MSS. we find here and there little sketches or suggestions for similar ornaments. Compare too G. MONGERI, L'Arte in Milano, p. 315 where an ornament of the same character is given from the old decorations of the vaulted ceiling of the Sacristy of S. Maria delle Grazie.]

[Footnote: 680, 17. The meaning in which the word coppi, literally pitchers, is here used I am unable to determine; but a change to copie seems to me too doubtful to be risked.]

681.

Stubborn rigour.
Doomed rigour.

[Footnote: See Pl. LXII, No. 2, the two upper pen and ink drawings. The originals, in the Windsor collection are slightly washed with colour. The background is blue sky; the plough and the instrument with the compass are reddish brown, the sun is tinted yellow].

682.

Obstacles cannot crush me
Every obstacle yields to stern resolve
He who is fixed to a star does not change
his mind.

[Footnote: This text is written to elucidate two sketches which were obviously the first sketches for the drawings reproduced on PL LXII, No. 2.]

683.

Ivy is [a type] of longevity.

[Footnote: In the original there is, near this text, a sketch of a coat wreathed above the waist with ivy.]

684.

Truth   the sun.
falsehood   a mask.
innocence,
malignity.
Fire destroys falsehood,
that is sophistry, and
restores truth, driving out
darkness.
Fire may be represented as the destroy of
all sophistry, and as the
image and demonstration of truth;
because it is light and drives
out darkness which conceals
all essences [or subtle things].

[Footnote: See Pl. LXIII. L. 1-8 are in the middle of the page; 1. 9-14 to the right below; 1. 15-22 below in the middle column. The rest of the text is below the sketches on the left. There are some other passages on this page relating to geometry.]

TRUTH.

Fire destroys all sophistry, that is deceit;
and maintains truth alone, that is gold.
Truth at last cannot be hidden.
Dissimulation is of no avail. Dissimulation is
to no purpose before
so great a judge.
Falsehood puts on a mask.
Nothing is hidden under the sun.
Fire is to represent truth because it
destroys all sophistry and lies; and the
mask is for lying and falsehood

which conceal truth.

685.

Movement will cease before we are
weary
of being useful.
Movement will fail sooner than usefulness.
Death sooner than   I am never weary of
weariness.   being useful,
In serving others I   is a motto for carnval.
cannot do enough.   Without fatigue.
No labour is
sufficient to tire me.
Hands into which
ducats and precious
stones fall like snow; they
never become tired by serving,
but this service is only for its
utility and not for our   I am never weary
own benefit.   of being useful.
Naturally
nature has so disposed me.

686.

This shall be placed in the
hand of Ingratitude.
Wood nourishes the fire that
consumes it.

687.

TO REPRESENT INGRATITUDE.

When the sun appears
which dispels darkness in
general, you put out the
light which dispelled it
for you in particular
for your need and convenience.

688.

On this side Adam and Eve on the other;
O misery of mankind, of how many things do
you make yourself the slave for money!

[Footnote: See Pl. LXIV. The figures of Adam and Eve in the clouds here
alluded to would seem to symbolise their superiority to all earthly needs.]

689.

Thus are base unions sundered.

[Footnote: A much blurred sketch is on the page by this text. It seems to represent an unravelled plait or tissue.]

690.

> Constancy does not begin, but is that
> which perseveres.

[Footnote: A drawing in red chalk, also rubbed, which stands in the original in the middle of this text, seems to me to be intended for a sword hilt, held in a fist.]

691.

> Love, Fear, and Esteem,--
> Write these on three stones. Of servants.

692.

Prudence Strength.

693.

> Fame alone raises herself to Heaven,
> because virtuous things are in favour with God.
> Disgrace should be represented upside
> down, because all her deeds are contrary to
> God and tend to hell.

694.

Short liberty.

695.

> Nothing is so much to be feared as Evil
> Report.
> This Evil Report is born of life.

696.

Not to disobey.

697.

> A felled tree which is shooting
> again.
> I am still hopeful.
> A falcon,
> Time.

[Footnote: I. Albero tagliato. This emblem was displayed during the Carnival at Florence in 1513. See VASARI VI, 251, ed. MILANESI 1881. But the coincidence is probably accidental.]

698.

Truth here makes Falsehood torment
lying tongues.

699.

Such as harm is when it hurts me not,
is good which avails me not.

[Footnote: See Pl. LX, No. 2. Compare this sketch with that on Pl. LXII, No. 2. Below the two lines of the text there are two more lines: li guchi (giunchi) che ritego le paglucole (pagliucole) chelli (che li) anniegano.]

700.

He who offends others, does not secure himself.

[Footnote: See Pl. LX, No. 3.]

701.

Ingratitude.

[Footnote: See Pl. LX, No. 4. Below the bottom sketches are the unintelligible words "sta stilli." For "Ingratitudo" compare also Nos. 686 and 687.]

702.

One's thoughts turn towards Hope.

[Footnote: 702. By the side of this passage is a sketch of a cage with a bird sitting in it.]

Ornaments and Decorations for feasts (703-705).

703.

A bird, for a comedy.

[Footnote: The biographies say so much, and the author's notes say so little of the invention attributed to Leonardo of making artificial birds fly through the air, that the text here given is of exceptional interest from being accompanied by a sketch. It is a very slight drawing of a bird with outspread wings, which appears to be sliding down a stretched string. Leonardo's flying machines and his studies of the flight of birds will be referred to later.]

704.

A DRESS FOR THE CARNIVAL.

To make a beautiful dress cut it in thin cloth and give it an odoriferous varnish, made of oil of turpentine and of varnish in grain, with a pierced stencil, which must be wetted, that it may not stick to the cloth; and this stencil may be made in a pattern of knots which afterwards may be filled up with black and the ground with white millet.[Footnote 7: The grains of black and white millet would stick to the varnish and look like embroidery.]

[Footnote: Ser Giuliano, da Vinci the painter's brother, had been commissioned, with some others, to order and to execute the garments of the Allegorical figures for the Carnival at Florence in 1515--16; VASARI however is incorrect in saying of the Florentine Carnival of 1513: "equelli che feciono ed ordinarono gli abiti delle figure furono Ser Piero da Vinci, padre di Lonardo, e Bernardino di Giordano, bellissimi ingegni" (See MILANESI'S ed. Voi. VI, pg. 251.)]

705.

Snow taken from the high peaks of mountains might be carried to hot places and let to fall at festivals in open places at summer time.

End of Volume 1

Volume 2

XI. The notes on Sculpture.

Compared with the mass of manuscript treating of Painting, a very small number of passages bearing on the practice and methods of Sculpture are to be found scattered through the note books; these are here given at the beginning of this section (Nos. 706-709). There is less cause for surprise at finding that the equestrian statue of Francesco Sforza is only incidentally spoken of; for, although Leonardo must have worked at it for a long succession of years, it is not in the nature of the case that it could have given rise to much writing. We may therefore regard it as particularly fortunate that no fewer than thirteen notes in the master's handwriting can be brought together, which seem to throw light on the mysterious history of this famous work. Until now writers on Leonardo were acquainted only with the passages numbered 712, 719, 720, 722 and 723.

In arranging these notes on sculpture I have given the precedence to those which treat of the casting of the monument, not merely because they are the fullest, but more especially with a view to reconstructing the monument, an achievement which really almost lies within our reach by combining and comparing the whole of the materials now brought to light, alike in notes and in sketches.

A good deal of the first two passages, Nos. 710 and 711, which refer to this subject seems obscure and incomprehensible; still, they supplement each other and one contributes in no small degree to the comprehension of the other. A very interesting and instructive commentary on these passages may be found in the fourth chapter of Vasari's Introduzione della Scultura under the title "Come si fanno i modelli per fare di bronzo le figure grandi e picciole, e come le forme per buttarle; come si armino di ferri, e come si gettino di metallo," &c. Among the drawings of models of the moulds for casting we find only one which seems to represent the horse in the act of galloping--No. 713. All the other designs show the horse as pacing quietly and as these studies of the horse are accompanied by copious notes as to the method of casting, the question as to the position of the horse in the model finally selected, seems to be decided by preponderating evidence. "Il cavallo dello Sforza"--C. Boito remarks very appositely in the Saggio on page 26, "doveva sembrare fratello al cavallo del Colleoni. E si direbbe che questo fosse figlio del cavallo del Gattamelata, il quale pare figlio di uno dei quattro cavalli che stavano forse sull' Arco di Nerone in Roma" (now at Venice). The publication of the Saggio also contains the reproduction of a drawing in red chalk, representing a horse walking to the left and supported by a scaffolding, given here on Pl. LXXVI,

No. 1. It must remain uncertain whether this represents the model as it stood during the preparations for casting it, or whether--as seems to me highly improbable--this sketch shows the model as it was exhibited in 1493 on the Piazza del Castello in Milan under a triumphal arch, on the occasion of the marriage of the Emperor Maximilian to Bianca Maria Sforza. The only important point here is to prove that strong evidence seems to show that, of the numerous studies for the equestrian statue, only those which represent the horse pacing agree with the schemes of the final plans.

The second group of preparatory sketches, representing the horse as galloping, must therefore be considered separately, a distinction which, in recapitulating the history of the origin of the monument seems justified by the note given under No. 720.

Galeazza Maria Sforza was assassinated in 1476 before his scheme for erecting a monument to his father Francesco Sforza could be carried into effect. In the following year Ludovico il Moro the young aspirant to the throne was exiled to Pisa, and only returned to Milan in 1479 when he was Lord (Governatore) of the State of Milan, in 1480 after the minister Cecco Simonetta had been murdered. It may have been soon after this that Ludovico il Moro announced a competition for an equestrian statue, and it is tolerably certain that Antonio del Pollajuolo took part in it, from this passage in Vasari's Life of this artist: "E si trovo, dopo la morte sua, il disegno e modello che a Lodovico Sforza egli aveva fatto per la statua a cavallo di Francesco Sforza, duca di Milano; il quale disegno e nel nostro Libro, in due modi: in uno egli ha sotto Verona; nell'altro, egli tutto armato, e sopra un basamento pieno di battaglie, fa saltare il cavallo addosso a un armato; ma la cagione perche non mettesse questi disegni in opera, non ho gia potuto sapere." One of Pollajuolo's drawings, as here described, has lately been discovered by Senatore Giovanni Morelli in the Munich Pinacothek. Here the profile of the horseman is a portrait of Francesco Duke of Milan, and under the horse, who is galloping to the left, we see a warrior thrown and lying on the ground; precisely the same idea as we find in some of Leonardo's designs for the monument, as on Pl. LXVI, LXVII, LXVIII, LXIX and LXXII No. 1; and, as it is impossible to explain this remarkable coincidence by supposing that either artist borrowed it from the other, we can only conclude that in the terms of the competition the subject proposed was the Duke on a horse in full gallop, with a fallen foe under its hoofs.

Leonardo may have been in the competition there and then, but the means for executing the monument do not seem to have been at once forthcoming. It was not perhaps until some years later that Leonardo in a letter to the Duke (No. 719) reminded him of the project for the monument. Then, after he had obeyed a summons to Milan, the plan seems to have been so far modified, perhaps in consequence of a remonstrance on the part of the artist, that a pacing horse was substituted for one galloping, and it may have been at the same time that the colossal dimensions of the statue were first decided on. The designs given on Pl. LXX, LXXI, LXXII, 2 and 3, LXXIII and LXXIV and on pp. 4 and 24, as well as three sketches on Pl. LXIX may be studied with reference to the project in its new form, though it is hardly possible to believe that in either of these we see the design as it was actually carried out. It is probable that in Milan Leonardo worked less on drawings, than in making small models of wax and clay as preparatory to his larger model. Among the drawings enumerated above, one in black chalk, Pl. LXXIII--the upper sketch on the right hand side, reminds us strongly of the antique statue of Marcus Aurelius. If, as it would seem, Leonardo had not until then visited Rome, he might easily have known this statue from drawings by his former master and friend Verrocchio, for Verrocchio had been in Rome for a long time between 1470 and 1480. In 1473 Pope Sixtus IV had this antique equestrian statue restored and placed on a new pedestal in front of the church of San Giovanni in Luterano. Leonardo, although he was painting independently as early as in 1472 is still spoken of as working in Verrocchio's studio in 1477. Two years later the Venetian senate decided on erecting an equestrian statue to Colleoni; and as Verrocchio, to whom the work was entrusted, did not at once move from Florence to Venice--where he died in 1488 before the casting was completed--but on the contrary remained in Florence for some years, perhaps even till 1485, Leonardo probably had the opportunity of seeing all his designs for the equestrian statue at Venice and the red chalk drawing on Pl. LXXIV may be a reminiscence of it.

The pen and ink drawing on Pl. LXXII, No. 3, reminds us of Donatello's statue of Gattamelata at Padua. However it does not appear that Leonardo was ever at Padua before 1499, but we may conclude that he took a special interest in this early bronze statue and the reports he could procure of it, form an incidental remark which is to be found in C. A. 145a; 432a, and which will be given in Vol. II under Ricordi or Memoranda. Among the studies--in the widest sense of the word--made in preparation statue we may include the Anatomy of the Horse which Lomazzo and Vas mention; the most important parts of this work still exist in the Queen's Li Windsor. It was beyond a doubt compiled by Leonardo when at Milan; only interesting records to be found among these designs are reproduced in Nos. 716a but it must be pointed out that out of 40 sheets of studies of the movements of the belonging to that treatise, a horse in full gallop occurs but once.

If we may trust the account given by Paulus Jovius--about I527-- Leonardo's horse was represented as "vehementer incitatus et anhelatus". Jovius had probably seen the model exhibited at Milan; but, need we, in fact, infer from this description that the horse was galloping? Compare Vasari's description of the Gattamelata monument at Padua: "Egli [Donatello] vi ando ben volentieri, e fece il cavallo di bronzo, che e in sulla piazza di Sant Antonio, nel quale si dimostra lo sbuffamento ed il fremito del cavallo, ed il grande animo e la fierezza vivacissimamente espressa dall'arte nella figura che lo cavalca".

These descriptions, it seems to me, would only serve to mark the difference between the work of the middle ages and that of the renaissance.

We learn from a statement of Sabba da Castiglione that, when Milan was taken by the French in 1499, the model sustained some injury; and this informant, who, however is not invariably trustworthy, adds that Leonardo had devoted fully sixteen years to this work (la forma del cavallo, intorno a cui

Leonardo avea sedici anni continui consumati). This often-quoted passage has given ground for an assumption, which has no other evidence to support it, that Leonardo had lived in Milan ever since 1483. But I believe it is nearer the truth to suppose that this author's statement alludes to the fact that about sixteen years must have past since the competition in which Leonardo had taken part.

I must in these remarks confine myself strictly to the task in hand and give no more of the history of the Sforza monument than is needed to explain the texts and drawings I have been able to reproduce. In the first place, with regard to the drawings, I may observe that they are all, with the following two exceptions, in the Queen's Library at Windsor Castle; the red chalk drawing on Pl. LXXVI No. 1 is in the MS. C. A. (see No. 7l2) and the fragmentary pen and ink drawing on page 4 is in the Ambrosian Library. The drawings from Windsor on Pl. LXVI have undergone a trifling reduction from the size of the originals.

There can no longer be the slightest doubt that the well-known engraving of several horsemen (Passavant, Le Peintre-Graveur, Vol. V, p. 181, No. 3) is only a copy after original drawings by Leonardo, executed by some unknown engraver; we have only to compare the engraving with the facsimiles of drawings on Pl. LXV, No. 2, Pl. LXVII, LXVIII and LXIX which, it is quite evident, have served as models for the engraver.

On Pl. LXV No. 1, in the larger sketch to the right hand, only the base is distinctly visible, the figure of the horseman is effaced. Leonardo evidently found it unsatisfactory and therefore rubbed it out.

The base of the monument--the pedestal for the equestrian statue--is repeatedly sketched on a magnificent plan. In the sketch just mentioned it has the character of a shrine or aedicula to contain a sarcophagus. Captives in chains are here represented on the entablature with their backs turned to that portion of the monument which more

strictly constitutes the pedestal of the horse. The lower portion of the aedicula is surrounded by columns. In the pen and ink drawing Pl. LXVI--the lower drawing on the right hand side--the sarcophagus is shown between the columns, and above the entablature is a plinth on which the horse stands. But this arrangement perhaps seemed to Leonardo to lack solidity, and in the little sketch on the left hand, below, the sarcophagus is shown as lying under an arched canopy. In this the trophies and the captive warriors are detached from the angles. In the first of these two sketches the place for the trophies is merely indicated by a few strokes; in the third sketch on the left the base is altogether broader, buttresses and pinnacles having been added so as to form three niches. The black chalk drawing on Pl. LXVIII shows a base in which the angles are formed by niches with pilasters. In the little sketch to the extreme left on Pl. LXV, No. 1, the equestrian statue serves to crown a circular temple somewhat resembling Bramante's tempietto of San Pietro in Montario at Rome, while the sketch above to the right displays an arrangement faintly reminding us of the tomb of the Scaligers in Verona. The base is thus constructed of two platforms or slabs, the upper one considerably smaller than the lower one which is supported on flying buttresses with pinnacles.

On looking over the numerous studies in which the horse is not galloping but merely walking forward, we find only one drawing for the pedestal, and this, to accord with the altered character of the statue, is quieter and simpler in style (Pl. LXXIV). It rises almost vertically from the ground and is exactly as long as the pacing horse. The whole base is here arranged either as an independent baldaquin or else as a projecting canopy over a recess in which the figure of the deceased Duke is seen lying on his sarcophagus; in the latter case it was probably intended as a tomb inside a church. Here, too, it was intended to fill the angles with trophies or captive warriors. Probably only No. 724 in the text refers to the work for the base of the monument.

If we compare the last mentioned sketch with the description of a plan for an equestrian monument to Gian Giacomo Trivulzio (No. 725) it seems by no means impossible that this drawing is a preparatory study for the very monument concerning which the manuscript gives us detailed information. We have no historical record regarding this sketch nor do the archives in the Trivulzio Palace give us any information. The simple monument to the great general in San Nazaro Maggiore in Milan consists merely of a sarcophagus placed in recess high on the wall of an octagonal chapel. The figure of the warrior is lying on the sarcophagus, on which his name is inscribed; a piece of sculpture which is certainly not Leonardo's work. Gian Giacomo Trivulzio died at Chartres in 1518, only five months before Leonardo, and it seems to me highly improbable that this should have been the date of this sketch; under these circumstances it would have been done under the auspices of Francis I, but the Italian general was certainly not in favour with the French monarch at the time. Gian Giacomo Trivulzio was a sworn foe to Ludovico il Moro, whom he strove for years to overthrow. On the 6th September 1499 he marched victorious into Milan at the head of a French army. In a short time, however, he was forced to quit Milan again when Ludovico il Moro bore down upon the city with a force of Swiss troops. On the 15th of April following, after defeating Lodovico at Novara, Trivulzio once more entered Milan as a Conqueror, but his hopes of becoming Governatore of the place were soon wrecked by intrigue. This victory and triumph, historians tell us, were signalised by acts of vengeance against the dethroned Sforza, and it might have been particularly flattering to him that the casting and construction of the Sforza monument were suspended for the time.

It must have been at this moment--as it seems to me--that he commissioned the artist to prepare designs for his own monument, which he probably intended should find a place in the Cathedral or in some other church. He, the husband of Margherita di Nicolino Colleoni, would have thought that he had a claim to the same distinction and public homage as his less illustrious connection had received at the hands of the Venetian republic. It was at this very time that Trivulzio had a medal struck with a bust portrait of himself and the following remarkable inscription on the reverse: DEO FAVENTE--1499-- DICTVS--10--IA--EXPVLIT--LVDOVICV--SF-- (Sfortiam) DVC-- (ducem) MLI (Mediolani)--NOIE (nomine)--REGIS--FRANCORVM--EODEM--ANN --(anno)

RED'T (redit)--LVS (Ludovicus)--SVPERATVS ET CAPTVS--EST--AB--EO. In the Library of the Palazzo Trivulzio there is a MS. of Callimachus Siculus written at the end of the XVth or beginning of the XVIth century. At the beginning of this MS. there is an exquisite illuminated miniature of an equestrian statue with the name of the general on the base; it is however very doubtful whether this has any connection with Leonardo's design.

Nos. 731-740, which treat of casting bronze, have probably a very indirect bearing on the arrangements made for casting the equestrian statue of Francesco Sforza. Some portions evidently relate to the casting of cannon. Still, in our researches about Leonardo's work on the monument, we may refer to them as giving us some clue to the process of bronze casting at that period.

Some practical hints (706-709).

706.

OF A STATUE.

If you wish to make a figure in marble, first make one of clay, and when you have finished it, let it dry and place it in a case which should be large enough, after the figure is taken out of it, to receive also the marble, from which you intend to reveal the figure in imitation of the one in clay. After you have put the clay figure into this said case, have little rods which will exactly slip in to the holes in it, and thrust them so far in at each hole that each white rod may touch the figure in different parts of it. And colour the portion of the rod that remains outside black, and mark each rod and each hole with a countersign so that each may fit into its place. Then take the clay figure out of this case and put in your piece of marble, taking off so much of the marble that all your rods may be hidden in the holes as far as their marks; and to be the better able to do this, make the case so that it can be lifted up; but the bottom of it will always remain under the marble and in this way it can be lifted with tools with great ease.

707.

Some have erred in teaching sculptors to measure the limbs of their figures with threads as if they thought that these limbs were equally round in every part where these threads were wound about them.

708.

MEASUREMENT AND DIVISION OF A STATUE.

Divide the head into 12 degrees, and each degree divide into 12 points, and each point into 12 minutes, and the minutes into minims and the minims into semi minims.

Degree--point--minute--minim.

709.

Sculptured figures which appear in motion, will, in their standing position, actually look as if they were falling forward.

[Footnote: figure di rilievo. Leonardo applies this term exclusively to wholly detached figures, especially to those standing free. This note apparently refers to some particular case, though we have no knowledge of what that may have been. If we suppose it to refer to the first model of the equestrian statue of Francesco Sforza (see the introduction to the notes on Sculpture) this observation may be regarded as one of his arguments for abandoning the first scheme of the Sforza Monument, in which the horse was to be galloping (see page 2). It is also in favour of this theory that the note is written in a manuscript volume already completed in 1492. Leonardo's opinions as to the shortcomings of plastic works when compared with paintings are given under No. 655 and 656.]

Notes on the casting of the Sforza monument (710-715).

710.

Three braces which bind the mould.

[If you want to make simple casts quickly, make them in a box of river sand wetted with vinegar.]

[When you shall have made the mould upon the horse you must make the thickness of the metal in clay.]

Observe in alloying how many hours are wanted for each hundredweight. [In casting each one keep the furnace and its fire well stopped up.] [Let the inside of all the moulds be wetted with linseed oil or oil of turpentine, and then take a handful of powdered borax and Greek pitch with aqua vitae, and pitch the mould over outside so that being under ground the damp may not [damage it?]

[To manage the large mould make a model of the small mould, make a small room in proportion.]

[Make the vents in the mould while it is on the horse.]

Hold the hoofs in the tongs, and cast them with fish glue. Weigh the parts of the mould and the quantity of metal it will take to fill them, and give so much to the furnace that it may afford to each part its amount of metal; and this you may know by weighing the clay of each part of the mould to which the quantity in the furnace must correspond. And this is done in order that the furnace for the legs when filled may not have to furnish metal from the legs to help out the head, which would be impossible. [Cast at the same casting as the horse the little door]

[Footnote: The importance of the notes included under this number is not diminished by the fact that they have been lightly crossed out with red chalk. Possibly they were the first scheme for some fuller observations which no longer exist; or perhaps they were crossed out when Leonardo found himself obliged to give up the idea of casting the equestrian statue. In the original the first two sketches are above l. 1, and the third below l. 9.]

711.

THE MOULD FOR THE HORSE.

Make the horse on legs of iron, strong and well set on a good foundation; then grease it and cover it with a coating, leaving each coat to dry thoroughly layer by layer; and this will thicken it by the breadth of three fingers. Now fix and bind it with iron as may be necessary. Moreover take off the mould and then make the thickness. Then fill the mould by degrees and make it good throughout; encircle and bind it with its irons and bake it inside where it has to touch the bronze.

OF MAKING THE MOULD IN PIECES.

Draw upon the horse, when finished, all the pieces of the mould with which you wish to cover the horse, and in laying on the clay cut it in every piece, so that when the mould is finished you can take it off, and then recompose it in its former position with its joins, by the countersigns.

The square blocks a b will be between the cover and the core, that is in the hollow where the melted bronze is to be; and these square blocks of bronze will support the intervals between the mould and the cover at an equal distance, and for this reason these squares are of great importance.

The clay should be mixed with sand.

Take wax, to return [what is not used] and to pay for what is used.

Dry it in layers.

Make the outside mould of plaster, to save time in drying and the expense in wood; and with this plaster enclose the irons [props] both outside and inside to a thickness of two fingers; make terra cotta. And this mould can be made in one day; half a boat load of plaster will serve you.

Good.

Dam it up again with glue and clay, or white of egg, and bricks and rubbish.

[Footnote: See Pl. LXXV. The figure "40," close to the sketch in the middle of the page between lines 16 and 17 has been added by a collector's hand.

In the original, below line 21, a square piece of the page has been cut out about 9 centimetres by 7 and a blank piece has been gummed into the place.

Lines 22-24 are written on the margin. l. 27 and 28 are close to the second marginal sketch. l. 42 is a note written above the third marginal sketch and on the back of this sheet is the text given as No. 642. Compare also No. 802.]

712.

All the heads of the large nails.

[Footnote: See Pl. LXXVI, No. i. This drawing has already been published in the "Saggio delle Opere di L. da Vinci." Milano 1872, Pl. XXIV, No. i. But, for various reasons I cannot regard the editor's suggestions as satisfactory. He says: "Veggonsi le armature di legname colle quali forse venne sostenuto il modello, quando per le nozze di Bianca Maria Sforza con Massimiliano imperatore, esso fu collocato sotto un arco trionfale davanti al Castello."

713.

These bindings go inside.

714.

Salt may be made from human excrements, burnt and calcined, made into lees and dried slowly at a fire, and all the excrements produce salt in a similar way and these salts when distilled, are very strong.

[Footnote: VASARI repeatedly states, in the fourth chapter of his Introduzione della Scultura, that in preparing to cast bronze statues horse-dung was frequently used by sculptors. If, notwithstanding this, it remains doubtful whether I am justified in having introduced here this text of but little interest, no such doubt can be attached to the sketch which accompanies it.]

715.

METHOD OF FOUNDING AGAIN.

This may be done when the furnace is made [Footnote: this note is written below the sketches.] strong and bruised.

Models for the horse of the Sforza monument (716-718).

7l6.

Messer Galeazzo's big genet

717.

Messer Galeazzo's Sicilian horse.

[Footnote: These notes are by the side of a drawing of a horse with figured measurements.]

718.

Measurement of the Sicilian horse the leg from behind, seen in front, lifted and extended.

[Footnote: There is no sketch belonging to this passage. Galeazze here probably means Galeazze di San Severino, the famous captain who married Bianca the daughter of Ludovico il Moro.]

Occasional references to the Sforza monument (719-724).

719.

Again, the bronze horse may be taken in hand, which is to be to the immortal glory and eternal honour of the happy memory of the prince your father, and of the illustrious house of Sforza.

[Footnote: The letter from which this passage is here extracted will be found complete in section XXI. (see the explanation of it, on page 2).]

720.

On the 23rd of April 1490 I began this book, and recommenced the horse.

721.

There is to be seen, in the mountains of Parma and Piacenza, a multitude of shells and corals full of holes, still sticking to the rocks, and when I was at work on the great horse for Milan, a large sackful of them, which were found thereabout, was brought to me into my workshop, by certain peasants.

722.

Believe me, Leonardo the Florentine, who has to do the equestrian bronze statue of the Duke Francesco that he does not need to care about it, because he has work for all his life time, and, being so great a work, I doubt whether he can ever finish it. [Footnote: This passage is quoted from a letter to a committee at Piacenza for whom Leonardo seems to have undertaken to execute some work. The letter is given entire in section XXL; in it Leonardo remonstrates as to some unreasonable demands.]

723.

Of the horse I will say nothing because I know the times. [Footnote: This passage occurs in a rough copy of a letter to Ludovico il Moro, without date (see below among the letters).]

724.

During ten years the works on the marbles have been going on I will not wait for my payment beyond the time, when my works are finished. [Footnote: This possibly refers to the works for the pedestal of the equestrian statue concerning which we have no farther information in the MSS. See p. 6.]

The project of the Trivulzio monument.

725.

THE MONUMENT TO MESSER GIOVANNI JACOMO DA TREVULZO.

[2] Cost of the making and materials for the horse [5].

[Footnote: In the original, lines 2-5, 12-14, 33-35, are written on the margin. This passage has been recently published by G. Govi in Vol. V, Ser. 3a, of Transunti, Reale Accademia dei Linea, sed. del 5 Giugno, 1881, with the following introductory note: "Desidero intanto che siano stampati questi pochi frammenti perche so che sono stati trascritti ultimamente, e verranno messi in luce tra poco fuori d'Italia. Li ripubblichi pure chi vuole, ma si sappia almeno che anche tra noi si conoscevano, e s'eran raccolti da anni per comporne, quando che fosse, una edizione ordinata degli scritti di Leonardo."

The learned editor has left out line 22 and has written 3 pie for 8 piedi in line 25. There are other deviations of less importance from the original.]

A courser, as large as life, with the rider requires for the cost of the metal, duc. 500.

And for cost of the iron work which is inside the model, and charcoal, and wood, and the pit to cast it in, and for binding the mould, and including the furnace where it is to be cast ... duc. 200.

To make the model in clay and then in wax......... duc. 432.

To the labourers for polishing it when it is cast. .... duc. 450.

in all. . duc. 1582.

[12] Cost of the marble of the monument [14].

Cost of the marble according to the drawing. The piece of marble under the horse which is 4 braccia long, 2 braccia and 2 inches wide and 9 inches thick 58 hundredweight, at 4 Lire and 10 Soldi per hundredweight.. duc. 58.

And for 13 braccia and 6 inches of cornice, 7 in. wide and 4 in. thick, 24 hundredweight....... duc. 24.

And for the frieze and architrave, which is 4 br. and 6 in. long, 2 br. wide and 6 in. thick, 29 hundredweight., duc. 20.

And for the capitals made of metal, which are 8, 5 inches in. square and 2 in. thick, at the price of 15 ducats each, will come to...... duc. 122.

And for 8 columns of 2 br. 7 in., 4 1/2 in. thick, 20 hundredweight duc. 20.

And for 8 bases which are 5 1/2 in. square and 2 in. high 5 hund'.. duc. 5.

And for the slab of the tombstone 4 br. io in. long, 2 br. 4 1/2 in. wide 36 hundredweight....... duc. 36.

And for 8 pedestal feet each 8 br. long and 6 1/2 in. wide and 6 1/2 in. thick, 20 hundredweight come to... duc. 20.

And for the cornice below which is 4 br. and 10 in. long, and 2 br. and 5 in. wide, and 4 in. thick, 32 hund'.. duc. 32.

And for the stone of which the figure of the deceased is to be made which is 3 br. and 8 in. long, and 1 br. and 6 in. wide, and 9 in. thick, 30 hund'.. duc. 30.

And for the stone on which the figure lies which is 3 br. and 4 in. long and 1 br. and 2 in., wide and 4 1/2 in. thick duc. 16.

And for the squares of marble placed between the pedestals which are 8 and are 9 br. long and 9 in. wide, and 3 in. thick, 8 hundredweight . . . duc. 8. in all. . duc. 389.

[33]Cost of the work in marble[35].

Round the base on which the horse stands there are 8 figures at 25 ducats each .... duc. 200.

And on the same base there are 8 festoons with some other ornaments, and of these there are 4 at the price of 15 ducats each, and 4 at the price of 8 ducats each .... duc. 92.

And for squaring the stones duc. 6.

Again, for the large cornice which goes below the base on which the horse stands, which is 13 br. and 6 in., at 2 due. per br. ...... duc. 27.

And for 12 br. of frieze at 5 due. per br. .... duc. 60.

And for 12 br. of architrave at 1 1/2 duc. per br. .... duc. 18.

And for 3 rosettes which will be the soffit of the monument, at 20 ducats each .... duc. 60.

And for 8 fluted columns at 8 ducats each .... duc. 64.

And for 8 bases at 1 ducat each, duc. 8.

And for 8 pedestals, of which 4 are at 10 duc. each, which go above the angles; and 4 at 6 duc. each .. duc. 64.

And for squaring and carving the moulding of the pedestals at 2 duc. each, and there are 8 .... duc. 16.

And for 6 square blocks with figures and trophies, at 25 duc. each .. duc. 150.

And for carving the moulding of the stone under the figure of the deceased .... duc. 40.

For the statue of the deceased, to do it well .... duc. 100.

For 6 harpies with candelabra, at 25 ducats each .... duc. 150.

For squaring the stone on which the statue lies, and carving the moulding .... duc. 20.

in all .. duc. 1075.

The sum total of every thing added together amount to ...... duc. 3046.

726.

MINT AT ROME.

It can also be made without a spring. But the screw above must always be joined to the part of the movable sheath: [Margin note: The mint of Rome.] [Footnote: See Pl. LXXVI. This passage is taken from a note book which can be proved to have been used in Rome.]

All coins which do not have the rim complete, are not to be accepted as good; and to secure the perfection of their rim it is requisite that, in the first place, all the coins should be a perfect circle; and to do this a coin must before all be made perfect in weight, and size, and thickness. Therefore have several plates of metal made of the same size and thickness, all drawn through the same gauge so as to come out in strips. And out of [24] these strips you will stamp the coins, quite round, as sieves are made for sorting chestnuts [27]; and these coins can then be stamped in the way indicated above; &c.

[31] The hollow of the die must be uniformly wider than the lower, but imperceptibly [35].

This cuts the coins perfectly round and of the exact thickness, and weight; and saves the man who cuts and weighs, and the man who makes the coins round. Hence it passes only through the hands of the gauger and of the stamper, and the coins are very superior. [Footnote: See Pl. LXXVI No. 2. The text of lines 31-35 stands parallel 1. 24-27.

Farther evidence of Leonardo's occupations and engagements at Rome under Pope Leo X. may be gathered from some rough copies of letters which will be found in this volume. Hitherto nothing has been known of his work in Rome beyond some doubtful, and perhaps mythical, statements in Vasari.]

727.

POWDER FOR MEDALS.

The incombustible growth of soot on wicks reduced to powder, burnt tin and all the metals, alum, isinglass, smoke from a brass forge, each ingredient to be moistened, with aqua vitae or malmsey or strong malt vinegar, white wine or distilled extract of turpentine, or oil; but there should be little moisture, and cast in moulds. [Margin note: On the coining of medals (727. 728).] [Footnote: The meaning of scagliuolo in this passage is doubtful.]

728.

OF TAKING CASTS OF MEDALS.

A paste of emery mixed with aqua vitae, or iron filings with vinegar, or ashes of walnut leaves, or ashes of straw very finely powdered.

[Footnote: The meaning of scagliuolo in this passage is doubtful.]

The diameter is given in the lead enclosed; it is beaten with a hammer and several times extended; the lead is folded and kept wrapped up in parchment so that the powder may not be spilt; then melt the lead, and the powder will be on the top of the melted lead, which must then be rubbed between two plates of steel till it is thoroughly pulverised; then wash it with aqua fortis, and the blackness of the iron will be dissolved leaving the powder clean.

Emery in large grains may be broken by putting it on a cloth many times doubled, and hit it sideways with the hammer, when it will break up; then mix it little by little and it can be founded with ease; but if you hold it on the anvil you will never break it, when it is large.

Any one who grinds smalt should do it on plates of tempered steel with a cone shaped grinder; then put it in aqua fortis, which melts away the steel that may have been worked up and mixed with the smalt, and which makes it black; it then remains purified and clean; and if you grind it on porphyry the porphyry will work up and mix with the smalt and spoil it, and aqua fortis will never remove it because it cannot dissolve the porphyry.

If you want a fine blue colour dissolve the smalt made with tartar, and then remove the salt.

Vitrified brass makes a fine red.

729.

STUCCO.

Place stucco over the prominence of the..... which may be composed of Venus and Mercury, and lay it well over that prominence of the thickness of the side of a knife, made with the ruler and cover this with the bell of a still, and you will have again the moisture with which you applied the paste. The rest you may dry [Margin note: On stucco (729. 730).] [Footnote: In this passage a few words have been written in a sort of cipher--that is to say backwards; as in l. 3 erenev for Venere, l. 4 oirucrem for Mercurio, l. 12 il orreve co ecarob for il everro (?) co borace. The meaning of the word before "di giesso" in l. 1 is unknown; and the sense, in which sagoma is used here and in other passages is obscure.-- Venere and Mercurio may mean 'marble' and 'lime', of which stucco is composed.

12. The meaning of orreve is unknown.]

well; afterwards fire it, and beat it or burnish it with a good burnisher, and make it thick towards the side.

STUCCO.

Powder ... with borax and water to a paste, and make stucco of it, and then heat it so that it may dry, and then varnish it, with fire, so that it shines well.

730.

STUCCO FOR MOULDING.

Take of butter 6 parts, of wax 2 parts, and as much fine flour as when put with these 2 things melted, will make them as firm as wax or modelling clay.

GLUE.

Take mastic, distilled turpentine and white lead.

On bronze casting generally (731-740).

731.

TO CAST.

Tartar burnt and powdered with plaster and cast cause the plaster to hold together when it is mixed up again; and then it will dissolve in water.

732.

TO CAST BRONZE IN PLASTER.

Take to every 2 cups of plaster 1 of ox-horns burnt, mix them together and make your cast with it.

733.

When you want to take a cast in wax, burn the scum with a candle, and the cast will come out without bubbles.

734.

2 ounces of plaster to a pound of metal;-- walnut, which makes it like the curve.

[Footnote: The second part of this is quite obscure.]

735.

[Dried earth 16 pounds, 100 pounds of metal wet clay 20,--of wet 100,-half,-which increases 4 lbs. of water,--1 of wax, 1 lb. of metal, a little less,-the scrapings of linen with earth, measure for measure.] [Footnote: The translation is given literally, but the meaning is quite obscure.]

736.

Such as the mould is, so will the cast be.

737.

HOW CASTS OUGHT TO BE POLISHED.

Make a bunch of iron wire as thick as thread, and scrub them with [this and] water; hold a bowl underneath that it may not make a mud below.

HOW TO REMOVE THE ROUGH EDGES FROM BRONZE.

Make an iron rod, after the manner of a large chisel, and with this rub over those seams on the bronze which remain on the casts of the guns, and which are caused by the joins in the mould; but make the tool heavy enough, and let the strokes be long and broad.

TO FACILITATE MELTING.

First alloy part of the metal in the crucible, then put it in the furnace, and this being in a molten state will assist in beginning to melt the copper.

TO PREVENT THE COPPER COOLING IN THE FURNACE.

When the copper cools in the furnace, be ready, as soon as you perceive it, to cut it with a long stick while it is still in a paste; or if it is quite cold cut it as lead is cut with broad and large chisels.

IF YOU HAVE TO MAKE A LARGE CAST.

If you have to make a cast of a hundred thousand pounds do it with two furnaces and with 2000 pounds in each, or as much as 3000 pounds at most.

738.

HOW TO PROCEED TO BREAK A LARGE MASS OF BRONZE.

If you want to break up a large mass of bronze, first suspend it, and then make round it a wall on the four sides, like a trough of bricks, and make a great fire therein. When it is quite red hot give it a blow with a heavy weight raised above it, and with great force.

739.

TO COMBINE LEAD WITH OTHER METAL.

If you wish for economy in combining lead with the metal in order to lessen the amount of tin which is necessary in the metal, first alloy the lead with the tin and then add the molten copper.

How TO MELT [METAL] IN A FURNACE.

The furnace should be between four well founded pillars.

OF THE THICKNESS OF THE COATING.

The coating should not be more than two fingers thick, it should be laid on in four thicknesses over fine clay and then well fixed, and it should be fired only on the inside and then carefully covered with ashes and cow's dung.

OF THE THICKNESS OF THE GUN.

The gun being made to carry 600 lbs. of ball and more, by this rule you will take the measure of the diameter of the ball and divide it into 6 parts and one of these parts will be its thickness at the muzzle; but at the breech it must always be half. And if the ball is to be 700 lbs., 1/7th of the diameter of the ball must be its thickness in front; and if the ball is to be 800, the eighth of its diameter in front; and if 900, 1/8th and 1/2 [3/16], and if 1000, 1/9th.

OF THE LENGTH OF THE BODY OF THE GUN.

If you want it to throw a ball of stone, make the length of the gun to be 6, or as much as 7 diameters of the ball; and if the ball is to be of iron make it as much as 12 balls, and if the ball is to be of lead, make it as much as 18 balls. I mean when the gun is to have the mouth fitted to receive 600 lbs. of stone ball, and more.

OF THE THICKNESS OF SMALL GUNS.

The thickness at the muzzle of small guns should be from a half to one third of the diameter of the ball, and the length from 30 to 36 balls.

740.

OF LUTING THE FURNACE WITHIN.

The furnace must be luted before you put the metal in it, with earth from Valenza, and over that with ashes.

[Footnote 1. 2.: Terra di Valenza.--Valenza is north of Alessandria on the Po.]

OF RESTORING THE METAL WHEN IT IS BECOMING COOL.

When you see that the bronze is congealing take some willow-wood cut in small chips and make up the fire with it.

THE CAUSE OF ITS CURDLING.

I say that the cause of this congealing often proceeds from too much fire, or from ill-dried wood.

TO KNOW THE CONDITION OF THE FIRE.

You may know when the fire is good and fit for your purpose by a clear flame, and if you see the tips of the flames dull and ending in much smoke do not trust it, and particularly when the flux metal is almost fluid.

OF ALLOYING THE METAL.

Metal for guns must invariably be made with 6 or even 8 per cent, that is 6 of tin to one hundred of copper, for the less you put in, the stronger will the gun be.

WHEN THE TIN SHOULD BE ADDED TO THE COPPER.

The tin should be put in with the copper when the copper is reduced to a fluid.

HOW TO HASTEN THE MELTING.

You can hasten the melting when 2/3ds of the copper is fluid; you can then, with a stick of chestnut-wood, repeatedly stir what of copper remains entire amidst what is melted.

Introductory Observations on the Architectural Designs (XII), and Writings on Architecture (XIII).

Until now very little has been known regarding Leonardo's labours in the domain of Architecture. No building is known to have been planned and executed by him, though by some contemporary writers incidental allusion is made to his occupying himself with architecture, and his famous letter to Lodovico il Moro,--which has long been a well-known document,--in which he offers his service as an architect to that prince, tends to confirm the belief that he was something more than an amateur of the art. This hypothesis has lately been confirmed by the publication of certain documents, preserved at Milan, showing that Leonardo was not only employed in preparing plans but that he took an active part, with much credit, as member of a commission on public buildings; his name remains linked with the history of the building of the Cathedral at Pavia and that of the Cathedral at Milan.

Leonardo's writings on Architecture are dispersed among a large number of MSS., and it would be scarcely possible to master their contents without the opportunity of arranging, sorting and comparing the whole mass of materials, so as to have some comprehensive idea of the whole. The sketches, when isolated and considered by themselves, might appear to be of but little value; it is not till we understand their general purport, from comparing them with each other, that we can form any just estimate of their true worth.

Leonardo seems to have had a project for writing a complete and separate treatise on Architecture, such as his predecessors and contemporaries had composed--Leon Battista Alberti, Filarete, Francesco di Giorgio and perhaps also Bramante. But, on the other hand, it cannot be denied that possibly no such scheme was connected with the isolated notes and researches, treating on special questions, which are given in this work; that he was merely working at problems in which, for some reason or other he took a special interest.

A great number of important buildings were constructed in Lombardy during the period between 1472 and 1499, and among them there are several by unknown architects, of so high an artistic merit, that it is certainly not improbable that either Bramante or Leonardo da Vinci may have been, directly or indirectly, concerned in their erection.

Having been engaged, for now nearly twenty years, in a thorough study of Bramante's life and labours, I have taken a particular interest in detecting the distinguishing marks of his style as compared with Leonardo's. In 1869 I made researches about the architectural drawings of the latter in the Codex Atlanticus at Milan, for the purpose of finding out, if possible the original plans and sketches of the churches of Santa Maria delle Grazie at Milan, and of the Cathedral at Pavia, which buildings have been supposed to be the work both of Bramante and of Leonardo. Since 1876 I have repeatedly examined Leonardo's architectural studies in the collection of his manuscripts in the Institut de France, and some of these I have already given to the public in my work on "Les Projets Primitifs pour la Basilique de St. Pierre de Rome", P1. 43. In 1879 I had the opportunity of examining the manuscript in the Palazzo Trivulzio at Milan, and in 1880 Dr Richter showed me in London the manuscripts in the possession of Lord Ashburnham, and those in the British Museum. I have thus had opportunities of seeing most of Leonardo's architectural drawings in the original, but of the manuscripts tliemselves I have deciphered only the notes which accompany the sketches. It is to Dr Richter's exertions that we owe the collected texts on Architecture which are now published, and while he has undertaken to be responsible for the correct reading of the original texts, he has also made it his task to extract the whole of the materials from the various MSS. It has been my task to arrange and elucidate the texts under the heads which have been adopted in this work. MS. B. at Paris and the Codex Atlanticus at Milan are the chief sources of our knowledge of Leonardo as an architect, and I have recently subjected these to a thorough re-investigation expressly with a view to this work.

A complete reproduction of all Leonardo's architectural sketches has not, indeed, been possible, but as far as the necessarily restricted limits of the work have allowed, the utmost completeness has been aimed at, and no efforts have been spared to include every thing that can contribute to a knowledge of Leonardo's style. It would have been very interesting, if it had been possible, to give some general account at least of Leonardo's work and studies in engineering, fortification, canal-making and the like, and it is only on mature reflection that we have reluctantly abandoned this idea. Leonardo's occupations in these departments have by no means so close a relation to literary work, in the strict sense of the word as we are fairly justified in attributing to his numerous notes on Architecture.

Leonardo's architectural studies fall naturally under two heads:

I. Those drawings and sketches, often accompanied by short remarks and explanations, which may be regarded as designs for buildings or monuments intended to be built. With these there are occasionally explanatory texts.

II. Theoretical investigations and treatises. A special interest attaches to these because they discuss a variety of questions which are of practical importance to this day. Leonardo's theory as to the origin and progress of cracks in buildings is perhaps to be considered as unique in its way in the literature of Architecture.

HENRY DE GEYMULLER

Study for the Sforza Monument, drawn with the silverpoint on bluish tinted paper

XII. Architectural Designs.

I. Plans for towns.

A. Sketches for laying out a new town with a double system of high- level and low-level road-ways.

Pl. LXXVII, No. 1 (MS. B, 15b). A general view of a town, with the roads outside it sloping up to the high-level ways within.

Pl. LXXVII, No. 3 (MS. B, 16b. see No. 741; and MS. B. 15b, see No. 742) gives a partial view of the town, with its streets and houses, with explanatory references.

Pl. LXXVII, No. 2 (MS. B, 15b; see No. 743). View of a double staircaise with two opposite flights of steps.

Pl. LXXVIII, Nos. 2 and 3 (MS. B, 37a). Sketches illustrating the connection of the two levels of roads by means of steps. The lower galleries are lighted by openings in the upper roadway.

B. Notes on removing houses (MS. Br. M., 270b, see No. 744).

741.

The roads m are 6 braccia higher than the roads p s, and each road must be 20 braccia wide and have 1/2 braccio slope from the sides towards the middle; and in the middle let there be at every braccio an opening, one braccio long and one finger wide, where the rain water may run off into hollows made on the same level as p s. And on each side at the extremity of the width of the said road let there be an arcade, 6 braccia broad, on columns; and understand that he who would go through the whole place by the high level streets can use them for this purpose, and he who would go by the low level can do the same. By the high streets no vehicles and similar objects should circulate, but they are exclusively for the use of gentlemen. The carts and burdens for the use and convenience of the inhabitants have to go by the low ones. One house must turn its back to the other, leaving the lower streets between them. Provisions, such as wood, wine and such things are carried in by the doors n, and privies, stables and other fetid matter must be emptied away underground. From one arch to the next

742.

must be 300 braccia, each street receiving its light through the openings of the upper streets, and at each arch must be a winding stair on a circular plan because the corners of square ones are always fouled; they must be wide, and at the first vault there must be a door entering into public privies and the said stairs lead from the upper to the lower streets and the high level streets begin outside the city gates and slope up till at these gates they have attained the height of 6 braccia. Let such a city be built near the sea or a large river in order that the dirt of the city may be carried off by the water.

743.

The construction of the stairs: The stairs c d go down to f g, and in the same way f g goes down to h k.

744.

ON MOVING HOUSES.

Let the houses be moved and arranged in order; and this will be done with facility because such houses are at first made in pieces on the open places, and can then be fitted together with their timbers in the site where they are to be permanent.

[9] Let the men of the country [or the village] partly inhabit the new houses when the court is absent [12].

[Footnote: On the same page we find notes referring to Romolontino and Villafranca with a sketch-map of the course of the "Sodro" and the "(Lo)cra" (both are given in the text farther on). There can hardly be a doubt that the last sentence of the passage given above, refers to the court of Francis I. King of France.--L.9-13 are written inside the larger sketch, which, in the original, is on the right hand side of the page by the side of lines 1-8. The three smaller sketches are below. J. P. R.]

II. Plans for canals and streets in a town.

Pl. LXXIX, 1. and 2, (MS. B, 37b, see No. 745, and MS. B. 36a, see No. 746). A Plan for streets and canals inside a town, by which the cellars of the houses are made accessible in boats.

The third text given under No. 747 refers to works executed by Leonardo in France.

745.

The front a m will give light to the rooms; a e will be 6 braccia--a b 8 braccia --b e 30 braccia, in order that the rooms under the porticoes may be lighted; c d f is the place where the boats come to the houses to be unloaded. In order to render this arrangement practicable, and in order that the inundation of the rivers may not penetrate into the cellars, it is necessary to chose an appropriate situation, such as a spot near a river which can be diverted into canals in which the level of the water will not vary either by inundations or drought. The construction is shown below; and make choice of a fine river, which the rains do not render muddy, such as the Ticino, the Adda and many others. [Footnote 12: Tesino, Adda e molti altri, i.e. rivers coming from the mountains and flowing through lakes.] The construction to oblige the waters to keep constantly at the same level will be a sort of dock, as shown below, situated at the entrance of the town; or better still, some way within, in order that the enemy may not destroy it [14].

[Footnote: L. 1-4 are on the left hand side and within the sketch given on Pl. LXXIX, No. I. Then follows after line 14, the drawing of a sluicegate--conca--of which the use is explained in the text below it. On the page 38a, which comes next in the original MS. is the sketch of an oval plan of a town over which is written "modo di canali per la citta" and through the longer axis of it "canale magior" is written with "Tesino" on the prolongation of the canal. J. P. R.]

746.

Let the width of the streets be equal to the average height of the houses.

747.

The main underground channel does not receive turbid water, but that water runs in the ditches outside the town with four mills at the entrance and four at the outlet; and this may be done by damming the water above Romorantin.

[11]There should be fountains made in each piazza[13].

[Footnote: In the original this text comes immediately after the passage given as No. 744. The remainder of the writing on the same page refers to the construction of canals and is given later, in the "Topographical Notes".

Lines 1-11 are written to the right of the plan lines 11-13 underneath it. J. P. R.]

[Footnote 10: Romolontino is Romorantin, South of Orleans in France.]

III. Castles and Villas.

A. Castles.

Pl. LXXX, No. 1 (P. V. fol. 39b; No. d'ordre 2282). The fortified place here represented is said by Vallardi to be the "castello" at Milan, but without any satisfactory reason. The high tower behind the "rivellino" ravelin--seems to be intended as a watch-tower.

Pl. LXXX, No. 2 (MS. B, 23b). A similarly constructed tower probably intended for the same use.

Pl. LXXX, No. 3 (MS. B). Sketches for corner towers with steps for a citadel.

Pl. LXXX, No. 4 (W. XVI). A cupola crowning a corner tower; an interesting example of decorative fortification. In this reproduction of the original pen and ink drawing it appears reversed.

B. Projects for Palaces.

Pl. LXXXI, No. 2 (MS. C. A, 75b; 221a, see No. 748). Project for a royal residence at Amboise in France.

Pl. LXXXII, No. 1 (C. A 308a; 939a). A plan for a somewhat extensive residence, and various details; but there is no text to elucidate it; in courts are written the three names:

Sam cosi giova

    (St. Mark)   (Cosmo)   (John),

arch mo nino

C. Plans for small castles or Villas.

The three following sketches greatly resemble each other. Pl. LXXXII, No. 2 (MS. K3 36b; see No. 749).

Pl. LXXXII, No. 3 (MS. B 60a; See No. 750).

Pl. LXXXIII (W. XVII). The text on this sheet refers to Cyprus (see Topographical Notes No. 1103), but seems to have no direct connection with the sketches inserted between.

Pl. LXXXVIII, Nos. 6 and 7 (MS. B, 12a; see No. 751). A section of a circular pavilion with the plan of a similar building by the side of it. These two drawings have a special historical interest because the text written below mentions the Duke and Duchess of Milan.

The sketch of a villa on a terrace at the end of a garden occurs in C. A. 150; and in C. A. 77b; 225b is another sketch of a villa somewhat resembling the Belvedere of Pope Innocent VIII, at Rome. In C. A. 62b; 193b there is a Loggia.

Pl. LXXXII, No. 4 (C. A. 387a; 1198a) is a tower-shaped Loggia above a fountain. The machinery is very ingeniously screened from view.

748.

The Palace of the prince must have a piazza in front of it.

Houses intended for dancing or any kind of jumping or any other movements with a multitude of people, must be on the ground- floor; for I have already witnessed the destruction of some, causing death to many persons, and above all let every wall, be it ever so thin, rest on the ground or on arches with a good foundation.

Let the mezzanines of the dwellings be divided by walls made of very thin bricks, and without wood on account of fire.

Let all the privies have ventilation [by shafts] in the thickness of the walls, so as to exhale by the roofs.

The mezzanines should be vaulted, and the vaults will be stronger in proportion as they are of small size.

The ties of oak must be enclosed in the walls in order to be protected from fire.

[Footnote: The remarks accompanying the plan reproduced on Pl. LXXXI, No. 2 are as follows: Above, to the left: "in a angholo stia la guardia de la sstalla" (in the angle a may be the keeper of the stable). Below are the words "strada dabosa" (road to Amboise), parallel with this "fossa br 40" (the moat 40 braccia) fixing the width of the moat. In the large court surrounded by a portico "in terre No.--Largha br.80 e lugha br 120." To the right of the castle is a large basin for aquatic sports with the words "Giostre colle nave cioe li giostra li stieno sopra le na" (Jousting in boats that is the men are to be in boats). J. P. R.]

The privies must be numerous and going one into the other in order that the stench may not penetrate into the dwellings., and all their doors must shut off themselves with counterpoises.

The main division of the facade of this palace is into two portions; that is to say the width of the court-yard must be half the whole facade; the 2nd ...

749.

30 braccia wide on each side; the lower entrance leads into a hall 10 braccia wide and 30 braccia long with 4 recesses each with a chimney.

[Footnote: On each side of the castle, Pl. LXXXII. No. 2 there are drawings of details, to the left "Camino" a chimney, to the right the central lantern, sketched in red "8 lati" i.e. an octagon.]

750.

The firststorey [or terrace] must be entirely solid.

751.

The pavilion in the garden of the Duchess of Milan.

The plan of the pavilion which is in the middle of the labyrinth of the Duke of Milan.

[Footnote: This passage was first published by AMORETTI in Memorie Storiche Cap. X: Una sua opera da riportarsi a quest' anno fu il bagno fatto per la duchessa Beatrice nel parco o giardino del Castello. Lionardo non solo ne disegno il piccolo edifizio a foggia di padiglione, nel cod. segnato Q. 3, dandone anche separatamente la pianta; ma sotto vi scrisse: Padiglione del giardino della duchessa; e sotto la pianta: Fondamento del padiglione ch'e nel mezzo del labirinto del duca di Milano; nessuna data e presso il padiglione, disegnato nella pagina 12, ma poco sopra fra molti circoli intrecciati vedesi = 10 Luglio 1492 = e nella pagina 2 presso ad alcuni disegni di legumi qualcheduno ha letto Settembre 1482 in vece di 1492, come dovea scriverevi, e probabilmente scrisse Lionardo.

The original text however hardly bears the interpretation put upon it by AMORETTI. He is mistaken as to the mark on the MS. as well as in his statements as to the date, for the MS. in question has no date; the date he gives occurs, on the contrary, in another note-book. Finally, it appears to me quite an open question whether Leonardo was the architect who carried out the construction of the dome-like Pavilion here shown in section, or of the ground plan of the Pavilion drawn by the side of it. Must we, in fact, suppose that "il duca di Milano" here mentioned was, as has been generally assumed, Ludovico il Moro? He did not hold this title from the Emperor before 1494; till that date he was only called Governatore and Leonardo in speaking of him, mentions him generally as "il Moro" even after 1494. On January 18, 1491, he married Beatrice d'Este the daughter of Ercole I, Duke of Ferrara. She died on the 2nd January 1497, and for the reasons I have given it seems improbable that it should be this princess who is here spoken of as the "Duchessa di Milano". From the style of the handwriting it appears to me to be beyond all doubt that the MS. B, from which this passage is taken, is older than the dated MSS. of 1492 and 1493. In that case the Duke of Milan here mentioned would be Gian Galeazzo (1469-1494) and the Duchess would be his wife Isabella of Aragon, to whom he was married on the second February 1489. J. P. R.]

752.

The earth that is dug out from the cellars must be raised on one side so high as to make a terrace garden as high as the level of the hall; but between the earth of the terrace and the wall of the house, leave an interval in order that the damp may not spoil the principal walls.

IV. Ecclesiastical Architecture.

A. General Observations.

753.

A building should always be detached on all sides so that its form may be seen.

[Footnote: The original text is reproduced on Pl. XCII, No. 1 to the left hand at the bottom.]

754.

Here there cannot and ought not to be any campanile; on the contrary it must stand apart like that of the Cathedral and of San Giovanni at Florence, and of the Cathedral at Pisa, where the campanile is quite detached as well as the dome. Thus each can display its own perfection. If however you wish to join it to the church, make the lantern serve for the campanile as in the church at Chiaravalle.

[Footnote: This text is written by the side of the plan given on Pl. XCI. No. 2.]

[Footnote 12: The Abbey of Chiaravalle, a few miles from Milan, has a central tower on the intersection of the cross in the style of that of the Certosa of Pavia, but the style is mediaeval (A. D. 1330). Leonardo seems here to mean, that in a building, in which the circular form is strongly conspicuous, the campanile must either be separated, or rise from the centre of the building and therefore take the form of a lantern.]

755.

It never looks well to see the roofs of a church; they should rather be flat and the water should run off by gutters made in the frieze.

[Footnote: This text is to the left of the domed church reproduced on Pl. LXXXVII, No. 2.]

B. The theory of Dome Architecture.

This subject has been more extensively treated by Leonardo in drawings than in writing. Still we may fairly assume that it was his purpose, ultimately to embody the results of his investigation in a "Trattato delle Cupole." The amount of materials is remarkably extensive. MS. B is particularly rich in plans and elevations of churches with one or more domes--from the simplest form to the most complicated that can be imagined. Considering the evident connexion between a great number of these sketches, as well as the impossibility of seeing in them designs or preparatory sketches for any building intended to be erected, the conclusion is obvious that they were not designed for any particular monument, but were theoretical and ideal researches, made in order to obtain a clear understanding of the laws which must govern the construction of a great central dome, with smaller ones grouped round it; and with or without the addition of spires, so that each of these parts by itself and in its juxtaposition to the other parts should produce the grandest possible effect.

In these sketches Leonardo seems to have exhausted every imaginable combination. [Footnote 1: In MS. B, 32b (see Pl. C III, No. 2) we find eight geometrical patterns, each drawn in a square; and in MS. C.A., fol. 87 to 98 form a whole series of patterns done with the same intention.] The results of some of these problems are perhaps not quite satisfactory; still they cannot be considered to give evidence of a want of taste or of any other defect in Leonardo s architectural capacity. They were no doubt intended exclusively for his own instruction, and, before all, as it seems, to illustrate the features or consequences resulting from a given principle.

I have already, in another place, [Footnote 1: Les Projets Primitifs pour la Basilique de St. Pierre de Rome, par Bramante, Raphael etc.,Vol. I, p. 2.] pointed out the law of construction for buildings crowned by a large dome: namely, that such a dome, to produce the greatest effect possible, should rise either from the centre of a Greek cross, or from the centre of a structure of which the plan has some symmetrical affinity to a circle, this circle being at the same time the centre of the whole plan of the building.

Leonardo's sketches show that he was fully aware, as was to be expected, of this truth. Few of them exhibit the form of a Latin cross, and when this is met with, it generally gives evidence of the determination to assign as prominent a part as possible to the dome in the general effect of the building.

While it is evident, on the one hand, that the greater number of these domes had no particular purpose, not being designed for execution, on the other hand several reasons may be found for Leonardo's perseverance in his studies of the subject.

Besides the theoretical interest of the question for Leonardo and his Trattato and besides the taste for domes prevailing at that time, it seems likely that the intended erection of some building of the first importance like the Duomos of Pavia and Como, the church of Sta. Maria delle Grazie at Milan, and the construction of a Dome or central Tower (Tiburio) on the cathedral of Milan, may have stimulated Leonardo to undertake a general and thorough investigation of the subject; whilst Leonardo's intercourse with Bramante for ten years or more, can hardly have remained without influence in this matter. In fact now that some of this great Architect's studies for S. Peter's at Rome have at last become known, he must be considered henceforth as the greatest master of Dome-Architecture that ever existed. His influence, direct or indirect even on a genius like Leonardo seems the more likely, since Leonardo's sketches reveal a style most similar to that of Bramante, whose name indeed, occurs twice in Leonardo's manuscript notes. It must not be forgotten that Leonardo was a Florentine; the characteristic form of the two principal domes of Florence, Sta. Maria del Fiore and the Battisterio, constantly appear as leading features in his sketches.

The church of San Lorenzo at Milan, was at that time still intact. The dome is to this day one of the most wonderful cupolas ever constructed, and with its two smaller domes might well attract the attention and study of a never resting genius such as Leonardo. A whole class of these sketches betray in fact the direct influence of the church of S. Lorenzo, and this also seems to have suggested the plan of Bramante's dome of St. Peter's at Rome.

In the following pages the various sketches for the construction of domes have been classified and discussed from a general point of view. On two sheets: Pl. LXXXIV (C.A. 354b; 118a) and Pl. LXXXV, Nos. 1-11 (Ash. II, 6b) we see various dissimilar types, grouped together; thus these two sheets may be regarded as a sort of nomenclature of the different types, on which we shall now have to treat.

1. Churches formed on the plan of a Greek cross.

Group I.

Domes rising from a circular base.

The simplest type of central building is a circular edifice.

Pl. LXXXIV, No. 9. Plan of a circular building surrounded by a colonnade.

Pl. LXXXIV, No. 8. Elevation of the former, with a conical roof.

Pl. XC. No. 5. A dodecagon, as most nearly approaching the circle.

Pl. LXXXVI, No. 1, 2, 3. Four round chapels are added at the extremities of the two principal axes;--compare this plan with fig. 1 on p. 44 and fig. 3 on p. 47 (W. P. 5b) where the outer wall is octagonal.

Group II.

Domes rising from a square base.

The plan is a square surrounded by a colonnade, and the dome seems to be octagonal.

Pl. LXXXIV. The square plan below the circular building No. 8, and its elevation to the left, above the plan: here the ground-plan is square, the upper storey octagonal. A further development of this type is shown in two sketches C. A. 3a (not reproduced here), and in

Pl. LXXXVI, No. 5 (which possibly belongs to No. 7 on Pl. LXXXIV).

Pl, LXXXV, No. 4, and p. 45, Fig. 3, a Greek cross, repeated p. 45, Fig. 3, is another development of the square central plan.

The remainder of these studies show two different systems; in the first the dome rises from a square plan,--in the second from an octagonal base.

Group III.

Domes rising from a square base and four pillars. [Footnote 1: The ancient chapel San Satiro, via del Falcone, Milan, is a specimen of this type.]

a) First type. A Dome resting on four pillars in the centre of a square edifice, with an apse in the middle, of each of the four sides. We have eleven variations of this type.

aa) Pl. LXXXVIII, No. 3.

bb) Pl. LXXX, No. 5.

cc) Pl. LXXXV, Nos. 2, 3, 5.

dd) Pl. LXXXIV, No. 1 and 4 beneath.

ee) Pl. LXXXV, Nos. 1, 7, 10, 11.

b) Second type. This consists in adding aisles to the whole plan of the first type; columns are placed between the apses and the aisles; the plan thus obtained is very nearly identical with that of S. Lorenzo at Milan.

Fig. 1 on p. 56. (MS. B, 75a) shows the result of this treatment adapted to a peculiar purpose about which we shall have to say a few words later on.

Pl. XCV, No. 1, shows the same plan but with the addition of a short nave. This plan seems to have been suggested by the general arrangement of S. Sepolcro at Milan.

MS. B. 57b (see the sketch reproduced on p.51). By adding towers in the four outer angles to the last named plan, we obtain a plan which bears the general features of Bramante's plans for S. Peter's at Rome. [Footnote 2: See Les projets primitifs etc., Pl. 9-12.] (See p. 51 Fig. 1.)

Group IV.

Domes rising from an octagonal base.

This system, developed according to two different schemes, has given rise to two classes with many varieties.

In a) On each side of the octagon chapels of equal form are added.

In b) The chapels are dissimilar; those which terminate the principal axes being different in form from those which are added on the diagonal sides of the octagon.

a. First Class.

The Chapel "degli Angeli," at Florence, built only to a height of about 20 feet by Brunellesco, may be considered as the prototype of this group; and, indeed it probably suggested it. The fact that we see in MS. B. 11b (Pl. XCIV, No. 3) by the side of Brunellesco's plan for the Basilica of Sto. Spirito at

Florence, a plan almost identical with that of the Capella degli Angeli, confirms this supposition. Only two small differences, or we may say improvements, have been introduced by Leonardo. Firstly the back of the chapels contains a third niche, and each angle of the Octagon a folded pilaster like those in Bramante's Sagrestia di S. M. presso San Satiro at Milan, instead of an interval between the two pilasters as seen in the Battistero at Florence and in the Sacristy of Sto. Spirito in the same town and also in the above named chapel by Brunellesco.

The first set of sketches which come under consideration have at first sight the appearance of mere geometrical studies. They seem to have been suggested by the plan given on page 44 Fig. 2 (MS. B, 55a) in the centre of which is written "Santa Maria in perticha da Pavia", at the place marked A on the reproduction.

a) (MS. B, 34b, page 44 Fig. 3). In the middle of each side a column is added, and in the axes of the intercolumnar spaces a second row of columns forms an aisle round the octagon. These are placed at the intersection of a system of semicircles, of which the sixteen columns on the sides of the octagon are the centres.

b) The preceding diagram is completed and becomes more monumental in style in the sketch next to it (MS. B, 35a, see p. 45 Fig. 1). An outer aisle is added by circles, having for radius the distance between the columns in the middle sides of the octagon.

c) (MS. B. 96b, see p. 45 Fig. 2). Octagon with an aisle round it; the angles of both are formed by columns. The outer sides are formed by 8 niches forming chapels. The exterior is likewise octagonal, with the angles corresponding to the centre of each of the interior chapels.

Pl. XCII, No. 2 (MS. B. 96b). Detail and modification of the preceding plan-- half columns against piers--an arrangement by which the chapels of the aisle have the same width of opening as the inner arches between the half columns. Underneath this sketch the following note occurs: questo vole - avere 12 facce - co 12 tabernaculi - come - a - b. (This will have twelve sides with twelve tabernacles as a b.) In the remaining sketches of this class the octagon is not formed by columns at the angles.

The simplest type shows a niche in the middle of each side and is repeated on several sheets, viz: MS. B 3; MS. C.A. 354b (see Pl. LXXXIV, No. 11) and MS. Ash II 6b; (see Pl. LXXXV, No. 9 and the elevations No. 8; Pl. XCII, No. 3; MS. B. 4b [not reproduced here] and Pl. LXXXIV, No. 2).

Pl. XCII, 3 (MS. B, 56b) corresponds to a plan like the one in MS. B 35a, in which the niches would be visible outside or, as in the following sketch, with the addition of a niche in the middle of each chapel.

Pl. XC, No. 6. The niches themselves are surrounded by smaller niches (see also No. 1 on the same plate).

Octagon expanded on each side.

A. by a square chapel:

MS. B. 34b (not reproduced here).

B. by a square with 3 niches:

MS. B. 11b (see Pl. XCIV, No. 3).

C. by octagonal chapels:

a) MS. B, 21a; Pl. LXXXVIII, No. 4.

b) No. 2 on the same plate. Underneath there is the remark: "quest'e come le 8 cappele ano a essere facte" (this is how the eight chapels are to be executed).

c) Pl. LXXXVIII, No. 5. Elevation to the plans on the same sheet, it is accompanied by the note: "ciasscuno de' 9 tiburi no'uole - passare l'alteza - di - 2 - quadri" (neither of the 9 domes must exceed the height of two squares).

d) Pl. LXXXVIII, No. 1. Inside of the same octagon. MS. B, 30a, and 34b; these are three repetitions of parts of the same plan with very slight variations.

D. by a circular chapel:

MS. B, 18a (see Fig. 1 on page 47) gives the plan of this arrangement in which the exterior is square on the ground floor with only four of the chapels projecting, as is explained in the next sketch.

Pl. LXXXIX, MS. B, 17b. Elevation to the preceding plan sketched on the opposite side of the sheet, and also marked A. It is accompanied by the following remark, indicating the theoretical character of these studies: questo - edifitio - anchora - starebbe - bene affarlo dalla linja - a - b - c - d - insu. ("This edifice would also produce a good effect if only the part above the lines a b, c d, were executed").

Pl. LXXXIV, No. 11. The exterior has the form of an octagon, but the chapels project partly beyond it. On the left side of the sketch they appear larger than on the right side.

Pl. XC, No. 1, (MS. B, 25b); Repetition of Pl. LXXXIV, No. 11.

Pl. XC, No. 2. Elevation to the plan No. 1, and also to No. 6 of the same sheet.

E. By chapels formed by four niches:

Pl. LXXXIV, No. 7 (the circular plan on the left below) shows this arrangement in which the central dome has become circular inside and might therefore be classed after this group. [Footnote 1: This plan and some others of this class remind us of the plan of the Mausoleum of Augustus as it is represented for instance by Durand. See Cab. des Estampes, Bibliotheque Nationale, Paris, Topographie de Rome, V, 6, 82.]

The sketch on the right hand side gives most likely the elevation for the last named plan.

F. By chapels of still richer combinations, which necessitate an octagon of larger dimensions:

Pl. XCI, No. 2 (MS. Ash. 11. 8b) [Footnote 2: The note accompanying this plan is given under No. 754.]; on this plan the chapels themselves appear to be central buildings formed like the first type of the third group. Pl. LXXXVIII, No. 3.

Pl. XCI, No. 2 above; the exterior of the preceding figure, particularly interesting on account of the alternation of apses and niches, the latter containing statues of a gigantic size, in proportion to the dimension of the niches.

b. Second Class.

Composite plans of this class are generally obtained by combining two types of the first class--the one worked out on the principal axes, the other on the diagonal ones.

MS. B. 22 shows an elementary combination, without any additions on the diagonal axes, but with the dimensions of the squares on the two principal axes exceeding those of the sides of the octagon.

In the drawing W. P. 5b (see page 44 Fig. 1) the exterior only of the edifice is octagonal, the interior being formed by a circular colonnade; round chapels are placed against the four sides of the principal axes.

The elevation, drawn on the same sheet (see page 47 Fig. 3), shows the whole arrangement which is closely related with the one on Pl. LXXXVI No. 1, 2.

MS. B. 21a shows:

a) four sides with rectangular chapels crowned by pediments Pl. LXXXVII No. 3 (plan and elevation);

b) four sides with square chapels crowned by octagonal domes. Pl. LXXXVII No. 4; the plan underneath.

MS. B. 18a shows a variation obtained by replacing the round chapels in the principal axes of the sketch MS. B. 18a by square ones, with an apse. Leonardo repeated both ideas for better comparison side by side, see page 47. Fig. 2.

Pl. LXXXIX (MS. B. 17b). Elevation for the preceding figure. The comparison of the drawing marked M with the plan on page 47 Fig. 2, bearing the same mark, and of the elevation on Pl. LXXXIX below (marked A) with the corresponding plan on page 47 is highly instructive, as illustrating the spirit in which Leonardo pursued these studies.

Pl. LXXXIV No. 12 shows the design Pl. LXXXVII No. 3 combined with apses, with the addition of round chapels on the diagonal sides.

Pl. LXXXIV No. 13 is a variation of the preceding sketch.

Pl. XC No. 3. MS. B. 25b. The round chapels of the preceding sketch are replaced by octagonal chapels, above which rise campaniles.

Pl. XC No. 4 is the elevation for the preceding plan.

Pl. XCII No. 1. (MS. B. 39b.); the plan below. On the principal as well as on the diagonal axes are diagonal chapels, but the latter are separated from the dome by semicircular recesses. The communication between these eight chapels forms a square aisle round the central dome.

Above this figure is the elevation, showing four campaniles on the angles. [Footnote 1: The note accompanying this drawing is reproduced under No. 753.]

Pl. LXXXIV No. 3. On the principal axes are square chapels with three niches; on the diagonals octagonal chapels with niches. Cod. Atl. 340b gives a somewhat similar arrangement.

MS. B. 30. The principal development is thrown on the diagonal axes by square chapels with three niches; on the principal axes are inner recesses communicating with outer ones.

The plan Pl. XCIII No. 2 (MS. B. 22) differs from this only in so far as the outer semicircles have become circular chapels, projecting from the external square as apses; one of them serves as the entrance by a semicircular portico.

The elevation is drawn on the left side of the plan.

MS. B. 19. A further development of MS. B. 18, by employing for the four principal chapels the type Pl. LXXXVIII No. 3, as we have already seen in Pl. XCI No. 2; the exterior presents two varieties.

a) The outer contour follows the inner. [Footnote 2: These chapels are here sketched in two different sizes; it is the smaller type which is thus formed.]

b) It is semicircular.

Pl. LXXXVII No. 2 (MS. B. 18b) Elevation to the first variation MS. B. 19. If we were not certain that this sketch was by Leonardo, we might feel tempted to take it as a study by Bramante for St. Peter's at Rome. [Footnote 3: See Les projets primitifs Pl. 43.]

MS. P. V. 39b. In the principal axes the chapels of MS. B. 19, and semicircular niches on the diagonals. The exterior of the whole edifice is also an octagon, concealing the form of the interior chapels, but with its angles on their axes.

Group V.

Suggested by San Lorenzo at Milan.

In MS. C. A. 266 IIb, 8l2b there is a plan almost identical with that of San Lorenzo. The diagonal sides of the irregular octagon are not indicated.

If it could be proved that the arches which, in the actual church, exist on these sides in the first story, were added in 1574 by Martimo Bassi, then this plan and the following section would be still nearer the original state of San Lorenzo than at present. A reproduction of this slightly sketched plan has not been possible. It may however be understood from Pl. LXXXVIII No. 3, by suppressing the four pillars corresponding to the apses.

Pl. LXXXVII No. 1 shows the section in elevation corresponding with the above-named plan. The recessed chapels are decorated with large shells in the halfdomes like the arrangement in San Lorenzo, but with proportions like those of Bramante's Sacristy of Santa Maria presso S. Satiro.

MS. C. A. 266; a sheet containing three views of exteriors of Domes. On the same sheet there is a plan similar to the one above-named but with uninterrupted aisles and with the addition of round chapels in the axes (compare Pl. XCVII No. 3 and page 44 Fig. 1), perhaps a reminiscence of the two chapels annexed to San Lorenzo.--Leonardo has here sketched the way of transforming this plan into a Latin cross by means of a nave with side aisles.

Pl. XCI No. 1. Plan showing a type deprived of aisles and comprised in a square building which is surrounded by a portico. It is accompanied by the following text:

756.

This edifice is inhabited [accessible] below and above, like San Sepolcro, and it is the same above as below, except that the upper story has the dome c d; and the [Footnote: The church of San Sepolcro at Milan, founded in 1030 and repeatedly rebuilt after the middle of the XVIth century, still stands over the crypt of the original structure.] lower has the dome a b, and when you enter into the crypt, you descend 10 steps, and when you mount into the upper you ascend 20 steps, which, with 1/3 braccio for each, make 10 braccia, and this is the height between one floor of the church and the other.

Above the plan on the same sheet is a view of the exterior. By the aid of these two figures and the description, sections of the edifice may easily be reconstructed. But the section drawn on the left side of the building seems not to be in keeping with the same plan, notwithstanding the explanatory note written underneath it: "dentro il difitio di sopra" (interior of the edifice above)[Footnote 1: The small inner dome corresponds to a b on the plan--it rises from the lower church into the upper-- above, and larger, rises the dome c d. The aisles above and below thus correspond (e di sopra come di sotto, salvoche etc.). The only difference is, that in the section Leonardo has not taken the trouble to make the form octagonal, but has merely sketched circular lines in perspective. J. P. R.].

Before leaving this group, it is well to remark that the germ of it seems already indicated by the diagonal lines in the plans Pl. LXXXV No. 11 and No. 7. We shall find another application of the same type to the Latin cross in Pl. XCVII No. 3.

2. Churches formed on the plan of a Latin cross.

We find among Leonardo's studies several sketches for churches on the plan of the Latin cross; we shall begin by describing them, and shall add a few observations.

A. Studies after existing Monuments.

Pl. XCIV No. 2. (MS. B. 11b.) Plan of Santo Spirito at Florence, a basilica built after the designs of Brunellesco.--Leonardo has added the indication of a portico in front, either his own invention or the reproduction of a now lost design.

Pl. XCV No. 2. Plan accompanied by the words: "A e santo sepolcro di milano di sopra"(A is the upper church of S. Sepolcro at Milan); although since Leonardo's time considerably spoilt, it is still the same in plan.

The second plan with its note: "B e la sua parte socto tera" (B is its subterranean part [the crypt]) still corresponds with the present state of this part of the church as I have ascertained by visiting the crypt with this plan. Excepting the addition of a few insignificant walls, the state of this interesting part of the church still conforms to Leonardo's sketch; but in the Vestibolo the two columns near the entrance of the winding stairs are absent.

B. Designs or Studies.

PL. XCV No. 1. Plan of a church evidently suggested by that of San Sepolcro at Milan. The central part has been added to on the principle of the second type of Group III. Leonardo has placed the "coro" (choir) in the centre.

Pl. XCVI No. 2. In the plan the dome, as regards its interior, belongs to the First Class of Group IV, and may be grouped with the one in MS. B. 35a. The nave seems to be a development of the type represented in Pl. XCV No. 2, B. by adding towers and two lateral porticos[Footnote 1: Already published in Les projets primitifs Pl. XLIII.].

On the left is a view of the exterior of the preceding plan. It is accompanied by the following note:

757.

This building is inhabited below and above; the way up is by the campaniles, and in going up one has to use the platform, where the drums of the four domes are, and this platform has a parapet in front, and none of these domes communicate with the church, but they are quite separate.

Pl. XCVI No. 1 (MS. C. A. 16b; 65a). Perspective view of a church seen from behind; this recalls the Duomo at Florence, but with two campaniles[Footnote 2: Already published in the Saggio Pl. IX.].

Pl. XCVII No. 3 (MS. B. 52a). The central part is a development of S. Lorenzo at Milan, such as was executed at the Duomo of Pavia. There is sufficient analogy between the building actually executed and this sketch to suggest a direct connection between them. Leonardo accompanied Francesco di Giorgio[Footnote 3: See MALASPINA, il Duomo di Pavia. Documents.] when the latter was consulted on June 21st, 1490 as to this church; the fact that the only word accompanying the plan is: "sagrestia", seems to confirm our supposition, for the sacristies were added only in 1492, i. e. four years after the beginning of the Cathedral, which at that time was most likely still sufficiently unfinished to be capable of receiving the form of the present sketch.

Pl. XCVII No. 2 shows the exterior of this design. Below is the note: edifitio al proposito del fodameto figurato di socto (edifice proper for the ground plan figured below).

Here we may also mention the plan of a Latin cross drawn in MS. C. A. fol. 266 (see p. 50).

Pl. XCIV No. 1 (MS. L. 15b). External side view of Brunellesco's Florentine basilica San Lorenzo, seen from the North.

Pl. XCIV No. 4 (V. A. V, 1). Principal front of a nave, most likely of a church on the plan of a Latin cross. We notice here not only the principal features which were employed afterwards in Alberti's front of S. Maria Novella, but even details of a more advanced style, such as we are accustomed to meet with only after the year 1520.

In the background of Leonardo's unfinished picture of St. Jerome (Vatican Gallery) a somewhat similar church front is indicated (see the accompanying sketch).

[Illustration with caption: The view of the front of a temple, apparently a dome in the centre of four corinthian porticos bearing pediments (published by Amoretti Tav. II. B as being by Leonardo), is taken from a drawing, now at the Ambrosian Gallery. We cannot consider this to be by the hand of the master.]

C. Studies for a form of a Church most proper for preaching.

The problem as to what form of church might answer the requirements of acoustics seems to have engaged Leonardo's very particular attention. The designation of "teatro" given to some of these sketches, clearly shows which plan seemed to him most favourable for hearing the preacher's voice.

Pl. XCVII, No. 1 (MS. B, 52). Rectangular edifice divided into three naves with an apse on either side, terminated by a semicircular theatre with rising seats, as in antique buildings. The pulpit is in the centre. Leonardo has written on the left side of the sketch: "teatro da predicare" (Theatre for preaching).

MS. B, 55a (see page 56, Fig. 1). A domed church after the type of Pl. XCV, No. 1, shows four theatres occupying the apses and facing the square "coro" (choir), which is in the centre between the four pillars of the dome.[Footnote 1: The note teatro de predicar, on the right side is, I believe, in the handwriting of Pompeo Leoni. J. P. R.] The rising arrangement of the seats is shown in the sketch above. At the place marked B Leonardo wrote teatri per uldire messa (rows of seats to hear mass), at T teatri, and at C coro (choir).

In MS. C.A. 260, are slight sketches of two plans for rectangular choirs and two elevations of the altar and pulpit which seem to be in connection with these plans.

In MS. Ash II, 8a (see p. 56 and 57. Fig. 2 and 3). "Locho dove si predica" (Place for preaching). A most singular plan for a building. The interior is a portion of a sphere, the centre of which is the summit of a column destined to serve as the preacher's pulpit. The inside is somewhat like a modern theatre, whilst the exterior and the galleries and stairs recall the ancient amphitheatres.

[Illustration with caption: Page 57, Fig. 4. A plan accompanying the two preceding drawings. If this gives the complete form Leonardo intended for the edifice, it would have comprised only about two thirds of the circle. Leonardo wrote in the centre "fondamento", a word he often employed for plans, and on the left side of the view of the exterior: locho dove si predicha (a place for preaching in).]

D. Design for a Mausoleum.

Pl. XCVIII (P. V., 182. No. d'ordre 2386). In the midst of a hilly landscape rises an artificial mountain in the form of a gigantic cone, crowned by an imposing temple. At two thirds of the height a terrace is cut out with six doorways forming entrances to galleries, each leading to three sepulchral halls, so constructed as to contain about five hundred funeral urns, disposed in the customary antique style. From two opposite sides steps ascend to the terrace in a single flight and beyond it to the temple above. A large circular opening, like that in the Pantheon, is in the dome above what may be the altar, or perhaps the central monument on the level of the terrace below.

The section of a gallery given in the sketch to the right below shows the roof to be constructed on the principle of superimposed horizontal layers, projecting one beyond the other, and each furnished with a sort of heel, which appears to be undercut, so as to give the appearance of a beam from within. Granite alone would be adequate to the dimensions here given to the key stone, as the thickness of the layers can hardly be considered to be less than a foot. In taking this as the basis of our calculation for the dimensions of the whole construction, the width of the chamber would be about 25 feet but, judging from the number of urns it contains--and there is no reason to suppose that these urns were larger than usual--it would seem to be no more than about 8 or 10 feet.

The construction of the vaults resembles those in the galleries of some etruscan tumuli, for instance the Regulini Galeassi tomb at Cervetri (lately discovered) and also that of the chamber and passages of the pyramid of Cheops and of the treasury of Atreus at Mycenae.

The upper cone displays not only analogies with the monuments mentioned in the note, but also with Etruscan tumuli, such as the Cocumella tomb at Vulci, and the Regulini Galeassi tomb[Footnote 1: See FERSGUSON, Handbook of Architecture, I, 291.]. The whole scheme is one of the most magnificent in the history of Architecture.

It would be difficult to decide as to whether any monument he had seen suggested this idea to Leonardo, but it is worth while to enquire, if any monument, or group of monuments of an earlier date may be supposed to have done so.[Footnote 2: There are, in Algiers, two Monuments, commonly called "Le Madracen" and "Le tombeau de la Chretienne," which somewhat resemble Leonardo's design. They are known to have served as the Mausolea of the Kings of Mauritania. Pomponius Mela, the geographer of the time of the Emperor Claudius, describes them as having been "Monumentum commune regiae gentis." See Le Madracen, Rapport fait par M. le Grand Rabbin AB. CAHEN, Constantine 1873--Memoire sur les fouilles executees au Madras'en .. par le Colonel BRUNON, Constantine 1873.--Deux Mausolees Africains, le Madracen et le tombeau de la Chretienne par M. J. DE LAURIERE, Tours 1874.--Le tombeau de la Chretienne, Mausolee des rois Mauritaniens par M. BERBRUGGER, Alger 1867.--I am indebted to M. LE BLANC, of the Institut, and M. LUD, LALANNE, Bibliothecaire of the Institut for having first pointed out to me the resemblance between these monuments; while M. ANT. HERON DE VILLEFOSSE of the Louvre was kind enough to place the abovementioned rare works at my disposal. Leonardo's observations on the coast of Africa are given later in this work. The Herodium near Bethlehem in Palestine (Jebel el Fureidis, the Frank Mountain) was, according to the latest researches, constructed on a very similar plan. See Der Frankenberg, von Baurath C. SCHICK in Jerusalem, Zeitschrift des Deutschen Palastina-Vereins, Leipzag 1880, Vol. III, pages 88-99 and Plates IV and V. J. P. R.]

E. Studies for the Central Tower, or Tiburio of Milan Cathedral.

Towards the end of the fifteenth century the Fabbricceria del Duomo had to settle on the choice of a model for the crowning and central part of this vast building. We learn from a notice published by G. L. Calvi [Footnote: G. L. CALVI, Notizie sulla vita e sulle opere dei principali architetti scultori e pittori che fiorirono in Milano, Part III, 20. See also: H. DE GEYMULLER, Les projets primitifs etc. I, 37 and 116-119.--The Fabbricceria of the Duomo has lately begun the publication of the archives, which may possibly tell us more about the part taken by Leonardo, than has hitherto been known.] that among the artists who presented models in the year 1488 were: Bramante, Pietro da Gorgonzola, Luca Paperio (Fancelli), and Leonardo da Vinci.--

Several sketches by Leonardo refer to this important project:

Pl. XCIX, No. 2 (MS. S. K. III, No. 36a) a small plan of the whole edifice.--The projecting chapels in the middle of the transept are wanting here. The nave appears to be shortened and seems to be approached by an inner "vestibolo".--

Pl. C, No. 2 (Tr. 21). Plan of the octagon tower, giving the disposition of the buttresses; starting from the eight pillars adjoining the four principal piers and intended to support the eight angles of the Tiburio. These buttresses correspond exactly with those described by Bramante as existing in the model presented by Omodeo. [Footnote: Bramante's opinion was first published by

G. MONGERI, Arch. stor. Lomb. V, fasc. 3 and afterwards by me in the publication mentioned in the preceding note.]

Pl. C, 3 (MS. Tr. 16). Two plans showing different arrangements of the buttresses, which seem to be formed partly by the intersection of a system of pointed arches such as that seen in **

Pl. C, No. 5 (MS. B, 27a) destined to give a broader base to the drum. The text underneath is given under No. 788.

MS. B, 3--three slight sketches of plans in connexion with the preceding ones.

Pl. XCIX, No.1 (MS. Tr. 15) contains several small sketches of sections and exterior views of the Dome; some of them show buttress-walls shaped as inverted arches. Respecting these Leonardo notes:

758.

L'arco rivescio e migliore per fare spalla che l'ordinario, perche il rovescio trova sotto se muro resistete alla sua debolezza, e l'ordinario no trova nel suo debole se non aria

The inverted arch is better for giving a shoulder than the ordinary one, because the former finds below it a wall resisting its weakness, whilst the latter finds in its weak part nothing but air.

[Footnote: Three slight sketches of sections on the same leaf--above those reproduced here--are more closely connected with the large drawing in the centre of Pl. C, No. 4 (M.S, Tr. 41) which shows a section of a very elevated dome, with double vaults, connected by ribs and buttresses ingeniously disposed, so as to bring the weight of the lantern to bear on the base of the dome.

A sketch underneath it shows a round pillar on which is indicated which part of its summit is to bear the weight: "il pilastro sara charicho in . a . b." (The column will bear the weight at a b.) Another note is above on the right side: Larcho regiera tanto sotto asse chome di sopra se (The arch supports as much below it [i. e. a hanging weight] as above it).

Pl. C, No. 1 (C. A. 303a). Larger sketch of half section of the Dome, with a very complicated system of arches, and a double vault. Each stone is shaped so as to be knit or dovetailed to its neighbours. Thus the inside of the Dome cannot be seen from below.

MS. C. A. 303b. A repetition of the preceding sketch with very slight modifications.]

[Figs. 1. and Fig. 2. two sketeches of the dome]

MS. Tr. 9 (see Fig. 1 and 2). Section of the Dome with reverted buttresses between the windows, above which iron anchors or chains seem to be intended. Below is the sketch of the outside.

Pl. XCIX, No. 3 (C. A., 262a) four sketches of the exterior of the Dome.

C. A. 12. Section, showing the points of rupture of a gothic vault, in evident connection with the sketches described above.

It deserves to be noticed how easily and apparently without effort, Leonardo manages to combine gothic details and structure with the more modern shape of the Dome.

The following notes are on the same leaf, oni cosa poderosa, and oni cosa poderosa desidera de(scendere); farther below, several multiplications most likely intended to calculate the weight of some parts of the Dome, thus 16 x 47 = 720; 720 x 800 = 176000, next to which is written: peso del pilastro di 9 teste (weight of the pillar 9 diameters high).

Below: 176000 x 8 = 1408000; and below:

Semjlio e se ce 80 (?) il peso del tiburio (six millions six hundred (?) 80 the weight of the Dome).

Bossi hazarded the theory that Leonardo might have been the architect who built the church of Sta. Maria delle Grazie, but there is no evidence to support this, either in documents or in the materials supplied by Leonardos manuscripts and drawings. The sketch given at the side shows the arrangement of the second and third socle on the apses of the choir of that church; and it is remarkable that those sketches, in MS. S. K. M. II2, 2a and Ib, occur with the passage given in Volume I as No. 665 and 666 referring to the composition of the Last Supper in the Refectory of that church.]

F. The Project for lifting up the Battistero of Florence and setting it on a basement.

Among the very few details Vasari gives as to the architectural studies of Leonardo, we read: "And among these models and designs there was one by way of which he showed several times to many ingenious citizens who then governed Florence, his readiness to lift up without ruining it, the church of San Giovanni in Florence (the Battistero, opposite the Duomo) in order to place under it the missing basement with steps; he supported his assertions with reasons so persuasive, that while he spoke the undertaking seemed feasable, although every one of his hearers, when he had departed, could see by himself the impossibility of so vast an undertaking."

[Footnote: This latter statement of Vasari's must be considered to be exaggerated. I may refer here to some data given by LIBRI, Histoire des sciences mathematiques en Italie (II, 216, 217): "On a cru dans ces derniers temps faire un miracle en mecanique en effectuant ce transport, et cependant des l'annee 1455, Gaspard Nadi et Aristote de Fioravantio avaient transporte, a une distance considerable, la tour de la Magione de Bologne, avec ses fondements, qui avait presque quatre-vingts pieds de haut. Le continuateur de la chronique de Pugliola dit que le trajet fut de 35 pieds et que durant le transport auquel le chroniqueur affirme avoir assiste, il arriva un accident grave qui fit pencher de trois pieds la tour pendant qu'elle etait suspendue, mais que cet accident fut promptement repare (Muratori, Scriptores rer. ital. Tom. XVIII, col. 717, 718). Alidosi a rapporte une note ou Nadi rend compte de ce transport avec une rare simplicite. D'apres cette note, on voit que les operations de ce genre n'etaient pas nouvelles. Celle-ci ne couta que 150 livres (monnaie d'alors) y compris le cadeau que le Legat fit aux deux mecaniciens. Dans la meme annee, Aristote redressa le clocher de Cento, qui penchait de plus de cinq pieds (Alidosi, instruttione p. 188-- Muratori, Scriptores rer. ital., tom. XXIII, col. 888.--Bossii, chronica Mediol., 1492, in-fol. ad ann. 1455). On ne concoit pas comment les historiens des beaux-arts ont pu negliger de tels hommes." J. P. R.]

In the MS. C. A. fol. 293, there are two sketches which possibly might have a bearing on this bold enterprise. We find there a plan of a circular or polygonal edifice surrounded by semicircular arches in an oblique position. These may be taken for the foundation of the steps and of the new platform. In the perspective elevation the same edifice, forming a polygon, is shown as lifted up and resting on a circle of inverted arches which rest on an other circle of arches in the ordinary position, but so placed that the inverted arches above rest on the spandrels of the lower range.

What seems to confirm the supposition that the lifting up of a building is here in question, is the indication of engines for winding up, such as jacks, and a rack and wheel. As the lifting apparatus represented on this sheet does not seem particularly applicable to an undertaking of such magnitude, we may consider it to be a first sketch or scheme for the engines to be used.

G. Description of an unknown Temple.

759.

Twelve flights of steps led up to the great temple, which was eight hundred braccia in circumference and built on an octagonal plan. At the eight corners were eight large plinths, one braccia and a half high, and three wide, and six long at the bottom, with an angle in the middle; on these were eight great pillars, standing on the plinths as a foundation, and twenty four braccia high. And on the top of these were eight capitals three braccia long and six wide, above which were the architrave frieze and cornice, four braccia and a half high, and this was carried on in a straight line from one pillar to the next and so, continuing for eight hundred braccia, surrounded the whole temple, from pillar to pillar. To support this entablature there were ten large columns of the same height as the pillars, three braccia thick above their bases which were one braccia and a half high.

The ascent to this temple was by twelve flights of steps, and the temple was on the twelfth, of an octagonal form, and at each angle rose a large pillar; and between the pillars were placed ten columns of the same height as the pillars, rising at once from the pavement to a height of twenty eight braccia and a half; and at this height the architrave, frieze and cornice were placed which surrounded the temple having a length of eight hundred braccia. At the same height, and within the temple at the same level, and all round the centre of the temple at a distance of 24 braccia farther in, are pillars corresponding to the eight pillars in the angles, and columns corresponding to those placed in the outer spaces. These rise to the same height as the former ones, and over these the continuous architrave returns towards the outer row of pillars and columns.

[Footnote: Either this description is incomplete, or, as seems to me highly probable, it refers to some ruin. The enormous dimensions forbid our supposing this to be any temple in Italy or Greece. Syria was the native land of colossal octagonal buildings, in the early centuries A. D. The Temple of Baalbek, and others are even larger than that here described. J. P. R.]

V. Palace architecture.

But a small number of Leonardo's drawings refer to the architecture of palaces, and our knowledge is small as to what style Leonardo might have adopted for such buildings.

Pl. CII No. 1 (W. XVIII). A small portion of a facade of a palace in two stories, somewhat resembling Alberti's Palazzo Rucellai.--Compare with this Bramante's painted front of the Casa Silvestri, and a painting by Montorfano in San Pietro in Gessate at Milan, third chapel on the left hand side and also with Bramante's palaces at Rome. The pilasters with arabesques, the rustica between them, and the figures over the window may be painted or in sgraffito. The original is drawn in red chalk.

Pl. LXXXI No. 1 (MS. Tr. 42). Sketch of a palace with battlements and decorations, most likely graffiti; the details remind us of those in the Castello at Vigevano. [Footnote 1: Count GIULIO PORRO, in his valuable contribution to the Archivio Storico Lombardo, Anno VIII, Fasc. IV (31 Dec. 1881): Leonardo da Vinci, Libro di Annotazioni e Memorie, refers to this in the following note: "Alla pag. 41 vi e uno schizzo di volta ed accanto scrisse: 'il pilastro sara charicho in su 6' e potrebbe darsi che si riferisse alla cupola della chiesa delle Grazie tanto piu che a pag. 42 vi e un disegno che rassomiglia assai al basamento che oggi si vede nella parte esterna del coro di quella chiesa." This may however be doubted. The drawing, here referred to, on page 41 of the same manuscript, is reproduced on Pl. C No. 4 and described on page 61 as being a study for the cupola of the Duomo of Milan. J. P. R.]

MS. Mz. 0", contains a design for a palace or house with a loggia in the middle of the first story, over which rises an attic with a Pediment reproduced on page 67. The details drawn close by on the left seem to indicate an arrangement of coupled columns against the wall of a first story.

Pl. LXXXV No. 14 (MS. S. K. M. III 79a) contains a very slight sketch in red chalk, which most probably is intended to represent the facade of a palace. Inside is the short note 7 he 7 (7 and 7).

MS. J2 8a (see pages 68 Fig. 1 and 2) contains a view of an unknown palace. Its plan is indicated at the side.

In MS. Br. M. 126a(see Fig. 3 on page 68) there is a sketch of a house, on which Leonardo notes; casa con tre terrazi (house with three terraces).

Pl. CX, No. 4 (MS. L. 36b) represents the front of a fortified building drawn at Cesena in 1502 (see No. 1040).

Here we may also mention the singular building in the allegorical composition represented on Pl. LVIII in Vol. I. In front of it appears the head of a sphinx or of a dragon which seems to be carrying the palace away.

The following texts refer to the construction of palaces and other buildings destined for private use:

760.

In the courtyard the walls must be half the height of its width, that is if the court be 40 braccia, the house must be 20 high as regards the walls of the said courtyard; and this courtyard must be half as wide as the whole front.

[Footnote: See Pl. CI, no. 1, and compare the dimensions here given, with No. 748 lines 26-29; and the drawing belonging to it Pl. LXXXI, no. 2.]

On the dispositions of a stable.

761.

FOR MAKING A CLEAN STABLE.

The manner in which one must arrange a stable. You must first divide its width in 3 parts, its depth matters not; and let these 3 divisions be equal and 6 braccia broad for each part and 10 high, and the middle part shall be for the use of the stablemasters; the 2 side ones for the horses, each of which must be 6 braccia in width and 6 in length, and be half a braccio higher at the head than behind. Let the manger be at 2 braccia from the ground, to the bottom of the rack, 3 braccia, and the top of it 4 braccia. Now, in order to attain to what I promise, that is to make this place, contrary to the general custom, clean and neat: as to the upper part of the stable, i. e. where the hay is, that part must have at its outer end a window 6 braccia high and 6 broad, through which by simple means the hay is brought up to the loft, as is shown by the machine E; and let this be erected in a place 6 braccia wide, and as long as the stable, as seen at k p. The other two parts, which are on either side of this, are again divided; those nearest to the hay-loft are 4 braccia, p s, and only for the use and circulation of the servants belonging to the stable; the other two which reach to the outer walls are 2 braccia, as seen at s k, and these are made for the purpose of giving hay to the mangers, by means of funnels, narrow at the top and wide over the manger, in order that the hay should not choke them. They must be well plastered and clean and are represented at 4 f s. As to the giving the horses water, the troughs must be of stone and above them [cisterns of] water. The mangers may be opened as boxes are uncovered by raising the lids. [Footnote: See Pl. LXXVIII, No.1.]

Decorations for feasts.

762.

THE WAY TO CONSTRUCT A FRAME-WORK FOR DECORATING BUILDINGS.

The way in which the poles ought to be placed for tying bunches of juniper on to them. These poles must lie close to the framework of the vaulting and tie the bunches on with osier withes, so as to clip them even afterwards with shears.

Let the distance from one circle to another be half a braccia; and the juniper [sprigs] must lie top downwards, beginning from below.

Round this column tie four poles to which willows about as thick as a finger must be nailed and then begin from the bottom and work upwards with bunches of juniper sprigs, the tops downwards, that is upside down. [Footnote: See Pl. CII, No. 3. The words here given as the title line, lines 1--4, are the last in the original MS.--Lines 5--16 are written under fig. 4.]

763.

The water should be allowed to fall from the whole circle a b. [Footnote: Other drawings of fountains are given on Pl. CI (W. XX); the original is a pen and ink drawing on blue paper; on Pl. CIII (MS. B.) and Pl. LXXXII.]

VI. Studies of architectural details.

Several of Leonardo's drawings of architectural details prove that, like other great masters of that period, he had devoted his attention to the study of the proportion of such details. As every organic being in nature has its law of construction and growth, these masters endeavoured, each in his way, to discover and prove a law of proportion in architecture. The following notes in Leonardo's manuscripts refer to this subject.

MS. S. K. M. III, 47b (see Fig. 1). A diagram, indicating the rules as given by Vitruvius and by Leon Battista Alberti for the proportions of the Attic base of a column.

MS. S. K. M. III 55a (see Fig. 2). Diagram showing the same rules.

764.

B toro superiore . . . . . toro superiore 2B nestroli . . . . . . astragali quadre 3B orbiculo . . . . troclea 4B nestroli . . . . . astragali quadre 5B toro iferiore . . . . . . toro iferiore 6B latastro . . . . plintho

[Footnote: No explanation can be offered of the meaning of the letter B, which precedes each name. It may be meant for basa (base). Perhaps it refers to some author on architecture or an architect (Bramante?) who employed the designations, thus marked for the mouldings. 3. troclea. Philander: Trochlea sive trochalia aut rechanum. 6. Laterculus or latastrum is the Latin name for Plinthus (pi lambda Xiv) but Vitruvius adopted this Greek name and "latastro" seems to have been little in use. It is to be found besides the text given above, as far as I am aware, only two drawings of the Uffizi Collection, where in one instance, it indicates the abacus of a Doric capital.]

765.

STEPS OF URRBINO.

The plinth must be as broad as the thickness of the wall against which the plinth is built. [Footnote: See Pl. CX No. 3. The hasty sketch on the right hand side illustrates the unsatisfactory effect produced when the plinth is narrower than the wall.]

766.

The ancient architects ...... beginning with the Egyptians (?) who, as Diodorus Siculus writes, were the first to build and construct large cities and castles, public and private buildings of fine form, large and well proportioned .....

The column, which has its thickness at the third part .... The one which would be thinnest in the middle, would break ...; the one which is of equal thickness and of equal strength, is better for the edifice. The second best as to the usefulness will be the one whose greatest thickness is where it joins with the base.

[Footnote: See Pl. CIII, No. 3, where the sketches belonging to lines 10--16 are reproduced, but reversed. The sketch of columns, here reproduced by a wood cut, stands in the original close to lines 5--8.]

The capital must be formed in this way. Divide its thickness at the top into 8; at the foot make it 5/7, and let it be 5/7 high and you will have a square; afterwards divide the height into 8 parts as you did for the column, and then take 1/8 for the echinus and another eighth for the thickness of the abacus on the top of the capital. The horns of the abacus of the capital have to project beyond the greatest width of the bell 2/7, i. e. sevenths of the top of the bell, so 1/7 falls to the projection of each horn. The truncated part of the horns must be as broad as it is high. I leave the rest, that is the ornaments, to the taste of the sculptors. But to return to the columns and in order to prove the reason of their strength or weakness according to their shape, I say that when the lines starting from the summit of the column and ending at its base and their direction and length ..., their distance apart or width may be equal; I say that this column ...

767.

The cylinder of a body columnar in shape and its two opposite ends are two circles enclosed between parallel lines, and through the centre of the cylinder is a straight line, ending at the centre of these circles, and called by the ancients the axis.

[Footnote: Leonardo wrote these lines on the margin of a page of the Trattato di Francesco di Giorgio, where there are several drawings of columns, as well as a head drawn in profile inside an outline sketch of a capital.]

768.

a b is 1/3 of n m; m o is 1/6 of r o. The ovolo projects 1/6 of r o; s 7 1/5 of r o, a b is divided into 9 1/2; the abacus is 3/9 the ovolo 4/9, the bead-moulding and the fillet 2/9 and 1/2.

[Footnote: See Pl. LXXXV, No. 16. In the original the drawing and writing are both in red chalk.]

Pl. LXXXV No. 6 (MS. Ash. II 6b) contains a small sketch of a capital with the following note, written in three lines: I chorni del capitelo deono essere la quarta parte d'uno quadro (The horns of a capital must measure the fourth part of a square).

MS. S. K. M. III 72b contains two sketches of ornamentations of windows.

In MS. C. A. 308a; 938a (see Pl. LXXXII No. 1) there are several sketches of columns. One of the two columns on the right is similar to those employed by Bramante at the Canonica di S. Ambrogio. The same columns appear in the sketch underneath the plan of a castle. There they appear coupled, and in two stories one above the other. The archivolls which seem to spring out of the columns, are shaped like twisted cords, meant perhaps to be twisted branches. The walls between the columns seem to be formed out of blocks of wood, the pedestals are ornamented with a reticulated pattern. From all this we may suppose that Leonardo here had in mind either some festive decoration, or perhaps a pavilion for some hunting place or park. The sketch of columns marked "35" gives an example of columns shaped like candelabra, a form often employed at that time, particularly in Milan, and the surrounding districts for instance in the Cortile di Casa Castiglione now Silvestre, in the cathedral of Como, at Porta della Rana &c.

769.

CONCERNING ARCHITRAVES OF ONE OR SEVERAL PIECES.

An architrave of several pieces is stronger than that of one single piece, if those pieces are placed with their length in the direction of the centre of the world. This is proved because stones have their grain or fibre generated in the contrary direction i. e. in the direction of the opposite horizons of the hemisphere, and this is contrary to fibres of the plants which have ...

[Footnote: The text is incomplete in the original.]

The Proportions of the stories of a building are indicated by a sketch in MS. S. K. M. II2 11b (see Pl. LXXXV No. 15). The measures are written on the left side, as follows: br 1 1/2--6 3/4--br 1/12--2 br--9 e 1/2--1 1/2--br 5--o 9--o 3 [br=braccia; o=oncie].

Pl. LXXXV No. 13 (MS. B. 62a) and Pl. XCIII No. 1. (MS. B. 15a) give a few examples of arches supported on piers.

XIII. Theoretical writings on Architecture.

Leonardo's original writings on the theory of Architecture have come down to us only in a fragmentary state; still, there seems to be no doubt that he himself did not complete them. It would seem that Leonardo entertained the idea of writing a large and connected book on Architecture; and it is quite evident that the materials we possess, which can be proved to have been written at different periods, were noted down with a more or less definite aim and purpose. They might all be collected under the one title: "Studies on the Strength of Materials". Among them the investigations on the subject of fissures in walls are particularly thorough, and very fully reported; these passages are also especially interesting, because Leonardo was certainly the first writer on architecture who ever treated the subject at all. Here, as in all other cases Leonardo carefully avoids all abstract argument. His data are not derived from the principles of algebra, but from the laws of mechanics, and his method throughout is strictly experimental.

Though the conclusions drawn from his investigations may not have that precision which we are accustomed to find in Leonardo's scientific labours, their interest is not lessened. They prove at any rate his deep sagacity and wonderfully clear mind. No one perhaps, who has studied these questions since Leonardo, has combined with a scientific mind anything like the artistic delicacy of perception which gives interest and lucidity to his observations.

I do not assert that the arrangement here adopted for the passages in question is that originally intended by Leonardo; but their distribution into five groups was suggested by the titles, or headings, which Leonardo himself prefixed to most of these notes. Some of the longer sections perhaps should not, to be in strict agreement with this division, have been reproduced in their entirety in the place where they occur. But the comparatively small amount of the materials we possess will render them, even so, sufficiently intelligible to the reader; it did not therefore seem necessary or desirable to subdivide the passages merely for the sake of strict classification.

The small number of chapters given under the fifth class, treating on the centre of gravity in roof-beams, bears no proportion to the number of drawings and studies which refer to the same subject. Only a small selection of these are reproduced in this work since the majority have no explanatory text.

I.

ON FISSURES IN WALLS.

770.

First write the treatise on the causes of the giving way of walls and then, separately, treat of the remedies.

Parallel fissures constantly occur in buildings which are erected on a hill side, when the hill is composed of stratified rocks with an oblique stratification, because water and other moisture often penetrates these oblique seams carrying in greasy and slippery soil; and as the strata are not continuous down to the bottom of the valley, the rocks slide in the direction of the slope, and the motion does not cease till they have reached the bottom of the valley, carrying with them, as though in a boat, that portion of the building which is separated by them from the rest. The remedy for this is always to build thick piers under the wall which is slipping, with arches from one to another, and with a good scarp and let the piers have a firm foundation in the strata so that they may not break away from them.

In order to find the solid part of these strata, it is necessary to make a shaft at the foot of the wall of great depth through the strata; and in this shaft, on the side from which the hill slopes, smooth and flatten a space one palm wide from the top to the bottom; and after some time this smooth portion made on the side of the shaft, will show plainly which part of the hill is moving.

[Footnote: See Pl. CIV.]

771.

The cracks in walls will never be parallel unless the part of the wall that separates from the remainder does not slip down.

WHAT IS THE LAW BY WHICH BUILDINGS HAVE STABILITY.

The stability of buildings is the result of the contrary law to the two former cases. That is to say that the walls must be all built up equally, and by degrees, to equal heights all round the building, and the whole thickness at once, whatever kind of walls they may be. And although a thin wall dries more quickly than a thick one it will not necessarily give way under the added weight day by day and thus, [16] although a thin wall dries more quickly than a thick one, it will not give way under the weight which the latter may acquire from day to day. Because if double the amount of it dries in one day, one of double the thickness will dry in two days or thereabouts; thus the small addition of weight will be balanced by the smaller difference of time [18].

The adversary says that a which projects, slips down.

And here the adversary says that r slips and not c.

HOW TO PROGNOSTICATE THE CAUSES OF CRACKS IN ANY SORT OF WALL.

The part of the wall which does not slip is that in which the obliquity projects and overhangs the portion which has parted from it and slipped down.

ON THE SITUATION OF FOUNDATIONS AND IN WHAT PLACES THEY ARE A CAUSE OF RUIN.

When the crevice in the wall is wider at the top than at the bottom, it is a manifest sign, that the cause of the fissure in the wall is remote from the perpendicular line through the crevice.

[Footnote: Lines 1-5 refer to Pl. CV, No. 2. Line 9 alle due anteciedete, see on the same page.

Lines 16-18. The translation of this is doubtful, and the meaning in any case very obscure.

Lines 19-23 are on the right hand margin close to the two sketches on Pl. CII, No. 3.]

772.

OF CRACKS IN WALLS, WHICH ARE WIDE AT THE BOTTOM AND NARROW AT THE TOP AND OF THEIR CAUSES.

That wall which does not dry uniformly in an equal time, always cracks.

A wall though of equal thickness will not dry with equal quickness if it is not everywhere in contact with the same medium. Thus, if one side of a wall were in contact with a damp slope and the other were in contact with the air, then this latter side would remain of the same size as before; that side which dries in the air will shrink or diminish and the side which is kept damp will not dry. And the dry portion will break away readily from the damp portion because the damp part not shrinking in the same proportion does not cohere and follow the movement of the part which dries continuously.

OF ARCHED CRACKS, WIDE AT THE TOP, AND NARROW BELOW.

Arched cracks, wide at the top and narrow below are found in walled-up doors, which shrink more in their height than in their breadth, and in proportion as their height is greater than their width, and as the joints of the mortar are more numerous in the height than in the width.

The crack diminishes less in r o than in m n, in proportion as there is less material between r and o than between n and m.

Any crack made in a concave wall is wide below and narrow at the top; and this originates, as is here shown at b c d, in the side figure.

1. That which gets wet increases in proportion to the moisture it imbibes.

2. And a wet object shrinks, while drying, in proportion to the amount of moisture which evaporates from it.

[Footnote: The text of this passage is reproduced in facsimile on Pl. CVI to the left. L. 36-40 are written inside the sketch No. 2. L. 41-46 are partly written over the sketch No. 3 to which they refer.]

773.

OF THE CAUSES OF FISSURES IN [THE WALLS OF] PUBLIC AND PRIVATE BUILDINGS.

The walls give way in cracks, some of which are more or less vertical and others are oblique. The cracks which are in a vertical direction are caused by the joining of new walls, with old walls, whether straight or with indentations fitting on to those of the old wall; for, as these indentations cannot bear the too great weight of the wall added on to them, it is inevitable that they should break, and give way to the settling of the new wall, which will shrink one braccia in every ten, more or less, according to the greater or smaller quantity of mortar used between the stones of the masonry, and whether this mortar is more or less liquid. And observe, that the walls should always be built first and then faced with the stones intended to face them. For, if you do not proceed thus, since the wall settles more than the stone facing, the projections left on the sides of the wall must inevitably give way; because the stones used for facing the wall being larger than those over which they are laid, they will necessarily have less mortar laid between the joints, and consequently they settle less; and this cannot happen if the facing is added after the wall is dry.

a b the new wall, c the old wall, which has already settled; and the part a b settles afterwards, although a, being founded on c, the old wall, cannot possibly break, having a stable foundation on the old wall. But only the remainder b of the new wall will break away, because it is built from top to bottom of the building; and the remainder of the new wall will overhang the gap above the wall that has sunk.

774.

A new tower founded partly on old masonry.

775.

OF STONES WHICH DISJOIN THEMSELVES FROM THEIR MORTAR.

Stones laid in regular courses from bottom to top and built up with an equal quantity of mortar settle equally throughout, when the moisture that made the mortar soft evaporates.

By what is said above it is proved that the small extent of the new wall between A and n will settle but little, in proportion to the extent of the same wall between c and d. The proportion will in fact be that of the thinness of the mortar in relation to the number of courses or to the quantity of mortar laid between the stones above the different levels of the old wall.

[Footnote: See Pl. CV, No. 1. The top of the tower is wanting in this reproduction, and with it the letter n which, in the original, stands above the letter A over the top of the tower, while c stands perpendicularly over d.]

776.

This wall will break under the arch e f, because the seven whole square bricks are not sufficient to sustain the spring of the arch placed on them. And these seven bricks will give way in their middle exactly as appears in a b. The reason is, that the brick a has above it only the weight a k, whilst the last brick under the arch has above it the weight c d x a.

c d seems to press on the arch towards the abutment at the point p but the weight p o opposes resistence to it, whence the whole pressure is transmitted to the root of the arch. Therefore the foot of the arch acts like 7 6, which is more than double of x z.

II.

ON FISSURES IN NICHES.

777.

ON FISSURES IN NICHES.

An arch constructed on a semicircle and bearing weights on the two opposite thirds of its curve will give way at five points of the curve. To prove this let the weights be at n m which will break the arch a, b, f. I say that, by the foregoing, as the extremities c and a are equally pressed upon by the thrust n, it follows, by the 5th, that the arch will give way at the point which is furthest from the two forces acting on them and that is the middle e. The same is to be understood of the opposite curve, d g b; hence the weights n m must sink, but they cannot sink by the 7th, without coming closer together, and they cannot come together unless the extremities of the arch between them come closer, and if these draw together the crown of the arch must break; and thus the arch will give way in two places as was at first said &c.

I ask, given a weight at a what counteracts it in the direction n f and by what weight must the weight at f be counteracted.

778.

ON THE SHRINKING OF DAMP BODIES OF DIFFERENT THICKNESS AND WIDTH.

The window a is the cause of the crack at b; and this crack is increased by the pressure of n and m which sink or penetrate into the soil in which foundations are built more than the lighter portion at b. Besides, the old foundation under b has already settled, and this the piers n and m have not yet done. Hence the part b does not settle down perpendicularly; on the contrary, it is thrown outwards obliquely, and it cannot on the contrary be thrown inwards, because a portion like this, separated from the main wall, is larger outside than inside and the main wall, where it is broken, is of the same shape and is also larger outside than inside; therefore, if this separate portion were to fall inwards the larger would have to pass through the smaller--which is impossible. Hence it is evident that the portion of the semicircular wall when disunited from the main wall will be thrust outwards, and not inwards as the adversary says.

When a dome or a half-dome is crushed from above by an excess of weight the vault will give way, forming a crack which diminishes towards the top and is wide below, narrow on the inner side and wide outside; as is the case with the outer husk of a pomegranate, divided into many parts lengthwise; for the more it is pressed in the direction of its length, that part of the joints will open most, which is most distant from the cause of the pressure; and for that reason the arches of the vaults of any apse should never be more loaded than the arches of the principal building. Because that which weighs most, presses most on the parts below, and they sink into the foundations; but this cannot happen to lighter structures like the said apses.

[Footnote: The figure on Pl. CV, No. 4 belongs to the first paragraph of this passage, lines 1-14; fig. 5 is sketched by the side of lines l5--and following.

The sketch below of a pomegranate refers to line 22. The drawing fig. 6 is, in the original, over line 37 and fig. 7 over line 54.]

Which of these two cubes will shrink the more uniformly: the cube A resting on the pavement, or the cube b suspended in the air, when both cubes are equal in weight and bulk, and of clay mixed with equal quantities of water?

The cube placed on the pavement diminishes more in height than in breadth, which the cube above, hanging in the air, cannot do. Thus it is proved. The cube shown above is better shown here below.

The final result of the two cylinders of damp clay that is a and b will be the pyramidal figures below c and d. This is proved thus: The cylinder a resting on block of stone being made of clay mixed with a great deal of water will sink by its weight, which presses on its base, and in proportion as it settles and spreads all the parts will be somewhat nearer to the base because that is charged with the whole weight.

III.

ON THE NATURE OF THE ARCH.

779.

WHAT IS AN ARCH?

The arch is nothing else than a force originated by two weaknesses, for the arch in buildings is composed of two segments of a circle, each of which being very weak in itself tends to fall; but as each opposes this tendency in the other, the two weaknesses combine to form one strength.

OF THE KIND OF PRESSURE IN ARCHES.

As the arch is a composite force it remains in equilibrium because the thrust is equal from both sides; and if one of the segments weighs more than the other the stability is lost, because the greater pressure will outweigh the lesser.

OF DISTRIBUTING THE PRESSURE ABOVE AN ARCH.

Next to giving the segments of the circle equal weight it is necessary to load them equally, or you will fall into the same defect as before.

WHERE AN ARCH BREAKS.

An arch breaks at the part which lies below half way from the centre.

SECOND RUPTURE OF THE ARCH.

If the excess of weight be placed in the middle of the arch at the point a, that weight tends to fall towards b, and the arch breaks at 2/3 of its height at c e; and g e is as many times stronger than e a, as m o goes into m n.

ON ANOTHER CAUSE OF RUIN.

The arch will likewise give way under a transversal thrust, for when the charge is not thrown directly on the foot of the arch, the arch lasts but a short time.

780.

ON THE STRENGTH OF THE ARCH.

The way to give stability to the arch is to fill the spandrils with good masonry up to the level of its summit.

ON THE LOADING OF ROUND ARCHES.

ON THE PROPER MANNER OF LOADING THE POINTED ARCH.

ON THE EVIL EFFECTS OF LOADING THE POINTED ARCH DIRECTLY ABOVE ITS CROWN.

ON THE DAMAGE DONE TO THE POINTED ARCH BY THROWING THE PRESSURE ON THE FLANKS.

An arch of small curve is safe in itself, but if it be heavily charged, it is necessary to strengthen the flanks well. An arch of a very large curve is weak in itself, and stronger if it be charged, and will do little harm to its abutments, and its places of giving way are o p.

[Footnote: Inside the large figure on the righi is the note: Da pesare la forza dell' archo.]

781.

ON THE REMEDY FOR EARTHQUAKES.

The arch which throws its pressure perpendicularly on the abutments will fulfil its function whatever be its direction, upside down, sideways or upright.

The arch will not break if the chord of the outer arch does not touch the inner arch. This is manifest by experience, because whenever the chord a o n of the outer arch n r a approaches the inner arch x b y the arch will be weak, and it will be weaker in proportion as the inner arch passes beyond that chord. When an arch is loaded only on one side the thrust will press on the top of the other side and be transmitted to the spring of the arch on that side; and it will break at a point half way between its two extremes, where it is farthest from the chord.

782.

A continuous body which has been forcibly bent into an arch, thrusts in the direction of the straight line, which it tends to recover.

783.

In an arch judiciously weighted the thrust is oblique, so that the triangle c n b has no weight upon it.

784.

I here ask what weight will be needed to counterpoise and resist the tendency of each of these arches to give way?

[Footnote: The two lower sketches are taken from the MS. S. K. M. III, 10a; they have there no explanatory text.]

785.

ON THE STRENGTH OF THE ARCH IN ARCHITECTURE.

The stability of the arch built by an architect resides in the tie and in the flanks.

ON THE POSITION OF THE TIE IN THE ABOVE NAMED ARCH.

The position of the tie is of the same importance at the beginning of the arch and at the top of the perpendicular pier on which it rests. This is proved by the 2nd "of supports" which says: that part of a support has least resistance which is farthest from its solid attachment; hence, as the top of the pier is farthest from the middle of its true foundation and the same being the case at the opposite extremities of the arch which are the points farthest from the middle, which is really its [upper] attachment, we have concluded that the tie a b requires to be in such a position as that its opposite ends are between the four above-mentioned extremes.

The adversary says that this arch must be more than half a circle, and that then it will not need a tie, because then the ends will not thrust outwards but inwards, as is seen in the excess at a c, b d. To this it must be answered that this would be a very poor device, for three reasons. The first refers to the strength of the arch, since it is proved that the circular parallel being composed of two semicircles will only break where these semicircles cross each other, as is seen in the figure n m; besides this it follows that there is a wider space between the extremes of the semicircle than between the plane of the walls; the third reason is that the weight placed to counterbalance the strength of the arch diminishes in proportion as the piers of the arch are wider than the space between the piers. Fourthly in proportion as the parts at c a b d turn outwards, the piers are weaker to support the arch above them. The 5th is that all the material and weight of the arch which are in excess of the semicircle are useless and indeed mischievous; and here it is to be noted that the weight placed above the arch will be more likely to break the arch at a b, where the curve of the excess begins that is added to the semicircle, than if the pier were straight up to its junction with the semicircle [spring of the arch].

AN ARCH LOADED OVER THE CROWN WILL GIVE WAY AT THE LEFT HAND AND RIGHT HAND QUARTERS.

This is proved by the 7th of this which says: The opposite ends of the support are equally pressed upon by the weight suspended to them; hence the weight shown at f is felt at b c, that is half at each extremity; and by the third which says: in a support of equal strength [throughout] that portion will give way soonest which is farthest from its attachment; whence it follows that d being equally distant from f, e .....

If the centering of the arch does not settle as the arch settles, the mortar, as it dries, will shrink and detach itself from the bricks between which it was laid to keep them together; and as it thus leaves them disjoined the vault will remain loosely built, and the rains will soon destroy it.

786.

ON THE STRENGTH AND NATURE OF ARCHES, AND WHERE THEY ARE STRONG OR WEAK; AND THE SAME AS TO COLUMNS.

That part of the arch which is nearer to the horizontal offers least resistance to the weight placed on it.

When the triangle a z n, by settling, drives backwards the 2/3 of each 1/2 circle that is a s and in the same way z m, the reason is that a is perpendicularly over b and so likewise z is above f.

Either half of an arch, if overweighted, will break at 2/3 of its height, the point which corresponds to the perpendicular line above the middle of its bases, as is seen at a b; and this happens because the weight tends to fall past the point r.--And if, against its nature it should tend to fall towards the point s the arch n s would break precisely in its middle. If the arch n s were of a single piece of timber, if the weight placed at n should tend to fall in the line n m, the arch would break in the middle of the arch e m, otherwise it will break at one third from the top at the point a because from a to n the arch is nearer to the horizontal than from a to o and from o to s, in proportion as p t is greater than t n, a o will be stronger than a n and likewise in proportion as s o is stronger than o a, r p will be greater than p t.

The arch which is doubled to four times of its thickness will bear four times the weight that the single arch could carry, and more in proportion as the diameter of its thickness goes a smaller number of times into its length. That is to say that if the thickness of the single arch goes ten times into its length, the thickness of the doubled arch will go five times into its length. Hence as the thickness of the double arch goes only half as many times into its length as that of the single arch does, it is reasonable that it should carry half as much more weight as it would have to carry if it were in direct proportion to the single arch. Hence as this double arch has 4 times the thickness of the single arch, it would seem that it ought to bear 4 times the weight; but by the above rule it is shown that it will bear exactly 8 times as much.

THAT PIER, WHICH is CHARGED MOST UNEQUALLY, WILL SOONEST GIVE WAY.

The column c b, being charged with an equal weight, [on each side] will be most durable, and the other two outward columns require on the part outside of their centre as much pressure as there is inside of their centre, that is, from the centre of the column, towards the middle of the arch.

Arches which depend on chains for their support will not be very durable.

THAT ARCH WILL BE OF LONGER DURATION WHICH HAS A GOOD ABUTMENT OPPOSED TO ITS THRUST.

The arch itself tends to fall. If the arch be 30 braccia and the interval between the walls which carry it be 20, we know that 30 cannot pass through the 20 unless 20 becomes likewise 30. Hence the arch being crushed by the excess of weight, and the walls offering insufficient resistance, part, and afford room between them, for the fall of the arch.

But if you do not wish to strengthen the arch with an iron tie you must give it such abutments as can resist the thrust; and you can do this thus: fill up the spandrels m n with stones, and direct the lines of the joints between them to the centre of the circle of the arch, and the reason why this makes the arch durable is this. We know very well that if the arch is loaded with an excess of weight above its quarter as a b, the wall f g will be thrust outwards because the arch would yield in that direction; if the other quarter b c were loaded, the wall f g would be thrust inwards, if it were not for the line of stones x y which resists this.

787.

PLAN.

Here it is shown how the arches made in the side of the octagon thrust the piers of the angles outwards, as is shown by the line h c and by the line t d which thrust out the pier m; that is they tend to force it away from the centre of such an octagon.

788.

An Experiment to show that a weight placed on an arch does not discharge itself entirely on its columns; on the contrary the greater the weight placed on the arches, the less the arch transmits the weight to the columns. The experiment is the following. Let a man be placed on a steel yard in the middle of the shaft of a well, then let him spread out his hands and feet between the walls of the well, and you will see him weigh much less on the steel yard; give him a weight on the shoulders, you will see by experiment, that the greater the weight you give him the greater effort he will make in spreading his arms and legs, and in pressing against the wall and the less weight will be thrown on the steel yard.

IV.

ON FOUNDATIONS, THE NATURE OF THE GROUND AND SUPPORTS.

789.

The first and most important thing is stability.

As to the foundations of the component parts of temples and other public buildings, the depths of the foundations must bear the same proportions to each other as the weight of material which is to be placed upon them.

Every part of the depth of earth in a given space is composed of layers, and each layer is composed of heavier or lighter materials, the lowest being the heaviest. And this can be proved, because these layers have been formed by the sediment from water carried down to the sea, by the current of rivers which flow into it. The heaviest part of this sediment was that which was first thrown down, and so on by degrees; and this is the action of water when it becomes stagnant, having first brought down the mud whence it first flowed. And such layers of soil are seen in the banks of rivers, where their constant flow has cut through them and divided one slope from the other to a great depth; where in gravelly strata the waters have run off, the materials have, in consequence, dried and been converted into hard stone, and this happened most in what was the finest mud; whence we conclude that every portion of the surface of the earth was once at the centre of the earth, and viceversa &c.

790.

The heaviest part of the foundations of buildings settles most, and leaves the lighter part above it separated from it.

And the soil which is most pressed, if it be porous yields most.

You should always make the foundations project equally beyond the weight of the walls and piers, as shown at m a b. If you do as many do, that is to say if you make a foundation of equal width from the bottom up to the surface of the ground, and charge it above with unequal weights, as shown at b e and at e o, at the part of the foundation at b e, the pier of the angle will weigh most and thrust its foundation downwards, which the wall at e o will not do; since it does not cover the whole of its foundation, and therefore thrusts less heavily and settles less. Hence, the pier b e in settling cracks and parts from the wall e o. This may be seen in most buildings which are cracked round the piers.

791.

The window a is well placed under the window c, and the window b is badly placed under the pier d, because this latter is without support and foundation; mind therefore never to make a break under the piers between the windows.

792.

OF THE SUPPORTS.

A pillar of which the thickness is increased will gain more than its due strength, in direct proportion to what its loses in relative height.

EXAMPLE.

If a pillar should be nine times as high as it is broad--that is to say, if it is one braccio thick, according to rule it should be nine braccia high--then, if you place 100 such pillars together in a mass this will be ten braccia broad and 9 high; and if the first pillar could carry 10000 pounds the second being only about as high as it is wide, and thus lacking 8 parts of its proper length, it, that is to say, each pillar thus united, will bear eight times more than when disconnected; that is to say, that if at first it would carry ten thousand pounds, it would now carry 90 thousand.

V.

ON THE RESISTANCE OF BEAMS.

793.

That angle will offer the greatest resistance which is most acute, and the most obtuse will be the weakest.

[Footnote: The three smaller sketches accompany the text in the original, but the larger one is not directly connected with it. It is to be found on fol. 89a of the same Manuscript and there we read in a note, written underneath, coverchio della perdicha del castello (roof of the flagstaff of the castle),-- Compare also Pl. XCIII, No. 1.]

794.

If the beams and the weight o are 100 pounds, how much weight will be wanted at ae to resist such a weight, that it may not fall down?

795.

ON THE LENGTH OF BEAMS.

That beam which is more than 20 times as long as its greatest thickness will be of brief duration and will break in half; and remember, that the part built into the wall should be steeped in hot pitch and filleted with oak boards likewise so steeped. Each beam must pass through its walls and be secured beyond the walls with sufficient chaining, because in consequence of earthquakes the beams are often seen to come out of the walls and bring down the walls and floors; whilst if they are chained they will hold the walls strongly together and the walls will hold the floors. Again I remind you never to put plaster over timber. Since by expansion and shrinking of the timber produced by damp and dryness such floors often crack, and once cracked their divisions gradually produce dust and an ugly effect. Again remember not to lay a floor on beams supported on arches; for, in time the floor which is made on beams settles somewhat in the middle while that part of the floor which rests on the arches remains in its place; hence, floors laid over two kinds of supports look, in time, as if they were made in hills [Footnote: 19 M. RAVAISSON, in his edition of MS. A gives a very different rendering of this passage translating it thus: Les planchers qui sont soutenus par deux differentes natures de supports paraissent avec le temps faits en voute a cholli.]

Remarks on the style of Leonardo's architecture.

A few remarks may here be added on the style of Leonardo's architectural studies. However incomplete, however small in scale, they allow us to establish a certain number of facts and probabilities, well worthy of consideration.

When Leonardo began his studies the great name of Brunellesco was still the inspiration of all Florence, and we cannot doubt that Leonardo was open to it, since we find among his sketches the plan of the church of Santo Spirito[Footnote 1: See Pl. XCIV, No. 2. Then only in course of erection after the designs of Brunellesco, though he was already dead; finished in 1481.] and a lateral view of San Lorenzo (Pl. XCIV No. 1), a plan almost identical with the chapel Degli Angeli, only begun by him (Pl. XCIV, No. 3) while among Leonardo's designs for domes several clearly betray the influence of

Brunellesco's Cupola and the lantern of Santa Maria del Fiore[Footnote 2: A small sketch of the tower of the Palazzo della Signoria (MS. C.A. 309) proves that he also studied mediaeval monuments.]

The beginning of the second period of modern Italian architecture falls during the first twenty years of Leonardo's life. However the new impetus given by Leon Battista Alberti either was not generally understood by his contemporaries, or those who appreciated it, had no opportunity of showing that they did so. It was only when taken up by Bramante and developed by him to the highest rank of modern architecture that this new influence was generally felt. Now the peculiar feature of Leonardo's sketches is that, like the works of Bramante, they appear to be the development and continuation of Alberti's.

But a question here occurs which is difficult to answer. Did Leonardo, till he quitted Florence, follow the direction given by the dominant school of Brunellesco, which would then have given rise to his "First manner", or had he, even before he left Florence, felt Alberti's influence--either through his works (Palazzo Ruccellai, and the front of Santa Maria Novella) or through personal intercourse? Or was it not till he went to Milan that Alberti's work began to impress him through Bramante, who probably had known Alberti at Mantua about 1470 and who not only carried out Alberti's views and ideas, but, by his designs for St. Peter's at Rome, proved himself the greatest of modern architects. When Leonardo went to Milan Bramante had already been living there for many years. One of his earliest works in Milan was the church of Santa Maria presso San Satiro, Via del Falcone[Footnote 1: Evidence of this I intend to give later on in a Life of Bramante, which I have in preparation.].

Now we find among Leonardos studies of Cupolas on Plates LXXXIV and LXXXV and in Pl. LXXX several sketches which seem to me to have been suggested by Bramante's dome of this church.

The MSS. B and Ash. II contain the plans of S. Sepolcro, the pavilion in the garden of the duke of Milan, and two churches, evidently inspired by the church of San Lorenzo at Milan.

MS. B. contains besides two notes relating to Pavia, one of them a design for the sacristy of the Cathedral at Pavia, which cannot be supposed to be dated later than 1492, and it has probably some relation to Leonardo's call to Pavia June 21, 1490[Footnote 2: The sketch of the plan of Brunellesco's church of Santo Spirito at Florence, which occurs in the same Manuscript, may have been done from memory.]. These and other considerations justify us in concluding, that Leonardo made his studies of cupolas at Milan, probably between the years 1487 and 1492 in anticipation of the erection of one of the grandest churches of Italy, the Cathedral of Pavia. This may explain the decidedly Lombardo-Bramantesque tendency in the style of these studies, among which only a few remind us of the forms of the cupolas of S. Maria del Fiore and of the Baptistery of Florence. Thus, although when compared with Bramante's work, several of these sketches plainly reveal that master's influence, we find, among the sketches of domes, some, which show already

Bramante's classic style, of which the Tempietto of San Pietro in Montorio, his first building executed at Rome, is the foremost example[Footnote 3: It may be mentioned here, that in 1494 Bramante made a similar design for the lantern of the Cupola of the Church of Santa Maria delle Grazie.].

On Plate LXXXIV is a sketch of the plan of a similar circular building; and the Mausoleum on Pl. XCVIII, no less than one of the pedestals for the statue of Francesco Sforza (Pl. LXV), is of the same type.

The drawings Pl. LXXXIV No. 2, Pl. LXXXVI No. 1 and 2 and the ground flour ("flour" sic but should be "floor" ?) of the building in the drawing Pl. XCI No. 2, with the interesting decoration by gigantic statues in large niches, are also, I believe, more in the style Bramante adopted at Rome, than in the Lombard style. Are we to conclude from this that Leonardo on his part influenced Bramante in the sense of simplifying his style and rendering it more congenial to antique art? The answer to this important question seems at first difficult to give, for we are here in presence of Bramante, the greatest of modern architects, and with Leonardo, the man comparable with no other. We have no knowledge of any buildings erected by Leonardo, and unless we admit personal intercourse--which seems probable, but of which there is no proof--, it would be difficult to understand how Leonardo could have affected Bramante's style. The converse is more easily to be admitted, since Bramante, as we have proved elsewhere, drew and built simultaneously in different manners, and though in Lombardy there is no building by him in his classic style, the use of brick for building, in that part of Italy, may easily account for it.

Bramante's name is incidentally mentioned in Leonardo's manuscripts in two passages (Nos. 1414 and 1448). On each occasion it is only a slight passing allusion, and the nature of the context gives us no due information as to any close connection between the two artists.

It might be supposed, on the ground of Leonardo's relations with the East given in sections XVII and XXI of this volume, that some evidence of oriental influence might be detected in his architectural drawings. I do not however think that any such traces can be pointed out with certainty unless perhaps the drawing for a Mausoleum, Pl. XC VIII.

Among several studies for the construction of cupolas above a Greek cross there are some in which the forms are decidedly monotonous. These, it is clear, were not designed as models of taste; they must be regarded as the results of certain investigations into the laws of proportion, harmony and contrast.

The designs for churches, on the plan of a Latin cross are evidently intended to depart as little as possible from the form of a Greek cross; and they also show a preference for a nave surrounded with outer porticos.

The architectural forms preferred by Leonardo are pilasters coupled (Pl. LXXXII No. 1; or grouped (Pl. LXXX No. 5 and XCIV No. 4), often combined with niches. We often meet with orders superposed, one in each story, or two small orders on one story, in combination with one great order (Pl. XCVI No. 2).

The drum (tamburo) of these cupolas is generally octagonal, as in the cathedral of Florence, and with similar round windows in its sides. In Pl. LXXXVII No. 2 it is circular like the model actually carried out by Michael Angelo at St. Peter's.

The cupola itself is either hidden under a pyramidal roof, as in the Baptistery of Florence, San Lorenzo of Milan and most of the Lombard churches (Pl. XCI No. 1 and Pl. XCII No. 1); but it more generally suggests the curve of Sta Maria del Fiore (Pl. LXXXVIII No. 5; Pl. XC No. 2; Pl. LXXXIX, M; Pl XC No. 4, Pl. XCVI No. 2). In other cases (Pl. LXXX No. 4; Pl. LXXXIX; Pl. XC No. 2) it shows the sides of the octagon crowned by semicircular pediments, as in Brunellesco's lantern of the Cathedral and in the model for the Cathedral of Pavia.

Finally, in some sketches the cupola is either semicircular, or as in Pl. LXXXVII No. 2, shows the beautiful line, adopted sixty years later by Michael Angelo for the existing dome of St. Peter's.

It is worth noticing that for all these domes Leonardo is not satisfied to decorate the exterior merely with ascending ribs or mouldings, but employs also a system of horizontal parallels to complete the architectural system. Not the least interesting are the designs for the tiburio (cupola) of the Milan Cathedral. They show some of the forms, just mentioned, adapted to the peculiar gothic style of that monument.

The few examples of interiors of churches recall the style employed in Lombardy by Bramante, for instance in S. Maria di Canepanuova at Pavia, or by Dolcebuono in the Monastero Maggiore at Milan (see Pl. CI No. 1 [C. A. 181b; 546b]; Pl. LXXXIV No. 10).

The few indications concerning palaces seem to prove that Leonardo followed Alberti's example of decorating the walls with pilasters and a flat rustica, either in stone or by graffitti (Pl. CII No. 1 and Pl. LXXXV No. 14).

By pointing out the analogies between Leonardo's architecture and that of other masters we in no way pretend to depreciate his individual and original inventive power. These are at all events beyond dispute. The project for the Mausoleum (Pl. XCVIII) would alone suffice to rank him among the greatest architects who ever lived. The peculiar shape of the tower (Pl. LXXX), of the churches for preaching (Pl. XCVII No. 1 and pages 56 and 57, Fig. 1-4), his curious plan for a city with high and low level streets (Pl. LXXVII and LXXVIII No. 2 and No. 3), his Loggia with fountains (Pl. LXXXII No. 4) reveal an originality, a power and facility of invention for almost any given problem, which are quite wonderful.

In addition to all these qualities he propably stood alone in his day in one department of architectural study,--his investigations, namely, as to the resistance of vaults, foundations, walls and arches.

As an application of these studies the plan of a semicircular vault (Pl. CIII No. 2) may be mentioned here, disposed so as to produce no thrust on the columns on which it rests: volta i botte e non ispignie ifori le colone. Above the geometrical patterns on the same sheet, close to a circle inscribed in a square is the note: la ragio d'una volta cioe il terzo del diamitro della sua ... del tedesco in domo.

There are few data by which to judge of Leonardo's style in the treatment of detail. On Pl. LXXXV No. 10 and Pl. CIII No. 3, we find some details of pillars; on Pl. CI No. 3 slender pillars designed for a fountain and on Pl. CIII No. 1 MS. B, is a pen and ink drawing of a vase which also seems intended for a fountain. Three handles seem to have been intended to connect the upper parts with the base. There can be no doubt that Leonardo, like Bramante, but unlike Michael Angelo, brought infinite delicacy of motive and execution to bear on the details of his work.

XIV. Anatomy, Zoology and Physiology.

Leonardo's eminent place in the history of medicine, as a pioneer in the sciences of Anatomy and Physiology, will never be appreciated till it is possible to publish the mass of manuscripts in which he largely treated of these two branches of learning. In the present work I must necessarily limit myself to giving the reader a general view of these labours, by publishing his introductory notes to the various books on anatomical subjects. I have added some extracts, and such observations as are scattered incidentally through these treatises, as serving to throw a light on Leonardo's scientific attitude, besides having an interest for a wider circle than that of specialists only.

VASARI expressly mentions Leonardo's anatomical studies, having had occasion to examine the manuscript books which refer to them. According to him Leonardo studied Anatomy in the companionship of Marc Antonio della Torre "aiutato e scambievolmente aiutando."--This learned Anatomist taught the science in the universities first of Padua and then of Pavia, and at Pavia he and Leonardo may have worked and studied together. We have no clue to any exact dates, but in the year 1506 Marc Antonio della Torre seems to have not yet left Padua. He was scarcely thirty years old when he died in 1512, and his writings on anatomy have not only never been published, but no manuscript copy of them is known to exist.

This is not the place to enlarge on the connection between Leonardo and Marc Antonio della Torre. I may however observe that I have not been able to discover in Leonardo's manuscripts on anatomy any mention of his younger contemporary. The few quotations which occur from writers on medicine-- either of antiquity or of the middle ages are printed in Section XXII. Here and there in the manuscripts mention is made of an anonymous "adversary" (avversario) whose views are opposed and refuted by Leonardo, but there is no ground for supposing that Marc Antonio della Torre should have been this "adversary".

Only a very small selection from the mass of anatomical drawings left by Leonardo have been published here in facsimile, but to form any adequate idea of their scientific merit they should be compared with the coarse and inadequate figures given in the published books of the early part of the XVI. century.

William Hunter, the great surgeon--a competent judge--who had an opportunity in the time of George III. of seeing the originals in the King's Library, has thus recorded his opinion: "I expected to see little more than such designs in Anatomy as might be useful to a painter in his own profession. But I saw, and indeed with astonishment, that Leonardo had been a general and deep student. When I consider what pains he has taken upon every part of the body, the superiority of his universal genius, his particular excellence in mechanics and hydraulics, and the attention with which such a man would examine and see objects which he has to draw, I am fully persuaded that Leonardo was the best Anatomist, at that time, in the world ... Leonardo was certainly the first man, we know of, who introduced the practice of making anatomical drawings" (Two introductory letters. London 1784, pages 37 and 39).

The illustrious German Naturalist Johan Friedrich Blumenback esteemed them no less highly; he was one of the privileged few who, after Hunter, had the chance of seeing these Manuscripts. He writes: Der Scharfblick dieses grossen Forschers und Darstellers der Natur hat schon auf Dinge geachtet, die noch Jahrhunderte nachher unbemerkt geblieben sind" (see Blumenbach's medicinische Bibliothek, Vol. 3, St. 4, 1795. page 728).

These opinions were founded on the drawings alone. Up to the present day hardly anything has been made known of the text, and, for the reasons I have given, it is my intention to reproduce here no more than a selection of extracts which I have made from the originals at Windsor Castle and elsewhere. In the Bibliography of the Manuscripts, at the end of this volume a short review is given of the valuable contents of these Anatomical note books which are at present almost all in the possession of her Majesty the Queen of England. It is, I believe, possible to assign the date with approximate accuracy to almost all the fragments, and I am thus led to conclude that the greater part of Leonardo's anatomical investigations were carried out after the death of della Torre.

Merely in reading the introductory notes to his various books on Anatomy which are here printed it is impossible to resist the impression that the Master's anatomical studies bear to a very great extent the stamp of originality and independent thought.

I.

ANATOMY.

796.

A general introduction

I wish to work miracles;--it may be that I shall possess less than other men of more peaceful lives, or than those who want to grow rich in a day. I may live for a long time in great poverty, as always happens, and to all eternity will happen, to alchemists, the would-be creators of gold and silver, and to engineers who would have dead water stir itself into life and perpetual motion, and to those supreme fools, the necromancer and the enchanter.

[Footnote 23: The following seems to be directed against students of painting and young artists rather than against medical men and anatomists.]

And you, who say that it would be better to watch an anatomist at work than to see these drawings, you would be right, if it were possible to observe all the things which are demonstrated in such drawings in a single figure, in which you, with all your cleverness, will not see nor obtain knowledge of more than some few veins, to obtain a true and perfect knowledge of which I have dissected more than ten human bodies, destroying all the other members, and removing the very minutest particles of the flesh by which these veins are surrounded, without causing them to bleed, excepting the insensible bleeding of the capillary veins; and as one single body would not last so long, since it was necessary to proceed with several bodies by degrees, until I came to an end and had a complete knowledge; this I repeated twice, to learn the differences [59].

[Footnote: Lines 1-59 and 60-89 are written in two parallel columns. When we here find Leonardo putting himself in the same category as the Alchemists and Necromancers, whom he elsewhere mocks at so bitterly, it is evidently meant ironically. In the same way Leonardo, in the introduction to the Books on Perspective sets himself with transparent satire on a level with other writers on the subject.]

And if you should have a love for such things you might be prevented by loathing, and if that did not prevent you, you might be deterred by the fear of living in the night hours in the company of those corpses, quartered and flayed and horrible to see. And if this did not prevent you, perhaps you might not be able to draw so well as is necessary for such a demonstration; or, if you had the skill in drawing, it might not be combined with knowledge of perspective; and if it were so, you might not understand the methods of geometrical demonstration and the method of the calculation of forces and of the strength of the muscles; patience also may be wanting, so that you lack perseverance. As to whether all these things were found in me or not [Footnote 84: Leonardo frequently, and perhaps habitually, wrote in note books of a very small size and only moderately thick; in most of those which have been preserved undivided, each contains less than fifty leaves. Thus a considerable number of such volumes must have gone to make up a volume of the bulk of the 'Codex Atlanticus' which now contains nearly 1200 detached leaves. In the passage under consideration, which was evidently written at a late period of his life, Leonardo speaks of his Manuscript note-books as numbering 120; but we should hardly be justified in concluding from this passage that the greater part of his Manuscripts were now missing (see Prolegomena, Vol. I, pp. 5-7).], the hundred and twenty books composed by me will give verdict Yes or No. In these I have been hindered neither by avarice nor negligence, but simply by want of time. Farewell [89].

Plans and suggestions for the arrangement of materials (797-802).

797.

OF THE ORDER OF THE BOOK.

This work must begin with the conception of man, and describe the nature of the womb and how the foetus lives in it, up to what stage it resides there, and in what way it quickens into life and feeds. Also its growth and what interval there is between one stage of growth and another. What it is that forces it out from the body of the mother, and for what reasons it sometimes comes out of the mother's womb before the due time.

Then I will describe which are the members, which, after the boy is born, grow more than the others, and determine the proportions of a boy of one year.

Then describe the fully grown man and woman, with their proportions, and the nature of their complexions, colour, and physiognomy.

Then how they are composed of veins, tendons, muscles and bones. This I shall do at the end of the book. Then, in four drawings, represent four universal conditions of men. That is, Mirth, with various acts of laughter, and describe the cause of laughter. Weeping in various aspects with its causes. Contention, with various acts of killing; flight, fear, ferocity, boldness, murder and every thing pertaining to such cases. Then represent Labour, with pulling, thrusting, carrying, stopping, supporting and such like things.

Further I would describe attitudes and movements. Then perspective, concerning the functions and effects of the eye; and of hearing--here I will speak of music--, and treat of the other senses.

And then describe the nature of the senses.

This mechanism of man we will demonstrate in ... figures; of which the three first will show the ramification of the bones; that is: first one to show their height and position and shape: the second will be seen in profile and will show the depth of the whole and of the parts, and their position. The third figure will be a demonstration of the bones of the backparts. Then I will make three other figures from the same point of view, with the bones sawn across, in which will be shown their thickness and hollowness. Three other figures of the bones complete, and of the nerves which rise from the nape of the neck, and in what limbs they ramify. And three others of the bones and veins, and where they ramify. Then three figures with the muscles and three with the skin, and their proper proportions; and three of woman, to illustrate the womb and the menstrual veins which go to the breasts.

[Footnote: The meaning of the word nervo varies in different passages, being sometimes used for muscolo (muscle).]

798.

THE ORDER OF THE BOOK.

This depicting of mine of the human body will be as clear to you as if you had the natural man before you; and the reason is that if you wish thoroughly to know the parts of man, anatomically, you--or your eye--require to see it from different aspects, considering it from below and from above and from its sides, turning it about and seeking the origin of each member; and in this way the natural anatomy is sufficient for your comprehension. But you must understand that this amount of knowledge will not continue to satisfy you; seeing the very great confusion that must result from the combination of tissues, with veins, arteries, nerves, sinews, muscles, bones, and blood which, of itself, tinges every part the same colour. And the veins, which discharge this blood, are not discerned by reason of their smallness. Moreover integrity of the tissues, in the process of the investigating the parts within them, is inevitably destroyed, and their transparent substance being tinged with blood does not allow you to recognise the parts covered by them, from the similarity of their blood-stained hue; and you cannot know everything of the one without confusing and destroying the other. Hence, some further anatomy drawings become necessary. Of which you want three to give full knowledge of the veins and arteries, everything else being destroyed with the greatest care. And three others to display the tissues; and three for the sinews and muscles and ligaments; and three for the bones and cartilages; and three for the anatomy of the bones, which have to be sawn to show which are hollow and which are not, which have marrow and which are spongy, and which are thick from the outside inwards, and which are thin. And some are extremely thin in some parts and thick in others, and in some parts hollow or filled up with bone, or full of marrow, or spongy. And all these conditions are sometimes found in one and the same bone, and in some bones none of them. And three you must have for the woman, in which there is much that is mysterious by reason of the womb and the foetus. Therefore by my drawings every part will be known to you, and all by means of demonstrations from three different points of view of each part; for when you have seen a limb from the front, with any muscles, sinews, or veins which take their rise from the opposite side, the same limb will be shown to you in a side view or from behind, exactly as if you had that same limb in your hand and were turning it from side to side until you had acquired a full comprehension of all you wished to know. In the same way there will be put before you three or four demonstrations of each limb, from various points of view, so that you will be left with a true and complete knowledge of all you wish to learn of the human figure[Footnote 35: Compare Pl. CVII. The original drawing at Windsor is 28 1/2 X 19 1/2 centimetres. The upper figures are slightly washed with Indian ink. On the back of this drawing is the text No. 1140.].

Thus, in twelve entire figures, you will have set before you the cosmography of this lesser world on the same plan as, before me, was adopted by Ptolemy in his cosmography; and so I will afterwards divide them into limbs as he divided the whole world into provinces; then I will speak of the function of each part in every direction, putting before your eyes a description of the whole form and substance of man, as regards his movements from place to place, by means of his different parts. And thus, if it please our great Author, I may demonstrate the nature of men, and their customs in the way I describe his figure.

And remember that the anatomy of the nerves will not give the position of their ramifications, nor show you which muscles they branch into, by means of bodies dissected in running water or in lime water; though indeed their origin and starting point may be seen without such water as well as with it. But their ramifications, when under running water, cling and unite--just like flat or hemp carded for spinning--all into a skein, in a way which makes it impossible to trace in which muscles or by what ramification the nerves are distributed among those muscles.

799.

THE ARRANGEMENT OF ANATOMY

First draw the bones, let us say, of the arm, and put in the motor muscle from the shoulder to the elbow with all its lines. Then proceed in the same way from the elbow to the wrist. Then from the wrist to the hand and from the hand to the fingers.

And in the arm you will put the motors of the fingers which open, and these you will show separately in their demonstration. In the second demonstration you will clothe these muscles with the secondary motors of the fingers and so proceed by degrees to avoid confusion. But first lay on the bones those muscles which lie close to the said bones, without confusion of other muscles; and with these you may put the nerves and veins which supply their nourishment, after having first drawn the tree of veins and nerves over the simple bones.

800.

Begin the anatomy at the head and finish at the sole of the foot.

801.

3 men complete, 3 with bones and nerves, 3 with the bones only. Here we have 12 demonstrations of entire figures.

802.

When you have finished building up the man, you will make the statue with all its superficial measurements.

[Footnote: Cresciere l'omo. The meaning of this expression appears to be different here and in the passage C.A. 157a, 468a (see No. 526, Note 1. 2). Here it can hardly mean anything else than modelling, since the sculptor forms the figure by degrees, by adding wet clay and the figure consequently increases or grows. Tu farai la statua would then mean, you must work out the figure in marble. If this interpretation is the correct one, this passage would have no right to find a place in the series on anatomical studies. I may say that it was originally inserted in this connection under the impression that di cresciere should be read descrivere.]

Plans for the representation of muscles by drawings (803-809).

803.

You must show all the motions of the bones with their joints to follow the demonstration of the first three figures of the bones, and this should be done in the first book.

804.

Remember that to be certain of the point of origin of any muscle, you must pull the sinew from which the muscle springs in such a way as to see that muscle move, and where it is attached to the ligaments of the bones.

NOTE.

You will never get any thing but confusion in demonstrating the muscles and their positions, origin, and termination, unless you first make a demonstration of thin muscles after the manner of linen threads; and thus you can represent them, one over another as nature has placed them; and thus, too, you can name them according to the limb they serve; for instance the motor of the point of the great toe, of its middle bone, of its first bone, &c. And when you have the knowledge you will draw, by the side of this, the true form and size and position of each muscle. But remember to give the threads which explain the situation of the muscles in the position which corresponds to the central line of each muscle; and so these threads will demonstrate the form of the leg and their distance in a plain and clear manner.

I have removed the skin from a man who was so shrunk by illness that the muscles were worn down and remained in a state like thin membrane, in such a way that the sinews instead of merging in muscles ended in wide membrane; and where the bones were covered by the skin they had very little over their natural size.

[Footnote: The photograph No. 41 of Grosvenor Gallery Publications: a drawing of the muscles of the foot, includes a complete facsimile of the text of this passage.]

805.

Which nerve causes the motion of the eye so that the motion of one eye moves the other?

Of frowning the brows, of raising the brows, of lowering the brows,--of closing the eyes, of opening the eyes,--of raising the nostrils, of opening the lips, with the teeth shut, of pouting with the lips, of smiling, of astonishment.--

Describe the beginning of man when it is caused in the womb and why an eight months child does not live. What sneezing is. What yawning is. Falling sickness, spasms, paralysis, shivering with cold, sweating, fatigue, hunger, sleepiness, thirst, lust.

Of the nerve which is the cause of movement from the shoulder to the elbow, of the movement from the elbow to the hand, from the joint of the hand to the springing of the fingers. From the springing of the fingers to the middle joints, and from the middle joints to the last.

Of the nerve which causes the movement of the thigh, and from the knee to the foot, and from the joint of the foot to the toes, and then to the middle of the toes and of the rotary motion of the leg.

806.

ANATOMY.

Which nerves or sinews of the hand are those which close and part the fingers and toes latteraly?

807.

Remove by degrees all the parts of the front of a man in making your dissection, till you come to the bones. Description of the parts of the bust and of their motions.

808.

Give the anatomy of the leg up to the hip, in all views and in every action and in every state; veins, arteries, nerves, sinews and muscles, skin and bones; then the bones in sections to show the thickness of the bones.

[Footnote: A straightened leg in profile is sketched by the side of this text.]

On corpulency and leanness (809-811).

809.

Make the rule and give the measurement of each muscle, and give the reasons of all their functions, and in which way they work and what makes them work &c.

[4] First draw the spine of the back; then clothe it by degrees, one after the other, with each of its muscles and put in the nerves and arteries and veins to each muscle by itself; and besides these note the vertebrae to which they are attached; which of the intestines come in contact with them; and which bones and other organs &c.

The most prominent parts of lean people are most prominent in the muscular, and equally so in fat persons. But concerning the difference in the forms of the muscles in fat persons as compared with muscular persons, it shall be described below.

[Footnote: The two drawings given on Pl. CVIII no. 1 come between lines 3 and 4. A good and very early copy of this drawing without the written text exists in the collection of drawings belonging to Christ's College Oxford, where it is attributed to Leonardo.]

810.

Describe which muscles disappear in growing fat, and which become visible in growing lean.

And observe that that part which on the surface of a fat person is most concave, when he grows lean becomes more prominent.

Where the muscles separate one from another you must give profiles and where they coalesce ...

811.

OF THE HUMAN FIGURE.

Which is the part in man, which, as he grows fatter, never gains flesh?

Or what part which as a man grows lean never falls away with a too perceptible diminution? And among the parts which grow fat which is that which grows fattest?

Among those which grow lean which is that which grows leanest?

In very strong men which are the muscles which are thickest and most prominent?

In your anatomy you must represent all the stages of the limbs from man's creation to his death, and then till the death of the bone; and which part of him is first decayed and which is preserved the longest.

And in the same way of extreme leanness and extreme fatness.

The divisions of the head (812. 813).

812.

ANATOMY.

There are eleven elementary tissues:-- Cartilage, bones, nerves, veins, arteries, fascia, ligament and sinews, skin, muscle and fat.

OF THE HEAD.

The divisions of the head are 10, viz. 5 external and 5 internal, the external are the hair, skin, muscle, fascia and the skull; the internal are the dura mater, the pia mater, [which enclose] the brain. The pia mater and the dura mater come again underneath and enclose the brain; then the rete mirabile, and the occipital bone, which supports the brain from which the nerves spring.

813.

a. hair

n. skin

c. muscle

m. fascia

o. skull i.e. bone

b. dura mater

d. pia mater

f. brain

r. pia mater, below

t. dura mater

l. rete mirablile

s. the occipitul bone.

[Footnote: See Pl. CVIII, No. 3.]

Physiological problems (814. 815).

814.

Of the cause of breathing, of the cause of the motion of the heart, of the cause of vomiting, of the cause of the descent of food from the stomach, of the cause of emptying the intestines.

Of the cause of the movement of the superfluous matter through the intestines.

Of the cause of swallowing, of the cause of coughing, of the cause of yawning, of the cause of sneezing, of the cause of limbs getting asleep.

Of the cause of losing sensibility in any limb.

Of the cause of tickling.

Of the cause of lust and other appetites of the body, of the cause of urine and also of all the natural excretions of the body.

[Footnote: By the side of this text stands the pen and ink drawing reproduced on Pl. CVIII, No. 4; a skull with indications of the veins in the fleshy covering.]

815.

The tears come from the heart and not from the brain.

Define all the parts, of which the body is composed, beginning with the skin with its outer cuticle which is often chapped by the influence of the sun.

II.

ZOOLOGY AND COMPARATIVE ANATOMY.

The divisions of the animal kingdom (816. 817).

816.

Man. The description of man, which includes that of such creatures as are of almost the same species, as Apes, Monkeys and the like, which are many,

The Lion and its kindred, as Panthers. [Footnote 3: Leonza--wild cat? "Secondo alcuni, lo stesso che Leonessa; e secondo altri con piu certezza, lo stesso che Pantera" FANFANI, Vocabolario page 858.] Wildcats (?) Tigers, Leopards, Wolfs, Lynxes, Spanish cats, common cats and the like.

The Horse and its kindred, as Mule, Ass and the like, with incisor teeth above and below.

The Bull and its allies with horns and without upper incisors as the Buffalo, Stag Fallow Deer, Wild Goat, Swine, Goat, wild Goats Muskdeers, Chamois, Giraffe.

817.

Describe the various forms of the intestines of the human species, of apes and such like. Then, in what way the leonine species differ, and then the bovine, and finally birds; and arrange this description after the manner of a disquisition.

Miscellaneous notes on the study of Zoology (818-821).

818.

Procure the placenta of a calf when it is born and observe the form of the cotyledons, if their cotyledons are male or female.

819.

Describe the tongue of the woodpecker and the jaw of the crocodile.

820.

Of the flight of the 4th kind of butterflies that consume winged ants. Of the three principal positions of the wings of birds in downward flight.

[Footnote: A passing allusion is all I can here permit myself to Leonardo's elaborate researches into the flight of birds. Compare the observations on this subject in the Introduction to section XVIII and in the Bibliography of Manuscripts at the end of the work.]

821.

Of the way in which the tail of a fish acts in propelling the fish; as in the eel, snake and leech.

[Footnote: A sketch of a fish, swimming upwards is in the original, inserted above this text.--Compare No. 1114.]

Comparative study of the structure of bones and of the action of muscles (822-826).

822.

OF THE PALM OF THE HAND.

Then I will discourse of the hands of each animal to show in what they vary; as in the bear, which has the ligatures of the sinews of the toes joined above the instep.

823.

A second demonstration inserted between anatomy and [the treatise on] the living being.

You will represent here for a comparison, the legs of a frog, which have a great resemblance to the legs of man, both in the bones and in the muscles. Then, in continuation, the hind legs of the hare, which are very muscular, with strong active muscles, because they are not encumbered with fat.

[Footnote: This text is written by the side of a drawing in black chalk of a nude male figure, but there is no connection between the sketch and the text.]

824.

Here I make a note to demonstrate the difference there is between man and the horse and in the same way with other animals. And first I will begin with the bones, and then will go on to all the muscles which spring from the bones without tendons and end in them in the same way, and then go on to those which start with a single tendon at one end.

[Footnote: See Pl. CVIII, No. 2.]

825.

Note on the bendings of joints and in what way the flesh grows upon them in their flexions or extensions; and of this most important study write a separate treatise: in the description of the movements of animals with four feet; among which is man, who likewise in his infancy crawls on all fours.

826.

OF THE WAY OF WALKING IN MAN.

The walking of man is always after the universal manner of walking in animals with 4 legs, inasmuch as just as they move their feet crosswise after the manner of a horse in trotting, so man moves his 4 limbs crosswise; that is, if he puts forward his right foot in walking he puts forward, with it, his left arm and vice versa, invariably.

III.

PHYSIOLOGY.

Comparative study of the organs of sense in men and animals.

827.

I have found that in the composition of the human body as compared with the bodies of animals the organs of sense are duller and coarser. Thus it is composed of less ingenious instruments, and of spaces less capacious for receiving the faculties of sense. I have seen in the Lion tribe that the sense of smell is connected with part of the substance of the brain which comes down the nostrils, which form a spacious receptacle for the sense of smell, which enters by a great number of cartilaginous vesicles with several passages leading up to where the brain, as before said, comes down.

The eyes in the Lion tribe have a large part of the head for their sockets and the optic nerves communicate at once with the brain; but the contrary is to be seen in man, for the sockets of the eyes are but a small part of the head, and the optic nerves are very fine and long and weak, and by the weakness of their action we see by day but badly at night, while these animals can see as well at night as by day. The proof that they can see is that they prowl for prey at night and sleep by day, as nocturnal birds do also.

Advantages in the structure of the eye in certain animals (828-831).

828.

Every object we see will appear larger at midnight than at midday, and larger in the morning than at midday.

This happens because the pupil of the eye is much smaller at midday than at any other time.

In proportion as the eye or the pupil of the owl is larger in proportion to the animal than that of man, so much the more light can it see at night than man can; hence at midday it can see nothing if its pupil does not diminish; and, in the same way, at night things look larger to it than by day.

829.

OF THE EYES IN ANIMALS.

The eyes of all animals have their pupils adapted to dilate and diminish of their own accord in proportion to the greater or less light of the sun or other luminary. But in birds the variation is much greater; and particularly in nocturnal birds, such as horned owls, and in the eyes of one species of owl; in these the pupil dilates in such away as to occupy nearly the whole eye, or diminishes to the size of a grain of millet, and always preserves the circular form. But in the Lion tribe, as panthers, pards, ounces, tigers, lynxes, Spanish cats and other similar animals the pupil diminishes from the perfect circle to the figure of a pointed oval such as is shown in the margin. But man having a weaker sight than any other animal is less hurt by a very strong light and his pupil increases but little in dark places; but in the eyes of these nocturnal animals, the horned owl--a bird which is the largest of all nocturnal birds--the power of vision increases so much that in the faintest nocturnal light (which we call darkness) it sees with much more distinctness than we do in the splendour of noon day, at which time these birds remain hidden in dark holes; or if indeed they are compelled to come out into the open air lighted up by the sun, they contract their pupils so much that their power of sight diminishes together with the quantity of light admitted.

Study the anatomy of various eyes and see which are the muscles which open and close the said pupils of the eyes of animals.

[Footnote: Compare No. 24, lines 8 and fol.]

830.

a b n is the membrane which closes the eye from below, upwards, with an opaque film, c n b encloses the eye in front and behind with a transparent membrane.

It closes from below, upwards, because it [the eye] comes downwards.

When the eye of a bird closes with its two lids, the first to close is the nictitating membrane which closes from the lacrymal duct over to the outer corner of the eye; and the outer lid closes from below upwards, and these two intersecting motions begin first from the lacrymatory duct, because we have already seen that in front and below birds are protected and use only the upper portion of the eye from fear of birds of prey which come down from above and behind; and they uncover first the membrane from the outer corner, because if the enemy comes from behind, they have the power of escaping to the front; and again the muscle called the nictitating membrane is transparent, because, if the eye had not such a screen, they could not keep it open against the wind which strikes against the eye in the rush of their rapid flight. And the pupil of the eye dilates and contracts as it sees a less or greater light, that is to say intense brilliancy.

831.

If at night your eye is placed between the light and the eye of a cat, it will see the eye look like fire.

Remarks on the organs of speech

(832. 833).

832.

a e i o u ba be bi bo bu ca ce ci co cu da de di do du fa fe fi fo fu ga ge gi go gu la le li lo lu ma me mi mo mu na ne ni no nu pa pe pi po pu qa qe qi qo qu ra re ri ro ru sa se si so su ta te ti to tu

The tongue is found to have 24 muscles which correspond to the six muscles which compose the portion of the tongue which moves in the mouth.

And when a o u are spoken with a clear and rapid pronunciation, it is necessary, in order to pronounce continuously, without any pause between, that the opening of the lips should close by degrees; that is, they are wide apart in saying a, closer in saying o, and much closer still to pronounce u.

It may be shown how all the vowels are pronounced with the farthest portion of the false palate which is above the epiglottis.

833.

If you draw in breath by the nose and send it out by the mouth you will hear the sound made by the division that is the membrane in [Footnote 5: The text here breaks off.]...

On the conditions of sight (834. 835).

834.

OF THE NATURE OF SIGHT.

I say that sight is exercised by all animals, by the medium of light; and if any one adduces, as against this, the sight of nocturnal animals, I must say that this in the same way is subject to the very same natural laws. For it will easily be understood that the senses which receive the images of things do not project from themselves any visual virtue [Footnote 4: Compare No. 68.]. On the contrary the atmospheric medium which exists between the object and the sense incorporates in itself the figure of things, and by its contact with the sense transmits the object to it. If the object--whether by sound or by odour--presents its spiritual force to the ear or the nose, then light is not required and does not act. The forms of objects do not send their images into the air if they are not illuminated [8]; and the eye being thus constituted cannot receive that from the air, which the air does not possess, although it touches its surface. If you choose to say that there are many animals that prey at night, I answer that when the little light which suffices the nature of their eyes is wanting, they direct themselves by their strong sense of hearing and of smell, which are not impeded by the darkness, and in which they are very far superior to man. If you make a cat leap, by daylight, among a quantity of jars and crocks you will see them remain unbroken, but if you do the same at night, many will be broken. Night birds do not fly about unless the moon shines full or in part; rather do they feed between sun-down and the total darkness of the night.

[Footnote 8: See No. 58-67.]

No body can be apprehended without light and shade, and light and shade are caused by light.

835.

WHY MEN ADVANCED IN AGE SEE BETTER AT A DISTANCE.

Sight is better from a distance than near in those men who are advancing in age, because the same object transmits a smaller impression of itself to the eye when it is distant than when it is near.

The seat of the common sense.

836.

The Common Sense, is that which judges of things offered to it by the other senses. The ancient speculators have concluded that that part of man which constitutes his judgment is caused by a central organ to which the other five senses refer everything by means of impressibility; and to this centre they have given the name Common Sense. And they say that this Sense is situated in the centre of the head between Sensation and Memory. And this name of Common Sense is given to it solely because it is the common judge of all the other five senses i.e. Seeing, Hearing, Touch, Taste and Smell. This Common Sense is acted upon by means of Sensation which is placed as a medium between it and the senses. Sensation is acted upon by means of the images of things presented to it by the external instruments, that is to say the senses which are the medium between external things and Sensation. In the same way the senses are acted upon by objects. Surrounding things transmit their images to the senses and the senses transfer them to the Sensation. Sensation sends them to the Common Sense, and by it they are stamped upon the memory and are there more or less retained according to the importance or force of the impression. That sense is most rapid in its function which is nearest to the sensitive medium and the eye, being the highest is the chief of the others. Of this then only we will speak, and the others we will leave in order not to make our matter too long. Experience tells us that the eye apprehends ten different natures of things, that is: Light and Darkness, one being the cause of the perception of the nine others, and the other its absence:-- Colour and substance, form and place, distance and nearness, motion and stillness [Footnote 15: Compare No. 23.].

On the origin of the soul.

837.

Though human ingenuity may make various inventions which, by the help of various machines answering the same end, it will never devise any inventions more beautiful, nor more simple, nor more to the purpose than Nature does; because in her inventions nothing is wanting, and nothing is superfluous, and she needs no counterpoise when she makes limbs proper for motion in the bodies of animals. But she puts into them the soul of the body, which forms them that is the soul of the mother which first constructs in the womb the form of the man and in due time awakens the soul that is to inhabit it. And this at first lies dormant and under the tutelage of the soul of the mother, who nourishes and vivifies it by the umbilical vein, with all its spiritual parts, and this happens because this umbilicus is joined to the placenta and the cotyledons, by which the child is attached to the mother. And these are the reason why a wish, a strong craving or a fright or any other mental suffering in the mother, has more influence on the child than on the mother; for there are many cases when the child loses its life from them, &c.

This discourse is not in its place here, but will be wanted for the one on the composition of animated bodies--and the rest of the definition of the soul I leave to the imaginations of friars, those fathers of the people who know all secrets by inspiration.

[Footnote 57: lettere incoronate. By this term Leonardo probably understands not the Bible only, but the works of the early Fathers, and all the books recognised as sacred by the Roman Church.] I leave alone the sacred books; for they are supreme truth.

On the relations of the soul to the organs of sense.

838.

HOW THE FIVE SENSES ARE THE MINISTERS OF THE SOUL.

The soul seems to reside in the judgment, and the judgment would seem to be seated in that part where all the senses meet; and this is called the Common Sense and is not all-pervading throughout the body, as many have thought. Rather is it entirely in one part. Because, if it were all-pervading and the same in every part, there would have been no need to make the instruments of the senses meet in one centre and in one single spot; on the contrary it would have sufficed that the eye should fulfil the function of its sensation on its surface only, and not transmit the image of the things seen, to the sense, by means of the optic nerves, so that the soul--for the reason given above-- may perceive it in the surface of the eye. In the same way as to the sense of hearing, it would have sufficed if the voice had merely sounded in the porous cavity of the indurated portion of the temporal bone which lies within the ear, without making any farther transit from this bone to the common sense, where the voice confers with and discourses to the common judgment. The sense of smell, again, is compelled by necessity to refer itself to that same judgment. Feeling passes through the perforated cords and is conveyed to this common sense. These cords diverge with infinite ramifications into the skin which encloses the members of the body and the viscera. The perforated cords convey volition and sensation to the subordinate limbs. These cords and the nerves direct the motions of the muscles and sinews, between which they are placed; these obey, and this obedience takes effect by reducing their thickness; for in swelling, their length is reduced, and the nerves shrink which are interwoven among the particles of the limbs; being extended to the tips of the fingers, they transmit to the sense the object which they touch.

The nerves with their muscles obey the tendons as soldiers obey the officers, and the tendons obey the Common [central] Sense as the officers obey the general. [27] Thus the joint of the bones obeys the nerve, and the nerve the muscle, and the muscle the tendon and the tendon the Common Sense. And the Common Sense is the seat of the soul [28], and memory is its ammunition, and the impressibility is its referendary since the sense waits on the soul and not the soul on the sense. And where the sense that ministers to the soul is not at the service of the soul, all the functions of that sense are also wanting in that man's life, as is seen in those born mute and blind.

[Footnote: The peculiar use of the words nervo, muscolo, corda, senso comune, which are here literally rendered by nerve, muscle cord or tendon and Common Sense may be understood from lines 27 and 28.]

On involuntary muscular action.

839.

HOW THE NERVES SOMETIMES ACT OF THEMSELVES WITHOUT ANY COMMANDS FROM THE OTHER FUNCTIONS OF THE SOUL.

This is most plainly seen; for you will see palsied and shivering persons move, and their trembling limbs, as their head and hands, quake without leave from their soul and their soul with all its power cannot prevent their members from trembling. The same thing happens in falling sickness, or in parts that have been cut off, as in the tails of lizards. The idea or imagination is the helm and guiding-rein of the senses, because the thing conceived of moves the sense. Pre-imagining, is imagining the things that are to be. Post-imagining, is imagining the things that are past.

Miscellaneous physiological observations (840-842).

840.

There are four Powers: memory and intellect, desire and covetousness. The two first are mental and the others sensual. The three senses: sight, hearing and smell cannot well be prevented; touch and taste not at all. Smell is connected with taste in dogs and other gluttonous animals.

841.

I reveal to men the origin of the first, or perhaps second cause of their existence.

842.

Lust is the cause of generation.

Appetite is the support of life. Fear or timidity is the prolongation of life and preservation of its instruments.

The laws of nutrition and the support of life (843-848).

843.

HOW THE BODY OF ANIMALS IS CONSTANTLY DYING AND BEING RENEWED.

The body of any thing whatever that takes nourishment constantly dies and is constantly renewed; because nourishment can only enter into places where the former nourishment has expired, and if it has expired it no longer has life. And if you do not supply nourishment equal to the nourishment which is gone, life will fail in vigour, and if you take away this nourishment, the life is entirely destroyed. But if you restore as much is destroyed day by day, then as much of the life is renewed as is consumed, just as the flame of the candle is fed by the nourishment afforded by the liquid of this candle, which flame continually with a rapid supply restores to it from below as much as is consumed in dying above: and from a brilliant light is converted in dying into murky smoke; and this death is continuous, as the smoke is continuous; and the continuance of the smoke is equal to the continuance of the nourishment, and in the same instant all the flame is dead and all regenerated, simultaneously with the movement of its own nourishment.

844.

King of the animals--as thou hast described him--I should rather say king of the beasts, thou being the greatest--because thou hast spared slaying them, in order that they may give thee their children for the benefit of the gullet, of which thou hast attempted to make a sepulchre for all animals; and I would say still more, if it were allowed me to speak the entire truth [5]. But we do not go outside human matters in telling of one supreme wickedness, which does not happen among the animals of the earth, inasmuch as among them are found none who eat their own kind, unless through want of sense (few indeed among them, and those being mothers, as with men, albeit they be not many in number); and this happens only among the rapacious animals, as with the leonine species, and leopards, panthers lynxes, cats and the like, who sometimes eat their children; but thou, besides thy children devourest father, mother, brothers and friends; nor is this enough for thee, but thou goest to the chase on the islands of others, taking other men and these half-naked, the ... and the ... thou fattenest, and chasest them down thy own throat[18]; now does not nature produce enough simples, for thee to satisfy thyself? and if thou art not content with simples, canst thou not by the mixture of them make infinite compounds, as Platina wrote[Footnote 21: Come scrisse il Platina (Bartolomeo Sacchi, a famous humanist). The Italian edition of his treatise De arte coquinaria, was published under the title De la honestra voluptate, e valetudine, Venezia 1487.], and other authors on feeding?

[Footnote: We are led to believe that Leonardo himself was a vegetarian from the following interesting passage in the first of Andrea Corsali's letters to Giuliano de'Medici: Alcuni gentili chiamati Guzzarati non si cibano di cosa, alcuna che tenga sangue, ne fra essi loro consentono che si noccia ad alcuna cosa animata, come il nostro Leonardo da Vinci.

5-18. Amerigo Vespucci, with whom Leonardo was personally acquainted, writes in his second letter to Pietro Soderini, about the inhabitants of the Canary Islands after having stayed there in 1503: "Hanno una scelerata liberta di viuere; ... si cibano di carne humana, di maniera che il padre magia il figliuolo, et all'incontro il figliuolo il padre secondo che a caso e per sorte auiene. Io viddi un certo huomo sceleratissimo che si vantaua, et si teneua a non piccola gloria di hauer mangiato piu di trecento huomini. Viddi anche vna certa citta, nella quale io dimorai forse ventisette giorni, doue le carni humane, hauendole salate, eran appicate alli traui, si come noi alli traui di cucina appicchiamo le carni di cinghali secche al sole o al fumo, et massimamente salsiccie, et altre simil cose: anzi si marauigliauano gradem ete che noi non magiaissimo della carne de nemici, le quali dicono muouere appetito, et essere di marauiglioso sapore, et le lodano come cibi soaui et delicati (Lettere due di Amerigo Vespucci Fiorentino drizzate al magnifico Pietro Soderini, Gonfaloniere della eccelsa Republica di Firenze; various editions).]

845.

Our life is made by the death of others.

In dead matter insensible life remains, which, reunited to the stomachs of living beings, resumes life, both sensual and intellectual.

846.

Here nature appears with many animals to have been rather a cruel stepmother than a mother, and with others not a stepmother, but a most tender mother.

847.

Man and animals are really the passage and the conduit of food, the sepulchre of animals and resting place of the dead, one causing the death of the other, making themselves the covering for the corruption of other dead [bodies].

On the circulation of the blood (848-850).

848.

Death in old men, when not from fever, is caused by the veins which go from the spleen to the valve of the liver, and which thicken so much in the walls that they become closed up and leave no passage for the blood that nourishes it.

[6]The incessant current of the blood through the veins makes these veins thicken and become callous, so that at last they close up and prevent the passage of the blood.

849.

The waters return with constant motion from the lowest depths of the sea to the utmost height of the mountains, not obeying the nature of heavier bodies; and in this they resemble the blood of animated beings which always moves from the sea of the heart and flows towards the top of the head; and here it may burst a vein, as may be seen when a vein bursts in the nose; all the blood rises from below to the level of the burst vein. When the water rushes out from the burst vein in the earth, it obeys the law of other bodies that are heavier than the air since it always seeks low places.

[Footnote: From this passage it is quite plain that Leonardo had not merely a general suspicion of the circulation of the blood but a very clear conception of it. Leonardo's studies on the muscles of the heart are to be found in the MS. W. An. III. but no information about them has hitherto been made public. The limits of my plan in this work exclude all purely anatomical writings, therefore only a very brief excerpt from this note book can be given here. WILLIAM HARVEY (born 1578 and Professor of Anatomy at Cambridge from 1615) is always considered to have been the discoverer of the circulation of the blood. He studied medicine at Padua in 1598, and in 1628 brought out his memorable and important work: De motu cordis et sanguinis.]

850.

That the blood which returns when the heart opens again is not the same as that which closes the valves of the heart.

Some notes on medicine (851-855).

851.

Make them give you the definition and remedies for the case ... and you will see that men are selected to be doctors for diseases they do not know.

852.

A remedy for scratches taught me by the Herald to the King of France. 4 ounces of virgin wax, 4 ounces of colophony, 2 ounces of incense. Keep each thing separate; and melt the wax, and then put in the incense and then the colophony, make a mixture of it and put it on the sore place.

853.

Medicine is the restoration of discordant elements; sickness is the discord of the elements infused into the living body.

854.

Those who are annoyed by sickness at sea should drink extract of wormwood.

855.

To keep in health, this rule is wise: Eat only when you want and relish food. Chew thoroughly that it may do you good. Have it well cooked, unspiced and undisguised. He who takes medicine is ill advised.

[Footnote: This appears to be a sketch for a poem.]

856.

I teach you to preserve your health; and in this you will succed better in proportion as you shun physicians, because their medicines are the work of alchemists.

[Footnote: This passage is written on the back of the drawing Pl. CVIII. Compare also No. 1184.]

XV. Astronomy.

Ever since the publication by Venturi in 1797 and Libri in 1840 of some few passages of Leonardo's astronomical notes, scientific astronomers have frequently expressed the opinion, that they must have been based on very important discoveries, and that the great painter also deserved a conspicuous place in the history of this science. In the passages here printed, a connected view is given of his astronomical studies as they lie scattered through the manuscripts, which have come down to us. Unlike his other purely scientific labours, Leonardo devotes here a good deal of attention to the opinions of the ancients, though he does not follow the practice universal in his day of relying on them as authorities; he only quotes them, as we shall see, in order to refute their arguments. His researches throughout have the stamp of independent thought. There is nothing in these writings to lead us to suppose that they were merely an epitome of the general learning common to the astronomers of the period. As early as in the XIVth century there were chairs of astronomy in the universities of Padua and Bologna, but so late as during the entire XVIth century Astronomy and Astrology were still closely allied.

It is impossible now to decide whether Leonardo, when living in Florence, became acquainted in his youth with the doctrines of Paolo Toscanelli the great astronomer and mathematician (died 1482), of whose influence and teaching but little is now known, beyond the fact that he advised and encouraged Columbus to carry out his project of sailing round the world. His name is nowhere mentioned by Leonardo, and from the dates of the manuscripts from which the texts on astronomy are taken, it seems highly probable that Leonardo devoted his attention to astronomical studies less in his youth than in his later years. It was evidently his purpose to treat of Astronomy in a connected form and in a separate work (see the beginning of Nos. 866 and 892; compare also No. 1167). It is quite in accordance with his general scientific thoroughness that he should propose to write a special treatise on Optics as an introduction to Astronomy (see Nos. 867 and 877). Some of the chapters belonging to this Section bear the title "Prospettiva" (see Nos. 869 and 870), this being the term universally applied at the time to Optics as well as Perspective (see Vol. I, p. 10, note to No. 13, l. 10).

At the beginning of the XVIth century the Ptolemaic theory of the universe was still universally accepted as the true one, and Leonardo conceives of the earth as fixed, with the moon and sun revolving round it, as they are represented in the diagram to No. 897. He does not go into any theory of the motions of the planets; with regard to these and the fixed stars he only investigates the phenomena of their luminosity. The spherical form of the earth he takes for granted as an axiom from the first, and he anticipates Newton by pointing out the universality of Gravitation not merely in the earth, but even in the moon. Although his acute research into the nature of the moon's light and the spots on the moon did not bring to light many results of lasting importance beyond making it evident that they were a refutation of the errors of his contemporaries, they contain various explanations of facts which modern science need not modify in any essential point, and discoveries which history has hitherto assigned to a very much later date.

The ingenious theory by which he tries to explain the nature of what is known as earth shine, the reflection of the sun's rays by the earth towards the moon, saying that it is a peculiar refraction, originating in the innumerable curved surfaces of the waves of the sea may be regarded as absurd; but it must not be forgotten that he had no means of detecting the fundamental error on which he based it, namely: the assumption that the moon was at a relatively short distance from the earth. So long as the motion of the earth round the sun remained unknown, it was of course impossible to form any estimate of the moon's distance from the earth by a calculation of its parallax.

Before the discovery of the telescope accurate astronomical observations were only possible to a very limited extent. It would appear however from certain passages in the notes here printed for the first time, that Leonardo was in a position to study the spots in the moon more closely than he could have done with the unaided eye. So far as can be gathered from the mysterious language in which the description of his instrument is wrapped, he made use of magnifying glasses; these do not however seem to have been constructed like a telescope--telescopes were first made about 1600. As LIBRI pointed out (Histoire des Sciences mathematiques III, 101) Fracastoro of Verona (1473-1553) succeeded in magnifying the moon's face by an arrangement of lenses (compare No. 910, note), and this gives probability to Leonardo's invention at a not much earlier date.

I.

THE EARTH AS A PLANET.

The earth's place in the universe (857. 858).

857.

The equator, the line of the horizon, the ecliptic, the meridian:

These lines are those which in all their parts are equidistant from the centre of the globe.

858.

The earth is not in the centre of the Sun's orbit nor at the centre of the universe, but in the centre of its companion elements, and united with them. And any one standing on the moon, when it and the sun are both beneath us, would see this our earth and the element of water upon it just as we see the moon, and the earth would light it as it lights us.

The fundamental laws of the solar system (859-864).

859.

Force arises from dearth or abundance; it is the child of physical motion, and the grand-child of spiritual motion, and the mother and origin of gravity. Gravity is limited to the elements of water and earth; but this force is unlimited, and by it infinite worlds might be moved if instruments could be made by which the force could be generated.

Force, with physical motion, and gravity, with resistance are the four external powers on which all actions of mortals depend.

Force has its origin in spiritual motion; and this motion, flowing through the limbs of sentient animals, enlarges their muscles. Being enlarged by this current the muscles are shrunk in length and contract the tendons which are connected with them, and this is the cause of the force of the limbs in man.

The quality and quantity of the force of a man are able to give birth to other forces, which will be proportionally greater as the motions produced by them last longer.

[Footnote: Only part of this passage belongs, strictly speaking, to this section. The principle laid down in the second paragraph is more directly connected with the notes given in the preceding section on Physiology.]

860.

Why does not the weight o remain in its place? It does not remain because it has no resistance. Where will it move to? It will move towards the centre [of gravity]. And why by no other line? Because a weight which has no support falls by the shortest road to the lowest point which is the centre of the world. And why does the weight know how to find it by so short a line? Because it is not independant and does not move about in various directions.

[Footnote: This text and the sketch belonging to it, are reproduced on Pl. CXXI.]

861.

Let the earth turn on which side it may the surface of the waters will never move from its spherical form, but will always remain equidistant from the centre of the globe.

Granting that the earth might be removed from the centre of the globe, what would happen to the water?

It would remain in a sphere round that centre equally thick, but the sphere would have a smaller diameter than when it enclosed the earth.

[Footnote: Compare No. 896, lines 48-64; and No. 936.]

862.

Supposing the earth at our antipodes which supports the ocean were to rise and stand uncovered, far out of the sea, but remaining almost level, by what means afterwards, in the course of time, would mountains and vallies be formed?

And the rocks with their various strata?

863.

Each man is always in the middle of the surface of the earth and under the zenith of his own hemisphere, and over the centre of the earth.

864.

Mem.: That I must first show the distance of the sun from the earth; and, by means of a ray passing through a small hole into a dark chamber, detect its real size; and besides this, by means of the aqueous sphere calculate the size of the globe ...

Here it will be shown, that when the sun is in the meridian of our hemisphere [Footnote 10: Antipodi orientali cogli occidentali. The word Antipodes does not here bear its literal sense, but--as we may infer from the simultaneous reference to inhabitants of the North and South-- is used as meaning men living at a distance of 90 degrees from the zenith of the rational horizon of each observer.], the antipodes to the East and to the West, alike, and at the same time, see the sun mirrored in their waters; and the same is equally true of the arctic and antarctic poles, if indeed they are inhabited.

How to prove that the earth is a planet (865-867).

865.

That the earth is a star.

866.

In your discourse you must prove that the earth is a star much like the moon, and the glory of our universe; and then you must treat of the size of various stars, according to the authors.

867.

THE METHOD OF PROVING THAT THE EARTH IS A STAR.

First describe the eye; then show how the twinkling of a star is really in the eye and why one star should twinkle more than another, and how the rays from the stars originate in the eye; and add, that if the twinkling of the stars were really in the stars --as it seems to be--that this twinkling appears to be an extension as great as the diameter of the body of the star; therefore, the star being larger than the earth, this motion effected in an instant would be a rapid doubling of the size of the star. Then prove that the surface of the air where it lies contiguous to fire, and the surface of the fire where it ends are those into which the solar rays penetrate, and transmit the images of the heavenly bodies, large when they rise, and small, when they are on the meridian. Let a be the earth and n d m the surface of the air in contact with the sphere of fire; h f g is the orbit of the moon or, if you please, of the sun; then I say that when the sun appears on the horizon g, its rays are seen passing through the surface of the air at a slanting angle, that is o m; this is not the case at d k. And so it passes through a greater mass of air; all of e m is a denser atmosphere.

868.

Beyond the sun and us there is darkness and so the air appears blue.

[Footnote: Compare Vol. I, No. 301.]

869.

PERSPECTIVE.

It is possible to find means by which the eye shall not see remote objects as much diminished as in natural perspective, which diminishes them by reason of the convexity of the eye which necessarily intersects, at its surface, the pyramid of every image conveyed to the eye at a right angle on its spherical surface. But by the method I here teach in the margin [9] these pyramids are intersected at right angles close to the surface of the pupil. The convex pupil of the eye can take in the whole of our hemisphere, while this will show only a single star; but where many small stars transmit their images to the surface of the pupil those stars are extremely small; here only one star is seen but it will be large. And so the moon will be seen larger and its spots of a more defined form [Footnote 20 and fol.: Telescopes were not in use till a century later. Compare No. 910 and page 136.]. You must place close to the eye a glass filled with the water of which mention is made in number 4 of Book 113 "On natural substances" [Footnote 23: libro 113. This is perhaps the number of a book in some library catalogue. But it may refer, on the other hand, to one of the 120 Books mentioned in No. 796. I. 84.]; for this water makes objects which are enclosed in balls of crystalline glass appear free from the glass.

OF THE EYE.

Among the smaller objects presented to the pupil of the eye, that which is closest to it, will be least appreciable to the eye. And at the same time, the experiments here made with the power of sight, show that it is not reduced to speck if the &c. [32][Footnote 32: Compare with this the passage in Vol. I, No. 52, written about twenty years earlier.].

Read in the margin.

[34]Those objects are seen largest which come to the eye at the largest angles.

But the images of the objects conveyed to the pupil of the eye are distributed to the pupil exactly as they are distributed in the air: and the proof of this is in what follows; that when we look at the starry sky, without gazing more fixedly at one star than another, the sky appears all strewn with stars; and their proportions to the eye are the same as in the sky and likewise the spaces between them [61].

[Footnote: 9. 32. in margine: lines 34-61 are, in the original, written on the margin and above them is the diagram to which Leonardo seems to refer here.]

870.

PERSPECTIVE.

Among objects moved from the eye at equal distance, that undergoes least diminution which at first was most remote.

When various objects are removed at equal distances farther from their original position, that which was at first the farthest from the eye will diminish least. And the proportion of the diminution will be in proportion to the relative distance of the objects from the eye before they were removed.

That is to say in the object t and the object e the proportion of their distances from the eye a is quintuple. I remove each from its place and set it farther from the eye by one of the 5 parts into which the proposition is divided. Hence it happens that the nearest to the eye has doubled the distance and according to the last proposition but one of this, is diminished by the half of its whole size; and the body e, by the same motion, is diminished 1/5 of its whole size. Therefore, by that same last proposition but one, that which is said in this last proposition is true; and this I say of the motions of the celestial bodies which are more distant by 3500 miles when setting than when overhead, and yet do not increase or diminish in any sensible degree.

871.

a b is the aperture through which the sun passes, and if you could measure the size of the solar rays at n m, you could accurately trace the real lines of the convergence of the solar rays, the mirror being at a b, and then show the reflected rays at equal angles to n m; but, as you want to have them at n m, take them at the. inner side of the aperture at cd, where they maybe measured at the spot where the solar rays fall. Then place your mirror at the distance a b, making the rays d b, c a fall and then be reflected at equal angles towards c d; and this is the best method, but you must use this mirror always in the same month, and the same day, and hour and instant, and this will be better than at no fixed time because when the sun is at a certain distance it produces a certain pyramid of rays.

872.

a, the side of the body in light and shade b, faces the whole portion of the hemisphere bed e f, and does not face any part of the darkness of the earth. And the same occurs at the point o; therefore the space a o is throughout of one and the same brightness, and s faces only four degrees of the hemisphere d e f g h, and also the whole of the earth s h, which will render it darker; and how much must be demonstrated by calculation. [Footnote: This passage, which has perhaps a doubtful right to its place in this connection, stands in the Manuscript between those given in Vol. I as No. 117 and No. 427.]

873.

THE REASON OF THE INCREASED SIZE OF THE SUN IN THE WEST.

Some mathematicians explain that the sun looks larger as it sets, because the eye always sees it through a denser atmosphere, alleging that objects seen through mist or through water appear larger. To these I reply: No; because objects seen through a mist are similar in colour to those at a distance; but not being similarly diminished they appear larger. Again, nothing increases in size in smooth water; and the proof of this may be seen by throwing a light on a board placed half under water. But the reason why the sun looks larger is that every luminous body appears larger in proportion as it is more remote. [Footnote: Lines 5 and 6 are thus rendered by M. RAVAISSON in his edition of MS. A. "De meme, aucune chose ne croit dans l'eau plane, et tu en feras l'experience en calquant un ais sous l'eau."--Compare the diagrams in Vol. I, p. 114.]

On the luminosity of the Earth in the universal space (874-878).

874.

In my book I propose to show, how the ocean and the other seas must, by means of the sun, make our world shine with the appearance of a moon, and to the remoter worlds it looks like a star; and this I shall prove.

Show, first that every light at a distance from the eye throws out rays which appear to increase the size of the luminous body; and from this it follows that 2 ...[Footnote 10: Here the text breaks off; lines 11 and fol. are written in the margin.].

[11]The moon is cold and moist. Water is cold and moist. Thus our seas must appear to the moon as the moon does to us.

875.

The waves in water magnify the image of an object reflected in it.

Let a be the sun, and n m the ruffled water, b the image of the sun when the water is smooth. Let f be the eye which sees the image in all the waves included within the base of the triangle c e f. Now the sun reflected in the unruffled surface occupied the space c d, while in the ruffled surface it covers all the watery space c e (as is proved in the 4th of my "Perspective") [Footnote 9: Nel quarto della mia prospettiva. If this reference is to the diagrams accompanying the text--as is usual with Leonardo--and not to some particular work, the largest of the diagrams here given must be meant. It is the lowest and actually the fifth, but he would have called it the fourth, for the text here given is preceded on the same page of the manuscript by a passage on whirlpools, with the diagram belonging to it also reproduced here. The words della mia prospettiva may therefore indicate that the diagram to the preceding chapter treating on a heterogeneal subject is to be excluded. It is a further difficulty that this diagram belongs properly to lines 9-10 and not to the preceding sentence. The reflection of the sun in water is also discussed in the Theoretical part of the Book on Painting; see Vol. I, No. 206, 207.] and it will cover more of the water in proportion as the reflected image is remote from the eye [10].

[Footnote: In the original sketch, inside the circle in the first diagram, is written Sole (sun), and to the right of it luna (moon). Thus either of these heavenly bodies may be supposed to fill that space. Within the lower circle is written simulacro (image). In the two next diagrams at the spot here marked L the word Luna is written, and in the last sole is written in the top circle at a.]

The image of the sun will be more brightly shown in small waves than in large ones--and this is because the reflections or images of the sun are more numerous in the small waves than in large ones, and the more numerous reflections of its radiance give a larger light than the fewer.

Waves which intersect like the scales of a fir cone reflect the image of the sun with the greatest splendour; and this is the case because the images are as many as the ridges of the waves on which the sun shines, and the shadows between these waves are small and not very dark; and the radiance of so many reflections together becomes united in the image which is transmitted to the eye, so that these shadows are imperceptible.

That reflection of the sun will cover most space on the surface of the water which is most remote from the eye which sees it.

Let a be the sun, p q the reflection of the sun; a b is the surface of the water, in which the sun is mirrored, and r the eye which sees this reflection on the surface of the water occupying the space o m. c is the eye at a greater distance from the surface of the water and also from the reflection; hence this reflection covers a larger space of water, by the distance between n and o.

876.

It is impossible that the side of a spherical mirror, illuminated by the sun, should reflect its radiance unless this mirror were undulating or filled with bubbles.

You see here the sun which lights up the moon, a spherical mirror, and all of its surface, which faces the sun is rendered radiant.

Whence it may be concluded that what shines in the moon is water like that of our seas, and in waves as that is; and that portion which does not shine consists of islands and terra firma.

This diagram, of several spherical bodies interposed between the eye and the sun, is given to show that, just as the reflection of the sun is seen in each of these bodies, in the same way that image may be seen in each curve of the waves of the sea; and as in these many spheres many reflections of the sun are seen, so in many waves there are many images, each of which at a great distance is much magnified to the eye. And, as this happens with each wave, the spaces interposed between the waves are concealed; and, for this reason, it looks as though the many suns mirrored in the many waves were but one continuous sun; and the shadows,, mixed up with the luminous images, render this radiance less brilliant than that of the sun mirrored in these waves.

[Footnote: In the original, at letter A in the diagram "Sole" (the sun) is written, and at o "occhio" (the eye).]

877.

This will have before it the treatise on light and shade.

The edges in the moon will be most strongly lighted and reflect most light, because, there, nothing will be visible but the tops of the waves of the water [Footnote 5: I have thought it unnecessary to reproduce the detailed explanation of the theory of reflection on waves contained in the passage which follows this.].

878.

The sun will appear larger in moving water or on waves than in still water; an example is the light reflected on the strings of a monochord.

II.

THE SUN.

The question of the true and of the apparent size of the sun (879-884).

879.

IN PRAISE OF THE SUN.

If you look at the stars, cutting off the rays (as may be done by looking through a very small hole made with the extreme point of a very fine needle, placed so as almost to touch the eye), you will see those stars so minute that it would seem as though nothing could be smaller; it is in fact their great distance which is the reason of their diminution, for many of them are very many times larger than the star which is the earth with water. Now reflect what this our star must look like at such a distance, and then consider how many stars might be added--both in longitude and latitude--between those stars which are scattered over the darkened sky. But I cannot forbear to condemn many of the ancients, who said that the sun was no larger than it appears; among these was Epicurus, and I believe that he founded his reason on the effects of a light placed in our atmosphere equidistant from the centre of the earth. Any one looking at it never sees it diminished in size at whatever distance; and the rea-

[Footnote 879-882: What Leonardo says of Epicurus-- who according to LEWIS, The Astronomy of the ancients, and MADLER, Geschichte der Himmelskunde, did not devote much attention to the study of celestial phenomena--, he probably derived from Book X of Diogenes Laertius, whose Vitae Philosophorum was not printed in Greek till 1533, but the Latin translation appeared in 1475.]

880.

sons of its size and power I shall reserve for Book 4. But I wonder greatly that Socrates

[Footnote 2: Socrates; I have little light to throw on this reference. Plato's Socrates himself declares on more than one occasion that in his youth he had turned his mind to the study of celestial phenomena (METEWPA) but not in his later years (see G. C. LEWIS, The Astronomy of the ancients, page 109; MADLER, Geschichte der Himmelskunde, page 41). Here and there in Plato's writings we find incidental notes on the sun and other heavenly bodies.

Leonardo may very well have known of these, since the Latin version by Ficinus was printed as early as 1491; indeed an undated edition exists which may very likely have appeared between 1480--90.

There is but one passage in Plato, Epinomis (p. 983) where he speaks of the physical properties of the sun and says that it is larger than the earth.

Aristotle who goes very fully into the subject says the same. A complete edition of Aristotele's works was first printed in Venice 1495-98, but a Latin version of the Books De Coelo et Mundo and De Physica had been printed in Venice as early as in 1483 (H. MULLER-STRUBING).]

should have depreciated that solar body, saying that it was of the nature of incandescent stone, and the one who opposed him as to that error was not far wrong. But I only wish I had words to serve me to blame those who are fain to extol the worship of men more than that of the sun; for in the whole universe there is nowhere to be seen a body of greater magnitude and power than the sun. Its light gives light to all the celestial bodies which are distributed throughout the universe; and from it descends all vital force, for the heat that is in living beings comes from the soul [vital spark]; and there is no other centre of heat and light in the universe as will be shown in Book 4; and certainly those who have chosen to worship men as gods--as Jove, Saturn, Mars and the like--have fallen into the gravest error, seeing that even if a man were as large as our earth, he would look no bigger than a little star which appears but as a speck in the universe; and seeing again that these men are mortal, and putrid and corrupt in their sepulchres.

Marcellus [Footnote 23: I have no means of identifying Marcello who is named in the margin. It may be Nonius Marcellus, an obscure Roman Grammarian of uncertain date (between the IInd and Vth centuries A. C.) the author of the treatise De compendiosa doctrina per litteras ad filium in which he treats de rebus omnibus et quibusdam aliis. This was much read in the middle ages. The editto princeps is dated 1470 (H. MULLER-STRUBING).] and many others praise the sun.

881.

Epicurus perhaps saw the shadows cast by columns on the walls in front of them equal in diameter to the columns from which the shadows were cast; and the breadth of the shadows being parallel from beginning to end, he thought he might infer that the sun also was directly opposite to this parallel and that consequently its breadth was not greater than that of the column; not perceiving that the diminution in the shadow was insensibly slight by reason of the remoteness of the sun. If the sun were smaller than the earth, the stars on a great portion of our hemisphere would have no light, which is evidence against Epicurus who says the sun is only as large as it appears.

[Footnote: In the original the writing is across the diagram.]

882.

Epicurus says the sun is the size it looks. Hence as it looks about a foot across we must consider that to be its size; it would follow that when the moon eclipses the sun, the sun ought not to appear the larger, as it does. Then, the moon being smaller than the sun, the moon must be less than a foot, and consequently when our world eclipses the moon, it must be less than a foot by a finger's breadth; inasmuch as if the sun is a foot across, and our earth casts a conical shadow on the moon, it is inevitable that the luminous cause of the cone of shadow must be larger than the opaque body which casts the cone of shadow.

883.

To measure how many times the diameter of the sun will go into its course in 24 hours.

Make a circle and place it to face the south, after the manner of a sundial, and place a rod in the middle in such a way as that its length points to the centre of this circle, and mark the shadow cast in the sunshine by this rod on the circumference of the circle, and this shadow will be--let us say-- as broad as from a to n. Now measure how many times this shadow will go into this circumference of a circle, and that will give you the number of times that the solar body will go into its orbit in 24 hours. Thus you may see whether Epicurus was [right in] saying that the sun was only as large as it looked; for, as the apparent diameter of the sun is about a foot, and as that sun would go a thousand times into the length of its course in 24 hours, it would have gone a thousand feet, that is 300 braccia, which is the sixth of a mile. Whence it would follow that the course of the sun during the day would be the sixth part of a mile and that this venerable snail, the sun will have travelled 25 braccia an hour.

884.

Posidonius composed books on the size of the sun. [Footnote: Poseidonius of Apamea, commonly called the Rhodian, because he taught in Rhodes, was a Stoic philosopher, a contemporary and friend of Cicero's, and the author of numerous works on natural science, among them.

Strabo quotes no doubt from one of his works, when he says that Poseidonius explained how it was that the sun looked larger when it was rising or setting than during the rest of its course (III, p. 135). Kleomedes, a later Greek Naturalist also mentions this observation of Poseidonius' without naming the title of his work; however, as Kleomedes' Cyclia Theorica was not printed till 1535, Leonardo must have derived his quotation from Strabo. He probably wrote this note in 1508, and as the original Greek was first printed in Venice in 1516, we must suppose him to quote here from the translation by Guarinus Veronensis, which was printed as early as 1471, also at Venice (H. MULLER-STRUBING).]

Of the nature of Sunlight.

885.

OF THE PROOF THAT THE SUN IS HOT BY NATURE AND NOT BY VIRTUE.

Of the nature of Sunlight.

That the heat of the sun resides in its nature and not in its virtue [or mode of action] is abundantly proved by the radiance of the solar body on which the human eye cannot dwell and besides this no less manifestly by the rays reflected from a concave mirror, which--when they strike the eye with such splendour that the eye cannot bear them--have a brilliancy equal to the sun in its own place. And that this is true I prove by the fact that if the mirror has its concavity formed exactly as is requisite for the collecting and reflecting of these rays, no created being could endure the heat that strikes from the reflected rays of such a mirror. And if you argue that the mirror itself is cold and yet send forth hot rays, I should reply that those rays come really from the sun and that it is the ray of the concave mirror after having passed through the window.

Considerations as to the size of the sun (886-891).

886.

The sun does not move. [Footnote: This sentence occurs incidentally among mathematical notes, and is written in unusually large letters.]

887.

PROOF THAT THE NEARER YOU ARE TO THE SOURCE OF THE SOLAR RAYS, THE LARGER WILL THE REFLECTION OF THE SUN FROM THE SEA APPEAR TO YOU.

[Footnote: Lines 4 and fol. Compare Vol. I, Nos. 130, 131.] If it is from the centre that the sun employs its radiance to intensify the power of its whole mass, it is evident that the farther its rays extend, the more widely they will be divided; and this being so, you, whose eye is near the water that mirrors the sun, see but a small portion of the rays of the sun strike the surface of the water, and reflecting the form of the sun. But if you were near to the sun--as would be the case when the sun is on the meridian and the sea to the westward--you would see the sun, mirrored in the sea, of a very great size; because, as you are nearer to the sun, your eye taking in the rays nearer to the point of radiation takes more of them in, and a great splendour is the result. And in this way it can be proved that the moon must have seas which reflect the sun, and that the parts which do not shine are land.

888.

Take the measure of the sun at the solstice in mid-June.

889.

WHY THE SUN APPEARS LARGER WHEN SETTING THAN AT NOON, WHEN IT IS NEAR TO US.

Every object seen through a curved medium seems to be of larger size than it is.

[Footnote: At A is written sole (the sun), at B terra (the earth).]

890.

Because the eye is small it can only see the image of the sun as of a small size. If the eye were as large as the sun it would see the image of the sun in water of the same size as the real body of the sun, so long as the water is smooth.

891.

A METHOD OF SEEING THE SUN ECLIPSED WITHOUT PAIN TO THE EYE.

Take a piece of paper and pierce holes in it with a needle, and look at the sun through these holes.

III.

THE MOON.

On the luminousity of the moon (892-901).

892.

OF THE MOON.

As I propose to treat of the nature of the moon, it is necessary that first I should describe the perspective of mirrors, whether plane, concave or convex; and first what is meant by a luminous ray, and how it is refracted by various kinds of media; then, when a reflected ray is most powerful, whether when the angle of incidence is acute, right, or obtuse, or from a convex, a plane, or a concave surface; or from an opaque or a transparent body. Besides this, how it is that the solar rays which fall on the waves of the sea, are seen by the eye of the same width at the angle nearest to the eye, as at the highest line of the waves on the horizon; but notwithstanding this the solar rays reflected from the waves of the sea assume the pyramidal form and consequently, at each degree of distance increase proportionally in size, although to our sight, they appear as parallel.

1st. Nothing that has very little weight is opaque.

2dly. Nothing that is excessively weighty can remain beneath that which is heavier.

3dly. As to whether the moon is situated in the centre of its elements or not.

And, if it has no proper place of its own, like the earth, in the midst of its elements, why does it not fall to the centre of our elements? [Footnote 26: The problem here propounded by Leonardo was not satisfactorily answered till Newton in 1682 formulated the law of universal attraction and gravitation. Compare No. 902, lines 5-15.]

And, if the moon is not in the centre of its own elements and yet does not fall, it must then be lighter than any other element.

And, if the moon is lighter than the other elements why is it opaque and not transparent?

When objects of various sizes, being placed at various distances, look of equal size, there must be the same relative proportion in the distances as in the magnitudes of the objects.

[Footnote: In the diagram Leonardo wrote sole at the place marked A.]

893.

OF THE MOON AND WHETHER IT IS POLISHED AND SPHERICAL.

The image of the sun in the moon is powerfully luminous, and is only on a small portion of its surface. And the proof may be seen by taking a ball of burnished gold and placing it in the dark with a light at some distance from it; and then, although it will illuminate about half of the ball, the eye will perceive its reflection only in a small part of its surface, and all the rest of the surface reflects the darkness which surrounds it; so that it is only in that spot that the image of the light is seen, and all the rest remains invisible, the eye being at a distance from the ball. The same thing would happen on the surface of the moon if it were polished, lustrous and opaque, like all bodies with a reflecting surface.

Show how, if you were standing on the moon or on a star, our earth would seem to reflect the sun as the moon does.

And show that the image of the sun in the sea cannot appear one and undivided, as it appears in a perfectly plane mirror.

894.

How shadows are lost at great distances, as is shown by the shadow side of the moon which is never seen. [Footnote: Compare also Vol. I, Nos. 175-179.]

895.

Either the moon has intrinsic luminosity or not. If it has, why does it not shine without the aid of the sun? But if it has not any light in itself it must of necessity be a spherical mirror; and if it is a mirror, is it not proved in Perspective that the image of a luminous object will never be equal to the extent of surface of the reflecting body that it illuminates? And if it be thus [Footnote 13: At A, in the diagram, Leonardo wrote "sole" (the sun), and at B "luna o noi terra" (the moon or our earth). Compare also the text of No. 876.], as is here shown at r s in the figure, whence comes so great an extent of radiance as that of the full moon as we see it, at the fifteenth day of the moon?

896.

OF THE MOON.

The moon has no light in itself; but so much of it as faces the sun is illuminated, and of that illumined portion we see so much as faces the earth. And the moon's night receives just as much light as is lent it by our waters as they reflect the image of the sun, which is mirrored in all those waters which are on the side towards the sun. The outside or surface of the waters forming the seas of the moon and of the seas of our globe is always ruffled little or much, or more or less--and this roughness causes an extension of the numberless images of the sun which are repeated in the ridges and hollows, the sides and fronts of the innumerable waves; that is to say in as many different spots on each wave as our eyes find different positions to view them from. This could not happen, if the aqueous sphere which covers a great part of the moon were uniformly spherical, for then the images of the sun would be one to each spectator, and its reflections would be separate and independent and its radiance would always appear circular; as is plainly to be seen in the gilt balls placed on the tops of high buildings. But if those gilt balls were rugged or composed of several little balls, like mulberries, which are a black fruit composed of minute round globules, then each portion of these little balls, when seen in the sun, would display to the eye the lustre resulting from the reflection of the sun, and thus, in one and the same body many tiny suns would be seen; and these often combine at a long distance and appear as one. The lustre of the new moon is brighter and stronger, than when the moon is full; and the reason of this is that the angle of incidence is more obtuse in the new than in the full moon, in which the angles [of incidence and reflection] are highly acute. The waves of the moon therefore mirror the sun in the hollows of the waves as well as on the ridges, and the sides remain in shadow. But at the sides of the moon the hollows of the waves do not catch the sunlight, but only their crests; and thus the images are fewer and more mixed up with the shadows in the hollows; and this intermingling of the shaded and illuminated spots comes to the eye with a mitigated splendour, so that the edges will be darker, because the curves of the sides of the waves are insufficient to reflect to the eye the rays that fall upon them. Now the new moon naturally reflects the solar rays more directly towards the eye from the crests of the waves than from any other part, as is shown by the form of the moon, whose rays a strike the waves b and are reflected in the line b d, the eye being situated at d. This cannot happen at the full moon, when the solar rays, being in the west, fall on the extreme waters of the moon to the East from n to m, and are not reflected to the eye in the West, but are thrown back eastwards, with but slight deflection from the straight course of the solar ray; and thus the angle of incidence is very wide indeed.

The moon is an opaque and solid body and if, on the contrary, it were transparent, it would not receive the light of the sun.

The yellow or yolk of an egg remains in the middle of the albumen, without moving on either side; now it is either lighter or heavier than this albumen, or equal to it; if it is lighter, it ought to rise above all the albumen and stop in contact with the shell of the egg; and if it is heavier, it ought to sink, and if it is equal, it might just as well be at one of the ends, as in the middle or below [54].

[Footnote 48-64: Compare No. 861.]

The innumerable images of the solar rays reflected from the innumerable waves of the sea, as they fall upon those waves, are what cause us to see the very broad and continuous radiance on the surface of the sea.

897.

That the sun could not be mirrored in the body of the moon, which is a convex mirror, in such a way as that so much of its surface as is illuminated by the sun, should reflect the sun unless the moon had a surface adapted to reflect it--in waves and ridges, like the surface of the sea when its surface is moved by the wind.

[Footnote: In the original diagrams sole is written at the place marked A; luna at C, and terra at the two spots marked B.]

The waves in water multiply the image of the object reflected in it.

These waves reflect light, each by its own line, as the surface of the fir cone does [Footnote 14: See the diagram p. 145.]

These are 2 figures one different from the other; one with undulating water and the other with smooth water.

It is impossible that at any distance the image of the sun cast on the surface of a spherical body should occupy the half of the sphere.

Here you must prove that the earth produces all the same effects with regard to the moon, as the moon with regard to the earth.

The moon, with its reflected light, does not shine like the sun, because the light of the moon is not a continuous reflection of that of the sun on its whole surface, but only on the crests and hollows of the waves of its waters; and thus the sun being confusedly reflected, from the admixture of the shadows that lie between the lustrous waves, its light is not pure and clear as the sun is.

[Footnote 38: This refers to the small diagram placed between B and B.--]. The earth between the moon on the fifteenth day and the sun. [Footnote 39: See the diagram below the one referred to in the preceding note.] Here the sun is in the East and the moon on the fifteenth day in the West. [Footnote 40.41: Refers to the diagram below the others.] The moon on the fifteenth [day] between the earth and the sun. [41]Here it is the moon which has the sun to the West and the earth to the East.

898.

WHAT SORT OF THING THE MOON IS.

The moon is not of itself luminous, but is highly fitted to assimilate the character of light after the manner of a mirror, or of water, or of any other reflecting body; and it grows larger in the East and in the West, like the sun and the other planets. And the reason is that every luminous body looks larger in proportion as it is remote. It is easy to understand that every planet and star is farther from us when in the West than when it is overhead, by about 3500 miles, as is proved on the margin [Footnote 7: refers to the first diagram.--A = sole (the sun), B = terra (the earth), C = luna (the moon).], and if you see the sun or moon mirrored in the water near to you, it looks to you of the same size in the water as in the sky. But if you recede to the distance of a mile, it will look 100 times larger; and if you see the sun reflected in the sea at sunset, its image would look to you more than 10 miles long; because that reflected image extends over more than 10 miles of sea. And if you could stand where the moon is, the sun would look to you, as if it were reflected from all the sea that it illuminates by day; and the land amid the water would appear just like the dark spots that are on the moon, which, when looked at from our earth, appears to men the same as our earth would appear to any men who might dwell in the moon.

[Footnote: This text has already been published by LIBRI: Histoire des Sciences, III, pp. 224, 225.]

OF THE NATURE OF THE MOON.

When the moon is entirely lighted up to our sight, we see its full daylight; and at that time, owing to the reflection of the solar rays which fall on it and are thrown off towards us, its ocean casts off less moisture towards us; and the less light it gives the more injurious it is.

899.

OF THE MOON.

I say that as the moon has no light in itself and yet is luminous, it is inevitable but that its light is caused by some other body.

900.

OF THE MOON.

All my opponent's arguments to say that there is no water in the moon. [Footnote: The objections are very minutely noted down in the manuscript, but they hardly seem to have a place here.]

901.

Answer to Maestro Andrea da Imola, who said that the solar rays reflected from a convex mirror are mingled and lost at a short distance; whereby it is altogether denied that the luminous side of the moon is of the nature of a mirror, and that consequently the light is not produced by the innumerable multitude of the waves of that sea, which I declared to be the portion of the moon which is illuminated by the solar rays.

Let o p be the body of the sun, c n s the moon, and b the eye which, above the base c n of the cathetus c n m, sees the body of the sun reflected at equal angles c n; and the same again on moving the eye from b to a. [Footnote: The large diagram on the margin of page 161 belongs to this chapter.]

Explanation of the lumen cinereum in the moon.

902.

OF THE MOON.

No solid body is less heavy than the atmosphere.

[Footnote: 1. On the margin are the words tola romantina, tola--ferro stagnato (tinned iron); romantina is some special kind of sheet-iron no longer known by that name.]

Having proved that the part of the moon that shines consists of water, which mirrors the body of the sun and reflects the radiance it receives from it; and that, if these waters were devoid of waves, it would appear small, but of a radiance almost like the sun; --[5] It must now be shown whether the moon is a heavy or a light body: for, if it were a heavy body--admitting that at every grade of distance from the earth greater levity must prevail, so that water is lighter than the earth, and air than water, and fire than air and so on successively--it would seem that if the moon had density as it really has, it would have weight, and having weight, that it could not be sustained in the space where it is, and consequently that it would fall towards the centre of the universe and become united to the earth; or if not the moon itself, at least its waters would fall away and be lost from it, and descend towards the centre, leaving the moon without any and so devoid of lustre. But as this does not happen, as might in reason be expected, it is a manifest sign that the moon is surrounded by its own elements: that is to say water, air and fire; and thus is, of itself and by itself, suspended in that part of space, as our earth with its element is in this part of space; and that heavy bodies act in the midst of its elements just as other heavy bodies do in ours [Footnote 15: This passage would certainly seem to establish Leonardo's claim to be regarded as the original discoverer of the cause of the ashy colour of the new moon (lumen cinereum). His observations however, having hitherto remained unknown to astronomers, Moestlin and Kepler have been credited with the discoveries which they made independently a century later.

Some disconnected notes treat of the same subject in MS. C. A. 239b; 718b and 719b; "Perche la luna cinta della parte alluminata dal sole in ponente, tra maggior splendore in mezzo a tal cerchio, che quando essa eclissava il sole. Questo accade perche nell' eclissare il sole ella ombrava il nostro oceano, il qual caso non accade essendo in ponente, quando il sole alluma esso oceano." The editors of the "Saggio" who first published this passage (page 12) add another short one about the seasons in the moon which I confess not to have seen in the original manuscript: "La luna ha ogni mese un verno e una state, e ha maggiori freddi e maggiori caldi, e i suoi equinozii son piu freddi de' nostri."]

When the eye is in the East and sees the moon in the West near to the setting sun, it sees it with its shaded portion surrounded by luminous portions; and the lateral and upper portion of this light is derived from the sun, and the lower portion from the ocean in the West, which receives the solar rays and reflects them on the lower waters of the moon, and indeed affords the part of the moon that is in shadow as much radiance as the moon gives the earth at midnight. Therefore it is not totally dark, and hence some have believed that the moon must in parts have a light of its own besides that which is given it by the sun; and this light is due, as has been said, to the above- mentioned cause,--that our seas are illuminated by the sun.

Again, it might be said that the circle of radiance shown by the moon when it and the sun are both in the West is wholly borrowed from the sun, when it, and the sun, and the eye are situated as is shown above.

[Footnote 23. 24: The larger of the two diagrams reproduced above stands between these two lines, and the smaller one is sketched in the margin. At the spot marked A Leonardo wrote corpo solare (solar body) in the larger diagram and Sole (sun) in the smaller one. At C luna (moon) is written and at B terra (the earth).]

Some might say that the air surrounding the moon as an element, catches the light of the sun as our atmosphere does, and that it is this which completes the luminous circle on the body of the moon.

Some have thought that the moon has a light of its own, but this opinion is false, because they have founded it on that dim light seen between the hornes of the new moon, which looks dark where it is close to the bright part, while against the darkness of the background it looks so light that many have taken it to be a ring of new radiance completing the circle where the tips of the horns illuminated by the sun cease to shine [Footnote 34: See Pl. CVIII, No. 5.]. And this difference of background arises from the fact that the portion of that background which is conterminous with the bright part of the moon, by comparison with that brightness looks darker than it is; while at the upper part, where a portion of the luminous circle is to be seen of uniform width, the result is that the moon, being brighter there than the medium or background on which it is seen by comparison with that darkness it looks more luminous at that edge than it is. And that brightness at such a time itself is derived from our ocean and other inland-seas. These are, at that time, illuminated by the sun which is already setting in such a way as that the sea then fulfils the same function to the dark side of the moon as the moon at its fifteenth day does to us when the sun is set. And the small amount of light which the dark side of the moon receives bears the same proportion to the light of that side which is illuminated, as that... [Footnote 42: Here the text breaks off; lines 43-52 are written on the margin.].

If you want to see how much brighter the shaded portion of the moon is than the background on which it is seen, conceal the luminous portion of the moon with your hand or with some other more distant object.

On the spots in the moon (903-907).

903.

THE SPOTS ON THE MOON.

Some have said that vapours rise from the moon, after the manner of clouds and are interposed between the moon and our eyes. But, if this were the case, these spots would never be permanent, either as to position or form; and, seeing the moon from various aspects, even if these spots did not move they would change in form, as objects do which are seen from different sides.

904.

OF THE SPOTS ON THE MOON.

Others say that the moon is composed of more or less transparent parts; as though one part were something like alabaster and others like crystal or glass. It would follow from this that the sun casting its rays on the less transparent portions, the light would remain on the surface, and so the denser part would be illuminated, and the transparent portions would display the shadow of their darker depths; and this is their account of the structure and nature of the moon. And this opinion has found favour with many philosophers, and particularly with Aristotle, and yet it is a false view--for, in the various phases and frequent changes of the moon and sun to our eyes, we should see these spots vary, at one time looking dark and at another light: they would be dark when the sun is in the West and the moon in the middle of the sky; for then the transparent hollows would be in shadow as far as the tops of the edges of those transparent hollows, because the sun could not then fling his rays into the mouth of the hollows, which however, at full moon, would be seen in bright light, at which time the moon is in the East and faces the sun in the West; then the sun would illuminate even the lowest depths of these transparent places and thus, as there would be no shadows cast, the moon at these times would not show us the spots in question; and so it would be, now more and now less, according to the changes in the position of the sun to the moon, and of the moon to our eyes, as I have said above.

905.

OF THE SPOTS ON THE MOON.

It has been asserted, that the spots on the moon result from the moon being of varying thinness or density; but if this were so, when there is an eclipse of the moon the solar rays would pierce through the portions which were thin as is alleged [Footnote 3-5: Eclissi. This word, as it seems to me, here means eclipses of the sun; and the sense of the passage, as I understand it, is that by the foregoing hypothesis the moon, when it comes between the sun and the earth must appear as if pierced,--we may say like a sieve.]. But as we do not see this effect the opinion must be false.

Others say that the surface of the moon is smooth and polished and that, like a mirror, it reflects in itself the image of our earth. This view is also false, inasmuch as the land, where it is not covered with water, presents various aspects and forms. Hence when the moon is in the East it would reflect different spots from those it would show when it is above us or in the West; now the spots on the moon, as they are seen at full moon, never vary in the course of its motion over our hemisphere. A second reason is that an object reflected in a convex body takes up but a small portion of that body, as is proved in perspective [Footnote 18: come e provato. This alludes to the accompanying diagram.]. The third reason is that when the moon is full, it only faces half the hemisphere of the illuminated earth, on which only the ocean and other waters reflect bright light, while the land makes spots on that brightness; thus half of our earth would be seen girt round with the brightness of the sea lighted up by the sun, and in the moon this reflection would be the smallest part of that moon. Fourthly, a radiant body cannot be reflected from another equally radiant; therefore the sea, since it borrows its brightness from the sun,--as the moon does--, could not cause the earth to be reflected in it, nor indeed could the body of the sun be seen reflected in it, nor indeed any star opposite to it.

906.

If you keep the details of the spots of the moon under observation you will often find great variation in them, and this I myself have proved by drawing them. And this is caused by the clouds that rise from the waters in the moon, which come between the sun and those waters, and by their shadow deprive these waters of the sun's rays. Thus those waters remain dark, not being able to reflect the solar body.

907.

How the spots on the moon must have varied from what they formerly were, by reason of the course of its waters.

On the moon's halo.

908.

OF HALOS ROUND THE MOON.

I have found, that the circles which at night seem to surround the moon, of various sizes, and degrees of density are caused by various gradations in the densities of the vapours which exist at different altitudes between the moon and our eyes. And of these halos the largest and least red is caused by the lowest of these vapours; the second, smaller one, is higher up, and looks redder because it is seen through two vapours. And so on, as they are higher they will appear smaller and redder, because, between the eye and them, there is thicker vapour. Whence it is proved that where they are seen to be reddest, the vapours are most dense.

On instruments for observing the moon (909. 910).

909.

If you want to prove why the moon appears larger than it is, when it reaches the horizon; take a lens which is highly convex on one surface and concave on the opposite, and place the concave side next the eye, and look at the object beyond the convex surface; by this means you will have produced an exact imitation of the atmosphere included beneath the sphere of fire and outside that of water; for this atmosphere is concave on the side next the earth, and convex towards the fire.

910.

Construct glasses to see the moon magnified.

[Footnote: See the Introduction, p. 136, Fracastoro says in his work Homocentres: "Per dua specilla ocularla si quis perspiciat, alteri altero superposito, majora multo et propinquiora videbit omnia.--Quin imo quaedam specilla ocularia fiunt tantae densitatis, ut si per ea quis aut lunam, aut aliud siderum spectet, adeo propinqua illa iudicet, ut ne turres ipsas excedant" (sect. II c. 8 and sect. III, c. 23).]

I. THE STARS. On the light of the stars (911-913). 911. The stars are visible by night and not by day, because we are eneath the dense atmosphere, which is full of innumerable articles of moisture, each of which independently, when the ays of the sun fall upon it, reflects a radiance, and so these umberless bright particles conceal the stars; and if it were not or this atmosphere the sky would always display the stars against ts darkness. [Footnote: See No. 296, which also refers to starlight.] 912. Whether the stars have their light from the sun or in themselves. Some say that they shine of themselves, alledging that if Venus nd Mercury had not a light of their own, when they come between ur eye and the sun they would darken so much of the sun as they ould cover from our eye. But this is false, for it is proved that

dark object against a luminous body is enveloped and entirely

oncealed by the lateral rays of the rest of that luminous body nd so remains invisible. As may be seen when the sun is seen hrough the boughs of trees bare of their leaves, at some distance he branches do not conceal any portion of the sun from our eye. he same thing happens with the above mentioned planets which, hough they have no light of their own, do not--as has been said-- onceal any part of the sun from our eye [18].

SECOND ARGUMENT.

Some say that the stars appear most brilliant at night in proportion as they are higher up; and that if they had no light of their own, the shadow of the earth which comes between them and the sun, would darken them, since they would not face nor be faced by the solar body. But those persons have not considered that the conical shadow of the earth cannot reach many of the stars; and even as to those it does reach, the cone is so much diminished that it covers very little of the star's mass, and all the rest is illuminated by the sun.

Footnote: From this and other remarks (see No. 902) it is clear hat Leonardo was familiar with the phenomena of Irradiation.]

13.

Why the planets appear larger in the East than they do overhead, whereas the contrary should be the case, as they are 3500 miles nearer to us when in mid sky than when on the horizon.

All the degrees of the elements, through which the images of the celestial bodies pass to reach the eye, are equal curves and the angles by which the central line of those images passes through them, are unequal angles [Footnote 13: inequali, here and elsewhere does not mean unequal in the sense of not being equal to each other, but angles which are not right angles.]; and the distance is greater, as is shown by the excess of a b beyond a d; and the enlargement of these celestial bodies on the horizon is shown by the 9th of the 7th.

Observations on the stars.

914.

To see the real nature of the planets open the covering and note at the base [Footnote 4: basa. This probably alludes to some instrument, perhaps the Camera obscura.] one single planet, and the reflected movement of this base will show the nature of the said planet; but arrange that the base may face only one at the time.

On history of astronomy.

915.

Cicero says in [his book] De Divinatione that Astrology has been practised five hundred seventy thousand years before the Trojan war.

57000.

[Footnote: The statement that CICERO, De Divin. ascribes the discovery of astrology to a period 57000 years before the Trojan war I believe to be quite erroneous. According to ERNESTI, Clavis Ciceroniana, CH. G. SCHULZ (Lexic. Cicer.) and the edition of De Divin. by GIESE the word Astrologia occurs only twice in CICERO: De Divin. II, 42. Ad Chaldaeorum monstra veniamus, de quibus Eudoxus, Platonis auditor, in astrologia judicio doctissimorum hominum facile princeps, sic opinatur (id quod scriptum reliquit): Chaldaeis in praedictione et in notatione cujusque vitae ex natali die minime esse credendum." He then quotes the condemnatory verdict of other philosophers as to the teaching of the Chaldaeans but says nothing as to the antiquity and origin of astronomy. CICERO further notes De oratore I, 16 that Aratus was "ignarus astrologiae" but that is all. So far as I know the word occurs nowhere else in CICERO; and the word Astronomia he does not seem to have used at all. (H. MULLER-STRUBING.)]

Of time and its divisions (916-918).

916.

Although time is included in the class of Continuous Quantities, being indivisible and immaterial, it does not come entirely under the head of Geometry, which represents its divisions by means of figures and bodies of infinite variety, such as are seen to be continuous in their visible and material properties. But only with its first principles does it agree, that is with the Point and the Line; the point may be compared to an instant of time, and the line may be likened to the length of a certain quantity of time, and just as a line begins and terminates in a point, so such a space of time. begins and terminates in an instant. And whereas a line is infinitely divisible, the divisibility of a space of time is of the same nature; and as the divisions of the line may bear a certain proportion to each other, so may the divisions of time.

[Footnote: This passage is repeated word for word on page 190b of the same manuscript and this is accounted for by the text in Vol. I, No. 4. Compare also No. 1216.]

917.

Describe the nature of Time as distinguished from the Geometrical definitions.

918.

Divide an hour into 3000 parts, and this you can do with a clock by making the pendulum lighter or heavier.

XVI. Physical Geography.

Leonardo's researches as to the structure of the earth and sea were made at a time, when the extended voyages of the Spaniards and Portuguese had also excited a special interest in geographical questions in Italy, and particularly in Tuscany. Still, it need scarcely surprise us to find that in deeper questions, as to the structure of the globe, the primitive state of the earth's surface, and the like, he was far in advance of his time.

The number of passages which treat of such matters is relatively considerable; like almost all Leonardo's scientific notes they deal partly with theoretical and partly with practical questions. Some of his theoretical views of the motion of water were collected in a copied manuscript volume by an early transcriber, but without any acknowledgment of the source whence they were derived. This copy is now in the Library of the Barberini palace at Rome and was published under the title: "De moto e misura dell'acqua," by FRANCESCO CARDINALI, Bologna 1828. In this work the texts are arranged under the following titles: Libr. I. Della spera dell'acqua; Libr. II. Del moto dell'acqua; Libr. III. Dell'onda dell'acqua; Libr. IV. Dei retrosi d'acqua; Libr. V. Dell'acqua cadente; Libr. VI. Delle rotture fatte dall'acqua; Libr. VII Delle cose portate dall'acqua; Libr. VIII. Dell'oncia dell'acqua e delle canne; Libr. IX. De molini e d'altri ordigni d'acqua.

The large number of isolated observations scattered through the manuscripts, accounts for our so frequently finding notes of new schemes for the arrangement of those relating to water and its motions, particularly in the Codex Atlanticus: I have printed several of these plans as an introduction to the Physical Geography, and I have actually arranged the texts in accordance with the clue afforded by one of them which is undoubtedly one of the latest notes referring to the subject (No. 920). The text given as No. 930 which is also taken from a late note-book of Leonardo's, served as a basis for the arrangement of the first of the seven books--or sections--, bearing the title: Of the Nature of Water (Dell'acque in se).

As I have not made it any part of this undertaking to print the passages which refer to purely physical principles, it has also been necessary to exclude those practical researches which, in accordance with indications given in 920, ought to come in as Books 13, 14 and 15. I can only incidentally mention here that Leonardo--as it seems to me, especially in his youth--devoted a great deal of attention to the construction of mills. This is proved by a number of drawings of very careful and minute execution, which are to be found in the Codex Atlanticus. Nor was it possible to include his considerations on the regulation of rivers, the making of canals and so forth (No. 920, Books 10, 11 and 12); but those passages in which the structure of a canal is directly connected with notices of particular places will be found duly inserted under section XVII (Topographical notes). In Vol. I, No. 5 the text refers to canal-making in general.

On one point only can the collection of passages included under the general heading of Physical Geography claim to be complete. When comparing and sorting the materials for this work I took particular care not to exclude or omit any text in which a geographical name was mentioned even incidentally, since in all such researches the chief interest, as it appeared to me, attached to the question whether these acute observations on the various local characteristics of mountains, rivers or seas, had been made by Leonardo himself, and on the spot. It is self-evident that the few general and somewhat superficial observations on the Rhine and the Danube, on England and Flanders, must have been obtained from maps or from some informants, and in the case of Flanders Leonardo himself acknowledges this (see No. 1008). But that most of the other and more exact observations were made, on the spot, by Leonardo himself, may be safely assumed from their method and the style in which he writes of them; and we should bear it in mind that in all investigations, of whatever kind, experience is always spoken of as the only basis on which he relies. Incidentally, as in No. 984, he thinks it necessary to allude to the total absence of all recorded observations.

I.

INTRODUCTION.

Schemes for the arrangement of the materials (919-928).

919.

These books contain in the beginning: Of the nature of water itself in its motions; the others treat of the effects of its currents, which change the world in its centre and its shape.

920.

DIVISIONS OF THE BOOK.

Book 1 of water in itself.

Book 2 of the sea.

Book 3 of subterranean rivers.

Book 4 of rivers.

Book 5 of the nature of the abyss.

Book 6 of the obstacles.

Book 7 of gravels.

Book 8 of the surface of water.

Book 9 of the things placed therein.

Book 10 of the repairing of rivers.

Book 11 of conduits.

Book 12 of canals.

Book 13 of machines turned by water.

Book 14 of raising water.

Book 15 of matters worn away by water.

921.

First you shall make a book treating of places occupied by fresh waters, and the second by salt waters, and the third, how by the disappearance of these, our parts of the world were made lighter and in consequence more remote from the centre of the world.

922.

First write of all water, in each of its motions; then describe all its bottoms and their various materials, always referring to the propositions concerning the said waters; and let the order be good, for otherwise the work will be confused.

Describe all the forms taken by water from its greatest to its smallest wave, and their causes.

923.

Book 9, of accidental risings of water.

924.

THE ORDER OF THE BOOK.

Place at the beginning what a river can effect.

925.

A book of driving back armies by the force of a flood made by releasing waters.

A book showing how the waters safely bring down timber cut in the mountains.

A book of boats driven against the impetus of rivers.

A book of raising large bridges higher. Simply by the swelling of the waters.

A book of guarding against the impetus of rivers so that towns may not be damaged by them.

926.

A book of the ordering of rivers so as to preserve their banks.

A book of the mountains, which would stand forth and become land, if our hemisphere were to be uncovered by the water.

A book of the earth carried down by the waters to fill up the great abyss of the seas.

A book of the ways in which a tempest may of itself clear out filled up sea-ports.

A book of the shores of rivers and of their permanency.

A book of how to deal with rivers, so that they may keep their bottom scoured by their own flow near the cities they pass.

A book of how to make or to repair the foundations for bridges over the rivers.

A book of the repairs which ought to be made in walls and banks of rivers where the water strikes them.

A book of the formation of hills of sand or gravel at great depths in water.

927.

Water gives the first impetus to its motion.

A book of the levelling of waters by various means,

A book of diverting rivers from places where they do mischief.

A book of guiding rivers which occupy too much ground.

A book of parting rivers into several branches and making them fordable.

A book of the waters which with various currents pass through seas.

A book of deepening the beds of rivers by means of currents of water.

A book of controlling rivers so that the little beginnings of mischief, caused by them, may not increase.

A book of the various movements of waters passing through channels of different forms.

A book of preventing small rivers from diverting the larger one into which their waters run.

A book of the lowest level which can be found in the current of the surface of rivers.

A book of the origin of rivers which flow from the high tops of mountains.

A book of the various motions of waters in their rivers.

928.

[1] Of inequality in the concavity of a ship. [Footnote 1: The first line of this passage was added subsequently, evidently as a correction of the following line.]

[1] A book of the inequality in the curve of the sides of ships.

[1] A book of the inequality in the position of the tiller.

[1] A book of the inequality in the keel of ships.

[2] A book of various forms of apertures by which water flows out.

[3] A book of water contained in vessels with air, and of its movements.

[4] A book of the motion of water through a syphon. [Footnote 7: cicognole, see No. 966, 11, 17.]

[5] A book of the meetings and union of waters coming from different directions.

[6] A book of the various forms of the banks through which rivers pass.

[7] A book of the various forms of shoals formed under the sluices of rivers.

[8] A book of the windings and meanderings of the currents of rivers.

[9] A book of the various places whence the waters of rivers are derived.

[10] A book of the configuration of the shores of rivers and of their permanency.

[11] A book of the perpendicular fall of water on various objects.

[12] Abook of the course of water when it is impeded in various places.

[12] A book of the various forms of the obstacles which impede the course of waters.

[13] A book of the concavity and globosity formed round various objects at the bottom.

[14] Abook of conducting navigable canals above or beneath the rivers which intersect them.

[15] A book of the soils which absorb water in canals and of repairing them.

[16] Abook of creating currents for rivers, which quit their beds, [and] for rivers choked with soil.

General introduction.

929.

THE BEGINNING OF THE TREATISE ON WATER.

By the ancients man has been called the world in miniature; and certainly this name is well bestowed, because, inasmuch as man is composed of earth, water, air and fire, his body resembles that of the earth; and as man has in him bones the supports and framework of his flesh, the world has its rocks the supports of the earth; as man has in him a pool of blood in which the lungs rise and fall in breathing, so the body of the earth has its ocean tide which likewise rises and falls every six hours, as if the world breathed; as in that pool of blood veins have their origin, which ramify all over the human body, so likewise the ocean sea fills the body of the earth with infinite springs of water. The body of the earth lacks sinews and this is, because the sinews are made expressely for movements and, the world being perpetually stable, no movement takes place, and no movement taking place, muscles are not necessary. --But in all other points they are much alike.

I.

OF THE NATURE OF WATER.

The arrangement of Book I.

930.

THE ORDER OF THE FIRST BOOK ON WATER.

Define first what is meant by height and depth; also how the elements are situated one inside another. Then, what is meant by solid weight and by liquid weight; but first what weight and lightness are in themselves. Then describe why water moves, and why its motion ceases; then why it becomes slower or more rapid; besides this, how it always falls, being in contact with the air but lower than the air. And how water rises in the air by means of the heat of the sun, and then falls again in rain; again, why water springs forth from the tops of mountains; and if the water of any spring higher than the ocean can pour forth water higher than the surface of that ocean. And how all the water that returns to the ocean is higher than the sphere of waters. And how the waters of the equatorial seas are higher than the waters of the North, and higher beneath the body of the sun than in any part of the equatorial circle; for experiment shows that under the heat of a burning brand the water near the brand boils, and the water surrounding this ebullition always sinks with a circular eddy. And how the waters of the North are lower than the other seas, and more so as they become colder, until they are converted into ice.

Definitions (931. 932).

931.

OF WHAT IS WATER.

Among the four elements water is the second both in weight and in instability.

932.

THE BEGINNING OF THE BOOK ON WATER.

Sea is the name given to that water which is wide and deep, in which the waters have not much motion.

[Footnote: Only the beginning of this passage is here given, the remainder consists of definitions which have no direct bearing on the subject.]

Of the surface of the water in relation to the globe (933-936).

933.

The centres of the sphere of water are two, one universal and common to all water, the other particular. The universal one is that which is common to all waters not in motion, which exist in great quantities. As canals, ditches, ponds, fountains, wells, dead rivers, lakes, stagnant pools and seas, which, although they are at various levels, have each in itself the limits of their superficies equally distant from the centre of the earth, such as lakes placed at the tops of high mountains; as the lake near Pietra Pana and the lake of the Sybil near Norcia; and all the lakes that give rise to great rivers, as the Ticino from Lago Maggiore, the Adda from the lake of Como, the Mincio from the lake of Garda, the Rhine from the lakes of Constance and of Chur, and from the lake of Lucerne, like the Tigris which passes through Asia Minor carrying with it the waters of three lakes, one above the other at different heights of which the highest is Munace, the middle one Pallas, and the lowest Triton; the Nile again flows from three very high lakes in Ethiopia.

[Footnote 5: Pietra Pana, a mountain near Florence. If for Norcia, we may read Norchia, the remains of the Etruscan city near Viterbo, there can be no doubt that by 'Lago della Sibilla'--a name not known elsewhere, so far as I can learn--Leonardo meant Lago di Vico (Lacus Ciminus, Aen. 7).]

934.

OF THE CENTRE OF THE OCEAN.

The centre of the sphere of waters is the true centre of the globe of our world, which is composed of water and earth, having the shape of a sphere. But, if you want to find the centre of the element of the earth, this is placed at a point equidistant from the surface of the ocean, and not equidistant from the surface of the earth; for it is evident that this globe of earth has nowhere any perfect rotundity, excepting in places where the sea is, or marshes or other still waters. And every part of the earth that rises above the water is farther from the centre.

935.

OF THE SEA WHICH CHANGES THE WEIGHT OF THE EARTH.

The shells, oysters, and other similar animals, which originate in sea-mud, bear witness to the changes of the earth round the centre of our elements. This is proved thus: Great rivers always run turbid, being coloured by the earth, which is stirred by the friction of their waters at the bottom and on their shores; and this wearing disturbs the face of the strata made by the layers of shells, which lie on the surface of the marine mud, and which were produced there when the salt waters covered them; and these strata were covered over again from time to time, with mud of various thickness, or carried down to the sea by the rivers and floods of more or less extent; and thus these layers of mud became raised to such a height, that they came up from the bottom to the air. At the present time these bottoms are so high that they form hills or high mountains, and the rivers, which wear away the sides of these mountains, uncover the strata of these shells, and thus the softened side of the earth continually rises and the antipodes sink closer to the centre of the earth, and the ancient bottoms of the seas have become mountain ridges.

936.

Let the earth make whatever changes it may in its weight, the surface of the sphere of waters can never vary in its equal distance from the centre of the world.

Of the proportion of the mass of water to that of the earth (937. 938).

937.

WHETHER THE EARTH IS LESS THAN THE WATER.

Some assert that it is true that the earth, which is not covered by water is much less than that covered by water. But considering the size of 7000 miles in diameter which is that of this earth, we may conclude the water to be of small depth.

938.

OF THE EARTH.

The great elevations of the peaks of the mountains above the sphere of the water may have resulted from this that: a very large portion of the earth which was filled with water that is to say the vast cavern inside the earth may have fallen in a vast part of its vault towards the centre of the earth, being pierced by means of the course of the springs which continually wear away the place where they pass.

Sinking in of countries like the Dead Sea in Syria, that is Sodom and Gomorrah.

It is of necessity that there should be more water than land, and the visible portion of the sea does not show this; so that there must be a great deal of water inside the earth, besides that which rises into the lower air and which flows through rivers and springs.

[Footnote: The small sketch below on the left, is placed in the original close to the text referring to the Dead Sea.]

The theory of Plato.

939.

THE FIGURES OF THE ELEMENTS.

Of the figures of the elements; and first as against those who deny the opinions of Plato, and who say that if the elements include one another in the forms attributed to them by Plato they would cause a vacuum one within the other. I say it is not true, and I here prove it, but first I desire to propound some conclusions. It is not necessary that the elements which include each other should be of corresponding magnitude in all the parts, of that which includes and of that which is included. We see that the sphere of the waters varies conspicuously in mass from the surface to the bottom, and that, far from investing the earth when that was in the form of a cube that is of 8 angles as Plato will have it, that it invests the earth which has innumerable angles of rock covered by the water and various prominences and concavities, and yet no vacuum is generated between the earth and water; again, the air invests the sphere of waters together with the mountains and valleys, which rise above that sphere, and no vacuum remains between the earth and the air, so that any one who says a vacuum is generated, speaks foolishly.

But to Plato I would reply that the surface of the figures which according to him the elements would have, could not exist.

That the flow of rivers proves the slope of the land.

940.

PROVES HOW THE EARTH IS NOT GLOBULAR AND NOT BEING GLOBULAR CANNOT HAVE A COMMON CENTRE.

We see the Nile come from Southern regions and traverse various provinces, running towards the North for a distance of 3000 miles and flow into the Mediterranean by the shores of Egypt; and if we will give to this a fall of ten braccia a mile, as is usually allowed to the course of rivers in general, we shall find that the Nile must have its mouth ten miles lower than its source. Again, we see the Rhine, the Rhone and the Danube starting from the German parts, almost the centre of Europe, and having a course one to the East, the other to the North, and the last to Southern seas. And if you consider all this you will see that the plains of Europe in their aggregate are much higher than the high peaks of the maritime mountains; think then how much their tops must be above the sea shores.

Theory of the elevation of water within the mountains.

941.

OF THE HEAT THAT IS IN THE WORLD.

Where there is life there is heat, and where vital heat is, there is movement of vapour. This is proved, inasmuch as we see that the element of fire by its heat always draws to itself damp vapours and thick mists as opaque clouds, which it raises from seas as well as lakes and rivers and damp valleys; and these being drawn by degrees as far as the cold region, the first portion stops, because heat and moisture cannot exist with cold and dryness; and where the first portion stops the rest settle, and thus one portion after another being added, thick and dark clouds are formed. They are often wafted about and borne by the winds from one region to another, where by their density they become so heavy that they fall in thick rain; and if the heat of the sun is added to the power of the element of fire, the clouds are drawn up higher still and find a greater degree of cold, in which they form ice and fall in storms of hail. Now the same heat which holds up so great a weight of water as is seen to rain from the clouds, draws them from below upwards, from the foot of the mountains, and leads and holds them within the summits of the mountains, and these, finding some fissure, issue continuously and cause rivers.

The relative height of the surface of the sea to that of the land (942-945).

942.

OF THE SEA, WHICH TO MANY FOOLS APPEARS TO BE HIGHER THAN THE EARTH WHICH FORMS ITS SHORE.

b d is a plain through which a river flows to the sea; this plain ends at the sea, and since in fact the dry land that is uncovered is not perfectly level--for, if it were, the river would have no motion--as the river does move, this place is a slope rather than a plain; hence this plain d b so ends where the sphere of water begins that if it were extended in a continuous line to b a it would go down beneath the sea, whence it follows that the sea a c b looks higher than the dry land.

Obviously no portions of dry land left uncovered by water can ever be lower than the surface of the watery sphere.

943.

OF CERTAIN PERSONS WHO SAY THE WATERS WERE HIGHER THAN THE DRY LAND.

Certainly I wonder not a little at the common opinion which is contrary to truth, but held by the universal consent of the judgment of men. And this is that all are agreed that the surface of the sea is higher than the highest peaks of the mountains; and they allege many vain and childish reasons, against which I will allege only one simple and short reason; We see plainly that if we could remove the shores of the sea, it would invest the whole earth and make it a perfect sphere. Now, consider how much earth would be carried away to enable the waves of the sea to cover the world; therefore that which would be carried away must be higher than the sea-shore.

944.

THE OPINION OF SOME PERSONS WHO SAY THAT THE WATER OF SOME SEAS IS HIGHER THAN THE HIGHEST SUMMITS OF MOUNTAINS; AND NEVERTHELESS THE WATER WAS FORCED UP TO THESE SUMMITS.

Water would not move from place to place if it were not that it seeks the lowest level and by a natural consequence it never can return to a height like that of the place where it first on issuing from the mountain came to light. And that portion of the sea which, in your vain imagining, you say was so high that it flowed over the summits of the high mountains, for so many centuries would be swallowed up and poured out again through the issue from these mountains. You can well imagine that all the time that Tigris and Euphrates

945.

have flowed from the summits of the mountains of Armenia, it must be believed that all the water of the ocean has passed very many times through these mouths. And do you not believe that the Nile must have sent more water into the sea than at present exists of all the element of water? Undoubtedly, yes. And if all this water had fallen away from this body of the earth, this terrestrial machine would long since have been without water. Whence we may conclude that the water goes from the rivers to the sea, and from the sea to the rivers, thus constantly circulating and returning, and that all the sea and the rivers have passed through the mouth of the Nile an infinite number of times [Footnote: Moti Armeni, Ermini in the original, in M. RAVAISSON'S transcript "monti ernini [le loro ruine?]". He renders this "Le Tigre et l'Euphrate se sont deverses par les sommets des montagnes [avec leurs eaux destructives?] on pent cro're" &c. Leonardo always writes Ermini, Erminia, for Armeni, Armenia (Arabic: Irminiah). M. RAVAISSON also deviates from the original in his translation of the following passage: "Or tu ne crois pas que le Nil ait mis plus d'eau dans la mer qu'il n'y en a a present dans tout l'element de l'eau. Il est certain que si cette eau etait tombee" &c.]

II.

ON THE OCEAN.

Refutation of Pliny's theory as to the saltness of the sea (946. 947).

946.

WHY WATER IS SALT.

Pliny says in his second book, chapter 103, that the water of the sea is salt because the heat of the sun dries up the moisture and drinks it up; and this gives to the wide stretching sea the savour of salt. But this cannot be admitted, because if the saltness of the sea were caused by the heat of the sun, there can be no doubt that lakes, pools and marshes would be so much the more salt, as their waters have less motion and are of less depth; but experience shows us, on the contrary, that these lakes have their waters quite free from salt. Again it is stated by Pliny in the same chapter that this saltness might originate, because all the sweet and subtle portions which the heat attracts easily being taken away, the more bitter and coarser part will remain, and thus the water on the surface is fresher than at the bottom [Footnote 22: Compare No. 948.]; but this is contradicted by the same reason given above, which is, that the same thing would happen in marshes and other waters, which are dried up by the heat. Again, it has been said that the saltness of the sea is the sweat of the earth; to this it may be answered that all the springs of water which penetrate through the earth, would then be salt. But the conclusion is, that the saltness of the sea must proceed from the many springs of water which, as they penetrate into the earth, find mines of salt and these they dissolve in part, and carry with them to the ocean and the other seas, whence the clouds, the begetters of rivers, never carry it up. And the sea would be salter in our times than ever it was at any time; and if the adversary were to say that in infinite time the sea would dry up or congeal into salt, to this I answer that this salt is restored to the earth by the setting free of that part of the earth which rises out of the sea with the salt it has acquired, and the rivers return it to the earth under the sea.

[Footnote: See PLINY, Hist. Nat. II, CIII [C]. Itaque Solis ardore siccatur liquor: et hoc esse masculum sidus accepimus, torrens cuncta sorbensque. (cp. CIV.) Sic mari late patenti saporem incoqui salis, aut quia exhausto inde dulci tenuique, quod facillime trahat vis ignea, omne asperius crassiusque linquatur: ideo summa aequorum aqua dulciorem profundam; hanc esse veriorem causam, quam quod mare terrae sudor sit aeternus: aut quia plurimum ex arido misceatur illi vapore: aut quia terrae natura sicut medicatas aquas inficiat ... (cp. CV): altissimum mare XV. stadiorum Fabianus tradit. Alii n Ponto coadverso Coraxorum gentis (vocant B Ponti) trecentis fere a continenti stadiis immensam altitudinem maris tradunt, vadis nunquam repertis. (cp. CVI [CIII]) Mirabilius id faciunt aquae dulces, juxta mare, ut fistulis emicantes. Nam nec aquarum natura a miraculis cessat. Dulces mari invehuntur, leviores haud dubie. Ideo et marinae, quarum natura gravior, magis invecta sustinent. Quaedam vero et dulces inter se supermeant alias.]

947.

For the third and last reason we will say that salt is in all created things; and this we learn from water passed over the ashes and cinders of burnt things; and the urine of every animal, and the superfluities issuing from their bodies, and the earth into which all things are converted by corruption.

But,--to put it better,--given that the world is everlasting, it must be admitted that its population will also be eternal; hence the human species has eternally been and would be consumers of salt; and if all the mass of the earth were to be turned into salt, it would not suffice for all human food [Footnote 27: That is, on the supposition that salt, once consumed, disappears for ever.]; whence we are forced to admit, either that the species of salt must be everlasting like the world, or that it dies and is born again like the men who devour it. But as experience teaches us that it does not die, as is evident by fire, which does not consume it, and by water which becomes salt in proportion to the quantity dissolved in it,--and when it is evaporated the salt always remains in the original quantity--it must pass through the bodies of men either in the urine or the sweat or other excretions where it is found again; and as much salt is thus got rid of as is carried every year into towns; therefore salt is dug in places where there is urine.-- Sea hogs and sea winds are salt.

We will say that the rains which penetrate the earth are what is under the foundations of cities with their inhabitants, and are what restore through the internal passages of the earth the saltness taken from the sea; and that the change in the place of the sea, which has been over all the mountains, caused it to be left there in the mines found in those mountains, &c.

The characteristics of sea water (948. 949).

948.

The waters of the salt sea are fresh at the greatest depths.

949.

THAT THE OCEAN DOES NOT PENETRATE UNDER THE EARTH.

The ocean does not penetrate under the earth, and this we learn from the many and various springs of fresh water which, in many parts of the ocean make their way up from the bottom to the surface. The same thing is farther proved by wells dug beyond the distance of a mile from the said ocean, which fill with fresh water; and this happens because the fresh water is lighter than salt water and consequently more penetrating.

Which weighs most, water when frozen or when not frozen?

FRESH WATER PENETRATES MORE AGAINST SALT WATER THAN SALT WATER AGAINST FRESH WATER.

That fresh water penetrates more against salt water, than salt water against fresh is proved by a thin cloth dry and old, hanging with the two opposite ends equally low in the two different waters, the surfaces of which are at an equal level; and it will then be seen how much higher the fresh water will rise in this piece of linen than the salt; by so much is the fresh lighter than the salt.

On the formation of Gulfs (950. 951).

950.

All inland seas and the gulfs of those seas, are made by rivers which flow into the sea.

951.

HERE THE REASON IS GIVEN OF THE EFFECTS PRODUCED BY THE WATERS IN THE ABOVE MENTIONED PLACE.

All the lakes and all the gulfs of the sea and all inland seas are due to rivers which distribute their waters into them, and from impediments in their downfall into the Mediterranean --which divides Africa from Europe and Europe from Asia by means of the Nile and the Don which pour their waters into it. It is asked what impediment is great enough to stop the course of the waters which do not reach the ocean.

On the encroachments of the sea on the land and vice versa (952-954).

952.

OF WAVES.

A wave of the sea always breaks in front of its base, and that portion of the crest will then be lowest which before was highest.

[Footnote: The page of FRANCESCO DI GIORGIO'S Trattato, on which Leonardo has written this remark, contains some notes on the construction of dams, harbours &c.]

953.

That the shores of the sea constantly acquire more soil towards the middle of the sea; that the rocks and promontories of the sea are constantly being ruined and worn away; that the Mediterranean seas will in time discover their bottom to the air, and all that will be left will be the channel of the greatest river that enters it; and this will run to the ocean and pour its waters into that with those of all the rivers that are its tributaries.

954.

How the river Po, in a short time might dry up the Adriatic sea in the same way as it has dried up a large part of Lombardy.

The ebb and flow of the tide (955-960).

955.

Where there is a larger quantity of water, there is a greater flow and ebb, but the contrary in narrow waters.

Look whether the sea is at its greatest flow when the moon is half way over our hemisphere [on the meridian].

956.

Whether the flow and ebb are caused by the moon or the sun, or are the breathing of this terrestrial machine. That the flow and ebb are different in different countries and seas.

[Footnote: 1. Allusion may here be made to the mythological explanation of the ebb and flow given in the Edda. Utgardloki says to Thor (Gylfaginning 48): "When thou wert drinking out of the horn, and it seemed to thee that it was slow in emptying a wonder befell, which I should not have believed possible: the other end of the horn lay in the sea, which thou sawest not; but when thou shalt go to the sea, thou shalt see how much thou hast drunk out of it. And that men now call the ebb tide."

Several passages in various manuscripts treat of the ebb and flow. In collecting them I have been guided by the rule only to transcribe those which named some particular spot.]

957.

Book 9 of the meeting of rivers and their flow and ebb. The cause is the same in the sea, where it is caused by the straits of Gibraltar. And again it is caused by whirlpools.

958.

OF THE FLOW AND EBB.

All seas have their flow and ebb in the same period, but they seem to vary because the days do not begin at the same time throughout the universe; in such wise as that when it is midday in our hemisphere, it is midnight in the opposite hemisphere; and at the Eastern boundary of the two hemispheres the night begins which follows on the day, and at the Western boundary of these hemispheres begins the day, which follows the night from the opposite side. Hence it is to be inferred that the above mentioned swelling and diminution in the height of the seas, although they take place in one and the same space of time, are seen to vary from the above mentioned causes. The waters are then withdrawn into the fissures which start from the depths of the sea and which ramify inside the body of the earth, corresponding to the sources of rivers, which are constantly taking from the bottom of the sea the water which has flowed into it. A sea of water is incessantly being drawn off from the surface of the sea. And if you should think that the moon, rising at the Eastern end of the Mediterranean sea must there begin to attract to herself the waters of the sea, it would follow that we must at once see the effect of it at the Eastern end of that sea. Again, as the Mediterranean sea is about the eighth part of the circumference of the aqueous sphere, being 3000 miles long, while the flow and ebb only occur 4 times in 24 hours, these results would not agree with the time of 24 hours, unless this Mediterranean sea were six thousand miles in length; because if such a superabundance of water had to pass through the straits of Gibraltar in running behind the moon, the rush of the water through that strait would be so great, and would rise to such a height, that beyond the straits it would for many miles rush so violently into the ocean as to cause floods and tremendous seething, so that it would be impossible to pass through. This agitated ocean would afterwards return the waters it had received with equal fury to the place they had come from, so that no one ever could pass through those straits. Now experience shows that at every hour they are passed in safety, but when the wind sets in the same direction as the current, the strong ebb increases [Footnote 23: In attempting to get out of the Mediterranean, vessels are sometimes detained for a considerable time; not merely by the causes mentioned by Leonardo but by the constant current flowing eastwards through the middle of the straits of Gibraltar.]. The sea does not raise the water that has issued from the straits, but it checks them and this retards the tide; then it makes up with furious haste for the time it has lost until the end of the ebb movement.

959.

That the flow and ebb are not general; for on the shore at Genoa there is none, at Venice two braccia, between England and Flanders 18 braccia. That in the straits of Sicily the current is very strong because all the waters from the rivers that flow into the Adriatic pass there.

[Footnote: A few more recent data may be given here to facilitate comparison. In the Adriatic the tide rises 2 and 1/2 feet, at Terracina 1 1/4. In the English channel between Calais and Kent it rises from 18 to 20 feet. In the straits of Messina it rises no more than 2 1/2 feet, and that only in stormy weather, but the current is all the stronger. When Leonardo accounts for this by the southward flow of all the Italian rivers along the coasts, the explanation is at least based on a correct observation; namely that a steady current flows southwards along the coast of Calabria and another northwards, along the shores of Sicily; he seems to infer, from the direction of the fust, that the tide in the Adriatic is caused by it.]

960.

In the West, near to Flanders, the sea rises and decreases every 6 hours about 20 braccia, and 22 when the moon is in its favour; but 20 braccia is the general rule, and this rule, as it is evident, cannot have the moon for its cause. This variation in the increase and decrease of the sea every 6 hours may arise from the damming up of the waters, which are poured into the Mediterranean by the quantity of rivers from Africa, Asia and Europe, which flow into that sea, and the waters which are given to it by those rivers; it pours them to the ocean through the straits of Gibraltar, between Abila and Calpe [Footnote 5: Abila, Lat. Abyla, Gr. , now Sierra Ximiera near Ceuta; Calpe, Lat. Calpe. Gr., now Gibraltar. Leonardo here uses the ancient names of the rocks, which were known as the Pillars of Hercules.]. That ocean extends to the island of England and others farther North, and it becomes dammed up and kept high in various gulfs. These, being seas of which the surface is remote from the centre of the earth, have acquired a weight, which as it is greater than the force of the incoming waters which cause it, gives this water an impetus in the contrary direction to that in which it came and it is borne back to meet the waters coming out of the straits; and this it does most against the straits of Gibraltar; these, so long as this goes on, remain dammed up and all the water which is poured out meanwhile by the aforementioned rivers, is pent up [in the Mediterranean]; and this might be assigned as the cause of its flow and ebb, as is shown in the 21st of the 4th of my theory.

III.

SUBTERRANEAN WATER COURSES.

Theory of the circulation of the waters (961. 962).

961.

Very large rivers flow under ground.

962.

This is meant to represent the earth cut through in the middle, showing the depths of the sea and of the earth; the waters start from the bottom of the seas, and ramifying through the earth they rise to the summits of the mountains, flowing back by the rivers and returning to the sea.

Observations in support of the hypothesis (963-969).

963.

The waters circulate with constant motion from the utmost depths of the sea to the highest summits of the mountains, not obeying the nature of heavy matter; and in this case it acts as does the blood of animals which is always moving from the sea of the heart and flows to the top of their heads; and here it is that veins burst--as one may see when a vein bursts in the nose, that all the blood from below rises to the level of the burst vein. When the water rushes out of a burst vein in the earth it obeys the nature of other things heavier than the air, whence it always seeks the lowest places. [7] These waters traverse the body of the earth with infinite ramifications.

[Footnote: The greater part of this passage has been given as No. 849 in the section on Anatomy.]

964.

The same cause which stirs the humours in every species of animal body and by which every injury is repaired, also moves the waters from the utmost depth of the sea to the greatest heights.

965.

It is the property of water that it constitutes the vital human of this arid earth; and the cause which moves it through its ramified veins, against the natural course of heavy matters, is the same property which moves the humours in every species of animal body. But that which crowns our wonder in contemplating it is, that it rises from the utmost depths of the sea to the highest tops of the mountains, and flowing from the opened veins returns to the low seas; then once more, and with extreme swiftness, it mounts again and returns by the same descent, thus rising from the inside to the outside, and going round from the lowest to the highest, from whence it rushes down in a natural course. Thus by these two movements combined in a constant circulation, it travels through the veins of the earth.

966.

WHETHER WATER RISES FROM THE SEA TO THE TOPS OF MOUNTAINS.

The water of the ocean cannot make its way from the bases to the tops of the mountains which bound it, but only so much rises as the dryness of the mountain attracts. And if, on the contrary, the rain, which penetrates from the summit of the mountain to the base, which is the boundary of the sea, descends and softens the slope opposite to the said mountain and constantly draws the water, like a syphon [Footnote 11: Cicognola, Syphon. See Vol. I, Pl. XXIV, No. 1.] which pours through its longest side, it must be this which draws up the water of the sea; thus if s n were the surface of the sea, and the rain descends from the top of the mountain a to n on one side, and on the other sides it descends from a to m, without a doubt this would occur after the manner of distilling through felt, or as happens through the tubes called syphons [Footnote 17: Cicognola, Syphon. See Vol. I, Pl. XXIV, No. 1.]. And at all times the water which has softened the mountain, by the great rain which runs down the two opposite sides, would constantly attract the rain a n, on its longest side together with the water from the sea, if that side of the mountain a m were longer than the other a n; but this cannot be, because no part of the earth which is not submerged by the ocean can be lower than that ocean.

967.

OF SPRINGS OF WATER ON THE TOPS OF MOUNTAINS.

It is quite evident that the whole surface of the ocean--when there is no storm--is at an equal distance from the centre of the earth, and that the tops of the mountains are farther from this centre in proportion as they rise above the surface of that sea; therefore if the body of the earth were not like that of man, it would be impossible that the waters of the sea--being so much lower than the mountains--could by their nature rise up to the summits of these mountains. Hence it is to be believed that the same cause which keeps the blood at the top of the head in man keeps the water at the summits of the mountains.

[Footnote: This conception of the rising of the blood, which has given rise to the comparison, was recognised as erroneous by Leonardo himself at a later period. It must be remembered that the MS. A, from which these passages are taken, was written about twenty years earlier than the MS. Leic. (Nos. 963 and 849) and twenty-five years before the MS. W. An. IV.

There is, in the original a sketch with No. 968 which is not reproduced. It represents a hill of the same shape as that shown at No. 982. There are veins, or branched streams, on the side of the hill, like those on the skull Pl. CVIII, No. 4]

968.

IN CONFIRMATION OF WHY THE WATER GOES TO THE TOPS OF MOUNTAINS.

I say that just as the natural heat of the blood in the veins keeps it in the head of man,--for when the man is dead the cold blood sinks to the lower parts-- and when the sun is hot on the head of a man the blood increases and rises so much, with other humours, that by pressure in the veins pains in the head are often caused; in the same way veins ramify through the body of the earth, and by the natural heat which is distributed throughout the containing body, the water is raised through the veins to the tops of mountains. And this water, which passes through a closed conduit inside the body of the mountain like a dead thing, cannot come forth from its low place unless it is warmed by the vital heat of the spring time. Again, the heat of the element of fire and, by day, the heat of the sun, have power to draw forth the moisture of the low parts of the mountains and to draw them up, in the same way as it draws the clouds and collects their moisture from the bed of the sea.

969.

That many springs of salt water are found at great distances from the sea; this might happen because such springs pass through some mine of salt, like that in Hungary where salt is hewn out of vast caverns, just as stone is hewn.

[Footnote: The great mine of Wieliczka in Galicia, out of which a million cwt. of rock-salt are annually dug out, extends for 3000 metres from West to East, and 1150 metres from North to South.]

IV.

OF RIVERS.

On the way in which the sources of rivers are fed.

970.

OF THE ORIGIN OF RIVERS.

The body of the earth, like the bodies of animals, is intersected with ramifications of waters which are all in connection and are constituted to give nutriment and life to the earth and to its creatures. These come from the depth of the sea and, after many revolutions, have to return to it by the rivers created by the bursting of these springs; and if you chose to say that the rains of the winter or the melting of the snows in summer were the cause of the birth of rivers, I could mention the rivers which originate in the torrid countries of Africa, where it never rains--and still less snows--because the intense heat always melts into air all the clouds which are borne thither by the winds. And if you chose to say that such rivers, as increase in July and August, come from the snows which melt in May and June from the sun's approach to the snows on the mountains of Scythia [Footnote 9: Scythia means here, as in Ancient Geography, the whole of the Northern part of Asia as far as India.], and that such meltings come down into certain valleys and form lakes, into which they enter by springs and subterranean caves to issue forth again at the sources of the Nile, this is false; because Scythia is lower than the sources of the Nile, and, besides, Scythia is only 400 miles from the Black sea and the sources of the Nile are 3000 miles distant from the sea of Egypt into which its waters flow.

The tide in estuaries.

971.

Book 9, of the meeting of rivers and of their ebb and flow. The cause is the same in the sea, where it is caused by the straits of Gibraltar; and again it is caused by whirlpools.

[3] If two rivers meet together to form a straight line, and then below two right angles take their course together, the flow and ebb will happen now in one river and now in the other above their confluence, and principally if the outlet for their united volume is no swifter than when they were separate. Here occur 4 instances.

[Footnote: The first two lines of this passage have already been given as No. 957. In the margin, near line 3 of this passage, the text given as No. 919 is written.]

On the alterations, caused in the courses of rivers by their confluence (972-974).

972.

When a smaller river pours its waters into a larger one, and that larger one flows from the opposite direction, the course of the smaller river will bend up against the approach of the larger river; and this happens because, when the larger river fills up all its bed with water, it makes an eddy in front of the mouth of the other river, and so carries the water poured in by the smaller river with its own. When the smaller river pours its waters into the larger one, which runs across the current at the mouth of the smaller river, its waters will bend with the downward movement of the larger river. [Footnote: In the original sketches the word Arno is written at the spot here marked A, at R. Rifredi, and at M. Mugnone.]

973.

When the fulness of rivers is diminished, then the acute angles formed at the junction of their branches become shorter at the sides and wider at the point; like the current a n and the current d n, which unite in n when the river is at its greatest fulness. I say, that when it is in this condition if, before the fullest time, d n was lower than a n, at the time of fulness d n will be full of sand and mud. When the water d n falls, it will carry away the mud and remain with a lower bottom, and the channel a n finding itself the higher, will fling its waters into the lower, d n, and will wash away all the point of the sand-spit b n c, and thus the angle a c d will remain larger than the angle a n d and the sides shorter, as I said before.

[Footnote: Above the first sketch we find, in the original, this note: "Sopra il pote rubaconte alla torricella"; and by the second, which represents a pier of a bridge, "Sotto l'ospedal del ceppo."]

974.

WATER.

OF THE MOVEMENT OF A SUDDEN RUSH MADE BY A RIVER IN ITS BED PREVIOUSLY DRY.

In proportion as the current of the water given forth by the draining of the lake is slow or rapid in the dry river bed, so will this river be wider or narrower, or shallower or deeper in one place than another, according to this proposition: the flow and ebb of the sea which enters the Mediterranean from the ocean, and of the rivers which meet and struggle with it, will raise their waters more or less in proportion as the sea is wider or narrower.

[Footnote: In the margin is a sketch of a river which winds so as to form islands.]

Whirlpools.

975.

Whirlpools, that is to say caverns; that is to say places left by precipitated waters.

On the alterations in the channels of rivers.

976.

OF THE VIBRATION OF THE EARTH.

The subterranean channels of waters, like those which exist between the air and the earth, are those which unceasingly wear away and deepen the beds of their currents.

The origin of the sand in rivers (977. 978).

977.

A river that flows from mountains deposits a great quantity of large stones in its bed, which still have some of their angles and sides, and in the course of its flow it carries down smaller stones with the angles more worn; that is to say the large stones become smaller. And farther on it deposits coarse gravel and then smaller, and as it proceeds this becomes coarse sand and then finer, and going on thus the water, turbid with sand and gravel, joins the sea; and the sand settles on the sea-shores, being cast up by the salt waves; and there results the sand of so fine a nature as to seem almost like water, and it will not stop on the shores of the sea but returns by reason of its lightness, because it was originally formed of rotten leaves and other very light things. Still, being almost--as was said--of the nature of water itself, it afterwards, when the weather is calm, settles and becomes solid at the bottom of the sea, where by its fineness it becomes compact and by its smoothness resists the waves which glide over it; and in this shells are found; and this is white earth, fit for pottery.

978.

All the torrents of water flowing from the mountains to the sea carry with them the stones from the hills to the sea, and by the influx of the sea-water towards the mountains; these stones were thrown back towards the mountains, and as the waters rose and retired, the stones were tossed about by it and in rolling, their angles hit together; then as the parts, which least resisted the blows, were worn off, the stones ceased to be angular and became round in form, as may be seen on the banks of the Elsa. And those remained larger which were less removed from their native spot; and they became smaller, the farther they were carried from that place, so that in the process they were converted into small pebbles and then into sand and at last into mud. After the sea had receded from the mountains the brine left by the sea with other humours of the earth made a concretion of these pebbles and this sand, so that the pebbles were converted into rock and the sand into tufa. And of this we see an example in the Adda where it issues from the mountains of Como and in the Ticino, the Adige and the Oglio coming from the German Alps, and in the Arno at Monte Albano [Footnote 13: At the foot of Monte Albano lies Vinci, the birth place of Leonardo. Opposite, on the other bank of the Arno, is Monte Lupo.], near Monte Lupo and Capraia where the rocks, which are very large, are all of conglomerated pebbles of various kinds and colours.

V.

ON MOUNTAINS.

The formation of mountains (979-983).

979.

Mountains are made by the currents of rivers.

Mountains are destroyed by the currents of rivers.

[Footnote: Compare 789.]

980.

That the Northern bases of some Alps are not yet petrified. And this is plainly to be seen where the rivers, which cut through them, flow towards the North; where they cut through the strata in the living stone in the higher parts of the mountains; and, where they join the plains, these strata are all of potter's clay; as is to be seen in the valley of Lamona where the river Lamona, as it issues from the Appenines, does these things on its banks.

That the rivers have all cut and divided the mountains of the great Alps one from the other. This is visible in the order of the stratified rocks, because from the summits of the banks, down to the river the correspondence of the strata in the rocks is visible on either side of the river. That the stratified stones of the mountains are all layers of clay, deposited one above the other by the various floods of the rivers. That the different size of the strata is caused by the difference in the floods--that is to say greater or lesser floods.

981.

The summits of mountains for a long time rise constantly.

The opposite sides of the mountains always approach each other below; the depths of the valleys which are above the sphere of the waters are in the course of time constantly getting nearer to the centre of the world.

In an equal period, the valleys sink much more than the mountains rise.

The bases of the mountains always come closer together.

In proportion as the valleys become deeper, the more quickly are their sides worn away.

982.

In every concavity at the summit of the mountains we shall always find the divisions of the strata in the rocks.

983.

OF THE SEA WHICH ENCIRCLES THE EARTH.

I find that of old, the state of the earth was that its plains were all covered up and hidden by salt water. [Footnote: This passage has already been published by Dr. M. JORDAN: Das Malerbuch des L. da Vinci, Leipzig 1873, p. 86. However, his reading of the text differs from mine.]

The authorities for the study of the structure of the earth.

984.

Since things are much more ancient than letters, it is no marvel if, in our day, no records exist of these seas having covered so many countries; and if, moreover, some records had existed, war and conflagrations, the deluge of waters, the changes of languages and of laws have consumed every thing ancient. But sufficient for us is the testimony of things created in the salt waters, and found again in high mountains far from the seas.

VI.

GEOLOGICAL PROBLEMS.

985.

In this work you have first to prove that the shells at a thousand braccia of elevation were not carried there by the deluge, because they are seen to be all at one level, and many mountains are seen to be above that level; and to inquire whether the deluge was caused by rain or by the swelling of the sea; and then you must show how, neither by rain nor by swelling of the rivers, nor by the overflow of this sea, could the shells--being heavy objects--be floated up the mountains by the sea, nor have carried there by the rivers against the course of their waters.

Doubts about the deluge.

986.

A DOUBTFUL POINT.

Here a doubt arises, and that is: whether the deluge, which happened at the time of Noah, was universal or not. And it would seem not, for the reasons now to be given: We have it in the Bible that this deluge lasted 40 days and 40 nights of incessant and universal rain, and that this rain rose to ten cubits above the highest mountains in the world. And if it had been that the rain was universal, it would have covered our globe which is spherical in form. And this spherical surface is equally distant in every part, from the centre of its sphere; hence the sphere of the waters being under the same conditions, it is impossible that the water upon it should move, because water, in itself, does not move unless it falls; therefore how could the waters of such a deluge depart, if it is proved that it has no motion? and if it departed how could it move unless it went upwards? Here, then, natural reasons are wanting; hence to remove this doubt it is necessary to call in a miracle to aid us, or else to say that all this water was evaporated by the heat of the sun.

[Footnote: The passages, here given from the MS. Leic., have hitherto remained unknown. Some preliminary notes on the subject are to be found in MS. F 8oa and 8ob; but as compared with the fuller treatment here given, they are, it seems to me, of secondary interest. They contain nothing that is not repeated here more clearly and fully. LIBRI, Histoire des Sciences mathematiques III, pages 218--221, has printed the text of F 80a and 80b, therefore it seemed desirable to give my reasons for not inserting it in this work.]

That marine shells could not go up the mountains.

987.

OF THE DELUGE AND OF MARINE SHELLS.

If you were to say that the shells which are to be seen within the confines of Italy now, in our days, far from the sea and at such heights, had been brought there by the deluge which left them there, I should answer that if you believe that this deluge rose 7 cubits above the highest mountains-- as he who measured it has written--these shells, which always live near the sea-shore, should have been left on the mountains; and not such a little way from the foot of the mountains; nor all at one level, nor in layers upon layers. And if you were to say that these shells are desirous of remaining near to the margin of the sea, and that, as it rose in height, the shells quitted their first home, and followed the increase of the waters up to their highest level; to this I answer, that the cockle is an animal of not more rapid movement than the snail is out of water, or even somewhat slower; because it does not swim, on the contrary it makes a furrow in the sand by means of its sides, and in this furrow it will travel each day from 3 to 4 braccia; therefore this creature, with so slow a motion, could not have travelled from the Adriatic sea as far as Monferrato in Lombardy [Footnote: Monferrato di Lombardia. The range of hills of Monferrato is in Piedmont, and Casale di Monferrato belonged, in Leonardo's time, to the Marchese di Mantova.], which is 250 miles distance, in 40 days; which he has said who took account of the time. And if you say that the waves carried them there, by their gravity they could not move, excepting at the bottom. And if you will not grant me this, confess at least that they would have to stay at the summits of the highest mountains, in the lakes which are enclosed among the mountains, like the lakes of Lario, or of Como and il Maggiore [Footnote: Lago di Lario. Lacus Larius was the name given by the Romans to the lake of Como. It is evident that it is here a slip of the pen since the the the words in the MS. are: "Come Lago di Lario o'l Magare e di Como," In the MS. after line 16 we come upon a digression treating of the weight of water; this has here been omitted. It is 11 lines long.] and of Fiesole, and of Perugia, and others.

And if you should say that the shells were carried by the waves, being empty and dead, I say that where the dead went they were not far removed from the living; for in these mountains living ones are found, which are recognisable by the shells being in pairs; and they are in a layer where there are no dead ones; and a little higher up they are found, where they were thrown by the waves, all the dead ones with their shells separated, near to where the rivers fell into the sea, to a great depth; like the Arno which fell from the Gonfolina near to Monte Lupo [Footnote: Monte Lupo, compare 970, 13; it is between Empoli and Florence.], where it left a deposit of gravel which may still be seen, and which has agglomerated; and of stones of various districts, natures, and colours and hardness, making one single conglomerate. And a little beyond the sandstone conglomerate a tufa has been formed, where it turned towards Castel Florentino; farther on, the mud was deposited in which the shells lived, and which rose in layers according to the levels at which the turbid Arno flowed into that sea. And from time to time the bottom of the sea was raised, depositing these shells in layers, as may be seen in the cutting at Colle Gonzoli, laid open by the Arno which is wearing away the base of it; in which cutting the said layers of shells are very plainly to be seen in clay of a bluish colour, and various marine objects are found there. And if the earth of our hemisphere is indeed raised by so much higher than it used to be, it must have become by so much lighter by the waters which it lost through the rift between Gibraltar and Ceuta; and all the more the higher it rose, because the weight of the waters which were thus lost would be added to the earth in the other hemisphere. And if the shells had been carried by the muddy deluge they would have been mixed up, and separated from each other amidst the mud, and not in regular steps and layers-- as we see them now in our time.

The marine shells were not produced away from the sea.

988.

As to those who say that shells existed for a long time and were born at a distance from the sea, from the nature of the place and of the cycles, which can influence a place to produce such creatures--to them it may be answered: such an influence could not place the animals all on one line, except those of the same sort and age; and not the old with the young, nor some with an operculum and others without their operculum, nor some broken and others whole, nor some filled with sea-sand and large and small fragments of other shells inside the whole shells which remained open; nor the claws of crabs without the rest of their bodies; nor the shells of other species stuck on to them like animals which have moved about on them; since the traces of their track still remain, on the outside, after the manner of worms in the wood which they ate into. Nor would there be found among them the bones and teeth of fish which some call arrows and others serpents' tongues, nor would so many [Footnote: I. Scilla argued against this hypothesis, which was still accepted in his days; see: La vana Speculazione, Napoli 1670.] portions of various animals be found all together if they had not been thrown on the sea shore. And the deluge cannot have carried them there, because things that are heavier than water do not float on the water. But these things could not be at so great a height if they had not been carried there by the water, such a thing being impossible from their weight. In places where the valleys have not been filled with salt sea water shells are never to be seen; as is plainly visible in the great valley of the Arno above Gonfolina; a rock formerly united to Monte Albano, in the form of a very high bank which kept the river pent up, in such a way that before it could flow into the sea, which was afterwards at its foot, it formed two great lakes; of which the first was where we now see the city of Florence together with Prato and Pistoia, and Monte Albano. It followed the rest of its bank as far as where Serravalle now stands. >From the Val d'Arno upwards, as far as Arezzo, another lake was formed, which discharged its waters into the former lake. It was closed at about the spot where now we see Girone, and occupied the whole of that valley above for a distance of 40 miles in length. This valley received on its bottom all the soil brought down by the turbid waters. And this is still to be seen at the foot of Prato Magno; it there lies very high where the rivers have not worn it away. Across this land are to be seen the deep cuts of the rivers that have passed there, falling from the great mountain of Prato Magno; in these cuts there are no vestiges of any shells or of marine soil. This lake was joined with that of Perugia [Footnote: See Pl. CXIII.]

A great quantity of shells are to be seen where the rivers flow into the sea, because on such shores the waters are not so salt owing to the admixture of the fresh water, which is poured into it. Evidence of this is to be seen where, of old, the Appenines poured their rivers into the Adriatic sea; for there in most places great quantities of shells are to be found, among the mountains, together with bluish marine clay; and all the rocks which are torn off in such places are full of shells. The same may be observed to have been done by the Arno when it fell from the rock of Gonfolina into the sea, which was not so very far below; for at that time it was higher than the top of San Miniato al Tedesco, since at the highest summit of this the shores may be seen full of shells and oysters within its flanks. The shells did not extend towards Val di Nievole, because the fresh waters of the Arno did not extend so far.

That the shells were not carried away from the sea by the deluge, because the waters which came from the earth although they drew the sea towards the earth, were those which struck its depths; because the water which goes down from the earth, has a stronger current than that of the sea, and in consequence is more powerful, and it enters beneath the sea water and stirs the depths and carries with it all sorts of movable objects which are to be found in the earth, such as the above-mentioned shells and other similar things. And in proportion as the water which comes from the land is muddier than sea water it is stronger and heavier than this; therefore I see no way of getting the said shells so far in land, unless they had been born there. If you were to tell me that the river Loire [Footnote: Leonardo has written Era instead of Loera or Loira--perhaps under the mistaken idea that Lo was an article.],which traverses France covers when the sea rises more than eighty miles of country, because it is a district of vast plains, and the sea rises about 20 braccia, and shells are found in this plain at the distance of 80 miles from the sea; here I answer that the flow and ebb in our Mediterranean Sea does not vary so much; for at Genoa it does not rise at all, and at Venice but little, and very little in Africa; and where it varies little it covers but little of the country.

The course of the water of a river always rises higher in a place where the current is impeded; it behaves as it does where it is reduced in width to pass under the arches of a bridge.

Further researches (989-991).

989.

A CONFUTATION OF THOSE WHO SAY THAT SHELLS MAY HAVE BEEN CARRIED TO A DISTANCE OF MANY DAYS' JOURNEY FROM THE SEA BY THE DELUGE, WHICH WAS SO HIGH AS TO BE ABOVE THOSE HEIGHTS.

I say that the deluge could not carry objects, native to the sea, up to the mountains, unless the sea had already increased so as to create inundations as high up as those places; and this increase could not have occurred because it would cause a vacuum; and if you were to say that the air would rush in there, we have already concluded that what is heavy cannot remain above what is light, whence of necessity we must conclude that this deluge was caused by rain water, so that all these waters ran to the sea, and the sea did not run up the mountains; and as they ran to the sea, they thrust the shells from the shore of sea and did not draw them to wards themselves. And if you were then to say that the sea, raised by the rain water, had carried these shells to such a height, we have already said that things heavier than water cannot rise upon it, but remain at the bottom of it, and do not move unless by the impact of the waves. And if you were to say that the waves had carried them to such high spots, we have proved that the waves in a great depth move in a contrary direction at the bottom to the motion at the top, and this is shown by the turbidity of the sea from the earth washed down near its shores. Anything which is lighter than the water moves with the waves, and is left on the highest level of the highest margin of the waves. Anything which is heavier than the water moves, suspended in it, between the surface and the bottom; and from these two conclusions, which will be amply proved in their place, we infer that the waves of the surface cannot convey shells, since they are heavier than water.

If the deluge had to carry shells three hundred and four hundred miles from the sea, it would have carried them mixed with various other natural objects heaped together; and we see at such distances oysters all together, and sea-snails, and cuttlefish, and all the other shells which congregate together, all to be found together and dead; and the solitary shells are found wide apart from each other, as we may see them on sea-shores every day. And if we find oysters of very large shells joined together and among them very many which still have the covering attached, indicating that they were left here by the sea, and still living when the strait of Gibraltar was cut through; there are to be seen, in the mountains of Parma and Piacenza, a multitude of shells and corals, full of holes, and still sticking to the rocks there. When I was making the great horse for Milan, a large sack full was brought to me in my workshop by certain peasants; these were found in that place and among them were many preserved in their first freshness.

Under ground, and under the foundations of buildings, timbers are found of wrought beams and already black. Such were found in my time in those diggings at Castel Fiorentino. And these had been in that deep place before the sand carried by the Arno into the sea, then covering the plain, had heen raised to such a height; and before the plains of Casentino had been so much lowered, by the earth being constantly carried down from them.

[Footnote: These lines are written in the margin.]

And if you were to say that these shells were created, and were continually being created in such places by the nature of the spot, and of the heavens which might have some influence there, such an opinion cannot exist in a brain of much reason; because here are the years of their growth, numbered on their shells, and there are large and small ones to be seen which could not have grown without food, and could not have fed without motion--and here they could not move [Footnote: These lines are written in the margin.]

990.

That in the drifts, among one and another, there are still to be found the traces of the worms which crawled upon them when they were not yet dry. And all marine clays still contain shells, and the shells are petrified together with the clay. From their firmness and unity some persons will have it that these animals were carried up to places remote from the sea by the deluge. Another sect of ignorant persons declare that Nature or Heaven created them in these places by celestial influences, as if in these places we did not also find the bones of fishes which have taken a long time to grow; and as if, we could not count, in the shells of cockles and snails, the years and months of their life, as we do in the horns of bulls and oxen, and in the branches of plants that have never been cut in any part. Besides, having proved by these signs the length of their lives, it is evident, and it must be admitted, that these animals could not live without moving to fetch their food; and we find in them no instrument for penetrating the earth or the rock where we find them enclosed. But how could we find in a large snail shell the fragments and portions of many other sorts of shells, of various sorts, if they had not been thrown there, when dead, by the waves of the sea like the other light objects which it throws on the earth? Why do we find so many fragments and whole shells between layer and layer of stone, if this had not formerly been covered on the shore by a layer of earth thrown up by the sea, and which was afterwards petrified? And if the deluge before mentioned had carried them to these parts of the sea, you might find these shells at the boundary of one drift but not at the boundary between many drifts. We must also account for the winters of the years during which the sea multiplied the drifts of sand and mud brought down by the neighbouring rivers, by washing down the shores; and if you chose to say that there were several deluges to produce these rifts and the shells among them, you would also have to affirm that such a deluge took place every year. Again, among the fragments of these shells, it must be presumed that in those places there were sea coasts, where all the shells were thrown up, broken, and divided, and never in pairs, since they are found alive in the sea, with two valves, each serving as a lid to the other; and in the drifts of rivers and on the shores of the sea they are found in fragments. And within the limits of the separate strata of rocks they are found, few in number and in pairs like those which were left by the sea, buried alive in the mud, which subsequently dried up and, in time, was petrified.

991.

And if you choose to say that it was the deluge which carried these shells away from the sea for hundreds of miles, this cannot have happened, since that deluge was caused by rain; because rain naturally forces the rivers to rush towards the sea with all the things they carry with them, and not to bear the dead things of the sea shores to the mountains. And if you choose to say that the deluge afterwards rose with its waters above the mountains, the movement of the sea must have been so sluggish in its rise against the currents of the rivers, that it could not have carried, floating upon it, things heavier than itself; and even if it had supported them, in its receding it would have left them strewn about, in various spots. But how are we to account for the corals which are found every day towards Monte Ferrato in Lombardy, with the holes of the worms in them, sticking to rocks left uncovered by the currents of rivers? These rocks are all covered with stocks and families of oysters, which as we know, never move, but always remain with one of their halves stuck to a rock, and the other they open to feed themselves on the animalcules that swim in the water, which, hoping to find good feeding ground, become the food of these shells. We do not find that the sand mixed with seaweed has been petrified, because the weed which was mingled with it has shrunk away, and this the Po shows us every day in the debris of its banks.

Other problems (992-994).

992.

Why do we find the bones of great fishes and oysters and corals and various other shells and sea-snails on the high summits of mountains by the sea, just as we find them in low seas?

993.

You now have to prove that the shells cannot have originated if not in salt water, almost all being of that sort; and that the shells in Lombardy are at four levels, and thus it is everywhere, having been made at various times. And they all occur in valleys that open towards the seas.

994.

>From the two lines of shells we are forced to say that the earth indignantly submerged under the sea and so the first layer was made; and then the deluge made the second.

[Footnote: This note is in the early writing of about 1470--1480. On the same sheet are the passages No. 1217 and 1219. Compare also No. 1339. All the foregoing chapters are from Manuscripts of about 1510. This explains the want of connection and the contradiction between this and the foregoing texts.]

VII.

ON THE ATMOSPHERE.

Constituents of the atmosphere.

995.

That the brightness of the air is occasioned by the water which has dissolved itself in it into imperceptible molecules. These, being lighted by the sun from the opposite side, reflect the brightness which is visible in the air; and the azure which is seen in it is caused by the darkness that is hidden beyond the air. [Footnote: Compare Vol. I, No. 300.]

On the motion of air (996--999).

996.

That the return eddies of wind at the mouth of certain valleys strike upon the waters and scoop them out in a great hollow, whirl the water into the air in the form of a column, and of the colour of a cloud. And I saw this thing happen on a sand bank in the Arno, where the sand was hollowed out to a greater depth than the stature of a man; and with it the gravel was whirled round and flung about for a great space; it appeared in the air in the form of a great bell-tower; and the top spread like the branches of a pine tree, and then it bent at the contact of the direct wind, which passed over from the mountains.

997.

The element of fire acts upon a wave of air in the same way as the air does on water, or as water does on a mass of sand --that is earth; and their motions are in the same proportions as those of the motors acting upon them.

998.

OF MOTION.

I ask whether the true motion of the clouds can be known by the motion of their shadows; and in like manner of the motion of the sun.

999.

To know better the direction of the winds. [Footnote: In connection with this text I may here mention a hygrometer, drawn and probably invented by Leonardo. A facsimile of this is given in Vol. I, p. 297 with the note: 'Modi di pesare l'arie eddi sapere quando s'a arrompere il tepo' (Mode of weighing the air and of knowing when the weather will change); by the sponge "Spugnea" is written.]

The globe an organism.

1000.

Nothing originates in a spot where there is no sentient, vegetable and rational life; feathers grow upon birds and are changed every year; hairs grow upon animals and are changed every year, excepting some parts, like the hairs of the beard in lions, cats and their like. The grass grows in the fields, and the leaves on the trees, and every year they are, in great part, renewed. So that we might say that the earth has a spirit of growth; that its flesh is the soil, its bones the arrangement and connection of the rocks of which the mountains are composed, its cartilage the tufa, and its blood the springs of water. The pool of blood which lies round the heart is the ocean, and its breathing, and the increase and decrease of the blood in the pulses, is represented in the earth by the flow and ebb of the sea; and the heat of the spirit of the world is the fire which pervades the earth, and the seat of the vegetative soul is in the fires, which in many parts of the earth find vent in baths and mines of sulphur, and in volcanoes, as at Mount Aetna in Sicily, and in many other places.

[Footnote: Compare No. 929.]

XVII. Topographical Notes.

A large part of the texts published in this section might perhaps have found their proper place in connection with the foregoing chapters on Physical Geography. But these observations on Physical Geography, of whatever kind they may be, as soon as they are localised acquire a special interest and importance and particularly as bearing on the question whether Leonardo himself made the observations recorded at the places mentioned or merely noted the statements from hearsay. In a few instances he himself tells us that he writes at second hand. In some cases again, although the style and expressions used make it seem highly probable that he has derived his information from others-- though, as it seems to me, these cases are not very numerous--we find, on the other hand, among these topographical notes a great number of observations, about which it is extremely difficult to form a decided opinion. Of what the Master's life and travels may have been throughout his sixty-seven years of life we know comparatively little; for a long course of time, and particularly from about 1482 to 1486, we do not even know with certainty that he was living in Italy. Thus, from a biographical point of view a very great interest attaches to some of the topographical notes, and for this reason it seemed that it would add to their value to arrange them in a group by themselves. Leonardo's intimate knowledge with places, some of which were certainly remote from his native home, are of importance as contributing to decide the still open question as to the extent of Leonardo's travels. We shall find in these notes a confirmation of the view, that the MSS. in which the Topographical Notes occur are in only a very few instances such diaries as may have been in use during a journey. These notes are mostly found in the MSS. books of his later and quieter years, and it is certainly remarkable that Leonardo is very reticent as to the authorities from whom he quotes his facts and observations: For instance, as to the Straits of Gibraltar, the Nile, the Taurus Mountains and the Tigris and Euphrates. Is it likely that he, who declared that in all scientific research, his own experience should be the foundation of his statements (see XIX Philosophy No. 987--991,) should here have made an exception to this rule without mentioning it?

As for instance in the discussion as to the equilibrium of the mass of water in the Mediterranean Sea--a subject which, it may be observed, had at that time attracted the interest and study of hardly any other observer. The acute remarks, in Nos. 985--993, on the presence of shells at the tops of mountains, suffice to prove--as it seems to me--that it was not in his nature to allow himself to be betrayed into wide generalisations, extending beyond the limits of his own investigations, even by such brilliant results of personal study.

Most of these Topographical Notes, though suggesting very careful and thorough research, do not however, as has been said, afford necessarily indisputable evidence that that research was Leonardo's own. But it must be granted that in more than one instance probability is in favour of this idea.

Among the passages which treat somewhat fully of the topography of Eastern places by far the most interesting is a description of the Taurus Mountains; but as this text is written in the style of a formal report and, in the original, is associated with certain letters which give us the history of its origin, I have thought it best not to sever it from that connection. It will be found under No. XXI (Letters).

That Florence, and its neighbourhood, where Leonardo spent his early years, should be nowhere mentioned except in connection with the projects for canals, which occupied his attention for some short time during the first ten years of the XVIth century, need not surprise us. The various passages relating to the construction of canals in Tuscany, which are put together at the beginning, are immediately followed by those which deal with schemes for canals in Lombardy; and after these come notes on the city and vicinity of Milan as well as on the lakes of North Italy.

The notes on some towns of Central Italy which Leonardo visited in 1502, when in the service of Cesare Borgia, are reproduced here in the same order as in the note book used during these travels (MS. L., Institut de France). These notes have but little interest in themselves excepting as suggesting his itinerary. The maps of the districts drawn by Leonardo at the time are more valuable (see No. 1054 note). The names on these maps are not written from right to left, but in the usual manner, and we are permitted to infer that they were made in obedience to some command, possibly for the use of Cesare Borgia himself; the fact that they remained nevertheless in Leonardo's hands is not surprising when we remember the sudden political changes and warlike events of the period. There can be no doubt that these maps, which are here published for the first time, are original in the strictest sense of the word, that is to say drawn from observations of the places themselves; this is proved by the fact--among others--that we find among his manuscripts not only the finished maps themselves but the rough sketches and studies for them. And it would perhaps be difficult to point out among the abundant contributions to geographical knowledge published during the XVIth century, any maps at all approaching these in accuracy and finish.

The interesting map of the world, so far as it was then known, which is among the Leonardo MSS. at Windsor (published in the 'Archaeologia' Vol. XI) cannot be attributed to the Master, as the Marchese Girolamo d'Adda has sufficiently proved; it has not therefore been reproduced here.

Such of Leonardo's observations on places in Italy as were made before or after his official travels as military engineer to Cesare Borgia, have been arranged in alphabetical order, under Nos. 1034-1054. The most interesting are those which relate to the Alps and the Appenines, Nos. 1057-1068.

Most of the passages in which France is mentioned have hitherto remained unknown, as well as those which treat of the countries bordering on the Mediterranean, which come at the end of this section. Though these may be regarded as of a more questionable importance in their bearing on the biography of the Master than those which mention places in France, it must be allowed that they are interesting as showing the prominent place which the countries of the East held in his geographical studies. He never once alludes to the discovery of America.

I.

ITALY.

Canals in connection with the Arno (1001-1008).

1001.

CANAL OF FLORENCE.

Sluices should be made in the valley of la Chiana at Arezzo, so that when, in the summer, the Arno lacks water, the canal may not remain dry: and let this canal be 20 braccia wide at the bottom, and at the top 30, and 2 braccia deep, or 4, so that two of these braccia may flow to the mills and the meadows, which will benefit the country; and Prato, Pistoia and Pisa, as well as Florence, will gain two hundred thousand ducats a year, and will lend a hand and money to this useful work; and the Lucchese the same, for the lake of Sesto will be navigable; I shall direct it to Prato and Pistoia, and cut through Serravalle and make an issue into the lake; for there will be no need of locks or supports, which are not lasting and so will always be giving trouble in working at them and keeping them up.

And know that in digging this canal where it is 4 braccia deep, it will cost 4 dinari the square braccio; for twice the depth 6 dinari, if you are making 4 braccia [Footnote: This passage is illustrated by a slightly sketched map, on which these places are indicated from West to East: Pisa, Luccha, Lago, Seravalle, Pistoja, Prato, Firenze.] and there are but 2 banks; that is to say one from the bottom of the trench to the surface of the edges of it, and the other from these edges to the top of the ridge of earth which will be raised on the margin of the bank. And if this bank were of double the depth only the first bank will be increased, that is 4 braccia increased by half the first cost; that is to say that if at first 4 dinari were paid for 2 banks, for 3 it would come to 6, at 2 dinari the bank, if the trench measured 16 braccia at the bottom; again, if the trench were 16 braccia wide and 4 deep, coming to 4 lire for the work, 4 Milan dinari the square braccio; a trench which was 32 braccia at the bottom would come to 8 dinari the square braccio.

1002.

>From the wall of the Arno at [the gate of] la Giustizia to the bank of the Arno at Sardigna where the walls are, to the mills, is 7400 braccia, that is 2 miles and 1400 braccia and beyond the Arno is 5500 braccia.

[Footnote: 2. Giustizia. By this the Porta della Giustizia seems to be meant; from the XVth to the XVIth centuries it was also commonly known as Porta Guelfa, Porta San Francesco del Renaio, Porta Nuova, and Porta Reale. It was close to the Arno opposite to the Porta San Niccolo, which still exists.]

1003.

By guiding the Arno above and below a treasure will be found in each acre of ground by whomsoever will.

1004.

The wall of the old houses runs towards the gate of San Nicolo.

[Footnote: By the side of this text there is an indistinct sketch, resembling that given under No.973. On the bank is written the word Casace. There then follows in the original a passage of 12 lines in which the consequences of the windings of the river are discussed. A larger but equally hasty diagram on the same page represents the shores of the Arno inside Florence as in two parallel lines. Four horizontal lines indicate the bridges. By the side these measures are stated in figures: I. (at the Ponte alla Carraja): 230--largho br. 12 e 2 di spoda e 14 di pile e a 4 pilastri; 2. (at the Ponte S. Trinita); 188--largho br. 15 e 2 di spode he 28 di pilastri for delle spode e pilastri so 2; 3. (at the Ponte vecchio); pote lung br. 152 e largo; 4. (at the Ponte alle Grazie): 290 ellargo 12 e 2 di spode e 6 di pili.

There is, in MS. W. L. 2l2b, a sketched plan of Florence, with the following names of gates: Nicholo--Saminiato--Giorgo--Ghanolini--Porta San Fredian --Prato--Faenza--Ghallo--Pinti--Giustitia.]

1005.

The ruined wall is 640 braccia; 130 is the wall remaining with the mill; 300 braccia were broken in 4 years by Bisarno.

1006.

They do not know why the Arno will never remain in a channel. It is because the rivers which flow into it deposit earth where they enter, and wear it away on the opposite side, bending the river in that direction. The Arno flows for 6 miles between la Caprona and Leghorn; and for 12 through the marshes, which extend 32 miles, and 16 from La Caprona up the river, which makes 48; by the Arno from Florence beyond 16 miles; to Vico 16 miles, and the canal is 5; from Florence to Fucechio it is 40 miles by the river Arno.

56 miles by the Arno from Florence to Vico; by the Pistoia canal it is 44 miles. Thus it is 12 miles shorter by the canal than by the Arno.

[Footnote: This passage is written by the side of a map washed in Indian ink, of the course of the Arno; it is evidently a sketch for a completer map.

These investigations may possibly be connected with the following documents. Francesco Guiducci alla Balia di Firenze. Dal Campo contro Pisa 24 Luglio 1503 (Archivio di Stato, Firenze, Lettere alla Balia; published by J. GAYE, Carteggio inedito d'Artisti, Firenze 1840, Tom. II, p. 62): Ex Castris, Franciscus Ghuiduccius, 24. Jul. 1503. Appresso fu qui hieri con una di V. Signoria Alexandro degli Albizi insieme con Leonardo da Vinci et certi altri, et veduto el disegno insieme con el ghovernatore, doppo molte discussioni et dubii conclusesi che l'opera fussi molto al proposito, o si veramente Arno volgersi qui, o restarvi con un canale, che almeno vieterebbe che le colline da nemici non potrebbono essere offese; come tucto referiranno loro a bocha V. S.

And, Archivio di Stato, Firenze, Libro d'Entrata e Uscita di cassa de' Magnifici Signori di luglio e agosto

1503 a 51 T.: Andata di Leonardo al Campo sotto Pisa. Spese extraordinarie dieno dare a di XXVI di luglio L. LVI sol. XII per loro a Giovanni Piffero; e sono per tanti, asegnia avere spexi in vetture di sei chavalli a spese di vitto per andare chon Lionardo da Vinci a livellare Arno in quello di Pisa per levallo del lilo suo. (Published by MILANESI, Archivio Storico Italiano, Serie III, Tom. XVI.} VASARI asserts: (Leonardo) fu il primo ancora, che giovanetto discorresse sopra il fiume d'Arno per metterlo in canale da Pisa a Fiorenza (ed. SANSONI, IV, 20).

The passage above is in some degree illustrated by the map on Pl. CXII, where the course of the Arno westward from Empoli is shown.]

1007.

The eddy made by the Mensola, when the Arno is low and the Mensola full.

[Footnote: Mensola is a mountain stream which falls into the Arno about a mile and a half above Florence.

A=Arno, I=Isola, M=Mvgone, P=Pesa, N=Mesola.]

1008.

That the river which is to be turned from one place to another must be coaxed and not treated roughly or with violence; and to do this a sort of floodgate should be made in the river, and then lower down one in front of it and in like manner a third, fourth and fifth, so that the river may discharge itself into the channel given to it, or that by this means it may be diverted from the place it has damaged, as was done in Flanders--as I was told by Niccolo di Forsore.

How to protect and repair the banks washed by the water, as below the island of Cocomeri.

Ponte Rubaconte (Fig. 1); below [the palaces] Bisticci and Canigiani (Fig. 2). Above the flood gate of la Giustizia (Fig. 3); a b is a sand bank opposite the end of the island of the Cocomeri in the middle of the Arno (Fig. 4). [Footnote: The course of the river Arno is also discussed in Nos. 987 and 988.]

Canals in the Milanese (1009-1013).

1009.

The canal of San Cristofano at Milan made May 3rd 1509. [Footnote: This observation is written above a washed pen and ink drawing which has been published as Tav. VI in the ,,Saggio." The editors of that work explain the drawing as "uno Studio di bocche per estrazione d'acqua."]

1010.

OF THE CANAL OF MARTESANA.

By making the canal of Martesana the water of the Adda is greatly diminished by its distribution over many districts for the irrigation of the fields. A remedy for this would be to make several little channels, since the water drunk up by the earth is of no more use to any one, nor mischief neither, because it is taken from no one; and by making these channels the water which before was lost returns again and is once more serviceable and useful to men.

[Footnote: "el navilio di Martagano" is also mentioned in a note written in red chalk, MS. H2 17a Leonardo has, as it seems, little to do with Lodovico il Moro's scheme to render this canal navigable. The canal had been made in 1460 by Bertonino da Novara. Il Moro issued his degree in 1493, but Leonardo's notes about this canal were, with the exception of one (No. 1343), written about sixteen years later.]

1011.

No canal which is fed by a river can be permanent if the river whence it originates is not wholly closed up, like the canal of Martesana which is fed by the Ticino.

1012.

>From the beginning of the canal to the mill.

>From the beginning of the canal of Brivio to the mill of Travaglia is 2794 trabochi, that is 11176 braccia, which is more than 3 miles and two thirds; and here the canal is 57 braccia higher than the surface of the water of the Adda, giving a fall of two inches in every hundred trabochi; and at that spot we propose to take the opening of our canal.

[Footnote: The following are written on the sketches: At the place marked N: navilio da dacquiue (canal of running water); at M: molin del Travaglia (Mill of Travaglia); at R: rochetta ssanta maria (small rock of Santa Maria); at A: Adda; at L: Lagho di Lecho ringorgato alli 3 corni in Adda,--Concha perpetua (lake of Lecco overflowing at Tre Corni, in Adda,-- a permanent sluice). Near the second sketch, referring to the sluice near Q: qui la chatena ttalie d'u peso (here the chain is in one piece). At M in the lower sketch: mol del travaglia, nel cavare la concha il tereno ara chotrapero co cassa d'acqua. (Mill of Travaglia, in digging out the sluice the soil will have as a counterpoise a vessel of water).]

1013.

If it be not reported there that this is to be a public canal, it will be necessary to pay for the land; [Footnote 3: il re. Louis XII or Francis I of France. It is hardly possible to doubt that the canals here spoken of were intended to be in the Milanese. Compare with this passage the rough copy of a letter by Leonardo, to the "Presidente dell' Ufficio regolatore dell' acqua" on No. 1350. See also the note to No. 745, 1. 12.] and the king will pay it by remitting the taxes for a year.

Estimates and preparatory studies for canals (1014. 1015).

1014.

CANAL.

The canal which may be 16 braccia wide at the bottom and 20 at the top, we may say is on the average 18 braccia wide, and if it is 4 braccia deep, at 4 dinari the square braccia; it will only cost 900 ducats, to excavate by the mile, if the square braccio is calculated in ordinary braccia; but if the braccia are those used in measuring land, of which every 4 are equal to 4 1/2 and if by the mile we understand three thousand ordinary braccia; turned into land braccia, these 3000 braccia will lack 1/4; there remain 2250 braccia, which at 4 dinari the braccio will amount to 675 ducats a mile. At 3 dinari the square braccio, the mile will amount to 506 1/4 ducats so that the excavation of 30 miles of the canal will amount to 15187 1/2 ducats.

1015.

To make the great canal, first make the smaller one and conduct into it the waters which by a wheel will help to fill the great one.

Notes on buildings in Milan (1016-1019)

1016.

Indicate the centre of Milan.

Moforte--porta resa--porta nova--strada nova--navilio--porta cumana--barco--porta giovia--porta vercellina--porta sco Anbrogio--porta Tesinese--torre dell' Imperatore-- porta Lodovica--acqua.

[Footnote: See Pl. CIX. The original sketch is here reduced to about half its size. The gates of the town are here named, beginning at the right hand and following the curved line. In the bird's eye view of Milan below, the cathedral is plainly recognisable in the middle; to the right is the tower of San Gottardo. The square, above the number 9147, is the Lazzaretto, which was begun in 1488. On the left the group of buildings of the 'Castello' will be noticed. On the sketched Plan of Florence (see No. 1004 note) Leonardo has written on the margin the following names of gates of Milan: Vercellina --Ticinese--Ludovica--Romana--Orientale-- Nova--Beatrice--Cumana--Compare too No. 1448, 11. 5, 12.]

1017.

The moat of Milan.

Canal 2 braccia wide.

The castle with the moats full.

The filling of the moats of the Castle of Milan.

1018.

THE BATH.

To heat the water for the stove of the Duchess take four parts of cold water to three parts of hot water.

[Footnote: Duchessa di Milano, Beatrice d'Este, wife of Ludovico il Moro to whom she was married, in 1491. She died in June 1497.]

1019.

In the Cathedral at the pulley of the nail of the cross.

Item.

To place the mass v r in the...

[Footnote: On this passage AMORETTI remarks (Memorie Storiche chap. IX): Nell'anno stesso lo veggiamo formare un congegno di carucole e di corde, con cui trasportare in piu venerabile e piu sicuro luogo, cioe nell'ultima arcata della nave di mezzo della metropolitana, la sacra reliquia del Santo Chiodo, che ivi ancor si venera. Al fol. 15 del codice segnato Q. R. in 16, egli ci ha lasciata di tal congegno una doppia figura, cioe una di quattro carucole, e una di tre colle rispettive corde, soggiugnandovi: in Domo alla carucola del Chiodo della Croce.

AMORETTI'S views as to the mark on the MS, and the date when it was written are, it may be observed, wholly unfounded. The MS. L, in which it occurs, is of the year 1502, and it is very unlikely that Leonardo was in Milan at that time; this however would not prevent the remark, which is somewhat obscure, from applying to the Cathedral at Milan.]

1020.

OF THE FORCE OF THE VACUUM FORMED IN A MOMENT.

I saw, at Milan, a thunderbolt fall on the tower della Credenza on its Northern side, and it descended with a slow motion down that side, and then at once parted from that tower and carried with it and tore away from that wall a space of 3 braccia wide and two deep; and this wall was 4 braccia thick and was built of thin and small old bricks; and this was dragged out by the vacuum which the flame of the thunderbolt had caused, &c.

[Footnote: With reference to buildings at Milan see also Nos. 751 and 756, and Pl. XCV, No. 2 (explained on p. 52), Pl. C (explained on pages 60-62). See also pages 25, 39 and 40.]

Remarks on natural phenomena in and near Milan (1021. 1022).

1021.

I have already been to see a great variety (of atmospheric effects). And lately over Milan towards Lago Maggiore I saw a cloud in the form of an immense mountain full of rifts of glowing light, because the rays of the sun, which was already close to the horizon and red, tinged the cloud with its own hue. And this cloud attracted to it all the little clouds that were near while the large one did not move from its place; thus it retained on its summit the reflection of the sunlight till an hour and a half after sunset, so immensely large was it; and about two hours after sunset such a violent wind arose, that it was really tremendous and unheard of.

[Footnote: di arie is wanting in the original but may safely be inserted in the context, as the formation of clouds is under discussion before this text.]

1022.

On the 10th day of December at 9 o'clock a. m. fire was set to the place.

On the 18th day of December 1511 at 9 o'clock a. m. this second fire was kindled by the Swiss at Milan at the place called DCXC. [Footnote: With these two texts, (l. 1--2 and l. 3--5 are in the original side by side) there are sketches of smoke wreaths in red chalk.]

Note on Pavia.

1023.

The chimneys of the castle of Pavia have 6 rows of openings and from each to the other is one braccio.

[Footnote: Other notes relating to Pavia occur on p. 43 and p. 53 (Pl. XCVIII, No. 3). Compare No. 1448, 26.]

Notes on the Sforzesca near Vigevano (1024-1028).

1024.

On the 2nd day of February 1494. At Sforzesca I drew twenty five steps, 2/3 braccia to each, and 8 braccia wide.

[Footnote: See Pl. CX, No. 2. The rest of the notes on this page refer to the motion of water. On the lower sketch we read: 4 br. (four braccia) and giara (for ghiaja, sand, gravel).]

1025.

The vineyards of Vigevano on the 20th day of March 1494.

[Footnote: On one side there is an effaced sketch in red chalk.]

1026.

To lock up a butteris at Vigevano.

1027.

Again if the lowest part of the bank which lies across the current of the waters is made in deep and wide steps, after the manner of stairs, the waters which, in their course usually fall perpendicularly from the top of such a place to the bottom, and wear away the foundations of this bank can no longer descend with a blow of too great a force; and I find the example of this in the stairs down which the water falls in the fields at Sforzesca at Vigevano over which the running water falls for a height of 50 braccia.

1028.

Stair of Vigevano below La Sforzesca, 130 steps, 1/4 braccio high and 1/2 braccio wide, down which the water falls, so as not to wear away anything at the end of its fall; by these steps so much soil has come down that it has dried up a pool; that is to say it has filled it up and a pool of great depth has been turned into meadows.

Notes on the North Italian lake. (1029-1033)

1029.

In many places there are streams of water which swell for six hours and ebb for six hours; and I, for my part, have seen one above the lake of Como called Fonte Pliniana, which increases and ebbs, as I have said, in such a way as to turn the stones of two mills; and when it fails it falls so low that it is like looking at water in a deep pit.

[Footnote: The fountain is known by this name to this day: it is near Torno, on the Eastern shore of Como. The waters still rise and fall with the flow and ebb of the tide as Pliny described it (Epist. IV, 30; Hist. Nat. II, 206).]

1030.

LAKE OF COMO. VALLEY OF CHIAVENNA.

Above the lake of Como towards Germany is the valley of Chiavenna where the river Mera flows into this lake. Here are barren and very high mountains, with huge rocks. Among these mountains are to be found the water-birds called gulls. Here grow fir trees, larches and pines. Deer, wildgoats, chamois, and terrible bears. It is impossible to climb them without using hands and feet. The peasants go there at the time of the snows with great snares to make the bears fall down these rocks. These mountains which very closely approach each other are parted by the river. They are to the right and left for the distance of 20 miles throughout of the same nature. >From mile to mile there are good inns. Above on the said river there are waterfalls of 400 braccia in height, which are fine to see; and there is good living at 4 soldi the reckoning. This river brings down a great deal of timber.

VAL SASINA.

Val Sasina runs down towards Italy; this is almost the same form and character. There grow here many mappello and there are great ruins and falls of water [Footnote 14: The meaning of mappello is unknown.].

VALLEY OF INTROZZO.

This valley produces a great quantity of firs, pines and larches; and from here Ambrogio Fereri has his timber brought down; at the head of the Valtellina are the mountains of Bormio, terrible and always covered with snow; marmots (?) are found there.

BELLAGGIO.

Opposite the castle Bellaggio there is the river Latte, which falls from a height of more than 100 braccia from the source whence it springs, perpendicularly, into the lake with an inconceivable roar and noise. This spring flows only in August and September.

VALTELLINA.

Valtellina, as it is called, is a valley enclosed in high and terrible mountains; it produces much strong wine, and there is so much cattle that the natives conclude that more milk than wine grows there. This is the valley through which the Adda passes, which first runs more than 40 miles through

Germany; this river breeds the fish temolo which live on silver, of which much is to be found in its sands. In this country every one can sell bread and wine, and the wine is worth at most one soldo the bottle and a pound of veal one soldo, and salt ten dinari and butter the same and their pound is 30 ounces, and eggs are one soldo the lot.

1031.

At BORMIO.

At Bormio are the baths;--About eight miles above Como is the Pliniana, which increases and ebbs every six hours, and its swell supplies water for two mills; and its ebbing makes the spring dry up; two miles higher up there is Nesso, a place where a river falls with great violence into a vast rift in the mountain. These excursions are to be made in the month of May. And the largest bare rocks that are to be found in this part of the country are the mountains of Mandello near to those of Lecco, and of Gravidona towards Bellinzona, 30 miles from Lecco, and those of the valley of Chiavenna; but the greatest of all is that of Mandello, which has at its base an opening towards the lake, which goes down 200 steps, and there at all times is ice and wind.

IN VAL SASINA.

In Val Sasina, between Vimognio and Introbbio, to the right hand, going in by the road to Lecco, is the river Troggia which falls from a very high rock, and as it falls it goes underground and the river ends there. 3 miles farther we find the buildings of the mines of copper and silver near a place called Pra' Santo Pietro, and mines of iron and curious things. La Grigna is the highest mountain there is in this part, and it is quite bare.

[Footnote: 1030 and 1031. From the character of the handwriting we may conclude that these observations were made in Leonardo's youth; and I should infer from their contents, that they were notes made in anticipation of a visit to the places here described, and derived from some person (unknown to us) who had given him an account of them.]

1032.

The lake of Pusiano flows into the lake of Segrino [Footnote 3: The statement about the lake Segrino is incorrect; it is situated in the Valle Assina, above the lake of Pusiano.] and of Annone and of Sala. The lake of Annone is 22 braccia higher at the surface of its water than the surface of the water of the lake of Lecco, and the lake of Pusiano is 20 braccia higher than the lake of Annone, which added to the afore said 22 braccia make 42 braccia and this is the greatest height of the surface of the lake of Pusiano above the surface of the lake of Lecco.

[Footnote: This text has in the original a slight sketch to illustrate it.]

1033.

At Santa Maria in the Valley of Ravagnate [Footnote 2: Ravagnate (Leonardo writes Ravagna) in the Brianza is between Oggiono and Brivio, South of the lake of Como. M. Ravaisson avails himself of this note to prove his hypothesis that Leonardo paid two visits to France. See Gazette des Beaux Arts, 1881 pag. 528:

Au recto du meme feuillet, on lit encore une note relative a une vallee "nemonti brigatia"; il me semble qu'il s'agit bien des monts de Briancon, le Brigantio des anciens. Briancon est sur la route de Lyon en Italie. Ce fut par le mont Viso que passerent, en aout 1515, les troupes francaises qui allaient remporter la victoire de Marignan.

Leonard de Vinci, ingenieur de Francois Ier, comme il l'avait ete de Louis XII, aurait-il ete pour quelque chose dans le plan du celebre passage des Alpes, qui eut lieu en aout 1515, et a la suite duquel on le vit accompagner partout le chevaleresque vainqueur? Auraitil ete appele par le jeune roi, de Rome ou l'artiste etait alors, des son avenement au trone?] in the mountains of Brianza are the rods of chestnuts of 9 braccia and one out of an average of 100 will be 14 braccia.

At Varallo di Ponbia near to Sesto on the Ticino the quinces are white, large and hard.

[Footnote 5: Varallo di Ponbia, about ten miles South of Arona is distinct from Varallo the chief town in the Val di Sesia.]

Notes on places in Central Italy, visited in 1502 (1034-1054).

1034.

Pigeon-house at Urbino, the 30th day of July 1502. [Footnote: An indistinct sketch is introduced with this text, in the original, in which the word Scolatoro (conduit) is written.]

1035.

Made by the sea at Piombino. [Footnote: Below the sketch there are eleven lines of text referring to the motion of waves.]

1036.

Acquapendente is near Orvieto. [Footnote: Acquapendente is about 10 miles West of Orvieto, and is to the right in the map on Pl. CXIII, near the lake of Bolsena.]

1037.

The rock of Cesena. [Footnote: See Pl. XCIV No. 1, the lower sketch. The explanation of the upper sketch is given on p. 29.]

1038.

Siena, a b 4 braccia, a c 10 braccia. Steps at [the castle of] Urbino. [Footnote: See Pl. CX No. 3; compare also No. 765.]

1039.

The bell of Siena, that is the manner of its movement, and the place of the attachment of the clapper. [Footnote: The text is accompanied by an indistinct sketch.]

1040.

On St. Mary's day in the middle of August, at Cesena, 1502. [Footnote: See Pl. CX, No. 4.]

1041.

Stairs of the [palace of the] Count of Urbino,--rough. [Footnote: The text is accompanied by a slight sketch.]

1042.

At the fair of San Lorenzo at Cesena. 1502.

1043.

Windows at Cesena. [Footnote: There are four more lines of text which refer to a slightly sketched diagram.]

1044.

At Porto Cesenatico, on the 6th of September 1502 at 9 o'clock a. m.

The way in which bastions ought to project beyond the walls of the towers to defend the outer talus; so that they may not be taken by artillery.

[Footnote: An indistinct sketch, accompanies this passage.]

1045.

The rock of the harbour of Cesena is four points towards the South West from Cesena.

1046.

In Romagna, the realm of all stupidity, vehicles with four wheels are used, of which O the two in front are small and two high ones are behind; an arrangement which is very unfavourable to the motion, because on the fore wheels more weight is laid than on those behind, as I showed in the first of the 5th on "Elements".

1047.

Thus grapes are carried at Cesena. The number of the diggers of the ditches is [arranged] pyramidically. [Footnote: A sketch, representing a hook to which two bunches of grapes are hanging, refers to these first two lines. Cesena is mentioned again Fol. 82a: Carro da Cesena (a cart from Cesena).]

1048.

There might be a harmony of the different falls of water as you saw them at the fountain of Rimini on the 8th day of August, 1502.

1049.

The fortress at Urbino. [Footnote: 1049. In the original the text is written inside the sketch in the place here marked n.]

1050.

Imola, as regards Bologna, is five points from the West, towards the North West, at a distance of 20 miles.

Castel San Piero is seen from Imola at four points from the West towards the North West, at a distance of 7 miles.

Faenza stands with regard to Imola between East and South East at a distance of ten miles. Forli stands with regard to Faenza between South East and East at a distance of 20 miles from Imola and ten from Faenza.

Forlimpopoli lies in the same direction at 25 miles from Imola.

Bertinoro, as regards Imola, is five points from the East to wards the South East, at 27 miles.

1051.

Imola as regards Bologna is five points from the West towards the North West at a distance of 20 miles.

Castel San Pietro lies exactly North West of Imola, at a distance of 7 miles.

Faenza, as regards Imola lies exactly half way between the East and South East at a distance of 10 miles; and Forli lies in the same direction from Imola at a distance of 20 miles; and Forlimpopolo lies in the same direction from Forli at a distance of 25 miles.

Bertinoro is seen from Imola two points from the East towards the South East at a distance of 27 miles.

[Footnote: Leonardo inserted this passage on the margin of the circular plan, in water colour, of Imola--see Pl. CXI No. 1.--In the original the fields surrounding the town are light green; the moat, which surrounds the fortifications and the windings of the river Santerno, are light blue. The parts, which have come out blackish close to the river are yellow ochre in the original. The dark groups of houses inside the town are red. At the four points of the compass drawn in the middle of the town Leonardo has written (from right to left): Mezzodi (South) at the top; to the left Scirocho (South east), levante (East), Greco (North East), Septantrione (North), Maesstro (North West), ponente (West) Libecco (South West). The arch in which the plan is drawn is, in the original, 42 centimetres across.

At the beginning of October 1502 Cesare Borgia was shut up in Imola by a sudden revolt of the Condottieri, and it was some weeks before he could release himself from this state of siege (see Gregorovius, Geschichte der Stadt Rom im Mittelalter, Vol. VII, Book XIII, 5, 5).

Besides this incident Imola plays no important part in the history of the time. I therefore think myself fully justified in connecting this map, which is at Windsor, with the siege of 1502 and with Leonardo's engagements in the service of Cesare Borgia, because a comparison of these texts, Nos. 1050 and 1051, raise, I believe, the hypothesis to a certainty.]

1052.

>From Bonconventi to Casa Nova are 10 miles, from Casa Nova to Chiusi 9 miles, from Chiusi to Perugia, from, Perugia to Santa Maria degli Angeli, and then to Fuligno. [Footnote: Most of the places here described lie within the district shown in the maps on Pl. CXIII.]

1053.

On the first of August 1502, the library at Pesaro.

1054.

OF PAINTING.

On the tops and sides of hills foreshorten the shape of the ground and its divisions, but give its proper shape to what is turned towards you. [Footnote: This passage evidently refers to the making of maps, such as Pl. CXII, CXIII, and CXIV. There is no mention of such works, it is true, excepting in this one passage of MS. L. But this can scarcely be taken as evidence against my view that Leonardo busied himself very extensively at that time in the construction of maps; and all the less since the foregoing chapters clearly prove that at a time so full of events Leonardo would only now and then commit his observations to paper, in the MS. L.

By the side of this text we find, in the original, a very indistinct sketch, perhaps a plan of a position. Instead of this drawing I have here inserted a much clearer sketch of a position from the same MS., L. 82b and 83a. They are the only drawings of landscape, it may be noted, which occur at all in that MS.]

Alessandria in Piedmont (1055. 1056).

1055.

At Candia in Lombardy, near Alessandria della Paglia, in making a well for Messer Gualtieri [Footnote 2: Messer Gualtieri, the same probably as is mentioned in Nos. 672 and 1344.] of Candia, the skeleton of a very large boat was found about 10 braccia underground; and as the timber was black and fine, it seemed good to the said Messer Gualtieri to have the mouth of the well lengthened in such a way as that the ends of the boat should be uncovered.

1056.

At Alessandria della Paglia in Lombardy there are no stones for making lime of, but such as are mixed up with an infinite variety of things native to the sea, which is now more than 200 miles away.

The Alps (1057-1062).

1057.

At Monbracco, above Saluzzo,--a mile above the Certosa, at the foot of Monte Viso, there is a quarry of flakey stone, which is as white as Carrara marble, without a spot, and as hard as porphyry or even harder; of which my worthy gossip, Master Benedetto the sculptor, has promised to give me a small slab, for the colours, the second day of January 1511.

[Footnote: Saluzzo at the foot of the Alps South of Turin.]

[Footnote 9. 10.: Maestro Benedetto scultore; probably some native of Northern Italy acquainted with the place here described. Hardly the Florentine sculptor Benedetto da Majano. Amoretti had published this passage, and M. Ravaisson who gave a French translation of it in the Gazette des Beaux Arts (1881, pag. 528), remarks as follows: Le maitre sculpteur que Leonard appelle son "compare" ne serait-il pas Benedetto da Majano, un de ceux qui jugerent avec lui de la place a donner au David de Michel-Ange, et de qui le Louvre a acquis recemment un buste d'apres Philippe Strozzi? To this it may be objected that Benedetto da Majano had already lain in his grave fourteen years, in the year 1511, when he is supposed to have given the promise to Leonardo. The colours may have been given to the sculptor Benedetto and the stone may have been in payment for them. >From the description of the stone here given we may conclude that it is repeated from hearsay of the sculptor's account of it. I do not understand how, from this observation, it is possible to conclude that Leonardo was on the spot.]

1058.

That there are springs which suddenly break forth in earthquakes or other convulsions and suddenly fail; and this happened in a mountain in Savoy where certain forests sank in and left a very deep gap, and about four miles from here the earth opened itself like a gulf in the mountain, and threw out a sudden and immense flood of water which scoured the whole of a little valley of the tilled soil, vineyards and houses, and did the greatest mischief, wherever it overflowed.

1059.

The river Arve, a quarter of a mile from Geneva in Savoy, where the fair is held on midsummerday in the village of Saint Gervais.

[Footnote: An indistinct sketch is to be seen by the text.]

1060.

And this may be seen, as I saw it, by any one going up Monbroso [Footnote: I have vainly enquired of every available authority for a solution of the mystery as to what mountain is intended by the name Monboso (Comp. Vol. I Nos. 300 and 301). It seems most obvious to refer it to Monte Rosa. ROSA derived from the Keltic ROS which survives in Breton and in Gaelic, meaning, in its first sense, a mountain spur, but which also--like HORN--means a very high peak; thus Monte Rosa would mean literally the High Peak.], a peak of the Alps which divide France from Italy. The base of this mountain gives birth to the 4 rivers which flow in four different directions through the whole of Europe. And no mountain has its base at so great a height as this, which lifts itself above almost all the clouds; and snow seldom falls there, but only hail in the summer, when the clouds are highest. And this hail lies [unmelted] there, so that if it were not for the absorption of the rising and falling clouds, which does not happen more than twice in an age, an enormous mass of ice would be piled up there by the layers of hail, and in the middle of July I found it very considerable; and I saw the sky above me quite dark, and the sun as it fell on the mountain was far brighter here than in the plains below, because a smaller extent of atmosphere lay between the summit of the mountain and the sun. [Footnote 6: in una eta. This is perhaps a slip of the pen on Leonardo's part and should be read estate (summer).]

Leic. 9b]

1061.

In the mountains of Verona the red marble is found all mixed with cockle shells turned into stone; some of them have been filled at the mouth with the cement which is the substance of the stone; and in some parts they have remained separate from the mass of the rock which enclosed them, because the outer covering of the shell had interposed and had not allowed them to unite with it; while in other places this cement had petrified those which were old and almost stripped the outer skin.

1062.

Bridge of Goertz-Wilbach (?).

[Footnote: There is a slight sketch with this text, Leonardo seems to have intended to suggest, with a few pen-strokes, the course of the Isonzo and of the Wipbach in the vicinity of Gorizia (Goerz). He himself says in another place that he had been in Friuli (see No. 1077 1. 19).]

The Appenins (1063-1068).

1063.

That part of the earth which was lightest remained farthest from the centre of the world; and that part of the earth became the lightest over which the greatest quantity of water flowed. And therefore that part became lightest where the greatest number of rivers flow; like the Alps which divide Germany and France from Italy; whence issue the Rhone flowing Southwards, and the Rhine to the North. The Danube or Tanoia towards the North East, and the Po to the East, with innumerable rivers which join them, and which always run turbid with the soil carried by them to the sea.

The shores of the sea are constantly moving towards the middle of the sea and displace it from its original position. The lowest portion of the Mediterranean will be reserved for the bed and current of the Nile, the largest river that flows into that sea. And with it are grouped all its tributaries, which at first fell into the sea; as may be seen with the Po and its tributaries, which first fell into that sea, which between the Appenines and the German Alps was united to the Adriatic sea.

That the Gallic Alps are the highest part of Europe.

1064.

And of these I found some in the rocks of the high Appenines and mostly at the rock of La Vernia. [Footnote 6: Sasso della Vernia. The frowning rock between the sources of the Arno and the Tiber, as Dante describes this mountain, which is 1269 metres in height.

This note is written by the side of that given as No. 1020; but their connection does not make it clear what Leonardo's purpose was in writing it.]

1065.

At Parma, at 'La Campana' on the twenty-fifth of October 1514. [Footnote 2: Capano, an Inn.]

A note on the petrifactions, or fossils near Parma will be found under No. 989.]

1066.

A method for drying the marsh of Piombino. [Footnote: There is a slight sketch with this text in the original.--Piombino is also mentioned in Nos. 609, I. 55-58 (compare Pl. XXXV, 3, below). Also in No. 1035.]

1067.

The shepherds in the Romagna at the foot of the Apennines make peculiar large cavities in the mountains in the form of a horn, and on one side they fasten a horn. This little horn becomes one and the same with the said cavity and thus they produce by blowing into it a very loud noise. [Footnote: As to the Romagna see also No. 1046.]

1068.

A spring may be seen to rise in Sicily which at certain times of the year throws out chesnut leaves in quantities; but in Sicily chesnuts do not grow, hence it is evident that that spring must issue from some abyss in Italy and then flow beneath the sea to break forth in Sicily. [Footnote: The chesnut tree is very common in Sicily. In writing cicilia Leonardo meant perhaps Cilicia.]

II.

FRANCE.

1069.

GERMANY.   FRANCE.

a. Austria, a. Picardy. b. Saxony. b. Normandy. c. Nuremberg. c. Dauphine. d. Flanders.

SPAIN.
a. Biscay.
b. Castille.
c. Galicia.
d. Portugal.
e. Taragona.

f. Granada.

[Footnote: Two slightly sketched maps, one of Europe the other of Spain, are at the side of these notes.]

1070.

Perpignan. Roanne. Lyons. Paris. Ghent. Bruges. Holland.

[Footnote: Roana does not seem to mean here Rouen in Normandy, but is probably Roanne (Rodumna) on the upper Loire, Lyonnais (Dep. du Loire). This town is now unimportant, but in Leonardo's time was still a place of some consequence.]

1071.

At Bordeaux in Gascony the sea rises about 40 braccia before its ebb, and the river there is filled with salt water for more than a hundred and fifty miles; and the vessels which are repaired there rest high and dry on a high hill above the sea at low tide. [Footnote 2: This is obviously an exaggeration founded on inaccurate information. Half of 150 miles would be nearer the mark.]

1072.

The Rhone issues from the lake of Geneva and flows first to the West and then to the South, with a course of 400 miles and pours its waters into the Mediterranean.

1073.

c d is the garden at Blois; a b is the conduit of Blois, made in France by Fra Giocondo, b c is what is wanting in the height of that conduit, c d is the height of the garden at Blois, e f is the siphon of the conduit, b c, e f, f g is where the siphon discharges into the river. [Footnote: The tenor of this note (see lines 2 and 3) seems to me to indicate that this passage was not written in France, but was written from oral information. We have no evidence as to when this note may have been written beyond the circumstance that Fra Giocondo the Veronese Architect left France not before the year 1505. The greater part of the magnificent Chateau of Blois has now disappeared. Whether this note was made for a special purpose is uncertain. The original form and extent of the Chateau is shown in Androvet, Les plus excellents Bastiments de France, Paris MDCVII, and it may be observed that there is in the middle of the garden a Pavilion somewhat similar to that shown on Pl. LXXXVIII No. 7.

See S. DE LA SAUSSAYE, Histoire du Chateau de Blois 4eme edition Blois et Paris p. 175: En mariant sa fille ainee a Francois, comte d'Angouleme, Louis XII lui avait constitue en dot les comtes de Blois, d'Asti, de Coucy, de Montfort, d'Etampes et de Vertus. Une ordonnance de Francois I. lui laissa en 1516 l'administration du comte de Blois.

Le roi fit commencer, dans la meme annee, les travaux de celle belle partie du chateau, connue sous le nom d'aile de Francois I, et dont nous avons donne la description au commencement de ce livre. Nous trouvons en effet, dans les archives du Baron de Foursanvault, une piece qui en fixe parfaitement la date. On y lit: "Je, Baymon Philippeaux, commis par le Roy a tenir le compte et fair le payement des bastiments, ediffices et reparacions que le dit seigneur fait faire en son chastu de Blois, confesse avoir eu et receu ... la somme de trois mille livres tournois ... le cinquieme jour de juillet, l'an mil cinq cent et seize. P. 24: Les jardins avaient ete decores avec beaucoup de luxe par les differents possesseurs du chateau. Il ne reste de tous les batiments qu'ils y eleverent que ceux des officiers charges de l'administration et de la culture des jardins, et un pavilion carre en pierre et en brique flanque de terrasses a chacun de ses angles. Quoique defigure par des mesures elevees sur les terrasses, cet edifice est tris-digne d'interet par l'originalite du plan, la decoration architecturale et le souvenir d'Anne de Bretagne qui le fit construire. Felibien describes the garden as follows: Le jardin haut etait fort bien dresse par grands compartimens de toutes sortes de figures, avec des allees de meuriers blancs et des palissades de coudriers. Deux grands berceaux de charpenterie separoient toute la longueur et la largeur du jardin, et dans les quatres angles des allees, ou ces berceaux se croissent, il y auoit 4 cabinets, de mesme charpenterie ... Il y a pas longtemps qu'il y auoit dans ce mesme jardin, a l'endroit ou se croissent les allees du milieu, un edifice de figure octogone, de plus de 7 thoises de diametre et de plus de neuf thoises de haut; avec 4 enfoncements en forme de niches dans les 4 angles des allies. Ce bastiment.... esloit de charpente mais d'un extraordinairement bien travaille. On y voyait particulierement la cordiliere qui regnati tout autour en forme de cordon. Car la Reyne affectait de la mettre nonseulement a ses armes et a ses chiffres mais de la faire representer en divers manieres dans tous les ouvrages qu'on lui faisait pour elle ... le bastiment estati couvert en forme de dome qui dans son milieu avait encore un plus petit dome, ou lanterne vitree au-dessus de laquelle estait une figure doree representant Saint Michel. Les deux domes estoient proprement couvert d'ardoise et de plomb dore par dehors; par dedans ils esloient lambrissez d'une menuiserie tres delicate. Au milieu de ce Salon il y avait un grand bassin octogone de marbre blanc, dont toutes les faces estoient enrichies de differentes sculptures, avec les armes et les chiffres du Roy Louis XII et de la Reine Anne, Dans ce bassin il y en avait un autre pose sur un piedestal lequel auoit sept piedz de diametre. Il estait de figure ronde a godrons, avec des masques et d'autres ornements tres scauamment taillez. Du milieu de ce deuxiesme bassin s'y levoit un autre petit piedestal qui portait un troisiesme bassin de trois pieds de diametre, aussy parfaitement bien taille; c'estoit de ce dernier bassin que jallissoit l'eau qui se rependoit en suitte dans les deux autres bassins. Les beaux ouvrages faits d'un marbre esgalement blanc et poli, furent brisez par la pesanteur de tout l'edifice, que les injures de l'air renverserent de fond en comble.]

1074.

The river Loire at Amboise.

The river is higher within the bank b d than outside that bank.

The island where there is a part of Amboise.

This is the river that passes through Amboise; it passes at a b c d, and when it has passed the bridge it turns back, against the original current, by the channel d e, b f in contact with the bank which lies between the two contrary currents of the said river, a b, c d, and d e, b f. It then turns down again by the channel f l, g h, n m, and reunites with the river from which it was at first separated, which passes by k n, which makes k m, r t. But when the river is very full it flows all in one channel passing over the bank b d. [Footnote: See Pl. CXV. Lines 1-7 are above, lines 8-10 in the middle of the large island and the word Isola is written above d in the smaller island; a is written on the margin on the bank of the river above 1. l; in the reproduction it is not visible. As may be seen from the last sentence, the observation was made after long study of the river's course, when Leonardo had resided for some time at, or near, Amboise.]

1075.

The water may be dammed up above the level of Romorantin to such a height, that in its fall it may be used for numerous mills.

1075.

The river at Villefranche may be conducted to Romorantin which may be done by the inhabitants; and the timber of which their houses are built may be carried in boats to Romorantin [Footnote: Compare No. 744.]. The river may be dammed up at such a height that the waters may be brought back to Romorantin with a convenient fall.

1076.

As to whether it is better that the water should all be raised in a single turn or in two?

The answer is that in one single turn the wheel could not support all the water that it can raise in two turns, because at the half turn of the wheel it would be raising 100 pounds and no more; and if it had to raise the whole, 200 pounds in one turn, it could not raise them unless the wheel were of double the diameter and if the diameter were doubled, the time of its revolution would be doubled; therefore it is better and a greater advantage in expense to make such a wheel of half the size (?) the land which it would water and would render the country fertile to supply food to the inhabitants, and would make navigable canals for mercantile purposes.

The way in which the river in its flow should scour its own channel.

By the ninth of the third; the more rapid it is, the more it wears away its channel; and, by the converse proposition, the slower the water the more it deposits that which renders it turbid.

And let the sluice be movable like the one I arranged in Friuli [Footnote 19: This passage reveals to us the fact that Leonardo had visited the country of Friuli and that he had stayed there for some time. Nothing whatever was known of this previously.], where when one sluice was opened the water which passed through it dug out the bottom. Therefore when the rivers are flooded, the sluices of the mills ought to be opened in order that the whole course of the river may pass through falls to each mill; there should be many in order to give a greater impetus, and so all the river will be scoured. And below the site of each of the two mills there may be one of the said sluice falls; one of them may be placed below each mill.

1078.

A trabocco is four braccia, and one mile is three thousand of the said braccia. Each braccio is divided into 12 inches; and the water in the canals has a fall in every hundred trabocchi of two of these inches; therefore 14 inches of fall are necessary in two thousand eight hundred braccia of flow in these canals; it follows that 15 inches of fall give the required momentum to the currents of the waters in the said canals, that is one braccio and a half in the mile. And from this it may be concluded that the water taken from the river of Ville-franche and lent to the river of Romorantin will..... Where one river by reason of its low level cannot flow into the other, it will be necessary to dam it up, so that it may acquire a fall into the other, which was previously the higher.

The eve of Saint Antony I returned from Romorantin to Amboise, and the King went away two days before from Romorantin.

>From Romorantin as far as the bridge at Saudre it is called the Saudre, and from that bridge as far as Tours it is called the Cher.

I would test the level of that channel which is to lead from the Loire to Romorantin, with a channel one braccio wide and one braccio deep.

[Footnote: Lines 6-18 are partly reproduced in the facsimile on p. 254, and the whole of lines 19-25.

The following names are written along the rivers on the larger sketch, era f (the Loire) scier f (the Cher) three times. Pote Sodro (bridge of the Soudre). Villa francha (Villefranche) banco (sandbank) Sodro (Soudre). The circle below shows the position of Romorantin. The words 'orologio del sole' written below do not belong to the map of the rivers. The following names are written by the side of the smaller sketch-map:--tors (Tours), Abosa (Amboise) bres-- for Bles (Blois) mo rica (Montrichard). Lione (Lyons). This map was also published in the 'Saggio' (Milano, 1872) Pl. XXII, and the editors remark: Forse la linia retta che va da Amboise a Romorantin segna l'andamento proposto d'un Canale, che poi rembra prolungarsi in giu fin dove sta scritto Lione.

M. Ravaisson has enlarged on this idea in the Gazette des Beaux Arts (1881 p. 530): Les traces de Leonard permettent d'entrevoir que le canal commencant soit aupres de Tours, soit aupres de Blois et passant par Romorantin, avec port d'embarquement a Villefranche, devait, au dela de Bourges, traverser l'Allier au-dessous des affluents de la Dore et de la Sioule, aller par Moulins jusqu' a Digoin; enfin, sur l'autre rive de la Loire, depasser les monts du Charolais et rejoindre la Saone aupres de Macon. It seems to me rash, however, to found so elaborate an hypothesis on these sketches of rivers. The slight stroke going to Lione is perhaps only an indication of the direction.--With regard to the Loire compare also No. 988. I. 38.]

1079.

THE ROAD TO ORLEANS

At 1/4 from the South to the South East. At 1/3 from the South to the South East. At 1/4 from the South to the South East. At 1/5 from the South to the South East. Between the South West and South, to the East bearing to the South; from the South towards the East 1/8; thence to the West, between the South and South West; at the South.

[Footnote: The meaning is obscure; a more important passage referring to France is to be found under No. 744]

On the Germans (1080. 1081).

1080.

The way in which the Germans closing up together cross and interweave their broad leather shields against the enemy, stooping down and putting one of the ends on the ground while they hold the rest in their hand. [Footnote: Above the text is a sketch of a few lines crossing each other and the words de ponderibus. The meaning of the passage is obscure.]

1081.

The Germans are wont to annoy a garrison with the smoke of feathers, sulphur and realgar, and they make this smoke last 7 or 8 hours. Likewise the husks of wheat make a great and lasting smoke; and also dry dung; but this must be mixed with olive husks, that is olives pressed for oil and from which the oil has been extracted. [Footnote: There is with this passage a sketch of a round tower shrouded in smoke.]

The Danube.

1082.

That the valleys were formerly in great part covered by lakes the soil of which always forms the banks of rivers,--and by seas, which afterwards, by the persistent wearing of the rivers, cut through the mountains and the wandering courses of the rivers carried away the other plains enclosed by the mountains; and the cutting away of the mountains is evident from the strata in the rocks, which correspond in their sections as made by the courses of the rivers [Footnote 4: Emus, the Balkan; Dardania, now Servia.], The Haemus mountains which go along Thrace and Dardania and join the Sardonius mountains which, going on to the westward change their name from Sardus to Rebi, as they come near Dalmatia; then turning to the West cross Illyria, now called Sclavonia, changing the name of Rebi to Albanus, and going on still to the West, they change to Mount Ocra in the North; and to the South above Istria they are named Caruancas; and to the West above Italy they join the Adula, where the Danube rises [8], which stretches to the East and has a course of 1500 miles; its shortest line is about l000 miles, and the same or about the same is that branch of the Adula mountains changed as to their name, as before mentioned. To the North are the Carpathians, closing in the breadth of the valley of the Danube, which, as I have said extends eastward, a length of about 1000 miles, and is sometimes 200 and in some places 300 miles wide; and in the midst flows the Danube, the principal river of Europe as to size. The said Danube runs through the middle of Austria and Albania and northwards through Bavaria, Poland, Hungary, Wallachia and Bosnia and then the Danube or Donau flows into the Black Sea, which formerly extended almost to Austria and occupied the plains through which the Danube now courses; and the evidence of this is in the oysters and cockle shells and scollops and bones of great fishes which are still to be found in many places on the sides of those mountains; and this sea was formed by the filling up of the spurs of the Adula mountains which then extended to the East joining the spurs of the Taurus which extend to the West. And near Bithynia the waters of this Black Sea poured into the Propontis [Marmora] falling into the Aegean Sea, that is the Mediterranean, where, after a long course, the spurs of the Adula mountains became separated from those of the Taurus. The Black Sea sank lower and laid bare the valley of the Danube with the above named countries, and the whole of Asia Minor beyond the Taurus range to the North, and the plains from mount Caucasus to the Black Sea to the West, and the plains of the Don this side--that is to say, at the foot of the Ural mountains. And thus the Black Sea must have sunk about 1000 braccia to uncover such vast plains.

[Footnote 8: Danubio, in the original Reno; evidently a mistake as we may infer from come dissi l. 10 &c.]

III.

THE COUNTRIES OF THE WESTERN END OF THE MEDITERRANEAN.

The straits of Gibraltar (1083-1085).

1083.

WHY THE SEA MAKES A STRONGER CURRENT IN THE STRAITS OF SPAIN THAN ELSEWHERE.

A river of equal depth runs with greater speed in a narrow space than in a wide one, in proportion to the difference between the wider and the narrower one.

This proposition is clearly proved by reason confirmed by experiment. Supposing that through a channel one mile wide there flows one mile in length of water; where the river is five miles wide each of the 5 square miles will require 1/5 of itself to be equal to the square mile of water required in the sea, and where the river is 3 miles wide each of these square miles will require the third of its volume to make up the amount of the square mile of the narrow part; as is demonstrated in f g h at the mile marked n.

[Footnote: In the place marked A in the diagram Mare Mediterano (Mediterranean Sea) is written in the original. And at B, stretto di Spugna (straits of Spain, i.e. Gibraltar). Compare No. 960.]

1084.

WHY THE CURRENT OF GIBRALTAR IS ALWAYS GREATER TO THE WEST THAN TO THE EAST.

The reason is that if you put together the mouths of the rivers which discharge into the Mediterranean sea, you would find the sum of water to be larger than that which this sea pours through the straits into the ocean. You see Africa discharging its rivers that run northwards into this sea, and among them the Nile which runs through 3000 miles of Africa; there is also the Bagrada river and the Schelif and others. [Footnote 5: Bagrada (Leonardo writes Bragada) in Tunis, now Medscherda; Mavretano, now Schelif.] Likewise Europe pours into it the Don and the Danube, the Po, the Rhone, the Arno, and the Tiber, so that evidently these rivers, with an infinite number of others of less fame, make its great breadth and depth and current; and the sea is not wider than 18 miles at the most westerly point of land where it divides Europe from Africa.

1085.

The gulf of the Mediterranean, as an inland sea, received the principal waters of Africa, Asia and Europe that flowed towards it; and its waters came up to the foot of the mountains that surrounded it and made its shores. And the summits of the Apennines stood up out of this sea like islands, surrounded by salt water. Africa again, behind its Atlas mountains did not expose uncovered to the sky the surface of its vast plains about 3000 miles in length, and Memphis [Footnote 6: Mefi. Leonardo can only mean here the citadel of Cairo on the Mokattam hills.] was on the shores of this sea, and above the plains of Italy, where now birds fly in flocks, fish were wont to wander in large shoals.

1086.

Tunis.

The greatest ebb made anywhere by the Mediterranean is above Tunis, being about two and a half braccia and at Venice it falls two braccia. In all the rest of the Mediterranean sea the fall is little or none.

1087.

Libya.

Describe the mountains of shifting deserts; that is to say the formation of waves of sand borne by the wind, and of its mountains and hills, such as occur in Libya. Examples may be seen on the wide sands of the Po and the Ticino, and other large rivers.

1088.

Majorca.

Circumfulgore is a naval machine. It was an invention of the men of Majorca. [Footnote: The machine is fully described in the MS. and shown in a sketch.]

1089.

The Tyrrhene Sea.

Some at the Tyrrhene sea employ this method; that is to say they fastened an anchor to one end of the yard, and to the other a cord, of which the lower end was fastened to an anchor; and in battle they flung this anchor on to the oars of the opponent's boat and by the use of a capstan drew it to the side; and threw soft soap and tow, daubed with pitch and set ablaze, on to that side where the anchor hung; so that in order to escape that fire, the defenders of that ship had to fly to the opposite side; and in doing this they aided to the attack, because the galley was more easily drawn to the side by reason of the counterpoise. [Footnote: This text is illustrated in the original by a pen and ink sketch.]

IV.

THE LEVANT.

The Levantine Sea.

1090.

On the shores of the Mediterranean 300 rivers flow, and 40, 200 ports. And this sea is 3000 miles long. Many times has the increase of its waters, heaped up by their backward flow and the blowing of the West winds, caused the overflow of the Nile and of the rivers which flow out through the Black Sea, and have so much raised the seas that they have spread with vast floods over many countries. And these floods take place at the time when the sun melts the snows on the high mountains of Ethiopia that rise up into the cold regions of the air; and in the same way the approach of the sun acts on the mountains of Sarmatia in Asia and on those in Europe; so that the gathering together of these three things are, and always have been, the cause of tremendous floods: that is, the return flow of the sea with the West wind and the melting of the snows. So every river will overflow in Syria, in Samaria, in Judea between Sinai and the Lebanon, and in the rest of Syria between the Lebanon and the Taurus mountains, and in Cilicia, in the Armenian mountains, and in Pamphilia and in Lycia within the hills, and in Egypt as far as the Atlas mountains. The gulf of Persia which was formerly a vast lake of the Tigris and discharged into the Indian Sea, has now worn away the mountains which formed its banks and laid them even with the level of the Indian ocean. And if the Mediterranean had continued its flow through the gulf of Arabia, it would have done the same, that is to say, would have reduced the level of the Mediterranean to that of the Indian Sea.

The Red Sea. (1091. 1092).

1091.

For a long time the water of the Mediterranean flowed out through the Red Sea, which is 100 miles wide and 1500 long, and full of reefs; and it has worn away the sides of Mount Sinai, a fact which testifies, not to an inundation from the Indian sea beating on these coasts, but to a deluge of water which carried with it all the rivers which abound round the Mediterranean, and besides this there is the reflux of the sea; and then, a cutting being made to the West 3000 miles away from this place, Gibraltar was separated from Ceuta, which had been joined to it. And this passage was cut very low down, in the plains between Gibraltar and the ocean at the foot of the mountain, in the low part, aided by the hollowing out of some valleys made by certain rivers, which might have flowed here. Hercules [Footnote 9: Leonardo seems here to mention Hercules half jestingly and only in order to suggest to the reader an allusion to the legend of the pillars of Hercules.] came to open the sea to the westward and then the sea waters began to pour into the Western Ocean; and in consequence of this great fall, the Red Sea remained the higher; whence the water, abandoning its course here, ever after poured away through the Straits of Spain.

1092.

The surface of the Red Sea is on a level with the ocean.

A mountain may have fallen and closed the mouth of the Red Sea and prevented the outlet of the Mediterranean, and the Mediterranean Sea thus overfilled had for outlet the passage below the mountains of Gades; for, in our own times a similar thing has been seen [Footnote 6: Compare also No. 1336, II. 30, 35 and 36.-- Paolo Giovio, the celebrated historian (born at Como in 1483) reports that in 1513 at the foot of the Alps, above Bellinzona, on the road to Switzerland, a mountain fell with a very great noise, in consequence of an earthquake, and that the mass of rocks, which fell on the left (Western) side blocked the river Breno (T. I p. 218 and 345 of D. Sauvage's French edition, quoted in ALEXIS PERCY, Memoire des tremblements de terre de la peninsule italique; Academie Royale de Belgique. T. XXII).--]; a mountain fell seven miles across a valley and closed it up and made a lake. And thus most lakes have been made by mountains, as the lake of Garda, the lakes of Como and Lugano, and the Lago Maggiore. The Mediterranean fell but little on the confines of Syria, in consequence of the Gaditanean passage, but a great deal in this passage, because before this cutting was made the Mediterranean sea flowed to the South East, and then the fall had to be made by its run through the Straits of Gades.

At a the water of the Mediterranean fell into the ocean.

All the plains which lie between the sea and mountains were formerly covered with salt water.

Every valley has been made by its own river; and the proportion between valleys is the same as that between river and river.

The greatest river in our world is the Mediterranean river, which moves from the sources of the Nile to the Western ocean.

And its greatest height is in Outer Mauritania and it has a course of ten thousand miles before it reunites with its ocean, the father of the waters.

That is 3000 miles for the Mediterranean, 3000 for the Nile, as far as discovered and 3000 for the Nile which flows to the East, &c.

[Footnote: See Pl. CXI 2, a sketch of the shores of the Mediterranean Sea, where lines 11 to 16 may be seen. The large figures 158 are not in Leonardo's writing. The character of the writing leads us to conclude that this text was written later than the foregoing. A slight sketch of the Mediterranean is also to be found in MS. I', 47a.]

The Nile (1093-1098).

1093.

Therefore we must conclude those mountains to be of the greatest height, above which the clouds falling in snow give rise to the Nile.

1094.

The Egyptians, the Ethiopians, and the Arabs, in crossing the Nile with camels, are accustomed to attach two bags on the sides of the camel's bodies that is skins in the form shown underneath.

In these four meshes of the net the camels for baggage place their feet.

[Footnote: Unfortunately both the sketches which accompany this passage are too much effaced to be reproduced. The upper represents the two sacks joined by ropes, as here described, the other shows four camels with riders swimming through a river.]

1095.

The Tigris passes through Asia Minor and brings with it the water of three lakes, one after the other of various elevations; the first being Munace and the middle Pallas and the lowest Triton. And the Nile again springs from three very high lakes in Ethiopia, and runs northwards towards the sea of Egypt with a course of 4000 miles, and by the shortest and straightest line it is 3000 miles. It is said that it issues from the Mountains of the Moon, and has various unknown sources. The said lakes are about 4000 braccia above the surface of the sphere of water, that is 1 mile and 1/3, giving to the Nile a fall of 1 braccia in every mile.

[Footnote 5: Incogniti principio. The affluents of the lakes are probably here intended. Compare, as to the Nile, Nos. 970, 1063 and 1084.]

1096.

Very many times the Nile and other very large rivers have poured out their whole element of water and restored it to the sea.

1097.

Why does the inundation of the Nile occur in the summer, coming from torrid countries?

1098.

It is not denied that the Nile is constantly muddy in entering the Egyptian sea and that its turbidity is caused by soil that this river is continually bringing from the places it passes; which soil never returns in the sea which receives it, unless it throws it on its shores. You see the sandy desert beyond Mount Atlas where formerly it was covered with salt water.

Customs of Asiatic Nations (1099. 1100).

1099.

The Assyrians and the people of Euboea accustom their horses to carry sacks which they can at pleasure fill with air, and which in case of need they carry instead of the girth of the saddle above and at the side, and they are well covered with plates of cuir bouilli, in order that they may not be perforated by flights of arrows. Thus they have not on their minds their security in flight, when the victory is uncertain; a horse thus equipped enables four or five men to cross over at need.

1100.

SMALL BOATS.

The small boats used by the Assyrians were made of thin laths of willow plaited over rods also of willow, and bent into the form of a boat. They were daubed with fine mud soaked with oil or with turpentine, and reduced to a kind of mud which resisted the water and because pine would split; and always remained fresh; and they covered this sort of boats with the skins of oxen in safely crossing the river Sicuris of Spain, as is reported by Lucant; [Footnote 7: See Lucan's Pharsalia IV, 130: Utque habuit ripas Sicoris camposque reliquit, Primum cana salix madefacto vimine parvam Texitur in puppim, calsoque inducto juvenco Vectoris patiens tumidum supernatat amnem. Sic Venetus stagnante Pado, fusoque Britannus Navigat oceano, sic cum tenet omnia Nilus, Conseritur bibula Memphitis cymbo papyro. His ratibus transjecta manus festinat utrimque Succisam cavare nemus]

The Spaniards, the Scythians and the Arabs, when they want to make a bridge in haste, fix hurdlework made of willows on bags of ox-hide, and so cross in safety.

Rhodes (1101. 1102).

1101.

In [fourteen hundred and] eighty nine there was an earthquake in the sea of Atalia near Rhodes, which opened the sea--that is its bottom--and into this opening such a torrent of water poured that for more than three hours the bottom of the sea was uncovered by reason of the water which was lost in it, and then it closed to the former level.

[Footnote: Nello ottanto 9. It is scarcely likely that Leonardo should here mean 89 AD. Dr. H. MULLER- STRUBING writes to me as follows on this subject: "With reference to Rhodes Ross says (Reise auf den Griechischen Inseln, III 70 ff. 1840), that ancient history affords instances of severe earthquakes at Rhodes, among others one in the second year of the 138th Olympiad=270 B. C.; a remarkably violent one under Antoninus Pius (A. D. 138-161) and again under Constantine and later. But Leonardo expressly speaks of an earthquake "nel mar di Atalia presso a Rodi", which is singular. The town of

Attalia, founded by Attalus, which is what he no doubt means, was in Pamphylia and more than 150 English miles East of Rhodes in a straight line. Leake and most other geographers identify it with the present town of Adalia. Attalia is rarely mentioned by the ancients, indeed only by Strabo and Pliny and no earthquake is spoken of. I think therefore you are justified in assuming that Leonardo means 1489". In the elaborate catalogue of earthquakes in the East by Sciale Dshelal eddin Sayouthy (an unpublished Arabic MS. in the possession of Prof. SCHEFER, (Membre de l'Institut, Paris) mention is made of a terrible earthquake in the year 867 of the Mohamedan Era corresponding to the year 1489, and it is there stated that a hundred persons were killed by it in the fortress of Kerak. There are three places of this name. Kerak on the sea of Tiberias, Kerak near Tahle on the Libanon, which I visited in the summer of 1876--but neither of these is the place alluded to. Possibly it may be the strongly fortified town of Kerak=Kir Moab, to the West of the Dead Sea. There is no notice about this in ALEXIS PERCY, Memoire sur les tremblements de terres ressentis dans la peninsule turco- hellenique et en Syrie (Memoires couronnes et memoires des savants etrangers, Academie Royale de Belgique, Tome XXIII).]

1102.

Rhodes has in it 5000 houses.

Cyprus (1103. 1104).

1103.

SITE FOR [A TEMPLE OF] VENUS.

You must make steps on four sides, by which to mount to a meadow formed by nature at the top of a rock which may be hollowed out and supported in front by pilasters and open underneath in a large portico,

[Footnote: See Pl. LXXXIII. Compare also p. 33 of this Vol. The standing male figure at the side is evidently suggested by Michael Angelo's David. On the same place a slight sketch of horses seems to have been drawn first; there is no reason for assuming that the text and this sketch, which have no connection with each other, are of the same date.

Sito di Venere. By this heading Leonardo appears to mean Cyprus, which was always considered by the ancients to be the home and birth place of Aphrodite (Kirpic in Homer).]

in which the water may fall into various vases of granite, porphyryand serpentine, within semi-circular recesses; and the water may overflow from these. And round this portico towards the North there should be a lake with a little island in the midst of which should be a thick and shady wood; the waters at the top of the pilasters should pour into vases at their base, from whence they should flow in little channels.

Starting from the shore of Cilicia towards the South you discover the beauties of the island of Cyprus.

The Caspian Sea (1105. 1106).

1104.

>From the shore of the Southern coast of Cilicia may be seen to the South the beautiful island of Cyprus, which was the realm of the goddess Venus, and many navigators being attracted by her beauty, had their ships and rigging broken amidst the reefs, surrounded by the whirling waters. Here the beauty of delightful hills tempts wandering mariners to refresh themselves amidst their flowery verdure, where the winds are tempered and fill the island and the surrounding seas with fragrant odours. Ah! how many a ship has here been sunk. Ah! how many a vessel broken on these rocks. Here might be seen barks without number, some wrecked and half covered by the sand; others showing the poop and another the prow, here a keel and there the ribs; and it seems like a day of judgment when there should be a resurrection of dead ships, so great is the number of them covering all the Northern shore; and while the North gale makes various and fearful noises there.

1105.

Write to Bartolomeo the Turk as to the flow and ebb of the Black sea, and whether he is aware if there be such a flow and ebb in the Hyrcanean or Caspian sea. [Footnote: The handwriting of this note points to a late date.]

1106.

WHY WATER IS FOUND AT THE TOP OF MOUNTAINS.

>From the straits of Gibraltar to the Don is 3500 miles, that is one mile and 1/6, giving a fall of one braccio in a mile to any water that moves gently. The Caspian sea is a great deal higher; and none of the mountains of Europe rise a mile above the surface of our seas; therefore it might be said that the water which is on the summits of our mountains might come from the height of those seas, and of the rivers which flow into them, and which are still higher.

The sea of Azov.

1107.

Hence it follows that the sea of Azov is the highest part of the Mediterranean sea, being at a distance of 3500 miles from the Straits of Gibraltar, as is shown by the map for navigation; and it has 3500 braccia of descent, that is, one mile and 1/6; therefore it is higher than any mountains which exist in the West.

[Footnote: The passage before this, in the original, treats of the exit of the waters from Lakes in general.]

The Dardanelles.

1108.

In the Bosphorus the Black Sea flows always into the Egean sea, and the Egean sea never flows into it. And this is because the Caspian, which is 400 miles to the East, with the rivers which pour into it, always flows through subterranean caves into this sea of Pontus; and the Don does the same as well as the Danube, so that the waters of Pontus are always higher than those of the Egean; for the higher always fall towards the lower, and never the lower towards the higher.

Constantinople.

1109.

The bridge of Pera at Constantinople, 40 braccia wide, 70 braccia high above the water, 600 braccia long; that is 400 over the sea and 200 on the land, thus making its own abutments.

[Footnote: See Pl. CX No. 1. In 1453 by order of Sultan Mohamed II. the Golden Horn was crossed by a pontoon bridge laid on barrels (see Joh. Dukas' History of the Byzantine Empire XXXVIII p. 279). --The biographers of Michelangelo, Vasari as well as Condivi, relate that at the time when Michelangelo suddenly left Rome, in 1506, he entertained some intention of going to Constantinople, there to serve the Sultan, who sought to engage him, by means of certain Franciscan Monks, for the purpose of constructing a bridge to connect Constantinople with Pera. See VASARI, Vite (ed. Sansoni VII, 168): Michelangelo, veduto questa furia del papa, dubitando di lui, ebbe, secondo che si dice, voglia di andarsene in Gostantinopoli a servire il Turco, per mezzo di certi frati di San Francesco, che desiderava averlo per fare un ponte che passassi da Gostantinopoli a Pera. And CONDIVI, Vita di M. Buonaroti chap. 30; Michelangelo allora vedendosi condotto a questo, temendo dell'ira del papa, penso d'andarsene in Levante; massimamente essendo stato dal Turco ricercato con grandissime promesse per mezzo di certi frati di San Francesco, per volersene servire in fare un ponte da Costantinopoli a Pera ed in altri affari. Leonardo's plan for this bridge was made in 1502. We may therefore conclude that at about that time the Sultan Bajazet II. had either announced a competition in this matter, or that through his agents Leonardo had first been called upon to carry out the scheme.]

The Euphrates.

1110.

If the river will turn to the rift farther on it will never return to its bed, as the Euphrates does, and this may do at Bologna the one who is disappointed for his rivers.

Centrae Asia.

1111.

Mounts Caucasus, Comedorum, and Paropemisidae are joined together between Bactria and India, and give birth to the river Oxus which takes its rise in these mountains and flows 500 miles towards the North and as many towards the West, and discharges its waters into the Caspian sea; and is accompanied by the Oxus, Dargados, Arthamis, Xariaspes, Dargamaim, Ocus and Margus, all very large rivers. From the opposite side towards the South rises the great river Indus which sends its waters for 600 miles Southwards and receives as tributaries in this course the rivers Xaradrus, Hyphasis, Vadris, Vandabal Bislaspus to the East, Suastes and Coe to the

West, uniting with these rivers, and with their waters it flows 800 miles to the West; then, turning back by the Arbiti mountains makes an elbow and turns Southwards, where after a course of about 100 miles it finds the Indian Sea, in which it pours itself by seven branches. On the side of the same mountains rises the great Ganges, which river flows Southwards for 500 miles and to the Southwest a thousand ... and Sarabas, Diarnuna, Soas and Scilo, Condranunda are its tributaries. It flows into the Indian sea by many mouths.

On the natives of hot countries.

1112.

Men born in hot countries love the night because it refreshes them and have a horror of light because it burns them; and therefore they are of the colour of night, that is black. And in cold countries it is just the contrary.

[Footnote: The sketch here inserted is in MS. H3 55b.]

XVIII. Naval Warfare. Mechanical Appliances. Music.

Such theoretical questions, as have been laid before the reader in Sections XVI and XVII, though they were the chief subjects of Leonardo's studies of the sea, did not exclusively claim his attention. A few passages have been collected at the beginning of this section, which prove that he had turned his mind to the practical problems of navigation, and more especially of naval warfare. What we know for certain of his life gives us no data, it is true, as to when or where these matters came under his consideration; but the fact remains certain both from these notes in his manuscripts, and from the well known letter to Ludovico il Moro (No. 1340), in which he expressly states that he is as capable as any man, in this very department.

The numerous notes as to the laws and rationale of the flight of birds, are scattered through several note-books. An account of these is given in the Bibliography of the manuscripts at the end of this work. It seems probable that the idea which led him to these investigations was his desire to construct a flying or aerial machine for man. At the same time it must be admitted that the notes on the two subjects are quite unconnected in the manuscripts, and that those on the flight of birds are by far the most numerous and extensive. The two most important passages that treat of the construction of a flying machine are those already published as Tav. XVI, No. 1 and Tav. XVIII in the "Saggio delle opere di Leonardo da Vinci" (Milan 1872). The passages--Nos. 1120-1125--here printed for the first time and hitherto unknown--refer to the same subject and, with the exception of one already published in the Saggio-- No. 1126--they are, so far as I know, the only notes, among the numerous observations on the flight of birds, in which the phenomena are incidentally and expressly connected with the idea of a flying machine.

The notes on machines of war, the construction of fortifications, and similar matters which fall within the department of the Engineer, have not been included in this work, for the reasons given on page 26 of this Vol. An exception has been made in favour of the passages Nos. 1127 and 1128, because they have a more general interest, as bearing on the important question: whence the Master derived his knowledge of these matters. Though it would be rash to assert that Leonardo was the first to introduce the science of mining into Italy, it may be confidently said that he is one of the earliest writers who can be proved to have known and understood it; while, on the other hand, it is almost beyond doubt that in the East at that time, the whole science of besieging towns and mining in particular, was far more advanced than in Europe. This gives a peculiar value to the expressions used in No. 1127.

I have been unable to find in the manuscripts any passage whatever which throws any light on Leonardo's great reputation as a musician. Nothing therein illustrates VASARPS well-known statement: Avvenne che morto Giovan Galeazze duca di Milano, e creato Lodovico Sforza nel grado medesimo anno 1494, fu condotto a Milano con gran riputazione Lionardo al duca, il quale molto si dilettava del suono della lira, perche sonasse; e Lionardo porto quello strumento ch'egli aveva di sua mano fabbricato d'argento gran parte, in forma d'un teschio di cavallo, cosa bizzarra e nuova, acciocche l'armonia fosse con maggior tuba e piu sonora di voce; laonde supero tutti i musici che quivi erano concorsi a sonare.

The only notes on musical matters are those given as Nos. 1129 and 1130, which explain certain arrangements in instruments.

The ship's logs of Vitruvius, of Alberti and of Leonardo

1113.

ON MOVEMENTS;--TO KNOW HOW MUCH A SHIP ADVANCES IN AN HOUR.

The ancients used various devices to ascertain the distance gone by a ship each hour, among which Vitruvius [Footnote 6: See VITRUVIUS, De Architectura lib. X. C. 14 (p. 264 in the edition of Rose and Muller- Strubing). The German edition published at Bale in 1543 has, on fol. 596, an illustration of the contrivance, as described by Vitruvius.] gives one in his work on Architecture which is just as fallacious as all the others; and this is a mill wheel which touches the waves of the sea at one end and in each complete revolution describes a straight line which represents the circumference of the wheel extended to a straightness. But this invention is of no worth excepting on the smooth and motionless surface of lakes. But if the water moves together with the ship at an equal rate, then the wheel remains motionless; and if the motion of the water is more or less rapid than that of the ship, then neither has the wheel the same motion as the ship so that this invention is of but little use. There is another method tried by experiment with a known distance between one island and another; and this is done by a board or under the pressure of wind which strikes on it with more or less swiftness. This is in Battista Alberti [Footnote 25: LEON BATTISTA ALBERTI, De Architectura lib. V., c. 12 treats 'de le navi e parti loro', but there is no reference to the machine, mentioned by Leonardo. Alberti says here: Noi abbiamo trattato lungamente in altro luogo de' modi de le navi, ma in questo luogo ne abbiamo detto quel tanto che si bisogna. To this the following note is added in the most recent Italian edition: Questo libro e tuttora inedito e porta il titolo, secondo Gesnero di 'Liber navis'.].

Battista Alberti's method which is made by experiment on a known distance between one island and another. But such an invention does not succeed excepting on a ship like the one on which the experiment was made, and it must be of the same burden and have the same sails, and the sails in the same places, and the size of the waves must be the same. But my method will serve for any ship, whether with oars or sails; and whether it be small or large, broad or long, or high or low, it always serves [Footnote 52: Leonardo does not reveal the method invented by him.].

Methods of staying and moving in water

1114.

How an army ought to cross rivers by swimming with air-bags ... How fishes swim [Footnote 2: Compare No. 821.]; of the way in which they jump out of the water, as may be seen with dolphins; and it seems a wonderful thing to make a leap from a thing which does not resist but slips away. Of the swimming of animals of a long form, such as eels and the like. Of the mode of swimming against currents and in the rapid falls of rivers. Of the mode of swimming of fishes of a round form. How it is that animals which have not long hind quartres cannot swim. How it is that all other animals which have feet with toes, know by nature how to swim, excepting man. In what way man ought to learn to swim. Of the way in which man may rest on the water. How man may protect himself against whirlpools or eddies in the water, which drag him down. How a man dragged to the bottom must seek the reflux which will throw him up from the depths. How he ought to move his arms. How to swim on his back. How he can and how he cannot stay under water unless he can hold his breath [13]. How by means of a certain machine many people may stay some time under water. How and why I do not describe my method of remaining under water, or how long I can stay without eating; and I do not publish nor divulge these by reason of the evil nature of men who would use them as means of destruction at the bottom of the sea, by sending ships to the bottom, and sinking them together with the men in them. And although I will impart others, there is no danger in them; because the mouth of the tube, by which you breathe, is above the water supported on bags or corks [19].

[Footnote: L. 13-19 will also be found in Vol. I No. 1.]

On naval warfare (1115. 1116).

1115.

Supposing in a battle between ships and galleys that the ships are victorious by reason of the high of heir tops, you must haul the yard up almost to the top of the mast, and at the extremity of the yard, that is the end which is turned towards the enemy, have a small cage fastened, wrapped up below and all round in a great mattress full of cotton so that it may not be injured by the bombs; then, with the capstan, haul down the opposite end of this yard and the top on the opposite side will go up so high, that it will be far above the round-top of the ship, and you will easily drive out the men that are in it. But it is necessary that the men who are in the galley should go to the opposite side of it so as to afford a counterpoise to the weight of the men placed inside the cage on the yard.

1116.

If you want to build an armada for the sea employ these ships to ram in the enemy's ships. That is, make ships 100 feet long and 8 feet wide, but arranged so that the left hand rowers may have their oars to the right side of the ship, and the right hand ones to the left side, as is shown at M, so that the leverage of the oars may be longer. And the said ship may be one foot and a half thick, that is made with cross beams within and without, with planks in contrary directions. And this ship must have attached to it, a foot below the water, an iron-shod spike of about the weight and size of an anvil; and this, by force of oars may, after it has given the first blow, be drawn back, and driven forward again with fury give a second blow, and then a third, and so many as to destroy the other ship.

The use of swimming belts.

1117.

A METHOD OF ESCAPING IN A TEMPEST AND SHIPWRECK AT SEA.

Have a coat made of leather, which must be double across the breast, that is having a hem on each side of about a finger breadth. Thus it will be double from the waist to the knee; and the leather must be quite air-tight. When you want to leap into the sea, blow out the skirt of your coat through the double hems of the breast; and jump into the sea, and allow yourself to be carried by the waves; when you see no shore near, give your attention to the sea you are in, and always keep in your mouth the air-tube which leads down into the coat; and if now and again you require to take a breath of fresh air, and the foam prevents you, you may draw a breath of the air within the coat.

[Footnote: AMORETTI, Memorie Storiche, Tav. II. B. Fig. 5, gives the same figure, somewhat altered. 6. La canna dell' aria. Compare Vol. I. No. I. Note]

On the gravity of water.

1118.

If the weight of the sea bears on its bottom, a man, lying on that bottom and having l000 braccia of water on his back, would have enough to crush him.

Diving apparatus and Skating (1119-1121).

1119.

Of walking under water. Method of walking on water.

[Footnote: The two sketches belonging to this passage are given by AMORETTI, Memorie Storiche. Tav. II, Fig. 3 and 4.]

1120.

Just as on a frozen river a man may run without moving his feet, so a car might be made that would slide by itself.

[Footnote: The drawings of carts by the side of this text have no direct connection with the problem as stated in words.--Compare No. 1448, l. 17.]

1121.

A definition as to why a man who slides on ice does not fall. [Footnote: An indistinct sketch accompanies the passage, in the original.]

On Flying machines (1122-1126).

1122.

Man when flying must stand free from the waist upwards so as to be able to balance himself as he does in a boat so that the centre of gravity in himself and in the machine may counterbalance each other, and be shifted as necessity demands for the changes of its centre of resistance.

1123.

Remember that your flying machine must imitate no other than the bat, because the web is what by its union gives the armour, or strength to the wings.

If you imitate the wings of feathered birds, you will find a much stronger structure, because they are pervious; that is, their feathers are separate and the air passes through them. But the bat is aided by the web that connects the whole and is not pervious.

1124.

TO ESCAPE THE PERIL OF DESTRUCTION.

Destruction to such a machine may occur in two ways; of which the first is the breaking of the machine. The second would be when the machine should turn on its edge or nearly on its edge, because it ought always to descend in a highly oblique direction, and almost exactly balanced on its centre. As regards the first--the breaking of the machine--, that may be prevented by making it as strong as possible; and in whichever direction it may tend to turn over, one centre must be very far from the other; that is, in a machine 30 braccia long the centres must be 4 braccia one from the other.

[Footnote: Compare No. 1428.]

1125.

Bags by which a man falling from a height of 6 braccia may avoid hurting himself, by a fall whether into water or on the ground; and these bags, strung together like a rosary, are to be fixed on one's back.

1126.

An object offers as much resistance to the air as the air does to the object. You may see that the beating of its wings against the air supports a heavy eagle in the highest and rarest atmosphere, close to the sphere of elemental fire. Again you may see the air in motion over the sea, fill the swelling sails and drive heavily laden ships. From these instances, and the reasons given, a man with wings large enough and duly connected might learn to overcome the resistance of the air, and by conquering it, succeed in subjugating it and rising above it. [Footnote: A parachute is here sketched, with an explanatory remark. It is reproduced on Tav. XVI in the Saggio, and in: Leonardo da Vinci als Ingenieur etc., Ein Beitrag zur Geschichte der Technik und der induktiven Wissenschaften, von Dr. Hermann Grothe, Berlin 1874, p. 50.]

Of mining.

1127.

If you want to know where a mine runs, place a drum over all the places where you suspect that it is being made, and upon this drum put a couple of dice, and when you are over the spot where they are mining, the dice will jump a little on the drum at every blow which is given underground in the mining.

There are persons who, having the convenience of a river or a lake in their lands, have made, close to the place where they suspect that a mine is being made, a great reservoir of water, and have countermined the enemy, and having found them, have turned the water upon them and destroyed a great number in the mine.

Of Greek fire.

1128.

GREEK FIRE.

Take charcoal of willow, and saltpetre, and sulphuric acid, and sulphur, and pitch, with frankincense and camphor, and Ethiopian wool, and boil them all together. This fire is so ready to burn that it clings to the timbers even under water. And add to this composition liquid varnish, and bituminous oil, and turpentine and strong vinegar, and mix all together and dry it in the sun, or in an oven when the bread is taken out; and then stick it round hempen or other tow, moulding it into a round form, and studding it all over with very sharp nails. You must leave in this ball an opening to serve as a fusee, and cover it with rosin and sulphur.

Again, this fire, stuck at the top of a long plank which has one braccio length of the end pointed with iron that it may not be burnt by the said fire, is good for avoiding and keeping off the ships, so as not to be overwhelmed by their onset.

Again throw vessels of glass full of pitch on to the enemy's ships when the men in them are intent on the battle; and then by throwing similar burning balls upon them you have it in your power to burn all their ships.

[Footnote: Venturi has given another short text about the Greek fire in a French translation (Essai Section XIV). He adds that the original text is to be found in MS. B. 30 (?). Libri speaks of it in a note as follows (Histoire des sciences mathematiques en Italie Vol. II p. 129): La composition du feu gregeois est une des chases qui ont ete les plus cherchees et qui sont encore les plus douteuses. On dit qu'il fut invente au septieme siecle de l'ere chretienne par l'architecte Callinique (Constantini Porphyrogenetae opera, Lugd. Batav. 1617,-- in-8vo; p. 172, de admin, imper. exp. 48), et il se trouve souvent mentionne par les Historiens Byzantins. Tantot on le langait avec des machines, comme on lancerait une banche, tantot on le soufflait avec de longs tubes, comme on soufflerait un gaz ou un liquide enflamme (Annae Comnenae Alexias, p. 335, lib. XI.--Aeliani et Leonis, imperatoris tactica, Lugd.-Bat. 1613, in-4. part. 2 a, p. 322, Leonis tact. cap. I9.--Joinville, histoire du Saint Louis collect. Petitot tom. II, p. 235). Les ecrivains contemporains disent que l'eau ne pouvait pas eteindre ce feu, mais qu'avec du vinaigre et du sable on y parvenait. Suivant quelques historiens le feu gregeois etait compose de soufre et de resine. Marcus Graecus (Liber ignium, Paris, 1804, in-40) donne plusieurs manieres de le faire qui ne sont pas tres intelligibles, mais parmi lesquelles on trouve la composition de la poudre a canon. Leonard de Vinci (MSS. de Leonard de Vinci, vol. B. f. 30,) dit qu'on le faisait avec du charbon de saule, du salpetre, de l'eau de vie, de la resine, du soufre, de la poix et du camphre. Mais il est probable que nous ne savons pas qu'elle etait sa composition, surtout a cause du secret qu'en faisaient les Grecs. En effet, l'empereur Constantin Porphyrogenete recommende a son fils de ne jamais en donner aux Barbares, et de leur reponndre, s'ils en demandaient, qu'il avait ete apporti du ciel par un ange et que le secret en avait ete confie aux Chretiens (Constantini Porphyrogennetae opera, p. 26-27, de admin. imper., cap. 12).]

Of Music (1129. 1130).

1129.

A drum with cogs working by wheels with springs [2].

[Footnote: This chapter consists of explanations of the sketches shown on Pl. CXXI. Lines 1 and 2 of the text are to be seen at the top at the left hand side of the first sketch of a drum. Lines 3-5 refer to the sketch immediately below this. Line 6 is written as the side of the seventh sketch, and lines 7 and 8 at the side of the eighth. Lines 9-16 are at the bottom in the middle. The remainder of the text is at the side of the drawing at the bottom.]

A square drum of which the parchment may be drawn tight or slackened by the lever a b [5].

A drum for harmony [6].

[7] A clapper for harmony; that is, three clappers together.

[9] Just as one and the same drum makes a deep or acute sound according as the parchments are more or less tightened, so these parchments variously tightened on one and the same drum will make various sounds [16].

Keys narrow and close together; (bicchi) far apart; these will be right for the trumpet shown above.

a must enter in the place of the ordinary keys which have the ... in the openings of a flute.

1130.

Tymbals to be played like the monochord, or the soft flute.

[6] Here there is to be a cylinder of cane after the manner of clappers with a musical round called a Canon, which is sung in four parts; each singer singing the whole round. Therefore I here make a wheel with 4 teeth so that each tooth takes by itself the part of a singer.

[Footnote: In the original there are some more sketches, to which the text, from line 6, refers. They are studies for a contrivance exactly like the cylinder in our musical boxes.]

1131.

Of decorations.

White and sky-blue cloths, woven in checks to make a decoration.

Cloths with the threads drawn at a b c d e f g h i k, to go round the decoration.

XIX. Philosophical Maxims. Morals. Polemics and Speculations.

Vasari indulges in severe strictures on Leonardo's religious views. He speaks, among other things, of his "capricci nel filosofar delle cose naturali" and says on this point: "Per il che fece nell'animo un concetto si eretico che e' non si accostava a qualsi voglia religione, stimando per avventura assai piu lo esser filosofo che cristiano" (see the first edition of 'Le Vite'). But this accusation on the part of a writer in the days of the Inquisition is not a very serious one--and the less so, since, throughout the manuscripts, we find nothing to support it.

Under the heading of "Philosophical Maxims" I have collected all the passages which can give us a clear comprehension of Leonardo's ideas of the world at large. It is scarcely necessary to observe that there is absolutely nothing in them to lead to the inference that he was an atheist. His views of nature and its laws are no doubt very unlike those of his contemporaries, and have a much closer affinity to those which find general acceptance at the present day. On the other hand, it is obvious from Leonardo's will (see No. 1566) that, in the year before his death, he had professed to adhere to the fundamental doctrines of the Roman Catholic faith, and this evidently from his own personal desire and impulse.

The incredible and demonstrably fictitious legend of Leonardo's death in the arms of Francis the First, is given, with others, by Vasari and further embellished by this odious comment: "Mostrava tuttavia quanto avea offeso Dio e gli uomini del mondo, non avendo operato nell'arte come si conveniva." This last accusation, it may be remarked, is above all evidence of the superficial character of the information which Vasari was in a position to give about Leonardo. It seems to imply that Leonardo was disdainful of diligent labour. With regard to the second, referring to Leonardo's morality and dealings with his fellow men, Vasari himself nullifies it by asserting the very contrary in several passages. A further refutation may be found in the following sentence from the letter in which Melsi, the young Milanese nobleman, announces the Master's death to Leonardo's brothers: Credo siate certificati della morte di Maestro Lionardo fratello vostro, e mio quanto optimo padre, per la cui morte sarebbe impossibile che io potesse esprimere il dolore che io ho preso; e in mentre che queste mia membra si sosterranno insieme, io possedero una perpetua infelicita, e meritamente perche sviscerato et ardentissimo amore mi portava giornalmente. E dolto ad ognuno la perdita di tal uomo, quale non e piu in podesta della natura, ecc.

It is true that, in April 1476, we find the names of Leonardo and Verrocchio entered in the "Libro degli Uffiziali di notte e de' Monasteri" as breaking the laws; but we immediately after find the note "Absoluti cum condizione ut retamburentur" (Tamburini was the name given to the warrant cases of the night police). The acquittal therefore did not exclude the possibility of a repetition of the charge. It was in fact repeated, two months later, and on this occasion the Master and his pupil were again fully acquitted. Verrocchio was at this time forty and Leonardo four-and-twenty. The documents referring to this affair are in the State Archives of Florence; they have been withheld from publication, but it seemed to me desirable to give the reader this brief account of the leading facts of the story, as the vague hints of it, which have recently been made public, may have given to the incident an aspect which it had not in reality, and which it does not deserve.

The passages here classed under the head "Morals" reveal Leonardo to us as a man whose life and conduct were unfailingly governed by lofty principles and aims. He could scarcely have recorded his stern reprobation and unmeasured contempt for men who do nothing useful and strive only for riches, if his own life and ambitions had been such as they have so often been misrepresented.

At a period like that, when superstition still exercised unlimited dominion over the minds not merely of the illiterate crowd, but of the cultivated and learned classes, it was very natural that Leonardo's views as to Alchemy, Ghosts, Magicians, and the like should be met with stern reprobation whenever and wherever he may have expressed them; this accounts for the argumentative tone of all his utterances on such subjects which I have collected in Subdivision III of this section. To these I have added some passages which throw light on Leonardo's personal views on the Universe. They are, without exception, characterised by a broad spirit of naturalism of which the principles are more strictly applied in his essays on Astronomy, and still more on Physical Geography.

To avoid repetition, only such notes on Philosophy, Morals and Polemics, have been included in this section as occur as independent texts in the original MSS. Several moral reflections have already been given in Vol. I, in section "Allegorical representations, Mottoes and Emblems". Others will be found in the following section. Nos. 9 to 12, Vol. I, are also passages of an argumentative character. It did not seem requisite to repeat here these and similar passages, since their direct connection with the context is far closer in places where they have appeared already, than it would be here.

I. PHILOSOPHICAL MAXIMS
Prayers to God (1132-1133)

1132.

I obey Thee Lord, first for the love I ought, in all reason to bear Thee; secondly for that Thou canst shorten or prolong the lives of men.

1133.

A PRAYER.

Thou, O God, dost sell us all good things at the price of labour.

The powers of Nature (1134-1139)

1134.

O admirable impartiality of Thine, Thou first Mover; Thou hast not permitted that any force should fail of the order or quality of its necessary results.

1135.

Necessity is the mistress and guide of nature.

Necessity is the theme and the inventress, the eternal curb and law of nature.

1136.

In many cases one and the same thing is attracted by two strong forces, namely Necessity and Potency. Water falls in rain; the earth absorbs it from the necessity for moisture; and the sun evaporates it, not from necessity, but by its power.

1137.

Weight, force and casual impulse, together with resistance, are the four external powers in which all the visible actions of mortals have their being and their end.

1138.

Our body is dependant on heaven and heaven on the Spirit.

1139.

The motive power is the cause of all life.

Psychology (1140-1147)

1140.

And you, O Man, who will discern in this work of mine the wonderful works of Nature, if you think it would be a criminal thing to destroy it, reflect how much more criminal it is to take the life of a man; and if this, his external form, appears to thee marvellously constructed, remember that it is nothing as compared with the soul that dwells in that structure; for that indeed, be it what it may, is a thing divine. Leave it then to dwell in His work at His good will and pleasure, and let not your rage or malice destroy a life--for indeed, he who does not value it, does not himself deserve it [Footnote 19: In MS. II 15a is the note: chi no stima la vita, non la merita.].

[Footnote: This text is on the back of the drawings reproduced on Pl. CVII. Compare No. 798, 35 note on p. 111: Compare also No. 837 and 838.]

1141.

The soul can never be corrupted with the corruption of the body,, but is in the body as it were the air which causes the sound of the organ, where when a pipe bursts, the wind would cease to have any good effect. [Footnote: Compare No. 845.]

1142.

The part always has a tendency to reunite with its whole in order to escape from its imperfection.

The spirit desires to remain with its body, because, without the organic instruments of that body, it can neither act, nor feel anything.

1143.

If any one wishes to see how the soul dwells in its body, let him observe how this body uses its daily habitation; that is to say, if this is devoid of order and confused, the body will be kept in disorder and confusion by its soul.

1144.

Why does the eye see a thing more clearly in dreams than with the imagination being awake?

1145.

The senses are of the earth; Reason, stands apart in contemplation.

[Footnote: Compare No. 842.]

1146.

Every action needs to be prompted by a motive.

To know and to will are two operations of the human mind.

Discerning, judging, deliberating are acts of the human mind.

1147.

All our knowledge has its origin in our preceptions.

Science, its principles and rules (1148-1161)

1148.

Science is the observation of things possible, whether present or past; prescience is the knowledge of things which may come to pass, though but slowly.

1149.

Experience, the interpreter between formative nature and the human race, teaches how that nature acts among mortals; and being constrained by necessity cannot act otherwise than as reason, which is its helm, requires her to act.

1150.

Wisdom is the daughter of experience.

1151.

Nature is full of infinite causes that have never occured in experience.

1152.

Truth was the only daughter of Time.

1153.

Experience never errs; it is only your judgments that err by promising themselves effects such as are not caused by your experiments.

Experience does not err; only your judgments err by expecting from her what is not in her power. Men wrongly complain of Experience; with great abuse they accuse her of leading them astray but they set Experience aside, turning from it with complaints as to our ignorance causing us to be carried away by vain and foolish desires to promise ourselves, in her name, things that are not in her power; saying that she is fallacious. Men are unjust in complaining of innocent Experience, constantly accusing her of error and of false evidence.

1154.

Instrumental or mechanical science is of all the noblest and the most useful, seeing that by means of this all animated bodies that have movement perform all their actions; and these movements are based on the centre of gravity which is placed in the middle dividing unequal weights, and it has dearth and wealth of muscles and also lever and counterlever.

1155.

OF MECHANICS.

Mechanics are the Paradise of mathematical science, because here we come to the fruits of mathematics. [Footnote: Compare No. 660, 11. 19--22 (Vol. I., p. 332). 1156.

Every instrument requires to be made by experience.

1157.

The man who blames the supreme certainty of mathematics feeds on confusion, and can never silence the contradictions of sophistical sciences which lead to an eternal quackery.

1158.

There is no certainty in sciences where one of the mathematical sciences cannot be applied, or which are not in relation with these mathematics.

1159.

Any one who in discussion relies upon authority uses, not his understanding, but rather his memory. Good culture is born of a good disposition; and since the cause is more to be praised than the effect, I will rather praise a good disposition without culture, than good culture without the disposition.

1160.

Science is the captain, and practice the soldiers.

1161.

OF THE ERRORS OF THOSE WHO DEPEND ON PRACTICE WITHOUT SCIENCE.

Those who fall in love with practice without science are like a sailor who enters a ship without a helm or a compass, and who never can be certain whither he is going.

II. MORALS
What is life? (1162-1163)

1162.

Now you see that the hope and the desire of returning home and to one's former state is like the moth to the light, and that the man who with constant longing awaits with joy each new spring time, each new summer, each new month and new year--deeming that the things he longs for are ever too late in coming--does not perceive that he is longing for his own destruction. But this desire is the very quintessence, the spirit of the elements, which finding itself imprisoned with the soul is ever longing to return from the human body to its giver. And you must know that this same longing is that quintessence, inseparable from nature, and that man is the image of the world.

1163.

O Time! consumer of all things; O envious age! thou dost destroy all things and devour all things with the relentless teeth of years, little by little in a slow death. Helen, when she looked in her mirror, seeing the withered wrinkles made in her face by old age, wept and wondered why she had twice been carried away.

O Time! consumer of all things, and O envious age! by which all things are all devoured.

Death.

1164.

Every evil leaves behind a grief in our memory, except the supreme evil, that is death, which destroys this memory together with life.

How to spend life (1165-1170).

1165.

0 sleepers! what a thing is slumber! Sleep resembles death. Ah, why then dost thou not work in such wise as that after death thou mayst retain a resemblance to perfect life, when, during life, thou art in sleep so like to the hapless dead? [Footnote: Compare No. 676, Vol. I. p. 353.]

1166.

One pushes down the other.

By these square-blocks are meant the life and the studies of men.

1167.

The knowledge of past times and of the places on the earth is both an ornament and nutriment to the human mind.

1168.

To lie is so vile, that even if it were in speaking well of godly things it would take off something from God's grace; and Truth is so excellent, that if it praises but small things they become noble.

Beyond a doubt truth bears the same relation to falsehood as light to darkness; and this truth is in itself so excellent that, even when it dwells on humble and lowly matters, it is still infinitely above uncertainty and lies, disguised in high and lofty discourses; because in our minds, even if lying should be their fifth element, this does not prevent that the truth of things is the chief nutriment of superior intellects, though not of wandering wits.

But you who live in dreams are better pleased by the sophistical reasons and frauds of wits in great and uncertain things, than by those reasons which are certain and natural and not so far above us.

1169.

Avoid studies of which the result dies with the worker.

1170.

Men are in error when they lament the flight of time, accusing it of being too swift, and not perceiving that it is sufficient as it passes; but good memory, with which nature has endowed us, causes things long past to seem present.

1171.

Learning acquired in youth arrests the evil of old age; and if you understand that old age has wisdom for its food, you will so conduct yourself in youth that your old age will not lack for nourishment.

1172.

The acquisition of any knowledge is always of use to the intellect, because it may thus drive out useless things and retain the good.

For nothing can be loved or hated unless it is first known.

1173.

As a day well spent procures a happy sleep, so a life well employed procures a happy death.

1174.

The water you touch in a river is the last of that which has passed, and the first of that which is coming. Thus it is with time present.

Life if well spent, is long.

1175.

Just as food eaten without caring for it is turned into loathsome nourishment, so study without a taste for it spoils memory, by retaining nothing which it has taken in.

1176.

Just as eating against one's will is injurious to health, so study without a liking for it spoils the memory, and it retains nothing it takes in.

1177.

On Mount Etna the words freeze in your mouth and you may make ice of them.[Footnote 2: There is no clue to explain this strange sentence.]

Just as iron rusts unless it is used, and water putrifies or, in cold, turns to ice, so our intellect spoils unless it is kept in use.

You do ill if you praise, and still worse if you reprove in a matter you do not understand.

When Fortune comes, seize her in front with a sure hand, because behind she is bald.

1178.

It seems to me that men of coarse and clumsy habits and of small knowledge do not deserve such fine instruments nor so great a variety of natural mechanism as men of speculation and of great knowledge; but merely a sack in which their food may be stowed and whence it may issue, since they cannot be judged to be any thing else than vehicles for food; for it seems to me they have nothing about them of the human species but the voice and the figure, and for all the rest are much below beasts.

1179.

Some there are who are nothing else than a passage for food and augmentors of excrement and fillers of privies, because through them no other things in the world, nor any good effects are produced, since nothing but full privies results from them.

On foolishness and ignorance (1180-1182)

1180.

The greatest deception men suffer is from their own opinions.

1181.

Folly is the shield of shame, as unreadiness is that of poverty glorified.

1182.

Blind ignorance misleads us thus and delights with the results of lascivious joys.

Because it does not know the true light. Because it does not know what is the true light.

Vain splendour takes from us the power of being .... behold! for its vain splendour we go into the fire, thus blind ignorance does mislead us. That is, blind ignorance so misleads us that ...

O! wretched mortals, open your eyes.

On riches (1183-1187)

1183.

That is not riches, which may be lost; virtue is our true good and the true reward of its possessor. That cannot be lost; that never deserts us, but when life leaves us. As to property and external riches, hold them with trembling; they often leave their possessor in contempt, and mocked at for having lost them.

1184.

Every man wishes to make money to give it to the doctors, destroyers of life; they then ought to be rich. [Footnote 2: Compare No. 856.]

Man has much power of discourse which for the most part is vain and false; animals have but little, but it is useful and true, and a small truth is better than a great lie.

1185.

He who possesses most must be most afraid of loss.

1186.

He who wishes to be rich in a day will be hanged in a year.

1187.

That man is of supreme folly who always wants for fear of wanting; and his life flies away while he is still hoping to enjoy the good things which he has with extreme labour acquired.

Rules of Life (1188-1202)

1188.

If you governed your body by the rules of virtue you would not walk on all fours in this world.

You grow in reputation like bread in the hands of a child. [Footnote: The first sentence is obscure. Compare Nos. 825, 826.]

1189.

Savage he is who saves himself.

1190.

We ought not to desire the impossible. [Footnote: The writing of this note, which is exceedingly minute, is reproduced in facsimile on Pl. XLI No. 5 above the first diagram.

1191.

Ask counsel of him who rules himself well.

Justice requires power, insight, and will; and it resembles the queen-bee.

He who does not punish evil commands it to be done.

He who takes the snake by the tail will presently be bitten by it.

The grave will fall in upon him who digs it.

1192.

The man who does not restrain wantonness, allies himself with beasts.

You can have no dominion greater or less than that over yourself.

He who thinks little, errs much.

It is easier to contend with evil at the first than at the last.

No counsel is more loyal than that given on ships which are in peril: He may expect loss who acts on the advice of an inexperienced youth.

1193.

Where there is most feeling, there is the greatest martyrdom;--a great martyr.

1194.

The memory of benefits is a frail defence against ingratitude.

Reprove your friend in secret and praise him openly.

Be not false about the past.

1195.

A SIMILE FOR PATIENCE.

Patience serves us against insults precisely as clothes do against the cold. For if you multiply your garments as the cold increases, that cold cannot hurt you; in the same way increase your patience under great offences, and they cannot hurt your feelings.

1196.

To speak well of a base man is much the same as speaking ill of a good man.

1197.

Envy wounds with false accusations, that is with detraction, a thing which scares virtue.

1198.

We are deceived by promises and time disappoints us ... [Footnote 2: The rest of this passage may be rendered in various ways, but none of them give a satisfactory meaning.]

1199.

Fear arises sooner than any thing else.

1200.

Just as courage imperils life, fear protects it.

Threats alone are the weapons of the threatened man.

Wherever good fortune enters, envy lays siege to the place and attacks it; and when it departs, sorrow and repentance remain behind.

He who walks straight rarely falls.

It is bad if you praise, and worse if you reprove a thing, I mean, if you do not understand the matter well.

It is ill to praise, and worse to reprimand in matters that you do not understand.

1201.

Words which do not satisfy the ear of the hearer weary him or vex him, and the symptoms of this you will often see in such hearers in their frequent yawns; you therefore, who speak before men whose good will you desire, when you see such an excess of fatigue, abridge your speech, or change your discourse; and if you do otherwise, then instead of the favour you desire, you will get dislike and hostility.

And if you would see in what a man takes pleasure, without hearing him speak, change the subject of your discourse in talking to him, and when you presently see him intent, without yawning or wrinkling his brow or other actions of various kinds, you may be certain that the matter of which you are speaking is such as is agreeable to him &c.

1202.

The lover is moved by the beloved object as the senses are by sensible objects; and they unite and become one and the same thing. The work is the first thing born of this union; if the thing loved is base the lover becomes base.

When the thing taken into union is perfectly adapted to that which receives it, the result is delight and pleasure and satisfaction.

When that which loves is united to the thing beloved it can rest there; when the burden is laid down it finds rest there.

Politics (1203-1204)

1203.

There will be eternal fame also for the inhabitants of that town, constructed and enlarged by him.

All communities obey and are led by their magnates, and these magnates ally themselves with the lords and subjugate them in two ways: either by consanguinity, or by fortune; by consanguinity, when their children are, as it were, hostages, and a security and pledge of their suspected fidelity; by property, when you make each of these build a house or two inside your city which may yield some revenue and he shall have...; 10 towns, five thousand houses with thirty thousand inhabitants, and you will disperse this great congregation of people which stand like goats one behind the other, filling every place with fetid smells and sowing seeds of pestilence and death;

And the city will gain beauty worthy of its name and to you it will be useful by its revenues, and the eternal fame of its aggrandizement.

[Footnote: These notes were possibly written in preparation for a letter. The meaning is obscure.]

1204.

To preserve Nature's chiefest boon, that is freedom, I can find means of offence and defence, when it is assailed by ambitious tyrants, and first I will speak of the situation of the walls, and also I shall show how communities can maintain their good and just Lords.

[Footnote: Compare No. 1266.]

III. POLEMICS

SPECULATION.

Against Speculators (1205-1206)

1205.

Oh! speculators on things, boast not of knowing the things that nature ordinarily brings about; but rejoice if you know the end of those things which you yourself devise.

1206.

Oh! speculators on perpetual motion how many vain projects of the like character you have created! Go and be the companions of the searchers for gold. [Footnote: Another short passage in MS. I, referring also to speculators, is given by LIBRI (Hist, des Sciences math. III, 228): Sicche voi speculatori non vi fidate delli autori che anno sol col immaginatione voluto farsi interpreti tra la natura e l'omo, ma sol di quelli che non coi cienni della natura, ma cogli effetti delle sue esperienze anno esercitati i loro ingegni.]

Against alchemists (1207-1208)

1207.

The false interpreters of nature declare that quicksilver is the common seed of every metal, not remembering that nature varies the seed according to the variety of the things she desires to produce in the world.

1208.

And many have made a trade of delusions and false miracles, deceiving the stupid multitude.

Against friars

1209.

Pharisees--that is to say, friars.

[Footnote: Compare No. 837, 11. 54-57, No. 1296 (p. 363 and 364), and No. 1305 (p. 370).]

Against writers of epitomes

1210.

Abbreviators do harm to knowledge and to love, seeing that the love of any thing is the offspring of this knowledge, the love being the more fervent in proportion as the knowledge is more certain. And this certainty is born of a complete knowledge of all the parts, which, when combined, compose the totality of the thing which ought to be loved. Of what use then is he who abridges the details of those matters of which he professes to give thorough information, while he leaves behind the chief part of the things of which the whole is composed? It is true that impatience, the mother of stupidity, praises brevity, as if such persons had not life long enough to serve them to acquire a complete knowledge of one single subject, such as the human body; and then they want to comprehend the mind of God in which the universe is included, weighing it minutely and mincing it into infinite parts, as if they had to dissect it!

Oh! human stupidity, do you not perceive that, though you have been with yourself all your life, you are not yet aware of the thing you possess most of, that is of your folly? and then, with the crowd of sophists, you deceive yourselves and others, despising the mathematical sciences, in which truth dwells and the knowledge of the things included in them. And then you occupy yourself with miracles, and write that you possess information of those things of which the human mind is incapable and which cannot be proved by any instance from nature. And you fancy you have wrought miracles when you spoil a work of some speculative mind, and do not perceive that you are falling into the same error as that of a man who strips a tree of the ornament of its branches covered with leaves mingled with the scented blossoms or fruit....... [Footnote 48: Givstino, Marcus Junianus Justinus, a Roman historian of the second century, who compiled an epitome from the general history written by Trogus Pompeius, who lived in the time of Augustus. The work of the latter writer no longer exist.] as Justinus did, in abridging the histories written by Trogus Pompeius, who had written in an ornate style all the worthy deeds of his forefathers, full of the most admirable and ornamental passages; and so composed a bald work worthy only of those impatient spirits, who fancy they are losing as much time as that which they employ usefully in studying the works of nature and the deeds of men. But these may remain in company of beasts; among their associates should be dogs and other animals full of rapine and they may hunt with them after...., and then follow helpless beasts, which in time of great snows come near to your houses asking alms as from their master....

On spirits (1211-1213)

1211.

O mathematicians shed light on this error.

The spirit has no voice, because where there is a voice there is a body, and where there is a body space is occupied, and this prevents the eye from seeing what is placed behind that space; hence the surrounding air is filled by the body, that is by its image.

1212.

There can be no voice where there is no motion or percussion of the air; there can be no percussion of the air where there is no instrument, there can be no instrument without a body; and this being so, a spirit can have neither voice, nor form, nor strength. And if it were to assume a body it could not penetrate nor enter where the passages are closed. And if any one should say that by air, compressed and compacted together, a spirit may take bodies of various forms and by this means speak and move with strength--to him I reply that when there are neither nerves nor bones there can be no force exercised in any kind of movement made by such imaginary spirits.

Beware of the teaching of these speculators, because their reasoning is not confirmed by experience.

1213.

Of all human opinions that is to be reputed the most foolish which deals with the belief in Necromancy, the sister of Alchemy, which gives birth to simple and natural things. But it is all the more worthy of reprehension than alchemy, because it brings forth nothing but what is like itself, that is, lies; this does not happen in Alchemy which deals with simple products of nature and whose function cannot be exercised by nature itself, because it has no organic instruments with which it can work, as men do by means of their hands, who have produced, for instance, glass &c. but this Necromancy the flag and flying banner, blown by the winds, is the guide of the stupid crowd which is constantly witness to the dazzling and endless effects of this art; and there are books full, declaring that enchantments and spirits can work and speak without tongues and without organic instruments-- without which it is impossible to speak-- and can carry heaviest weights and raise storms and rain; and that men can be turned into cats and wolves and other beasts, although indeed it is those who affirm these things who first became beasts.

And surely if this Necromancy did exist, as is believed by small wits, there is nothing on the earth that would be of so much importance alike for the detriment and service of men, if it were true that there were in such an art a power to disturb the calm serenity of the air, converting it into darkness and making coruscations or winds, with terrific thunder and lightnings rushing through the darkness, and with violent storms overthrowing high buildings and rooting up forests; and thus to oppose armies, crushing and annihilating them; and, besides these frightful storms may deprive the peasants of the reward of their labours.--Now what kind of warfare is there to hurt the enemy so much as to deprive him of the harvest? What naval warfare could be compared with this? I say, the man who has power to command the winds and to make ruinous gales by which any fleet may be submerged, --surely a man who could command such violent forces would be lord of the nations, and no human ingenuity could resist his crushing force. The hidden treasures and gems reposing in the body of the earth would all be made manifest to him. No lock nor fortress, though impregnable, would be able to save any one against the will of the necromancer. He would have himself carried through the air from East to West and through all the opposite sides of the universe. But why should I enlarge further upon this? What is there that could not be done by such a craftsman? Almost nothing, except to escape death. Hereby I have explained in part the mischief and the usefulness, contained in this art, if it is real; and if it is real why has it not remained among men who desire it so much, having nothing to do with any deity? For I know that there are numberless people who would, to satisfy a whim, destroy God and all the universe; and if this necromancy, being, as it were, so necessary to men, has not been left among them, it can never have existed, nor will it ever exist according to the definition of the spirit, which is invisible in substance; for within the elements there are no incorporate things, because where there is no body, there is a vacuum; and no vacuum can exist in the elements because it would be immediately filled up. Turn over.

1214.

OF SPIRITS.

We have said, on the other side of this page, that the definition of a spirit is a power conjoined to a body; because it cannot move of its own accord, nor can it have any kind of motion in space; and if you were to say that it moves itself, this cannot be within the elements. For, if the spirit is an incorporeal quantity, this quantity is called a vacuum, and a vacuum does not exist in nature; and granting that one were formed, it would be immediately filled up by the rushing in of the element in which the vacuum had been generated. Therefore, from the definition of weight, which is this--Gravity is an accidental power, created by one element being drawn to or suspended in another--it follows that an element, not weighing anything compared with itself, has weight in the element above it and lighter than it; as we see that the parts of water have no gravity or levity compared with other water, but if you draw it up into the air, then it would acquire weight, and if you were to draw the air beneath the water then the water which remains above this air would acquire weight, which weight could not sustain itself by itself, whence collapse is inevitable. And this happens in water; wherever the vacuum may be in this water it will fall in; and this would happen with a spirit amid the elements, where it would continuously generate a vacuum in whatever element it might find itself, whence it would be inevitable that it should be constantly flying towards the sky until it had quitted these elements.

AS TO WHETHER A SPIRIT HAS A BODY AMID THE ELEMENTS.

We have proved that a spirit cannot exist of itself amid the elements without a body, nor can it move of itself by voluntary motion unless it be to rise upwards. But now we will say how such a spirit taking an aerial body would be inevitably melt into air; because if it remained united, it would be separated and fall to form a vacuum, as is said above; therefore it is inevitable, if it is to be able to remain suspended in the air, that it should absorb a certain quantity of air; and if it were mingled with the air, two difficulties arise; that is to say: It must rarefy that portion of the air with which it mingles; and for this cause the rarefied air must fly up of itself and will not remain among the air that is heavier than itself; and besides this the subtle spiritual essence disunites itself, and its nature is modified, by which that nature loses some of its first virtue. Added to these there is a third difficulty, and this is that such a body formed of air assumed by the spirits is exposed to the penetrating winds, which are incessantly sundering and dispersing the united portions of the air, revolving and whirling amidst the rest of the atmosphere; therefore the spirit which is infused in this

1215.

air would be dismembered or rent and broken up with the rending of the air into which it was incorporated.

AS TO WHETHER THE SPIRIT, HAVING TAKEN THIS BODY OF AIR, CAN MOVE OF ITSELF OR NOT.

It is impossible that the spirit infused into a certain quantity of air, should move this air; and this is proved by the above passage where it is said: the spirit rarefies that portion of the air in which it incorporates itself; therefore this air will rise high above the other air and there will be a motion of the air caused by its lightness and not by a voluntary movement of the spirit, and if this air is encountered by the wind, according to the 3rd of this, the air will be moved by the wind and not by the spirit incorporated in it.

AS TO WHETHER THE SPIRIT CAN SPEAK OR NOT.

In order to prove whether the spirit can speak or not, it is necessary in the first place to define what a voice is and how it is generated; and we will say that the voice is, as it were, the movement of air in friction against a dense body, or a dense body in friction against the air,--which is the same thing. And this friction of the dense and the rare condenses the rare and causes resistance; again, the rare, when in swift motion, and the rare in slow motion condense each other when they come in contact and make a noise and very great uproar; and the sound or murmur made by the rare moving through the rare with only moderate swiftness, like a great flame generating noises in the air; and the tremendous uproar made by the rare mingling with the rare, and when that air which is both swift and rare rushes into that which is itself rare and in motion, it is like the flame of fire which issues from a big gun and striking against the air; and again when a flame issues from the cloud, there is a concussion in the air as the bolt is generated. Therefore we may say that the spirit cannot produce a voice without movement of the air, and air in it there is none, nor can it emit what it has not; and if desires to move that air in which it is incorporated, it is necessary that the spirit should multiply itself, and that cannot multiply which has no quantity. And in the 4th place it is said that no rare body can move, if it has not a stable spot, whence it may take its motion; much more is it so when an element has to move within its own element, which does not move of itself, excepting by uniform evaporation at the centre of the thing evaporated; as occurs in a sponge squeezed in the hand held under water; the water escapes in every direction with equal movement through the openings between the fingers of the hand in which it is squeezed.

As to whether the spirit has an articulate voice, and whether the spirit can be heard, and what hearing is, and seeing; the wave of the voice passes through the air as the images of objects pass to the eye.

Nonentity.

1216.

Every quantity is intellectually conceivable as infinitely divisible.

[Amid the vastness of the things among which we live, the existence of nothingness holds the first place; its function extends over all things that have no existence, and its essence, as regards time, lies precisely between the past and the future, and has nothing in the present. This nothingness has the part equal to the whole, and the whole to the part, the divisible to the indivisible; and the product of the sum is the same whether we divide or multiply, and in addition as in subtraction; as is proved by arithmeticians by their tenth figure which represents zero; and its power has not extension among the things of Nature.]

[What is called Nothingness is to be found only in time and in speech. In time it stands between the past and future and has no existence in the present; and thus in speech it is one of the things of which we say: They are not, or they are impossible.]

With regard to time, nothingness lies between the past and the future, and has nothing to do with the present, and as to its nature it is to be classed among things impossible: hence, from what has been said, it has no existence; because where there is nothing there would necessarily be a vacuum.

[Footnote: Compare No. 916.]

Reflections on Nature (1217-1219)

1217.

EXAMPLE OF THE LIGHTNING IN CLOUDS.

[O mighty and once living instrument of formative nature. Incapable of availing thyself of thy vast strength thou hast to abandon a life of stillness and to obey the law which God and time gave to procreative nature.]

Ah! how many a time the shoals of terrified dolphins and the huge tunny-fish were seen to flee before thy cruel fury, to escape; whilst thy fulminations raised in the sea a sudden tempest with buffeting and submersion of ships in the great waves; and filling the uncovered shores with the terrified and desperate fishes which fled from thee, and left by the sea, remained in spots where they became the abundant prey of the people in the neighbourhood.

O time, swift robber of all created things, how many kings, how many nations hast thou undone, and how many changes of states and of various events have happened since the wondrous forms of this fish perished here in this cavernous and winding recess. Now destroyed by time thou liest patiently in this confined space with bones stripped and bare; serving as a support and prop for the superimposed mountain.

[Footnote: The character of the handwriting points to an early period of Leonardo's life. It has become very indistinct, and is at present exceedingly difficult to decipher. Some passages remain doubtful.]

[Footnote: Compare No. 1339, written on the same sheet.]

1218.

The watery element was left enclosed between the raised banks of the rivers, and the sea was seen between the uplifted earth and the surrounding air which has to envelope and enclose the complicated machine of the earth, and whose mass, standing between the water and the element of fire, remained much restricted and deprived of its indispensable moisture; the rivers will be deprived of their waters, the fruitful earth will put forth no more her light verdure; the fields will no more be decked with waving corn; all the animals, finding no fresh grass for pasture, will die and food will then be lacking to the lions and wolves and other beasts of prey, and to men who after many efforts will be compelled to abandon their life, and the human race will die out. In this way the fertile and fruitful earth will remain deserted, arid and sterile from the water being shut up in its interior, and from the activity of nature it will continue a little time to increase until the cold and subtle air being gone, it will be forced to end with the element of fire; and then its surface will be left burnt up to cinder and this will be the end of all terrestrial nature. [Footnote: Compare No. 1339, written on the same sheet.]

1219.

Why did nature not ordain that one animal should not live by the death of another? Nature, being inconstant and taking pleasure in creating and making constantly new lives and forms, because she knows that her terrestrial materials become thereby augmented, is more ready and more swift in her creating, than time in his destruction; and so she has ordained that many animals shall be food for others. Nay, this not satisfying her desire, to the same end she frequently sends forth certain poisonous and pestilential vapours upon the vast increase and congregation of animals; and most of all upon men, who increase vastly because other animals do not feed upon them; and, the causes being removed, the effects would not follow. This earth therefore seeks to lose its life, desiring only continual reproduction; and as, by the argument you bring forward and demonstrate, like effects always follow like causes, animals are the image of the world.

XX. Humorous Writings.

Just as Michaelangelo's occasional poems reflect his private life as well as the general disposition of his mind, we may find in the writings collected in this section, the transcript of Leonardo's fanciful nature, and we should probably not be far wrong in assuming, that he himself had recited these fables in the company of his friends or at the court festivals of princes and patrons. Era tanto piacevole nella conversazione-- so relates Vasari--che tirava a se gli animi delle genti. And Paulus Jovius says in his short biography of the artist: Fuit ingenio valde comi, nitido, liberali, vultu autem longe venustissimo, et cum elegantiae omnis deliciarumque maxime theatralium mirificus inventor ac arbiter esset, ad lyramque scito caneret, cunctis per omnem aetatem principibus mire placuit. There can be no doubt that the fables are the original offspring of Leonardo's brain, and not borrowed from any foreign source; indeed the schemes and plans for the composition of fables collected in division V seem to afford an external proof of this, if the fables themselves did not render it self-evident. Several of them-- for instance No. l279--are so strikingly characteristic of Leonardo's views of natural science that we cannot do them justice till we are acquainted with his theories on such subjects; and this is equally true of the 'Prophecies'.

I have prefixed to these quaint writings the 'Studies on the life and habits of animals' which are singular from their peculiar aphoristic style, and I have transcribed them in exactly the order in which they are written in MS. H. This is one of the very rare instances in which one subject is treated in a consecutive series of notes, all in one MS., and Leonardo has also departed from his ordinary habits, by occasionally not completing the text on the page it is begun. These brief notes of a somewhat mysterious bearing have been placed here, simply because they may possibly have been intended to serve as hints for fables or allegories. They can scarcely be regarded as preparatory for a natural history, rather they would seem to be extracts. On the one hand the names of some of the animals seem to prove that Leonardo could not here be recording observations of his own; on the other hand the notes on their habits and life appear to me to dwell precisely on what must have interested him most--so far as it is possible to form any complete estimate of his nature and tastes.

In No. 1293 lines 1-10, we have a sketch of a scheme for grouping the Prophecies. I have not however availed myself of it as a clue to their arrangement here because, in the first place, the texts are not so numerous as to render the suggested classification useful to the reader, and, also, because in reading the long series, as they occur in the original, we may follow the author's mind; and here and there it is not difficult to see how one theme suggested another. I have however regarded Leonardo's scheme for the classification of the Prophecies as available for that of the Fables and Jests, and have adhered to it as far as possible.

Among the humourous writings I might perhaps have included the 'Rebusses', of which there are several in the collection of Leonardo's drawings at Windsor; it seems to me not likely that many or all of them could be solved at the present day and the MSS. throw no light on them. Nor should I be justified if I intended to include in the literary works the well-known caricatures of human faces attributed to Leonardo-- of which, however, it may be incidentally observed, the greater number are in my opinion undoubtedly spurious. Two only have necessarily been given owing to their presence in text, which it was desired to reproduce: Vol. I page 326, and Pl. CXXII. It can scarcely be doubted that some satirical intention is conveyed by the drawing on Pl. LXIV (text No. 688).

My reason for not presenting Leonardo to the reader as a poet is the fact that the maxims and morals in verse which have been ascribed to him, are not to be found in the manuscripts, and Prof. Uzielli has already proved that they cannot be by him. Hence it would seem that only a few short verses can be attributed to him with any certainty.

I.

STUDIES ON THE LIFE AND HABITS OF ANIMALS.

1220.

THE LOVE OF VIRTUE.

The gold-finch is a bird of which it is related that, when it is carried into the presence of a sick person, if the sick man is going to die, the bird turns away its head and never looks at him; but if the sick man is to be saved the bird never loses sight of him but is the cause of curing him of all his sickness.

Like unto this is the love of virtue. It never looks at any vile or base thing, but rather clings always to pure and virtuous things and takes up its abode in a noble heart; as the birds do in green woods on flowery branches. And this Love shows itself more in adversity than in prosperity; as light does, which shines most where the place is darkest.

1221.

ENVY.

We read of the kite that, when it sees its young ones growing too big in the nest, out of envy it pecks their sides, and keeps them without food.

CHEERFULNESS.

Cheerfulness is proper to the cock, which rejoices over every little thing, and crows with varied and lively movements.

SADNESS.

Sadness resembles the raven, which, when it sees its young ones born white, departs in great grief, and abandons them with doleful lamentations, and does not feed them until it sees in them some few black feathers.

1222.

PEACE.

We read of the beaver that when it is pursued, knowing that it is for the virtue [contained] in its medicinal testicles and not being able to escape, it stops; and to be at peace with its pursuers, it bites off its testicles with its sharp teeth, and leaves them to its enemies.

RAGE.

It is said of the bear that when it goes to the haunts of bees to take their honey, the bees having begun to sting him he leaves the honey and rushes to revenge himself. And as he seeks to be revenged on all those that sting him, he is revenged on none; in such wise that his rage is turned to madness, and he flings himself on the ground, vainly exasperating, by his hands and feet, the foes against which he is defending himself.

1223.

GRATITUDE.

The virtue of gratitude is said to be more [developed] in the birds called hoopoes which, knowing the benefits of life and food, they have received from their father and their mother, when they see them grow old, make a nest for them and brood over them and feed them, and with their beaks pull out their old and shabby feathers; and then, with a certain herb restore their sight so that they return to a prosperous state.

AVARICE.

The toad feeds on earth and always remains lean; because it never eats enough:-- it is so afraid lest it should want for earth.

1224.

INGRATITUDE.

Pigeons are a symbol of ingratitude; for when they are old enough no longer to need to be fed, they begin to fight with their father, and this struggle does not end until the young one drives the father out and takes the hen and makes her his own.

CRUELTY.

The basilisk is so utterly cruel that when it cannot kill animals by its baleful gaze, it turns upon herbs and plants, and fixing its gaze on them withers them up.

1225.

GENEROSITY.

It is said of the eagle that it is never so hungry but that it will leave a part of its prey for the birds that are round it, which, being unable to provide their own food, are necessarily dependent on the eagle, since it is thus that they obtain food.

DISCIPLINE.

When the wolf goes cunningly round some stable of cattle, and by accident puts his foot in a trap, so that he makes a noise, he bites his foot off to punish himself for his folly.

1226.

FLATTERERS OR SYRENS.

The syren sings so sweetly that she lulls the mariners to sleep; then she climbs upon the ships and kills the sleeping mariners.

PRUDENCE.

The ant, by her natural foresight provides in the summer for the winter, killing the seeds she harvests that they may not germinate, and on them, in due time she feeds.

FOLLY.

The wild bull having a horror of a red colour, the hunters dress up the trunk of a tree with red and the bull runs at this with great frenzy, thus fixing his horns, and forthwith the hunters kill him there.

1227.

JUSTICE.

We may liken the virtue of Justice to the king of the bees which orders and arranges every thing with judgment. For some bees are ordered to go to the flowers, others are ordered to labour, others to fight with the wasps, others to clear away all dirt, others to accompagny and escort the king; and when he is old and has no wings they carry him. And if one of them fails in his duty, he is punished without reprieve.

TRUTH.

Although partridges steal each other's eggs, nevertheless the young born of these eggs always return to their true mother.

1228.

FIDELITY, OR LOYALTY.

The cranes are so faithful and loyal to their king, that at night, when he is sleeping, some of them go round the field to keep watch at a distance; others remain near, each holding a stone in his foot, so that if sleep should overcome them, this stone would fall and make so much noise that they would wake up again. And there are others which sleep together round the king; and this they do every night, changing in turn so that their king may never find them wanting.

FALSEHOOD.

The fox when it sees a flock of herons or magpies or birds of that kind, suddenly flings himself on the ground with his mouth open to look as he were dead; and these birds want to peck at his tongue, and he bites off their heads.

1229.

LIES.

The mole has very small eyes and it always lives under ground; and it lives as long as it is in the dark but when it comes into the light it dies immediately, because it becomes known;--and so it is with lies.

VALOUR.

The lion is never afraid, but rather fights with a bold spirit and savage onslaught against a multitude of hunters, always seeking to injure the first that injures him.

FEAR OR COWARDICE.

The hare is always frightened; and the leaves that fall from the trees in autumn always keep him in terror and generally put him to flight.

1230.

MAGNANIMITY.

The falcon never preys but on large birds; and it will let itself die rather than feed on little ones, or eat stinking meat.

VAIN GLORY.

As regards this vice, we read that the peacock is more guilty of it than any other animal. For it is always contemplating the beauty of its tail, which it spreads in the form of a wheel, and by its cries attracts to itself the gaze of the creatures that surround it.

And this is the last vice to be conquered.

1231.

CONSTANCY.

Constancy may be symbolised by the phoenix which, knowing that by nature it must be resuscitated, has the constancy to endure the burning flames which consume it, and then it rises anew.

INCONSTANCY.

The swallow may serve for Inconstancy, for it is always in movement, since it cannot endure the smallest discomfort.

CONTINENCE.

The camel is the most lustful animal there is, and will follow the female for a thousand miles. But if you keep it constantly with its mother or sister it will leave them alone, so temperate is its nature.

1232.

INCONTINENCE.

The unicorn, through its intemperance and not knowing how to control itself, for the love it bears to fair maidens forgets its ferocity and wildness; and laying aside all fear it will go up to a seated damsel and go to sleep in her lap, and thus the hunters take it.

HUMILITY.

We see the most striking example of humility in the lamb which will submit to any animal; and when they are given for food to imprisoned lions they are as gentle to them as to their own mother, so that very often it has been seen that the lions forbear to kill them.

1233.

PRIDE.

The falcon, by reason of its haughtiness and pride, is fain to lord it and rule over all the other birds of prey, and longs to be sole and supreme; and very often the falcon has been seen to assault the eagle, the Queen of birds.

ABSTINENCE.

The wild ass, when it goes to the well to drink, and finds the water troubled, is never so thirsty but that it will abstain from drinking, and wait till the water is clear again.

GLUTTONY.

The vulture is so addicted to gluttony that it will go a thousand miles to eat a carrion [carcase]; therefore is it that it follows armies.

1234.

CHASTITY.

The turtle-dove is never false to its mate; and if one dies the other preserves perpetual chastity, and never again sits on a green bough, nor ever again drinks of clear water.

UNCHASTITY.

The bat, owing to unbridled lust, observes no universal rule in pairing, but males with males and females with females pair promiscuously, as it may happen.

MODERATION.

The ermine out of moderation never eats but once in the day; it will rather let itself be taken by the hunters than take refuge in a dirty lair, in order not to stain its purity.

1235.

THE EAGLE.

The eagle when it is old flies so high that it scorches its feathers, and Nature allowing that it should renew its youth, it falls into shallow water [Footnote 5:

The meaning is obscure.]. And if its young ones cannot bear to gaze on the sun [Footnote 6: The meaning is obscure.]--; it does not feed them with any bird, that does not wish to die. Animals which much fear it do not approach its nest, although it does not hurt them. It always leaves part of its prey uneaten.

LUMERPA,--FAME.

This is found in Asia Major, and shines so brightly that it absorbs its own shadow, and when it dies it does not lose this light, and its feathers never fall out, but a feather pulled out shines no longer.

1236.

THE PELICAN.

This bird has a great love for its young; and when it finds them in its nest dead from a serpent's bite, it pierces itself to the heart, and with its blood it bathes them till they return to life.

THE SALAMANDER.

This has no digestive organs, and gets no food but from the fire, in which it constantly renews its scaly skin.

The salamander, which renews its scaly skin in the fire,--for virtue.

THE CAMELEON.

This lives on air, and there it is the prey of all the birds; so in order to be safer it flies above the clouds and finds an air so rarefied that it cannot support the bird that follows it.

At that height nothing can go unless it has a gift from Heaven, and that is where the chameleon flies.

1237.

THE ALEPO, A FISH.

The fish alepo does not live out of water.

THE OSTRICH.

This bird converts iron into nourishment, and hatches its eggs by its gaze;-- Armies under commanders.

THE SWAN.

The swan is white without any spot, and it sings sweetly as it dies, its life ending with that song.

THE STORK.

This bird, by drinking saltwater purges itself of distempers. If the male finds his mate unfaithful, he abandons her; and when it grows old its young ones brood over it, and feed it till it dies.

1238.

THE GRASSHOPPER.

This silences the cuckoo with its song. It dies in oil and revives in vinegar. It sings in the greatest heats

THE BAT.

The more light there is the blinder this creature becomes; as those who gaze most at the sun become most dazzled.--For Vice, that cannot remain where Virtue appears.

THE PARTRIDGE.

This bird changes from the female into the male and forgets its former sex; and out of envy it steals the eggs from others and hatches them, but the young ones follow the true mother.

THE SWALLOW.

This bird gives sight to its blind young ones by means of celandine.

1239.

THE OYSTER.--FOR TREACHERY.

This creature, when the moon is full opens itself wide, and when the crab looks in he throws in a piece of rock or seaweed and the oyster cannot close again, whereby it serves for food to that crab. This is what happens to him who opens his mouth to tell his secret. He becomes the prey of the treacherous hearer.

THE BASILISK.--CRUELTY.

All snakes flie from this creature; but the weasel attacks it by means of rue and kills it.

THE ASP.

This carries instantaneous death in its fangs; and, that it may not hear the charmer it stops its ears with its tail.

1240.

THE DRAGON.

This creature entangles itself in the legs of the elephant which falls upon it, and so both die, and in its death it is avenged.

THE VIPER.

She, in pairing opens her mouth and at last clenches her teeth and kills her husband. Then the young ones, growing within her body rend her open and kill their mother.

THE SCORPION.

Saliva, spit out when fasting will kill a scorpion. This may be likened to abstinence from greediness, which removes and heals the ills which result from that gluttony, and opens the path of virtue.

1241.

THE CROCODILE. HYPOCRISY.

This animal catches a man and straightway kills him; after he is dead, it weeps for him with a lamentable voice and many tears. Then, having done lamenting, it cruelly devours him. It is thus with the hypocrite, who, for the smallest matter, has his face bathed with tears, but shows the heart of a tiger and rejoices in his heart at the woes of others, while wearing a pitiful face.

THE TOAD.

The toad flies from the light of the sun, and if it is held there by force it puffs itself out so much as to hide its head below and shield itself from the rays. Thus does the foe of clear and radiant virtue, who can only be constrainedly brought to face it with puffed up courage.

1242.

THE CATERPILLAR.--FOR VIRTUE IN GENERAL.

The caterpillar, which by means of assiduous care is able to weave round itself a new dwelling place with marvellous artifice and fine workmanship, comes out of it afterwards with painted and lovely wings, with which it rises towards Heaven.

THE SPIDER.

The spider brings forth out of herself the delicate and ingenious web, which makes her a return by the prey it takes.

[Footnote: Two notes are underneath this text. The first: 'nessuna chosa e da ttemere piu che lla sozza fama' is a repetition of the first line of the text given in Vol. I No. 695.

The second: faticha fugga cholla fama in braccio quasi ochultata c is written in red chalk and is evidently an incomplete sentence.]

1243.

THE LION.

This animal, with his thundering roar, rouses his young the third day after they are born, teaching them the use of all their dormant senses and all the wild things which are in the wood flee away.

This may be compared to the children of Virtue who are roused by the sound of praise and grow up in honourable studies, by which they are more and more elevated; while all that is base flies at the sound, shunning those who are virtuous.

Again, the lion covers over its foot tracks, so that the way it has gone may not be known to its enemies. Thus it beseems a captain to conceal the secrets of his mind so that the enemy may not know his purpose.

1244.

THE TARANTULA.

The bite of the tarantula fixes a man's mind on one idea; that is on the thing he was thinking of when he was bitten.

THE SCREECH-OWL AND THE OWL.

These punish those who are scoffing at them by pecking out their eyes; for nature has so ordered it, that they may thus be fed.

1245.

THE ELEPHANT.

The huge elephant has by nature what is rarely found in man; that is Honesty, Prudence, Justice, and the Observance of Religion; inasmuch as when the moon is new, these beasts go down to the rivers, and there, solemnly cleansing themselves, they bathe, and so, having saluted the planet, return to the woods. And when they are ill, being laid down, they fling up plants towards Heaven as though they would offer sacrifice. --They bury their tusks when they fall out from old age.--Of these two tusks they use one to dig up roots for food; but they save the point of the other for fighting with; when they are taken by hunters and when worn out by fatigue, they dig up these buried tusks and ransom themselves.

1246.

They are merciful, and know the dangers, and if one finds a man alone and lost, he kindly puts him back in the road he has missed, if he finds the footprints of the man before the man himself. It dreads betrayal, so it stops and blows, pointing it out to the other elephants who form in a troop and go warily.

These beasts always go in troops, and the oldest goes in front and the second in age remains the last, and thus they enclose the troop. Out of shame they pair only at night and secretly, nor do they then rejoin the herd but first bathe in the river. The females do not fight as with other animals; and it is so merciful that it is most unwilling by nature ever to hurt those weaker than itself. And if it meets in the middle of its way a flock of sheep

1247.

it puts them aside with its trunk, so as not to trample them under foot; and it never hurts any thing unless when provoked. When one has fallen into a pit the others fill up the pit with branches, earth and stones, thus raising the bottom that he may easily get out. They greatly dread the noise of swine and fly in confusion, doing no less harm then, with their feet, to their own kind than to the enemy. They delight in rivers and are always wandering about near them, though on account of their great weight they cannot swim. They devour stones, and the trunks of trees are their favourite food. They have a horror of rats. Flies delight in their smell and settle on their back, and the beast scrapes its skin making its folds even and kills them.

1248.

When they cross rivers they send their young ones up against the stream of the water; thus, being set towards the fall, they break the united current of the water so that the current does not carry them away. The dragon flings itself under the elephant's body, and with its tail it ties its legs; with its wings and with its arms it also clings round its ribs and cuts its throat with its teeth, and the elephant falls upon it and the dragon is burst. Thus, in its death it is revenged on its foe.

THE DRAGON.

These go in companies together, and they twine themselves after the manner of roots, and with their heads raised they cross lakes, and swim to where they find better pasture; and if they did not thus combine

1249.

they would be drowned, therefore they combine.

THE SERPENT.

The serpent is a very large animal. When it sees a bird in the air it draws in its breath so strongly that it draws the birds into its mouth too. Marcus Regulus, the consul of the Roman army was attacked, with his army, by such an animal and almost defeated. And this animal, being killed by a catapult, measured 123 feet, that is 64 1/2 braccia and its head was high above all the trees in a wood.

THE BOA(?)

This is a very large snake which entangles itself round the legs of the cow so that it cannot move and then sucks it, in such wise that it almost dries it up. In the time of Claudius the Emperor, there was killed, on the Vatican Hill,

1250.

one which had inside it a boy, entire, that it had swallowed.

THE MACLI.--CAUGHT WHEN ASLEEP.

This beast is born in Scandinavia. It has the shape of a great horse, excepting that the great length of its neck and of its ears make a difference. It feeds on grass, going backwards, for it has so long an upper lip that if it went forwards it would cover up the grass. Its legs are all in one piece; for this reason when it wants to sleep it leans against a tree, and the hunters, spying out the place where it is wont to sleep, saw the tree almost through, and then, when it leans against it to sleep, in its sleep it falls, and thus the hunters take it. And every other mode of taking it is in vain, because it is incredibly swift in running.

1251.

THE BISON WHICH DOES INJURY IN ITS FLIGHT.

This beast is a native of Paeonia and has a neck with a mane like a horse. In all its other parts it is like a bull, excepting that its horns are in a way bent inwards so that it cannot butt; hence it has no safety but in flight, in which it flings out its excrement to a distance of 400 braccia in its course, and this burns like fire wherever it touches.

LIONS, PARDS, PANTHERS, TIGERS.

These keep their claws in the sheath, and never put them out unless they are on the back of their prey or their enemy.

THE LIONESS.

When the lioness defends her young from the hand of the hunter, in order not to be frightened by the spears she keeps her eyes on the ground, to the end that she may not by her flight leave her young ones prisoners.

1252.

THE LION.

This animal, which is so terrible, fears nothing more than the noise of empty carts, and likewise the crowing of cocks. And it is much terrified at the sight of one, and looks at its comb with a frightened aspect, and is strangely alarmed when its face is covered.

THE PANTHER IN AFRICA.

This has the form of the lioness but it is taller on its legs and slimmer and long bodied; and it is all white and marked with black spots after the manner of rosettes; and all animals delight to look upon these rosettes, and they would always be standing round it if it were not for the terror of its face;

1253.

therefore knowing this, it hides its face, and the surrounding animals grow bold and come close, the better to enjoy the sight of so much beauty; when suddenly it seizes the nearest and at once devours it.

CAMELS.

The Bactrian have two humps; the Arabian one only. They are swift in battle and most useful to carry burdens. This animal is extremely observant of rule and measure, for it will not move if it has a greater weight than it is used to, and if it is taken too far it does the same, and suddenly stops and so the merchants are obliged to lodge there.

1254.

THE TIGER.

This beast is a native of Hyrcania, and it is something like the panther from the various spots on its skin. It is an animal of terrible swiftness; the hunter when he finds its young ones carries them off hastily, placing mirrors in the place whence he takes them, and at once escapes on a swift horse. The panther returning finds the mirrors fixed on the ground and looking into them believes it sees its young; then scratching with its paws it discovers the cheat. Forthwith, by means of the scent of its young, it follows the hunter, and when this hunter sees the tigress he drops one of the young ones and she takes it, and having carried it to the den she immediately returns to the hunter and does

1255.

the same till he gets into his boat.

CATOBLEPAS.

It is found in Ethiopia near to the source Nigricapo. It is not a very large animal, is sluggish in all its parts, and its head is so large that it carries it with difficulty, in such wise that it always droops towards the ground; otherwise it would be a great pest to man, for any one on whom it fixes its eyes dies immediately. [Footnote: Leonardo undoubtedly derived these remarks as to the Catoblepas from Pliny, Hist. Nat. VIII. 21 (al. 32): Apud Hesperios Aethiopas fons est Nigris (different readings), ut plerique existimavere, Nili caput.-----Juxta hunc fera appellatur catoblepas, modica alioquin, ceterisque membris iners, caput tantum praegrave aegre ferens; alias internecio humani generis, omnibus qui oculos ejus videre, confestim morientibus. Aelian, Hist. An. gives a far more minute description of the creature, but he says that it poisons beasts not by its gaze, but by its venomous breath. Athenaeus 221 B, mentions both. If Leonardo had known of these two passages, he would scarcely have omitted the poisonous breath. (H. MULLER-STRUBING.)]

THE BASILISK.

This is found in the province of Cyrenaica and is not more than 12 fingers long. It has on its head a white spot after the fashion of a diadem. It scares all serpents with its whistling. It resembles a snake, but does not move by wriggling but from the centre forwards to the right. It is said that one

1256.

of these, being killed with a spear by one who was on horse-back, and its venom flowing on the spear, not only the man but the horse also died. It spoils the wheat and not only that which it touches, but where it breathes the grass dries and the stones are split.

THE WEASEL.

This beast finding the lair of the basilisk kills it with the smell of its urine, and this smell, indeed, often kills the weasel itself.

THE CERASTES.

This has four movable little horns; so, when it wants to feed, it hides under leaves all of its body except these little horns which, as they move, seem to the birds to be some small worms at play. Then they immediately swoop down to pick them and the Cerastes suddenly twines round them and encircles and devours them.

1257.

THE AMPHISBOENA.

This has two heads, one in its proper place the other at the tail; as if one place were not enough from which to fling its venom.

THE IACULUS.

This lies on trees, and flings itself down like a dart, and pierces through the wild beast and kills them.

THE ASP.

The bite of this animal cannot be cured unless by immediately cutting out the bitten part. This pestilential animal has such a love for its mate that they always go in company. And if, by mishap, one of them is killed the other, with incredible swiftness, follows him who has killed it; and it is so determined and eager for vengeance that it overcomes every difficulty, and passing by every troop it seeks to hurt none but its enemy. And it will travel any distance, and it is impossible to avoid it unless by crossing water and by very swift flight. It has its eyes turned inwards, and large ears and it hears better than it sees.

1258.

THE ICHNEUMON.

This animal is the mortal enemy of the asp. It is a native of Egypt and when it sees an asp near its place, it runs at once to the bed or mud of the Nile and with this makes itself muddy all over, then it dries itself in the sun, smears itself again with mud, and thus, drying one after the other, it makes itself three or four coatings like a coat of mail. Then it attacks the asp, and fights well with him, so that, taking its time it catches him in the throat and destroys him.

THE CROCODILE.

This is found in the Nile, it has four feet and lives on land and in water. No other terrestrial creature but this is found to have no tongue, and it only bites by moving its upper jaw. It grows to a length of forty feet and has claws and is armed with a hide that will take any blow. By day it is on land and at night in the water. It feeds on fishes, and going to sleep on the bank of the Nile with its mouth open, a bird called

1259.

trochilus, a very small bird, runs at once to its mouth and hops among its teeth and goes pecking out the remains of the food, and so inciting it with voluptuous delight tempts it to open the whole of its mouth, and so it sleeps. This being observed by the ichneumon it flings itself into its mouth and perforates its stomach and bowels, and finally kills it.

THE DOLPHIN.

Nature has given such knowledge to animals, that besides the consciousness of their own advantages they know the disadvantages of their foes. Thus the dolphin understands what strength lies in a cut from the fins placed on his chine, and how tender is the belly of the crocodile; hence in fighting with him it thrusts at him from beneath and rips up his belly and so kills him.

The crocodile is a terror to those that flee, and a base coward to those that pursue him.

1260.

THE HIPPOPOTAMUS.

This beast when it feels itself over-full goes about seeking thorns, or where there may be the remains of canes that have been split, and it rubs against them till a vein is opened; then when the blood has flowed as much as he needs, he plasters himself with mud and heals the wound. In form he is something like a horse with long haunches, a twisted tail and the teeth of a wild boar, his neck has a mane; the skin cannot be pierced, unless when he is bathing; he feeds on plants in the fields and goes into them backwards so that it may seem, as though he had come out.

THE IBIS.

This bird resembles a crane, and when it feels itself ill it fills its craw with water, and with its beak makes an injection of it.

THE STAG.

These creatures when they feel themselves bitten by the spider called father-long-legs, eat crabs and free themselves of the venom.

1261.

THE LIZARD.

This, when fighting with serpents eats the sow-thistle and is free.

THE SWALLOW.

This [bird] gives sight to its blind young ones, with the juice of the celandine.

THE WEASEL.

This, when chasing rats first eats of rue.

THE WILD BOAR.

This beast cures its sickness by eating of ivy.

THE SNAKE.

This creature when it wants to renew itself casts its old skin, beginning with the head, and changing in one day and one night.

THE PANTHER.

This beast after its bowels have fallen out will still fight with the dogs and hunters.

1262.

THE CHAMELEON.

This creature always takes the colour of the thing on which it is resting, whence it is often devoured together with the leaves on which the elephant feeds.

THE RAVEN.

When it has killed the Chameleon it takes laurel as a purge.

1263.

Moderation checks all the vices. The ermine will die rather than besmirch itself.

OF FORESIGHT.

The cock does not crow till it has thrice flapped its wings; the parrot in moving among boughs never puts its feet excepting where it has first put its beak. Vows are not made till Hope is dead.

Motion tends towards the centre of gravity.

1264.

MAGNANIMITY.

The falcon never seizes any but large birds and will sooner die than eat [tainted] meat of bad savour.

II.

FABLES.

Fables on animals (1265-1270).

1265.

A FABLE.

An oyster being turned out together with other fish in the house of a fisherman near the sea, he entreated a rat to take him to the sea. The rat purposing to eat him bid him open; but as he bit him the oyster squeezed his head and closed; and the cat came and killed him.

1266.

A FABLE.

The thrushes rejoiced greatly at seeing a man take the owl and deprive her of liberty, tying her feet with strong bonds. But this owl was afterwards by means of bird-lime the cause of the thrushes losing not only their liberty, but their life. This is said for those countries which rejoice in seeing their governors lose their liberty, when by that means they themselves lose all succour, and remain in bondage in the power of their enemies, losing their liberty and often their life.

1267.

A FABLE.

A dog, lying asleep on the fur of a sheep, one of his fleas, perceiving the odour of the greasy wool, judged that this must be a land of better living, and also more secure from the teeth and nails of the dog than where he fed on the dog; and without farther reflection he left the dog and went into the thick wool. There he began with great labour to try to pass among the roots of the hairs; but after much sweating had to give up the task as vain, because these hairs were so close that they almost touched each other, and there was no space where fleas could taste the skin. Hence, after much labour and fatigue, he began to wish to return to his dog, who however had already departed; so he was constrained after long repentance and bitter tears, to die of hunger.

1268.

A FABLE.

The vain and wandering butterfly, not content with being able to fly at its ease through the air, overcome by the tempting flame of the candle, decided to fly into it; but its sportive impulse was the cause of a sudden fall, for its delicate wings were burnt in the flame. And the hapless butterfly having dropped, all scorched, at the foot of the candlestick, after much lamentation and repentance, dried the tears from its swimming eyes, and raising its face exclaimed: O false light! how many must thou have miserably deceived in the past, like me; or if I must indeed see light so near, ought I not to have known the sun from the false glare of dirty tallow?

A FABLE.

The monkey, finding a nest of small birds, went up to it greatly delighted. But they, being already fledged, he could only succeed in taking the smallest; greatly delighted he took it in his hand and went to his abode; and having begun to look at the little bird he took to kissing it, and from excess of love he kissed it so much and turned it about and squeezed it till he killed it. This is said for those who by not punishing their children let them come to mischief.

1269.

A FABLE.

A rat was besieged in his little dwelling by a weasel, which with unwearied vigilance awaited his surrender, while watching his imminent peril through a little hole. Meanwhile the cat came by and suddenly seized the weasel and forthwith devoured it. Then the rat offered up a sacrifice to Jove of some of his store of nuts, humbly thanking His providence, and came out of his hole to enjoy his lately lost liberty. But he was instantly deprived of it, together with his life, by the cruel claws and teeth of the lurking cat.

1270.

A FABLE.

The ant found a grain of millet. The seed feeling itself taken prisoner cried out to her: "If you will do me the kindness to allow me accomplish my function of reproduction, I will give you a hundred such as I am." And so it was.

A Spider found a bunch of grapes which for its sweetness was much resorted to by bees and divers kinds of flies. It seemed to her that she had found a most convenient spot to spread her snare, and having settled herself on it with her delicate web, and entered into her new habitation, there, every day placing herself in the openings made by the spaces between the grapes, she fell like a thief on the wretched creatures which were not aware of her. But, after a few days had passed, the vintager came, and cut away the bunch of grapes and put it with others, with which it was trodden; and thus the grapes were a snare and pitfall both for the treacherous spider and the betrayed flies.

An ass having gone to sleep on the ice over a deep lake, his heat dissolved the ice and the ass awoke under water to his great grief, and was forthwith drowned.

A falcon, unable to endure with patience the disappearance of a duck, which, flying before him had plunged under water, wished to follow it under water, and having soaked his feathers had to remain in the water while the duck rising to the air mocked at the falcon as he drowned.

The spider wishing to take flies in her treacherous net, was cruelly killed in it by the hornet.

An eagle wanting to mock at the owl was caught by the wings in bird-lime and was taken and killed by a man.

Fables on lifeless objects (1271--1274).

1271.

The water finding that its element was the lordly ocean, was seized with a desire to rise above the air, and being encouraged by the element of fire and rising as a very subtle vapour, it seemed as though it were really as thin as air. But having risen very high, it reached the air that was still more rare and cold, where the fire forsook it, and the minute particles, being brought together, united and became heavy; whence its haughtiness deserting it, it betook itself to flight and it fell from the sky, and was drunk up by the dry earth, where, being imprisoned for a long time, it did penance for its sin.

1272.

A FABLE.

The razor having one day come forth from the handle which serves as its sheath and having placed himself in the sun, saw the sun reflected in his body, which filled him with great pride. And turning it over in his thoughts he began to say to himself: "And shall I return again to that shop from which I have just come? Certainly not; such splendid beauty shall not, please God, be turned to such base uses. What folly it would be that could lead me to shave the lathered beards of rustic peasants and perform such menial service! Is this body destined for such work? Certainly not. I will hide myself in some retired spot and there pass my life in tranquil repose." And having thus remained hidden for some months, one day he came out into the air, and issuing from his sheath, saw himself turned to the similitude of a rusty saw while his surface no longer reflected the resplendent sun. With useless repentance he vainly deplored the irreparable mischief saying to himself: "Oh! how far better was it to employ at the barbers my lost edge of such exquisite keenness! Where is that lustrous surface? It has been consumed by this vexatious and unsightly rust."

The same thing happens to those minds which instead of exercise give themselves up to sloth. They are like the razor here spoken of, and lose the keenness of their edge, while the rust of ignorance spoils their form.

A FABLE.

A stone of some size recently uncovered by the water lay on a certain spot somewhat raised, and just where a delightful grove ended by a stony road; here it was surrounded by plants decorated by various flowers of divers colours. And as it saw the great quantity of stones collected together in the roadway below, it began to wish it could let itself fall down there, saying to itself: "What have I to do here with these plants? I want to live in the company of those, my sisters." And letting itself fall, its rapid course ended among these longed for companions. When it had been there sometime it began to find itself constantly toiling under the wheels of the carts the iron-shoed feet of horses and of travellers. This one rolled it over, that one trod upon it; sometimes it lifted itself a little and then it was covered with mud or the dung of some animal, and it was in vain that it looked at the spot whence it had come as a place of solitude and tranquil place.

Thus it happens to those who choose to leave a life of solitary comtemplation, and come to live in cities among people full of infinite evil.

1273.

Some flames had already lasted in the furnace of a glass-blower, when they saw a candle approaching in a beautiful and glittering candlestick. With ardent longing they strove to reach it; and one of them, quitting its natural course, writhed up to an unburnt brand on which it fed and passed at the opposite end out by a narrow chink to the candle which was near. It flung itself upon it, and with fierce jealousy and greediness it devoured it, having reduced it almost to death, and, wishing to procure the prolongation of its life, it tried to return to the furnace whence it had come. But in vain, for it was compelled to die, the wood perishing together with the candle, being at last converted, with lamentation and repentance, into foul smoke, while leaving all its sisters in brilliant and enduring life and beauty.

1274.

A small patch of snow finding itself clinging to the top of a rock which was lying on the topmost height of a very high mountain and being left to its own imaginings, it began to reflect in this way, saying to itself: "Now, shall not I be thought vain and proud for having placed myself--such a small patch of snow--in so lofty a spot, and for allowing that so large a quantity of snow as I have seen here around me, should take a place lower than mine? Certainly my small dimensions by no means merit this elevation. How easily may I, in proof of my insignificance, experience the same fate as that which the sun brought about yesterday to my companions, who were all, in a few hours, destroyed by the sun. And this happened from their having placed themselves higher than became them. I will flee from the wrath of the sun, and humble myself and find a place befitting my small importance." Thus, flinging itself down, it began to descend, hurrying from its high home on to the other snow; but the more it sought a low place the more its bulk increased, so that when at last its course was ended on a hill, it found itself no less in size than the hill which supported it; and it was the last of the snow which was destroyed that summer by the sun. This is said for those who, humbling themselves, become exalted.

Fables on plants (1275-1279).

1275.

The cedar, being desirous of producing a fine and noble fruit at its summit, set to work to form it with all the strength of its sap. But this fruit, when grown, was the cause of the tall and upright tree-top being bent over.

The peach, being envious of the vast quantity of fruit which she saw borne on the nut-tree, her neighbour, determined to do the same, and loaded herself with her own in such a way that the weight of the fruit pulled her up by the roots and broke her down to the ground.

The nut-tree stood always by a road side displaying the wealth of its fruit to the passers by, and every one cast stones at it.

The fig-tree, having no fruit, no one looked at it; then, wishing to produce fruits that it might be praised by men, it was bent and broken down by them.

The fig-tree, standing by the side of the elm and seeing that its boughs were bare of fruit, yet that it had the audacity to keep the Sun from its own unripe figs with its branches, said to it: "Oh elm! art thou not ashamed to stand in front of me. But wait till my offspring are fully grown and you will see where you are!" But when her offspring were mature, a troop of soldiers coming by fell upon the fig-tree and her figs were all torn off her, and her boughs cut away and broken. Then, when she was thus maimed in all her limbs, the elm asked her, saying: "O fig-tree! which was best, to be without offspring, or to be brought by them into so miserable a plight!"

1276.

The plant complains of the old and dry stick which stands by its side and of the dry stakes that surround it.

One keeps it upright, the other keeps it from low company.

1277.

A FABLE.

A nut, having been carried by a crow to the top of a tall campanile and released by falling into a chink from the mortal grip of its beak, it prayed the wall by the grace bestowed on it by God in allowing it to be so high and thick, and to own such fine bells and of so noble a tone, that it would succour it, and that, as it had not been able to fall under the verdurous boughs of its venerable father and lie in the fat earth covered up by his fallen leaves it would not abandon it; because, finding itself in the beak of the cruel crow, it had there made a vow that if it escaped from her it would end its life in a little hole. At these words the wall, moved to compassion, was content to shelter it in the spot where it had fallen; and after a short time the nut began to split open and put forth roots between the rifts of the stones and push them apart, and to throw out shoots from its hollow shell; and, to be brief, these rose above the building and the twisted roots, growing thicker, began to thrust the walls apart, and tear out the ancient stones from their old places. Then the wall too late and in vain bewailed the cause of its destruction and in a short time, it wrought the ruin of a great part of it.

1278.

A FABLE.

The privet feeling its tender boughs loaded with young fruit, pricked by the sharp claws and beak of the insolent blackbird, complained to the blackbird with pitious remonstrance entreating her that since she stole its delicious fruits she should not deprive it of the leaves with which it preserved them from the burning rays of the sun, and that she should not divest it of its tender bark by scratching it with her sharp claws. To which the blackbird replied with angry upbraiding: "O, be silent, uncultured shrub! Do you not know that Nature made you produce these fruits for my nourishment; do you not see that you are in the world [only] to serve me as food; do you not know, base creature, that next winter you will be food and prey for the Fire?" To which words the tree listened patiently, and not without tears. After a short time the blackbird was taken in a net and boughs were cut to make a cage, in which to imprison her. Branches were cut, among others from the pliant privet, to serve for the small rods of the cage; and seeing herself to be the cause of the Blackbird's loss of liberty it rejoiced and spoke as follows: "O Blackbird, I am here, and not yet burnt by fire as you said. I shall see you in prison before you see me burnt."

A FABLE.

The laurel and the myrtle seeing the pear tree cut down cried out with a loud voice: "O pear-tree! whither are you going? Where is the pride you had when you were covered with ripe fruits? Now you will no longer shade us with your mass of leaves." Then the pear-tree replied: "I am going with the husbandman who has cut me down and who will take me to the workshop of a good sculptor who by his art will make me take the form of Jove the god; and I shall be dedicated in a temple and adored by men in the place of Jove, while you are bound always to remain maimed and stripped of your boughs, which will be placed round me to do me honour.

A FABLE.

The chestnut, seeing a man upon the fig-tree, bending its boughs down and pulling off the ripe fruits, which he put into his open mouth destroying and crushing them with his hard teeth, it tossed its long boughs and with a noisy rustle exclaimed: "O fig! how much less are you protected by nature than I. See how in me my sweet offspring are set in close array; first clothed in soft wrappers over which is the hard but softly lined husk; and not content with taking this care of me, and having given them so strong a shelter, on this she has placed sharp and close-set spines so that the hand of man cannot hurt me." Then the fig-tree and her offspring began to laugh and having laughed she said: "I know man to be of such ingenuity that with rods and stones and stakes flung up among your branches he will bereave you of your fruits; and when they are fallen, he will trample them with his feet or with stones, so that your offspring will come out of their armour, crushed and maimed; while I am touched carefully by their hands, and not like you with sticks and stones."

1279.

The hapless willow, finding that she could not enjoy the pleasure of seeing her slender branches grow or attain to the height she wished, or point to the sky, by reason of the vine and whatever other trees that grew near, but was always maimed and lopped and spoiled, brought all her spirits together and gave and devoted itself entirely to imagination, standing plunged in long meditation and seeking, in all the world of plants, with which of them she might ally herself and which could not need the help of her withes. Having stood for some time in this prolific imagination, with a sudden flash the gourd presented itself to her thoughts and tossing all her branches with extreme delight, it seemed to her that she had found the companion suited to her purpose, because the gourd is more apt to bind others than to need binding; having come to this conclusion she awaited eagerly some friendly bird who should be the mediator of her wishes. Presently seeing near her the magpie she said to him: "O gentle bird! by the memory of the refuge which you found this morning among my branches, when the hungry cruel, and rapacious falcon wanted to devour you, and by that repose which you have always found in me when your wings craved rest, and by the pleasure you have enjoyed among my boughs, when playing with your companions or making love--I entreat you find the gourd and obtain from her some of her seeds, and tell her that those that are born of them I will treat exactly as though they were my own flesh and blood; and in this way use all the words you can think of, which are of the same persuasive purport; though, indeed, since you are a master of language, I need not teach you. And if you will do me this service I shall be happy to have your nest in the fork of my boughs, and all your family without payment of any rent." Then the magpie, having made and confirmed certain new stipulations with the willow,--and principally that she should never admit upon her any snake or polecat, cocked his tail, and put down his head, and flung himself from the bough, throwing his weight upon his wings; and these, beating the fleeting air, now here, now there, bearing about inquisitively, while his tail served as a rudder to steer him, he came to a gourd; then with a handsome bow and a few polite words, he obtained the required seeds, and carried them to the willow, who received him with a cheerful face. And when he had scraped away with his foot a small quantity of the earth near the willow, describing a circle, with his beak he planted the grains, which in a short time began to grow, and by their growth and the branches to take up all the boughs of the willow, while their broad leaves deprived it of the beauty of the sun and sky. And not content with so much evil, the gourds next began, by their rude hold, to drag the ends of the tender shoots down towards the earth, with strange twisting and distortion.

Then, being much annoyed, it shook itself in vain to throw off the gourd. After raving for some days in such plans vainly, because the firm union forbade it, seeing the wind come by it commended itself to him. The wind flew hard and opened the old and hollow stem of the willow in two down to the roots, so that it fell into two parts. In vain did it bewail itself recognising that it was born to no good end.

III.

JESTS AND TALES.

1280.

A JEST.

A priest, making the rounds of his parish on Easter Eve, and sprinkling holy water in the houses as is customary, came to a painter's room, where he sprinkled the water on some of his pictures. The painter turned round, somewhat angered, and asked him why this sprinkling had been bestowed on his pictures; then said the priest, that it was the custom and his duty to do so, and that he was doing good; and that he who did good might look for good in return, and, indeed, for better, since God had promised that every good deed that was done on earth should be rewarded a hundred-fold from above. Then the painter, waiting till he went out, went to an upper window and flung a large pail of water on the priest's back, saying: "Here is the reward a hundred-fold from above, which you said would come from the good you had done me with your holy water, by which you have damaged my pictures."

1281.

When wine is drunk by a drunkard, that wine is revenged on the drinker.

1282.

Wine, the divine juice of the grape, finding itself in a golden and richly wrought cup, on the table of Mahomet, was puffed up with pride at so much honour; when suddenly it was struck by a contrary reflection, saying to itself: "What am I about, that I should rejoice, and not perceive that I am now near to my death and shall leave my golden abode in this cup to enter into the foul and fetid caverns of the human body, and to be transmuted from a fragrant and delicious liquor into a foul and base one. Nay, and as though so much evil as this were not enough, I must for a long time lie in hideous receptacles, together with other fetid and corrupt matter, cast out from human intestines." And it cried to Heaven, imploring vengeance for so much insult, and that an end might henceforth be put to such contempt; and that, since that country produced the finest and best grapes in the whole world, at least they should not be turned into wine. Then Jove made that wine drunk by Mahomet to rise in spirit to his brain; and that in so deleterious a manner that it made him mad, and gave birth to so many follies that when he had recovered himself, he made a law that no Asiatic should drink wine, and henceforth the vine and its fruit were left free.

As soon as wine has entered the stomach it begins to ferment and swell; then the spirit of that man begins to abandon his body, rising as it were skywards, and the brain finds itself parting from the body. Then it begins to degrade him, and make him rave like a madman, and then he does irreparable evil, killing his friends.

1283.

An artizan often going to visit a great gentleman without any definite purpose, the gentleman asked him what he did this for. The other said that he came there to have a pleasure which his lordship could not have; since to him it was a satisfaction to see men greater than himself, as is the way with the populace; while the gentleman could only see men of less consequence than himself; and so lords and great men were deprived of that pleasure.

1284.

Franciscan begging Friars are wont, at certain times, to keep fasts, when they do not eat meat in their convents. But on journeys, as they live on charity, they have license to eat whatever is set before them. Now a couple of these friars on their travels, stopped at an inn, in company with a certain merchant, and sat down with him at the same table, where, from the poverty of the inn, nothing was served to them but a small roast chicken. The merchant, seeing this to be but little even for himself, turned to the friars and said: "If my memory serves me, you do not eat any kind of flesh in your convents at this season." At these words the friars were compelled by their rule to admit, without cavil, that this was the truth; so the merchant had his wish, and eat the chicken and the friars did the best they could. After dinner the messmates departed, all three together, and after travelling some distance they came to a river of some width and depth. All three being on foot--the friars by reason of their poverty, and the other from avarice--it was necessary by the custom of company that one of the friars, being barefoot, should carry the merchant on his shoulders: so having given his wooden shoes into his keeping, he took up his man. But it so happened that when the friar had got to the middle of the river, he again remembered a rule of his order, and stopping short, he looked up, like Saint Christopher, to the burden on his back and said: "Tell me, have you any money about you?"--"You know I have", answered the other, "How do you suppose that a Merchant like me should go about otherwise?" "Alack!" cried the friar, "our rules forbid as to carry any money on our persons," and forthwith he dropped him into the water, which the merchant perceived was a facetious way of being revenged on the indignity he had done them; so, with a smiling face, and blushing somewhat with shame, he peaceably endured the revenge.

1285.

A JEST.

A man wishing to prove, by the authority of Pythagoras, that he had formerly been in the world, while another would not let him finish his argument, the first speaker said to the second: "It is by this token that I was formerly here, I remember that you were a miller." The other one, feeling himself stung by these words, agreed that it was true, and that by the same token he remembered that the speaker had been the ass that carried the flour.

A JEST.

It was asked of a painter why, since he made such beautiful figures, which were but dead things, his children were so ugly; to which the painter replied that he made his pictures by day, and his children by night.

1286.

A man saw a large sword which another one wore at his side. Said he "Poor fellow, for a long time I have seen you tied to that weapon; why do you not release yourself as your hands are untied, and set yourself free?" To which the other replied: "This is none of yours, on the contrary it is an old story." The former speaker, feeling stung, replied: "I know that you are acquainted with so few things in this world, that I thought anything I could tell you would be new to you."

1287.

A man gave up his intimacy with one of his friends because he often spoke ill of his other friends. The neglected friend one day lamenting to this former friend, after much complaining, entreated him to say what might be the cause that had made him forget so much friendship. To which he answered: "I will no longer be intimate with you because I love you, and I do not choose that you, by speaking ill of me, your friend, to others, should produce in others, as in me, a bad impression of yourself, by speaking evil to them of me, your friend. Therefore, being no longer intimate together, it will seem as though we had become enemies; and in speaking evil of me, as is your wont, you will not be blamed so much as if we continued intimate.

1288.

A man was arguing and boasting that he knew many and various tricks. Another among the bystanders said: "I know how to play a trick which will make whomsoever I like pull off his breeches." The first man-- the boaster-- said: "You won't make me pull off mine, and I bet you a pair of hose on it." He who proposed the game, having accepted the offer, produced breeches and drew them across the face of him who bet the pair of hose and won the bet [4].

A man said to an acquaintance: "Your eyes are changed to a strange colour." The other replied: "It often happens, but you have not noticed it." "When does it happen?" said the former. "Every time that my eyes see your ugly face, from the shock of so unpleasing a sight they suddenly turn pale and change to a strange colour."

A man said to another: "Your eyes are changed to a strange colour." The other replied: "It is because my eyes behold your strange ugly face."

A man said that in his country were the strangest things in the world. Another answered: "You, who were born there, confirm this as true, by the strangeness of your ugly face."

[Footnote: The joke turns, it appears, on two meanings of trarre and is not easily translated.]

1289.

An old man was publicly casting contempt on a young one, and boldly showing that he did not fear him; on which the young man replied that his advanced age served him better as a shield than either his tongue or his strength.

1290.

A JEST.

A sick man finding himself in articulo mortis heard a knock at the door, and asking one of his servants who was knocking, the servant went out, and answered that it was a woman calling herself Madonna Bona. Then the sick man lifting his arms to Heaven thanked God with a loud voice, and told the servants that they were to let her come in at once, so that he might see one good woman before he died, since in all his life he had never yet seen one.

1291.

A JEST.

A man was desired to rise from bed, because the sun was already risen. To which he replied: "If I had as far to go, and as much to do as he has, I should be risen by now; but having but a little way to go, I shall not rise yet."

1292.

A man, seeing a woman ready to hold up the target for a jousting match, exclaimed, looking at the shield, and considering his spear: "Alack! this is too small a workman for so great a business."

IV.

PROPHECIES.

1293.

THE DIVISION OF THE PROPHECIES.

First, of things relating to animals; secondly, of irrational creatures; thirdly of plants; fourthly, of ceremonies; fifthly, of manners; sixthly, of cases or edicts or quarrels; seventhly, of cases that are impossible in nature [paradoxes], as, for instance, of those things which, the more is taken from them, the more they grow. And reserve the great matters till the end, and the small matters give at the beginning. And first show the evils and then the punishment of philosophical things.

(Of Ants.)

These creatures will form many communities, which will hide themselves and their young ones and victuals in dark caverns, and they will feed themselves and their families in dark places for many months without any light, artificial or natural.

[Footnote: Lines 1--5l are in the original written in one column, beginning with the text of line 11. At the end of the column is the programme for the arrangement of the prophecies, placed here at the head: Lines 56--79 form a second column, lines 80--97 a third one (see the reproduction of the text on the facsimile Pl. CXVIII).

Another suggestion for the arrangement of the prophecies is to be found among the notes 55--57 on page 357.]

(Of Bees.)

And many others will be deprived of their store and their food, and will be cruelly submerged and drowned by folks devoid of reason. Oh Justice of God! Why dost thou not wake and behold thy creatures thus ill used?

(Of Sheep, Cows, Goats and the like.)

Endless multitudes of these will have their little children taken from them ripped open and flayed and most barbarously quartered.

(Of Nuts, and Olives, and Acorns, and Chesnuts, and such like.)

Many offspring shall be snatched by cruel thrashing from the very arms of their mothers, and flung on the ground, and crushed.

(Of Children bound in Bundles.)

O cities of the Sea! In you I see your citizens--both females and males--tightly bound, arms and legs, with strong withes by folks who will not understand your language. And you will only be able to assuage your sorrows and lost liberty by means of tearful complaints and sighing and lamentation among yourselves; for those who will bind you will not understand you, nor will you understand them.

(Of Cats that eat Rats.)

In you, O cities of Africa your children will be seen quartered in their own houses by most cruel and rapacious beasts of your own country.

(Of Asses that are beaten.)

[Footnote 48: Compare No. 845.] O Nature! Wherefore art thou so partial; being to some of thy children a tender and benign mother, and to others a most cruel and pitiless stepmother? I see children of thine given up to slavery to others, without any sort of advantage, and instead of remuneration for the good they do, they are paid with the severest suffering, and spend their whole life in benefitting those who ill treat them.

(Of Men who sleep on boards of Trees.)

Men shall sleep, and eat, and dwell among trees, in the forests and open country.

(Of Dreaming.)

Men will seem to see new destructions in the sky. The flames that fall from it will seem to rise in it and to fly from it with terror. They will hear every kind of animals speak in human language. They will instantaneously run in person in various parts of the world, without motion. They will see the greatest splendour in the midst of darkness. O! marvel of the human race! What madness has led you thus! You will speak with animals of every species and they with you in human speech. You will see yourself fall from great heights without any harm and torrents will accompany you, and will mingle with their rapid course.

(Of Christians.)

Many who hold the faith of the Son only build temples in the name of the Mother.

(Of Food which has been alive.)

[84] A great portion of bodies that have been alive will pass into the bodies of other animals; which is as much as to say, that the deserted tenements will pass piecemeal into the inhabited ones, furnishing them with good things, and carrying with them their evils. That is to say the life of man is formed from things eaten, and these carry with them that part of man which dies . . .

1294.

(Of Funeral Rites, and Processions, and Lights, and Bells, and Followers.)

The greatest honours will be paid to men, and much pomp, without their knowledge.

[Footnote: A facsimile of this text is on Pl. CXVI below on the right, but the writing is larger than the other notes on the same sheet and of a somewhat different style. The ink is also of a different hue, as may be seen on the original sheet at Milan.]

1295.

(Of the Avaricious.)

There will be many who will eagerly and with great care and solicitude follow up a thing, which, if they only knew its malignity, would always terrify them.

(Of those men, who, the older they grow, the more avaricious they become, whereas, having but little time to stay, they should become more liberal.)

We see those who are regarded as being most experienced and judicious, when they least need a thing, seek and cherish it with most avidity.

(Of the Ditch.)

Many will be busied in taking away from a thing, which will grow in proportion as it is diminished.

(Of a Weight placed on a Feather-pillow.)

And it will be seen in many bodies that by raising the head they swell visibly; and by laying the raised head down again, their size will immediately be diminished.

(Of catching Lice.)

And many will be hunters of animals, which, the fewer there are the more will be taken; and conversely, the more there are, the fewer will be taken.

(Of Drawing Water in two Buckets with a single Rope.)

And many will be busily occupied, though the more of the thing they draw up, the more will escape at the other end.

(Of the Tongues of Pigs and Calves in Sausage-skins.)

Oh! how foul a thing, that we should see the tongue of one animal in the guts of another.

(Of Sieves made of the Hair of Animals.)

We shall see the food of animals pass through their skin everyway excepting through their mouths, and penetrate from the outside downwards to the ground.

(Of Lanterns.)

[Footnote 35: Lanterns were in Italy formerly made of horn.] The cruel horns of powerful bulls will screen the lights of night against the wild fury of the winds.

(Of Feather-beds.)

Flying creatures will give their very feathers to support men.

(Of Animals which walk on Trees--wearing wooden Shoes.)

The mire will be so great that men will walk on the trees of their country.

(Of the Soles of Shoes, which are made from the Ox.)

And in many parts of the country men will be seen walking on the skins of large beasts.

(Of Sailing in Ships.)

There will be great winds by reason of which things of the East will become things of the West; and those of the South, being involved in the course of the winds, will follow them to distant lands.

(Of Worshipping the Pictures of Saints.)

Men will speak to men who hear not; having their eyes open, they will not see; they will speak to these, and they will not be answered. They will implore favours of those who have ears and hear not; they will make light for the blind.

(Of Sawyers.)

There will be many men who will move one against another, holding in their hands a cutting tool. But these will not do each other any injury beyond tiring each other; for, when one pushes forward the other will draw back. But woe to him who comes between them! For he will end by being cut in pieces.

(Of Silk-spinning.)

Dismal cries will be heard loud, shrieking with anguish, and the hoarse and smothered tones of those who will be despoiled, and at last left naked and motionless; and this by reason of the mover, which makes every thing turn round.

(Of putting Bread into the Mouth of the Oven and taking it out again.)

In every city, land, castle and house, men shall be seen, who for want of food will take it out of the mouths of others, who will not be able to resist in any way.

(Of tilled Land.)

The Earth will be seen turned up side down and facing the opposite hemispheres, uncovering the lurking holes of the fiercest animals.

(Of Sowing Seed.)

Then many of the men who will remain alive, will throw the victuals they have preserved out of their houses, a free prey to the birds and beasts of the earth, without taking any care of them at all.

(Of the Rains, which, by making the Rivers muddy, wash away the Land.)

[Footnote 81: Compare No. 945.] Something will fall from the sky which will transport a large part of Africa which lies under that sky towards Europe, and that of Europe towards Africa, and that of the Scythian countries will meet with tremendous revolutions [Footnote 84: Compare No. 945.].

(Of Wood that burns.)

The trees and shrubs in the great forests will be converted into cinder.

(Of Kilns for Bricks and Lime.)

Finally the earth will turn red from a conflagration of many days and the stones will be turned to cinders.

(Of boiled Fish.)

The natives of the waters will die in the boiling flood.

(Of the Olives which fall from the Olive trees, shedding oil which makes light.)

And things will fall with great force from above, which will give us nourishment and light.

(Of Owls and screech owls and what will happen to certain birds.)

Many will perish of dashing their heads in pieces, and the eyes of many will jump out of their heads by reason of fearful creatures come out of the darkness.

(Of flax which works the cure of men.)

That which was at first bound, cast out and rent by many and various beaters will be respected and honoured, and its precepts will be listened to with reverence and love.

(Of Books which teach Precepts.)

Bodies without souls will, by their contents give us precepts by which to die well.

(Of Flagellants.)

Men will hide themselves under the bark of trees, and, screaming, they will make themselves martyrs, by striking their own limbs.

(Of the Handles of Knives made of the Horns of Sheep.)

We shall see the horns of certain beasts fitted to iron tools, which will take the lives of many of their kind.

(Of Night when no Colour can be discerned.)

There will come a time when no difference can be discerned between colours, on the contrary, everything will be black alike.

(Of Swords and Spears which by themselves never hurt any one.)

One who by himself is mild enough and void of all offence will become terrible and fierce by being in bad company, and will most cruelly take the life of many men, and would kill many more if they were not hindered by bodies having no soul, that have come out of caverns--that is, breastplates of iron.

(Of Snares and Traps.)

Many dead things will move furiously, and will take and bind the living, and will ensnare them for the enemies who seek their death and destruction.

(Of Metals.)

That shall be brought forth out of dark and obscure caves, which will put the whole human race in great anxiety, peril and death. To many that seek them, after many sorrows they will give delight, and to those who are not in their company, death with want and misfortune. This will lead to the commission of endless crimes; this will increase and persuade bad men to assassinations, robberies and treachery, and by reason of it each will be suspicious of his partner. This will deprive free cities of their happy condition; this will take away the lives of many; this will make men torment each other with many artifices deceptions and treasons. O monstrous creature! How much better would it be for men that every thing should return to Hell! For this the vast forests will be devastated of their trees; for this endless animals will lose their lives.

(Of Fire.)

One shall be born from small beginnings which will rapidly become vast. This will respect no created thing, rather will it, by its power, transform almost every thing from its own nature into another.

(Of Ships which sink.)

Huge bodies will be seen, devoid of life, carrying, in fierce haste, a multitude of men to the destruction of their lives.

(Of Oxen, which are eaten.)

The masters of estates will eat their own labourers.

(Of beating Beds to renew them.)

Men will be seen so deeply ungrateful that they will turn upon that which has harboured them, for nothing at all; they will so load it with blows that a great part of its inside will come out of its place, and will be turned over and over in its body.

(Of Things which are eaten and which first are killed.)

Those who nourish them will be killed by them and afflicted by merciless deaths.

(Of the Reflection of Walls of Cities in the Water of their Ditches.)

The high walls of great cities will be seen up side down in their ditches.

(Of Water, which flows turbid and mixed with Soil and Dust; and of Mist, which is mixed with the Air; and of Fire which is mixed with its own, and each with each.)

All the elements will be seen mixed together in a great whirling mass, now borne towards the centre of the world, now towards the sky; and now furiously rushing from the South towards the frozen North, and sometimes from the East towards the West, and then again from this hemisphere to the other.

(The World may be divided into two Hemispheres at any Point.)

All men will suddenly be transferred into opposite hemispheres.

(The division of the East from the West may be made at any point.)

All living creatures will be moved from the East to the West; and in the same way from North to South, and vice versa.

(Of the Motion of Water which carries wood, which is dead.)

Bodies devoid of life will move by themselves and carry with them endless generations of the dead, taking the wealth from the bystanders.

(Of Eggs which being eaten cannot form Chickens.)

Oh! how many will they be that never come to the birth!

(Of Fishes which are eaten unborn.)

Endless generations will be lost by the death of the pregnant.

(Of the Lamentation on Good Friday.)

Throughout Europe there will be a lamentation of great nations over the death of one man who died in the East.

(Of Dreaming.)

Men will walk and not stir, they will talk to those who are not present, and hear those who do not speak.

(Of a Man's Shadow which moves with him.)

Shapes and figures of men and animals will be seen following these animals and men wherever they flee. And exactly as the one moves the other moves; but what seems so wonderful is the variety of height they assume.

(Of our Shadow cast by the Sun, and our Reflection in the Water at one and the same time.)

Many a time will one man be seen as three and all three move together, and often the most real one quits him.

(Of wooden Chests which contain great Treasures.)

Within walnuts and trees and other plants vast treasures will be found, which lie hidden there and well guarded.

(Of putting out the Light when going to Bed.)

Many persons puffing out a breath with too much haste, will thereby lose their sight, and soon after all consciousness.

(Of the Bells of Mules, which are close to their Ears.)

In many parts of Europe instruments of various sizes will be heard making divers harmonies, with great labour to those who hear them most closely.

(Of Asses.)

The severest labour will be repaid with hunger and thirst, and discomfort, and blows, and goadings, and curses, and great abuse.

(Of Soldiers on horseback.)

Many men will be seen carried by large animals, swift of pace, to the loss of their lives and immediate death.

In the air and on earth animals will be seen of divers colours furiously carrying men to the destruction of their lives.

(Of the Stars of Spurs.)

By the aid of the stars men will be seen who will be as swift as any swift animal.

(Of a Stick, which is dead.)

The motions of a dead thing will make many living ones flee with pain and lamentation and cries.

(Of Tinder.)

With a stone and with iron things will be made visible which before were not seen.

1296.

(Of going in Ships.)

We shall see the trees of the great forests of Taurus and of Sinai and of the Appenines and others, rush by means of the air, from East to West and from North to South; and carry, by means of the air, great multitudes of men. Oh! how many vows! Oh! how many deaths! Oh! how many partings of friends and relations! Oh! how many will those be who will never again see their own country nor their native land, and who will die unburied, with their bones strewn in various parts of the world!

(Of moving on All Saints' Day.)

Many will forsake their own dwellings and carry with them all their belongings and will go to live in other parts.

(Of All Souls' Day.)

How many will they be who will bewail their deceased forefathers, carrying lights to them.

(Of Friars, who spending nothing but words, receive great gifts and bestow Paradise.)

Invisible money will procure the triumph of many who will spend it.

(Of Bows made of the Horns of Oxen.)

Many will there be who will die a painful death by means of the horns of cattle.

(Of writing Letters from one Country to another.)

Men will speak with each other from the most remote countries, and reply.

(Of Hemispheres, which are infinite; and which are divided by an infinite number of Lines, so that every Man always has one of these Lines between his Feet.)

Men standing in opposite hemispheres will converse and deride each other and embrace each other, and understand each other's language.

(Of Priests who say Mass.)

There will be many men who, when they go to their labour will put on the richest clothes, and these will be made after the fashion of aprons [petticoats].

(Of Friars who are Confessors.)

And unhappy women will, of their own free will, reveal to men all their sins and shameful and most secret deeds.

(Of Churches and the Habitations of Friars.)

Many will there be who will give up work and labour and poverty of life and goods, and will go to live among wealth in splendid buildings, declaring that this is the way to make themselves acceptable to God.

(Of Selling Paradise.)

An infinite number of men will sell publicly and unhindered things of the very highest price, without leave from the Master of it; while it never was theirs nor in their power; and human justice will not prevent it.

(Of the Dead which are carried to be buried.)

The simple folks will carry vast quantities of lights to light up the road for those who have entirely lost the power of sight.

(Of Dowries for Maidens.)

And whereas, at first, maidens could not be protected against the violence of Men, neither by the watchfulness of parents nor by strong walls, the time will come when the fathers and parents of those girls will pay a large price to a man who wants to marry them, even if they are rich, noble and most handsome. Certainly this seems as though nature wished to eradicate the human race as being useless to the world, and as spoiling all created things.

(Of the Cruelty of Man.)

Animals will be seen on the earth who will always be fighting against each other with the greatest loss and frequent deaths on each side. And there will be no end to their malignity; by their strong limbs we shall see a great portion of the trees of the vast forests laid low throughout the universe; and, when they are filled with food the satisfaction of their desires will be to deal death and grief and labour and wars and fury to every living thing; and from their immoderate pride they will desire to rise towards heaven, but the too great weight of their limbs will keep them down. Nothing will remain on earth, or under the earth or in the waters which will not be persecuted, disturbed and spoiled, and those of one country removed into another. And their bodies will become the sepulture and means of transit of all they have killed.

O Earth! why dost thou not open and engulf them in the fissures of thy vast abyss and caverns, and no longer display in the sight of heaven such a cruel and horrible monster.

1297.

PROPHECIES.

There will be many which will increase in their destruction.

(The Ball of Snow rolling over Snow.)

There will be many who, forgetting their existence and their name, will lie as dead on the spoils of other dead creatures.

(Sleeping on the Feathers of Birds.)

The East will be seen to rush to the West and the South to the North in confusion round and about the universe, with great noise and trembling or fury.

(In the East wind which rushes to the West.)

The solar rays will kindle fire on the earth, by which a thing that is under the sky will be set on fire, and, being reflected by some obstacle, it will bend downwards.

(The Concave Mirror kindles a Fire, with which we heat the oven, and this has its foundation beneath its roof.)

A great part of the sea will fly towards heaven and for a long time will not return. (That is, in Clouds.)

There remains the motion which divides the mover from the thing moved.

Those who give light for divine service will be destroyed.(The Bees which make the Wax for Candles)

Dead things will come from underground and by their fierce movements will send numberless human beings out of the world. (Iron, which comes from under ground is dead but the Weapons are made of it which kill so many Men.)

The greatest mountains, even those which are remote from the sea shore, will drive the sea from its place.

(This is by Rivers which carry the Earth they wash away from the Mountains and bear it to the Sea-shore; and where the Earth comes the sea must retire.)

The water dropped from the clouds still in motion on the flanks of mountains will lie still for a long period of time without any motion whatever; and this will happen in many and divers lands.

(Snow, which falls in flakes and is Water.)

The great rocks of the mountains will throw out fire; so that they will burn the timber of many vast forests, and many beasts both wild and tame.

(The Flint in the Tinder-box which makes a Fire that consumes all the loads of Wood of which the Forests are despoiled and with this the flesh of Beasts is cooked.)

Oh! how many great buildings will be ruined by reason of Fire.

(The Fire of great Guns.)

Oxen will be to a great extent the cause of the destruction of cities, and in the same way horses and buffaloes.

(By drawing Guns.)

1298.

The Lion tribe will be seen tearing open the earth with their clawed paws and in the caves thus made, burying themselves together with the other animals that are beneath them.

Animals will come forth from the earth in gloomy vesture, which will attack the human species with astonishing assaults, and which by their ferocious bites will make confusion of blood among those they devour.

Again the air will be filled with a mischievous winged race which will assail men and beasts and feed upon them with much noise-- filling themselves with scarlet blood.

1299.

Blood will be seen issuing from the torn flesh of men, and trickling down the surface.

Men will have such cruel maladies that they will tear their flesh with their own nails. (The Itch.)

Plants will be seen left without leaves, and the rivers standing still in their channels.

The waters of the sea will rise above the high peaks of the mountains towards heaven and fall again on to the dwellings of men. (That is, in Clouds.)

The largest trees of the forest will be seen carried by the fury of the winds from East to West. (That is across the Sea.)

Men will cast away their own victuals. (That is, in Sowing.)

1300.

Human beings will be seen who will not understand each other's speech; that is, a German with a Turk.

Fathers will be seen giving their daughters into the power of man and giving up all their former care in guarding them. (When Girls are married.)

Men will come out their graves turned into flying creatures; and they will attack other men, taking their food from their very hand or table. (As Flies.)

Many will there be who, flaying their mother, will tear the skin from her back. (Husbandmen tilling the Earth.)

Happy will they be who lend ear to the words of the Dead. (Who read good works and obey them.)

1031.

Feathers will raise men, as they do birds, towards heaven (that is, by the letters which are written with quills.)

The works of men's hands will occasion their death. (Swords and Spears.)

Men out of fear will cling to the thing they most fear. (That is they will be miserable lest they should fall into misery.)

Things that are separate shall be united and acquire such virtue that they will restore to man his lost memory; that is papyrus [sheets] which are made of separate strips and have preserved the memory of the things and acts of men.

The bones of the Dead will be seen to govern the fortunes of him who moves them. (By Dice.)

Cattle with their horns protect the Flame from its death. (In a Lantern [Footnote 13: See note page 357.].)

The Forests will bring forth young which will be the cause of their death. (The handle of the hatchet.)

1302.

Men will deal bitter blows to that which is the cause of their life. (In thrashing Grain.)

The skins of animals will rouse men from their silence with great outcries and curses. (Balls for playing Games.)

Very often a thing that is itself broken is the occasion of much union. (That is the Comb made of split Cane which unites the threads of Silk.)

The wind passing through the skins of animals will make men dance. (That is the Bag-pipe, which makes people dance.)

1303.

(Of Walnut trees, that are beaten.)

Those which have done best will be most beaten, and their offspring taken and flayed or peeled, and their bones broken or crushed.

(Of Sculpture.)

Alas! what do I see? The Saviour cru- cified anew.

(Of the Mouth of Man, which is a Sepulchre.)

Great noise will issue from the sepulchres of those who died evil and violent deaths.

(Of the Skins of Animals which have the sense of feeling what is in the things written.)

The more you converse with skins covered with sentiments, the more wisdom will you acquire.

(Of Priests who bear the Host in their body.)

Then almost all the tabernacles in which dwells the Corpus Domini, will be plainly seen walking about of themselves on the various roads of the world.

1304.

And those who feed on grass will turn night into day (Tallow.)

And many creatures of land and water will go up among the stars (that is Planets.)

The dead will be seen carrying the living (in Carts and Ships in various places.)

Food shall be taken out of the mouth of many (the oven's mouth.)

And those which will have their food in their mouth will be deprived of it by the hands of others (the oven.)

1305.

(Of Crucifixes which are sold.)

I see Christ sold and crucified afresh, and his Saints suffering Martyrdom.

(Of Physicians, who live by sickness.)

Men will come into so wretched a plight that they will be glad that others will derive profit from their sufferings or from the loss of their real wealth, that is health.

(Of the Religion of Friars, who live by the Saints who have been dead a great while.)

Those who are dead will, after a thou- sand years be those who will give a livelihood to many who are living.

(Of Stones converted into Lime, with which prison walls are made.)

Many things that have been before that time destroyed by fire will deprive many men of liberty.

1306.

(Of Children who are suckled.)

Many Franciscans, Dominicans and Benedictines will eat that which at other times was eaten by others, who for some months to come will not be able to speak.

(Of Cockles and Sea Snails which are thrown up by the sea and which rot inside their shells.)

How many will there be who, after they are dead, will putrefy inside their own houses, filling all the surrounding air with a fetid smell.

1307.

(Of Mules which have on them rich burdens of silver and gold.)

Much treasure and great riches will be laid upon four-footed beasts, which will convey them to divers places.

1308.

(Of the Shadow cast by a man at night with a light.)

Huge figures will appear in human shape, and the nearer you get to them, the more will their immense size diminish.

[Footnote page 1307: It seems to me probable that this note, which occurs in the note book used in 1502, when Leonardo, in the service of Cesare Borgia, visited Urbino, was suggested by the famous pillage of the riches of the palace of Guidobaldo, whose treasures Cesare Borgia at once had carried to Cesena (see GREGOROVIUS, Geschichte der Stadt Rom im Mittelalter. XIII, 5, 4).]

1309.

(Of Snakes, carried by Storks.)

Serpents of great length will be seen at a great height in the air, fighting with birds.

(Of great guns, which come out of a pit and a mould.)

Creatures will come from underground which with their terrific noise will stun all who are near; and with their breath will kill men and destroy cities and castles.

1310.

(Of Grain and other Seeds.)

Men will fling out of their houses those victuals which were intended to sustain their life.

(Of Trees, which nourish grafted shoots.)

Fathers and mothers will be seen to take much more delight in their step-children then in their own children.

(Of the Censer.)

Some will go about in white garments with arrogant gestures threatening others with metal and fire which will do no harm at all to them.

1311.

(Of drying Fodder.)

Innumerable lives will be destroyed and innumerable vacant spaces will be made on the earth.

(Of the Life of Men, who every year change their bodily substance.)

Men, when dead, will pass through their own bowels.

1312.

(Shoemakers.)

Men will take pleasure in seeing their own work destroyed and injured.

1313.

(Of Kids.)

The time of Herod will come again, for the little innocent children will be taken from their nurses, and will die of terrible wounds inflicted by cruel men.

V.

DRAUGHTS AND SCHEMES FOR THE HUMOROUS WRITINGS.

Schemes for fables, etc. (1314-1323).

1314.

A FABLE.

The crab standing under the rock to catch the fish which crept under it, it came to pass that the rock fell with a ruinous downfall of stones, and by their fall the crab was crushed.

THE SAME.

The spider, being among the grapes, caught the flies which were feeding on those grapes. Then came the vintage, and the spider was cut down with the grapes.

The vine that has grown old on an old tree falls with the ruin of that tree, and through that bad companionship must perish with it.

The torrent carried so much earth and stones into its bed, that it was then constrained to change its course.

The net that was wont to take the fish was seized and carried away by the rush of fish.

The ball of snow when, as it rolls, it descends from the snowy mountains, increases in size as it falls.

The willow, which by its long shoots hopes as it grows, to outstrip every other plant, from having associated itself with the vine which is pruned every year was always crippled.

1315.

Fable of the tongue bitten by the teeth.

The cedar puffed up with pride of its beauty, separated itself from the trees around it and in so doing it turned away towards the wind, which not being broken in its fury, flung it uprooted on the earth.

The traveller's joy, not content in its hedge, began to fling its branches out over the high road, and cling to the opposite hedge, and for this it was broken away by the passers by.

1316.

The goldfinch gives victuals to its caged young. Death rather than loss of liberty. [Footnote: Above this text is another note, also referring to liberty; see No. 694.]

1317.

(Of Bags.)

Goats will convey the wine to the city.

1318.

All those things which in winter are hidden under the snow, will be uncovered and laid bare in summer. (for Falsehood, which cannot remain hidden).

1319.

A FABLE.

The lily set itself down by the shores of the Ticino, and the current carried away bank and the lily with it.

1320.

A JEST.

Why Hungarian ducats have a double cross on them.

1321.

A SIMILE.

A vase of unbaked clay, when broken, may be remoulded, but not a baked one.

1322.

Seeing the paper all stained with the deep blackness of ink, it he deeply regrets it; and this proves to the paper that the words, composed upon it were the cause of its being preserved.

1323.

The pen must necessarily have the penknife for a companion, and it is a useful companionship, for one is not good for much without the other.

Schemes for prophecies (1324-1329).

1324.

The knife, which is an artificial weapon, deprives man of his nails, his natural weapons.

The mirror conducts itself haughtily holding mirrored in itself the Queen. When she departs the mirror remains there ...

1325.

Flax is dedicated to death, and to the corruption of mortals. To death, by being used for snares and nets for birds, animals and fish; to corruption, by the flaxen sheets in which the dead are wrapped when they are buried, and who become corrupt in these winding sheets.-- And again, this flax does not separate its fibre till it has begun to steep and putrefy, and this is the flower with which garlands and decorations for funerals should be made.

1326.

(Of Peasants who work in shirts)

Shadows will come from the East which will blacken with great colour darkness the sky that covers Italy.

(Of the Barbers.)

All men will take refuge in Africa.

1327.

The cloth which is held in the hand in the current of a running stream, in the waters of which the cloth leaves all its foulness and dirt, is meant to signify this &c.

By the thorn with inoculated good fruit is signified those natures which of themselves were not disposed towards virtue, but by the aid of their preceptors they have the repudation of it.

1328.

A COMMON THING.

A wretched person will be flattered, and these flatterers are always the deceivers, robbers and murderers of the wretched person.

The image of the sun where it falls appears as a thing which covers the person who attempts to cover it.

(Money and Gold.)

Out of cavernous pits a thing shall come forth which will make all the nations of the world toil and sweat with the greatest torments, anxiety and labour, that they may gain its aid.

(Of the Dread of Poverty.)

The malicious and terrible [monster] will cause so much terror of itself in men that they will rush together, with a rapid motion, like madmen, thinking they are escaping her boundless force.

(Of Advice.)

The man who may be most necessary to him who needs him, will be repaid with ingratitude, that is greatly contemned.

1329.

(Of Bees.)

They live together in communities, they are destroyed that we may take the honey from them. Many and very great nations will be destroyed in their own dwellings.

1330.

WHY DOGS TAKE PLEASURE IN SMELLING AT EACH OTHER.

This animal has a horror of the poor, because they eat poor food, and it loves the rich, because they have good living and especially meat. And the excrement of animals always retains some virtue of its origin as is shown by the faeces ...

Now dogs have so keen a smell, that they can discern by their nose the virtue remaining in these faeces, and if they find them in the streets, smell them and if they smell in them the virtue of meat or of other things, they take them, and if not, they leave them: And to return to the question, I say that if by means of this smell they know that dog to be well fed, they respect him, because they judge that he has a powerful and rich master; and if they discover no such smell with the virtue of meet, they judge that dog to be of small account and to have a poor and humble master, and therefore they bite that dog as they would his master.

1331.

The circular plans of carrying earth are very useful, inasmuch as men never stop in their work; and it is done in many ways. By one of these ways men carry the earth on their shoulders, by another in chests and others on wheelbarrows. The man who carries it on his shoulders first fills the tub on the ground, and he loses time in hoisting it on to his shoulders. He with the chests loses no time. [Footnote: The subject of this text has apparently no connection with the other texts of this section.]

Irony (1332).

1332.

If Petrarch was so fond of bay, it was because it is of a good taste in sausages and with tunny; I cannot put any value on their foolery. [Footnote: Conte Porro has published these lines in the Archivio Stor. Lombarda VIII, IV; he reads the concluding line thus: I no posso di loro gia (sic) co' far tesauro.-- This is known to be by a contemporary poet, as Senatore Morelli informs me.]

Tricks (1333-1335).

1333.

We are two brothers, each of us has a brother. Here the way of saying it makes it appear that the two brothers have become four.

1334.

TRICKS OF DIVIDING.

Take in each hand an equal number; put 4 from the right hand into the left; cast away the remainder; cast away an equal number from the left hand; add 5, and now you will find 13 in this [left] hand; that is-I made you put 4 from the right hand into the left, and cast away the remainder; now your right hand has 4 more; then I make you throw away as many from the right as you threw away from the left; so, throwing from each hand a quantity of which the remainder may be equal, you now have 4 and 4, which make 8, and that the trick may not be detec- ted I made you put 5 more, which made 13.

TRICKS OF DIVIDING.

Take any number less than 12 that you please; then take of mine enough to make up the number 12, and that which remains to me is the number which you at first had; because when I said, take any number less than 12 as you please, I took 12 into my hand, and of that 12 you took such a number as made up your number of 12; and what you added to your number, you took from mine; that is, if you had 8 to go as far as to 12, you took of my 12, 4; hence this 4 transferred from me to you reduced my 12 to a remainder of 8, and your 8 became 12; so that my 8 is equal to your 8, before it was made 12.

[Footnote 1334: G. Govi says in the 'Saggio' p. 22: Si dilett Leonarda, di giuochi di prestigi e molti (?) ne descrisse, che si leggono poi riportati dal Paciolo nel suo libro: de Viribus Quantitatis, e che, se non tutti, sono certo in gran parte invenzioni del Vinci.]

1335.

If you want to teach someone a subject you do not know yourself, let him measure the length of an object unknown to you, and he will learn the measure you did not know before;--Master Giovanni da Lodi.

XXI. Letters. Personal Records. Dated Notes.

When we consider how superficial and imperfect are the accounts of Leonardo's life written some time after his death by Vasari and others, any notes or letters which can throw more light on his personal circumstances cannot fail to be in the highest degree interesting. The texts here given as Nos. 1351--1353, set his residence in Rome in quite a new aspect; nay, the picture which irresistibly dwells in our minds after reading these details of his life in the Vatican, forms a striking contrast to the contemporary life of Raphael at Rome.

I have placed foremost of these documents the very remarkable letters to the Defterdar of Syria. In these Leonardo speaks of himself as having staid among the mountains of Armenia, and as the biographies of the master tell nothing of any such distant journeys, it would seem most obvious to treat this passage as fiction, and so spare ourselves the onus of proof and discussion. But on close examination no one can doubt that these documents, with the accompanying sketches, are the work of Leonardo's own hand. Not merely is the character of the handwriting his, but the spelling and the language are his also. In one respect only does the writing betray any marked deviation from the rest of the notes, especially those treating on scientific questions; namely, in these observations he seems to have taken particular pains to give the most distinct and best form of expression to all he had to say; we find erasures and emendations in almost every line. He proceeded, as we shall see, in the same way in the sketches for letters to Giuliano de' Medici, and what can be more natural, I may ask, than to find the draft of a letter thus altered and improved when it is to contain an account of a definite subject, and when personal interests are in the scale? The finished copies as sent off are not known to exist; if we had these instead of the rough drafts, we might unhesitatingly have declared that some unknown Italian engineer must have been, at that time, engaged in Armenia in the service of the Egyptian Sultan, and that Leonardo had copied his documents. Under this hypothesis however we should have to state that this unknown writer must have been so far one in mind with Leonardo as to use the same style of language and even the same lines of thought. This explanation might--as I say--have been possible, if only we had the finished letters. But why should these rough drafts of letters be regarded as anything else than what they actually and obviously are? If Leonardo had been a man of our own time, we might perhaps have attempted to account for the facts by saying that Leonardo, without having been in the East himself, might have undertaken to write a Romance of which the scene was laid in Armenia, and at the desire of his publisher had made sketches of landscape to illustrate the text.

I feel bound to mention this singular hypothesis as it has actually been put forward (see No. 1336 note 5); and it would certainly seem as though there were no other possible way of evading the conclusion to which these letters point, and their bearing on the life of the master,--absurd as the alternative is. But, if, on a question of such importance, we are justified in suggesting theories that have no foundation in probability, I could suggest another which, as compared with that of a Fiction by Leonardo, would be neither more nor less plausible; it is, moreover the only other hypothesis, perhaps, which can be devised to account for these passages, if it were possible to prove that the interpretation that the documents themselves suggest, must be rejected a priori; viz may not Leonardo have written them with the intention of mystifying those who, after his death, should try to decipher these manuscripts with a view to publishing them? But if, in fact, no objection that will stand the test of criticism can be brought against the simple and direct interpretation of the words as they stand, we are bound to regard Leonardo's travels in the East as an established fact. There is, I believe nothing in what we know of his biography to negative such a fact, especially as the details of his life for some few years are wholly unknown; nor need we be at a loss for evidence which may serve to explain--at any rate to some extent--the strangeness of his undertaking such a journey. We have no information as to Leonardo's history between 1482 and 1486; it cannot be proved that he was either in Milan or in Florence. On the other hand the tenor of this letter does not require us to assume a longer absence than a year or two. For, even if his appointment (offitio) as Engineer in Syria had been a permanent one, it might have become untenable--by the death perhaps of the Defterdar, his patron, or by his removal from office--, and Leonardo on his return home may have kept silence on the subject of an episode which probably had ended in failure and disappointment.

From the text of No. 1379 we can hardly doubt that Leonardo intended to make an excursion secretly from Rome to Naples, although so far as has hitherto been known, his biographers never allude to it. In another place (No. 1077) he says that he had worked as an Engineer in Friuli. Are we to doubt this statement too, merely because no biographer has hitherto given us any information on the matter? In the geographical notes Leonardo frequently speaks of the East, and though such passages afford no direct proof of his having been there, they show beyond a doubt that, next to the Nile, the Euphrates, the Tigris and the Taurus mountains had a special interest in his eyes. As a still further proof of the futility of the argument that there is nothing in his drawings to show that he had travelled in the East, we find on Pl. CXX a study of oriental heads of Armenian type,--though of course this may have been made in Italy.

If the style of these letters were less sober, and the expressions less strictly to the point throughout, it miglit be possible to regard them as a romantic fiction instead of a narrative of fact. Nay, we have only to compare them with such obviously fanciful passages as No. 1354, Nos. 670-673, and the Fables and Prophecies. It is unnecessary to discuss the subject any further here; such explanations as the letter needs are given in the foot notes.

The drafts of letters to Lodovico il Moro are very remarkable. Leonardo and this prince were certainly far less closely connected, than has hitherto been supposed. It is impossible that Leonardo can have remained so long in the service of this prince, because the salary was good, as is commonly stated. On the contrary, it would seem, that what kept him there, in spite of his sore need of the money owed him by the prince, was the hope of some day being able to carry out the project of casting the 'gran cavallo'.

Drafts of Letters and Reports referring to Armenia (1336. 1337).

1336.

To THE DEVATDAR OF SYRIA, LIEUTENANT OF THE SACRED SULTAN OF BABYLON.

[3] The recent disaster in our Northern parts which I am certain will terrify not you alone but the whole world, which

[Footnote: Lines 1-52 are reproduced in facsimile on Pl. CXVI.

1. Diodario. This word is not to be found in any Italian dictionary, and for a long time I vainly sought an explanation of it. The youthful reminiscences of my wife afforded the desired clue. The chief town of each Turkish Villayet, or province --such as Broussa, for instance, in Asia Minor, is the residence of a Defterdar, who presides over the financial affairs of the province. Defterdar hane was, in former times, the name given to the Ministry of Finance at Constantinople; the Minister of Finance to the Porte is now known as the Mallie-Nazri and the Defterdars are his subordinates. A Defterdar, at the present day is merely the head of the finance department in each Provincial district. With regard to my suggestion that Leonardo's Diodario might be identical with the Defterdar of former times, the late M. C. DEFREMERIE, Arabic Professor, and Membre de l'Institut de France wrote to me as follows: Votre conjecture est parfaitement fondee; diodario est Vequivalent de devadar ou plus exactement devatdar, titre d'une importante dignite en Egypt'e, sous les Mamlouks.

The word however is not of Turkish, but of Perso-Arabie derivation. [Defter written in arab?] literally Defter (Arabic) meaning folio; for dar (Persian) Bookkeeper or holder is the English equivalent; and the idea is that of a deputy in command. During the Mamelook supremacy over Syria, which corresponded in date with Leonardo's time, the office of Defterdar was the third in importance in the State.

Soltano di Babilonia. The name of Babylon was commonly applied to Cairo in the middle ages. For instance BREIDENBACH, Itinerarium Hierosolyma p. 218 says: "At last we reached Babylon. But this is not that Babylon which stood on the further shore of the river Chober, but that which is called the Egyptian Babylon. It is close by Cairo and the twain are but one and not two towns; one half is called Cairo and the other Babylon, whence they are called together Cairo-Babylon; originally the town is said to have been named Memphis and then Babylon, but now it is called Cairo." Compare No. 1085, 6.

Egypt was governed from 1382 till 1517 by the Borgite or Tcherkessian dynasty of the Mamelook Sultans. One of the most famous of these, Sultan Kait Bey, ruled from 1468-1496 during whose reign the Gama (or Mosque) of Kait Bey and tomb of Kait Bey near the Okella Kait Bey were erected in Cairo, which preserve his name to this day. Under the rule of this great and wise prince many foreigners, particularly Italians, found occupation in Egypt, as may be seen in the 'Viaggio di Josaphat Barbaro', among other travellers. "Next to Leonardo (so I learn from Prof. Jac. Burckhardt of Bale) Kait Bey's most helpful engineer was a German who in about 1487, superintended the construction of the Mole at Alexandria. Felix Fabri knew him and mentions him in his Historia Suevorum, written in 1488."

3. Il nuovo accidente accaduto, or as Leonardo first wrote and then erased, e accaduto un nuovo accidente. From the sequel this must refer to an earthquake, and indeed these were frequent at that period, particularly in Asia Minor, where they caused immense mischief. See No. 1101 note.]

shall be related to you in due order, showing first the effect and then the cause. [Footnote 4: The text here breaks off. The following lines are a fresh beginning of a letter, evidently addressed to the same person, but, as it would seem, written at a later date than the previous text. The numerous corrections and amendments amply prove that it is not a copy from any account of a journey by some unknown person; but, on the contrary, that Leonardo was particularly anxious to choose such words and phrases as might best express his own ideas.]

Finding myself in this part of Armenia [Footnote 5: Parti d'Erminia. See No. 945, note. The extent of Armenia in Leonardo's time is only approximately known. In the XVth century the Persians governed the Eastern, and the Arabs the Southern portions. Arabic authors--as, for instance Abulfeda--include Cilicia and a part of Cappadocia in Armenia, and Greater Armenia was the tract of that country known later as Turcomania, while Armenia Minor was the territory between Cappadocia and the Euphrates. It was not till 1522, or even 1574 that the whole country came under the dominion of the Ottoman Turks, in the reign of Selim I.

The Mamelook Sultans of Egypt seem to have taken a particular interest in this, the most Northern province of their empire, which was even then in danger of being conquered by the Turks. In the autumn of 1477 Sultan Kait Bey made a journey of inspection, visiting Antioch and the valleys of the Tigris and Euphrates with a numerous and brilliant escort. This tour is briefly alluded to by Moodshireddin p. 561; and by WEIL, Geschichte der Abbasiden V, p. 358. An anonymous member of the suite wrote a diary of the expedition in Arabic, which has been published by R. V. LONZONE ('Viaggio in Palestina e Soria di Kaid Ba XVIII sultano della II dinastia mamelucca, fatto nel 1477. Testo arabo. Torino 1878', without notes or commentary). Compare the critique on this edition, by J. GILDEMEISTER in Zeitschrift des Deutschen Palaestina Vereins (Vol. III p. 246--249). Lanzone's edition seems to be no more than an abridged copy of the original. I owe to Professor Sche'fer, Membre de l'Institut, the information that he is in possession of a manuscript in which the text is fuller, and more correctly given. The Mamelook dynasty was, as is well known, of Circassian origin, and a large proportion of the Egyptian Army was recruited in Circassia even so late as in the XVth century. That was a period of political storms in Syria and Asia Minor and it is easy to suppose that the Sultan's minister, to whom Leonardo addresses his report as his superior, had a special interest in the welfare of those frontier provinces. Only to mention a few historical events of Sultan Kait Bey's reign, we find that in 1488 he assisted the Circassians to resist the encroachments of

Alaeddoulet, an Asiatic prince who had allied himself with the Osmanli to threaten the province; the consequence was a war in Cilicia by sea and land, which broke out in the following year between the contending powers. Only a few years earlier the same province had been the scene of the so-called Caramenian war in which the united Venetian, Neapolitan and Sclavonic fleets had been engaged. (See CORIALANO CIPPICO, Della guerra dei Veneziani nell' Asia dal 1469--1474. Venezia 1796, p. 54) and we learn incidentally that a certain Leonardo Boldo, Governor of Scutari under Sultan Mahmoud,--as his name would indicate, one of the numerous renegades of Italian birth--played an important part in the negotiations for peace.

Tu mi mandasti. The address tu to a personage so high in office is singular and suggests personal intimacy; Leonardo seems to have been a favourite with the Diodario. Compare lines 54 and 55.

I have endeavoured to show, and I believe that I am also in a position to prove with regard to these texts, that they are draughts of letters actually written by Leonardo; at the same time I must not omit to mention that shortly after I had discovered

these texts in the Codex Atlanticus and published a paper on the subject in the Zeitschrift fur bildende Kunst (Vol. XVI), Prof. Govi put forward this hypothesis to account for their origin:

"Quanto alle notizie sul monte Tauro, sull'Armenia e sull' Asia minore che si contengono negli altri frammenti, esse vennero prese da qualche geografro o viaggiatore contemporaneo. Dall'indice imperfetto che accompagna quei frammenti, si potrebbe dedurre che Leonardo volesse farne un libro, che poi non venne compiuto. A ogni modo, non e possibile di trovare in questi brani nessun indizio di un viaggio di Leonardo in oriente, ne della sua conversione alla religione di Maometto, come qualcuno pretenderebbe. Leonardo amava con passione gli studi geografici, e nel suoi scritti s'incontran spesso itinerart, indicazioni, o descrizioni di luoghi, schizzi di carte e abbozzi topografici di varie regioni, non e quindi strano che egli, abile narratore com'era, si fosse proposto di scrivere una specie di Romanzo in forma epistolare svolgendone Pintreccio nell'Asia Minore, intorno alla quale i libri d'allora, e forse qualche viaggiatore amico suo, gli avevano somministrato alcuni elementi piu o meno fantastici. (See Transunti della Reale Accademia dei Lincei Voi. V Ser. 3).

It is hardly necessary to point out that Prof. Govi omits to name the sources from which Leonardo could be supposed to have drawn his information, and I may leave it to the reader to pronounce judgment on the anomaly which is involved in the hypothesis that we have here a fragment of a Romance, cast in the form of a correspondence. At the same time, I cannot but admit that the solution of the difficulties proposed by Prof. Govi is, under the circumstances, certainly the easiest way of dealing with the question. But we should then be equally justified in supposing some more of Leonardo's letters to be fragments of such romances; particularly those of which the addresses can no longer be named. Still, as regards these drafts of letters to the Diodario, if we accept the Romance theory, as pro- posed by Prof. Govi, we are also compelled to assume that Leonardo purposed from the first to illustrate his tale; for it needs only a glance at the sketches on Pl. CXVI to CXIX to perceive that they are connected with the texts; and of course the rest of Leonardo's numerous notes on matters pertaining to the East, the greater part of which are here published for the first time, may also be somehow connected with this strange romance.

7. Citta de Calindra (Chalindra). The position of this city is so exactly determined, between the valley of the Euphrates and the Taurus range that it ought to be possible to identify it. But it can hardly be the same as the sea port of Cilicia with a somewhat similar name Celenderis, Kelandria, Celendria, Kilindria, now the Turkish Gulnar. In two Catalonian Portulans in the Bibliotheque Natio- nale in Paris-one dating from the XV'h century, by Wilhelm von Soler, the other by Olivez de Majorca, in I584-I find this place called Calandra. But Leonardo's Calindra must certainly have lain more to the North West, probably somewhere in Kurdistan. The fact that the geographical position is so care- fully determined by Leonardo seems to prove that it was a place of no great importance and little known. It is singular that the words first written in 1. 8 were divisa dal lago (Lake Van?), altered afterwards to dall'Eitfrates.

Nostri confini, and in 1. 6 proposito nostro. These refer to the frontier and to the affairs of the Mamelook Sultan, Lines 65 and 66 throw some light on the purpose of Leonardo's mission.

8. I corni del gra mote Tauro. Compare the sketches Pl. CXVI-CXVIII. So long as it is im- possible to identify the situation of Calindra it is most difficult to decide with any certainty which peak of the Taurus is here meant; and I greatly regret that I had no foreknowledge of this puzzling topographical question when, in 1876, I was pursuing archaeological enquiries in the Provinces of Aleppo and Cilicia, and had to travel for some time in view of the imposing snow-peaks of Bulghar Dagh and Ala Tepessi.

9-10. The opinion here expressed as to the height of the mountain would be unmeaning, unless it had been written before Leonardo moved to Milan, where Monte Rosa is so conspicuous an object in the landscape. 4 ore inanzi seems to mean, four hours before the sun's rays penetrate to the bottom of the valleys.]

to carry into effect with due love and care the task for which you sent me [Footnote:][6]; and to make a beginning in a place which seemed to me to be most to our purpose, I entered into the city of Calindrafy[7], near to our frontiers. This city is situated at the base of that part of the Taurus mountains which is divided from the Euphrates and looks towards the peaks of the great Mount Taurus [8] to the West [9]. These peaks are of such a height that they seem to touch the sky, and in all the world there is no part of the earth, higher than its summit[10], and the rays of the sun always fall upon it on its East side, four hours before day-time, and being of the whitest stone [Footnote 11:Pietra bianchissima. The Taurus Mountains consist in great part of limestone.] it shines resplendently and fulfils the function to these Armenians which a bright moon-light would in the midst of the darkness; and by its great height it outreaches the utmost level of the clouds by a space of four miles in a straight line. This peak is seen in many places towards the West, illuminated by the sun after its setting the third part of the night. This it is, which with you [Footnote 14: Appresso di voi. Leonardo had at first written noi as though his meaning had, been: This peak appeared to us to be a comet when you and I observed it in North Syria (at Aleppo? at Aintas?). The description of the curious reflection in the evening, resembling the "Alpine-glow" is certainly not an invented fiction, for in the next lines an explanation of the phenomenon is offered, or at least attempted.] we formerly in calm weather had supposed to be a comet, and appears to us in the darkness of night, to change its form, being sometimes divided in two or three parts, and sometimes long and sometimes short. And this is caused by the clouds on the horizon of the sky which interpose between part of this mountain and the sun, and by cutting off some of the solar rays the light on the mountain is intercepted by various intervals of clouds, and therefore varies in the form of its brightness.

THE DIVISIONS OF THE BOOK [Footnote 19: The next 33 lines are evidently the contents of a connected Report or Book, but not of one which he had at hand; more probably, indeed, of one he purposed writing.].

The praise and confession of the faith [Footnote 20: Persuasione di fede, of the Christian or the Mohammedan faith? We must suppose the latter, at the beginning of a document addressed to so high a Mohammedan official. Predica probably stands as an abbreviation for predicazione (lat. praedicatio) in the sense of praise or glorification; very probably it may mean some such initial doxology as we find in Mohammedan works. (Comp. 1. 40.)].

The sudden inundation, to its end.

[23] The destruction of the city.

[24]The death of the people and their despair.

The preacher's search, his release and benevolence [Footnote 28: The phraseology of this is too general for any conjecture as to its meaning to be worth hazarding.]

Description of the cause of this fall of the mountain [Footnote 30: Ruina del monte. Of course by an earthquake. In a catalogue of earthquakes, entitled kechf aussalssaleb an auasf ezzel-zeleh, and written by Djelal eddin].

The mischief it did.

[32] Fall of snow.

The finding of the prophet [33].

His prophesy.

[35] The inundation of the lower portion of Eastern Armenia, the draining of which was effected by the cutting through the Taurus Mountains.

How the new prophet showed [Footnote 40:Nova profeta, 1. 33, profeta. Mohammed. Leonardo here refers to the Koran:

In the name of the most merciful God.--When the earth shall be shaken by an earthquake; and the earth shall cast forth her burdens; and a man shall say, what aileth her? On that day the earth shall declare her tidings, for that thy Lord will inspire her. On that day men shall go forward in distinct classes, that they may behold their works. And whoever shall have wrought good of the weight of an ant, shall behold the same. And whoever shall have wrought evil of the weight of an ant, shall behold the same. (The Koran, translated by G. Sale, Chapter XCIX, p. 452).] that this destruction would happen as he had foretold.

Description of the Taurus Mountains [43] and the river Euphrates.

Why the mountain shines at the top, from half to a third of the night, and looks like a comet to the inhabitants of the West after the sunset, and before day to those of the East.

Why this comet appears of variable forms, so that it is now round and now long, and now again divided into two or three parts, and now in one piece, and when it is to be seen again.

OF THE SHAPE OF THE TAURUS MOUNTAINS [Footnote 53-94: The facsimile of this passage is given on Pl. CXVII.].

I am not to be accused, Oh Devatdar, of idleness, as your chidings seem to hint; but your excessive love for me, which gave rise to the benefits you have conferred on me [Footnote 55] is that which has also compelled me to the utmost painstaking in seeking out and diligently investigating the cause of so great and stupendous an effect. And this could not be done without time; now, in order to satisfy you fully as to the cause of so great an effect, it is requisite that I should explain to you the form of the place, and then I will proceed to the effect, by which I believe you will be amply satisfied.

[Footnote 36: Tagliata di Monte Tauro. The Euphrates flows through the Taurus range near the influx of the Kura Shai; it rushes through a rift in the wildest cliffs from 2000 to 3000 feet high and runs on for 90 miles in 300 falls or rapids till it reaches Telek, near which at a spot called Gleikash, or the Hart's leap, it measures only 35 paces across. Compare the map on Pl. CXIX and the explanation for it on p. 391.]

[Footnote 54: The foregoing sketch of a letter, lines 5. 18, appears to have remained a fragment when Leonardo received pressing orders which caused him to write immediately and fully on the subject mentioned in line 43.]

[Footnote 59: This passage was evidently intended as an improvement on that immediately preceding it. The purport of both is essentially the same, but the first is pitched in a key of ill-disguised annoyance which is absent from the second. I do not see how these two versions can be reconciled with the romance-theory held by Prof. Govi.] Do not be aggrieved, O Devatdar, by my delay in responding to your pressing request, for those things which you require of me are of such a nature that they cannot be well expressed without some lapse of time; particularly because, in order to explain the cause of so great an effect, it is necessary to describe with accuracy the nature of the place; and by this means I can afterwards easily satisfy your above-mentioned request. [Footnote 62: This passage was evidently intended as an improvement on that immediately preceding it. The purport of both is essentially the same, but the first is pitched in a key of ill-disguised annoyance which is absent from the second. I do not see how these two versions can be reconciled with the romance-theory held by Prof. Govi.]

I will pass over any description of the form of Asia Minor, or as to what seas or lands form the limits of its outline and extent, because I know that by your own diligence and carefulness in your studies you have not remained in ignorance of these matters [65]; and I will go on to describe the true form of the Taurus Mountain which is the cause of this stupendous and harmful marvel, and which will serve to advance us in our purpose [66]. This Taurus is that mountain which, with many others is said to be the ridge of Mount Caucasus; but wishing to be very clear about it, I desired to speak to some of the inhabitants of the shores of the Caspian sea, who give evidence that this must be the true Caucasus, and that though their mountains bear the same name, yet these are higher; and to confirm this in the Scythian tongue Caucasus means a very high [Footnote 68: Caucasus; Herodot Kaoxaais; Armen. Kaukaz.] peak, and in fact we have no information of there being, in the East or in the West, any mountain so high. And the proof of this is that the inhabitants of the countries to the West see the rays of the sun illuminating a great part of its summit for as much as a quarter of the longest night. And in the same way, in those countries which lie to the East.

OF THE STRUCTURE AND SIZE OF MOUNT TAURUS.

[Footnote 73: The statements are of course founded on those of the 'inhabitants' spoken of in 1. 67.] The shadow of this ridge of the Taurus is of such a height that when, in the middle of June, the Sun is at its meridian, its shadow extends as far as the borders of Sarmatia, twelve days off; and in the middle of December it extends as far as the Hyperborean mountains, which are at a month's journey to the North [75]. And the side which faces the wind is always free from clouds and mists, because the wind which is parted in beating on the rock, closes again on the further side of that rock, and in its motion carries with it the clouds from all quarters and leaves them where it strikes. And it is always full of thunderbolts from the great quantity of clouds which accumulate there, whence the rock is all riven and full of huge debris [Footnote 77: Sudden storms are equally common on the heights of Ararat. It is hardly necessary to observe that Ararat cannot be meant here. Its summit is formed like the crater of Vesuvius. The peaks sketched on Pl. CXVI-CXVIII are probably views of the same mountain, taken from different sides. Near the solitary peak, Pl. CXVIII these three names are written goba, arnigasar, caruda, names most likely of different peaks. Pl. CXVI and CXVII are in the original on a single sheet folded down the middle, 30 centimetres high and 43 1/2 wide. On the reverse of one half of the sheet are notes on peso and bilancia (weight and balance), on the other are the 'prophecies' printed under Nos. 1293 and 1294. It is evident from the arrangement that these were written subsequently, on the space which had been left blank. These pages are facsimiled on Pl. CXVIII. In Pl. CXVI-CXVIII the size is smaller than in the original; the map of Armenia, Pl. CXVIII, is on Pl. CXIX slightly enlarged. On this map we find the following names, beginning from the right hand at the top: pariardes mo (for Paryadres Mons, Arm. Parchar, now Barchal or Kolai Dagh; Trebizond is on its slope).

Aquilone --North, Antitaurus Antitaurus psis mo (probably meant for Thospitis = Lake Van, Arm. Dgov Vanai, Tospoi, and the Mountain range to the South); Gordis mo (Mountains of Gordyaea), the birth place of the Tigris; Oriente -- East; Tigris, and then, to the left, Eufrates. Then, above to the left Argeo mo (now Erdshigas, an extinct volcano, 12000 feet high); Celeno mo (no doubt Sultan Dagh in Pisidia). Celeno is the Greek town of KeAouvat-- see Arian I, 29, I--now the ruins of Dineir); oriente --East; africo libezco (for libeccio--South West). In the middle of the Euphrates river on this small map we see a shaded portion surrounded by mountains, perhaps to indicate the inundation mentioned in l. 35. The affluent to the Euphrates shown as coming with many windings from the high land of 'Argeo' on the West, is the Tochma Su, which joins the main river at Malatie. I have not been able to discover any map of Armenia of the XVth or XVIth century in which the course of the Euphrates is laid down with any thing like the correctness displayed in this sketch. The best I have seen is the Catalonian Portulan of Olivez de Majorca, executed in 1584, and it is far behind Leonardo's.]. This mountain, at its base, is inhabited by a very rich population and is full of most beautiful springs and rivers, and is fertile and abounding in all good produce, particularly in those parts which face to the South. But after mounting about three miles we begin to find forests of great fir trees, and beech and other similar trees; after this, for a space of three more miles, there are meadows and vast pastures; and all the rest, as far as the beginning of the Taurus, is eternal snows which never disappear at any time, and extend to a height of about fourteen miles in all. From this beginning of the Taurus up to the height of a mile the clouds never pass away; thus we have fifteen miles, that is, a height of about five miles in a straight line; and the summit of the peaks of the Taurus are as much, or about that. There, half way up, we begin to find a scorching air and never feel a breath of wind; but nothing can live long there; there nothing is brought forth save a few birds of prey which breed in the high fissures of Taurus and descend below the clouds to seek their prey. Above the wooded hills all is bare rock, that is, from the clouds upwards; and the rock is the purest white. And it is impossible to walk to the high summit on account of the rough and perilous ascent.

1337.

[Footnote: 1337. On comparing this commencement of a letter l. 1-2 with that in l. 3 and 4 of No. 1336 it is quite evident that both refer to the same event. (Compare also No. 1337 l. 10-l2 and 17 with No. 1336 l. 23, 24 and 32.) But the text No. 1336, including the fragment l. 3-4, was obviously written later than the draft here reproduced. The Diodario is not directly addressed--the person addressed indeed is not known--and it seems to me highly probable that it was written to some other patron and friend whose name and position are not mentioned.]

Having often made you, by my letters, acquainted with the things which have happened, I think I ought not to be silent as to the events of the last few days, which--[2]...

Having several times--

Having many times rejoiced with you by letters over your prosperous fortunes, I know now that, as a friend you will be sad with me over the miserable state in which I find myself; and this is, that during the last few days I have been in so much trouble, fear, peril and loss, besides the miseries of the people here, that we have been envious of the dead; and certainly I do not believe that since the elements by their separation reduced the vast chaos to order, they have ever combined their force and fury to do so much mischief to man. As far as regards us here, what we have seen and gone through is such that I could not imagine that things could ever rise to such an amount of mischief, as we experienced in the space of ten hours. In the first place we were assailed and attacked by the violence and fury of the winds [10]; to this was added the falling of great mountains of snow which filled up all this valley, thus destroying a great part of our city [Footnote 11: Della nostra citta (Leonardo first wrote di questa citta). From this we may infer that he had at some time lived in the place in question wherever it might be.]. And not content with this the tempest sent a sudden flood of water to submerge all the low part of this city [12]; added to which there came a sudden rain, or rather a ruinous torrent and flood of water, sand, mud, and stones, entangled with roots, and stems and fragments of various trees; and every kind of thing flying through the air fell upon us; finally a great fire broke out, not brought by the wind, but carried as it would seem, by ten thousand devils, which completely burnt up all this neighbourhood and it has not yet ceased. And those few who remain unhurt are in such dejection and such terror that they hardly have courage to speak to each other, as if they were stunned. Having abandoned all our business, we stay here together in the ruins of some churches, men and women mingled together, small and great [Footnote 17: Certe ruine di chiese. Either of Armenian churches or of Mosques, which it was not unusual to speak of as churches.

Maschi e femmini insieme unite, implies an infringement of the usually strict rule of the separation of the sexes.], just like herds of goats. The neighbours out of pity succoured us with victuals, and they had previously been our enemies. And if

[Footnote 18: I vicini, nostri nimici. The town must then have stood quite close to the frontier of the country. Compare 1336. L. 7. vicini ai nostri confini. Dr. M. JORDAN has already published lines 4-13 (see Das Malerbuch, Leipzig, 1873, p. 90:--his reading differs from mine) under the title of "Description of a landscape near Lake Como". We do in fact find, among other loose sheets in the Codex Atlanticus, certain texts referring to valleys of the Alps (see Nos. 1030, 1031 and note p. 237) and in the arrangement of the loose sheets, of which the Codex Atlanticus has been formed, these happen to be placed close to this text. The compiler stuck both on the same folio sheet; and if this is not the reason for Dr. JORDAN'S choosing such a title (Description &c.) I cannot imagine what it can have been. It is, at any rate, a merely hypothetical statement. The designation of the population of the country round a city as "the enemy" (nemici) is hardly appropriate to Italy in the time of Leonardo.]

it had not been for certain people who succoured us with victuals, all would have died of hunger. Now you see the state we are in. And all these evils are as nothing compared with those which are promised to us shortly.

I know that as a friend you will grieve for my misfortunes, as I, in former letters have shown my joy at your prosperity ...

Notes about events observed abroad (1338-1339).

1338.

BOOK 43. OF THE MOVEMENT OF AIR ENCLOSED IN WATER.

I have seen motions of the air so furious that they have carried, mixed up in their course, the largest trees of the forest and whole roofs of great palaces, and I have seen the same fury bore a hole with a whirling movement digging out a gravel pit, and carrying gravel, sand and water more than half a mile through the air.

[Footnote: The first sixteen lines of this passage which treat of the subject as indicated on the title line have no place in this connexion and have been omitted.]

[Footnote 2: Ho veduto movimenti &c. Nothing of the kind happened in Italy during Leonardo's lifetime, and it is therefore extremely probable that this refers to the natural phenomena which are so fully described in the foregoing passage. (Compare too, No. 1021.) There can be no doubt that the descriptions of the Deluge in the Libro di Pittura (Vol. I, No. 607-611), and that of the fall of a mountain No. 610, I. 17-30 were written from the vivid impressions derived from personal experience. Compare also Pl. XXXIV-XL.]

1339.

[Footnote: It may be inferred from the character of the writing, which is in the style of the note in facsimile Vol. I, p. 297, that this passage was written between 1470 and 1480. As the figure 6 at the end of the text indicates, it was continued on another page, but I have searched in vain for it. The reverse of this leaf is coloured red for drawing in silver point, but has not been used for that purpose but for writing on, and at about the same date. The passages are given as Nos. 1217, 1218, 1219, 1162 and No. 994 (see note page 218). The text given above is obviously not a fragment of a letter, but a record of some personal experience. No. 1379 also seems to refer to Leonardo's journeys in Southern Italy.]

Like a whirling wind which rushes down a sandy and hollow valley, and which, in its hasty course, drives to its centre every thing that opposes its furious course ...

No otherwise does the Northern blast whirl round in its tempestuous progress ...

Nor does the tempestuous sea bellow so loud, when the Northern blast dashes it, with its foaming waves between Scylla and Charybdis; nor Stromboli, nor Mount Etna, when their sulphurous flames, having been forcibly confined, rend, and burst open the mountain, fulminating stones and earth through the air together with the flames they vomit.

Nor when the inflamed caverns of Mount Etna [Footnote 13: Mongibello is a name commonly given in Sicily to Mount Etna (from Djebel, Arab.=mountain). Fr. FERRARA, Descrizione dell' Etna con la storia delle eruzioni (Palermo, 1818, p. 88) tells us, on the authority of the Cronaca del Monastero Benedettino di Licordia of an eruption of the Volcano with a great flow of lava on Sept. 21, 1447. The next records of the mountain are from the years 1533 and 1536. A. Percy neither does mention any eruptions of Etna during the years to which this note must probably refer Memoire des tremblements de terre de la peninsule italique, Vol. XXII des Memoires couronnees et Memoires des savants etrangers. Academie Royal de Belgique).

A literal interpretation of the passage would not, however, indicate an allusion to any great eruption; particularly in the connection with Stromboli, where the periodical outbreaks in very short intervals are very striking to any observer, especially at night time, when passing the island on the way from Naples to Messina.], rejecting the ill-restained element vomit it forth, back to its own region, driving furiously before it every obstacle that comes in the way of its impetuous rage ...

Unable to resist my eager desire and wanting to see the great ... of the various and strange shapes made by formative nature, and having wandered some distance among gloomy rocks, I came to the entrance of a great cavern, in front of which I stood some time, astonished and unaware of such a thing. Bending my back into an arch I rested my left hand on my knee and held my right hand over my down-cast and contracted eye brows: often bending first one way and then the other, to see whether I could discover anything inside, and this being forbidden by the deep darkness within, and after having remained there some time, two contrary emotions arose in me, fear and desire--fear of the threatening dark cavern, desire to see whether there were any marvellous thing within it ...

Drafts of Letters to Lodovico il Moro (1340-1345).

1340.

[Footnote: The numerous corrections, the alterations in the figures (l. 18) and the absence of any signature prove that this is merely the rough draft of a letter to Lodovico il Moro. It is one of the very few manuscripts which are written from left to right--see the facsimile of the beginning as here reproduced. This is probably the final sketch of a document the clean of which copy was written in the usual manner. Leonardo no doubt very rarely wrote so, and this is probably the reason of the conspicuous dissimilarity in the handwriting, when he did. (Compare Pl. XXXVIII.) It is noteworthy too that here the orthography and abbreviations are also exceptional. But such superficial peculiarities are not enough to stamp the document as altogether spurious. It is neither a forgery nor the production of any artist but Leonardo himself. As to this point the contents leave us no doubt as to its authenticity, particularly l. 32 (see No. 719, where this passage is repeated). But whether the fragment, as we here see it, was written from Leonardo's dictation--a theory favoured by the orthography, the erasures and corrections--or whether it may be a copy made for or by Melzi or Mazenta is comparatively unimportant. There are in the Codex Atlanticus a few other documents not written by Leonardo himself, but the notes in his own hand found on the reverse pages of these leaves amply prove that they were certainly in Leonardo's possession. This mark of ownership is wanting to the text in question, but the compilers of the Codex Atlanticus; at any rate, accepted it as a genuine document.

With regard to the probable date of this projected letter see Vol. II, p. 3.]

Most illustrious Lord, Having now sufficiently considered the specimens of all those who proclaim themselves skilled contrivers of instruments of war, and that the invention and operation of the said instruments are nothing different to those in common use: I shall endeavour, without prejudice to any one else, to explain myself to your Excellency showing your Lordship my secrets, and then offering them to your best pleasure and approbation to work with effect at opportune moments as well as all those things which, in part, shall be briefly noted below.

1) I have a sort of extremely light and strong bridges, adapted to be most easily carried, and with them you may pursue, and at any time flee from the enemy; and others, secure and indestructible by fire and battle, easy and convenient to lift and place. Also methods of burning and destroying those of the enemy.

2) I know how, when a place is besieged, to take the water out of the trenches, and make endless variety of bridges, and covered ways and ladders, and other machines pertaining to such expeditions.

3) Item. If, by reason of the height of the banks, or the strength of the place and its position, it is impossible, when besieging a place, to avail oneself of the plan of bombardment, I have methods for destroying every rock or other fortress, even if it were founded on a rock, &c.

4) Again I have kinds of mortars; most convenient and easy to carry; and with these can fling small stones almost resembling a storm; and with the smoke of these causing great terror to the enemy, to his great detriment and confusion.

9) [8] And when the fight should be at sea I have kinds of many machines most efficient for offence and defence; and vessels which will resist the attack of the largest guns and powder and fumes.

5) Item. I have means by secret and tortuous mines and ways, made without noise to reach a designated [spot], even if it were needed to pass under a trench or a river.

6) Item. I will make covered chariots, safe and unattackable which, entering among the enemy with their artillery, there is no body of men so great but they would break them. And behind these, infantry could follow quite unhurt and without any hindrance.

7) Item. In case of need I will make big guns, mortars and light ordnance of fine and useful forms, out of the common type.

8) Where the operation of bombardment should fail, I would contrive catapults, mangonels, trabocchi and other machines of marvellous efficacy and not in common use. And in short, according to the variety of cases, I can contrive various and endless means of offence and defence.

10) In time of peace I believe I can give perfect satisfaction and to the equal of any other in architecture and the composition of buildings public and private; and in guiding water from one place to another.

Item: I can carry out sculpture in marble, bronze or clay, and also in painting whatever may be done, and as well as any other, be he whom he may.

[32] Again, the bronze horse may be taken in hand, which is to be to the immortal glory and eternal honour of the prince your father of happy memory, and of the illustrious house of Sforza.

And if any one of the above-named things seem to any one to be impossible or not feasible, I am most ready to make the experiment in your park, or in whatever place may please your Excellency--to whom I commend myself with the utmost humility &c.

1341.

To my illustrious Lord, Lodovico, Duke of Bari, Leonardo da Vinci of Florence-- Leonardo.

[Footnote: Evidently a note of the superscription of a letter to the Duke, and written, like the foregoing from left to right. The manuscript containing it is of the year 1493. Lodovico was not proclaimed and styled Duke of Milan till September 1494. The Dukedom of Bari belonged to the Sforza family till 1499.]

1342.

You would like to see a model which will prove useful to you and to me, also it will be of use to those who will be the cause of our usefulness.

[Footnote: 1342. 1343. These two notes occur in the same not very voluminous MS. as the former one and it is possible that they are fragments of the same letter. By the Modello, the equestrian statue is probably meant, particularly as the model of this statue was publicly exhibited in this very year, 1493, on tne occasion of the marriage of the Emperor Maximilian with Bianca Maria Sforza.]

1343.

There are here, my Lord, many gentlemen who will undertake this expense among them, if they are allowed to enjoy the use of admission to the waters, the mills, and the passage of vessels and when it is sold to them the price will be repaid to them by the canal of Martesana.

1344.

I am greatly vexed to be in necessity, but I still more regret that this should be the cause of the hindrance of my wish which is always disposed to obey your Excellency.

Perhaps your Excellency did not give further orders to Messer Gualtieri, believing that I had money enough.

I am greatly annoyed that you should have found me in necessity, and that my having to earn my living should have hindered me ...

[12] It vexes me greatly that having to earn my living has forced me to interrupt the work and to attend to small matters, instead of following up the work which your Lordship entrusted to me. But I hope in a short time to have earned so much that I may carry it out quietly to the satisfaction of your Excellency, to whom I commend myself; and if your Lordship thought that I had money, your Lordship was deceived. I had to feed 6 men for 56 months, and have had 50 ducats.

1345.

And if any other comission is given me

by any ...

of the reward of my service. Because I am

not [able] to be ...

things assigned because meanwhile they

have ... to them ...

... which they well may settle rather than I ... not my art which I wish to change and ... given some clothing if I dare a sum ...

My Lord, I knowing your Excellency's

mind to be occupied ...

to remind your Lordship of my small matters

and the arts put to silence

that my silence might be the cause of making

your Lordship scorn ...

my life in your service. I hold myself ever

in readiness to obey ...

[Footnote 11: See No. 723, where this passage is repeated.]

Of the horse I will say nothing because

I know the times [are bad]

to your Lordship how I had still to receive

two years' salary of the ...

with the two skilled workmen who are constantly in my pay and at my cost that at last I found myself advanced the

said sum about 15 lire ...

works of fame by which I could show to

those who shall see it that I have been

everywhere, but I do not know where I could bestow my work [more] ...

[Footnote 17: See No. 1344 l. 12.] I, having been working to gain my

living ...

I not having been informed what it is, I find

myself ...

[Footnote 19: In April, 1498, Leonardo was engaged in painting the Saletta Nigra of the Castello at Milan. (See G. MONGERI, l'Arte in Milano, 1872, p. 417.)]

remember the commission to paint the

rooms ...

I conveyed to your Lordship only requesting

you ...

[Footnote: The paper on which this is written is torn down the middle; about half of each line remains.]

Draft of letter to be sent to Piacenza (1346. 1347).

[Footnote: 1346. 1347. Piacenza belonged to Milan. The Lord spoken of in this letter, is no doubt Lodovico il Moro. One may infer from the concluding sentence (No. 1346, l. 33. 34 and No. 1347), that Leonardo, who no doubt compiled this letter, did not forward it to Piacenza himself, but gave it to some influential patron, under whose name and signature a copy of it was sent to the Commission.]

1346.

Magnificent Commissioners of Buildings I, understanding that your Magnificencies have made up your minds to make certain great works in bronze, will remind you of certain things: first that you should not be so hasty or so quick to give the commission, lest by this haste it should become impossible to select a good model and a good master; and some man of small merit may be chosen, who by his insufficiency may cause you to be abused by your descendants, judging that this age was but ill supplied with men of good counsel and with good masters; seeing that other cities, and chiefly the city of the Florentines, has been as it were in these very days, endowed with beautiful and grand works in bronze; among which are the doors of their Baptistery. And this town of Florence, like Piacenza, is a place of intercourse, through which many foreigners pass; who, seeing that the works are fine and of good quality, carry away a good impression, and will say that that city is well filled with worthy inhabitants, seeing the works which bear witness to their opinion; and on the other hand, I say seeing so much metal expended and so badly wrought, it were less shame to the city if the doors had been of plain wood; because, the material, costing so little, would not seem to merit any great outlay of skill...

Now the principal parts which are sought for in cities are their cathedrals, and of these the first things which strike the eye are the doors, by which one passes into these churches.

Beware, gentlemen of the Commission, lest too great speed in your determination, and so much haste to expedite the entrusting of so great a work as that which I hear you have ordered, be the cause that that which was intended for the honour of God and of men should be turned to great dishonour of your judgments, and of your city, which, being a place of mark, is the resort and gathering-place of innumerable foreigners. And this dishonour would result if by your lack of diligence you were to put your trust in some vaunter, who by his tricks or by favour shown to him here should obtain such work from you, by which lasting and very great shame would result to him and to you. Thus I cannot help being angry when I consider what men those are who have conferred with you as wishing to undertake this great work without thinking of their sufficiency for it, not to say more. This one is a potter, that one a maker of cuirasses, this one is a bell-founder, another a bell ringer, and one is even a bombardier; and among them one in his Lordship's service, who boasted that he was the gossip of Messer Ambrosio Ferrere [Footnote 26: Messer Ambrogio Ferrere was Farmer of the Customs under the Duke. Piacenza at that time belonged to Milan.], who has some power and who has made him some promises; and if this were not enough he would mount on horseback, and go to his Lord and obtain such letters that you could never refuse [to give] him the work. But consider where masters of real talent and fit for such work are brought when they have to compete with such men as these. Open your eyes and look carefully lest your money should be spent in buying your own disgrace. I can declare to you that from that place you will procure none but average works of inferior and coarse masters. There is no capable man,--[33] and you may believe me,--except Leonardo the Florentine, who is making the equestrian statue in bronze of the Duke Francesco and who has no need to bring himself into notice, because he has work for all his life time; and I doubt, whether being so great a work, he will ever finish it [34].

The miserable painstakers ... with what hope may they expect a reward of their merit?

1347.

There is one whom his Lordship invited from Florence to do this work and who is a worthy master, but with so very much business he will never finish it; and you may imagine that a difference there is to be seen between a beautiful object and an ugly one. Quote Pliny.

Letter to the Cardinal Ippolito d' Este.

1348.

[Footnote: This letter addressed to the Cardinal Ippolito d'Este is here given from Marchese G. CAMPORI'S publication: Nuovi documenti per la Vita di Leonardo da Vinci. Atti e Memorie delle R. R. Deputazioni di Storia patria per la provincie modenesi e parmenesi, Vol. III. It is the only text throughout this work which I have not myself examined and copied from the original. The learned discoverer of this letter--the only letter from Leonardo hitherto known as having been sent--adds these interesting remarks: Codesto Cardinale nato ad Ercole I. nel 1470, arcivescovo di Strigonia a sette anni, poi d'Agra, aveva conseguito nel 1497 la pingue ed ambita cattedra di Milano, la dove avra conosciuto il Vinci, sebbene il poco amore ch'ei professava alle arti lasci credere che le proteste di servitu di Leonardo piu che a gratitudine per favori ricevuti e per opere a lui allogate, accennino a speranza per un favore che si aspetta. Notabile e ancora in questo prezioso documento la ripetuta signatura del grande artista 'che si scrive Vincio e Vincius, non da Vinci come si tiene comunemente, sebbene l'una e l'altra possano valere a significare cosi il casato come il paese; restando a sapere se il nome del paese di Vinci fosse assunto a cognome della famiglia di Leonardo nel qual supposto piu propriamento avrebbe a chiamarsi Leonardo Vinci, o Vincio (latinamente Vincius) com'egli stesso amo segnarsi in questa lettera, e come scrissero parecchi contenporanei di lui, il Casio, il Cesariano, Geoffrey Tory, il Gaurico, il Bandello, Raffaelle Maffei, il Paciolo. Per ultimo non lascero d'avvertire come la lettera del Vinci e assai ben conservata, di nitida e larga scrittura in forma pienemente corrispondente a quella dei suoi manoscritti, vergata all'uso comune da sinistra a destra, anziche contrariamente come fu suo costume; ma indubbiamente autentica e fornita della menzione e del suggello che fresca ancora conserva l'impronta di una testa di profilo da un picciolo antico cammeo. (Compare No. 1368, note.)]

Most Illustrious and most Reverend Lord.

> The Lord Ippolito, Cardinal of Este
> at Ferrare.

Most Illustrious and most Reverend Lord.

I arrived from Milan but a few days since and finding that my elder brother refuses to carry into effect a will, made three years ago when my father died--as also, and no less, because I would not fail in a matter I esteem most important--I cannot forbear to crave of your most Reverend Highness a letter of recommendation and favour to Ser Raphaello Hieronymo, at present one of the illustrious members of the Signoria before whom my cause is being argued; and more particularly it has been laid by his Excellency the Gonfaloniere into the hands of the said Ser Raphaello, that his Worship may have to decide and end it before the festival of All Saints. And therefore, my Lord, I entreat you, as urgently as I know how and am able, that your Highness will write a letter to the said Ser Raphaello in that admirable and pressing manner which your Highness can use, recommending to him Leonardo Vincio, your most humble servant as I am, and shall always be; requesting him and pressing him not only to do me justice but to do so with despatch; and I have not the least doubt, from many things that I hear, that Ser Raphaello, being most affectionately devoted to your Highness, the matter will issue ad votum. And this I shall attribute to your most Reverend Highness' letter, to whom I once more humbly commend myself. Et bene valeat.

Florence XVIIIa 7bris 1507. E. V. R. D.

your humble servant Leonardus Vincius, pictor.

Draft of Letter to the Governor of Milan.

1349.

I am afraid lest the small return I have made for the great benefits, I have received from your Excellency, have not made you somewhat angry with me, and that this is why to so many letters which I have written to your Lordship I have never had an answer. I now send Salai to explain to your Lordship that I am almost at an end of the litigation I had with my brother; that I hope to find myself with you this Easter, and to carry with me two pictures of two Madonnas of different sizes. These were done for our most Christian King, or for whomsoever your Lordship may please. I should be very glad to know on my return thence where I may have to reside, for I would not give any more trouble to your Lordship. Also, as I have worked for the most Christian King, whether my salary is to continue or not. I wrote to the President as to that water which the king granted me, and which I was not put in possession of because at that time there was a dearth in the canal by reason of the great droughts and because [Footnote:Compare Nos. 1009 and 1010. Leonardo has noted the payment of the pension from the king in 1505.] its outlets were not regulated; but he certainly promised me that when this was done I should be put in possession. Thus I pray your Lordship that you will take so much trouble, now that these outlets are regulated, as to remind the President of my matter; that is, to give me possession of this water, because on my return I hope to make there instruments and other things which will greatly please our most Christian King. Nothing else occurs to me. I am always yours to command. [Footnote:1349. Charles d'Amboise, Marechal de Chaumont, was Governor of Milan under Louis XII. Leonardo was in personal communication with him so early as in 1503. He was absent from Milan in the autumn of 1506 and from October I5I0--when he besieged Pope Julius II. in Bologna--till his death, which took place at Correggio, February 11, 1511. Francesco Vinci, Leonardo's uncle, died--as Amoretti tells us--in the winter of I5I0-11 (or according to Uzielli in 1506?), and Leonardo remained in Florence for business connected with his estate. The letter written with reference to this affair, No. 1348, is undoubtedly earlier than the letters Nos. 1349 and 1350. Amoretti tells us, Memorie Storiche, ch. II, that the following note existed on the same leaf in MS. C. A. I have not however succeeded in finding it. The passage runs thus: Jo sono quasi al fine del mio letizio che io o con mie fratetgli ... Ancora ricordo a V. Excia la facenda che o cum Ser Juliana mio Fratello capo delli altri fratelli ricordandoli come se offerse di conciar le cose nostre fra noi fratelli del comune della eredita de mio Zio, e quelli costringa alla expeditione, quale conteneva la lettera che lui me mando.]

Drafts of Letters to the Superintendent of Canals and to Fr. Melzi.

1350.

Magnificent President, I am sending thither Salai, my pupil, who is the bearer of this, and from him you will hear by word of mouth the cause of my...

Magnificent President, I...

Magnificent President:--Having ofttimes remembered the proposals made many times to me by your Excellency, I take the liberty of writing to remind your Lordship of the promise made to me at my last departure, that is the possession of the twelve inches of water granted to me by the most Christian King. Your Lordship knows that I did not enter into possession, because at that time when it was given to me there was a dearth of water in the canal, as well by reason of the great drought as also because the outlets were not regulated; but your Excellency promised me that as soon as this was done, I should have my rights. Afterwards hearing that the canal was complete I wrote several times to your Lordship and to Messer Girolamo da Cusano, who has in his keeping the deed of this gift; and so also I wrote to Corigero and never had a reply. I now send thither Salai, my pupil, the bearer of this, to whom your Lordship may tell by word of mouth all that happened in the matter about which I petition your Excellency. I expect to go thither this Easter since I am nearly at the end of my lawsuit, and I will take with me two pictures of our Lady which I have begun, and at the present time have brought them on to a very good end; nothing else occurs to me.

My Lord the love which your Excellency has always shown me and the benefits that I have constantly received from you I have hitherto...

I am fearful lest the small return I have made for the great benefits I have received from your Excellency may not have made you somewhat annoyed with me. And this is why, to many letters which I have written to your Excellency I have never had an answer. I now send to you Salai to explain to your Excellency that I am almost at the end of my litigation with my brothers, and that I hope to be with you this Easter and carry with me two pictures on which are two Madonnas of different sizes which I began for the most Christian King, or for whomsoever you please. I should be very glad to know where, on my return from this place, I shall have to reside, because I do not wish to give more trouble to your Lordship; and then, having worked for the most Christian King, whether my salary is to be continued or not. I write to the President as to the water that the king granted me of which I had not been put in possession by reason of the dearth in the canal, caused by the great drought and because its outlets were not regulated; but he promised me certainly that as soon as the regulation was made, I should be put in possession of it; I therefore pray you that, if you should meet the said President, you would be good enough, now that the outlets are regulated, to remind the said President to cause me to be put in possession of that water, since I understand it is in great measure in his power. Nothing else occurs to me; always yours to command.

Good day to you Messer Francesco. Why, in God's name, of all the letters I have written to you, have you never answered one. Now wait till I come, by God, and I shall make you write so much that perhaps you will become sick of it.

Dear Messer Francesco. I am sending thither Salai to learn from His Magnificence the President to what end the regulation of the water has come since, at my departure this regulation of the outlets of the canal had been ordered, because His Magnificence the President promised me that as soon as this was done I should be satisfied. It is now some time since I heard that the canal was in order, as also its outlets, and I immediately wrote to the President and to you, and then I repeated it, and never had an answer. So you will have the goodness to answer me as to that which happened, and as I am not to hurry the matter, would you take the trouble, for the love of me, to urge the President a little, and also Messer Girolamo Cusano, to whom you will commend me and offer my duty to his Magnificence.

[Footnote: 1350. 28-36. Draft of a letter to Francesco Melzi, born 1493--a youth therefore of about 17 in 1510. Leonardo addresses his young friend as "Messer", as being the son of a noble house. Melzi practised art under Leonardo as a dilettante and not as a pupil, like Cesare da Sesto and others (See LERMOLIEFF, Die Galerien &c., p. 476).]

Drafts of a letter to Giuliano de' Medici (1351-1352).

1351.

[Most illustrious Lord. I greatly rejoice most Illustrious Lord at your...]

I was so greatly rejoiced, most illustrious Lord, by the desired restoration of your health, that it almost had the effect that [my own health recovered]--[I have got through my illness]--my own illness left me-- --of your Excellency's almost restored health. But I am extremely vexed that I have not been able completely to satisfy the wishes of your Excellency, by reason of the wickedness of that deceiver, for whom I left nothing undone which could be done for him by me and by which I might be of use to him; and in the first place his allowances were paid to him before the time, which I believe he would willingly deny, if I had not the writing signed by myself and the interpreter. And I, seeing that he did not work for me unless he had no work to do for others, which he was very careful in solliciting, invited him to dine with me, and to work afterwards near me, because, besides the saving of expense, he

[Footnote 1351. 1353: It is clear from the contents of this notes that they refer to Leonardo's residence in Rome in 1513-1515. Nor can there be any doubt that they were addressed to Leonardo's patron at the time: Giuliano de' Medici, third son of Lorenzo the Magnificent and brother of Pope Leo X (born 1478). In 1512 he became the head of the Florentine Republic. The Pope invited him to Rome, where he settled; in 1513 he was named patrician with much splendid ceremonial. The medal struck in honour of the event bears the words MAG. IVLIAN. MEDICES. Leonardo too uses the style "Magnifico", in his letter. Compare also No. 1377.

GINO CAPPONI (Storia della Repubblica di Firenze, Vol. III, p. 139) thus describes the character of Giuliano de' Medici, who died in 1516: Era il migliore della famiglia, di vita placida, grande spenditore, tenendo intorno a se uomini ingegnosi, ed ogni nuova cosa voleva provare.

See too GREGOROVIUS, Geschichte der Stadi Rom, VIII (book XIV. III, 2): Die Luftschlosser furstlicher Grosse, wozu ihn der Papst hatte erheben wollen zerfielen. Julian war der edelste aller damaligen Medici, ein Mensch von innerlicher Richtung, unbefriedigt durch das Leben, mitten im Sonnenglanz der Herrlichkeit Leo's X. eine dunkle Gestalt die wie ein Schatten voruberzog. Giuliano lived in the Vatican, and it may be safely inferred from No. 1352 l. 2, and No. 1353 l. 4, that Leonardo did the same.

From the following unpublished notice in the Vatican archives, which M. Eug. Muntz, librarian of the Ecole des Beaux arts, Paris, has done me the favour to communicate to me, we get a more accurate view of Leonardo's relation to the often named GIORGIO TEDESCO:

Nota delle provisione (sic) a da pagare per me in nome del nostro ill. S. Bernardo Bini e chompa di Roma, e prima della illma sua chonsorte ogni mese d. 800.

A Ldo da Vinci per sua provisione d. XXXIII, e piu d. VII al detto per la provisione di Giorgio tedescho, che sono in tutto d. 40.

From this we learn, that seven ducats formed the German's monthly wages, but according to No. 1353 l. 7 he pretended that eight ducats had been agreed upon.]

would acquire the Italian language. He always promised, but would never do so. And this I did also, because that Giovanni, the German who makes the mirrors, was there always in the workshop, and wanted to see and to know all that was being done there and made it known outside ... strongly criticising it; and because he dined with those of the Pope's guard, and then they went out with guns killing birds among the ruins; and this went on from after dinner till the evening; and when I sent Lorenzo to urge him to work he said that he would not have so many masters over him, and that his work was for your Excellency's Wardrobe; and thus two months passed and so it went on; and one day finding Gian Niccolo of the Wardrobe and asking whether the German had finished the work for your Magnificence, he told me this was not true, but only that he had given him two guns to clean. Afterwards, when I had urged him farther, be left the workshop and began to work in his room, and lost much time in making another pair of pincers and files and other tools with screws; and there he worked at mills for twisting silk which he hid when any one of my people went in, and with a thousand oaths and mutterings, so that none of them would go there any more.

I was so greatly rejoiced, most Illustrious Lord, by the desired restoration of your health, that my own illness almost left me. But I am greatly vexed at not having been able to completely satisfy your Excellency's wishes by reason of the wickedness of that German deceiver, for whom I left nothing undone by which I could have hope to please him; and secondly I invited him to lodge and board with me, by which means I should constantly see the work he was doing and with greater ease correct his errors while, besides this, he would learn the Italian tongue, by means of which be could with more ease talk without an interpreter; his moneys were always given him in advance of the time when due. Afterwards he wanted to have the models finished in wood, just as they were to be in iron, and wished to carry them away to his own country. But this I refused him, telling him that I would give him, in drawing, the breadth, length, height and form of what he had to do; and so we remained in ill-will.

The next thing was that he made himself another workshop and pincers and tools in his room where he slept, and there he worked for others; afterwards he went to dine with the Swiss of the guard, where there are idle fellows, in which he beat them all; and most times they went two or three together with guns, to shoot birds among the ruins, and this went on till evening.

At last I found how this master Giovanni the mirror-maker was he who had done it all, for two reasons; the first because he had said that my coming here had deprived him of the countenance and favour of your Lordship which always... The other is that he said that his iron-workers' rooms suited him for working at his mirrors, and of this he gave proof; for besides making him my enemy, he made him sell all he had and leave his workshop to him, where he works with a number of workmen making numerous mirrors to send to the fairs.

1352.

I was so greatly rejoiced, most Illustrious Lord, by the wished for recovery of your health, that my own ills have almost left me; and I say God be praised for it. But it vexes me greatly that I have not been able completely to satisfy your Excellency's wishes by reason of the wickedness of that German deceiver, for whom I left nothing undone by which I could hope to please him; and secondly I invited him to lodge and board with me, by which means I should see constantly the work he was doing, for which purpose I would have a table fixed at the foot of one of these windows, where he could work with the file and finish the things made below; and so I should constantly see the work he might do, and it could be corrected with greater ease.

Draft of letter written at Rome.

1353.

This other hindered me in anatomy, blaming it before the Pope; and likewise at the hospital; and he has filled [4] this whole Belvedere with workshops for mirrors; and he did the same thing in Maestro Giorgio's room. He said that he had been promised [7] eight ducats every month, beginning with the first day, when he set out, or at latest when he spoke with you; and that you agreed.

Seeing that he seldom stayed in the workshop, and that he ate a great deal, I sent him word that, if he liked I could deal with him separately for each thing that he might make, and would give him what we might agree to be a fair valuation. He took counsel with his neighbour and gave up his room, selling every thing, and went to find...

Miscellaneous Records (1354. 1355).

1354.

[Footnote: A puzzling passage, meant, as it would seem, for a jest. Compare the description of Giants in Dante, Inf. XXI and XXII. Perhaps Leonardo had the Giant Antaeus in his mind. Of him the myth relates that he was a son of Ge, that he fed on lions; that he hunted in Libya and killed the inhabitants. He enjoyed the peculiarity of renewing his strength whenever he fell and came in contact with his mother earth; but that Hercules lifted him up and so conquered and strangled him. Lucan gives a full account of the struggle. Pharsalia IV, 617. The reading of this passage, which is very indistinctly written, is in many places doubtful.]

Dear Benedetto de' Pertarti. When the proud giant fell because of the bloody and miry state of the ground it was as though a mountain had fallen so that the country shook as with an earthquake, and terror fell on Pluto in hell. From the violence of the shock he lay as stunned on the level ground. Suddenly the people, seeing him as one killed by a thunderbolt, turned back; like ants running wildly over the body of the fallen oak, so these rushing over his ample limbs.......... them with frequent wounds; by which, the giant being roused and feeling himself almost covered by the multitude, he suddenly perceives the smarting of the stabs, and sent forth a roar which sounded like a terrific clap of thunder; and placing his hands on the ground he raised his terrible face: and having lifted one hand to his head he found it full of men and rabble sticking to it like the minute creatures which not unfrequently are found there; wherefore with a shake of his head he sends the men flying through the air just as hail does when driven by the fury of the winds. Many of these men were found to be dead; stamping with his feet.

And clinging to his hair, and striving to hide in it, they behaved like sailors in a storm, who run up the ropes to lessen the force of the wind [by taking in sail].

News of things from the East.

Be it known to you that in the month of June there appeared a Giant, who came from the Lybian desert... mad with rage like ants.... struck down by the rude.

This great Giant was born in Mount Atlas and was a hero ... and had to fight against the Egyptians and Arabs, Medes and Persians. He lived in the sea on whales, grampuses and ships.

Mars fearing for his life took refuge under the... of Jove.

And at the great fall it seemed as though the whole province quaked.

1355.

This spirit returns to the brain whence it had departed, with a loud voice and with these words, it moved...

And if any man though he may have wisdom or goodness ....

[Footnote: This passage, very difficult to decipher, is on the reverse of a drawing at Windsor, Pl. CXXII, which possibly has some connection with it. The drawing is slightly reduced in this reproduction; the original being 25 cm. high by 19 cm. wide.]

O blessed and happy spirit whence comest thou? Well have I known this man, much against my will. This one is a receptacle of villainy; he is a perfect heap of the utmost ingratitude combined with every vice. But of what use is it to fatigue myself with vain words? Nothing is to be found in them but every form of sin ... And if there should be found among them any that possesses any good, they will not be treated differently to myself by other men; and in fine, I come to the conclusion that it is bad if they are hostile, and worse if they are friendly.

Miscellaneous drafts of letters and personal records (1356--1368).

1356.

All the ills that are or ever were, if they could be set to work by him, would not satisfy the desires of his iniquitous soul; and I could not in any length of time describe his nature to you, but I conclude...

1357.

I know one who, having promised me much, less than my due, being disappointed of his presumptuous desires, has tried to deprive me of all my friends; and as he has found them wise and not pliable to his will, he has menaced me that, having found means of denouncing me, he would deprive me of my benefactors. Hence I have informed your Lordship of this, to the end [that this man who wishes to sow the usual scandals, may find no soil fit for sowing the thoughts and deeds of his evil nature] so that he, trying to make your Lordship, the instrument of his iniquitous and maliceous nature may be disappointed of his desire.

1358.

[Footnote: Below this text we read gusstino--Giustino and in another passage on the same page Justin is quoted (No. 1210, 1. 48). The two have however no real connection.]

And in this case I know that I shall make few enemies seeing that no one will believe what I can say of him; for they are but few whom his vices have disgusted, and he only dislikes those men whose natures are contrary to those vices. And many hate their fathers, and break off friendship with those who reprove their vices; and he will not permit any examples against them, nor any advice.

If you meet with any one who is virtuous do not drive him from you; do him honour, so that he may not have to flee from you and be reduced to hiding in hermitages, or caves or other solitary places to escape from your treachery; if there is such an one among you do him honour, for these are our Saints upon earth; these are they who deserve statues from us, and images; but remember that their images are not to be eaten by you, as is still done in some parts of India [Footnote 15: In explanation of this passage I have received the following communication from Dr. G. W. LEITNER of Lahore: "So far as Indian customs are known to us, this practice spoken of by Leonardo as 'still existing in some parts of India' is perfectly unknown; and it is equally opposed to the spirit of Hinduism, Mohammedanism and Sikhism. In central Thibet the ashes of the dead, when burnt, are mixed with dough, and small figures--usually of Buddha--are stamped out of them and some are laid in the grave while others are distributed among the relations. The custom spoken of by Leonardo may have prevailed there but I never heard of it." Possibly Leonardo refers here to customs of nations of America.] where, when the images have according to them, performed some miracle, the priests cut them in pieces, being of wood, and give them to all the people of the country, not without payment; and each one grates his portion very fine, and puts it upon the first food he eats; and thus believes that by faith he has eaten his saint who then preserves him from all perils. What do you think here, Man, of your own species? Are you so wise as you believe yourselves to be? Are these things to be done by men?

1359.

As I told you in past days, you know that I am without any.... Francesco d'Antonio. Bernardo di Maestro Jacopo.

1360.

Tell me how the things happened.

1361.

j lorezo\\\ 2 inbiadali\\\ 3 inferri de\\\ 4in lorezo\\\ 5[inno abuil]\\ 6 in acocatu\\\ 7 per la sella\\\ 8colte di lor\\\ 9v cavallott\\\ l0el uiagg\\\ lIal\\\ l2a lurez\\\ 13in biada\\\ 14inferri\\\\ 15abuss\\\ 16in viagg\\\ 17alorz\\\ [Footnote: This seems to be the beginning of a letter, but only the first words of the lines have been preserved, the leaf being torn down the middle. No translation is possible.]

1362.

And so may it please our great Author that I may demonstrate the nature of man and his customs, in the way I describe his figure.

[Footnote: A preparatory note for the passage given as No. 798, 11. 41--42.]

1363.

This writing distinctly about the kite seems to be my destiny, because among the first recollections of my infancy, it seemed to me that, as I was in my cradle, a kite came to me and opened my mouth with its tail, and struck me several times with its tail inside my lips.

[Footnote: This note probably refers to the text No. 1221.]

1364.

[When I did well, as a boy you used to put me in prison. Now if I do it being grown up, you will do worse to me.]

1365.

Tell me if anything was ever done.

1366.

Tell me if ever I did a thing which me ....

1367.

Do not reveal, if liberty is precious to you; my face is the prison of love.

[Footnote: This note seems to be a quotation.]

1368.

Maestro Leonardo of Florence.

[Footnote: So Leonardo writes his name on a sheet with sundry short notes, evidently to try a pen. Compare the signature with those in Nos. 1341, 1348 and 1374 (see also No. 1346, l. 33). The form "Lionardo" does not occur in the autographs. The Portrait of the Master in the Royal Library at Turin, which is reproduced--slightly diminished--on Pl. I, has in the original two lines of writing underneath; one in red chalk of two or three words is partly effaced: lionardo it... lm (or lai?); the second written in pencil is as follows: fatto da lui stesso assai vecchio. In both of these the writing is very like the Master's, but is certainly only an imitation.]

Notes bearing Dates (1369--1378).

1369.

The day of Santa Maria della Neve [of the Snows] August the 2nd 1473. [Footnote: W. An. I. 1368. 1369. This date is on a drawing of a rocky landscape. See Chronique des Arts 1881 no. 23: Leonard de Vinci a-t-il ete au Righi le 5 aout 1473? letter by H. de Geymuller. The next following date in the MSS. is 1478 (see No. 663).

1370.

On the 2nd of April 1489, book entitled 'Of the human figure'. [Footnote: While the letters in the MS. notes of 1473 and 1478 are very ornate, this note and the texts on anatomy on the same sheet (for instance No. 805) are in the same simple hand as we see on Pl. CXVI and CXIX. No 1370 is the only dated note of the years between 1480 and 1489, and the characters are in all essential points identical with those that we see in the latest manuscripts written in France (compare the facsimiles on Pl. CXV and p. 254), so that it is hardly possible to determine exactly the date of a manuscript from the style of the handwriting, if it does not betray the peculiarities of style as displayed in the few notes dated previous to l480.--Compare the facsimile of the manuscripts 1479 on Pl.LXII, No. 2; No. 664, note, Vol. I p. 346. This shows already a marked simplicity as compared with the calligraphy of l478.

The text No. 720 belongs to the year 1490; No. 1510 to the year 1492; No. 1459, No. 1384 and No. 1460 to the year 1493; No. 1463, No. 1517, No. 1024, 1025 and 1461 to the year 1494; Nos. 1523 and 1524 to the year 1497.

1371.

On the 1st of August 1499, I wrote here of motion and of weight.

[Footnote:1371. Scrissi qui. Leonardo does not say where; still we may assume that it was not in Milan. Amoretti writes, Memorie Storiche, chap. XIX: Sembra pertanto che non nel 1499 ma nel 1500, dopo il ritorno e la prigionia del duca, sia da qui partito Lionardo per andare a Firenze; ed e quindi probabile, che i mesi di governo nuovo e incerto abbia passati coll' amico suo Francesco Melzi a Vaprio, ove meglio che altrove studiar potea la natura, e soprattutta le acque, e l'Adda specialmente, che gia era stato l'ogetto delle sue idrostatiche ricerche. At that time Melzi was only six years of age. The next date is 1502; to this year belong No. 1034, 1040, 1042, 1048 and 1053. The note No. 1525 belongs to the year 1503.]

1372.

On the 9th of July 1504, Wednesday, at seven o'clock, died Ser Piero da Vinci, notary at the Palazzo del Podesta, my father, --at seven o'clock, being eighty years old, leaving behind ten sons and two daughters.

[Footnote: This statement of Ser Piero's age contradicts that of the Riassunto della portata di Antonio da Vinci (Leonardo's grandfather), who speaks of Ser Piero as being thirty years old in 1457; and that of the Riassunto della portata di Ser Piero e Francesco, sons of Antonia da Vinci, where Ser Piero is mentioned as being forty in 1469. These documents were published by G. UZIELLI, Ricerche intorno a L. da Vinci, Firenze, 1872, pp. 144 and 146. Leonardo was, as is well known, a natural son. His mother 'La Catarina' was married in 1457 to Acchattabriga di Piero del Vaccha da Vinci. She died in 1519. Leonardo never mentions her in the Manuscripts. In the year of Leonardo's birth Ser Piero married Albiera di Giovanni Amadoci, and after her death at the age of thirty eight he again married, Francesca, daughter of Ser Giovanni Lanfredi, then only fifteen. Their children were Leonardo's halfbrothers, Antonio (b. 1476), Ser Giuliano (b. 1479), Lorenzo (b. 1484), a girl, Violante (b. 1485), and another boy Domenico (b. 1486); Domenico's descendants still exist as a family. Ser Piero married for the third time Lucrezia di Guglielmo Cortigiani by whom he had six children: Margherita (b. 1491), Benedetto (b. 1492), Pandolfo (b. 1494), Guglielmo (b. 1496), Bartolommeo (b. 1497), and Giovanni) date of birth unknown). Pierino da Vinci the sculptor (about 1520-1554) was the son of Bartolommeo, the fifth of these children. The dates of their deaths are not known, but we may infer from the above passage that they were all still living in 1505.]

1373.

On Wednesday at seven o'clock died Ser Piero da Vinci on the 9th of July 1504.

[Footnote: This and the previous text it may be remarked are the only mention made by Leonardo of his father; Nos. 1526, 1527 and No. 1463 are of the year 1504.]

1374.

Begun by me, Leonardo da Vinci, on the l2th of July 1505.

[Footnote: Thus he writes on the first page of the MS. The title is on the foregoing coversheet as follows: Libro titolato disstrafformatione coe (cioe) d'un corpo nvn (in un) altro sanza diminuitione e acresscemento di materia.]

1375.

Begun at Milan on the l2th of September 1508.

[Footnote: No. 1528 and No. 1529 belong to the same year. The text Vol. I, No. 4 belongs to the following year 1509 (1508 old style); so also does No. 1009.-- Nos. 1022, 1057 and 1464 belong to 1511.]

1376.

On the 9th of January 1513.

[Footnote: No. 1465 belongs to the same year. No. 1065 has the next date 1514.]

1377.

The Magnifico Giuliano de' Medici left Rome on the 9th of January 1515, just at daybreak, to take a wife in Savoy; and on the same day fell the death of the king of France.

[Footnote: Giuliano de Medici, brother to Pope Leo X.; see note to Nos. 1351-1353. In February, 1515, he was married to Filiberta, daughter of Filippo, Duke of Savoy, and aunt to Francis I, Louis XII's successor on the throne of France. Louis XII died on Jan. 1st, and not on Jan. 9th as is here stated.-- This addition is written in paler ink and evidently at a later date.]

1378.

On the 24th of June, St John's day, 1518 at Amboise, in the palace of...

[Footnote: Castello del clli. The meaning of this word is obscure; it is perhaps not written at full length.]

XXII. Miscellaneous Notes.

The incidental memoranda scattered here and there throughout the MSS. can have been for the most part intelligible to the writer only; in many cases their meaning and connection are all the more obscure because we are in ignorance about the persons with whom Leonardo used to converse nor can we say what part he may have played in the various events of his time. Vasari and other early biographers give us a very superficial and far from accurate picture of Leonardo's private life. Though his own memoranda, referring for the most part to incidents of no permanent interest, do not go far towards supplying this deficiency, they are nevertheless of some importance and interest as helping us to solve the numerous mysteries in which the history of Leonardo's long life remains involved. We may at any rate assume, from Leonardo's having committed to paper notes on more or less trivial matters on his pupils, on his house-keeping, on various known and unknown personages, and a hundred other trifies--that at the time they must have been in some way important to him.

I have endeavoured to make these 'Miscellaneous Notes' as complete as possible, for in many cases an incidental memorandum will help to explain the meaning of some other note of a similar kind. The first portion of these notes (Nos. l379--l457), as well as those referring to his pupils and to other artists and artificers who lived in his house (1458--1468,) are arranged in chronological order. A considerable proportion of these notes belong to the period between 1490 and 1500, when Leonardo was living at Milan under the patronage of Lodovico il Moro, a time concerning which we have otherwise only very scanty information. If Leonardo did really--as has always been supposed,--spend also the greater part of the preceding decade in Milan, it seems hardly likely that we should not find a single note indicative of the fact, or referring to any event of that period, on the numerous loose leaves in his writing that exist. Leonardo's life in Milan between 1489 and 1500 must have been comparatively uneventful. The MSS. and memoranda of those years seem to prove that it was a tranquil period of intellectual and artistic labour rather than of bustling court life. Whatever may have been the fate of the MSS. and note books of the foregoing years--whether they were destroyed by Leonardo himself or have been lost--it is certainly strange that nothing whatever exists to inform us as to his life and doings in Milan earlier than the consecutive series of manuscripts which begin in the year 1489.

There is nothing surprising in the fact that the notes regarding his pupils are few and meagre. Excepting for the record of money transactions only very exceptional circumstances would have prompted him to make any written observations on the persons with whom he was in daily intercourse, among whom, of course, were his pupils. Of them all none is so frequently mentioned as Salai, but the character of the notes does not--as it seems to me--justify us in supposing that he was any thing more than a sort of factotum of Leonardo's (see 1519, note).

Leonardo's quotations from books and his lists of titles supply nothing more than a hint as to his occasional literary studies or recreations. It was evidently no part of his ambition to be deeply read (see Nrs. 10, 11, 1159) and he more than once expressly states (in various passages which will be found in the foregoing sections) that he did not recognise the authority of the Ancients, on scientific questions, which in his day was held paramount. Archimedes is the sole exception, and Leonardo frankly owns his admiration for the illustrious Greek to whose genius his own was so much akin (see No. 1476). All his notes on various authors, excepting those which have already been inserted in the previous section, have been arranged alphabetically for the sake of convenience (1469--1508).

The passages next in order contain accounts and inventories principally of household property. The publication of these--often very trivial entries--is only justifiable as proving that the wealth, the splendid mode of life and lavish expenditure which have been attributed to Leonardo are altogether mythical; unless we put forward the very improbable hypothesis that these notes as to money in hand, outlay and receipts, refer throughout to an exceptional state of his affairs, viz. when he was short of money.

The memoranda collected at the end (No. 1505--1565) are, in the original, in the usual writing, from left to right. Besides, the style of the handwriting is at variance with what we should expect it to be, if really Leonardo himself had written these notes. Most of them are to be found in juxtaposition with undoubtedly authentic writing of his. But this may be easily explained, if we take into account the fact, that Leonardo frequently wrote on loose sheets. He may therefore have occasionally used paper on which others had made short memoranda, for the most part as it would seem, for his use. At the end of all I have given Leonardo's will from the copy of it preserved in the Melzi Library. It has already been printed by Amoretti and by Uzielli. It is not known what has become of the original document.

Memoranda before 1500 (1379-l413).

1379.

Find Longhi and tell him that you wait for him at Rome and will go with him to Naples; make you pay the donation [Footnote 2: Libro di Vitolone see No. 1506 note.] and take the book by Vitolone, and the measurements of the public buildings. [3] Have two covered boxes made to be carried on mules, but bed-covers will be best; this makes three, of which you will leave one at Vinci. [4] Obtain the............. from Giovanni Lombardo the linen draper of Verona. Buy handkerchiefs and towels,.... and shoes, 4 pairs of hose, a jerkin of... and skins, to make new ones; the lake of Alessandro. [Footnote: 7 and fol. It would seem from the text that Leonardo intended to have instructions in painting on paper. It is hardly necessary to point out that the Art of illuminating was quite separate from that of painting.]

Sell what you cannot take with you. Get from Jean de Paris the method of painting in tempera and the way of making white [Footnote: The mysterious looking words, quite distinctly written, in line 1: ingol, amor a, ilopan a and on line 2: enoiganod al are obviously in cipher and the solution is a simple one; by reading them backwards we find for ingol: logni-probably longi, evidently the name of a person; for amor a: a Roma, for ilopan a: a Napoli. Leonardo has done the same in two passages treating on some secrets of his art Nos. 641 and 729, the only other places in which we find this cipher employed; we may therefore conclude that it was for the sake of secrecy that he used it.

There can be no doubt, from the tenor of this passage, that Leonardo projected a secret excursion to Naples. Nothing has hitherto been known of this journey, but the significance of the passage will be easily understood by a reference to the following notes, from which we may infer that Leonardo really had at the time plans for travelling further than Naples. From lines 3, 4 and 7 it is evident that he purposed, after selling every thing that was not easily portable, to leave a chest in the care of his relations at Vinci. His luggage was to be packed into two trunks especially adapted for transport by mules. The exact meaning of many sentences in the following notes must necessarily remain obscure. These brief remarks on small and irrelevant affairs and so forth are however of no historical value. The notes referring to the preparations for his journey are more intelligible.]

salt, and how to make tinted paper; sheets of paper folded up; and his box of colours; learn to work flesh colours in tempera, learn to dissolve gum lac, linseed ... white, of the garlic of Piacenza; take 'de Ponderibus'; take the works of Leonardo of Cremona. Remove the small furnace ... seed of lilies and of... Sell the boards of the support. Make him who stole it, give you the ... learn levelling and how much soil a man can dig out in a day.

1380.

This was done by Leone in the piazza of the castle with a chain and an arrow. [Footnote: This note must have been made in Milan; as we know from the date of the MS.]

1381.

NAMES OF ENGINEERS.

Callias of Rhodes, Epimachus the Athenian, Diogenes, a philosopher, of Rhodes, Calcedonius of Thrace, Febar of Tyre, Callimachus the architect, a master of fires. [Footnote: Callias, Architect of Aradus, mentioned by Vitruvius (X, 16, 5).--Epimachus, of Athens, invented a battering-enginee for Demetrius Poliorketes (Vitruvius X, 16, 4).--Callimachus, the inventor of the Corinthian capital (Vitr. IV, I, 9), and of the method of boring marble (Paus. I, 26, 7), was also famous for his casts in bronze (Plin. XXXIV, 8, 19). He invented a lamp for the temple of Athene Polias, on the Acropolis of Athens (Paus. I, 26, 7)-- The other names, here mentioned, cannot be identified.]

1382.

Ask maestro Lodovico for 'the conduits of water'. [Footnote: Condotti d'acqua. Possibly a book, a MS. or a map.]

1383.

... at Pistoja, Fioravante di Domenico at Florence is my most beloved friend, as though he were my [brother]. [Footnote: On the same sheet is the text No. 663.]

1384.

On the 16th day of July.

Caterina came on 16th day of July, 1493.

Messer Mariolo's Morel the Florentin, has a big horse with a fine neck and a beautiful head.

The white stallion belonging to the falconer has fine hind quarters; it is behind the Comasina Gate.

The big horse of Cermonino, of Signor Giulio. [Footnote: Compare Nos. 1522 and 1517. Caterina seems to have been his housekeeper.]

1385.

OF THE INSTRUMENT.

Any one who spends one ducat may take the instrument; and he will not pay more than half a ducat as a premium to the inventor of the instrument and one grosso to the workman every year. I do not want sub-officials. [Footnote: Refers perhaps to the regulation of the water in the canals.]

1386.

Maestro Giuliano da Marliano has a fine herbal. He lives opposite to Strami the Carpenters. [Footnote: Compare No. 616, note. 4. legnamiere (milanese dialect) = legnajuolo.]

1387.

Christofano da Castiglione who lives at the Pieta has a fine head.

1388.

Work of ... of the stable of Galeazzo; by the road of Brera [Footnote 4: Brera, see No. 1448, II, 13]; benefice of Stanghe [Footnote 5:Stanghe, see No. 1509.]; benefice of Porta Nuova; benefice of Monza; Indaco's mistake; give first the benefices; then the works; then ingratitude, indignity and lamentations.

1389.

Chiliarch--captain of 1000.

Prefects--captains.

A legion, six thousand and sixty three men.

1390.

A nun lives at La Colomba at Cremona; she works good straw plait, and a friar of Saint Francis. [Footnote: La Colomba is to this day the name of a small house at Cremona, decorated with frescoes.]

1391.

Needle,--Niccolao,--thread,--Ferrando, -Iacopo Andrea,--canvas,--stone,-- colours, --brushes,--pallet,--sponge,--the panel of the Duke.

1392.

Messer Gian Domenico Mezzabarba and Messer Giovanni Franceso Mezzabarba. By the side of Messer Piero d'Anghiera.

1393.

Conte Francesco Torello.

1394.

Giuliano Trombetta,--Antonio di Ferrara, --Oil of .... [Footnote: Near this text is the sketch of a head drawn in red chalk.]

1395.

Paul was snatched up to heaven. [Footnote: See the facsimile of this note on Pl. XXIII No. 2.]

1396.

Giuliano da Maria, physician, has a steward without hands.

1397.

Have some ears of corn of large size sent from Florence.

1398.

See the bedstead at Santa Maria. Secret.

1399.

Arrigo is to have 11 gold Ducats. Arrigo is to have 4 gold ducats in the middle of August.

1400.

Give your master the instance of a captain who does not himself win the victory, but the soldiers do by his counsels; and so he still deserves the reward.

1401.

Messer Pier Antonio.

1402.

Oil,--yellow,--Ambrosio,--the mouth, --the farmhouse.

1403.

My dear Alessandro from Parma, by the hand of ...

1404.

Giovannina, has a fantastic face,--is at Santa Caterina, at the Hospital. [Footnote: Compare the text on the same page: No. 667.]

1405.

24 tavole make 1 perch. 4 trabochi make 1 tavola. 4 braccia and a half make a trabocco. A perch contains 1936 square braccia, or 1944.

1406.

The road of Messer Mariolo is 13 1/4 braccia wide; the House of Evangelista is 75.

It enters 7 1/2 braccia in the house of Mariolo. [Footnote: On this page and that which faces it, MS.I2 7la, are two diagrams with numerous reference numbers, evidently relating to the measurements of a street.]

1407.

I ask at what part of its curved motion the moving cause will leave the thing moved and moveable.

Speak to Pietro Monti of these methods of throwing spears.

1408.

Antonio de' Risi is at the council of Justice.

1409.

Paolo said that no machine that moves another .... [Footnote: The passage, of which the beginning is here given, deals with questions in mechanics. The instances in which Leonardo quotes the opinions of his contemporaries on scientific matters are so rare as to be worth noticing. Compare No. 901.]

1410.

Caravaggio. [Footnote: Caravaggio, a village not far from the Adda between Milan and Brescia, where Polidoro and Michelangelo da Caravaggio were born. This note is given in facsimile on Pl. XIII, No. I (above, to the left). On Pl. XIII, No. 2 above to the right we read cerovazo.]

1411.

Pulleys,--nails,--rope,--mercury,--cloth, Monday.

1412.

MEMORANDUM.

Maghino, Speculus of Master Giovanni the Frenchman; Galenus on utility.

1413.

Near to Cordusio is Pier Antonio da Tossano and his brother Serafino. [Footnote: This note is written between lines 23 and 24 of the text No. 710. Corduso, Cordusio (curia ducis) = Cordus in the Milanese dialect, is the name of a Piazza between the Via del Broletto and the Piazza de' Mercanti at Milan.. In the time of il Moro it was the centre of the town. The persons here named were members of the noble Milanese family de'Fossani; Ambrogio da Possano, the contemporary painter, had no connection with them.]

1414.

Memoranda after 1500 (1414--1434)

1414.

Paul of Vannochio at Siena ... The upper chamber for the apostles.

[4] Buildings by Bramante.

The governor of the castle made a prisoner.

[6] Visconti carried away and his son killed. [Footnote 6: Visconti. Chi fosse quel Visconte non sapremmo indovinare fra tanti di questo nome. Arluno narra che allora atterrate furono le case de' Viconti, de' Castiglioni, de' Sanseverini, e de' Botta e non e improbabile che ne fossero insultati e morti i padroni. Molti Visconti annovera lo stesso Cronista che per essersi rallegrati del ritorno del duca in Milano furono da' Francesi arrestati, e strascinati in Francia come prigionieri di stato; e fra questi Messer Francesco Visconti, e suo figliuolo Battista. (AMORETTI, Mem. Stor. XIX.).]

Giovanni della Rosa deprived of his money.

Borgonzio began ....; and moreover his fortunes fled. [Footnote 8: Borgonzio o Brugonzio Botta fu regolatore delle ducali entrate sotto il Moro, alla cui fuga la casa sua fu pur messa a sacco da' partitanti francesi. (AMORETTI, I. c.)]

The Duke has lost the state, property and liberty and none of his entreprises was carried out by him.

[Footnote: I. 4--10 This passage evidently refers to events in Milan at the time of the overthrow of Ludovico il Moro. Amoretti published it in the 'Memorie Storiche' and added copious notes.]

1415.

Ambrosio Petri, St. Mark, 4 boards for the window, 2 ..., 3 the saints of chapels, 5 the Genoese at home.

1416.

Piece of tapestry,--pair of compasses,-- Tommaso's book,--the book of Giovanni Benci,--the box in the custom-house,--to cut the cloth,--the sword-belt,--to sole the boots, --a light hat,--the cane from the ruined houses,--the debt for the table linen, --swimming-belt,--a book of white paper for drawing,--charcoal.--How much is a florin ...., a leather bodice.

1417.

Borges shall get for you the Archimedes from the bishop of Padua, and Vitellozzo the one from Borgo a San Sepolcro [Footnote 3: Borgo a San Sepolcro, where Luca Paciolo, Leonardo's friend, was born.]

[Footnote: Borges. A Spanish name.]

1418.

Marzocco's tablet.

1419.

Marcello lives in the house of Giacomo da Mengardino.

1420.

Where is Valentino?--boots,--boxes in the custom-house,...,--[Footnote 5: Carmine. A church and monastery at Florence.] the monk at the Carmine,--squares,--[Footnotes 7 and 8: Martelli, Borgherini; names of Florentine families. See No. 4.] Piero Martelli,--[8] Salvi Borgherini,--send back the bags,--a support for the spectacles,--[Footnote 11: San Gallo; possibly Giuliano da San Gallo, the Florentine architect.] the nude study of San Gallo,--the cloak. Porphyry,--groups,--square,--[Footnote 16: Pandolfini, see No. 1544 note.] Pandolfino. [Footnote: Valentino. Cesare Borgia is probably meant. After being made Archbishop of Valence by Alexander VI he was commonly called Valentinus or Valentino. With reference to Leonardo's engagements by him see pp. 224 and 243, note.]

1421.

Concave mirrors; philosophy of Aristotle;[Footnote 2: Avicenna (Leonardo here writes it Avinega) the Arab philosopher, 980-1037, for centuries the unimpeachable authority on all medical questions. Leonardo possibly points here to a printed edition: Avicennae canonum libri V, latine 1476 Patavis. Other editions are, Padua 1479, and Venice 1490.] the books of Avicenna Italian and Latin vocabulary; Messer Ottaviano Palavicino or his Vitruvius [Footnote 3: Vitruvius. See Vol. I, No. 343 note.]. bohemian knives; Vitruvius[Footnote 6: Vitruvius. See Vol. I, No. 343 note.]; go every Saturday to the hot bath where you will see naked men;

'Meteora' [Footnote 7: Meteora. See No. 1448, 25.],

Archimedes, on the centre of gravity; [Footnote 9: The works of Archimedes were not printed during Leonardo's life-time.] anatomy [Footnote 10: Compare No. 1494.] Alessandro Benedetto; The Dante of Niccolo della Croce; Inflate the lungs of a pig and observe whether they increase in width and in length, or in width diminishing in length.

[Footnote 14: Johannes Marliani sua etate philosophorum et medicorum principis et ducalis phisic. primi de proportione motuum velocitate questio subtilissima incipit ex ejusdem Marliani originali feliciter extracta, M(ilano) 1482.

Another work by him has the title: Marlianus mediolanensis. Questio de caliditate corporum humanorum tempore hiemis ed estatis et de antiparistasi ad celebrem philosophorum et medicorum universitatem ticinensem. 1474.] Marliano, on Calculation, to Bertuccio. Albertus, on heaven and earth [Footnote 15: See No. 1469, 1. 7.], [from the monk Bernardino]. Horace has written on the movements of the heavens.

[Footnote: Filosofia d'Aristotele see No. 1481 note.]

1422.

Of the three regular bodies as opposed to some commentators who disparage the Ancients, who were the originators of grammar and the sciences and ...

1423.

The room in the tower of Vaneri.

[Footnote: This note is written inside the sketch of a plan of a house. On the same page is the date 1513 (see No. 1376).]

1424.

The figures you will have to reserve for the last book on shadows that they may appear in the study of Gerardo the illuminator at San Marco at Florence.

[Go to see Melzo, and the Ambassador, and Maestro Bernardo].

[Footnote: L. 1-3 are in the original written between lines 3 and 4 of No. 292. But the sense is not clear in this connection. It is scarcely possible to devine the meaning of the following sentence.

2. 3. Gherardo Miniatore, a famous illuminator, 1445-1497, to whom Vasari dedicated a section of his Lives (Vol. II pp. 237-243, ed. Sansoni 1879).

5. Bernardo, possibly the painter Bernardo Zenale.]

1425.

Hermes the philosopher.

1426.

Suisset, viz. calculator,--Tisber, --Angelo Fossobron,--Alberto.

1427.

The structure of the drawbridge shown me by Donnino, and why c and d thrust downwards.

[Footnote: The sketch on the same page as this text represents two poles one across the other. At the ends of the longest are the letter c and d. The sense of the passage is not rendered any clearer.]

1428.

The great bird will take its first flight;-- on the back of his great swan,--filling the universe with wonders; filling all writings with his fame and bringing eternal glory to his birthplace.

[Footnote: This seems to be a speculation about the flying machine (compare p. 271).]

1429.

This stratagem was used by the Gauls against the Romans, and so great a mortality ensued that all Rome was dressed in mourning.

[Footnote: Leonardo perhaps alludes to the Gauls under Brennus, who laid his sword in the scale when the tribute was weighed.]

1430.

Alberto da Imola;--Algebra, that is, the demonstration of the equality of one thing to another.

1431.

Johannes Rubicissa e Robbia.

1432.

Ask the wife of Biagio Crivelli how the capon nurtures and hatches the eggs of the hen,--he being drunk.

1433.

The book on Water to Messer Marco Antonio.

[Footnote: Possibly Marc-Antonio della Torre, see p. 97.]

1434.

Have Avicenna's work on useful inventions translated; spectacles with the case, steel and fork and...., charcoal, boards, and paper, and chalk and white, and wax;.... .... for glass, a saw for bones with fine teeth, a chisel, inkstand .... three herbs, and Agnolo Benedetto. Get a skull, nut,--mustard.

Boots,--gloves, socks, combs, papers, towels, shirts,.... shoe-tapes,--..... shoes, penknife, pens. A skin for the chest.

[Footnote: 4. Lapis. Compare Condivi, Vita di Michelagnolo Buonarotti, Chap. XVIII.: Ma egli (Michelangelo) non avendo che mostrare, prese una penna (percioche in quel tempo il lapis non era in uso) e con tal leggiadria gli dipinse una mano ecc. The incident is of the year l496.--Lapis means pencil, and chalk (matita). Between lines 7 and 8 are the texts given as Nos. 819 and No. 7.]

Undated memoranda (1435-1457).

1435.

The book of Piero Crescenze,--studies from the nude by Giovanni Ambrosio,--compasses, --the book of Giovanni Giacomo.

1436.

MEMORARDUM.

To make some provisions for my garden, --Giordano, De Ponderibus[Footnote 3: Giordano. Jordanus Nemorarius, a mathematician of the beginning of the XIIIth century. No particulars of his life are known. The title of his principal work is: Arithmetica decem libris demonstrata, first published at Paris 1496. In 1523 appeared at Nuremberg: Liber Jordani Nemorarii de ponderibus, propositiones XIII et earundem demonstrationes, multarumque rerum rationes sane pulcherrimas complectens, nunc in lucem editus.],--the peacemaker, the flow and ebb of the sea,--have two baggage trunks made, look to Beltraffio's [Footnote 6: Beltraffio, see No. 465, note 2.

There are sketches by the side of lines 8 and 10.] lathe and have taken the stone,--out leave the books belonging to Messer Andrea the German,-- make scales of a long reed and weigh the substance when hot and again when cold. The mirror of Master Luigi; A b the flow and ebb of the water is shown at the mill of Vaprio,--a cap.

1437.

Giovanni Fabre,--Lazaro del Volpe,-- the common,--Ser Piero.

[Footnote: These names are inserted on a plan of plots of land adjoining the Arno.]

1438.

[Lactantius], [the book of Benozzo], groups,--to bind the book,--a lantern,--Ser Pecantino,--Pandolfino.--[Rosso]--a square, --small knives,--carriages,--curry combs-- cup.

1439.

Quadrant of Carlo Marmocchi,--Messer Francesco Araldo,--Ser Benedetto d'Accie perello,--Benedetto on arithmetic,--Maestro Paulo, physician,-- Domenico di Michelino,-- ...... of the Alberti,--Messer Giovanni Argimboldi.

1440.

Colours, formula,--Archimedes,--Marcantonio.

Tinned iron,--pierced iron.

1441.

See the shop that was formerly Bartolommeo's, the stationer.

[Footnote: 6. Marc Antonio, see No. 1433.]

1442.

The first book is by Michele di Francesco Nabini; it treats on science.

1443.

Messer Francesco, physician of Lucca, with the Cardinal Farnese.

[Footnote: Alessandro Farnese, afterwards Pope Paul III was created in 1493 Cardinal di San Cosimo e San Damiano, by Alexander VI.]

1444.

Pandolfino's book [Footnote 1: Pandolfino, Agnolo, of Florence. It is to this day doubtful whether he or L. B. Alberti was the author of the famous work 'Del Governo della Famiglia'. It is the more probable that Leonardo should have meant this work by the words il libro, because no other book is known to have been written by Pandolfino. This being the case this allusion of Leonardo's is an important evidence in favour of Pandolfino's authorship (compare No. 1454, line 3).],--knives,--a pen for ruling,--to have the vest dyed,--The library at St.-Mark's,--The library at Santo Spirito,--Lactantius of the Daldi [Footnote 7: The works of Lactantius were published very often in Italy during Leonardo's lifetime. The first edition published in 1465 "in monastero sublacensi" was also the first book printed in Italy.],--Antonio Covoni,--A book by Maestro Paolo Infermieri, --Boots, shoes and hose,-- (Shell)lac, --An apprentice to do the models for me. Grammar, by Lorenzo de Medici,--Giovanni del Sodo,--Sansovino, [Footnote 15: Sansovino, Andrea--the sculptor; 1460-1529.]--a ruler,--a very sharp knife,--Spectacles,--fractions...., --repair..........,--Tomaso's book,-- Michelagnolo's little chain; Learn the multiplication of roots from Maestro Luca;--my map of the world which Giovanni Benci has [Footnote 25: Leonardo here probably alludes to the map, not executed by him (See p. 224), which is with the collection of his MSS. at Windsor, and was published in the Archaeologia Vol. XI (see p. 224).];-Socks,--clothes from the customhouse-officier,--Red Cordova leather,--The map of the world, of Giovanni Benci,--a print, the districts about Milan--Market book.

Get the Friar di Brera to show you [the book] 'de Ponderibus' [Footnote 11: Brera, now Palazzo delle Scienze ed Arti. Until 1571 it was the monastery of the order of the Umiliati and afterwards of the Jesuits.

De ponderibus, compare No. 1436, 3.],--

Of the measurement of San Lorenzo,--

I lent certain groups to Fra Filippo de Brera, [Footnote 13: Brera, now Palazzo delle Scienze ed Arti. Until 1571 it was the monastery of the order of the Umiliati and afterwards of the Jesuits.

De ponderibus, compare No. 1436, 3.]--

Memorandum: to ask Maestro Giovannino as to the mode in which the tower of Ferrara is walled without loopholes,--

Ask Maestro Antonio how mortars are placed on bastions by day or by night,--

Ask Benedetto Portinari how the people go on the ice in Flanders,--

On proportions by Alchino, with notes by Marliano, from Messer Fazio,--

The measurement of the sun, promised me by Maestro Giovanni, the Frenchman,--

The cross bow of Maestro Gianetto,--

The book by Giovanni Taverna that Messer Fazio,--

You will draw Milan [21],--

The measurement of the canal, locks and supports, and large boats; and the expense,--

Plan of Milan [Footnote 23: Fondamento is commonly used by Leonardo to mean ground-plan. See for instance p. 53.],--

Groups by Bramante [Footnote 24: Gruppi. See Vol. I p. 355, No. 600, note 9.],--

The book on celestial phenomena by Aristoteles, in Italian [Footnote 25: Meteora. By this Leonardo means no doubt the four books. He must refer here to a MS. translation, as no Italian translation is known to have been published (see No. 1477 note).],--

Try to get Vitolone, which is in the library at Pavia [Footnote 26: Vitolone see No. 1506, note.

Libreria di Pavia. One of the most famous of Italian libraries. After the victory of Novara in April 1500, Louis XII had it conveyed to France, 'come trofeo di vittoria'!] and which treats of Mathematics,--He had a master [learned] in waterworks and get him to explain the repairs and the costs, and a lock and a canal and a mill in the Lombard fashion.

A grandson of Gian Angelo's, the painter has a book on water which was his fathers.

Paolino Scarpellino, called Assiolo has great knowledge of water works.

[Footnote 12: Sco Lorenzo. A church at Milan, see pp. 39, 40 and 50.]

[Footnote 13. 24: Gruppi. See Vol. I p. 355, No. 600, note 9.]

[Footnote 16: The Portinari were one of the great merchant- families of Florence.]

1449.

Francesco d'Antonio at Florence.

1450.

Giuliano Condi[1],--Tomaso Ridolfi,-- Tomaso Paganelli,--Nicolo del Nero,--Simone Zasti,--Nasi,--the heir of Lionardo Manelli, --Guglielmo di Ser Martino,--Bartolomeo del Tovaglia,--Andrea Arrigucci,-- Nicolo Capponi,--Giovanni Portinari.

[Footnote: I. Guiliano Gondi. Ser Piero da Vinci, Leonardo's father, lived till 1480, in a house belonging to Giuliano Gondi. In 1498 this was pulled down to make room for the fine Palazzo built on the Piazza San Firenze by Giuliano di San Gallo, which still exists. In the Riassunto del Catasto di Ser Piero da Vinci, 1480, Leonardo is not mentioned; it is evident therefore that he was living elsewhere. It may be noticed incidentally that in the Catasto di Giuliano Gondi of the same year the following mention is made of his four eldest sons:

Lionardo mio figliuolo d'eta d'anni 29, non fa nulla, Giovambatista d'eta d'anni 28 in Ghostantinopoli, Billichozo d'eta d'anni 24 a Napoli, Simone d'eta d'anni 23 in Ungheria.

He himself was a merchant of gold filigree (facciamo lavorare una bottegha d'arte di seta ... facciamo un pocho di trafico a Napoli}. As he was 59 years old in 1480, he certainly would not have been alive at the time of Leonardo's death. But Leonardo must have been on intimate terms with the family till the end of his life, for in a letter dated June 1. 1519, in which Fr. Melzi, writing from Amboise, announces Leonardo's death to Giuliano da Vinci at Florence (see p. 284), he says at the end "Datemene risposta per i Gondi" (see UZIELLI, Ricerche, passim).

Most of the other names on the list are those of well-known Florentine families.]

1451.

Pandolfino.

1452.

Vespuccio will give me a book of Geometry.

[Footnote: See No. 844, note, p. 130.]

1453.

Marcantonio Colonna at Santi Apostoli.

[Footnote: In July 1506 Pope Julius II gave Donna Lucrezia della Rovere, the daughter of his sister Lucchina, in marriage to the youthful Marcantonio Colonna, who, like his brothers Prospero and Fabrizio, became one of the most famous Captains of his family. He gave to him Frascati and made him a present of the palazzo he had built, when Cardinal, near the church of Santi Apostoli which is now known as the Palazzo Colonna (see GREGOROVIUS, Gesch. der Stadt Rom. Vol. VIII, book XIV I, 3. And COPPI, Mem. Colonnesi p. 251).]

1454.

A box, a cage,-- A square, to make the bird [Footnote 2: Vasari states that Leonardo invented mechanical birds which moved through the air. Compare No. 703.],-- Pandolfino's book, mortar [?],-- Small knives, Venieri for the

[Footnote: Much of No. 1444 is repeated in this memorandum.]

Pen for ruling, stone,--star,--

To have the vest dyed, Alfieri's tazza,--

The Libraries, the book on celestial

        phenomena,--

Lactantius of the go to the house of Daldi,-- the Pazzi,

Book from Maestro small box,-- Paolo Infermieri,--

Boots, shoes and small gimlet,-- hose,

Lac, ...,--

An apprentice for .....,-- models,

Grammar of Lo- the amount of the renzo de' Medici, ...

Giovanni del Sodo ..... for...,--the broken

Sansovino, the....

Piero di Cosino the wings,--

[Footnote 16: Pier di Cosimo the well known Florentine painter 1462-1521. See VASARI, Vite (Vol. IV, p. 134 ed. Sansoni 1880) about Leonardo's influence on Piero di Cosimo's style of painting.]

Filippo and Lorenzo [Footnote 17: Filippo e Lorenzo; probably the painters Filippino Lippi and Lorenzo di Credi. L. di Credi's pictures and Vasari's history of that painter bear ample evidence to his intimate relations with Leonardo.],-- A ruler-,-- Spectacles,--to do the..... again,--Tomaso's book,--Michelagnolo's chain,--The multiplication of roots,--Of the bow and strinch,--The map of the world from Benci,-- Socks,--The clothes from the custom-house officier,-- Cordova leather,--Market books, --waters of Cronaca,--waters of Tanaglino..., --the caps,--Rosso's mirror; to see him make it,--1/3 of which I have 5/6,--on the celestial phenomena, by Aristotle [Footnote 36: Meteora. See No. 1448, 25.],--boxes of Lorenzo di Pier Francesco [Footnote 37: Lorenzo di Pier Francesco and his brother Giovanni were a lateral branch of the Medici family and changed their name for that of Popolani.],--Maestro Piero of the Borgo,-- To have my book bound,--Show the book to Serigatto,-- and get the rule of the clock [Footnote 41: Possibly this refers to the clock on the tower of the Palazzo Vecchio at Florence. In February 1512 it had been repaired, and so arranged as to indicate the hours after the French manner (twelve hours a. m. and as many p. m.).],-- ring,--nutmeg,--gum,--the square,--Giovan' Batista at the piazza, de' Mozzi,--Giovanni Benci has my book and jaspers,--brass for the spectacles.

1455.

Search in Florence for......

1456.

Bernardo da Ponte ... Val di Lugano ... many veins for anatomical demonstration.

[Footnote: This fragmentary note is written on the margin of a drawing of two legs.]

1457.

Paolo of Tavechia, to see the marks in the German stones.

[Footnote: This note occurs on a pen and ink drawing made by Leonardo as a sketch for the celebrated large cartoon in the possession of the Royal Academy of Arts, in London. This cartoon is commonly supposed to be identical with that described and lauded by Vasari, which was exhibited in Florence at the time and which now seems to be lost. Mr. Alfred Marks, of Long Ditton, in his valuable paper (read before the Royal Soc. of Literature, June 28, 1882) "On the St. Anne of Leonardo da Vinci", has adduced proof that the cartoon now in the Royal Academy was executed earlier at Milan. The note here given, which is written on the sheet containing the study for the said cartoon, has evidently no reference to the drawing on which it is written but is obviously of the same date. Though I have not any opening here for discussing this question of the cartoon, it seemed to me important to point out that the character of the writing in this note does not confirm the opinion hitherto held that the Royal Academy cartoon was the one described by Vasari, but, on the contrary, supports the hypothesis put forward by Mr. Marks.]

Notes on pupils (1458-1468.)

1458.

Giacomo came to live with me on St.-Mary Magdalen's[Footnote: Il di della Maddalena. July 22.] day, 1490, aged 10 years. The second day I had two shirts cut out for him, a pair of hose, and a jerkin, and when I put aside some money to pay for these things he stole 4 lire the money out of the purse; and I could never make him confess, though I was quite certain of the fact.--Thief, liar, obstinate, glutton.

The day after, I went to sup with Giacomo Andrea, and the said Giacomo supped for two and did mischief for four; for he brake 3 cruets, spilled the wine, and after this came to sup where I ....

Item: on the 7th day of September he stole a silver point of the value of 22 soldi from Marco[Footnote 6: Marco, probably Leonardo's pupil Marco d'Oggionno; 1470 is supposed to be the date of his birth and 1540 of his death.

Che stava con meco. We may infer from this that he left the master shortly after this, his term of study having perhaps expired.] who was living with me, 4 lire this being of silver; and he took it from his studio, and when the said Marco had searched for it a long while he found it hidden in the said Giacomo's box 4 lire.

Item: on the 26th January following, I, being in the house of Messer Galeazzo da San Severino [Footnote 9: Galeazzo. See No. 718 note.], was arranging the festival for his jousting, and certain footmen having undressed to try on some costumes of wild men for the said festival, Giacomo went to the purse of one of them which lay on the bed with other clothes, 2 lire 4 S, and took out such money as was in it.

Item: when I was in the same house, Maestro Agostino da Pavia gave to me a Turkish hide to have (2 lire.) a pair of short boots made of it; this Giacomo stole it of me within a month and sold it to a cobbler for 20 soldi, with which money, by his own confession, he bought anise comfits.

Item: again, on the 2nd April, Giovan Antonio [Footnote 16: Giovan Antonio, probably Beltraffio, 1467 to 1516.] having left a silver point on a drawing of his, Giacomo stole it, and this was of the value of 24 soldi (1 lira 4 S.)

The first year-

A cloak, 2 lire, 6 shirts, 4 lire, 3 jerkins, 6 lire, 4 pairs of hose, 7 lire 8 soldi, 1 lined doublet, 5 lire, 24 pairs of shoes, 6 lire 5 soldi, A cap, 1 lira, laces, 1 lira.

[Footnote: Leonardo here gives a detailed account not only of the loss he and others incurred through Giacomo but of the wild tricks of the youth, and we may therefore assume that the note was not made merely as a record for his own use, but as a report to be forwarded to the lad's father or other responsible guardian.]

1459.

On the last day but one of September;

Thursday the 27th day of September Maestro Tommaso came back and worked for himself until the last day but one of February. On the 18th day of March, 1493, Giulio, a German, came to live with me,--Lucia, Piero, Leonardo.

On the 6th day of October.

1460.

1493. On the 1st day of November we settled accounts. Giulio had to pay 4 months; and Maestro Tommaso 9 months; Maestro Tommaso afterwards made 6 candlesticks, 10 days' work; Giulio some fire-tongs 15 days work. Then he worked for himself till the 27th May, and worked for me at a lever till the 18th July; then for himself till the 7th of August, and for one day, on the fifteenth, for a lady. Then again for me at 2 locks until the 20th of August.

1461.

On the 23rd day of August, 12 lire from Pulisona. On the 14th of March 1494, Galeazzo came to live with me, agreeing to pay 5 lire a month for his cost paying on the l4th day of each month.

His father gave me 2 Rhenish florins.

On the l4th of July, I had from Galeazzo 2 Rhenish florins.

1462.

On the 15th day of September Giulio began the lock of my studio 1494.

1463.

Saturday morning the 3rd of August 1504 Jacopo the German came to live with me in the house, and agreed with me that I should charge him a carlino a day.

1464.

1511. On the 26th of September Antonio broke his leg; he must rest 40 days.

[Footnote: This note refers possibly to Beltraffio.]

1465.

I left Milan for Rome on the 24th day of September, 1513, with Giovanni [Footnote 2: Giovan; it is not likely that Leonardo should have called Giovan' Antonio Beltraffio at one time Giovanni, as in this note and another time Antonio, as in No. 1464 while in No. 1458 l. 16 we find Giovan'Antonio, and in No. 1436, l.6 Beltraffio. Possibly the Giovanni here spoken of is Leonardo's less known pupil Giovan Pietrino (see No. 1467, 5).], Francesco di Melzi [Footnote 2,3: Francesco de' Melzi is often mentioned, see Nos. 1350.], Salai [Footnote 3: Salai. See No. 1519 note.], Lorenzo and il Fanfoia.

[Footnote 4: Lorenzo. See No. 1351, l. 10 (p. 408). Amoretti gives the following note in Mem. Stor. XXIII: 1505. Martedi--sera a di 14 d'aprile. Venne Lorenzo a stare con mecho: disse essere d'eta d'anni 17 .. a di 15 del detto aprile ebbi scudi 25 d'oro dal chamerlingo di Santa Maria nuova. This, he asserts is derived from a MS. marked S, in quarto. This MS. seems to have vanished and left no trace behind; Amoretti himself had not seen it, but copied from a selection of extracts made by Oltrocchi before the Leonardo MSS. were conveyed to Paris on the responsibility of the first French Republic. Lorenzo, by this, must have been born in 1487. The sculptor Lorenzetto was born in 1490. Amoretti has been led by the above passage to make the following absurd observations:

Cotesto Lorenzo, che poi gli fu sempre compagno, almeno sin che stette in Italia, sarebb' egli Lorenzo Lotto bergamasco? Sappiamo essere stato questo valente dipintore uno de'bravi scolari del Vinci (?).

Il Fafoia, perhaps a nickname. Cesare da Sesto, Leonardo's pupil, seems to have been in Rome in these years, as we learn from a drawing by him in the Louvre.

1466.

On the 3rd day of January.

Benedetto came on the 17th of October; he stayed with me two months and 13 days of last year, in which time he earned 38 lire, 18 soldi and 8 dinari; he had of this 26 lire and 8 soldi, and there remains to be paid for the past year 12 lire 10 soldi.

Giodatti (?) came on the 8th day of September, at 4 soldi a month, and stayed with me 3 months and 24 days, and earned 59 lire 14 soldi and 8 dinari; he has had 43 lire, 4 soldi, there remains to pay 16 lire, 10 soldi and 8 dinari.

Benedetto, 24 grossoni.

[Footnote: This seems to be an account for two assistants. The name of the second is scarcely legible. The year is not given. The note is nevertheless of chronological value. The first line tells us the date when the note was registered, January 3d, and the observations that follow refer to events of the previous month 'of last year' (dell'anno passato). Leonardo cannot therefore have written thus in Florence where the year was, at that period, calculated as beginning in the month of March (see Vol. I, No. 4, note 2). He must then have been in Milan. What is more important is that we thus learn how to date the beginning of the year in all the notes written at Milan. This clears up Uzielli's doubts: A Milano facevasi cominciar l'anno ab incarnatione, cioe il 25 Marzo e a nativitate, cioe il 25 Decembre. Ci sembra probabile che Leonardo dovesse prescegliere lo stile che era in uso a Firenze. (Ricerche, p. 84, note.)]

1467.

Gian Maria 4, Benedetto 4, Gian Pietro [5] 3, Salai 3, Bartolomeo 3, Gherardo 4.

1468.

Salai, 20 lire, Bonifacio, 2 lire, Bartolomeo, 4 lire, Arrigo [Harry], 15 lire.

Quotations and notes on books and authors (1469-1508).

1469.

Book on Arithmetic [Footnote 1: "La nobel opera de arithmethica ne la qual se tracta tute cosse amercantia pertinente facta & compilata per Piero borgi da Veniesia", in-40. In fine: "Nela inclita cita di Venetia a corni. 2 augusto. 1484. fu imposto fine ala presente opera." Segn. a--p. quaderni. V'ha pero un' altra opera simile di Filippo Calandro, 1491. E da consultarsi su quest' ultimo, Federici: Memorie Trevigiane, Fiore di virtu: pag. 73. "Libricciuolo composto di bello stile verso il 1320 e piu volte impresso nel secolo XV (ristampato poi anche piu tardi). Gli accademici della Crusca lo ammettono nella serie dei testi di lingua. Vedasi Gamba, Razzolini, Panzer, Brunet, Lechi, ecc. (G. D'A.)], 'Flowers of Virtue',

Pliny [Footnote 2: "Historia naturale di C. Plinio Secondo, tradocta di lingua latina in fiorentina per Christophoro Laudino & Opus Nicolai Jansonis gallici imp. anno salutis M.CCCC.LXXVI. Venetiis" in-fol.--Diogene Laertio. Incomincia: "El libro de la vita de philosophi etc.: Impressum Venetiis" per Bernardinum Celerium de Luere, 1480", in-40 (G. D'A.).], 'Lives of the Philosophers',

The Bible [Footnote 3: "La Bibia volgare historiata (per Nicolo di Mallermi) Venecia ... M.CCCC.LXXI in kalende di Augusto (per Vindelino de Spira)" 2 vol. in-fol. a 2 col. di 50 lin,; od altra ediz. della stessa versione del Mallermi, Venetia 1471, e sempre: "Venecia per Gabriel de Piero 1477," in-fol.; 2 vol.; Ottavio Scotto da Modoetia 1481," "Venetia 1487 per Joan Rosso Vercellese," "1490 Giovanni Ragazo di Monteferato a instantia di Luchanthonio di Giunta, ecc."--Lapidario Teofrasto? Mandebille: "Le grand lapidaire," versione italiana ms.?... Giorgio Agricola non puo essere, perche nato nel 1494, forse Alberto Magno: de mineralibus. Potrebbe essere una traduzione del poema latino (Liber lapidum seu de gemmis) di Marbordio Veterio di Rennes (morto nel 1123 da lui stesso tradotto in francese dal greco di Evao re d'Arabia celebre medico che l'aveva composto per l'imperatore Tiberio. Marbodio scrisse il suo prima per Filippo Augusto re di Francia. Vi sono anche traduzioni in prosa. "Il lapidario o la forza e la virtu delle pietre preziose, delle Erbe e degli Animali." (G. D'A.)], 'Lapidary',

'On warfare' [Footnote 4: Il Vegezio? ... Il Frontino? ... Il Cornazzano?... Noi crediamo piuttosto il Valturio. Questo libro doveva essere uno de'favoriti di Leonardo poiche libro di scienza e d'arte nel tempo stesso.], 'Epistles of Filelfo',

[Footnote: The late Marchese Girolamo d'Adda published a highly valuable and interesting disquisition on this passage under the title: Leonardo da Vinci e la sua Libreria, note di un bibliofilo (Milano 1873. Ed. di soli 75 esemplari; privately printed). In the autumn of 1880 the Marchese d'Adda showed me a considerable mass of additional notes prepared for a second edition. This, as he then intended, was to come out after the publication of this work of mine. After the much regretted death of the elder Marchese, his son, the Marchese Gioachino d'Adda was so liberal as to place these MS. materials at my disposal for the present work, through the kind intervention of Signor Gustavo Frizzoni. The following passages, with the initials G. d'A. are prints from the valuable notes in that publication, the MS. additions I have marked. I did not however think myself justified in reproducing here the acute and interesting observations on the contents of most of the rare books here enumerated.]

[Footnote: 1467. 5. See No. 1465, 2.]

The first decade, [5] 'On the preservation of health', The third decade, [6] Ciecho d'Ascoli, The fourth decade, [7] Albertus Magnus, Guido, [8] New treatise on rhetorics, Piero Crescentio, [9] Cibaldone, 'Quadriregio', [10] Aesop,

Donato, [Footnote 11: "Donatus latine & italice: Impressum Venetiis impensis Johannis Baptistae de Sessa anno 1499, in-4deg.".-- "El Psalterio de David in lingua volgare (da Malermi Venetia nel M.CCCC.LXXVI," in-fol. s. n. (G. D'A.)] Psalms,

Justinus, [Footnote 12: Compare No. 1210, 48.--La versione di Girolamo Squarzafico: "Il libro di Justino posto diligentemente in materna lingua. Venetia ale spesse (sic) di Johane de Colonia & Johane Gheretze ... I477," in-fol.--"Marsilii Ficini, Theologia platonica, sive de animarum immortalitate, Florentine, per Ant. Misconimum 1482," in-fol., ovvero qualche versione italiana di questo stesso libro, ms. (G. D'A.)] 'On the immortality of the soul,

Guido [Footnote 13: Forse "la Historia Trojana Guidonis" od il "manipulus" di "Guido da Monterocherii" ma piu probabilmente "Guido d'Arezzo" il di cui libro: "Micrologus, seu disciplina artis musicae" poteva da Leonardo aversi ms.; di questi ne esistono in molto biblioteche, e fu poi impresso nel 1784 dal Gerbert.

Molte sono le edizione dei sonetti di Burchiello Fiorentino, impresse nel secolo XV. La prima e piu rara e recercata: "Incominciano li sonetti, ecc. (per

Christoforo Arnaldo)", in-4deg. senza numeri, richiami o segnature, del 1475, e fors' anche del 1472, secondo Morelli e Dibdin, ecc. (G. D'A.)] Burchiello,

'Doctrinale' [Footnote 14: Versione italiana det "Doctrinal de Sapience" di Guy de Roy, e foris'anche l'originale in lingua francese.--

Di Pulci Luigi, benche nell' edizione: "Florentiae 1479" in-4deg. si dica: "Il Driadeo composto in rima octava per Lucio Pulcro" Altre ediz, del secolo XV, "Florentie Miscomini 1481, in-40, Firenze, apud S. Jacob, de Ripoli, 1483," in-4deg. e "Antoni de Francesco, 1487," in-4deg. e Francesco di Jacopo 1489,in-4deg. ed altre ancora di Venezia e senza alcuna nota ecc. (G. D'A.)] Driadeo,

Morgante [Footnote 15: Una delle edizioni del Morgante impresse nel secolo XV, ecc.--

Quale delle opere di Francesco Petrarca, sarebbe malagevole l'indovinare, ma probabilmente il Canzoniere. (G. D'A.)] Petrarch.

John de Mandeville [Footnote 16: Sono i viaggi del cavaliere "Mandeville" gentiluomo inglese. Scrisse il suo libro in lingua francese. Fu stampato replicatamente nel secolo XV in francese, in inglese ed in italiano ed in tedesco; del secolo XV ne annoverano forse piu di 27 edizioni, di cui ne conosciamo 8 in francese, quattro in latino, sei in tedesco e molte altre in volgare. (G. D'A.)]

'On honest recreation' [Footnote 17: Il Platina (Bartolomeo Sacchi) la versione italiana "de la honesta voluptate, & valetudine (& de li obsonnii) Venetia (senza nome di tipografo) 1487," piccolo in-4deg. gotico. (G. D'A.)--Compare No. 844, 21.]

Manganello, [Footnote 18: Il Manganello: Satira eccessivamente vivace contro le donne ad imitazione della Sesta di Giovenale. Manganello non e soltanto il titolo del libricino, sua ben anche il nome dell'autore ch'era un "milanese". Di questo libercolo rarissimo, che sembra impresso a Venezia dallo Zoppino (Nicolo d'Aristotile detto il), senza data, ma dei primissimi anni del secolo XVI, e forse piu antico, come vedremo in appresso, non se ne conoscono fra biblioteche pubbliche e private che due soli esemplari in Europa. (G. D'A.)]

The Chronicle of Isidoro, [Footnote 19: "Cronica desidero", sembra si deggia leggere piuttosto "cronico disidoro"; ed in questo caso s'intenderebbe la "cronica d'Isidoro" tanto in voga a quel tempo "Comenza la Cronica di Sancto Isidoro menore con alchune additione cavate del testo & istorie de la Bibia & del libro di Paulo Oroso .... Impresso in Ascoli in casa del reverendo misser Pascale ..... per mano di Guglielmo de Linis de Alamania M.CCCC.LXXVII" in-4deg. di 157 ff. E il primo libro impresso ad Ascoli e l'edizione principe di questa cronica in oggi assai rara. Non lo e meno l'edizione di Cividal del Friuli, 1480, e quella ben anche di Aquila, 1482, sempre in-4deg.. Vedasi Panzer, Hain, Brunet e P. Dechamps. (G. D'A.)]

The Epistles of Ovid, [Footnote 20: "Le pistole di Ovidio tradotte in prosa. Napoli Sixt. Riessinger", in-4deg., oppure: "Epistole volgarizzate 1489," in-

4deg. a due col. "impresse ne la cita (sic) di Bressa per pre: Baptista de Farfengo," (in ottave) o: "El libro dele Epistole di Ovidio in rima volgare per messere Dominico de Monticelli toschano. Brescia Farfengo," in-4deg. got. (in rima volgare), 1491, ed anche la versione di Luca Pulci. Firenze, Mischomini, 1481, in-4deg.. (G. D'A.)]

Epistles of Filelfo, [Footnote 21: See l. 4.]

Sphere, [Footnote 22: "Jo: de Sacrobusto," o "Goro Dati," o "Tolosano da Colle" di cui molteplici edizioni del secolo XV. (G. D'A.)]

The Jests of Poggio, [Footnote 23: Tre edizioni delle facezie del Poggio abbiamo in lingua italiana della fine del secolo XV, tutte senza data. "Facetie de Poggio fiorentino traducte de latino in vulgare ornatissimo," in-40, segn. a-- e in caratteri romani; l'altra: "Facetie traducte de latino in vulgare," in-40, caratteri gotici, ecc. (G. D'A.)] Chiromancy, [Footnote 24: "Die Kunst Cyromantia etc, in tedesco. 26 ff. di testo e figure il tutte eseguito su tavole di legno verso la fine del secolo XV da Giorgio Schapff". Dibdin, Heinecken, Sotheby e Chatto ne diedero una lunga descrizione; i primi tre accompagnati da fac-simili. La data 1448 che si legge alla fine del titolo si riferisce al periodo della composizione del testo, non a quello della stampa del volume benche tabellario. Altri molti libri di Chiromanzia si conoscono di quel tempo e sarebbe opera vana il citarli tutti. (G. D'A.)]

Formulary of letters, [Footnote 25: Miniatore Bartolomeo. "Formulario de epistole vulgare missive e responsive, & altri fiori de ornali parlamenti al principe Hercule d'Esti ecc. composto ecc. Bologna per Ugo di Rugerii," in-40, del secolo XV. Altra edizione di "Venetia Bernardino di Novara, 1487" e "Milano per Joanne Angelo Scinzenzeler 1500," in-40. (G. D'A.)

Five books out of this list are noted by Leonardo in another MS. (Tr. 3): donato, -- lapidario, -- plinio, -- abacho, -- morgante.]

1470.

Nonius Marcellus, Festus Pompeius, Marcus Varro.

[Footnote: Nonius Marcellus and Sextus Pompeius Festus were Roman grammarians of about the fourth century A. D. Early publications of the works of Marcellus are: De proprietate sermonis, Romae (about 1470), and 1471 (place of publication unknown). Compendiosa doctrina, ad filium, de proprietate sermonum. Venice, 1476. BRUNET, Manuel du libraire (IV, p. 97) notes: Le texte de cet ancien grammairien a ete reimprime plusieurs fois a la fin du XVe siecle, avec ceux de Pomponius Festus et de Terentius Varro. La plus ancienne edition qui reunisse ces trois auteurs est celle de Parme, 1480 ... Celles de Venise, 1483, 1490, 1498, et de Milan, 1500, toutes in-fol., ont peu de valeur.]

1471.

Map of Elephanta in India which Antonello Merciaio has from maestro Maffeo;--there for seven years the earth rises and for seven years it sinks;-- Enquire at the stationers about Vitruvius.

1472.

See 'On Ships' Messer Battista, and Frontinus 'On Acqueducts' [Footnote 2: 2. Vitruvius de Arch., et Frontinus de Aquedoctibus. Florence, 1513.--This is the earliest edition of Frontinus.--The note referring to this author thus suggests a solution of the problem of the date of the Leicester Manuscript.].

[Footnote: Compare No. 1113, 25.]

1473.

Anaxagoras: Every thing proceeds from every thing, and every thing becomes every thing, and every thing can be turned into every thing else, because that which exists in the elements is composed of those elements.

1474.

The Archimedes belonging to the Bishop of Padua.

[Footnote: See No. 1421, 1. 3, 6 and Vol. I, No. 343.]

1475.

Archimedes gave the quadrature of a polygonal figure, but not of the circle. Hence Archimedes never squared any figure with curved sides. He squared the circle minus the smallest portion that the intellect can conceive, that is the smallest point visible.

[Footnote: Compare No. 1504.]

1476.

If any man could have discovered the utmost powers of the cannon, in all its various forms and have given such a secret to the Romans, with what rapidity would they have conquered every country and have vanquished every army, and what reward could have been great enough for such a service! Archimedes indeed, although he had greatly damaged the Romans in the siege of Syracuse, nevertheless did not fail of being offered great rewards from these very Romans; and when Syracuse was taken, diligent search was made for Archimedes; and he being found dead greater lamentation was made for him by the Senate and people of Rome than if they had lost all their army; and they did not fail to honour him with burial and with a statue. At their head was Marcus Marcellus. And after the second destruction of Syracuse, the sepulchre of Archimedes was found again by Cato[25], in the ruins of a temple. So Cato had the temple restored and the sepulchre he so highly honoured.... Whence it is written that Cato said that he was not so proud of any thing he had done as of having paid such honour to Archimedes.

[Footnote: Where Leonardo found the statement that Cato had found and restored the tomb of Archimedes, I do not know. It is a merit that Cicero claims as his own (Tusc. V, 23) and certainly with a full right to it. None of Archimedes' biographers --not even the diligent Mazzucchelli, mentions any version in which Cato is named. It is evidently a slip of the memory on Leonardo's part. Besides, according to the passage in Cicero, the grave was not found 'nelle ruine d'un tempio'--which is highly improbable as relating to a

Greek--but in an open spot (H. MULLER-STRUBING).--See too, as to Archimedes, No. 1417.

Leonardo says somewhere in MS. C.A.: Architronito e una macchina di fino rame, invenzlon d' Archimede (see 'Saggio', p. 20).]

1477.

Aristotle, Book 3 of the Physics, and Albertus Magnus, and Thomas Aquinas and the others on the rebound of bodies, in the 7th on Physics, on heaven and earth.

1478.

Aristotle says that if a force can move a body a given distance in a given time, the same force will move half the same body twice as far in the same time.

1479.

Aristotle in Book 3 of the Ethics: Man merits praise or blame solely in such matters as lie within his option to do or not to do.

1480.

Aristotle says that every body tends to maintain its nature.

1481.

On the increase of the Nile, a small book by Aristotle. [Footnote: De inundatione Nili, is quoted here and by others as a work of Aristotle. The Greek original is lost, but a Latin version of the beginning exists (Arist. Opp. IV p. 213 ed. Did. Par.).

In his quotations from Aristotle Leonardo possibly refers to one of the following editions: Aristotelis libri IV de coelo et mundo; de anima libri III; libri VIII physi- corum; libri de generatione et corruptione; de sensu et sensato... omnia latine, interprete Averroe, Venetiis 1483 (first Latin edition). There is also a separate edition of Liber de coelo et mundo, dated 1473.]

1482.

Avicenna will have it that soul gives birth to soul as body to body, and each member to itself.

[Footnote: Avicenna, see too No. 1421, 1. 2.]

1483.

Avicenna on liquids.

1484.

Roger Bacon, done in print. [Footnote: The earliest printed edition known to Brunet of the works of Roger Bacon, is a French translation, which appeared about fourty years after Leonardo's death.]

1485.

Cleomedes the philosopher.

[Footnote: Cleomede. A Greek mathematician of the IVth century B. C. We have a Cyclic theory of Meteorica by him. His works were not published before Leonardo's death.]

1486.

CORNELIUS CELSUS.

The highest good is wisdom, the chief evil is suffering in the body. Because, as we are composed of two things, that is soul and body, of which the first is the better, the body is the inferior; wisdom belongs to the better part, and the chief evil belongs to the worse part and is the worst of all. As the best thing of all in the soul is wisdom, so the worst in the body is suffering. Therefore just as bodily pain is the chief evil, wisdom is the chief good of the soul, that is with the wise man; and nothing else can be compared with it.

[Footnote: Aulus Cornelius Celsus, a Roman physician, known as the Roman Hippocrates, probably contemporary with Augustus. Only his eight Books 'De Medicina', are preserved. The earliest editions are: Cornelius Celsus, de medicina libr. VIII., Milan 1481 Venice 1493 and 1497.]

1487.

Demetrius was wont to say that there was no difference between the speech and words of the foolish and ignorant, and the noises and rumblings of the wind in an inflated stomach. Nor did he say so without reason, for he saw no difference between the parts whence the noise issued; whether their lower parts or their mouth, since one and the other were of equal use and importance.

[Footnote: Compare Vol. I, No. 10.]

1488.

Maestro Stefano Caponi, a physician, lives at the piscina, and has Euclid De Ponderibus.

1489.

5th Book of Euclid. First definition: a part is a quantity of less magnitude than the greater magnitude when the less is contained a certain number of times in the greater.

A part properly speaking is that which may be multiplied, that is when, being multiplied by a certain number, it forms exactly the whole. A common aggregate part ...

Second definition. A greater magnitude is said to be a multiple of a less, when the greater is measured by the less.

By the first we define the lesser [magnitude] and by the second the greater is defined. A part is spoken

1490.

of in relation to the whole; and all their relations lie between these two extremes, and are called multiples.

1491.

Hippocrates says that the origin of men's sperm derives from the brain, and from the lungs and testicles of our parents, where the final decocture is made, and all the other limbs transmit their substance to this sperm by means of expiration, because there are no channels through which they might come to the sperm.

[Footnote: The works of Hippocrates were printed first after Leonardo's death.]

1492.

Lucretius in his third [book] 'De Rerum Natura'. The hands, nails and teeth were (165) the weapons of ancient man.

They also use for a standard a bunch of grass tied to a pole (167).

[Footnote: Lucretius, de rerum natura libri VI were printed first about 1473, at Verona in 1486, at Brescia in 1495, at Venice in 1500 and in 1515, and at Florence in 1515. The numbers 165 and 167 noted by Leonardo at the end of the two passages seem to indicate pages, but if so, none of the editions just mentioned can here be meant, nor do these numbers refer to the verses in the poems of Lucretius.]

1493.

Ammianus Marcellinus asserts that seven hundred thousand volumes of books were burnt in the siege of Alexandria in the time of Julius Cesar.

[Footnote: Ammiani Marcellini historiarum libri qui extant XIII, published at Rome in 1474.]

1494.

Mondino says that the muscles which raise the toes are in the outward side of the thigh, and he adds that there are no muscles in the back [upper side] of the feet, because nature desired to make them light, so as to move with ease; and if they had been fleshy they would be heavier; and here experience shows ...

[Footnote: "Mundini anatomia. Mundinus, Anothomia (sic). Mundini praestantissimorum doctorum almi studii ticiensis (sic) cura diligentissime emendata. Impressa Papiae per magistrum Antonium de Carfano 1478," in-fol.; ristampata: "Bononiae Johan. de Noerdlingen, 1482," in-fol.; "Padova per Mattheum Cerdonis de Vuindischgretz, 1484," in-40; "Lipsia, 1493," in-40; "Venezia, 1494," in-40 e ivi "1498," con fig. Queste figure per altro non sono, come si e preteso, le prime che fossero introdotte in un trattato di Notamia. Nel 'fasciculus Medicinae' di Giovanni Ketham, che riproduce lAnatomia' del Mundinus, impresso pure a Venezia da J. e G. de Gregoriis, 1491, in-fol., contengonsi intagli in legno (si vogliono disegnati non gia incisi da Andrea Mantegna) di grande dimensione, e che furono piu volte riprodotti negli anni successivi. Quest' edizione del "fasciculus" del 1491, sta fra nostri libri e potrebbe benissimo essere il volume d'Anatomia notato da Leonardo. (G. D'A.)]

1495.

Of the error of those who practice without knowledge;--[3] See first the 'Ars poetica' of Horace [5].

[Footnote: A 3-5 are written on the margin at the side of the title line of the text given, entire as No. 19]

1496.

The heirs of Maestro Giovanni Ghiringallo have the works of Pelacano.

1497.

The catapult, as we are told by Nonius and Pliny, is a machine devised by those &c.

[Footnote: Plinius, see No. 946.]

1498.

I have found in a history of the Spaniards that in their wars with the English Archimedes of Syracuse who at that time was living at the court of Ecliderides, King of the Cirodastri. And in maritime warfare he ordered that the ships should have tall masts, and that on their tops there should be a spar fixed [Footnote 6: Compare No. 1115.] of 40 feet long and one third of a foot thick. At one end of this was a small grappling iron and at the other a counterpoise; and there was also attached 12 feet of chain; and, at the end of this chain, as much rope as would reach from the chain to the base of the top, where it was fixed with a small rope; from this base it ran down to the bottom of the mast where a very strong spar was attached and to this was fastened the end of the rope. But to go on to the use of his machine; I say that below this grappling iron was a fire [Footnote 14: Compare No. 1128.] which, with tremendous noise, threw down its rays and a shower of burning pitch; which, pouring down on the [enemy's] top, compelled the men who were in it to abandon the top to which the grappling-iron had clung. This was hooked on to the edges of the top and then suddenly the cord attached at the base of the top to support the cord which went from the grappling iron, was cut, giving way and drawing in the enemy's ship; and if the anchor--was cast ...

[Footnote: Archimedes never visited Spain, and the names here mentioned cannot be explained. Leonardo seems to quote here from a book, perhaps by some questionable mediaeval writer. Prof. C. Justi writes to me from Madrid, that Spanish savants have no knowledge of the sources from which this story may have been derived.]

1499.

Theophrastus on the ebb and flow of the tide, and of eddies, and on water. [Footnote: The Greek philosophers had no opportunity to study the phenomenon of the ebb and flow of the tide and none of them wrote about it.

The movement of the waters in the Euripus however was to a few of them a puzzling problem.]

1500.

Tryphon of Alexandria, who spent his life at Apollonia, a city of Albania (163). [Footnote: Tryphon of Alexandria, a Greek Grammarian of the time of Augustus. His treatise TtaOY Aeijecu appeared first at Milan in 1476, in Constantin Laskaris's Greek Grammar.]

1501.

Messer Vincenzio Aliprando, who lives near the Inn of the Bear, has Giacomo Andrea's Vitruvius.

1502.

Vitruvius says that small models are of no avail for ascertaining the effects of large ones; and I here propose to prove that this conclusion is a false one. And chiefly by bringing forward the very same argument which led him to this conclusion; that is, by an experiment with an auger. For he proves that if a man, by a certain exertion of strength, makes a hole of a given diameter, and afterwards another hole of double the diameter, this cannot be made with only double the exertion of the man's strength, but needs much more. To this it may very well be answered that an auger

1503.

of double the diameter cannot be moved by double the exertion, be- cause the superficies of a body of the same form but twice as large has four times the extent of the superficies of the smaller, as is shown in the two figures a and n.

1504.

OF SQUARING THE CIRCLE, AND WHO IT WAS THAT FIRST DISCOVERED IT BY ACCIDENT.

Vitruvius, measuring miles by means of the repeated revolutions of the wheels which move vehicles, extended over many Stadia the lines of the circumferences of the circles of these wheels. He became aware of them by the animals that moved the vehicles. But he did not discern that this was a means of finding a square equal to a circle. This was first done by Archimedes of Syracuse, who by multiplying the second diameter of a circle by half its circumference produced a rectangular quadrilateral equal figure to the circle [Footnote 10: Compare No. 1475.].

[Footnote: Vitruvius, see also Nos. 1113 and 343.]

1505.

Virgil says that a blank shield is devoid of merit because among the people of Athens the true recognition confirmed by testimonies ...

[Footnote: The end of the text cannot be deciphered.]

1506.

In Vitolone there are 805 conclusions [problems] in perspective.

[Footnote: (Witelo, Vitellion, Vitellon) Vitellione. E da vedersi su questo ottico prospettico del secolo XIII Luca Pacioli, Paolo Lomazzo, Leonardo da Vinci, ecc. e fra i moderni il Graesse, il Libri, il Brunet, e le Memorie pubblicate dal principe Boncompagni, e 'Sur l' orthographe du nom et sur la patrie de Witelo (Vitellion) note de Maximilien Curtze, professeur a Thorn', ove sono descritti i molti codici esistenti nelle biblioteche d' Europa. Bernardino Baldi nelle sue 'Vite de'matematici', manoscritto presso il principe Boncompagni, ha una biografia del Vitellione. Questo scritto del Baldi reca la data 25 agosto 1588. Discorsero poi di lui Federigo Risnerio e Giovanni di Monteregio nella prefazione dell' Alfagrano, Giovanni Boteone, Girolamo Cardano, 'De subtilitate', che nota gli errori di Vitellione. Visse, secondo il Baldi, intorno all' anno 1269, ma secondo il Reinoldo fioriva nel 1299, avendo dedicata la sua opera ad un frate Guglielmo di Monteca, che visse di que' tempi.

Intorno ad un manoscritto dell' ottica di Vitellione, citato da Luca Pacioli v'ha un secondo esemplare del Kurlz, con aggiunte del principe Boncompagni, e le illustrazioni del cav. Enrico Narducci. Nel 'Catalogo di manoscritti' posseduti da D. Baldassare de' principi Boncompagni, compilato da esso Narducci, Roma, 1862, sotto al n. 358, troviamo citato: Vitellio, 'Perspectiva', manoscritto del secolo XIV. La 'Prospettiva di Vitelleone' (sic) Thuringo-poloni e citata due volte da Paolo Lomazzo nel Trattato dell' arte della pittura. Vitellio o Vitello o Witelo. Il suo libro fu impresso in foglio a Norimberga nel 1535; la seconda edizione e del 1551, sempre di Norimberga, ed una terza di Basilea, 1572. (See Indagini Storiche ... sulla Libreria-Visconteo-Sforzesca del Castello di Pavia ... per cura di G. D'A., Milano 1879. P. I. Appendice p. 113. 114).]

1507.

Vitolone, at Saint Mark's.

[Footnote: Altro codice di cotesta 'Prospettiva' del Vitolone troviamo notato nel 'Canone bibliographico di Nicolo V', conservato alla, Magliabecchiana, in copia dell' originale verosimilmente inviato dal Parentucelli a Cosimo de' Medici (Magliab. cod. segn. 1 VII, 30 carte da 193 a 198). Proviene dal Convento di San Marco e lo aveva trascritto frate Leonardo Scruberti fiorentino, dell' ordine dei predicatori che fu anche bibliotecario della Medicea pubblica in San Marco (See Indagini Storiche ... per cura di G. D'A. Parte I, p. 97).]

1508.

How this proposition of Xenophon is false.

If you take away unequal quantities from unequal quantities, but in the same proportion, &c. [Footnote: Xenophon's works were published several times during Leonardo's lifetime.]

Inventories and accounts (1509--1545).

1509.

On the 28th day of April I received from the Marchesino 103 lire and 12 dinari. [Footnote: Instead of the indication of the year there is a blank space after d'aprile.--Marchesino Stange was one of Lodovico il Moro's officials.-- Compare No. 1388.]

1510.

On the 10th day of July 1492 in 135 Rhenish florins 1. 445 in dinari of 6 soldi 1. 112 S 16 in dinari of 5 1/2 soldi 1. 29 S 13 9 in gold and 3 scudi 1. 53

----

1. 811 in all

1511.

On the first day of February, lire 1200.

1512.

The hall towards the court is 126 paces long and 27 braccia wide.

1513.

The narrow cornice above the hall lire 30.

The cornice beneath that, being one for each picture, lire 7, and for the cost of blue, gold, white, plaster, indigo and glue 3 lire; time 3 days.

The pictures below these mouldings with their pilasters, 12 lire each.

I calculate the cost for smalt, blue and gold and other colours at 1 1/2 lire.

The days I calculate at 3, for the invention of the composition, pilasters and other things.

1514.

Item for each vault 7 lire

outlay for blue and gold 3 1/2

time, 4 days

for the windows 1 1/2

The cornice below the windows 16 soldi per braccio

item for 24 pictures of Roman history 14 lire each

The philosophers 10 lire

the pilasters, one ounce of blue 10 soldi

for gold 15 soldi

Total 2 and 1/2 lire.

1515.

The cornice above lire 30

The cornice below lire 7

The compositions, one with another lire 13

1516.

Salai, 6 lire ... 4 soldi ... 10 soldi for a chain;--

On the l4th of March I had 13 lire S. 4; 16 lire remain.

1517.

How many braccia high is the level of the walls?--

123 braccia

How large is the hall?

How large is the garland?

30 ducats.

On the 29th day of January, 1494

cloth for hose lire 4 S 3

lining S 16

making S 8

to Salai S 3

a jasper ring S 13

a sparkling stone S 11

to Caterina S 10

to Caterina S 10

1518.

The wheel lire 7

the tire lire 10

the shield lire 4

the cushion lire 8

the ends of the axle-tree lire 2

bed and frame lire 30

conduit lire 10

S.K.M.II.2 4a]

1519.

Parsley 10 parts

mint 1 part

thyme 1 part

Vinegar ... and a little salt two pieces of canvas for Salai.

[Footnote: This note, of about the year 1494, is the earliest mention of Salai, and the last is of the year 1513 (see No. 1465, 3). From the various notes in the MSS. he seems to have been Leonardo's assistant and keeper only, and scarcely himself a painter. At any rate no signed or otherwise authenticated picture by him is known to exist. Vasari speaks somewhat doubtfully on this point.]

1520.

On Tuesday I bought wine for morning [drinking]; on Friday the 4th day of September the same.

[Footnote: This note enables us to fix the date of the Manuscript, in which it is to be found. In 1495 the 4th of September fell on a Friday; the contents of the Manuscript do not permit us to assign it to a much earlier or later date (Compare No. 1522, and Note).]

1521.

The cistern ... at the Hospital, --2 ducats, --beans, --white maize, --red maize, --millet, --buckwheat, --kidney beans, --beans, --peas.

1522.

EXPENSES OF THE INTERMENT OF CATERINA.

For the 3 lbs of tapers 27 S For the bier 8 S A pall over the bier 12 S For bearing and placing the cross 4 S For bearing the body 8 S For 4 priests and 4 clerks 20 S Bell, book and sponge 2 S For the gravediggers 16 S To the senior 8 S For a license from the authorities 1 S 106 S

The doctor 2 S Sugar and candles 12 S 120 S

[Footnote: See Nos. 1384 and 1517.]

1523.

Salai's cloak, the 4th of April 1497. 4 braccia of silver cloth l. 15 S 4 green velvet to trim it l. 9 S -- binding l.-- S 9 loops l.-- S 12 the making l. 1 S 5 binding for the front l.-- S 5 stitching here are 13 grossoni of his l. 26 S 5 Salai stole the soldi.

1524.

On Monday I bought 4 braccia of cloth lire 13 S 14 1/2 on the 17th of, October 1497.

1525.

Memorandum. That on the 8th day of April 1503, I, Leonardo da Vinci, lent to Vante, miniature painter 4 gold ducats, in gold. Salai carried them to him and gave them into his own hand, and he said he would repay within the space of 40 days.

Memorandum. That on the same day I paid to Salai 3 gold ducats which he said he wanted for a pair of rose-coloured hose with their trimming; and there remain 9 ducats due to him--excepting that he owes me 20 ducats, that is 17 I lent him at Milan, and 3 at Venice.

Memorandum. That I gave Salai 21 braccia of cloth to make a shirt, at 10 soldi the braccio, which I gave him on the 20th day of April 1503.

[Footnote: With regard to Vante or Attavante, the miniature painter (not Nanni as I formerly deciphered this name, which is difficult to read; see Zeitschrift fur Bild. Kunst, 1879, p. 155), and Vasari, Lives of Frate Giovanni da Fiesole, of Bartolommeo della Gatta, and of Gherardo, miniatore. He, like Leonardo, was one of the committee of artists who, in 1503, considered the erection and placing of Michel Angelo's David. The date of his death is not known; he was of the same age as Leonardo. Further details will be found in 'Notizie di Attavante miniatore, e di alcuni suoi lavori' (Milanese's ed. of Vasari, III, 231-235).]

1526.

On the morning of San Peter's day, June 29th, 1504, I took io ducats, of which I gave one to Tommaso my servant to spend.

On Monday morning 1 florin to Salai to spend on the house.

On Thursday I took 1 florin for my own spending.

Wednesday evening 1 florin to Tommaso, before supper.

Saturday morning 1 florin to Tommaso.

Monday morning 1 florin less 10 soldi.

Thursday to Salai 1 florin less 10 soldi.

For a jerkin, 1 florin.

For a jerkin And a cap 2 florins.

To the hosier, 1 florin.

To Salai, 1 florin.

Friday morning, the 19th of July, 1 florin, less 6 soldi. I have 7 fl. left, and 22 in the box.

Tuesday, the 23th day of July, 1 florin to Tommaso.

Monday morning, to Tommaso 1 florin.

[Wednesday morning 1 fl. to Tommaso.]

Thursday morning the 1st day of August 1 fl. to Tommaso.

Sunday, the 4th of August, 1 florin.

Friday, the 9th day of August 1504, I took 10 ducats out of the box.

1527.

1504. On the 9th day of August, 1504, I took 10 florins in gold[2] ... [3] on Friday the 9th day of August fifteen grossoni that is fl. 5 S 5 ... given to me 1 florin in gold on the 12th day of August [4] ... on the 14th of August, 32 grossoni to Tommaso. On the 18th of the same 5 grossoni to Salai. On the 8th of September 6 grossoni to the workman to spend; that is on the day of our Lady's birth. On the 16th day of September I gave 4 grossoni to Tommaso: on a Sunday.

[Footnote: In the original, the passage given as No. 1463 is written between lines 2 and 3 of this text, and it is possible that the entries in lines 3 and 4 refer to the payments of Jacopo Tedesco, who is there mentioned. The first words of these lines are very illegible.]

[Footnote 7: Al fattore. Il Fattore, was, as is well known, the nick-name of Giovanni Franceso Penni, born in Florence in 1486, and subsequently a pupil of Raphael's. According to Vasari he was known by it even as a boy. Whether he is spoken of in this passage, or whether the word Fattore should be translated literally, I will not undertake to decide. The latter seems to me more probably right.]

1528.

On the day of October, 1508, I had 30 scudi; 13 I lent to Salai to make up his sister's dowry, and 17 I have left.

1529.

Memorandum of the money I have had from the King as my salary from July 1508 till April next 1509. First 100 scudi, then 70, then 50, then 20 and then 200 florins at 48 soldi the florin. [Footnote: Compare No. 1350 and 1561.]

1530.

Saturday the 2nd day of March I had from Santa Maria Novella 5 gold ducats, leaving 450. Of these I gave 2 the same day to Salai, who had lent them to me. [Footnote: See 'Conto corrente di Leonardo da Vinci con lo Spedale di S. Maria Nuova' [1500 a 1507, 1513-1520] published by G. UZIELLI, Ricerche intorno a Leonardo da Vinci, Firenze, 1872, pp. 164, 165, 218 and 219. The date here given by Leonardo does not occur in either of the accounts.]

1531.

Thursday, the eighth day of June, I took 17 grossoni, 18 soldi; on the same Thursday in the morning I gave to Salai 22 soldi for the expenses.

1532.

To Salai 4 grossoni, and for one braccio of velvet, 5 lire, and 1/2; viz. 10 soldi for loops of silver; Salai 14 soldi for binding, the making of the cloak 25 soldi. [Footnote: Compare No. 1523.]

1533.

I gave to Salai 93 lire 6 soldi, of which I have had 67 lire and there remain 26 lire 6 soldi.

1534.

To Salai S 42

2 dozen of laces S 8

for papers S 3 d 8

a pair of shoes S 14

for velvet S 14

a sword and knife S 21

to the barber S 11

to Paolo for a ... S 20

For having his fortune told S 6

1535.

On Friday morning, one florin to Salai to spend; 3 soldi received

bread S.. d

wine S.. d

grapes S.. d

mushrooms S.. d

fruit S.. d

[Footnote 6: Compare Nos. 1545, l. 4 and 5, with similar entries for horse's fodder.] bran S.. d

at the barber's S.. d

for shoes S.. d

1536.

On Thursday morning one florin.

1537.

On Saint Ambrose's day from the morning to Thursday 36 soldi.

1538.

The moneys I have had from Ser Matteo; first 20 grassoni, then on 13 occasions 3 f. and then 61 grassoni, then 3, and then 33; 46 soldi 12 grossoni.

1539.

For paper S 18

for canvas S 30

for paper S 10 d 19

Total S 73

1540.

20 pounds of German blue, at one ducat the pound lire 80 S d

60 pounds of white, S.. the pound lire 15 S d

1 1/2 pound at 4 S the pound lire 6 S d

2 pounds of cinnabar at S 18 the pound lire 1 S 16 d

6 pounds of green at S 12 the pound lire 3 S 12 d

4 pounds of yellow at S 12 the pound lire 2 S 8 d

1 pound of minium at S 8 the pound lire 0 S 8 d

4 pounds of ... at S 2 the pound lire 0 S 8 d

6 pounds of ochre at S 1 the pound lire 0 S 6 d

black ... at S 2 the pound for 20 lire 2 S 0 d

wax to make the stars 29 pounds at S--the pound lire 0 S 0 d

40 pounds of oil for painting at 5 soldi the pound lire 10 S 0 d

Altogether lire 120 d 18 without the gold. 18

tin for putting on the gold 120 18

58

1541.

Two large hatchets and one very small one, 8 brass spoons, 4 tablecloths, 2 towels, 15 small napkins, 2 coarse napkins, 2 coarse cloths, 2 wrappers, 3 pairs of sheets, 2 pairs new and 1 old.

1542.

Bed 7 0 S

ring 7 0

crockery 2 5

gardener 1 2

..... 2 8

porters 2 1

glasses 1

fuel 3 6

a lock 1

Section title: Miscellaneous Notes.

1543.

New tin-ware 3 pairs of sheets 6 small bowls, each of 4 breadths, 6 bowls, 2 small sheets, 2 large dishes, 2 tablecloths and 1/2, 2 dishes medium size, 16 coarse cloths, 2 small ones 8 shirts,

Old tin-ware   9 napkins,

3 small bowls, 2 hand-towels. 4 bowls, 3 square stones, 2 small bowls, 1 large bowl, 1 platter, 4 candlesticks, 1 small candlestick.

1544.

Hose S 40 straw S 60 wheat S 42 wine S 54 bread S 18 meat S 54 eggs S 5 salad S 3 the Barber S 2 d 6 horses S 1

1545.

Sunday

meat S 10 d wine S 12 d bran S 5 d 4 herbs S 10 d buttermilk S 4 d 4 melon S 3 d bread S 3 d 1

Monday S 9 8

..... S 6 d wine S 12 d bran S 9 d 4 buttermilk S 4 d 4 herbs S 8 d

Tuesday S   d

meat S 0 d 8 wine S 12 d bread S 3 d meal S 5 d 4 herbs S 8 d

Wednesday

wine S 5 d melon S 2 d meal S 5 d 4 vegetables S 8

Notes by unknown persons among the MSS. (1546-1565).

1546.

Miseracione divina sacro sancte Romane ecclesie tituli n cardinalis 2wulgariter nuncupatus venerabili religioso fratri Johanni Mair d'Nustorf 3ordinis praedicatorum provintie teutonie (?) conventus Wiennensis capellano 4 nostro commensali salutem in dno sempiternam Religione zelus rite ac in [ferite?] 5honestas aliarumque laudabilium probitatis et virtutum merita quibus apud nos fide 6digno commendationis testimonio Magistri videlicet ordinis felicis recordacionis Leonardi de 7Mansuetis de Perusio sigillo suo ... us dans tibi ad ... opera virtutum comen(salem)? 8 locum et tempus success(ores) cujus similiter officium ministratus qui praedecessoris sui donum (?) 9confirmavit et de novo dedit aliorumque plurima [laudatis] qui opera tua laudant 10nos inducunt ut tibi (?) reddamus ad gratiam liberalem hinc est quod nos cupientes. [Footnote: The meaning of this document, which is very difficult to decipher, and is written in unintelligible Latin, is, that Leonardo di Mansuetis recommends the Rev. Mair of Nusdorf, chaplain at Vienna, to some third person; and says also that something, which had to be proved, has been proved. The rest of the passages on the same leaf are undoubtedly in Leonardo's hand. (Nos. 483, 661, 519, 578, 392, 582, 887 and 894.)]

1547.

Johannes Antonius di Johannes Ambrosius de Bolate. He who lets time pass and does not grow in virtue, the more I think of it the more I grieve. No man has it in him to be virtuous who will give up honour for gain. Good fortune is valueless to him who knows not toil. The man becomes happy who follows Christ. There is no perfect gift without great suffering. Our glories and our triumphs pass away. Foul lust, and dreams, and luxury, and sloth have banished every virtue from the world; so that our Nature, wandering and perplexed, has almost lost the old and better track. Henceforth it were well to rouse thyself from sleep. The master said that lying in down will not bring thee to Fame; nor staying beneath the quilts. He who, without Fame, burns his life to waste, leaves no more vestige of himself on earth than wind-blown smoke, or the foam upon the sea. [Footnote: From the last sentence we may infer that this text is by the hand of a pupil of Leonardo's.-- On the same sheet are the notes Nos.1175 and 715 in Leonardo's own handwriting.]

1548.

On the morning of Santo Zanobio the 29th of May 1504, I had from Lionardo Vinci 15 gold ducats and began to spend them. to Mona Margarita S 62 d 4 to remake the ring S 19 d 8 clothes S 13 good beef S 4 eggs S 6 debt at the bank S 7 velvet S 12 wine S 6 d 4 meat S 4 mulberries S 2 d 4 mushrooms S 3 d 4 salad S 1 fruit S 1 d 4 candles S 3 ... S 1 flour S 2

     Sunday   198 8

bread S 6 wine S 9 d 4 meat S 7 soup S 2 fruit S 3 d 4 candles S 3 d

Monday 31

bread S 6 d 4 meat S 10 d 8 wine S 9 d 4 fruit S 4 soup S 1 d 8

        32

1549.

Tuesday

bread S 6 meat S 11 wine S 7 fruit S 9 soup S 2 salad S 1

[Footnote 1548 and 1549: On the same sheet is the text No. 1015 in Leonardo's own handwriting.]

1550.

To Monna Margarita S 5 to Tomaso S 14 to Monna Margarita d 5 S 2 on the day of San Zanobi left ... after payment d 13 S 2 d 4 of Monna Margarita

     altogether   d 14 S 5 d 4

1551.

On Monday, the l3th of February, I lent lire S 7 to Lionardo to spend, Friday d 7.

[Footnote: This note is followed by an account very like the one given as No. 1549.]

1552.

Stephano Chigi, Canonico ..., servant of the honorable Count Grimani at S. Apostoli.

[Footnote: Compare No. 674, 21-23.]

1553.

Having become anxious ... Bernardo di Simone, Silvestro di Stefano, Bernardo di Jacopo, Francesco di Matteo Bonciani, Antonio di Giovanni Ruberti, Antonio da Pistoia.... Antonio; He who has time and waits for time, will lose his friends and his money.

1554.

Reverend Maestro, Domino Giovanni, I spoke to Maestro Zacaria as a brother about this business, and I made him satisfied with the arrangement that I had wished; that is, as regards the commission that I had from the parties and I say that between us there is no need to pay money down, as regard the pictures of the ...

1555.

Of things seen through a mist that which is nearest its farthest limit will be least visible, and all the more so as they are more remote.

1556.

Theodoricus Rex Semper Augustus.

1557.

Either you say Hesperia alone, and it will mean Italy, or you add ultima, and it will mean Spain. Umbria, part of Tuscany.

[Footnote: The notes in Greek, Nos. 1557, 1558 and 1562 stand in close connection with each other, but the meaning of some words is very doubtful, and a translation is thus rendered impossible.]

1558.

[Footnote: Greek Characters]

1559.

Canonica of ... on the 5th of July 1507; my dearly beloved mother, sisters and cousin I herewith inform you that thanks to God I am ... about the sword which I ... bring it to Maso at the piazza ... and I will settle the business of Piero so that ...

[Footnote: AMORETTI, Mem. Stor. XXIV, quotes the first three lines of this letter as by Leonardo. The character of the writing however does not favour this hypothesis, and still less the contents. I should regard it rather a rough draft of a letter by young Melzi. I have not succeeded in deciphering completely the 13 lines of this text. Amoretti reads at the beginning Canonica di Vaprio, but Vaprio seems to me a very doubtful reading.]

1560.

Ut bene respondet Naturae ars docta! dedisset
　Vincius, ut tribuit cetera - sic animam -
Noluit ut similis magis haec foret: altera sic est:
　Possidet illius Maurus amans animam.

[Footnote: These three epigrams on the portrait of Lucrezia Crivelli, a picture by Leonardo which must have been lost at a very early date, seem to have been dedicated to Leonardo by the poet. Leonardo used the reverse of the sheet for notes on geometry.]

Hujus quam cernis nomen Lucretia, Divi Omnia cui larga contribuere manu. Rara huic forma data est; pinxit Leonardos, amavit Maurus, pictorum primus hic, ille ducum.

Naturam, ac superas hac laesit imagine Divas Pictor: tantum hominis posse manum haec doluit, Illae longa dari tam magnae tempera formae, Quae spatio fuerat deperitura brevi.

1561.

Egidius Romanus on the formation of the human body in the mother's womb [Footnote 1: Liber magistri Egidii de pulsibus matrice conipositus (cum commentario Gentilis de Fulgineo) published in 1484 at Padova, in 1494 and in 1514 at Venice, and in 1505 at Lyons.].

[Footnote 2:2. This text appears to be in a handwriting different from that in the note, l. 1. Here the reading is not so simple as AMORETTI gave it, Mem. Star. XXV: A Monsieur Lyonard Peintre du Roy pour Amboyse. He says too that this address is of the year 1509, and Mr. Ravaisson remarks: "De cette suscription il semble qu'on peut inferer que Leonard etait alors en France, a la cour de Louis XII ... Pour conclure je crois qu'il n'est pas prouve que Leonard de Vinci n'ait pas fait un voyage de quelques mois en France sous Louis XII, entre le printemps de 1509 et l'automne de 1510."--I must confess that I myself have not succeeded in deciphering completely this French writing of which two words remain to me doubtful. But so much seems to be quite evident that this is not an address of a letter at all, but a certificate or note. Amboise[l. 6] I believe to be the signature of Charles d'Amboise the Governor of Milan. If this explanation is the right one, it can be easily explained by the contents of Nos. 1350 and 1529. The note, line 1, was perhaps added later by another hand; and Leonardo himself wrote afterwards on the same sheet some geometrical explanations. I must also point out that the statement that this sheet belongs to the year 1509 has absolutely no foundation in fact. There is no clue whatever for giving a precise date to this note.] To Monsieur le Vinci,--the horses of the king's equerry.... Continue the payment to Ms. Lyonard, Painter to the King.

[6] Amboise.

1562.

[Footnote: Greek Characters]

1563.

Memorandum to Maestro Lionardo to have ... the state of Florence.

1564.

To remind your Excellency that Ridolfo Manini brought to Florence a quantity of crystal besides other stones such as are ...

1565.

XVI C. 6 de Ciuitate Dei, se Antipodes.

[Footnote: A facsimile of this note, which refers to a well known book by St. Augustin, is given on page 254.]

1566.

Leonardo's Will.

Be it known to all persons, present and to come that at the court of our Lord the King at Amboise before ourselves in person, Messer Leonardo da Vinci painter to the King, at present staying at the place known as Cloux near Amboise, duly considering the certainty of death and the uncertainty of its time, has acknowledged and declared in the said court and before us that he has made, according to the tenor of these presents, his testament and the declaration of his last will, as follows. And first he commends his soul to our Lord, Almighty God, and to the Glorious Virgin Mary, and to our lord Saint Michael, to all the blessed Angels and Saints male and female in Paradise.

Item. The said Testator desires to be buried within the church of Saint Florentin at Amboise, and that his body shall be borne thither by the chaplains of the church.

Item. That his body may be followed from the said place to the said church of Saint Florentin by the collegium of the said church, that is to say by the rector and the prior, or by their vicars and chaplains of the church of Saint Denis of Amboise, also the lesser friars of the place, and before his body shall be carried to the said church this Testator desires, that in the said church of Saint Florentin three grand masses shall be celebrated by the deacon and sub-deacon and that on the day when these three high masses are celebrated, thirty low masses shall also be performed at Saint Gregoire.

Item. That in the said church of Saint Denis similar services shall be performed, as above.

Item. That the same shall be done in the church of the said friars and lesser brethren.

Item. The aforesaid Testator gives and bequeaths to Messer Francesco da Melzo, nobleman, of Milan, in remuneration for services and favours done to him in the past, each

[Footnote: See page 420.]

and all of the books the Testator is at present possessed of, and the instruments and portraits appertaining to his art and calling as a painter.

Item. The same Testator gives and bequeaths henceforth for ever to Battista de Vilanis his servant one half, that is the moity, of his garden which is outside the walls of Milan, and the other half of the same garden to Salai his servant; in which garden aforesaid Salai has built and constructed a house which shall be and remain henceforth in all perpetuity the property of the said Salai, his heirs and successors; and this is in remuneration for the good and kind services which the said de Vilanis and Salai, his servants have done him in past times until now.

Item. The said Testator gives to Maturina his waiting woman a cloak of good black cloth lined with fur, a ... of cloth and two ducats paid once only; and this likewise is in remuneration for good service rendered to him in past times by the said Maturina.

Item. He desires that at his funeral sixty tapers shall be carried which shall be borne by sixty poor men, to whom shall be given money for carrying them; at the discretion of the said Melzo, and these tapers shall be distributed among the four above mentioned churches.

Item. The said Testator gives to each of the said churches ten lbs. of wax in thick tapers, which shall be placed in the said churches to be used on the day when those said services are celebrated.

Item. That alms shall be given to the poor of the Hotel-Dieu, to the poor of Saint Lazare d'Amboise and, to that end, there shall be given and paid to the treasurers of that same fraternity the sum and amount of seventy soldi of Tours.

Item. The said Testator gives and bequeaths to the said Messer Francesco Melzo, being present and agreeing, the remainder of his pension and the sums of money which are owing to him from the past time till the day of his death by the receiver or treasurer-general M. Johan Sapin, and each and every sum of money that he has already received from the aforesaid Sapin of his said pension, and in case he should die before the said Melzo and not otherwise; which moneys are at present in the possession of the said Testator in the said place called Cloux, as he says. And he likewise gives and bequeaths to the said Melzo all and each of his clothes which he at present possesses at the said place of Cloux, and all in remuneration for the good and kind services done by him in past times till now, as well as in payment for the trouble and annoyance he may incur with regard to the execution of this present testament, which however, shall all be at the expense of the said Testator.

And he orders and desires that the sum of four hundred scudi del Sole, which he has deposited in the hands of the treasurer of Santa Maria Nuova in the city of Florence, may be given to his brothers now living in Florence with all the interest and usufruct that may have accrued up to the present time, and be due from the aforesaid treasurer to the aforesaid Testator on account of the said four hundred crowns, since they were given and consigned by the Testator to the said treasurers.

Item. He desires and orders that the said Messer Francesco de Melzo shall be and remain the sole and only executor of the said will of the said Testator; and that the said testament shall be executed in its full and complete meaning and according to that which is here narrated and said, to have, hold, keep and observe, the said Messer Leonardo da Vinci, constituted Testator, has obliged and obliges by these presents the said his heirs and successors with all his goods moveable and immoveable present and to come, and has renounced and expressly renounces by these presents all and each of the things which to that are contrary. Given at the said place of Cloux in the presence of Magister Spirito Fieri vicar, of the church of Saint Denis at Amboise, of M. Guglielmo Croysant priest and chaplain, of Magister Cipriane Fulchin, Brother Francesco de Corion, and of Francesco da Milano, a brother of the Convent of the Minorites at Amboise, witnesses summoned and required to that end by the indictment of the said court in the presence of the aforesaid M. Francesco de Melze who accepting and agreeing to the same has promised by his faith and his oath which he has administered to us personally and has sworn to us never to do nor say nor act in any way to the contrary. And it is sealed by his request with the royal seal apposed to legal contracts at Amboise, and in token of good faith.

Given on the XXIIIrd day of April MDXVIII, before Easter.

And on the XXIIIrd day of this month of April MDXVIII, in the presence of M. Guglielmo Borian, Royal notary in the court of the bailiwick of Amboise, the aforesaid M. Leonardo de Vinci gave and bequeathed, by his last will and testament, as aforesaid, to the said M. Baptista de Vilanis, being present and agreeing, the right of water which the King Louis XII, of pious memory lately deceased gave to this same de Vinci, the stream of the canal of Santo Cristoforo in the duchy of Milan, to belong to the said Vilanis for ever in such wise and manner that the said gentleman made him this gift in the presence of M. Francesco da Melzo, gentleman, of Milan and in mine.

And on the aforesaid day in the said month of April in the said year MDXVIII the same M. Leonardo de Vinci by his last will and testament gave to the aforesaid M. Baptista de Vilanis, being present and agreeing, each and all of the articles of furniture and utensils of his house at present at the said place of Cloux, in the event of the said de Vilanis surviving the aforesaid M. Leonardo de Vinci, in the presence of the said M. Francesco Melzo and of me Notary &c. Borean.